CENTRAL-EASTERN EUROPE

CRUCIBLE OF WORLD WARS

CENTRAL-EASTERN EUROPE

CRUCIBLE OF WORLD WARS

By JOSEPH S. ROUCEK, *Ph.D.*

AND ASSOCIATES

MITCHELL P. BRIGGS, *Ph.D., Fresno State College.*

FLOYD A. CAVE, *Ph.D., San Francisco State College.*

KIMON A. DOUKAS, *Ph.D., formerly of Indiana University.*

WIKTOR J. EHRENPREIS, *Jur.D., formerly of "Poland Fights."*

FELIKS GROSS, *Jur.M., Jur.D., New York University and University of Wyoming.*

E. C. HELMREICH, *Ph.D., Bowdoin College.*

T. V. KALIJARVI, *Ph.D., New Hampshire State Planning and Development Commission.*

MANFRED KRIDL, *Ph.D., Smith College.*

HANS KOHN, *Jur.D., Smith College.*

JOSEPH S. ROUCEK, *Ph.D., Hofstra College.*

ERNEST ŠTURC, *Ph.D., Czechoslovak Information Service.*

New York PRENTICE-HALL, INC. *1946*

Copyright, 1946, by

PRENTICE-HALL, INC.

70 Fifth Avenue, New York

Printed in the United States of America

DEDICATED TO
MY BELOVED FRIEND
GRANT MITCHELL
FOR HIS CONTRIBUTIONS
TO BROADWAY AND HOLLYWOOD

PREFACE

BOTH World War I and World War II originated in the region that can roughly be defined as Central-Eastern Europe. Although the sparks of the conflagrations in that area eventually menaced the very existence of the British Empire and even set the United States ablaze, the region is "terra incognita" to most Anglo-Saxons. American political writers are unfortunately inclined to underestimate the complex realities of Central-Eastern Europe. Their ignorance of those realities was aptly illustrated by Prime Minister Chamberlain's statement about the Czechoslovak crisis in 1938: "How terrible, fantastic, incredible it is that we should be digging trenches and trying on gas masks here because of a quarrel in a faraway country between people of whom we know nothing."

One cause of Anglo-American indifference is the influence exerted in the United States and in Anglo-Saxon historiography by the concepts of "Western Civilization" and the related tendencies rooted in German scholarship. Most of the founders of the graduate departments of history in American universities either received their training in Germany or eventually came under the spell of its traditions. Ranke's earlier view that the Germanic and Romance nations form a distinct cultural unit with a common history to be identified with the history of Europe has been accepted by the entire German historiography. It has also been followed, to a considerable degree, in the United States. For a long time America and Western Europe have thought of Western civilization as being somehow identical with universal history. This concept has been bolstered by innumerable textbooks on "The Development of Western Civilization," with the result that the graduates of our institutions of learning have had a very definite impression that all important history was made by the larger nations of Western Europe. Thus Central-Eastern Europe has been generally lost in the shuffle.

The period after 1918 only strengthened this tendency. Because the war originated in the Balkans, those states acquired an unfortunate reputation as an element of eternal dissension, a source of evil and upheaval, and a constant, ever-threatening danger to European peace. German propaganda was only too glad to foster such ideas, especially since it served Berlin's purposes to attack the results of the Versailles Treaty and the other peace treaties which created a "new order" in Central-Eastern Europe that Germany did not like. This strange propaganda against the peace treaties was repeated diligently year in and year out by American and English people who had never read a line of the treaty and perhaps did not even know the names of its makers. Those people utterly ignored the achievement of the peace treaties in liberating the smaller nations of Central-Eastern Europe and greatly exaggerated the hardships inflicted on Germany by the economic clauses (which, for the most part, were completely inoperative). The Central-Eastern European states were thus regarded with the utmost suspicion, particularly since the liberals of the generation regarded "nationalism" as the source of all evils. As conditions in Europe deteriorated, innumerable people sighed: "Ah, it's the fault of those small nations." They apparently failed to realize that the mailed fist was not shaken by the small nations, but first by Italy and then by Nazi Germany.

After a brief resurgence of democracy and a spread of representative government and parliamentary forms, the glittering phrases of constitutionalism and parliamentarianism proved to be illusory. When democratic machinery broke down in several of the Central-Eastern European states, the disillusionment became even more pronounced. During this period, the critics failed to understand that rationalism can project a Utopia but cannot make it a reality.

However, it should be emphasized that the Central-Eastern European nations have by no means been faultless. But whatever their faults or their contributions to "Western" civilization, knowledge of conditions in that region is of paramount importance. This has been particularly exemplified in the case of Russia, a veritable "enigma" to most people during the last two decades and especially puzzling to those who cannot overcome their surprise that Communist Russia was the first nation to stop Hitler's hordes. The Russians were helped by their allies, of course, but still they had that signal honor.

From this discussion, it is only logical to assume that a more definite knowledge of the backgrounds and current problems of the Central-Eastern European states is urgently desirable. The present book is one of the first to try to present fair and reliable information on the historical development of those nations, with particular emphasis on the period following the First World War, in a single volume. The result is, therefore, a harvest of studies aiming to synthesize, summarize, and reinterpret available knowledge about the region. Each chapter is accordingly designed to bring into sharp focus the main trends involved in the national development of each country. The editor is particularly proud to have been able to secure the co-authors of this volume as his collaborators. The frequently observed inclination of a single author to be panoramic is a notable eccentricity in our age of specialists. This book is the result of the coöperation of a number of distinguished collaborators, in recognition of the reality that it is no longer possible for one man to digest all the facts and to present reliable and useful conclusions therefrom.

It is the hope of the editor and his collaborators that a better understanding of Central-Eastern Europe will go a long way to clarify the reasons why both our enemies and our friends are so powerful. It is also hoped that it will suggest methods of integrating states into the world community, if that particular task should fall to us.

The individual chapters of this book were written by the authors to whom they are ascribed in the Table of Contents. The editor, however, has taken the liberty of adding material to some of the chapters in order to amplify and harmonize their relationship with one another and to bring the material up to date.

The editor wishes to express special appreciation to Dr. Feliks Gross, General Secretary of the former Central and Eastern European Planning Board, for invaluable help in developing and completing the project. He also wishes to thank James C. McMullin, publisher of *The Interpreter,* for his assistance in revising the manuscript for publication.

Joseph S. Roucek

TABLE OF CONTENTS

TABLE OF CONTENTS

LIST OF MAPS

PART I

CHAPTER I

CENTRAL-EASTERN EUROPE IN WORLD HISTORY

Historic Background

THE aphorism that all reasonable hopes of the future depend upon a sound understanding of the past applies with particular force to Central-Eastern Europe. Both World Wars started there, and the solution of the problems arising in this region will determine whether Russia's collaboration with the Western Allies will have a permanent foundation. Moreover, the key to an understanding of titanic modern struggles can be found in the forces of history which have perpetuated a disequilibrium in the no man's land of Central-Eastern Europe, where Western and Eastern influences in European and Asiatic history have remained locked in a stalemate.

The strip of territory lying between the Baltic and the Aegean is certainly not a homogeneous region in any ordinary historical or geographic sense. Yet the most important features in the life of all the countries of this area are the same—a great diversity of nationality and religion, a predominantly agricultural economy, and a history of domination or conquest from one direction or another. This territory comprises the borderlands between the great national states of Western Europe and the Slavic power of Russia. Two significant factors in the history of these lands have been the development of national consciousness and the relation of the smaller Slavic nationalities to the growing Russian state.

The Central-Eastern European region seems to have been predestined to endless conflicts by the very geography of the area. The core of the region, the Danube, has always afforded a most favorable avenue for military operations, whether the invasion came from the east or from the west. In the first thousand years of our era, the Romans were the lords of Danubia for five centuries. During the second five hundred years, domination of the Danube basin continually changed hands. In modern times the Turkish thrust, which for centuries had been directed northwestward along the Danube, was replaced in the eight-

3

eenth century by German pressure exerted in the opposite direction. After the liquidation of the Napoleonic menace, German and Austro-Hungarian pressure down the Danube to the Balkans was opposed by two other forces—one, growing out of the *risorgimento* of Italy, from the southwest along the old Roman routes; the other a Russian drive toward the Balkans and against Turkey around the Black Sea.

Meanwhile the problem of the Baltic Sea had already become a problem of international concern in the sixteenth century. Even then the interests of the Baltic riparian states and other European states were interwoven. This became especially clear after Muscovy conquered the Livonian port of Barva (on Estonian territory) at the mouth of the Narva river in 1558. The Narva was connected by inland waterways with the Finnish Gulf. The rise of Russia's power drove her eventually to become the master of all the Baltic and created Russo-German rivalry which was to make the Baltic a battleground between these two nations. The struggle between the Germanic and Russian states for power in the region led to the first partition of Poland between Prussia, Russia, and Austria in 1772. The eighteenth century showed that the balance of power in Central-Eastern Europe had definitely tipped in Russia's favor. Peter the Great conquered the Baltic provinces and his advance toward the Black Sea helped to encircle Poland, whose destruction was accomplished at the end of the eighteenth century by Catherine II. Russia then became the only European power east of Germany.

A very interesting "racial" aspect of history appears in the development of Central-Eastern Europe. This entire area is predominantly Slavic. It has never achieved any real unity based on the Slavic element, yet Slavic feelings of racial solidarity have never died out. The Czechoslovaks, Poles, Yugoslavs, and Bulgarians all have tried, at one time or another, to make historical decisions based on Pan-Slav considerations. These Pan-Slavic ideas were used by the Russians to help to liberate the Balkan Slavs during the nineteenth century and to agitate the Slavs of the Austro-Hungarian Empire before 1914. In addition, these Pan-Slavic ideals made the Germans see their history as an eternal conflict between the Teutonic and Slavic worlds.

Along with the "racial" trends of Central-Eastern European history, we must also note important religious factors. The forces of Protestantism encountered the forces of Catholicism along the Danube, and Mohammedanism and the Greek Orthodox Church also came into conflict here. In fact, the cultural and religious trends stemming from Byzantium at a time when some of the Slavic peoples were already in contact with the Latin West militated strongly against the achievement of Slavic unity. All of the northwestern Slavs (Poles, Czechs, and Slovaks) and even some of the southern Slavs (Croats and Slovenes) joined the Roman Catholic Church, whereas the Serbs and Bulgars joined the Greek Orthodox Church. These divisions, together with the complications of Protestantism in the case of the Czechoslovaks, have always had repercussions among the Slavs, creating misunderstandings and sometimes vigorous hostility between closely related Slavic populations.

By the nineteenth century, Central-Eastern Europe was living under the domination of the Russian, German, Austro-Hungarian, and Turkish Empires, all competing for power in the region. The Austro-Hungarian Empire was unwilling to let the Tsar's armies march into the Balkan Peninsula and thus block the empire's access to the Black Sea or the Aegean, or to continue inspiring the Slavs of the Habsburg domain and the Balkans to tear the Dual Monarchy apart by their nationalistic ambitions. By this time, the Habsburg Monarchy was seething with dissatisfied nationalities, rebellious against the rule of the German and Hungarian minorities. In the last quarter of the nineteenth century, the Italians also began casting a covetous eye on the Balkans as a part of the world that was once Roman. Italian aspirations encountered major opposition from two quarters: Russian Pan-Slavism, which was used to dismember Turkey by supporting Turkey's Slavic subjects against Constantinople, and also Pan-Germanism. By the end of the century, Germany had convinced herself that the Balkans were the necessary springboard for her world power ambitions. The German-Austro-Hungarian alliance insured Berlin's connections with the Balkan Peninsula and across it to Asia Minor.

German foreign policy was motivated by a beautiful dream called "Mitteleuropa." It envisioned a mighty German Empire whose political and economic tentacles would stretch from the North Sea and the Baltic through Central Europe to the Bosporus and across it to Baghdad, the key to the Near East. German goods would be carried through the Balkans to Constantinople and beyond. They would be sold in the vast markets of Arabia despite the French, and in India despite the British, as well as in the markets of a dozen economically undeveloped countries in between. Germany would thus really dominate Europe and later the Orient—and perhaps eventually the entire world.

The First World War was the direct fruit of these ambitions and dragged in all four of the empires mentioned above. When the smoke cleared away from the battlefields of World War I, Austria-Hungary had disappeared, Russia was impotent and in the throes of a Communist revolution, and Turkey was not a "sick man" but a dead man so far as the Ottoman Empire was concerned. Germany, by attempting to conquer Central-Eastern Europe and expedite the fulfillment of her dream, was defeated. She was to make another try in 1938—only to find that such attempts always end in disaster.[1]

* * * * * * * * * *

The Settlement of Central-Eastern Europe

Early migrations. Although most of the peoples of this region have remained fairly stationary since approximately the tenth century, certain groups seem to be more indigenous than others to the areas where they center today.[2] Starting in the Balkans, we have the Greeks, the scattered Kutzo-Vlachs in Macedonia, who are best identified today with the modern Romanians, and the Albanians. Although the matter is a subject of much dispute among anthropologists and historians, some of them also place the Romanians of the Carpathian area in the same category. We are on surer ground when we come to the Baltic littoral. Here the related Finns, Estonians, and Livonians have resided since very early times, along with another group, the Latvians and Lithuanians. The Germans and Slavs have a more varied history. They are indigenous to certain areas, but were more inclined to wander, and at different times in history they occupied and dominated vastly different territories.

At about the beginning of the Christian era, the various German tribes occupied not only the territory beyond the Rhine-Danube frontier of the Roman Empire but were also in control fairly well down the valley of the Vistula toward the Black Sea. Driven by an increase in population, the need for better grazing and hunting preserves, and urged on by the inroads of enemies and the desire for plunder, these tribes began to move about. This migration of nations (*Völkerwanderung*) was primarily concentrated in the fourth and fifth centuries, although the process continued well beyond that period. It had catastrophic effects on the old Roman Empire and eventually led to the establishment of new Germanic kingdoms in Western Europe. The direction of the migration was south and, as the Germanic tribes moved

---

[1] The above section, "Historic Background," has been prepared by the editor.

[2] See particularly Macartney, C. A., *National States and National Minorities* (London: Oxford University Press, 1934), Ch. III; Josef Hanč, *Tornado Across Eastern Europe* (New York: The Greystone Press, 1942), Part I.

out, their places were taken by Slavs and newcomers from the Asiatic reservoir of humanity. The gap between the Urals and the Caspian, leading to the flat plains to the north of the Black Sea and the beckoning Danube valley, formed a broad highway into the heart of Europe and along this highway, in the fifth century, came Attila and his Hunnish bands, soon to be followed by the Avars. These were to be absorbed by later arrivals, and today, as a synonym for complete oblivion, there is the proverb "to perish like the Avars without leaving a trace."

The expansion of the Slavs was less spectacular but more enduring than the advent of the Huns and the Avars. The best that ethnographers can do to locate the early Slavs is to place them in the region northeast of the Carpathians in the upper basins of the Vistula, Pripet, Dniester, and Dnieper rivers—a region about halfway between the Baltic and Black Seas in what is sometimes referred to as the Isthmus of Europe. From here the Slavs radiated like spokes in a wheel. To the east went what were later to be known as the White Russians and the Great Russians, to the south and west went the Little Russians (Ruthenians), the principal inhabitants of modern Galicia and the Ukraine. The main direction of Slav migration in this early period was westward, and the Slavs soon overran Central Europe, reaching even beyond the Elbe and to the classic frontiers of Italy and Greece.

The claims of the Slavs to Central and Eastern Europe were not, however, to go unchallenged. The Germans reversed their westward migratory trend and began to erect a series of barriers (marches) against them. Charlemagne (800-814) was the first ruler to do this on a grand scale. His biographer enumerates no less than four wars against the Slavs.

The Danubian basin. The Slav expansion to the west and south was challenged not only by the Germans but by a new series of Asiatic invaders. Toward the end of the seventh century the Bulgars, an Asiatic-Turanian tribe akin to the Huns and Avars and to the modern Finns, Estonians, and Magyars, crossed the Danube delta and spread into the Balkans. Although they conquered the Slavs, who by that time had taken possession of these lands, they were absorbed in turn, so that today they are Slavs with little but their name to remind them of their ancient origin. By the eighth century, the Khazars had established a strong kingdom north and east of the Black Sea. The conversion of their Khan to Judaism, even though the majority of the Khazars later accepted Mohammedanism, indicates the extent of Jewish influence in this area. More important than the Bulgars and

Khazars were the Magyars, who settled in the great Danubian Plain (Alföld) in the ninth century and extended their conquests up to the southeastern German marches.[3]

The great body of Slavs was thus permanently divided into two sections, for to the east of the Magyars the breach was continued by the Romanians, with their basic Latin culture. The Slavic group to the north and west consisted of the Wends, the Sorbs, the Czechs, the Slovaks, and the Poles. The southern group consisted of the Slovenes, the Croatians, the Slavonians, and the Serbs. Of these groups, the Wends (near Berlin) and the Sorbs (in Silesia) have been entirely absorbed by the Germans. The Slavonians are really Serbs who reside in a region known as Slavonia and have a history quite distinct from that of the other Serbians. In this they resemble the Montenegrins, who are racially among the purest Serbs, but who receive special mention because they inhabit the territory of the Cernagora (Black Mountain) and have a distinct regional history.

Later invasions. Following the Magyars, additional invaders swept westward across the vast steppes of southern Russia. As conquerors they influenced the history of this region, although in most cases they founded no modern national groups of significance. More important than the Petchenegs in the tenth century and the Cumans in the eleventh century were the Mongols. Having created a vast empire under Genghiz Khan in Central Asia and China, they raided Europe, reaching Bohemia in 1241. Destruction and disorganization were left in the wake of their armies. Under Batu they established an "Empire of the Golden Horde," with its capital at Sarai on the Volga, from which they ruled a large part of Eastern Europe.

Not all invaders followed the easy route north of the Black Sea. The Seljuk Turks struck south into Anatolia, revitalized the Mohammedan Saracenic Empire, and soon challenged the power of the Byzantine Empire at Constantinople. This threat furnished the pretext for the Crusades (1095-1270), with their great influence not only on Western Europe but on the East as well. More important than the Seljuks were the Ottoman Turks who replaced them and who were to become the founders and organizers of the great Turkish Empire. Although the Ottoman Turks extended their power up to the gates of

---

[3] "The Székely, or Szeklers, who inhabit the eastern valleys of Transylvania, are now completely Magyarized, but it is most probable that they are in origin a pre-Magyar Turkish people (perhaps Avars). In the Middle Ages they were free peasants, preserving their own constitution which was tribal and closely akin to that of the early Magyars and subject only to the Székely-Graf, or Count of the Székely, who was directly responsible to the Crown." Macartney, *National States and National Minorities*, p. 62.

Vienna, and thus had a tremendous effect on the peoples of South-eastern Europe, they ruled as conquerors. They established no large Turkish national groups, but only small minorities here and there to add to the babel of tongues.

Colonization. A consideration of early indigenous groups and groups which became indigenous as a result of somewhat later mass migrations does not suffice to account historically for the mosaic of peoples which is the most fundamental characteristic of Central and Eastern Europe. This must be traced also to an important colonization movement into the region throughout the course of history.

Under the Roman Empire the province of Dacia was colonized, and the modern Romanians claim they are the descendants of these colonists and of the tribes originally occupying this area. Traders in the Middle Ages established small national colonies in remote regions. This type of colonization is well illustrated by the settlements of the German merchants of the Hanseatic League in the Baltic States. Colonists also followed the Cross: witness the activity of the Teutonic Knights in the Baltic regions of East Prussia, Estonia, and Latvia, and the German settlers who followed the German missionaries into Bohemia. In later years many groups of settlers migrated to escape religious persecution, either Mohammedan, Roman Catholic, Greek Orthodox, or Protestant. Conquest of new territories also brought new colonists, as illustrated by Swedish expansion along the shores of the Baltic, German expansion into the eastern marches, and Russian expansion into the Baltic and Black Sea regions.

Colonization by groups of nationals was, however, largely the result of direct invitation by ruling princes who wanted settlers to work the lands, businessmen to conduct the trade of the cities, and soldiers to protect the frontiers. This process has gone on continually. Such settlers obtained not only special land grants but, equally important, special governing privileges. The large immigration of Saxons into Transylvania in the twelfth century is a perfect example of this type of colonization. These famous Siebenbürgen Saxons were recognized as a separate nation by their overlords and were granted autonomy. They have jealously guarded these rights and in part maintained them to this day.

After the devastation of the series of wars in the seventeenth and eighteenth centuries when the Turks were gradually driven back beyond the Danube, the Habsburg rulers regularly invited peoples to settle in this area. Many of the settlers who responded were Germans, but there were also many Slovaks and Serbs. The Swabians along the lower Danube for the most part migrated to this region in the eighteenth and nineteenth centuries. The Cossacks, with their historic special privileges in the Ukraine, originated as a group of frontier guards. The Habsburgs down to 1867 maintained against the Turks a special Military Frontier staffed largely by Croats and Serbs who had special privileges and were subject directly to the Ministry of War in Vienna.

The reason for these grants of special privilege to colonists is not hard to find. They arose primarily out of the need to entice immigrants to increase the prosperity and wealth of the ruler's domains. Colonists would not come unless they were accorded special rights because they were often accustomed to a more highly developed state of law in their mother country than existed in the regions to which they were migrating. This was especially true with regard to towns, which accounts for the fact that many German communities in Eastern Europe (notably in Poland) were governed by German municipal codes. In fact, *Magdeburger Recht* did not disappear from Russian Poland until 1831. This recognition of special legal systems had the same purpose as the capitulations in Turkey and extraterritorial rights in China and Japan. In addition, there was the concept of personality of law so prevalent in mediaeval Europe, especially among the Germans, according to which a man took his law (the law of his tribe or nation) with him wherever he went and expected to be tried and judged by it.

By granting such legal and other privileges, the ruling prince sought also to win the support of the immigrants against his obstreperous nobility or the majority nationality. But while special minority privileges satisfied and pacified their recipients, they also often antagonized the more numerous native population. The greater centralization of the state in recent years and the passing of power to majority groups through the democratization of government have resulted in the curtailment of special minority privileges, a fact that accounts in part for the acuteness of minority problems today.

Among the racial and religious minorities who were often granted special privileges were the Jews. These grants did not have to be extensive to attract the Jews, who were generally under severe persecution in Western Europe. A number of rulers in fourteenth-century Poland and Lithuania were especially well disposed toward them, however, and many Jews came to live in these territories. Later, these Jews were restricted to certain areas, which became known as the "Pale." But there were also many Jews scattered beyond the Pale, particularly in the rest of Galicia, Hungary, and Romania. Eastern Europe thus became the world center of Jewish population.

Religious Development

The great variety of peoples is naturally a divisive force in Central and Eastern Europe. The same is true of religion, which has often been closely associated with nationality in this region. In the Middle Ages there were two main missionary centers: Rome and Constantinople. Roman Catholicism spread from the first; Eastern Orthodoxy from the second. The former brought with it a western orientation, western culture, and the use of the Latin alphabet. Eastern Orthodoxy brought about contacts with the civilization of the Byzantine Empire and, except in the case of the Romanians, the use of the Cyrillic alphabet. After the Mohammedan conquest of Constantinople (1453) and the Balkans, the isolation of the Eastern churches from the rest of Christendom was increased.

On the eastern (i.e., Greek Orthodox) side of the religious demarcation line which extends vertically across Europe are the Greeks, the Bulgars, about one-third of the Albanians, the Serbs, a greater part of the Romanians, and the Russians. To the west, and predominantly Roman Catholic, are the Poles, Czechs, Slovaks, Magyars, Austrians, Slovenes, and Croats. Constituting a sort of border line in Galicia and sections of Romania are the Uniates: Catholics in full communion with Rome but following Eastern rites of worship.[4]

This religious division of Central-Eastern Europe was disturbed but not materially changed by the Protestant Reformation. Although the Protestant movement originally swept large sections of Bohemia, Slovakia, Austria, Hungary, and Poland, the reaction of the Counter-Reformation regained much of this territory for Roman Catholicism. In the north, where Protestant Sweden controlled Finland, Estonia, and Courland, Lutheranism was introduced and remains the dominant religion. The secularization of the Teutonic Order left Protestantism in control in East Prussia and in portions of the Baltic littoral. In Hungary, Protestantism was able to preserve itself in some places against the Catholic power of the Habsburgs, particularly in the eastern sections which remained longer under Turkish rule, and in Transylvania, which enjoyed a peculiar autonomous status. In this region, as early as 1571, Roman Catholicism, Lutheranism, Calvinism, and Uni-

---

[4] Attwater, Donald. *The Catholic Eastern Churches* (Milwaukee: Bruce Publishing Co., 1935), Chs. III, IV, V.

tarianism received official recognition and toleration. The Orthodox faith, however, remained outside the fold.[5] The Turkish conquest of Southeastern Europe brought with it Mohammedanism and added a new divisive element. This was important in its day but has no marked present significance.

Economic Development

The diversity found in race and religion in Central-Eastern Europe is not paralleled in its economic life. In the past and even today, the whole region remains fundamentally a rural area. The existence of age-old manufacturing centers in Bohemia, Austria, and Greece does not change this basic generalization. In recent years there has been some industrialization in all the states in this part of Europe, except perhaps Albania. But here again, the movement is so universal that the economies remain essentially parallel and not complementary in relation to one another. True, a measure of economic interdependence can be discerned in certain regions, but this is not sufficiently widespread to bring about economic unity in Central-Eastern Europe.

It is by no means certain, as is so often supposed, that economically this region was better off when it was under two or three sovereign states than when it was divided among the numerous states of post-World War I Europe. It is war which from time immemorial has retarded the economy of these borderlands.

Political Development to 1450

General pattern. It is difficult to work out a coherent political pattern for Central-Eastern Europe. At the time when the Balkan Peninsula was the home of Greek civilization, the territory from the Danube to the Baltic was inhabited by unknown wandering tribes. The Roman Empire extended its control somewhat beyond the Danube, but essentially it remained a Mediterranean power. Nevertheless the influence of the Roman Empire, with its heritage from Greece, eventually spread throughout Central-Eastern Europe. Insofar as that influence derived directly from Rome, it was similar to the heritage of Western Europe where the Church asserted supremacy over the State.

To a great extent, however, Central-Eastern Europe derives from Constantinople, where Roman and Greek traditions merged into the civilization of the Byzantine Empire. It was from Constantinople that the first missionaries were sent to the Slavs and with them

---

[5] Macartney, C. A., *Hungary and Her Successors. The Treaty of Trianon and Its Consequences, 1919-1937* (London: Oxford University Press, 1937), p. 260.

went the concept that the State was not only closely related to the Church, but was dominant over it. Often the ruling prince took the lead in bringing his people into the Christian fold and, having done so, retained a directing hand over the Church. *Cuius regio eius religio* was a doctrine enforced in Central-Eastern Europe long before the Reformation wrote into the public law of the Germanies that a prince should determine the religion of his subjects.

From Rome the imperial tradition was passed on to the Germans, from Constantinople to the Russians. Some of the people who separated the two—Poles, Hungarians, Serbs, Bulgarians—were also inspired by the imperial concept and at various times attempted to establish empires of their own. Yet on the whole these peoples, as will be pointed out below, became the parts out of which rival imperial states were built. The persistence of the imperial idea in Central-Eastern Europe was in part due to the relatively late rise of nationalism and democracy there. Although these forces did in time disrupt the established imperial states, they did not end the imperial tradition—a fact amply demonstrated by contemporary world politics.

By about 1350 a turning point in the history of Central-Eastern Europe can be discerned. To the east the Mongols, the last invaders to sweep across the steppes of Russia, were still firmly established on the Volga. To the southeast, the Byzantine Empire was in the throes of revolution. In 1354, the Ottoman Turks established their first foothold in Europe. Already beset by the Black Death, which ravaged Europe about 1350, the people were soon to add to their litanies a prayer for protection against this new scourge. Between these powers on the east and the states of Western Europe, Central-Eastern Europe consisted of a number of independent or semi-independent states which owed their freedom largely to the weakness of their neighbors. To the west lay an enormous and grasping but weakly organized empire.

The Holy Roman Empire. The Holy Roman Empire was a loose confederation of feudal states, mostly Germanic. The Emperor, who laid claim to universal rule as heir of the Roman emperors, always had difficulty in controlling both his Italian and his German subjects. The emperorship was an elective office, a fact which frequently led to bitter rivalries. In the famous Golden Bull of 1356, the election procedure was formally organized by assigning the task to seven electors. Three of them were ecclesiastics: the Archbishops of Mainz, Trier, and Cologne. The other four were lay rulers: the Count Palatine of the Rhine, the Duke of Saxony, the Margrave of Brandenburg, and the King

of Bohemia. Bohemia had become a recognized part of the Holy
Roman Empire after Boleslav I had been forced to accept German
suzerainty in 950. When the line of succession failed in Bohemia in
1526, the crown passed to the Habsburgs.

The fact that the Catholic Habsburgs could thus always unite with
the three ecclesiastical electors to assure the election of a Habsburg
emperor was of fateful significance to the history of all Europe. Vague
and shadowy as the power of the emperors came to be, the Habsburgs
would have cut a relatively minor figure in Eastern European history
had they not been backed by the influence, prestige, and power that
they obtained as emperors of the Holy Roman Empire. Equally fateful was the fact that at times the welfare of Central-Eastern Europe
was sacrificed to support Habsburg policies in Germany, Spain, and
Italy. Via the Habsburgs and the Empire, the wars and troubles of
Western, Central, and Southeastern Europe were to be inextricably intermingled. Thus the states of Central-Eastern Europe led a precarious existence between their imperialistic neighbors.

The Baltic region. In the far north, the Swedes had conquered the
Finns in the twelfth century, but the Finns nevertheless maintained a
high degree of autonomy. The loose organization of the Swedish
kingdom and its complex relationship to the other Scandinavian kingdoms in this period made Swedish suzerainty little more than nominal.
Along the Baltic littoral and in the islands of the Baltic, the Hanseatic
League maintained important trading centers which actually served as
German outposts. The Peace of Stralsund (1370) between the League
and Sweden marked the high point of the power of the Hansa in this
area. Strong though it was, however, the Hansa was forced to share
its control of the Baltic with the Teutonic Knights. In 1200 the Pope
had proclaimed a Crusade against the Baltic heathen, and the German
Knights of the Sword (joined later by the Teutonic Knights) had
responded eagerly to this summons to "Christian warfare." The
Knights had colonized and Christianized East Prussia and, then expanding their rule northward from their base at Riga, had finally won
Estonia from its Danish overlords in 1346.

The Order of Teutonic Knights also sent its colonists deep into Poland and into Lithuania, but they were never able to subjugate these
territories. At this time Lithuania was the most powerful state in
Eastern Europe, and in 1386 the Duke of Lithuania brought about a
federation with Poland by a marriage alliance. The allies were able
to defeat the Teutonic Order in the famous battle of Tannenberg in
1410. This defeat marked the beginning of the end for the Teutonic

Order and the corresponding rise of the Polish-Lithuanian state, which in the sixteenth century was to control the vast territory from the Baltic to the Black Sea and from east of the Oder River and the Carpathians to the headwaters of the Volga.

Bohemia-Moravia. Before and after the Polish-Lithuanian federation, Poland at various times entered into relations with Bohemia and Hungary, which lay beyond its southern mountain frontier. In Bohemia the Czechs had established a state as early as the seventh century, only to be absorbed by the kindred state of Moravia in the tenth century. As mentioned above, Bohemia in 950 became a recognized part of the Holy Roman Empire. This tie with the government of Germany, often very tenuous, was nevertheless to last in one fashion or another down to the rupture of the Germanic Confederation in 1866 and, through the continuing connection of Bohemia with Austria, even longer.

The middle of the fourteenth century is often regarded as the Golden Age of Bohemia. Under its King Charles I (1347-1378), the famous Charles IV of the Empire, Bohemia took the lead in imperial affairs. The University of Prague was founded in 1348 and soon it nourished a national-religious leader in the person of John Hus (1369-1415). He was to pay with his life for his denunciations of abuses within the Catholic Church and of German dominance in Bohemia. His death at the stake by order of the Council of Constance (1415) unleashed the civil conflicts known as the Hussite Wars (1420-1433) and laid the basis for the bitter religious-national struggles against the Habsburgs in the seventeenth century. Failure of a direct line of succession united Bohemia through dynastic ties with Hungary and, as we have seen, in 1526 with the Austrian Habsburgs.

Hungary. The Magyars, who had reached the Danubian plain in 896, organized and obtained Western recognition of their state of Hungary in the year 1001, when King Stephen was crowned with a special crown blessed by the Pope. Certainly by the end of the tenth century the Magyars were in control of modern Slovakia, which remained from that time until 1918, except for a very brief episode or two, an integral part of the Hungarian state. In this period Hungary also held modern Transylvania, but here a varying degree of autonomy was always the rule until 1867. Croatia-Slavonia, which Hungary conquered in the eleventh century, likewise enjoyed a measure of autonomy under the crown of St. Stephen.

Under Louis the Great (1342-1382), mediaeval Hungary reached the peak of its power. Louis forced the princes of Serbia, Wallachia, and

Moldavia to recognize his suzerainty, established control over Ragusa and most of Dalmatia, and even was elected King of Poland. But this great Hungarian-dominated federation, extending from close to the Baltic to the Mediterranean and Black Seas, was only a flash in the pan, for it centered too much in the person of the king. Poland, after its union with Lithuania (1386), became a dangerous rival. Moreover, the princes to the southeast took their oaths of allegiance lightly, and the inroads of the Turks soon placed the Hungarian kings on the defensive.

The Slovenes. While the Croats came under Magyar rule, the Slovenes were conquered by the Germans in the ninth century and, like the Czechs, were to be associated thenceforth with the history of the Holy Roman Empire. Their territories (mainly Carinthia, Carniola, and Styria) were ruled by different princes subject to varied allegiances, but in the course of the thirteenth and fourteenth centuries all of them came into the hands of the Habsburgs, who had won possession of the neighboring territory of Austria under Rudolf I (1273-1291). This long association of the Slovenes with Vienna and with the Habsburg champions of Catholic Christianity has profoundly affected their cultural and economic development.

The Balkans. The hundred years from 1350 to 1450 brought tremendous changes south of the lower Danube. The Bulgarian Empire had collapsed under the attack of the Byzantine emperor in 1018, and for the following century and a half Bulgaria had been an integral part of the Eastern Empire. In 1186 a second Bulgarian Empire had arisen and had maintained a precarious existence for two centuries. In the middle of the fourteenth century, the Bulgarian Tsar married the daughter of Stephen Dushan (1331-1355), the greatest of Serb rulers. Under Dushan, the Serbs dominated the Balkan Peninsula for a few brief years. In 1389, however, the Ottoman Turks defeated a coalition of Balkan armies in the famous battle of Kossovo. This victory marked the first great Turkish success in Europe. After conquering most of the Balkan Peninsula, the Turks turned to besiege Constantinople, which they had originally by-passed. With the capture of this city in 1453, the Byzantine Empire came to an end. Within the next few years the Turks completed their conquest of the Balkans, mopping up the few remaining Greek outposts in Morea and extending their control to Wallachia (1462), Bosnia (1463), and Albania (1479).

The fall of the Byzantine Empire marks an epoch in world history. Now the Roman Empire had truly come to an end, the control of the holy places had definitely passed into Moslem hands, and the Cathedral of St. Sophia, the symbol of the leadership of Eastern Orthodoxy, was converted into a mosque. At the same time Christian Europe, itself beset with ever increasing religious controversy, was confronted by a powerful new ideological foe. In the east a rising new power, the Principality of Moscow, laid ominous claim to the imperial heritage of the Byzantine emperors.

Russia. By the middle of the ninth century, a number of important city states were located along the so-called eastern water route from the Baltic to the Black Sea—Novgorod in the north, Smolensk in the middle, and Kiev in the south. These cities controlled the important trade with Constantinople. Kiev, thanks to the aid of certain Viking invaders (known as *Varangians* in Russian history), established its supremacy in the period 882-1132. During this time of Kiev's dominance, the Russians received Christianity as taught by the Church at Constantinople. Subsequent invasions, particularly the Mongolian incursions, caused the Kiev state to disintegrate into many principalities. The rulers of the Golden Horde exercised only weak control over the more westerly sections of their Empire. By the middle of the fourteenth century, the Dukes of Lithuania extended their dominance to the plains of the Black Sea. Many of these peoples were only too glad to come under the protection of Christian Polish or Lithuanian princes in order to escape the harsher levies of the Tartar Khans.

To the east of the Lithuanian state, the Principality of Moscow began to achieve prominence. Its first ruler of significance was Ivan I (1325-1341), who received the surname Kalita (Moneybag) because of his parsimony. He purchased special privileges from his Tartar overlords and in turn was commissioned by them to collect tribute from other princes. "To him who hath shall be given," and the princes of Moscow prospered, gradually adding one bit of territory after another to their domain. The creation of modern Russia is an expansion of the Principality of Moscow, much as the creation of modern France is a result of additions of territory to the Capetian possession of the *Ile de France*.

In 1462 Ivan III, to be known in history as "Ivan the Great" and as the first sovereign of the modern Russian state, became Prince of Moscow. The Khans of the Golden Horde had already been weakened by new attacks from Asia under Timur the Great (1369-1405), and Ivan now broke their domination in Russia. In 1472 he married the niece of the last Byzantine emperor and announced himself heir of the Roman emperors and Protector of the Orthodox Church. The double eagle of the Byzantine Empire was adopted as the Russian coat of arms.

Genealogists went so far as to trace Ivan's descent, by a stretch of imagination, back to Caesar Augustus. Ivan also challenged the power of his western neighbors, Poland-Lithuania, without much success, although this presages the next historical period to be surveyed.

Political Development, 1450-1700

General pattern. The next political epoch which lends itself to summation ends with the seventeenth century. In this period, from about 1450 to 1700, much of Central-Eastern Europe was divided among three great imperial states: the strong Swedish power in the north, the Polish-Lithuanian state in the center and east, and the vastly expanded Ottoman Empire in the southeast. Equally important was the foundation in this period of the power of three border states, Romanov Russia, Habsburg Austria and Hungary, and Hohenzollern Prussia, which in the eighteenth century were substantially to liquidate the above-mentioned states and establish a new imperialism of their own. It is also significant that at this time the future boundaries of Roman Catholicism, Greek Orthodoxy, and Protestantism were drawn.

Sweden. In 1523 Sweden broke away from Denmark and Norway, with which she had been joined since the Union of Kalmar of 1387. Under the leadership of the House of Vasa, Sweden now successfully challenged the trade monopoly exercised by the Hanseatic League in the Baltic. In fact, the League disappeared as an international power in the seventeenth century. Already in possession of Finland, Sweden acquired Estonia, Livonia, and important sections of northern Germany (Pomerania) in the course of the sixteenth and seventeenth centuries. In this period, Sweden was by far the strongest power in the Baltic region. As a leading Protestant state, Sweden took a prominent part in the last phases of the Thirty Years' War, which devastated Germany in 1618-1648. Having adopted Lutheranism, Sweden furthered this religion in the areas under its control. In accord with the doctrines of the universal priesthood of all believers and that a person should seek his own salvation in the Scriptures, the Lutheran clergy did much to encourage native schools. This resulted in a high degree of literacy in Finland, Estonia, and Livonia which is noteworthy even to the present day. On the whole, Swedish dominance, in comparison with what existed before and what was to follow, provided an era of enlightened government and administration.

Poland-Lithuania. The Polish-Lithuanian personal union inaugurated in 1386 by the marriage of Jagiello of Lithuania and Jadwiga of Poland was consolidated in 1569 by the Union of Lublin. The Poles had gradually become the dominant partner. Henceforth Lithuania and Poland were to have a common sovereign and a common Diet, although Lithuania was still to have its separate administrative system and its own army. In 1466 Poland had again defeated the Order of Teutonic Knights, and this time the territories of the Knights were divided. Poland received West Prussia, including the city of Danzig, while the Order retained East Prussia, including Memel, as a fief of the Polish kingdom.

Here was a fundamental division of territory that was to cause much difficulty in subsequent years. In 1525, under the leadership of Albert of Hohenzollern, the lands of the Order were secularized, but they still remained a fief of Poland. In 1618, through a marriage alliance, East Prussia came into the possession of a branch of the Hohenzollern family that was ruling in Brandenburg. At about the same time, these Hohenzollerns also obtained possession of Cleve and its dependencies of Mark and Ravensberg on the Rhine, thus becoming involved in Western as well as Eastern European affairs. The growth of Prussian power is largely the story of the territorial unification of these three territorial areas: Cleve, Brandenburg, and East Prussia. It was a long historic process, and it ran counter to Poland's historic claim to a share of the Baltic coast. In 1657 the Polish king was forced to relinquish his claim of suzerainty over East Prussia, and this territory became the first bit of land held by the Hohenzollern family without any obligations to a superior sovereignty. For this reason, when the Hohenzollerns were granted the title of "King" by the Emperor in 1701, they chose to be known as "Kings in Prussia." "Kings *in* Prussia," rather than "Kings *of* Prussia," because as yet there were important Prussian territories under the Polish crown.

The defeat and liquidation of the Teutonic Order ended German eastward expansion. The Poles gradually replaced many of the German colonists. During the sixteenth century, Poland followed one of the most liberal religious policies of any state. More Jews sought its protection and Protestantism spread throughout the land. In the seventeenth century, the country was won back to Catholicism, largely through the energetic efforts of the Jesuits. The fact that the Poles and Lithuanians remained Roman Catholic in the end has had important effects on the later relations of Poland to Protestant Prussia to the north and west, and to Orthodox Russia to the east.

The Polish-Lithuanian state on the whole held its own against the rising power of the Princes of Moscow up to the end of the seventeenth century. During the Time of Troubles (1604-1613), a period of civil warfare in Russia, a Polish candidate for the Russian throne achieved his brief day of glory. Although there were many wars, the only territory that Poland lost was the city of Kiev and a small surrounding area. Under the able leadership of King John Sobieski (1674-1696), the Poles successfully withstood Turkish onslaughts from the south and in 1683 broke the second Turkish siege of Vienna.

This rescue of Western Christian civilization from Turkish conquest marks the apogee of Polish power. The Polish kingdom was already stricken with grave internal weakness. The nobility in Poland had long possessed special powers which they began to use more and more for their own feudal class interests and less for the nation as a whole. Poland had long been an elective monarchy, and each election was apt to bring civil strife and more privileges for the group of nobles who won. The seventeenth century ended with Augustus II (1697-1732), elector of Saxony, on the Polish throne. Already involved in German politics via Prussian territories, Poland was thus drawn in still further.

The expansion of the Turkish Empire. The capture of Constantinople in 1453 gave great impetus to Turkish expansion. In 1516-1517 the Turks conquered Syria and Egypt, in 1534 they won Tunis, and in the next year they overran the territory around the Red Sea, extending their power even into Persia. In Europe they continued their drive beyond the Danube, and in 1526 they decisively defeated the Hungarians in the battle of Mohács. In this battle Louis, King of Hungary as well as of Bohemia, was killed, and Ferdinand of Habsburg, Archduke of Austria, was elected to both vacant thrones. Ferdinand was the brother of Emperor Charles V, who controlled not only the Germanies, the Lowlands, and large portions of Italy, but Spain and vast territories in America as well. The desire to obtain Habsburg aid against the Turkish invaders no doubt played a part in Ferdinand's election to the Bohemian and Hungarian thrones. This fateful choice laid the foundation for Habsburg domination of the Danube valley in the following centuries. After the battle of Mohács, the Turks pressed on to besiege Vienna in 1529. Unable to take the city, they returned to Hungary, where a peace negotiated in 1533 left only the western fringe of his Hungarian possessions to Ferdinand. Peace did not last along the frontier, and the chronicle of Habsburg-led expeditions against the Turks is a long one. Gradually one bit of territory after another was won back.

In this period Transylvania, under Turkish suzerainty, asserted its greatest degree of independence. With the end of the Thirty Years' War in 1648, the Habsburg rulers were able to devote more attention to their eastern possessions. Their policy of restoring Catholicism by force brought with it one of the bitterest periods of persecution for the Hungarians, who had quite generally accepted Protestantism. Catholicism and German control came to be considered synonymous, and tremendous anti-German feeling was aroused in Hungary. Transylvania, still under Turkish control, was less affected by this strife. The renewed aggressive eastern policy of the rulers at Vienna, however, roused the Turks to action. As already indicated, they were again at the gates of Vienna in 1683. Finally, by the Treaty of Karlowitz (1699) they were forced to retreat behind the Save-Danube frontier. They still controlled the Banat of Temesvár, Wallachia, Moldavia, and the territory around the Black Sea, but Russia, under the vigorous leadership of Peter the Great, was ready to take up the gage that was slipping from the hands of the Polish king.

The subjection of the Balkans and much of Central Europe to Turkish domination laid a blight on these regions. There was no great amount of religious persecution and Christians were generally left unmolested as long as they paid their taxes. On the other hand, Christians could not participate in governmental affairs or share in the many privileges which resulted from service in the army unless they accepted Mohammedanism. In Bosnia-Herzegovina, especially, a number of the nobility took this way out to regain their former position of influence. The people themselves were often subject to harsh rule by local petty governors, who were given a free hand by the government at Constantinople. The Janissaries, a special Turkish military corps partly recruited from Christian children who were separated from their parents, often established local despotisms. Being an Asiatic-North African power as well, Turkey introduced many practices and customs of this area into Europe. Little effort was made to improve industrial or agricultural methods, while culture and education were neglected.

The Greeks had some advantages possessed by none of the other nationalities. Very early the Turkish Government negotiated an agreement whereby the Greek Patriarch at Constantinople represented all the Christian subjects within the Ottoman Empire. Greeks gravitated into many positions of importance. For many years the Sultan appointed Phanariot Greeks (who took their name from the district of Constantinople where they lived) to act as provincial governors, notably in Moldavia and Wallachia. Their rapacious collection of taxes naturally aroused intense hatred, and this resentment is sometimes advanced as the reason why the Greek revolt of 1821 aroused so little enthusiasm in other Balkan lands.

Summary. In general, the period from the fifteenth to the seventeenth century established the three powers of Sweden, Poland-Lithuania, and Turkey as dominant in Central-Eastern Europe. But, as is always true in history, these centuries also nourished the seeds of future change. Reference has already been made to the foundation of the power of Hohenzollern Prussia and Habsburg Austria, Bohemia, and Hungary. A brief word remains to be said about Romanov Russia.

The Tsars who succeeded Ivan III, the real founder of modern Russia, were kept busy fighting for supremacy over the landed nobility. They also continually challenged the authority of Poland. Ivan IV (1535-1584), surnamed "the Terrible" because of his ruthless policy against certain groups of his nobility, is especially to be remembered for inaugurating a western policy for Russia. Disputes over succession to the throne led to a period of disintegration and strife known as the "Time of Troubles" that lasted until the election of Michael Romanov as Tsar in 1613. At the beginning of the eighteenth century, one of the most remarkable rulers in world history reached the throne of Russia. Peter I, the Great, was bent on westernizing his country and undertook an aggressive policy of expansion. Russia and all of Europe entered upon a new era, for Peter's reign coincided with the end of the reign of Louis XIV in France. Henceforth Russia was involved in the general wars of Europe, and all the territories of Central-Eastern Europe took on new significance in the high diplomacy of European chancellors.

Political Development, the Eighteenth Century

General pattern. The eighteenth century was an era of power politics par excellence. Religion played a much less important role in the wars of this period, and only at the end of the century did the revolutionary conflicts introduce a certain ideological bias. It was the Age of the Philosophers and of the Enlightened Despots, whose reforms were not always well received by the old privileged groups. This was particularly true of the work of Joseph II in Austria. But even the most enlightened despots believed that natural law gave right to the stronger and acted accordingly.

The century started with the liquidation of Sweden as a great power. Through the Great Northern War (1700-1721), Peter the Great established Russia's future position in the Baltic and brought the Estonians and many of the Latvians under his control. As he favored the German Baltic barons, the native Estonians and Letts became more than ever hewers of wood and drawers of water.

Under Frederick the Great (1740-1786), Prussia rose to the rank of a great European power and a challenge to Habsburg control of Central Europe. Poland, beset by internal difficulties, became a disturbing factor in European politics largely because of its elective crown. Various countries tried to win control of this valuable land by establishing their own puppets on the Polish throne. As a result, there were German, Swedish, French, and Russian candidates for what should have been a purely Polish office. French support of Stanislas Lesczynski in the War of the Polish Succession (1733-1735) was the real start of a long history of Franco-Polish friendship, a friendship resting on the basis of mutual antagonism to a strong German power.

Russia, Prussia, and Austria boldly and unscrupulously carved up the ancient Polish-Lithuanian state in the famous three Partitions of Poland in 1772, 1793, and 1795. Hardly were these partitions completed when Napoleon set about redrawing the map of Europe. In 1807 he resurrected Poland by establishing a Duchy of Warsaw. Napoleon did not separate East Prussia from the rest of the Prussian state by giving the Poles access to the sea, but established a landlocked Polish duchy. No attempt was made to restore Poland as it existed before the partitions. A fifth settlement of Poland was soon to follow, at the Congress of Vienna. The Congress Kingdom of Poland, included within the Russian Empire, constituted most of the old Duchy of Warsaw, although significant Polish minorities were left to Austria and Prussia.

In addition to these vast Polish territories in the north and west, Russia under Catherine the Great (1762-1796) won from Turkey the shores of the Black Sea. During the French Revolutionary Wars, Russian acquisitions were rounded out by the conquest of Bessarabia in the south and of Finland in the north. After 1815 Russia was to expand no further westward until her seizure of the Bukovina in 1940.

What influence Austria lost in German affairs in the eighteenth century through the ascendancy of Prussia was compensated for by the acquisition of areas from Poland and the consolidation of Habsburg territories to the south and east. By 1815 Turkey, while retaining the Balkan Peninsula inclusive of Bosnia-Herzegovina, had lost all territories beyond the Danube except for certain rights of suzerainty over Wallachia and Moldavia.

The eighteenth century, which of necessity must be extended to the close of the Napoleonic Era in 1815, thus witnessed great changes in Central-Eastern Europe. Russia, Prussia, and Austria now stood face to face, having appropriated the former borderlands with their peoples. Turkey was already considered the sick man of Europe, and it was not beyond the realm of possibility that Russia and Austria might administer the same medicine to Turkey that they had used for Poland.

Political Development, 1815-1918

General pattern. After 1815 other forces appeared which tended to prevent the use in European Turkey of methods similar to those used in Poland. First of all, Turkey was not left to Russia and Austria to settle between themselves, because Great Britain and France as maritime powers were determined to have a word to say in this area, especially in regard to the Straits. Then, too, this region was profoundly affected by the awakening of democracy and nationalism that took place in Europe after the French Revolution. This movement not only stimulated the people of the Balkans to fight for their own independence as national states, but also threatened the stability of the great powers and in a measure tamed their aggressive foreign policies. After the national revolutionary upheavals of nineteenth century Europe, incorporation of new minority groups within a body politic did not seem so attractive as it once did. This was particularly true when the existence of many national groups within a state made it more and more difficult to satisfy the growing demands of the people for more democratic governments.

Even if outright annexation of territory was to be impossible, the big powers were not willing to let the small nations alone. Now more than ever it became important, either through aid or by threats, to win a position of influence in the capitals of the small states. This was a game of power politics, which could be played by remote control. England, France, modern Germany, and Italy all played a hand, although they could claim no interests growing out of direct geographic propinquity, as could Russia or Austria-Hungary. Nor should it be forgotten that the small nations all too often called in foreign aid and tied themselves to the apron strings of some great foreign power in order to obtain some momentary advantage, very often against a neighboring small nationality. In 1815 and for some time after, Russians, Austrians, and Turks generally called the tunes to which the peoples of Central-Eastern Europe danced. In some regions more than others, the people joined in the choruses, if indeed they did not choose the theme song.

Russia. In the far north, Finland as a separate grand duchy of Russia had unusual liberties due to its special status of autonomy. Only at the end of the century were these curtailed. The Poles, because they had the courage to raise the standard of rebellion (in 1830, and in 1863), found that their privileges were progressively restricted. The policy of Russification that was pushed with renewed vigor in the last decades of the nineteenth century bore heavily on all the submerged nationalities of Russia.

Austria-Hungary. In 1867 the Magyars were able to win an equal status with the Austrians, when the dual monarchy of Austria-Hungary was organized. But the privileges they obtained at the expense of the Germans of Austria, the Magyars in turn were unwilling to share with the Slovakians, Romanians, and Serbs under their rule. Only the Croats were able to maintain a precarious measure of autonomy. In the Austrian section of the empire, the smaller nationalities remained unsatisfied although they had more privileges than were possessed by the minority nationalities in Hungary, in Russia, or, at a later period, in some of the post-war states.

Turkey. If the Turkish Empire was not entirely carved up *à la* Poland in this period, it nevertheless was well liquidated. The process started when the Greeks obtained their independence in 1829. At the same time, Serbia, Wallachia, and Moldavia received a status of autonomy, to be followed by recognition of their independence at the Congress of Berlin in 1878. Montenegro, never fully subjugated by the Turks, was also awarded full recognition as an independent state, while Bulgaria had to wait until 1908. Finally, as a result of the Balkan Wars of 1912-1913, when Turkish territory was restricted to the very tip of the Balkan Peninsula opposite the Bosporus and the Dardanelles, an independent Albania was created.

The great powers also shared in the spoils of the Turkish Empire. Austria-Hungary in 1878 obtained a protectorate over the provinces of Bosnia-Herzegovina, which in 1908 were definitely annexed. France acquired Tunis in 1882; Italy obtained Libya and the Dodecanese Islands in 1912; England got Cyprus in 1878 and control over the Suez Canal (1875) and Egypt (1882). In addition to these territorial acquisitions, all the great powers obtained from Turkey vast economic concessions which, indirectly at least, jeopardized her independence.

First World War. The First World War (1914-1918) continued the process of the liberation of small nationalities and the creation of national states which was so characteristic of the nineteenth century. It was now time for the Habsburg, Hohenzollern, and Romanov stars to set. Now, at long last, self-government was restored to a large part of Central-Eastern Europe. Whereas in 1815 Germans, Russians, and Turks dominated this region, these three now had to share power with an independent Finland, Estonia, Latvia, Lithuania, Poland, Czechoslovakia, Austria, Hungary, Romania, Yugoslavia, Bulgaria, Albania, and Greece. Only Montenegro disappeared from the map, having been incorporated into the newly created South Slav state.

But independence did not bring unity or harmony to Central-Eastern Europe. Austria was forced by the larger powers to stand alone, whereas in 1919 most Austrians would have preferred to unite with republican Germany. Boundaries were not always wisely drawn, and a whole new crop of minority problems were born. Communication systems built in the old era did not always serve well under the new dispensation. Old trading relations had to be revised and new ones created. Age-old territorial rivalries were not quelled, and in some cases imperialistic appetites were whetted. Hungary and Bulgaria had been forced to pay the historic price for defeat in extensive territorial cessions and consequently were particularly bitter. Nor were the great powers removed from the scene. Long historical processes and interests are not easily severed. Above all, Germany and Russia never renounced their interest in these neighboring areas which they had dominated for so many years and with which they were so closely associated. France and England also continued to play power politics and made use of some of the smaller powers to further their own interests.

Conclusion

Basic to the study of the history of Central-Eastern Europe is a knowledge of how these territories came to be settled by the mosaic of nationalities which have remained fairly stationary there since the eleventh century. In the Middle Ages, many of these peoples at one time or another set up their independent governments, only to be absorbed into larger and stronger imperial states. These in turn were subject to liquidation and reshuffling, but the peoples remained rooted in their good earth, to emerge in 1918, at least for a time, as captains of their own destinies.

Religion and political dominance have divided the peoples and have given to certain of them a more western orientation than to others. Yet none of them have lived apart from the general stream of European and world history. This is especially true in the more modern period, with its expansion of trade, its better means of communication, its rapid expansion of literacy, its great exchange of ideas. None of these peoples remained untouched by the ideals of the French Revolution, which acted as a tremendous stimulus to them throughout the nineteenth century. Finally coming to fruition in 1918, western liberalism profoundly affected the new governments which the peoples gave themselves and to which they paid sincere homage for at least a brief period.

Bibliography

Bell, H. T. Montague, *The Near East Year Book 1931-2* (London: The Near East, 1931). Along with a mass of information on modern conditions, this book contains excellent descriptive accounts of geography, population, climate, flora, fauna, and so forth. The chapters on religion are particularly useful.

Halecki, Oskar, "The Historical Role of Central-Eastern Europe," *The Annals of the American Academy of Political and Social Science,* Vol. CCXXXII (March, 1944), pp. 9-18.

Hanč, Josef, *Tornado Across Eastern Europe. The Path of Nazi Destruction from Poland to Greece* (New York: Greystone Press, 1942). Also published, with different pagination, as *Eastern Europe* (London: Museum Press, 1943). While dealing primarily with the history of Eastern Europe since World War I, it has a good introduction on the land and peoples of this region. Contains a useful general bibliography.

Jászi, Oscar, *The Dissolution of the Hapsburg Monarchy* (Chicago: University of Chicago Press, 1929). A mine of information.

Jordan, Peter, *Central Union of Europe* (New York: Robert M. McBride & Co., 1944). A plea for the establishment of a federation made up of the states between Germany and Russia. No plans are divulged as to how this federation is to be administered.

Kohn, Hans, *The Idea of Nationalism. A Study in Its Origins and Background* (New York: Macmillan, 1944).

Macartney, C. A., *Hungary and Her Successors. The Treaty of Trianon and Its Consequences* (London: Oxford University Press, 1937). The general introduction and the summary of the history of each of the provinces lost by Hungary after World War I are especially useful.

————, *National States and National Minorities* (London: Oxford University Press, 1934). Part I is the best account available of the development of national minorities in Europe. Part II is devoted to minorities treaties under the League of Nations.

————, *Problems of the Danube Basin* (Cambridge: University Press, 1942). An excellent short summary in the *Current Problems* series edited by Ernest Barker.

Possony, Stefan T., "Political and Military Geography of Central, Balkan, and Eastern Europe," *The Annals of the American Academy of Political and Social Science,* Vol. CCXXXII (March, 1944), pp. 1-8.

Reddaway, W. F., *Problems of the Baltic* (Cambridge: University Press, 1940). A volume in the *Current Problems* series.

Royal Institute of International Affairs, *Nationalism* (London: Oxford University Press, 1939). Prepared by a group of scholars, this book deals with the growth of nationalism among the different peoples of Europe.

Taylor, D. P. Stephen, ed., *Handbook of Central and East Europe* (Zurich: Central European Times Publishing Co., first ed., 1932/33). Contains convenient historical summaries along with a variety of information on geography, climate, flora, mineral deposits, and so forth, of the various countries.

Wanklyn, H. G., *The Eastern Marchlands of Europe* (London: George Philip & Son, 1941). Written by a geographer, this book contains many valuable maps and much pertinent information on Finland, Estonia, Latvia, Lithuania, Poland, Czechoslovakia, Hungary, and Yugoslavia.

Wiskemann, Elizabeth, *Czechs and Germans. A Study of the Struggle in the Historic Provinces of Bohemia and Moravia* (London: Oxford University Press, 1938). A very fine study of this problem issued under the auspices of the Royal Institute of International Affairs.

See bibliographies of later chapters for books on separate countries.

PART II

PART II

CHAPTER II

AUSTRIA-HUNGARY

The Anachronism of Austria

THE Austrian Empire was the creation of one family. In the course of its six centuries of existence, the Habsburg dynasty built up around the middle Danube a state which was held together largely by loyalty to the ruling family, a dynastic estate rather than a nation-state in the sense of Britain or France or Sweden. Dynastic motives and the incidents of history gathered together a territory where many races, nationalities, and languages intermingled. Only in the nineteenth century did it become a constitutional unit, the Austrian (and, after 1867, the Austro-Hungarian) monarchy. Its new form coincided with the rise of nationalism in Central Europe, which in many ways rendered the Austrian monarchy an anachronism bitterly contested by its component nationalities, German and Magyar, Czech and Croat, Polish and Italian. Throughout the nineteenth century, from the end of the Napoleonic wars to the end of the First World War, the monarchy stood out as a conservative force against the new movements of the period which threatened its existence. During this whole century it showed a surprising continuity, for it was truly ruled by two statesmen only: by Prince Metternich from 1815 to 1848, by Emperor Francis Joseph from 1848 to 1916. Both visualized their task as the preservation of the heritage of the past, though the methods they employed changed with the changing social and intellectual climate of the period.

The strange political structure of the Habsburg monarchy fulfilled a unifying and civilizing mission in its early history, not without some success and some dignity. In the nineteenth century it lacked the surging vitality of some of the more progressive countries like modern Germany, but its slower and quieter pace of life had a mellow and melancholic charm. Within the vast realm, with its surprising diversity of folkways, tongues, and creeds, of landscape and climate, a traditional civilization formed a uniform surface beneath which the energies of

rising classes and young national movements, released by the forces of
the new age, clamored for greater scope than the old structure was able
or willing to allow them. The lands of the monarchy formed a geographic and economic unit. Their united forces had protected Europe
against the Turks in the sixteenth and seventeenth centuries and served
as a bulwark against Prussian and Russian expansion in the nineteenth
century. It is possible that such a union in the twentieth century
could have accomplished an important task for the stabilization of
Europe by providing strategic security and economic well-being for its
members. But the domineering egoism of the Magyars and Germans
did not allow the transformation of the ancient monarchy into the
modern federation of free and equal peoples which a great Czech patriot, František Palacký, had proposed in the middle of the nineteenth
century. Nationalism, especially among the Magyars and Germans,
became too fierce a force to allow the full working of that spirit of
compromise and toleration that was noticeable after 1867 in the administration of the Austrian or western part of the dual monarchy of
Austria-Hungary.

Though their nationalism was young and exuberant in the nineteenth century, the peoples composing the monarchy were old. Their
history, full of bitter conflicts with their neighbors, goes back for a
thousand years. Their generations have grown up with all the rancor
of the past in their hearts, always conscious of memories of defeat and
victory, of oppression and triumph. The peoples of Central Europe
are profoundly history-minded. The shadows of the past loom large
over these ancient battlegrounds of races, creeds, and civilizations.
Their present aspirations are understandable only with a knowledge of
the past in which the Habsburg empire, now irrevocably gone, has
played so great a role.

The Habsburgs and Austria

In the year 1273 Rudolf, a scion of the southwestern German noble
house of Habsburg, was elected Emperor of Germany. He met successfully the challenge of Přemysl Otakar II, the powerful King of Bohemia, whose influence reached from the Baltic to the Adriatic and
who wished to secure the crown of the Holy Roman Empire for himself. Rudolf's victory in 1278 not only confirmed his royal position but
gave him the opportunity to establish his family along the middle Danube in Austria, Styria, and Carinthia. Austria, which until then had
been an eastern German outpost against Avars and Magyars, now be-

came the center of an agglomeration of power which finally included the ancient kingdoms of Bohemia and Hungary.

These beginnings of Habsburg Austria coincided with a momentous shift in German development. Before 1300, Germany had looked to the south and west. Its conquering armies marched in that direction, and from there higher forms of civilization and economic wealth enriched the relatively backward lands east of the Rhine. But in the thirteenth century, the Germans turned eastward to expand into lands which were culturally and economically weaker than their own. Though Germany's cultural and economic strength remained in the west, where the fertilizing ideas of Western civilization could enter more easily from France and Italy, the seat of German political power in Germany shifted to the east. There dynasties from western Germany, the Habsburgs in Austria, the Luxemburgs in Bohemia, and later the Hohenzollerns in Brandenburg and Prussia, tried to secure the leadership of Germany and to raise their capitals into centers of influence. The first universities in Central Europe were founded in Prague and Vienna, which became the early seats of the new learning which began to cross the Alps.

Origins of Hungary

From the beginning, Austria had been an eastern march (*Ostmark*) of Germany, first established by Charlemagne as a defense against the Avars. The Avars were one of the three nomadic peoples of the Ural-Altaic race group who had, in successive waves, made their headquarters in the fertile plains between the middle Danube and the Theiss rivers. The first wave was formed by the Huns, who overran Europe in the fourth and fifth centuries. The Avars followed in the eighth century. But only the third wave, the Magyars under the leadership of Arpad, the founder of their ruling dynasty, were able to establish a permanent government and to live a settled national existence. They had come to Hungary at the end of the ninth century, destroyed the great Moravian kingdom, and subjugated the Slav and Wallachian peoples who lived in the semicircle of the Carpathian mountains surrounding the Danube valley in the north. Their westward raids were stopped by the battle of Augsburg in 955, after which Austria reestablished its eastern bulwark against them. Whereas Vienna was changed during the Babenberg dynasty (976-1246) from a frontier post to a flourishing center of poetry and court life, Hungary, under its two great rulers Geza (972-997) and Stephen (997-1038), was Christianized and opened to the influx of Western civilization. Stephen was crowned king in 1001 with a crown sent by the Pope, and later canonized by the Church as the patron saint of his country. Under his successors, the frontier regions were protected by military settlements; German colonists, the so-called Saxons, were invited to settle in the Zips in northern Slovakia and in southern Transylvania; and Croatia was conquered by Ladislas I (1077-1095). It joined with Hungary in 1102 in a dynastic union. In the thirteenth century, Hungary declined as the power of the feudal nobility which gained control of the country increased and as the Mongol incursions became more numerous.

The Flowering of the Habsburgs

At the beginning of the fourteenth century, the national dynasties which had founded the kingdoms of Bohemia, Hungary, and Poland were extinguished. Thereafter, princes often ascended the thrones of these countries through intermarriage. In the following centuries, Bohemia, Austria, Hungary, and frequently Poland were repeatedly ruled by kings of the same house, and several attempts were made to unite them permanently, with either Prague, Budapest, or Vienna as the common capital. The Habsburgs finally succeeded in that task, thanks to their felicitous policy of wise marriage and to the crown of the Holy Roman Empire, which they possessed without interruption—except for the five years 1740-1745—from 1438 until 1806. "Emperor" and "Habsburg" became almost synonymous. Vienna grew into a truly imperial city where the great routes of Central Europe crossed and where the cultural influences of Spain and Italy, of Germany and the East, freely mingled.

This cosmopolitan atmosphere mirrored the world-wide ties of the Habsburg family. Frederick III (1440-1493) married his son Maximilian I (1493-1519) to the heiress of Burgundy and the Netherlands; their son in turn married the heiress of Aragon and Castile, who brought to the Habsburg family the possession of a united Spain and of its vast dominions in the New World. But Maximilian did not overlook the older Central European aspirations. He concluded an agreement with Ladislas II, a scion of the Lithuanian-Polish royal house of Jagiello and King of Bohemia (1471-1516) and of Hungary (1490-1516), by which Maximilian or his descendants would inherit the crowns of Bohemia and Hungary in case of the extinction of Ladislas' line. Ladislas' only son, Louis II, King of Bohemia and Hungary (1516-1526), fell at the age of twenty in the disastrous battle of Mohács against the Turks. Maximilian's younger son Ferdinand I, who inherited the Austrian lands after his father's death (1519) and followed his older brother as emperor (1556), married Louis' sister Anne and was elected King of Bohemia and of Hungary in 1526.

Thus began the union which was to last until 1918. "Bella gerant alii, tu felix Austria nube!"—a happy family policy had brought immense domains from the Pacific to the border of Turkey under Habsburg sway. But the eastern borders of the vast realm were far from safe. As the result of their victory at Mohács, the Turks occupied most of Hungary, including the capital, Ofen. For two hundred years thereafter the Habsburgs had to fight the Turks, who laid siege to Vienna for the first time in 1529. The defensive warfare lasted until 1683. In that year the Turks appeared at the gates of Vienna for the second and last time. The city was valiantly defended by its garrison under Rüdiger von Starhemberg and was relieved by German and Polish armies under Charles of Lorraine and Jan Sobieski. This event marked the turning point of Austro-Turkish relations. The Turkish danger to Europe had passed; the Turkish retreat began under Austrian and soon also under Russian pressure. In 1687 the Austrians defeated the Turks in the second battle of Mohács, and the Hungarian Diet in Pressburg elected the Habsburgs hereditary rulers of Hungary. The treaty of Karlowitz (1699) confirmed Austria's possession of Hungary, Transylvania, Croatia, and Slavonia. Fifteen years later, the Austrians resumed the war and Eugene of Savoy captured Belgrade (1717). The long-drawn-out wars between Austria and Turkey ended only in 1791, a little more than a century after the last Turkish siege of Vienna. The Austrian frontier toward the Balkans had been stabilized for the nineteenth century, corresponding roughly with the boundary between the spheres of Roman and Greek Christendom.

Before the Turkish menace had receded, the Habsburg monarchy successfully weathered the threat of religious diversity. The Thirty Years' War (1618-1648), which began in Bohemia as a conflict between Catholic and Protestant Europe, added religious uniformity to the dynastic tie as a foundation of the Habsburg realm. Ferdinand II (1619-1637) promoted the Counter Reformation most actively throughout his domain. Higher education was entrusted to the Jesuits, and the monumental style of the triumphant Church—the baroque—became dominant in the architecture and music of the period, impressing itself upon the face of Austrian cities and the rhythm of Austrian life.

The male line of the Habsburgs came to an end with Charles VI (1711-1740). The order of succession which he established, under the name of "Pragmatic Sanction," called to the throne, in the absence of male heirs, his oldest daughter Maria Theresa. In 1736, she married Francis of Lorraine, later grand duke of Tuscany and, as the "prince-consort" of the Habsburg heiress, German emperor (1745-1765). At the same time, the Pragmatic Sanction declared for the first time that the different lands ruled by the Habsburgs were an indivisible unit. A common name was still lacking: Charles VI was Archduke of Austria, King of Bohemia, King of Hungary, and so forth, and international usage spoke of the "maison d'Autriche." During the eighteenth century, the enlightened absolutism of the period endowed the various countries under Habsburg rule with centralized institutions and a modern bureaucracy. Maria Theresa (1740-1780) and her two sons, Joseph II (1780-1790) and Leopold II (1790-1792), promoted the welfare of the people in the spirit of the age, alleviated the condition of the peasantry, modernized and broadened the educational system, and reformed judicial procedure. Joseph II, a typical representative of the rational Enlightenment, granted civic rights to non-Catholics in his edict of tolerance (1781). His controversial innovations, aimed at a thorough modernization and a higher efficiency of the administration, provoked the resistance of the estates which represented the privileged classes and their traditional "liberties." His plans for a regeneration of the German Empire and a stronger position for its head were thwarted by Prussia.

Under the leadership of Frederick William I (1713-1740) and of his son Frederick II (1740-1786), Prussia had concentrated all the resources of the state upon building an army which surpassed all others in efficiency and preparedness.[1] With its help Frederick II, with the aim of annexing the rich province of Silesia, successfully attacked Austria in 1740. In three wars, of which the third or Seven Years' War (1756-1763) widened the conflict, through alliances, into a world war fought in Europe, America, and India, Prussia was able to retain Silesia. From then on, Prussia competed with Austria for the leadership of Germany in a bitter struggle lasting for more than a century. Prussia gained ad-

---

[1] On the foundation of Prussian power, see Robert Ergang, *The Potsdam Führer Frederick William I, Father of Prussian Militarism* (New York: Columbia University Press, 1941). The best recent judgment on the reign of Frederick II is in Leo Gershoy, *From Despotism to Revolution* (New York: Harper, 1944): "In a world moving toward the liberating play of bourgeois enterprise and free international exchange, Prussian purposes and ends remained, theory notwithstanding, outmoded and reactionary in practice . . . Frederick was enlightened but not liberal. The Gallic veneer of his personal surroundings was a thin gloss over a great body of barrack brutality." (p. 88f) "Least enlightened was the Prussian embodiment of the mandates of the age. Measured in terms of progressive social aspirations it was a dismal failure." (p. 321) See also Hans Kohn, *The Idea of Nationalism* (New York: Macmillan, 1944), pp. 356-369, and F. W. Foerster, *Europe and the German Question* (New York: Sheed & Ward, 1940).

ditional strength by the acquisition of Polish lands in the east and of the Rhineland in the west. The dismemberment of Poland, a measure originally suggested by Frederick II of Prussia, brought to Austria as her share in the first (1772) and third (1795) partitions Little Poland and Red Russia, the latter largely inhabited by Ukrainians (sometimes called *Ruthenians*). After the Napoleonic wars, Austria retained only the part acquired in the first partition—the province of Galicia, the basin of the upper Vistula, and upper Dniester rivers.[2]

The Monarchy in Modern Times

In the eighteenth century, the Pragmatic Sanction made the Habsburg lands a legal unit, which Maria Theresa and Joseph II provided with a single and coherent administration, but only in 1804 did this factual unity receive an official name. In that year Francis (1792-1835), the last ruler of the Holy Roman Empire—which came to an end in 1806—assumed the title of Francis I, Emperor of Austria. Henceforth Austria embraced all the different lands which, through the fortunes of centuries, the Habsburgs had gathered around their original hereditary possession, the Archduchy of Austria. The Napoleonic wars brought many changes in the position and composition of Austria—for example, Francis, whose aunt had been the wife of Louis XVI, had to accept Napoleon as a son-in-law—but this mediocre and uninspired monarch was able to weather the storms of the French Revolution, which twice almost destroyed Austria. After the defeat of Napoleon, the Habsburgs lost their last outlying dependencies, the Austrian Netherlands and the possessions on the upper Rhine; but in exchange they were confirmed in their acquisition of the legacy of Venice, and their territories for the first time formed a consolidated and unbroken whole. Austria in 1815 not only was the strongest power on the Danube, but exercised preponderant and unchallenged influence in Germany and in Italy and was firmly entrenched at the gateway to the Balkans, where Turkish power continued to disintegrate. No external enemy seemed to threaten her existence. The frontiers of Austria as determined in 1815 remained virtually unchanged until 1918. In that period, Austria lost Lombardy (1859) and Venetia (1866) in Italy; but she also acquired the small republic of Cracow (1846) and the Turkish provinces of Bosnia and Herzegovina, which came under Austrian administration in 1878 and were annexed in 1908.

---

[2] The Austrian Poles enjoyed much greater liberties and an infinitely wider scope of national development than those in Prussia and Russia. In fact, in Austria they belonged to the ruling and most privileged national groups. Galicia, in spite of its very large Ukrainian population, was practically under a Polish administration.

In 1815, Austria's leading position was generally recognized. The peace congress following the Napoleonic wars assembled in Austria's capital, and her foreign minister, Prince Metternich, became the leading European statesman.[3] Born in 1773 in the Rhineland, he became Austrian foreign minister at a critical hour for the empire in 1809. He retained the office, combined after 1821 with the chancellorship, until 1848. He strove for the preservation of the legitimate order and for European solidarity and remained always an eighteenth-century aristocrat, cultured and skeptical, without understanding the new forces which began to undermine the traditional structure of society and to stir deep emotions in the peoples, aroused from their age-old lethargy and unquestioning acceptance of authority. Metternich dimly perceived the need for reforms, but his half-hearted suggestions broke down before the stone wall of Francis' distrust of all new ideas and preference for petty bureaucratic measures which, with the centralization of all affairs at the Emperor's desk, necessarily led to inefficiency and incompetence.

The Habsburg monarchy lived on after 1814 in the bureaucratic forms of the eighteenth century without the reforming spirit and the modernizing energy of the great monarchs of the absolutist period. In that respect Francis' reign resembled that of Tsar Nicolai I of Russia. There was the same reluctance to appeal to the people and to make their support the firm foundation of the realm. Any move in that direction was entirely beyond the horizon of both rulers, who tried to concentrate all power in their own hands, and used the bureaucracy as a simple instrument of their will, allowing the officials no responsibility or initiative. Under these circumstances, the general confusion grew. Although the Austrian bureaucracy was on the whole more honest, much better educated, and even more efficient than the Russian, urgent measures were postponed again and again, so that finally the impression seemed to prevail that most problems could be solved by inaction. Life moved at a very slow pace, creative impulses were submerged, energy and innovations were distrusted. Austria, feverish with activities and ideals under Joseph II, became sleepy and slovenly under his nephew. Even so, life retained much of the softness and charm which made Austrian absolutism, tempered by inefficiency, so much less oppressive than other reigns of that kind.

Things grew much worse after the death of Francis I. His son and successor Ferdinand (1835-1848) was an idiot, incapable of understand-

---

[3] On Metternich (1773-1859), see Arthur Herman, *Metternich* (New York: Appleton-Century, 1932), and Helene du Coudray, *Metternich* (New Haven: Yale University Press, 1936).

ing the affairs of government or of making any decisions. The principle of legitimacy put him on the throne, but a regency or, as it was called, State Conference, governed in his name. It consisted of three elderly men, Metternich himself, the Bohemian Count Kolowrat, and Archduke Ludwig. Kolowrat, who hated Metternich, made himself indispensable by balancing the Austrian budget and by his understanding of financial affairs, the details of which bored Metternich and were beyond his grasp. The bitter hostility between these two men made any constructive work by the State Conference impossible. The third member, Archduke Ludwig, was weak and ineffectual. Metternich's remark that "Austria was administered, but not ruled," was too optimistic: it was not even administered properly, for the administration was paralyzed by a lack of coördination and of clear directives from the top.

Francis' principle of "changing nothing" remained supreme at the very time when the social structure of the empire began to change, when new ideas were penetrating from the West, and when national emotions for the first time began to stir the various peoples comprising the mass of the dynasty's subjects. As a remedy, Metternich tried to revive the ancient Diets of the various provinces, but these Diets themselves were antiquated representatives of privileged classes. Their revival would have marked a step backward from the administrative reforms of Maria Theresa and Joseph II. It was idle to appeal to the ghost of the past to banish the spirit of the new day.

When that day dawned in March, 1848, Metternich's system broke down. The liberals demanded his head, and the dynasty, hoping to save itself, dropped him without hesitation. When Metternich fled to England on March 13 after forty years of continuous leadership, the greatest defect of which lay in the very fact that it was no leadership, the *Vormärz* or pre-March period came to its end. But the general lethargy characteristic of the Metternich era had nowhere nurtured new forces strong enough to build a new structure on the ruins of the past. Ultimately the past, gaining fresh vigor in the revolutionary crisis, seemed to emerge victorious out of the welter of conflicting political ideas of the rising nationalities and classes.

Hungary's Nationalism and Constitutionalism

Of the many nationalities which formed the Austrian Empire, only one had maintained its historical structure unbroken. In Hungary, the constitutional forces of the past had preserved their vigor. Hungary for almost 900 years had formed a historical unit, based not upon language or race, but upon the symbol of the crown of St. Stephen and the privileges of the nobility, which recruited itself from many ethnic groups and used Latin as its official language. The Magyars formed only a minority in the Hungarian kingdom, but they were the largest single group and by far the wealthiest and best educated. Thus they attracted and assimilated the stronger and more progressive elements among the non-Magyar nationalities: the Slovaks, the Germans, the Romanians, and the southern Slavs.

Historically the land was divided into three parts, each with its own Diet: Hungary proper, Transylvania, and Croatia. The Hungarian Diet, which met at Pressburg on the western border of Hungary, only a short distance from Vienna, was the most important. This Diet drew much of its vitality from two sources. One was the charters of feudal privilege which, from the time of the Golden Bull (1222), gave rights to the nobility comparable to those granted in England's Magna Carta. The other was the self-government in the Hungarian counties or comitats, which was in no way democratic but confirmed the rule of the local gentry against the encroachments of a centralizing bureaucracy. But there the analogy with English history ends. In England, Parliament and local self-government became, with the growth of commerce and middle-class influence and under the impact of liberal ideas, the parents of democracy. In Hungary, they grew into a bulwark of the feudal reaction. The Diet consisted of a Table of Magnates representing the high nobility and princes of the Church, and a Table of Deputies elected by the county assemblies of the gentry. The few Hungarian cities were largely German in population and language; the peasants were oppressed and backward. A vigorous monarchy could have appealed to the middle classes, or even to the peasants, for support against the nobility. Joseph II had tried it prematurely; the Habsburgs of the nineteenth century were incapable of doing it. Thus the Hungarian nobility, adopting some of the outward forms of Western political development, could invoke middle-class nationalism and constitutionalism in support of their own power and thus win over the people for their own ends. Bismarck did the same thing in Germany.

After Francis I called the Diet in 1825, following several years of inactivity, the nobility began to make itself the spokesman of a rising Magyar nationalism. Liberal ideas beginning to penetrate from the West found their noblest advocate in Count Stephen Széchenyi, who called attention, after his visit to England, to the backwardness of the Hungarian people and the responsibility of its privileged classes. He pleaded for social reforms and popular education to precede any demand for independence. He also founded the Hungarian Academy of Sciences and promoted the growth of industrialism and modern capitalism.

But Széchenyi soon found himself in opposition to the more radical younger nationalists under Lajos Kossuth (1802-1894), with their spirit of Magyar chauvinism and intolerance toward the non-Magyar populations of Hungary. Of Slovak ancestry, Kossuth became the first representative of the new Magyar middle class who tried, like the German middle class of that period, to combine Western constitutionalism with ardent and expansive nationalism.[4] As a great orator and brilliant journalist, he won popular acclaim and broadened the narrow basis which so far had supported the reclamation of the Hungarian Diet. Under his leadership, an intransigeant demand for Hungarian independence and Magyar supremacy sprang up and grew. Latin was definitely replaced by Magyar as the official language in 1844. The elections to the Table of Deputies in 1847 brought a liberal majority which accepted a reform program of ten points proposed by Francis Deák, the leader of Hungarian liberalism.[5] This program abolished the worst surviving features of Hungarian feudalism, introduced modern constitutionalism, and demanded the incorporation of Transylvania into Hungary. The reforms, rejected by the Table of Magnates, formed the nucleus of the Hungarian constitution that was finally adopted in March, 1848, under the impact of the revolution.

Habsburg Subjects and the Growth of Nationalism

The other nationalities of the monarchy were in a less fortunate position than the Hungarians. German, Italian, and Polish subjects felt that they had ties with larger groups outside the Habsburg empire. German and Italian intellectuals outside the Habsburg frontiers were agitated by a rising nationalism. The Italian *risorgimento* found an echo in Milan and Venice, in Trieste and Trent. The German demand for political unity and cultural superiority reverberated in Vienna and Graz, in Eger and Linz. The Poles, longing for the national existence which they had lost at the end of the eighteenth century, found most of

---

[4] See the characterization of Kossuth in A. J. P. Taylor, *The Habsburg Monarchy 1815-1918* (London: Macmillan, 1941), p. 57. Much more favorable is Oscar Jászi in *Encyclopaedia of the Social Sciences,* Vol. VIII, p. 594.

[5] Arnold-Forster, Florence Mary, *Francis Deák, Hungarian Statesman: a memoir* (London: Macmillan, 1880). Another important liberal thinker was Josef Eötvös, whose satirical novel *The Village Notary* stressed the need for reforms of county administration and was translated into English (London, 1850).

their former territory merged into Russia and Prussia. They could therefore hardly expect to gain much from a disintegration of the Habsburg empire. But many German and Italian subjects of the Habsburgs, under the impact of the newly awakened national ardor, began to look more and more beyond the empire's frontiers.

The situation was different among the nationalities which had lost their historical continuity or had never possessed strong memories of national existence. These "submerged" nationalities, Czechs and Slovaks, Slovenes and Croats, Ukrainians and Romanians, were mostly peasants. Their languages had no literary standing and were spoken only by the uneducated masses. The middle classes spoke German, and the social rise of the peasants was accompanied by cultural assimilation into the dominant German civilization. Two of these submerged nationalities, the Czechs and the Croats, were, as a result of numbers and of past history, in a somewhat more fortunate position than the others. The first half of the nineteenth century brought them a national awakening through the cultural rediscovery of their traditions and the social rise of their peasantry.

The new cultural vitality owed much to the influence of German romanticism and especially to Johann Gottfried Herder,[6] who saw one of the greatest manifestations of the creative spirit in the language, folklore, and poetry of the common people. According to Herder, each people, even the smallest and least known, mirrored the idea of humanity in its own distinctive fashion. As a result, "the happiness of one people cannot be forced upon any other. The roses for the wreath of each nation's liberty must be picked with its own hands, and must grow happily out of its own wants, joys and love." Herder felt that a nationality lived above all in its civilization and its language: each man could be truly himself only by thinking and creating in his own mother tongue. Under Herder's influence, the young intellectuals of the submerged nationalities began to change their attitude toward their mother tongues. "A people, and especially a non-civilized one, has nothing dearer than the language of its fathers," Herder wrote. "Its whole spiritual wealth of tradition, all the fullness of life, all its heart and soul, lives in it. To deprive such a people of its language, or to minimize it, means to deprive it of the only immortal possession transmitted from parents to children." Under Herder's inspiration, folksongs were collected, national traditions revived, national history was written. Herder was especially fond of the Slavs, who in his opinion were an ideal, peaceful people living in a primitive democracy,

---

[6] Kohn, Hans, *The Idea of Nationalism*, pp. 427-451.

without a war-loving nobility, and who thus fell easy victims to German aggression and oppression. Herder predicted a glorious future for them when Europe should establish an age of law and peace.

This cultural renaissance aroused interest in the national past. Herder's conception influenced the Czech historian Palacký,[7] who began his *History of Bohemia* in 1836. It was first published in German and only in 1848 in Czech. To him, Czech history meant not so much a political or military struggle between the Czechs and the Germans as a conflict of moral ideas and national psychologies. The Czechs, like the Slavs in general, represented the primitive democracy of peaceful peasants and shepherds; the Germans, bellicose and well organized under aristocratic leadership, tried to gain their livelihood by conquest and the labor of the vanquished. The Czech striving for liberty reached its climax in Hussitism, which Palacký interpreted as the seedtime of democracy, a pioneer movement in humanity's struggle for freedom of conscience and the equality of men. Palacký's writings were only one outstanding example in a general rediscovery of the past which inspired the peoples not only in their national awakening, but also in their struggle for the reassertion of their "historical rights," claims which often conflicted with altered circumstances. In a curious way, romantic reminiscences of the past mingled with progressive aspirations for a liberal future.

These intellectual movements found a social foundation in the rise of the peasants. The progressive emancipation of the Austrian peasants, from the beneficial reforms of Joseph II to the final abolition of all feudal burdens in 1849, set free new energies which benefited the national awakening of the submerged nationalities. Not only did the peasants grow wealthier and better educated: their sons migrated to the cities, changed their ethnical composition, became members of the middle class, and insisted on a literature which would meet their cultural and social requirements in their own language. The last years of Metternich's rule therefore saw new forces arising among all the nationalities of the monarchy. The ideas of nationalism and liberalism, which the Congress of Vienna had tried to repress, gained strength under the deceptively calm surface of the pre-March days. When the vernal March winds carried seeds of the Parisian February days to central Europe, the "Spring of the Peoples"—a common name for the revolutionary year of 1848—called the nationalities of the monarchy to the realization of old dreams and new hopes.

[7] On Palacký (1798-1876), see Hans Kohn, *Not by Arms Alone* (Cambridge: Harvard University Press, 1940), pp. 65-83.

Habsburg Reaction

The revolution began in March, 1848. It ended in August, 1849, when the imperial armies liquidated the newly proclaimed republics in Hungary and Venetia. In reality there were many revolutions, conflicting in motives and interests and lacking any clear plan—national revolutions for independence of the various and often antagonistic nationalities, liberal revolutions for constitutionalism, and peasant revolts for social emancipation. The dynasty overcame the grave crisis by making use of the conflicting aspirations of nationalities and classes. After some initial weakness, the court which had fled from Vienna reasserted itself. Ferdinand abdicated on December 2, 1848. His nephew, Francis Joseph I, then eighteen years old, ascended the throne. Brought up in the Metternich era by his bigoted and ambitious mother, a Bavarian princess, and mounting the throne as the conqueror of the revolutionary movement of 1848, he devoted his long reign to the sole task of retaining the heritage of his ancestors intact. According to his lights, he was a model ruler, hard-working and dutiful, frugal and impersonal. If the empire, backed by the army, the bureaucracy, and the Church, could have been ruled from the desk of a conscientious autocrat, the ideal of Francis Joseph could have been realized. Despite his narrow intelligence and lack of creative imagination, he was yet, in his exemplary dignity and impersonal integrity, the last monarch in the true sense of the word. He disliked and distrusted all new ideas but was ready to accept or discard them with an open mind when the maintenance of his heritage seemed to demand changing devices.[8]

Of the nationalities in revolt in 1848, only the Magyars showed real strength. The situation of the Germans was difficult. Many of them looked to the German National Assembly in Frankfurt and to a future united Greater Germany, but when the Assembly chose the *kleindeutsch* or "little German" solution under Prussian leadership and thus left the Austrian Germans outside, their Austrian patriotism prevailed over their German nationalism. In Italy, Lombardy tried to gain her independence with the military help of Sardinia, while Venice rose and proclaimed the rebirth of her ancient republic. The Czechs of Bohemia, under the leadership of Palacký, rejected the invitation of the Frankfurt National Assembly to regard themselves as part of a resurrected and modernized German Reich; and Palacký stressed the ne-

[8] Tschuppik, Karl, *The Reign of Emperor Francis Joseph 1848-1916* (London: Bell, 1930); on his family life, see Egon Caesar Conte Corti, *Elizabeth, Empress of Austria* (New Haven: Yale University Press, 1936).

cessity of Austria's existence as a protector of the Austrian Slavs against
the German flood. A congress of the Austrian Slavs was called in
Prague to balance the Frankfurt Assembly. In Hungary, the Diet
voted the transfer of the capital to historic Budapest and the creation
of a unitary Magyar state of the lands of the crown of St. Stephen in
March, 1848. Though the Habsburgs were still recognized as kings,
the Hungarian state was to be practically independent. It was to include the non-Magyar nationalities, among them the Croats, who resisted the Magyar plans under Jellačić's leadership and were ready in
their own interest to defend the imperial unity against Magyar sep-
aratism.

More promising for the future than these disrupting and conflicting
tendencies was the convocation of an Austrian constituent assembly
which met first in Vienna and later at Kremsier in Moravia. Its
emancipation of the peasantry from the last feudal burdens (Sept. 7,
1848) was of lasting benefit, but its draft constitution of March 1, 1849,
which combined a liberal central authority with national autonomy of
the different peoples, unfortunately never went into effect. This constitution was the work of the best progressive minds among the Germans
and Czechs and offered a chance for the reconstruction of Austria on a
modern and healthy basis. But on March 4 the new prime minister,
Prince Felix Schwarzenberg, dissolved the constituent assembly. In
the intervening months, the Austrian army had reasserted the prestige
of the dynasty. Under General Radetzky it decisively defeated the
Sardinian army at Custozza and Novara and restored Austrian domination in Lombardy; under Prince Windischgrätz it occupied Budapest
and easily put down popular revolts in Prague and Vienna. But
Magyar resistance was not ended. The Hungarian Diet, meeting at
Debreczen in April, 1849, proclaimed a republic and elected Kossuth
governor-president. Nicolai I of Russia, afraid of revolutionary con-
tagion in his Polish lands, offered his help in suppressing the uprising.
In spite of a gallant defense under General Görgei, the Magyars were
defeated and surrendered in August at Világos. Kossuth fled abroad.
With the capture of Venice in the same month, peace was restored
throughout the Habsburg domain without any loss of territory. The
brief "Spring of the Peoples" had come to a tragic end and revealed all
the weaknesses and fatal tensions in the popular movements.

Prince Schwarzenberg, a man of great vigor, used the victory and
the prestige gained thereby to reaffirm the unity of the empire and
Austria's leadership in Germany. At Olmütz (November, 1850), he
forced Prussia to abandon her plans for a centralized Germany ruled

from Berlin. In 1851 he united all Habsburg lands through a strictly unitarian and absolutist regime. After his death in 1852, Alexander Bach carried on the same policy, based upon the army, the bureaucracy, and the Catholic Church. A concordat of 1855 gave wide powers to the Church, especially in the field of education. But Habsburg absolutism was fatally weakened by Austria's unfortunate foreign policy of abandoning the alliances on which Metternich had built her security. She antagonized Russia during the Crimean War. In 1859, Cavour's cunning maneuver provoked Austria into a conflict with France and Sardinia which cost her Lombardy. In 1866, Bismarck's unscrupulous diplomacy used an alliance with Italy and the preparedness of the Prussian army in a war against Austria and the German Confederation to drive Austria out of Germany and Italy. Defeated at Königgrätz (July 3, 1866), Austria had to agree to the dissolution of the German Confederation and to leave Germany to Prussia. Though victorious over Italy both on land and at sea (at Custozza and in the naval battle near Lissa), Austria had to cede Venetia to Italy. Thus the summer of 1866, which barred the Habsburgs from Germany and Italy, brought to an end a history of many centuries and demanded a reorganization of the Habsburg legacy.

Austria's Culture

Though political life was backward in Austria, the country had a right to be proud of its culture. Vienna was the great imperial capital, wide open to cultural influences from all sides and radiating a civilizing influence in all directions. It became not only the organizing and strategic center of the *Donauraum,* but knew itself to be the heart of the two great universal ideas of Western Christianity: the succession to the Roman Empire and the guardianship of the Catholic Church. Austrian civilization thus harmonized and acclimatized many elements stemming from different lands and different intellectual climates, assimilating them with such a degree of perfection that they developed into something entirely new and, at the same time, unique and typically Austrian. It was characteristic of Austria to avoid all extremes, to be well-tempered, to permeate her life with a broad-minded, tolerant ease. Its intellectual richness found expression more in the arts and letters than in science or scholarship. What Vienna produced was, above all, a mellow art of living.

Austria experienced its first cultural flourishing in the thirteenth century, when the court of Vienna was renowned for a splendor unsurpassed in central Europe. Here the famous *Minnesänger,* the knightly singers of love and beauty, found their home. Here the greatest of all of these singers, Walther von der Vogelweide (1170-1230), learned his art. His poems, to quote his English translator W. Allison Phillips, give us the picture not only of a great artistic genius, but of a strenuous, passionate, very human, and lovable character. In Austria the two greatest epics of German medieval literature, the *Nibelungenlied* and the *Gudrunlied,* received their definite poetical form. Next to poetry and music, architecture was a typical expression of the Austrian cultural climate, not only in the early period but also in the second stage of Austria's flowering, the period of the baroque.

The time of Austria's greatest development was the great age of the theater and opera, of Italian and Spanish influence. Lasting monuments of the sumptuous beauty of architecture of the period are the Charles Church and the Palace of Schönbrunn, built by Johann Fischer von Erlach; the Belvedere Palace, summer residence of Prince Eugene of Savoy, built by Lucas von Hildebrandt; and the Abbey of Melk, built by Jakob Prandtauer. In 1776 the famous *Burgtheater,* the imperial home of drama and comedy, was reorganized as Germany's foremost theater, and there Joseph Haydn (1732-1809) and Wolfgang Amadeus Mozart (1756-1791) made Vienna the music center of the world. Salzburg, where Mozart was born, vied on a smaller scale with Vienna in the glory of its baroque architecture and its natural setting.

The beginning of the nineteenth century added two more titles to Vienna's fame. The city became the center of German romantic poetry and letters of the later period, with their Catholic tendency, and it also grew, almost at the opposite pole of intellectual pursuits, to leadership in the medical world. Medical students from all over the world came to the university in Vienna, and later to the Universities of Prague and Graz. But the censorship of the pre-March period hindered the development of science and the free flow of creative art. It was 1846 when the Academy of Science was founded, with Joseph Baron Hammer-Purgstall, the most famous orientalist of his time, as its first president. Even the reaction could not entirely stifle intellectual life.

The greatest modern composer, Ludwig van Beethoven (1770-1827), spent all his creative life, from 1792 on, in Vienna. Here he conducted his *Seventh Symphony* in 1814, before the Congress of Vienna; here he completed in 1823 his greatest legacy, the *Missa Solemnis* and the *Ninth Symphony.* Franz Schubert (1797-1828), called by Franz Liszt the most poetical musician who has ever lived, wrote his famous romantic

Lieder in Vienna. Beethoven and Schubert conquered the world from Vienna; so on another level did the Viennese waltz, under its masters Joseph Lanner (1801-1843) and Johann Strauss, Sr. (1804-1849). The *Burgtheater* under the brilliant management of Josef Schreyvogel (1814-1832) and Heinrich Laube (1850-1867) became again the foremost stage of the German language. Laube trained a generation of great actors who formed one of the glories of Vienna and found worthy successors. Franz Grillparzer (1791-1872) wrote powerful tragedies and Eduard Bauernfeld (1802-1890) created brilliant comedies for the stage. But nearer to the heart of the people were the writers whose works were produced on the more popular stage—those like Ferdinand Raimund (1790-1836), perhaps the deepest and most characteristic representative of the Austrian mind; Johann Nestroy (1801-1862); and Ludwig Anzengruber (1839-1889). Of great writers outside the stage, the prose author Adalbert Stifter (1805-1868) and the poets Nikolaus Lenau (1820-1850) and Anastasius Grün (1806-1876) deserve mention.

The latter part of the nineteenth century brought a revival of architecture and the arts. Monumental buildings transformed Vienna into a city second only to Paris. In the twentieth century, many of the new ideas in architecture emanated from Vienna. Modern painting found a home among the *Sezession,* a group of advanced painters who broke with the conventional classicism in 1897 under the leadership of Gustav Klimt (1862-1918). Music again was even more prominent. The Philharmonic Orchestra, founded in 1860, and the Imperial Opera, reorganized in 1866 under Franz Dingelstedt as manager and Hans Richter as conductor, became the leading institutions of their kind. Johann Brahms (1833-1897) spent his later years in Vienna, conducting there for some time the concerts of the famous *Gesellschaft der Musikfreunde.* Anton Bruckner (1830-1904) was the last great master of the classical symphony; his disciples Gustav Mahler (1860-1911) and Hugo Wolf (1860-1903) found new forms of musical expression. Again, as at the beginning of the century, the lighter art of the operetta gained international fame from Vienna in the works of such Austrian composers as Johann Strauss, Jr. (1825-1899, *The Bat*) and Franz Lehár (b. 1870, *The Merry Widow*). In the field of literature, Marie von Ebner-Eschenbach (1830-1916) and Peter K. Rosegger (1843-1918) represented the older generation at its best, while the poets of Young Vienna, among them Hugo von Hofmannsthal (1874-1929) and the dramatist Arthur Schnitzler (1862-1931), enriched literature with a new depth of feeling and a new wealth of inner melody.

Hungary's Culture

Meanwhile Budapest had risen to the rank of a second capital, beautified after 1867 with many impressive buildings and enriched by the intense life of Hungarian letters. The end of the eighteenth century brought a revival of cultural life to Hungary. Ferencz Kazinczy (1759-1831) rejuvenated the Magyar language by many translations from foreign literature and by the rediscovery of many old Magyar words. The brothers Kisfaludy founded modern Magyar literature; Sándor wrote the first modern love lyrics; Károly prepared the first original Magyar dramas under romantic influence. The Academy of Science, after 1830, devoted its attention to the revival and improvement of the language and to the creation of a national drama. Alexander Petöfi (1823-1849) was as great a poet as a patriot. Of Croat descent, he Magyarized his original name, Petrovics, became prominent among the radical wing of the patriots in 1848, and fell in battle. His lyric talent was matched by the epic talent of Janos Arany (1817-1882), who edited translations of Shakespeare and wrote famous ballads of the national past. The great novelist of the period was Maurus Jókai (1825-1904), a writer of stupendous fertility and luxuriant imagination coupled with a true sense of humor. At the end of the century, Hungarian literature split into two schools: the Turanians, who stressed the Asiatic origin of the Magyars and emphasized an extreme nationalism, and the more cosmopolitan and progressive modernists, among whom was Endre Ady (1877-1919), a poet of genius.

As in Hungary, cultural progress among the other peoples of the monarchy developed rapidly. This progress made the transformation of Austria into a federation of its several peoples more and more a necessity.

The Ausgleich

Experiments in the federalization of Austria which started in 1860 were frustrated by the resistance of the Magyars. Their final outcome was the compromise of 1867, in which the Emperor accepted the Hungarian suggestions put forward by Francis Deák and supported by Count Julius Andrássy. This unfortunate step sacrificed the Austrian nationalities to the Magyars. It not only abandoned to Magyar rule all the lands of the crown of St. Stephen, but it made the Magyars the decisive element in the monarchy and gave Hungary an influence entirely out of proportion to its real importance. The Austrian empire was succeeded by the dual monarchy of Austria-Hungary, a union of two independent states held together by the hereditary dynasty, a common army, and a united foreign policy. The compromise provided for common ministers for foreign affairs and war, for the necessary finances, and for yearly meetings of the delegations of the two parliaments, deliberating separately but, if need be, voting together on all common affairs. Decennial treaties were to establish a unified policy in monetary and tariff matters.

Each half of the monarchy had its own parliament, consisting of two chambers and a cabinet responsible to it. But their structure differed fundamentally. Hungary had its distinct historic personality and an undisputed energetic leadership in the Magyar nobility. The limited suffrage subordinated the non-Magyar nationalities—the majority of the population—to the predominant Magyars. The western half of the dual monarchy, on the other hand, was an aggregate of historical units as different as Galicia and Dalmatia, or as Tyrol and Moravia. It lacked even a common name. The clumsy official title was "The Kingdoms and Lands Represented in the Imperial Council"; the unofficial name was Austria or Cis-Leithania.[9] Article 19 of the fundamental law of December 21, 1867, established, for the Austrian half of the dual monarchy, the complete equality of all ethnic groups and assured all of them of their inalienable right to preserve and promote their nationality and language. The equality of all languages was recognized, but the general principle was so vaguely expressed that it gave rise to innumerable disputes. Restricted suffrage gave the Germans and Poles a preponderant influence in the Austrian Parliament, the Imperial Council. In this rather complicated set-up, the Emperor safeguarded what he most wanted to preserve, the unity of the dynasty, army, and foreign policy. In both parts of the dual monarchy he now ruled as a constitutional monarch through parliamentary ministries.

Technically the monarchy was still the Austrian Empire and Francis Joseph was Emperor-King. But the Magyars tried more and more to emphasize Hungary's separateness and independence from Austria and to regard the Emperor of Austria (emperor of what was almost a foreign land) only as King of Hungary. Deák knew that Hungary was not a great state by itself and understood the need of the empire for Hungary's sake. But soon the radical element gained the upper hand. Overconfident of Hungary's strength and the Magyar mission, it demanded a completely independent Hungary under Magyar dominance

---

[9] Leitha is a river, a tributary of the Danube, separating Austria from Hungary (Trans-Leithania).

—a great Hungary in which Transylvania and Croatia, the latter with an autonomous status, had been incorporated in 1867. As long as Deák lived, he exercised a moderating influence, but he could not be fully replaced by Kálmán Tisza, who formed the Liberal Party and became prime minister of Hungary from 1875 to 1890. Under him the policy of Magyarization of the minorities was applied with growing vigor. It was in no way a policy of exclusion, aiming at their permanent subjection or liquidation: it sought rather to assimilate and absorb them into the ranks of the ruling nation. Yet this attempt foundered on the rock of the growing nationalism of the subject nationalities and on the inspiration which the southern Slavs and Romanians derived after 1878 from the existence of an independent Serbia and an independent Romania beyond Hungary's borders. In spite of the growing internal weakness of Hungary, the Magyars emphasized more and more their independence of Austria. They "treated their participation in the empire as a favor which had to be bought at an increasingly high price; and yet they insisted that the Emperor must serve their purposes only." [10] For many Magyars, the compromise of 1867 was not a settlement, but only a starting point; they attacked especially the common army with its German language of command.

This agitation gained added inspiration from Kossuth's death in exile in 1894 and the burial of his body, with great nationalist demonstrations, in his native land. His son Ferencz became the leader of the Hungarian Party of Independence, while Count István Tisza continued the more moderate policy of his father and stressed the need for a strong common army in view of the growing international tension. Only the Emperor's threat of introducing democratic suffrage into Hungary broke the intransigeance of the Party of Independence. Such a measure would have ended Magyar dominance in Hungary and would have forced a social transformation of its semifeudal social structure.

Such a transformation was achieved in Austria. Here the equality of all nationalities was recognized in principle, but, in spite of many efforts, no practical solution was found.[11] Each nationality was preoccupied with its own interests and none was ready for the spirit of

---

[10] Taylor, A. J. P., *op. cit.,* p. 165.

[11] See the recent standard work edited by Karl Gottfried Hugelmann *Das Nationalitätenrecht des alten Österreich* (Vienna: Braumüller, 1934). Successful solutions were found in some cases where historical claims did not interfere with a rational solution of present conditions looking toward the future, as in Moravia between Czechs and Germans and in Bukovina between Germans, Ukrainians, and Romanians. These two provinces became islands of national peace in spite of complex intermingling.

compromise which alone could have produced a durable understanding. From 1867 to 1878 the German liberal element predominated and suspended the concordat. But from 1879 to 1893 a coalition of conservative Czechs and Poles and German clericals provided Count Edward Taaffe with the opportunity of seeking a working agreement with the various nationalities, especially the Czechs. He himself consciously maintained the position of an imperial spokesman above the nationalities, impartial to all. As he said himself, he kept all nationalities equally in a state of moderate dissatisfaction and so gave to Austria fifteen years of relative peace, an Indian summer before the winter storms of nationalistic excitement broke. Meanwhile more radical elements came to the fore, especially in the German camp.

Pan-Germanism

Dissatisfied with the Slav and clerical majority behind Taaffe, a famous German program was drafted at Linz in 1880 by Heinrich Friedjung, later the foremost Austrian historian of his generation, Georg Schönerer, later the founder of the Pan-German Party, and Victor Adler, who was later to be the leader of the Austrian Social Democrats. It became the starting point for a radical German policy. This program demanded a centralized Austria, without Galicia and Dalmatia, under German leadership and linked with Germany by a perpetual alliance and customs union. By creating a German-led *Mittel-Europa*, the program was designed to bring about a *grossdeutsch* solution of German unity and at the same time to maintain Bismarck's achievements. "The two empires of the German nation are to be united as a firm bulwark of European peace." The program was adopted by the German Nationalist Party under Schönerer, a rabid anti-Semite. An article added to the program in 1885 demanded absolute eradication of the Jewish influence in all fields of public life. Schönerer's anti-Semitism found an enthusiastic following, especially among academic youth.

At the same time, Austrian Pan-Germanism assumed a violent anti-Habsburg and anti-Catholic attitude. It openly favored the destruction of the Habsburg empire and glorified Bismarck and the Hohenzollerns. Prussia's victories had been Protestant successes over Catholic lands, and the Catholic Church formed the main support of the Habsburg dynasty. Schönerer therefore propagated the *Los von Rom* movement, an appeal to leave the Roman Church. He had great success in the universities and in Bohemia and Styria, where the national struggle between Germans and Slavs was keenest. Schönerer, who first repre-

sented his native Lower Austrian district in parliament, later represented Eger in Bohemia. A Bohemian constituency also elected a
second Pan-German leader, Karl Hermann Wolf, who soon became
Schönerer's rival. This Austrian Pan-Germanism, with its hatred of
Habsburgs, Slavs, and Jews, deeply influenced Hitler in his youth.

While the Pan-Germans appealed to racial chauvinism and found
their following among the intellectuals and in national frontier districts, the Christian Social movement under Dr. Karl Lueger organized
the lower middle classes, especially in Vienna, by arousing their
hatred of both the capitalist bourgeoisie and the Socialist proletariat.
Hitler's demagogic methods were indebted to the example of Lueger,
whose party shared Schönerer's anti-Semitism but was deeply loyal to
the Habsburgs and faithfully Roman Catholic. The Pan-Germans and
the Christian Socials soon outnumbered the liberals in the German
ranks. They shared their hold over the masses with the Social Democrat Party, founded in 1889 by Victor Adler, a political leader of rare
integrity and deep humanitarianism. It could make its weight felt,
however, only after the introduction of universal suffrage, when the
first elections returned the Social Democrats, with 89 members,[12] as
the strongest party in parliament.

Monarchy's Nationalities Versus the Monarchy

A similar radicalization and differentiation of political life occurred
in the other nationalities, among whom the Czechs showed the greatest
social progress and the most intensive cultural life. The Czech-German struggle in Bohemia became the main problem of the monarchy.[13]
The conservative Old Czechs under the leadership of Palacký's son-
in-law, F. L. Rieger, ceded their leadership to the more radical Young
Czechs under Dr. Karel Kramář. The Young Czechs, in their turn,
were soon superseded by the mass appeal of the People's Socialist Party,
a non-Marxist, extremely nationalist group. The greatest statesman of
latter-day Austria, the Czech philosopher Thomas G. Masaryk, had a
following of only a few intellectuals among his own people. Born at
the Czecho-Slovak border, he tried to build a bridge from the progres-

---

[12] Of these 89 members, 52 were Germans, 24 Czechs, 6 Poles, 5 Italians, and 2 Ukrainians.
The Czech Social Democrats in 1911 separated from the United Social Democratic Party. The
"internationalism" of the party was faced in Austria, as it was in Russia, with the problem of
nationalism. From the Socialist side, solutions were proposed in Karl Renner, *Das Selbstbestim-
mungsrecht der Nationen in besonderer Anwendung auf Österreich* (Vienna: Deuticke, 1918),
and Otto Bauer, *Die Nationalitätenfrage und die Sozialdemokratie,* 2nd ed. (Vienna: Wiener
Volksbuchhandlung, 1924).

[13] Best brief discussion and history are found in Elizabeth Wiskemann, *Czechs and Germans*
(New York: Oxford University Press, 1938), pp. 1-86.

sive Czechs, who made full use of the opportunities of free development in Austria, to the backward Slovaks to whom, under Magyar domination, no such opportunities were given.

While in Hungary all non-Magyar nationalities were equally held down by Magyar supremacy, in Austria the nationalities found their adversary not solely and even not mainly in the Germans. The Ukrainians in eastern Galicia looked vainly to Vienna for protection against oppression by the Poles; the Slovenes found themselves less threatened by German encroachments in the north than by the strong Italian nationalism along the Adriatic coast. The Italians, in their *irredenta* (their "unredeemed" position outside the Italian kingdom), wished not only separation from Austria, but a dominant position based on supposed cultural superiority and historical rights all along the Adriatic coast. These Italian claims threatened not only the Slovenes but also the Croats. The latter had found it futile to appeal to Vienna for protection against the Magyars. Finally, overcoming a deep antagonism rooted in religious, cultural, and historical differences despite an identity of language and race, Croat and Serb leaders united on a program of Southern Slav unity and freedom which would include the lands from the Adriatic coast to the Romanian border. The program was drafted in October, 1905, at Fiume, a city that was to become the center and symbol of Italian-Croat conflict.

With these growing nationalist tensions, the conciliatory work of Taaffe soon ran into insurmountable difficulties and finally was wrecked by the coöperation of German and Czech extremists. Taaffe's successor, Casimar Badeni, a Polish aristocrat, published language ordinances for Bohemia on April 5, 1897, which aroused violent objections from the Germans. The latter, through widespread street demonstrations and noisy obstruction in the parliament, not only overthrew Badeni on November 28, 1897, but destroyed the parliamentary regime in Austria for which the German liberals had fought half a century before. The monarchy, which had tried after 1879 to win the Slavs to an active interest in and support of Austria's strength, now had to abandon its efforts. Thereafter it tried to preserve, as well as it could, the shaken and internally torn structure by a mere policy of "muddling through." It was a policy of imperial administration, not of constructive reform or strong rule.

The Austrian cabinets of the twentieth century no longer were presided over by members of the conservative high nobility, but by civil servants from the ranks of the leading bureaucracy. Two of them were men of great ability and liberal intentions, Ernest von Koerber and

Vladimir Beck. But their efforts were frustrated by the unwillingness
of the nationalities to compromise. Even the introduction of universal
equal and direct suffrage on January 26, 1907, did not advance the
parliamentary cause. Nationalistic grievances and pretensions, in-
flamed by appeals to history, were too deep-rooted to allow the normal
functioning of economic and social forces and motivations. The parliaments elected by democratic suffrage were as incapable of constructive work as their predecessors. The government was forced to rule
by expedients, using the famous paragraph 14 of the constitution which
allowed emergency decrees to assume the force of law. National pas-
sions and the unyielding opposition of the three privileged nationalities, Magyars, Germans, and Poles, blocked a rational solution of the
main problem of nineteenth century Austria: how to get neighboring
and intermingling nationalities to live together in a spirit of growing
liberty and tolerance.

Monarchy's Search for International Solutions

The domestic deadlock turned the attention of the monarchy again
to the foreign field for a possibility of asserting Austria's vitality. The
Habsburgs did not at first accept their exclusion from German affairs
in 1866 as final. After Prussia's victory, Francis Joseph appointed the
Saxon prime minister Friedrich Ferdinand von Beust, well known as
an enemy of Prussian leadership in Germany, as Austrian foreign
minister. In Austria he carried on that anti-Prussian policy until the
events of 1871 made it impossible. Then he was succeeded by Count
Julius Andrássy, a member of the high Magyar nobility.[14] The
monarchy now definitely accepted its exclusion from Germany and
Italy and sought a field of foreign activity, as in the eighteenth century,
in the legacy of the disintegrating Ottoman Empire. The Congress of
Berlin in 1878 gave Austria-Hungary the mandate to occupy, pacify,
and administer the Turkish provinces of Bosnia and Herzegovina with
their southern Slav population. As the two provinces were incorporated neither in Austria nor in Hungary, the monarchy now found
a common administrative task. It also received the right to military
occupation of the Turkish province of Novibazar, which formed a
wedge of Turkish territory between Serbia and Montenegro and the
direct route from Bosnia to Salonica on the Aegean Sea, to which
Austrian expansionist tendencies pointed.

[14] On Count Gyula (Julius) Andrássy (1823-1890), see Gyula Andrássy, *Bismarck, Andrássy
and their successors* (Boston: Houghton Mifflin, 1927), and David Harris, *A Diplomatic History of the Balkan Crisis of 1875-1878* (London: Oxford University Press, 1936).

Austria's Balkan position was strengthened by the conclusion of her alliance with Germany on October 7, 1879. This dual alliance—which in 1882 was expanded into a triple alliance by Italy's accession—reconstituted the link which had been broken in 1866. Germany, under Prussia's leadership, and Austria-Hungary now formed a strong bloc dominating *Mittel-Europa,* the strategic center of the continent. Count Andrássy sought the coöperation of the Germans, the Magyars, and the Turks, whom he regarded as races historically ruling the Slavs of the Danubian basin and the Balkans. This policy was not originally intended to be directed against Russia. The triple alliance wished "to fortify the monarchical principle and thereby to assure the unimpaired maintenance of the social and political order in their respective states." [15] Close coöperation with monarchical Russia was Bismarck's and Francis Joseph's ardent desire. The twenty years of conservative and pro-Slav cabinets in Austria at the end of the nineteenth century valued peaceful stability too much to risk any adventurous competition with Russia. The Germans and the Magyars in the monarchy were definitely opposed to any acquisition of territory which would increase the Slav element within the monarchy.

In the twentieth century, this situation changed. William II abandoned Bismarck's moderation and embarked upon a policy of unlimited aspirations which aroused deep fears in Russia and the West. Germany, growing in industrial power and prosperity and confident of possessing the best-prepared armed forces, the most efficient organization, and the highest national morality, rattled the saber. By controlling southeastern Europe and the Middle East, Germany expected to create a sufficient economic and strategic basis for world hegemony. She needed Austria's coöperation and strength to that end. The hopeless internal situation made Austria more inclined to adopt an active foreign policy. Count Alois Aehrenthal, Austrian ambassador to St. Petersburg (1899-1906), tried to carry out an active Balkan policy without endangering relations with Russia when he became foreign minister in October, 1906. The Turkish revolution of 1908 gave him the opportunity to annex Bosnia and Herzegovina against the opposition of the Serbs, who had hoped to incorporate the two provinces into their kingdom. At the same time Russia, after her defeat in the Far East in the war against Japan and after being weakened by the revolutionary turmoil of 1905, turned her attention to the Balkans and tried to regain prestige there by a reassertion of her

---

[15] Pribram, Alfred Francis, *The Secret Treaties of Austria-Hungary 1879-1914* (Cambridge: Harvard University Press, 1920), Vol. I, p. 65.

traditional policy of gaining Constantinople and protecting the Balkan Slavs. Thus Austrian policy, backed by Germany, soon clashed inevitably with Russia in the Balkans.

Throughout the crisis of 1908, Aehrenthal and his imperial master strove conscientiously to maintain peace. The chief of the general staff, Conrad von Hötzendorf, pleaded in vain for a preventive war, either against Serbia or against Italy. He believed that every passing year rendered the position of the monarchy more difficult and that postponement of the inevitable conflict diminished the prospects of a victory which alone would arrest the process of disintegration and thereby assure survival. But it was only under Aehrenthal's successor, Count Leopold von Berchtold (foreign minister 1912-1915), that these counsels began to prevail. The Balkan wars of 1912-1913, which ended in the vast territorial expansion of Serbia and completely changed the balance of power in the Near East to Germany's disadvantage, accelerated the decline of Austria-Hungary's prestige in the Balkans and intensified Serbia's agitation for the dismemberment of the monarchy and the inclusion of its Southern Slavs in a Greater Serbia.

The assassination of Francis Ferdinand,[16] heir to the Habsburg throne, by Serb nationalists at the Bosnian capital of Sarajevo on June 28, 1914, seemed to present Count Berchtold with the opportunity of settling the Serbian problem once and for all. Supported by Germany, Austria decided to force the issue,[17] even at the risk of a European war. Francis Joseph reluctantly agreed. When his ministers unleashed the war, the Habsburg heritage which he had faithfully guarded was at stake. He was not to witness its liquidation. Francis Joseph died on November 21, 1916, and his passing marked the end not only of an empire but of an epoch in central European history which had its roots deep in the past and of which he was the last representative survivor. His successor, Emperor Charles, tried to avert inescapable doom by con-

---

[16] The Emperor's only son, Rudolf, died by suicide on January 30, 1889, at the age of 31. He was a liberal, bitterly opposed to clericalism, anti-Semitism, and Pan-Germanism. "He regarded the (Bismarckian) German Empire only as a territory held together by Prussian bayonets and saw the possibility of a real union of all Germans only in a German republic" (Oskar Mitis in *Neue Österreichische Biographie,* Vol. II (Vienna: Amalthea Verlag, 1925), p. 21.) His suicide at Mayerling may have been caused by his despair over the political trends in Austria and his exclusion from participation in government affairs. Francis Ferdinand, who intended to ascend the throne as Francis II, had a personality much more akin to that of his uncle, Francis Joseph, than did the Emperor's own son. Francis Ferdinand was the oldest son of the Emperor's brother Charles Loui (d. 1896). After Francis Ferdinand's assassination, Charles Francis Joseph, the son of his brother Otto, became heir to the throne and in 1916 Emperor Charles I.

[17] On the outbreak of the war in 1914 and the immediate responsibilities for it, see Bernadotte E. Schmitt, "July 1914: Thirty Years After," *The Journal of Modern History,* Vol. XVI (September, 1944), pp. 169-204.

cluding peace and transforming the monarchy into a federation of free and equal peoples. He failed in both efforts. The manifesto of October 16, 1918, announced the decision of a federated Austria. Even then, three weeks before its complete collapse, the Magyars insisted on Hungary's inviolability, protested any concession to the other nationalities, and clung to their dominant position. It was, in any case, too late. History was taking its course; the surging forces of new classes and awakened nationalities which the Habsburgs did not understand and could not master engulfed the venerable crumbling structure. In the fall of 1918, it came to an end.[18] The last Habsburg emperor died in 1923 in exile. The nationalities carried on their ancient struggles in new forms on the ruins of the empire. The quest continued for a rational solution of their main problem, the collaboration of neighboring and intermingling nationalities in a spirit of growing liberty and tolerance.

Bibliography

Eisenmann, Louis, *Le Compromis austro-hongrois de 1867* (Paris: 1904). The book offers much more than the title indicates. It shows a deep understanding of the fundamental issues and forces involved.

Fischel, Alfred, *Der Panslavismus bis zum Weltkrieg* (Stuttgart: Cotta, 1919). An important survey, written from a hostile point of view.

Friedjung, Heinrich, *The Struggle for Supremacy in Germany 1859-1866* (London: Macmillan, 1935). An abbreviated translation of Friedjung's classic *Der Kampf um die Vorherrschaft in Deutschland 1859-1866* (1897), written with a warm enthusiasm for the German cause. Thoughtful introduction by A. J. P. Taylor.

Jászi, Oscar, *The Dissolution of the Habsburg Monarchy* (Chicago: University of Chicago Press, 1924). A profound and masterful analysis of the social, political, and intellectual trends of the monarchy, especially also of Hungary, in the last decades of its existence.

Kohn, Hans, "The Legacy of the Habsburgs," *Not by Arms Alone* (Cambridge: Harvard University Press, 1940), pp. 43-64. An attempt to analyze the Austrian idea.

Mayer-Kaindl-Pirchegger, *Geschichte und Kulturleben Deutsch-Österreichs von 1792 bis nach dem Weltkrieg* (Vienna: Braumüller, 1937). The new edition of an Austrian standard work, F. M. Mayer's *Geschichte*

---

[18] On the dissolution and last years of the monarchy, see the chapter "Downfall of the Habsburg Monarchy" in H. W. V. Temperley, *A History of the Peace Conference of Paris* (London: Henry Frowde, 1921), Vol. IV; Ottakar Count Czernin, *In the World War* (London: Cassell, 1919); Edmund von Glaise-Horstenau, *The Collapse of the Austro-Hungarian Empire* (London: Dent, 1930), one of the best accounts; Thomas G. Masaryk, *The Making of a State* (London: Allen & Unwin, 1927), indispensable; Arthur Count Potzer-Hoditz, *The Emperor Karl* (Boston: Houghton Mifflin, 1930), by a friend of the Emperor; David F. Strong, *Austria (October 1918-March 1919) Transition from Empire to Republic* (New York: Columbia University Press, 1939).

Osterreichs. This last (third) volume of the new edition is written by H. Pirchegger from the German-Austrian point of view.

Redlich, Joseph, *Emperor Francis Joseph of Austria* (New York: Macmillan, 1929). This biography is of special value for the period 1848 to 1867, where it relies on Prof. Redlich's great and exhaustive study *Das österreichische Staats- und Reichsproblem* (2 vols., 1920, 1926), and for the last years, in which Prof. Redlich himself actively participated.

Seton-Watson, R. W., *Racial Problems in Hungary* (London: Constable, 1908). This book and the book by Count Paul Teleki on Hungary's problems supplement one another and represent two different points of view.

————, *The Southern Slav Question in the Habsburg Monarchy* (London: Constable, 1911). The author is sympathetic to the Southern Slav aspirations. We owe to him also detailed studies on Slovakia and Romania.

Taylor, A. J. P., *The Habsburg Monarchy 1815-1918* (London: Macmillan, 1941). The best short survey with an emphasis on the internal developments and problems, well written and thoughtful.

Teleki, Count Paul, *The Evolution of Hungary and Its Place in European History* (New York: Macmillan, 1923).

Chapter III

CZECHOSLOVAKIA (UP TO 1918)

Who Are the Slavs?

VERY early in the history of Europe—around the sixth century—a sturdy Slav race came from the East and settled in the plain sheltered by the system of mountains between Germany and Czechoslovakia—one of the few natural frontiers of Europe. This branch of the Slavs was the foundation of what eventually became Czechoslovakia.

The Slavs are divided geographically and linguistically into three main groups: Eastern, Northwestern, and Southern. The Russians form the Eastern group, together with the Ruthenians, who constitute a wedge between the Poles and the Magyars. The Northwestern group includes the Poles, the Wends of Lusatia, and the Czechs; connecting the Ruthenians, Poles, and Moravians, but most closely akin to the latter, are the Slovaks.

The Southern Slavs—Slovenes, Serbo-Croats, and Bulgarians—are cut off from the main body by the Germans of Austria proper and the Magyars, both of whom occupy soil that was once Slavonic and have absorbed much Slavonic blood, and by the Romanians of Transylvania and the lower Danube.

The original home of the Slavs and the region from which their migrations began was the basin of the Dnieper and the area extending to the Carpathians and the Vistula. From these regions they spread to the west and southwest. At the present time, some eleven to fourteen languages, not including the extinct ones, can be reckoned as distinct Slavic tongues. It is often impossible to draw a definite line between one Slavonic people or language and another. The Great Russians, Poles, Czechs, and Bulgarians are universally admitted to be distinctive Slavonic peoples with distinct languages. The Little Russians and the White Russians tried at one time to develop into separate nationalities. This is also true of the Ruthenians in Czechoslovakia and of the Slovaks. The Moravians must be included in the Czech nation, because they themselves hold to this and there is no philological, political, or ethnographic reason to the contrary. The Slovaks of Moravia also consider themselves of Czech nationality. But it is difficult to draw a line between the Bulgarians and the Serbians in Macedonia. In racial and linguistic terms, the Croats and Serbs can be regarded as one nation; the same applies to the Czechs and Slovaks.

From a philological viewpoint, when the Slavs settled in the localities which they now occupy, they were a mass of tribes of closely allied tongues with slightly tribal differences. Later historical developments, the appearance of Slavic kingdoms, the growth of literary languages, and various civilizing influences resulted in the drawing of sharper distinctions in certain places and development of separate nationalities in different localities.

"Czech" refers to the principal people or language found in Bohemia and Moravia.[1] "Slovak" is the name given to the easternmost division of the Czech-speaking people. Protestant leaders and philologists have claimed that Slovak is merely Old Czech and have urged the use of Czech as the sole written language. The connection between the Slovak Protestants (one-fourth of the population) and the Moravian and Bohemian Brethren was close. On the other hand, Catholic writers have urged the literary development of various dialects spoken by the Slovaks.

The Origins of the Czech Nation

When the Czech tribes appeared on the stage of history in about the sixth century, their life was still semi-barbaric. Both Western and Byzantine historians have made this observation. By embracing Christianity in the ninth century, they escaped the fate of the Slavs then living along the Baltic Sea and the Elbe River.

The ninth century, which began with the coronation of Charlemagne as Roman Emperor, was characterized by the birth of the Great Moravian Empire (Moravia and Slovakia, 830-903) in the Czechoslovak territories in central Europe. Christianity was introduced in these countries in 863.

A Bohemian prince of the period was aware of the benefits of the Christianity preached by Western (German) priests. But there was the question of the Czech tongue, which had developed even up to the fourth and fifth centuries alongside of the Baltic tongues. Prince

---

[1] Seton-Watson, R. W., *A History of the Czechs and Slovaks* (London: Hutchinson & Co., 1943) is the best available introduction to the history of Czechoslovakia in English. Paul Selver, *Czechoslovak Literature* (London: George Allen & Unwin, 1942) is the best short introduction to the roots of Czechoslovak literary developments.

Rastislav appealed to Pope Nicholas I for apostles who knew the Slavonic language, but he turned down the request. Then Rastislav appealed to the Byzantine Emperor, Michael III, asking again for Christian teachers to instruct his people in their own tongue. Michael sent two brothers, known as Constantine (or Cyril) and Methodius. They were Greeks, not Slavs, who had learned the language of the Bulgarian people while mixing with them at Salonica (the "Thessalonica" of St. Paul). They translated parts of the Bible, for which purpose Constantine devised "Slavonic scripts" based on the Greek characters. They thus brought to the Moravians a liturgy in their own tongue as well as several books of the Bible. The Slav alphabet (the "glagolice" of Constantine), devised on the model of the Greek alphabet, and the Slav liturgy spread by St. Cyril and St. Methodius are, so to speak, the two columns upon which rests the civilization of all the Slav nations of the east and south. During the life of Methodius, the Slavonic liturgy penetrated into Bohemia, Poland, and Croatia, but all these countries finally accepted the Latin Church, and so were permanently cut off from the Orthodox Serbians, Bulgarians, and Russians.

In the following years, in the conflict between the Byzantine ecclesiastic tendency represented by St. Methodius and the German priests of the Latin rites, the Western forces triumphed. The disciples of Methodius, quitting Moravia, led missions to other Slav nations. The Czechoslovak tribes, already strongly attracted by the Western form of culture, were drawn definitely into its orbit.

The Separation of the Slovaks from the Czechs

The beginning of the tenth century saw the invasion of the Danubian countries by the Magyars. The Slav tribes of the west were cut off from those of the south (Yugoslavs and Bulgarians), and the Slovak branch was politically detached from the Czech branch. The Slovaks were driven northward into the confines of the Carpathians. In spite of heroic resistance, they were conquered and confined within the limits of present-day Slovakia, where for nearly a thousand years they were reduced to the status of an unwilling province of the Kingdom of Hungary. This enforced segregation of the Slovaks has had an important bearing upon their development and their relations with the Czechs. Cut off from intercourse with the other Slav peoples, their only defense against Magyar influences lay in their self-reliance. In religion they remained mainly Catholic, isolated alike from the Hussite Reformation which so profoundly stirred the Czechs (although the Hus influence was also felt among the Slovak Protestants) and from the Orthodoxy of the eastern Slavs. Similarly, the difficulty of intercourse with the Czechs has produced a divergence in what was originally a common language. The Slovak and Czech forms of the language differ in certain minor points to the present day, like two dialects of the same tongue spoken locally.

The Nucleus of National Consciousness

By joining the society of the Western nations, the Czech nation lived in a manner similar to theirs until the fourteenth century. The settlements scattered among forest swamps became villages, the nobles built themselves castles. Finally the kings, the nobles, and the Church, in the thirteenth century, founded a number of towns which they peopled almost exclusively with German colonists.

Before the fourteenth century, Czech history was merely a story of princes and kings; a story which includes many wars, a series of palace intrigues that were not without bloodshed, and attempts to form a great Czech state, at one time in the direction of Poland and again across the Danube as far as the Adriatic Sea.

In their mode of life, the Czechs linked themselves with the state and church institutions prevailing in Western Christian countries at that time. "This adoption of Western culture was even more advantageous to the Czech nation than the initial Byzantine influences of the apostles Cyril and Methodius, who introduced Christianity." [2] The early literature of the country reveals its international origin in its extant fragments—Latin, German, or French.

According to an ancient tradition, the first Czech prince, Přemysl, was called to the throne from the plough. Under the patriarchal rule of the Přemyslides, the nation made considerable progress. In its basinlike territory, surrounded and protected by mountains, the country maintained both its language and its prosperity, although it encountered some dangers because of the policies of the dynasty.

The Přemysl dynasty ended abruptly with the murder of Wenceslas III in 1305 by unknown assassins. We need to note the influence of one of the Přemyslides—"The good King Wenceslas" of the English Christmas carol—before turning to the next stage of Czech history.[3] Wenceslas I (928-935) lived during the period when the ideal of the Holy Roman Empire inspired a host of adventurous Counts of the Marches and other bearers of German culture to attempt inroads into

[2] Herben, Jan, *John Huss and his Followers* (London: Geoffrey Bles, 1926), p. 16.

[3] The words of the familiar Christmas carol about the "Good King Wenceslas" were written by Neale in recent times to a thirteenth-century melody. The correct version of this saintly prince's name is Václav (pronounced *Vatslav*).

territory inhabited by Slavonic tribes. The theory was that, as each
Slavonic tribe, principality, or kingdom adopted Christianity, it should
come under German domination and be held in trust for Mother
Church by German princes.

Wenceslas, who was never a king, by the way, but a prince, and who
certainly was not the bent, bearded figure of so many of our Christmas
illustrations, being quite young when he was murdered, adopted the
only course open to him. He bought off the German emperor by
promising to pay a yearly tribute of cattle. In return, the emperor
presented Wenceslas with a precious relic—a bone from the arm of St.
Vitus, which Wenceslas housed in a rich shrine.

This policy of appeasement did not please Wenceslas' hot-headed
brother Boleslav, who also strongly disapproved of his brother's Christian principles. So, early one morning, as Wenceslas approached the
chapel of Stará Boleslav to celebrate Mass, Boleslav leaped out on him
and stabbed him in the back as he clung to the iron knocker on the
door for sanctuary. After his murder, the Church of Rome canonized
Wenceslas as a saint, and the day is still kept sacred to the memory of
St. Wenceslas by the Czechs.

"Only after the extinction of the Přemyslid dynasty in 1305 did a
Czech nation finally emerge, that is, a nation with a full consciousness
of its Czech and Slavonic nationality and a typical national character." [4]

The best evidence of this national consciousness is provided by the
chronicles of Cosmas and Dalimil. Of the two, the first, written in
Latin, is of greater value. Although it is not always accurate and is
inclined to feature myths, especially with regard to the early period, it
gives a valuable description of the social and political conditions of
Cosmas' own times (up to 1125). Dalimil's work ends in 1310 and is
rhymed; it is the first historical work written in Czech. Largely based
on the work of Cosmas (a dean of Prague), it is written in a nationalistic spirit. ("Rather would I marry a Czech peasant girl than I
would take a German queen as my wife . . . .")

It is certain, at any rate, that toward the end of the Přemyslid era
the Czech language was already being adopted by scholars, that it
moved from the villages, towns, and castles into books, and that it even
began to replace both Latin and German.

Czech nationalism appears to have developed earlier than the nationalism of the Poles and Magyars. This was due to the continuous
series of conflicts between the Czechs and the Germans. The Přemyslides, closely bound up with the German princes through their

---

[4] Herben, *op. cit.*, pp. 16-17.

court, brought German colonists, such as skilled artisans and miners, into the country. They filled the Bishop's see in Prague with German prelates, handed over the monasteries to German monks, and used German clerks in their offices. The Czechs hated these Germans as a protected and privileged class.

The tension continued under the Luxemburg dynasty (1310-1347). The Czechs, after some confusion, elected the fourteen-year-old John of Luxemburg, the son of the German Emperor of that time, to be their ruler. John was an extravagant, adventurous knight who did not like his country and even offered it to Bavaria in exchange for the Palatinate. But he is important as an international figure. Expeditions to Hungary, Italy, and France and against the heathen Lithuanians all helped John to pass his time pleasurably and unprofitably. It then became a proverb that "nothing can be done without the help of God and of the king of Bohemia."

John, who proved an expensive luxury to Bohemia, reigned for 36 years. His nation must have been thankful when he was knocked on the head at Crécy—a story which is always told with pride in Czech history textbooks. King John had already lost the sight of one eye during a crusade against the Lithuanians and soon became totally blind, but this did not diminish his warlike ardor. In 1346 he hurried to the aid of the King of France against the English King Edward III and fell fighting on the field of Crécy, possibly making his oft-quoted statement when told to run for his life, as the battle was lost: "It has never happened that a Czech King should flee from a battle." Edward is said to have exclaimed, on hearing of his death, "The crown of chivalry has fallen to-day; never was anyone equal to this king of Bohemia." He also bequeathed the appropriate motto "Ich dien!" to the Black Prince.

Indeed, John had served every interest but his own. His son Charles, who was elected Emperor as the fourth of that name and the first as king of Bohemia, took the tangled coils of central European affairs into his own firm hands. Prague was the center of his activities.

Great were the number of enterprises by which Charles successfully improved the lands of the Bohemian crown and earned the title of "The Father of his Country." He enhanced the material wealth of the nation and enriched its moral and intellectual life by introducing a strict administration of justice and compelling respect for the law. Through his efforts, Prague became the junction for all the traffic of Central Europe. The southern Slavs gave it the name of "Zlatá Praha" (Golden Prague). Of greatest importance to the nationalistic and intellectual development of Bohemia was his founding of the Charles

University in Prague in 1348, which soon became worthy, by its surprising growth, of its older sisters of Bologna, Paris, and Oxford. (It is important to note the date, for, with the absorption of the remnants of Bohemia-Moravia by Germany in 1939, the German Protector proclaimed this university a German Institution on the theory that it was founded by Charles IV in his capacity as Holy Roman Emperor, although the university was chartered in 1348 and Charles did not become Holy Roman Emperor until seven years later, in 1355.)

John Hus

The greatest glory was bestowed upon the university by Magister John Hus, both as Rector and as a popular preacher at the Bethlehem Chapel, where the sermons were preached in Czech, although the German language was predominant both in public offices and in the churches and schools throughout the country. The efforts made by Hus for a reform of religious life resulted in the Czech Reformation.

Hus lived in a period characterized by the moral corruption of the Roman Catholic Church. The Emperor Charles, by his generous support of the Church and the clergy, had considerably increased its wealth and splendor. Hus castigated Church abuses in a general way at first, but was considered a heretic when he attacked the immoral life of the priests. Following his lengthy theological doubts and disputes, he sought information from the English heretic Wycliffe.

A sturdy peasant from southern Bohemia, Hus studied in Prague at the intermediate schools and at the university. In 1396, he became Master of Arts and began to lecture at the university. Entering the Church in 1400, it was his desire to become a Doctor of Theology. In 1402 he was elected not only Rector (President) but also preacher in the Bethlehem Chapel of Prague. The Bethlehem Chapel was built in 1391 by a Prague merchant and a country squire with the stipulation that the word of God be preached there exclusively in Czech. This requirement reveals to some extent the nationalistic feeling in Prague at that time. The majority of the parishes were either in the hands of German priests or those of Czech nationality who were bitterly hostile to the moral principles urged by Hus. The Bethlehem Chapel became a stronghold of the Church reform party. At the university, Hus taught the young Czech intelligentsia; in the Bethlehem Chapel, he spoke to burghers and nobles, to artisans and laborers, in rich, picturesque, and vivacious Czech.

The conflict of nationality between the Czechs and the Germans also became acute in Hus' time. The Czech "nation" became a factor at the university, and the Czechs bore with impatience their unjust representation there, which gave three votes to the foreign "nations" (allowing the Germans to dominate) while the Czechs had only one. On the surface these quarrels seemed to be merely secular, but the real dividing factor between Czech and German was the movement for religious reform. The Church was, in the true sense of the word, a state within a State, and the power of the hierarchy often even triumphed over the royal government.

Hus, the master of Charles' great university from 1401 to 1415, started as a religious reformer and gradually developed into the spokesman of the nationalists. He introduced a simplified spelling of the Czech language, giving the Roman letters newly devised accents to carry the soft sounds of the Slavonic tongue. But a controversy raged around him which darkened all Europe, and the teachings of Wycliffe took root in the halls of the university. When Rome was rent by the great schism and when all Europe was divided on points of theological doctrine, Bohemia solemnly declared that its own university should be an infallible authority in matters of dogma and faith. There was a Pope in Rome and another in Avignon, and the university of Hus decided to be independent of both.

In 1414 a Council met in Constance (Switzerland) to reform the Church in both head and limbs and to remove other serious disorders from which it was suffering. Hus was called to Constance; King Sigismund treacherously lured him into a trap. The Synod of Constance condemned him to be burned at the stake when he refused to renounce his opposition to the authority of the Church—to renounce the principle that the personal intellect and personal conviction of a Christian, supported by his conscience, could overrule the judgments of the Pope or the Council.

When Hus was burned at the stake in 1415, the whole Czech nation, almost to a man, placed itself behind Hus. The death of an innocent and pure-minded man aroused the common people; death for an ideal and the truth of the Scriptures appealed to the intelligentsia. Great gatherings took place in the mountains, which were given Biblical names. These new religious bodies signified nothing to the Church and state authorities but a rebellion. In 1419, at last, open rebellion broke out in Prague. The Hussites demanded that the Church should no longer withhold the sacramental wine from the worshippers. They adopted as their symbol the chalice, often carrying a stone cup at the head of their processions.

When the controversy overflowed beyond the Church and the university, it became Bohemia's battle against the encroachments of the Germans who pressed her from all sides. German Catholic miners of Kutná Hora threw Bohemian Protestants into the shafts and called the death trap Tábor in derision. The Hussites in turn nailed their Catholic prisoners in tarred beer barrels and rolled them into a bonfire, around which they sang the war psalms of King David. When all Europe rang with the controversy and the possession of fortified strongholds was a decisive matter, a great Hussite, Žižka, built his own fort on the hill of Tábor (1420). He made it a fortified city wherein every building was a "strong-point," the whole girded by two mighty walls within a moat. Here for a time a group of Hussites lived as the early Christians had done, possessing everything in common.

In battle after battle, the Hussites overthrew numerically superior forces hurled against the Czechs by the warriors of King Sigismund. Žižka was the first soldier to recognize the value of small firearms. Much of his success was due to his superlative courage, the courage of a general whose leadership was in no way impaired by the loss first of one eye, then of both. As a matter of fact, his blindness produced an uncanny terror in his adversaries. Above all, what made the ill-equipped, poorly-armed Hussite peasants invincible for so long was their determination, based upon their unshakable conviction that they were fighting for a just and righteous cause. Of course, their cause was helped not only by the "morale" element, but also by the new military tactics introduced by Žižka. Many of the Hussites were simple countryfolk who piled their families and household goods into their farm-carts and traveled around the country following Žižka's army. Their stout wagons, when armor-plated, became formidable "tanks."

The Hussite wars lasted 15 years (Žižka died in 1424). Under Prokop the Great, the Hussite armies undertook retaliatory expeditions into the German countries, penetrating as far as the Danube and the Baltic Sea, spreading abroad the terror of the Hussite name. The armies called themselves "fighters of the Lord," although they were also warring for the "Czech tongue," that is, for national rights against German usurpation. Thus Bohemia became a country of the Gospel and the Chalice, or Calixtines (or Utraquists, as the Holy Communion was introduced in the form of bread and wine).

The Meaning of Hussitism to the Czechs

The Hussites did not fight with the intention of creating a Czech state on a national basis.[5] They were burning to reform the faith and

---

[5] Kohn, Hans, *The Idea of Nationalism* (New York: The Macmillan Co., 1944), p. 109.

the true Church. But this religious movement coincided largely, though not entirely, with the Czech people; furthermore, the crusaders sent against them by Pope and Emperor were mostly Germans. Hence religious fervor became intermingled with national fervor and with a demand for social justice, the result of the resentment of the Czechs against the encroachment and growing influence of alien Germans in Bohemia.

The protracted wars between the Hussites and the Catholics naturally strengthened the antagonism between Czechs and Germans and made the Czechs aware of their affinity with other peoples speaking a similar Slavonic language. Under Žižka, the Hussites in 1420 went into the war "to liberate the truth of the Law of God and the Saints and to protect the faithful believers of the Church, and the Czech and Slavonic language." [6]

To this religious and linguistic antagonism was added a social conflict between the patriarchate and the lower urban classes. The economically weaker Czech artisans captured cities from the hands of the German burghers and many German towns came under Czech control. The Czech language and literature began to predominate and "the Czechs were thus the only people in Eastern Europe to develop their own urban middle classes before the nineteenth century. This educated Czech middle class tried to keep itself in the newly gained official positions by demanding a knowledge of Czech as a prerequisite for office and by trying generally to bar foreigners as far as possible from the privileges of government." [7]

What has Hussitism signified for the Czechs ever since? The day of Hus' martyrdom has become a national festival of remembrance and the Czechs love him more dearly than any other hero of the past. It was he who wrote, "Love the Truth, defend the Truth, speak the Truth, and hear the Truth," and it is significant that the motto of the Czech nation is, "Pravda Vítězí"—"Truth Prevails." It was this motto that was used as a national slogan during both World Wars.

The Czech nation has developed, especially under Masaryk's influence, the ideology of a nationalism based on Hus' preachings. To the Czech nationalist, the Czech nation took up as an inheritance from Hus the fight for truth, respect for personal conviction, loyalty to freedom, and a love of fraternity and democracy. His followers also like to emphasize that Hus' ideas traveled to Luther, from Luther to the era of enlightenment, and finally to the Declaration of Human

[6] *Ibid.*, p. 111.
[7] *Ibid.*

Rights on both shores of the Atlantic Ocean (in Virginia in 1776 and in Paris in 1793).

Other striking evidence of Hus' influence is found in the field of symbolism. One of the main things for which Hus contended was the right of all believing men and women to partake of the Cup in the Sacrament of the Lord's Supper, as against the Romanist practice of retaining it solely for the priests. No sooner had Hus been burned at Constance than the Czechs who favored his views adopted the Cup as their national symbol.

In the Great Square in Prague opposite the Town Hall, where 27 Protestant leaders were executed after the Battle of the White Mountain in 1621, visitors always notice the enormous and massive Memorial of John Hus. The martyr stands there amid a group of Czech patriots, calling on them to rise and be free. Some of the figures around him are still asleep, some are awakening, some are in the act of springing up, and some are fully erect with outstretched hands welcoming the new era of liberty.

This monument is a symbol of Czech nationalism. How the Germans were infuriated when the Czechs expressed opposition to their hated rule and paid symbolic allegiance to the ideals of Hus by "saying it with flowers" on Hus' Day (July 6, 1941), when the monument was literally drowned in flowers during the preceding night! At that time waves of intense emotion, religious fervor, and patriotic fervor were sweeping the German-occupied land and the utmost reverence was shown by almost all classes to the memory of the greatest man to which the Czech nation has given birth. John Hus has always lived on in the hearts, the lives, and the aspirations of millions of Czechs in Europe and across the seas.

Since the Church was unable to subdue the Hussites by arms, the Council of Basil recognized them as true sons of the Church, granting the Czech national Church four deviations from the ordinary Catholic confession and even permitting the Czechs to elect a Hussite archbishop. This agreement was known as the Compacts. After the death of Sigismund's grandson, the Czechs elected George of Podebrad as a king—the only Hussite king of Bohemia. He is known in Czech history as a successful ruler who brought back prosperity and who tried to introduce a League of Nations in Europe which would prevent future wars.

Soon Rome began to work against the Czech interests again by repealing the Compacts, refusing to acknowledge the Czech archbishop, and declaring King George's nation to be heretics. King George fought victoriously against his enemies, but he died in 1471. For a time two Polish kings of little ability occupied the throne of Bohemia; the second of them, Louis, was drowned in 1526 in the swamps near Mohács in Hungary on an expedition against the Turks.

During King George's reign, there arose in the Czech nation a new religious body called the Czech Brotherhood. Hus was burned at the stake on July 6, 1415, but those who silenced him could not unsay his message and at last in 1457, a little body of earnest men drew together. They agreed to accept the Bible as their only standard of faith and practice and to establish a strict discipline which would keep their lives in the simplicity, purity, and brotherly love of the Apostolic Church. The movement quickly interested thoughtful people in all classes of society, many of whom joined the ranks. The formal organization of the Unitas Fratrum (The Unity of Brethren) followed, and its preaching, theological publications, and educational work soon raised it to a great influence in Bohemia, Moravia, and Poland. The "Brothers" significantly enriched Czech literature and raised the standard of both education and art. In the sixteenth century, Bishop Blahoslav, with his disciples, translated the Scriptures from the original in a rendering called the "Králická Bible" after the town where it was printed. Its language was so beautiful that it has remained the standard of the Czech tongue to this day.

The End of Bohemia's Independence

Politically, the sixteenth century showed signs of the approaching decline of the following centuries. In 1536 the Czech Estates elected Ferdinand I, a Habsburg, to the throne. He succeeded in sowing discord between the nobles and the towns and between the Utraquists and the Catholics, in order to strengthen his power at the expense of the liberties of the Estates and to root out the nation's Hussite spirit. Calling Jesuits to Bohemia, he also established a Catholic archbishop in Prague, the first in 130 years.

The successors of Ferdinand carried on his policies, trying in vain to procure guarantees of religious liberty for the Protestants who formed the majority of the nation. They now consisted of the Utraquists, who had long ago broken with Rome due to Luther's influence, and the Czech Brethren. Eventually the Habsburg, prodded by the Spanish ambassadors, succeeded in driving the Czech Estates into rebellion (1618).

A definite act of imperial bad faith, following years of a policy in-

spired by malevolence and tempered by stupidity, brought matters to
a climax. A heated scene in the Council Chamber of the Castle of
Prague ended in what is described as the "Act of Defenestration":
the Emperor's lieutenants were thrown out of the window. Their
secretary, who protested, was treated in the same way. None of the
three was killed. A midden in the moat broke their fall and the
officials got safely away. This incident let loose all the horrors of the
Thirty Years' War. For the Czechs, as for those of Teutonic origin
who sympathized with the liberal movement of the time, the Battle of
the White Mountain and its tragic sequel on that June 21, 1620, was the
death knell of their hopes.

The Thirty Years' War was the last and worst of all the religious
wars which Europe suffered with the coming of the Reformation.
While it broke out first in Bohemia, it spread slowly over central Europe, gaining in fury and intensity. After Catholic and Protestant
Germans had mauled each other horribly, the war took on a political
significance in which all the greater powers of Europe gradually became embroiled. The Holy Roman Empire of the Habsburgs was
supported by Catholic Spain; against them in support of the Protestants
of Germany were finally ranged Sweden, Denmark, England, and
France.

The Darkest Period of Bohemian History

For the Bohemians, the Battle of the White Mountain was the most
tragic disaster. In 1500 the free Czech peasants had been deprived
of their rights and had become mere serfs. Since then they had lost
interest in the affairs of their country. The Hussite battles were won
by free peasants; the Battle of the White Mountain was lost by mercenaries.

In 1621, 27 of the leading noblemen, citizens, and learned men of
Bohemia who had supported the anti-Habsburg movement were be-
headed in the Old Town Square in Prague. Escorted by alien mercenaries, the martyrs were led to execution, and the rolling of drums
accompanied the scene until the last victim had been killed.[8] To the
present, on the anniversary of that day, patriotic Czechs have carried
wreaths to the graves of these men who died in the courage of their
convictions. This recalling of sad events in their history seems to be a

---

[8] Strange to relate, the sword that was used by the one executioner was discovered some
50 years ago in an Edinburgh curiosity shop. On its basket hilt are graven the names of the
Bohemian gentlemen who fell by it (three of the 27 were hanged), and under those names the
remark in the Czech language: "The 1st unhappy task on 21st June 1621. G.M."

peculiarly Slavonic trait. The Serbs still observe Vidovdan, the day of their disastrous defeat at Kosovo, where their chivalry succumbed in a sea of blood.

Emperor Ferdinand's saying gives the key to the Counter-Reformation period of Czech history: "Better no population at all than a population of heretics." At the beginning of the Thirty Years' War, there were 3,000,000 people in Bohemia, nearly all Protestants. At the end, there were only 800,000, all (nominally) Roman Catholics. One Jesuit priest boasted that he alone had burned 60,000 Czech books; the very possession of a Bible or hymnary was punishable with death.

The towns were repopulated by German immigrants belonging to the Church of Rome, and the estates of the nobles were confiscated and given to aliens. It was estimated that two-thirds of the estates passed to aliens in this way. Great numbers of the nobles and citizens went into exile rather than renounce their faith. The Czech language ceased to be the official language. Bohemia became a bilingual (Czecho-German) country—and eventually German became the dominant language. The Jesuits suppressed all literature, science, and the schools. They also changed the Czech calendar by adding to the patron saints of the country a new saint, John of Nepomuk, a fabulous figure but one nevertheless canonized by the Pope. This John was designed to eradicate John Hus from the memory of the people. The Jesuits even tried to suppress the language of the "Králická Bible" by creating a new so-called "St. Wenceslas tongue."

John Amos Comenius

In short, after 1627, the Bohemian nation lived spiritually only in exile (in Germany, Poland, and the Netherlands). The most famous of these exiles, John Amos Comenius (Komenský, 1592-1670), the last Bishop of the Bohemian Brotherhood, wandered for more than 40 years in exile and died in Amsterdam. He was welcome and honored in courts and universities, introducing new educational principles that revolutionized teaching methods. His real worth was recognized in his own day, as is witnessed by the opinions of the doughty Swedish chancellor, Oxenstierna, of Samuel Hartlib and his English group, and of his protectors, the two De Geers, as well as his numerous friends among the pedagogical reformers. How many elements of the modern educational system were advocated by Comenius! He advocated a free and universal system of education; education of both sexes; pre-school home training; instruction in the native tongue; graded subject matter adjusted to the psychological development of the pupils; dramatization of the subject; close correlation of thought with things; incorporation of history and geography, of drawing and manual training, in the curriculum.[9]

In 1650 Comenius wrote the pathetic "Bequest of the Dying Mother of the Unity of Brethren," in which occur the words quoted by President Masaryk on the memorable day when he read his first message to the National Assembly of the new Czechoslovak Republic, December, 1918: "I also believe before God that after the passing of the storms of wrath brought down upon our heads by our sins, the rule over thine own possessions shall be restored to thee, O Czech people!"

But when Comenius wrote these words, the nation was nearly dead. It was a period of intellectual as well as material decay. The Czech language became gradually subordinated to German; in about 1700, the Bohemian nobility was completely denationalized and the greater part of the country—the so-called German territory—was settled with Germans. The nation became disunited religiously—Hussite and Catholic. Numerically, these two Czech peoples had changed. From the time of the Hussite Wars to the Battle of the White Mountain (1620), the number of adherents of the Chalice reached 80 per cent in the Bohemian lands, while the Protestants numbered 10 per cent and Catholics 10 per cent.[10]

In the middle of the seventeenth century, Bohemia had about 800,-000 and Moravia barely 500,000 inhabitants, most of them Catholics. When the Emperor Joseph II issued his famous Patent concerning the toleration of Protestants in the Habsburg Empire, no more than 70,000 clandestine Protestants made their appearance. The Kingdom of Bohemia became in effect no more than a colony governed from an unfriendly Vienna; it was the taxes levied on the Czech nation which allowed that city to develop at the expense of Prague. In seeking the favors of the reigning dynasty, the Czech nobility which remained in the country were traitors to the national cause. From that time forward, the history of Bohemia was not a history of kings and nobles, but a history of an enslaved people who kept alive the national tradition only in memories of their former political independence. That nation which three centuries earlier had centered on itself the atten-

---

[9] Matthew Spinka, *John Amos Comenius, That Incomparable Moravian* (Chicago: University of Chicago Press, 1934), and bibliography, pp. 156-177. It is little known that Comenius is also the spiritual founder of modern Masonry—see: Joseph S. Roucek, "Freemasonry in Czechoslovakia," *The Builder*, Vol. XV (February, 1929), pp. 45ff.; (March, 1929) pp. 67ff.; (April, 1929) pp. 111ff.; and "The Pioneer and Founder of Modern Masonry, Jan Amos Komensky," *Square and Compass* (Denver, Colo.), Vol. XXXVIII (December, 1929), pp. 28ff.

[10] Herben, Jan, *op. cit.*, p. 205.

tion of all Europe and through its energy had carried human thought to its highest summits, seemed now condemned to irredeemable ruin and its name about to be erased from history.

Not until the eighteenth century was the work of destruction consummated. Systematically carried out, the work of Germanization and bureaucratic centralization attached the Kingdom of Bohemia to Vienna by chains which daily became heavier. The state began to disappear from the map of Europe; it became no more than a simple province within the empire of the Habsburgs. The economic and civil reforms of Habsburg Joseph II (1780-1790), inspired by the "enlightened" spirit of the times, brought relief to the laboring classes but could not raise the intellectual level of a nation deprived of its schools and leaders. Fortunately, Joseph at least stopped the missionary activity of the Jesuits in Bohemia, freed the peasants from serfdom, and gave his support to the schools.

National Revival

But even during those days of absolute abasement, a new life began to germinate in the depth of the Czech soul. The breath of liberty that blew from France across the whole of Europe in the second half of the eighteenth century, struck a still-sensitive chord in the nationalistic spirit of the Czechs. Thanks to certain men with a rare capacity for self-immolation and fittingly named the "Awakeners of the Nation," the old struggle in Bohemia for national culture and political independence was revived. At the outset, this struggle was restricted to the intellectual domain. In taking as a starting point those traditions piously preserved in certain of the anti-Reformation districts of Bohemia and in remote parts of Slovakia by a small number of priests, the Czech "Awakeners" devoted themselves, with the encouragement of a group of pro-Czech nobles, to the task of rekindling the flames of national sentiment among the masses. Historians began to rediscover both Hus and the religious Reformation, George of Podebrad as well as Comenius. The philologists studied the old foundations of the written language, as they were laid down by Hus and Blahoslav. The poet and journalist also popularized the findings.

The defeat of Czech Protestantism in 1620 put an end to the native Protestant aristocracy. Catholic noblemen from other countries took their places. Together with the Jesuits, who monopolized education, they introduced into Bohemia a flowering of Spanish and Italian baroque with its voluptuous wealth of architecture, its transcendental modes of thought, and its international outlook. In the eighteenth

century, the French Rococo and secular spirit replaced the baroque in
shaping the minds and lives of the Bohemian aristocracy. Fortunately
for the development of a progressive Czech nationalism, the Bohemian
aristocracy was a small class of wealthy magnates with not too narrow
an outlook.

Under the influence of the Enlightenment, this Bohemian aristocracy,
although rooted in other countries and races, produced in the second
half of the eighteenth century a patriotism based, "as in Ireland or
Belgium, upon the community of the historical territory, of the *nation
Bohemia,* without any clear realization that this nation consisted of
the two ethnic groups sharply differentiated in language and traditions, the Czechs and the Germans." [11] They looked to the Czech
historical traditions and rights of the Bohemian Kingdom as a guarantee of their privileges against the centralizing tendencies of the
Austro-Hungarian monarchy and started to foster interest in the history of Bohemia and in the life and language of its people.

This process paralleled the rise of the middle class in Bohemia, due
to the transition from an agrarian to an industrial society. The Czech
renaissance thus had as its fathers "historians imbued with enlightened
humanitarianism; practical reformers searching to improve agriculture
to exploit the natural resources of the country, and to stimulate manufacture and commerce; and educators." [12]

The educational reforms were important in this respect: the former
instruction in Bohemia, dominated by Jesuit scholasticism and carried
on exclusively in Latin, was modernized and German was introduced
as the language of teaching in the high schools. Empress Maria Theresa ordered more instruction in Czech so that officials might converse
with the people in their native tongue. In fact, a chair of Czech language and literature was founded in the University of Vienna in 1775
for the candidates for bureaucratic positions. As the century drew to
its close, the middle class was rising, the position of the peasantry was
alleviated, and economic life was mobilized. Joseph's emancipation of
the Protestants added a new and vigorous element to the Czech middle class—which still remembered the Hussite movement and the
Reformation.

But the first generation of the "Awakeners" of the Czech historical
consciousness were enlightened Catholic priests, Piarists, ex-Jesuits, inspired in their patriotism by classical humanism and later Western
influences, largely from Germany. In Germany, Herder expressed

great hope in the Slav future; Goethe loved the Slav folk songs; Schlozer fostered Slavonic studies and was a good friend of the Slavs. "As the Irish national awakening started under the influence of English political ideas and men of English descent, so the Czech national awakening partly began under the influence of cultural ideas coming from Germany and of men of German descent." [13]

The first generation of Czech patriots tried to prove that Czech history and cultural achievements were equal to those of the Germans and the Western nations, and formed the Society of Sciences in 1773 (named the "Royal Bohemian Society of Sciences"). They unearthed a Czech nation out of the documents of the past and built up a new appreciation of the Hussites. The use of the Czech tongue began to spread. It was employed in theatrical performances and a growing periodical literature. In March, 1792, 33 "Bohemian aborigines" (that is, Bohemians of Slavonic origin) petitioned the Bohemian Diet against the policy of Germanizing their compatriots, which had been steadily pursued under Joseph II. Somewhat later, the "nationality" idea was resuscitated by the majority of the Bohemian gentry in the Diet, as a card which could be effectively played in order to preserve their "historical rights" when purely political methods failed.

From 1792 to 1848, the Czech cause was promoted mostly by scholars of middle-class origin acting as tutors in the families of nobles who wished to promote the Czech nationalistic idea for personal reasons. Since they were incompetent themselves to use their native language effectively, they employed the practiced pens of scholars for the purpose. The transition period from the eighteenth century of enlightenment to the nineteenth century of nationalism is headed by four men: Joseph Dobrovský (1753-1829), Joseph Jungmann (1773-1847), Pavel Joseph Šafařík (1795-1861), and František Palacký (1798-1876).

Dobrovský, the founder of Slavonic studies, wrote a Czech grammar and also a grammar of Old Church Slavonic, and did much by his writings to promote a feeling of kinship between the different branches of the Slavic race. Jungmann, the son of a peasant from Central Bohemia, compiled a famous dictionary and translated Western European romantic literature. Šafařík was a Slovak, the son of a Protestant pastor. He is best known for his colossal work on *Slavonic Antiquity*, which won him wide fame in the world of letters although it was never finished.

Palacký formulated the first Czech political program and, after 1848, in company with his son-in-law Fr. L. Rieger, became the political

---

[13] *Ibid.*, pp. 553-554.

leader of the Czech nation. Born in Moravia, the son of a village schoolmaster in whose family the traditions of Hus had been preserved, he made friends while at college with an Irish jockey, who lent him Robertson's *History of Scotland.* This induced him to write a history of his own nation. At the invitation of Dobrovský he went to Prague, where he met several Czech noblemen greatly interested in his proposed undertaking. Through their help he carried on immense researches in the Czech archives hidden in old castles and mansions; later he was appointed historiographer to the Bohemain Estates. His *History of the Czech People in Bohemia and Moravia,* a great and scholarly work, became a truly inspiring influence upon the Czechs and earned for Palacký the title of the "Father of the Nation."

Palacký propounded that the core of Czech history could be found in the period of the Czech Reformation, or from Hus to the Bohemian Brethren, which was also the modern consummation of the original Slav character. He deduced that the Czechs were forerunners of Western liberalism who pioneered in the Hussite wars for humanitarian ideals, opposing authority and hierarchy and asking for the equality of men and freedom of conscience. For Palacký, the Hussite period was the root of the Reformation, and so of all growth of liberalism, the Puritan Revolution, and the American and French Revolutions. By basing their political ambitions on their deepest national traditions, the Czechs could progress by identifying themselves with the progressive West.

This interpretation of history placed the Czechs geographically as the eastern outpost of the liberal West instead of the western outpost of the Slavic East. "In these traditions the nation was born—and in his farewell message on relinquishing the presidency of the Czechoslovak Republic, Masaryk rightly pointed out that nations live and preserve themselves by the ideals out of which they were born." [14]

Notice that Palacký, wisely, did not look for the solution of the problems of his nation in Pan-Slavism, although an enthusiasm for solidarity of the Slavonic races started with the Czech "Awakeners" and has been popular with the Slavs, in one form or another, ever since.

Pan-Slavism—a movement to unite all Slav peoples under the leadership of Russia—would have become a powerful political factor if it had succeeded. If Poles, Czechs, Slovaks, Serbs, and Bulgarians had joined with the Russians in a single state or federation of states, they would have formed a huge and potent political unit. There are about 300 million Slavs in Europe, a population exceeded only by that of China

---

[14] *Ibid.,* p. 560.

and India. But Russian and Pan-Slav concepts of Pan-Slavism remained largely dreams—although Russia did succeed in aiding the Serbs and Bulgarians to throw off the rule of the Ottoman Empire and establish their own national states.[15]

Pan-Slavism was originally extra-political, an affair of scholars and students rather than of statesmen. From the first, it was a vague, dreamy affection for a Slavonic policy. After the long residence of the Russian "deliverers" at Prague in 1813, Russian officers and Czech professors kept up correspondence. The study of the Russian language was taken up with ardor. But there was an infinite distance between this intellectual Pan-Slavism and the later political Pan-Slavism, the fundamental promise of which was the union of all the Slavic races in a single state. The earlier stages of the movement were intimately associated with Dobrovský, Jungmann, and Palacký. While Dobrovský laid the foundation of historical science in Bohemia, Jungmann's great merit was the popularizing of the Czech language. His enthusiasm for Pan-Slavism made him comparatively indifferent to purely Czech aspirations—hence his *magnum opus* is not so much a Bohemian as a Slavonic lexicon. Palacký founded a learned periodical in 1827 to champion the cause of Czech autonomy against the out-and-out Pan-Slavism of such passionate nationalists as Václav Hánka (1791-1861).

The most extravagant member of the opposite camp was the Slovak poet and preacher, Jan Kollár (1793-1852), who carried Pan-Slavism to the verge of absurdity by trying to prove that Latin was an old Slavonic tongue corrupted by Greek influences or even maintaining that the aboriginal inhabitants of Italy were Slavs. Despite the eccentricity of his scholarship, Kollár enjoyed the extraordinary influence which must always belong to a man of genius who is also an ardent patriot. Palacký rejected these claims. His position was strengthened when, in 1831, he was appointed a director of the newly instituted Czech section of the National Bohemian Museum and a member of the society "Matice Česká," founded in the same year by Prince Rudolf Kinský for the promotion of Czech literature.

Palacký served his nation not only as a historian, but also as its politi-

---

[15] But this dream became a potent political element during Hitler's rise. The possible unification of all the Slavs did become one of the nightmares haunting the Germans soon after their own national unification in 1870, since they knew that they could not match the man-power of the Slavs, whom the Nazis regarded as an especially inferior race. The Russians, under Lenin and Stalin, did not pay much attention to the Pan-Slavonic weapon, since they found much more use for the Comintern International. But, following Germany's invasion of Russia in the summer of 1941, the Kremlin urged the coöperation of Slav peoples, who for the most part have a deep attachment for Russia although not for Communism.

cal leader and spokesman. He hoped and strove for the federalization of Austria. His opposition to any close union between Austria and Germany was expressed in his often quoted statement: "If there were no Austria, it would be necessary to create one." But there is a later saying, also by Palacký, which is in the form of prophecy, and which became a dictum during the Great Wars. "Before Austria was, we were; and when Austria no longer is, we still shall be." He had ceased to fix his hopes on the dream of a reformed Austria. In 1876, when his great history was completed, a banquet was held at Prague to celebrate the event. The substance of Palacký's speech, which he called his "testament," was: "We must educate ourselves and work."

This was also the keynote of the lifework of Karel Havlíček (1821-1856), who, as editor of the *National Newspaper,* exercised a strong influence over the masses, although he lived to be only thirty-five. His thesis bore fruit; the Czechs made use of modern methods, printed books and journals, established libraries and museums, took care of their schools, and turned to scientific labors.

The Czech politicians took over the trend only when the French revolution of February, 1848, began to advance eastward and also to set Vienna, Prague, and Budapest aflame. In that year, when the whole of Europe followed the example of France and broke the chains of archaic absolutism, Austria was forced to grant certain constitutional liberties to the nationalities which she oppressed. Thereafter the movement to rebuild the Czech nation expanded in an atmosphere noticeably more favorable to its growth. Although the revolution was suppressed (the Bohemian peasant alone gained his freedom by the abolition of socage) and punished by the stifling reaction of the years 1850-1860, the Czech politician was no longer absent from the Austrian political tribune. He offered to coöperate in building up a strong Austria if the latter would be just to the Czech nation on the basis of the program of Bohemian state rights—the restoration of the State of Bohemia, thus uniting Bohemia, Moravia, and Silesia. This plan was sponsored by the Czech aristocracy (Count Martinic) and the leader of the nation of that time, Dr. Rieger. But the throne was dominated by the German and Hungarian minorities, although the Czech lands paid the most taxes and although the Austrian state was formed in 1526 as a triple empire: German-Bohemian-Hungarian, with equal rights for all the three components. But the concept of centralization became the fixed idea of Austrian statesmen, and in 1867, in place of a confederation of states like the one demanded by the Czechs, they created a dual monarchy, one half dominated by the Germans (Austria) and the other by the Hungarians, with the Austro-Hungarian Empire working in concert with the new German Empire.

The Slovaks

This political rearrangement, so fatal for the Czechs, placed the Slovak branch of the nation in an even more deplorable position. The Slovaks settled their part of Europe about the same time as the Czechs and were closely associated with them. For instance, Samo, a Czech chieftain, in the seventh century formed a kingdom which included the Slovaks. Both formed what is sometimes known as the Great Moravian Empire (ninth century). In the tenth century, the Hungarians conquered the Slovaks and confined them within the limits of present-day Slovakia, where for nearly a thousand years they became an unwilling province of the Kingdom of Hungary. But the Slovaks remained a separate and distinct people, even though cut off from intercourse with other Slav peoples. They remained mainly Catholic and developed their language as a dialect of the Czech language.

Owing to the Magyar pressure on the Slovaks during the nineteenth century, and to the barrier raised against any form of intercommunication between the Czechs and Slovaks, a "literary" Slovak language was developed by certain Slovak patriots in the sixties.[16] The Hungarian Counter-Reformation had its seat in the Jesuit University at Tyrnava in Slovakia and succeeded in limiting the formerly strong influence of Protestantism in Slovakia. Yet Protestant influence remained, especially in Bratislava (Pressburg), and the Protestant Slovaks felt deeply their affinity with the Czechs and used the Czech literary language until the second half of the eighteenth century.

To combat these tendencies, the Catholic priest Antonin Bernolák (1762-1813) tried to create a separate Slovak literary language. But his and other similar efforts had no lasting effect because they used the western Slovak dialect, which was too close to Czech and too little understood in central and eastern Slovakia. After 1844, Ludevít Štur made the central Slovak dialect the literary language in an effort to establish Slovak culture and rights within Hungary and to increase the national consciousness of Hungarian Slovaks separated from the Austrian Czechs. This literary or written Slovak was not adopted by Slovaks living outside the borders of Slovakia, who continued to speak the Slovak dialect but to write in Czech. It was merely owing to the

---

[16] Street, C. J., *Slovakia Past and Present* (London: The Czech Society of Great Britain, n. d.), is a very convenient short introduction to Slovak history.

Magyar prohibition against writing Czech that the Slovaks in Slovakia were compelled to introduce written Slovak.

The Slovaks had to suffer continuous inroads on their culture and economic life. It became the policy of the Hungarian kings to introduce Germanic colonies into Slovakia in the hope that they would ultimately take the place of the irreconcilable Slovaks. By the fifteenth century there was scarcely a Slovak village without a group of German families. But the Slovaks showed the same ability to resist Germanization that they had shown in resisting Magyarization.

In the nineteenth century, the Magyars determined to take drastic steps to destroy the Slovak national consciousness. The popular Magyar proverb, "Tót nem émber" ("The Slovak is not a man") sufficiently illustrates this mentality. Until the first half of the last century, Latin had been the official language of the Kingdom of Hungary. The substitution of Magyar for Latin served as a pretext to make the use of the former language obligatory throughout the Hungarian state. Every citizen was forced to employ the Magyar language in the schools, the civil service, the army, and every branch of public life. This denationalizing policy drove even the simple and pastoral Slovaks into revolt. In 1848-1849, when the Magyars rebelled against the Habsburgs, the Slovaks threw their swords into the scale against the Magyars, whose revolution failed ignominiously.

The Magyars, instead of seeking an understanding with the nationalities, preferred to make their peace with the Habsburgs. By the Compromise of 1867, the Dual Monarchy was virtually divided between the Germans and the Magyars and the field was clear for a renewed policy of intensive Magyarization; thereafter the Slovaks found themselves at the mercy of the Hungarians, who forced upon them a regime of unprecedented oppression, a regime which sought to detach the Slovak branch completely from the Czech branch and to Magyarize it from the standpoint of both intellectual and political life. If a Slovak was content to enroll himself as a Magyar, well and good. If not, he could either emigrate or he must resign himself to a condition which justified the proverb, "Tót nem émber." He was denied the advantages of education and representation, and he was subject to police persecution if he dared evince the slightest signs of Slovak consciousness. During the forty years preceding World War I, no fewer than 793,665 Slovaks emigrated, mostly to the United States. Even the writings of Dr. Seton-Watson and others did not seem to be able to save the Slovaks from national extinction. Their only hope of regeneration lay in deliverance from Magyar rule. The prospects, however, appeared remote when the Dual Monarchy, impelled by Germany, plunged Europe into World War I and so rushed headlong to its inevitable doom.

But the liberation of Slovakia—as well as the lands of Bohemia—was on the way through T. G. Masaryk. The Czech political parties before 1914 had always been ready to discuss with Austria their demands for equal rights, but got nowhere fighting the centralistic government of Austria. Masaryk laid before his followers—and there were not too many of them before World War I—a program of work designed to build up inner national strength. At first Masaryk emphasized education and moral principles rather than politics. He tried to do away with absolutism and to transform Austria into a progressive state. But when Austria-Hungary entered World War I, he changed his platform to revolution.

Thomas G. Masaryk

Three men were finally responsible for shaking off the yoke of Austro-Hungarian oppression: Thomas G. Masaryk, a Moravian Slovak; Edward Beneš, a Bohemian; and Milán R. Štefánik, a Slovak. Masaryk, an aged philosopher, returned as the President of the new state four years to the day after he had fled from his country. His fellow-worker Beneš headed the Czechoslovak Foreign Ministry (in addition to holding other portfolios) uninterruptedly from that time until he became Masaryk's successor as President. The third conspirator, Štefánik, a young astronomer who represented the Slovaks in their rebellion against Habsburg rule, returned as a general of the French Army. His plane crashed over the very frontier of his native land. The Czechs still retain the distinction of selecting their national leaders according to Plato's recipe for the ideal state: from among professors —Hus, Komenský, Palacký, Masaryk, Beneš, and then Hodža and others.

Few prominent Europeans had more intimate connections with America than the founder and president of the Czechoslovak Republic. From the time when he first visited the United States to claim as his bride the American girl with whom he had fallen in love in Leipzig to the day when he last left its shores accompanied by all the honors due the head of a sovereign state, he maintained a most active interest in the United States. American institutions and experience were frequently used to point his writings. The son of a Slovak teamster on an imperial estate in Eastern Slovakia, Masaryk was born (1850) at a time when serfdom, although officially abolished a few years before, was still in practical effect. Work as a smith at home was interrupted by the interest of one of Masaryk's former teachers, who arranged for him to go on with his studies. From that time on, Masaryk paid for his high school and college education by his own earnings. Even after his marriage, life as an assistant professor in Vienna and later in Prague was a bitter struggle for a living. Masaryk began to fight against the authoritarian regime of Austria-Hungary while he was still in school. When he declared certain manuscripts to be forgeries in 1876, many of his people turned against him for questioning these so-called proofs of an early Czech culture. But he held firm against the opposition and vituperation of his own countrymen. No nation's reputation, he asserted, could be built upon a falsehood. Thirteen years later, when he protested an injustice to a Jewish tramp, he was branded a traitor to Christianity and nearly mobbed in the university when he tried to resume his lectures. There were other conflicts in which he participated in the twenty years before the war. Most of them took place in the Parliament of Vienna. By 1914 he was the recognized champion of minority rights in the whole Austro-Hungarian Empire, an object of hatred and persecution by the government.

One of the most fascinating romances of modern times is the story of how Masaryk, setting out alone in December, 1914, came back after four years of exile as the head of a new and independent Czechoslovak state. England helped him almost from the first and he was later Professor of Slav Research at King's College in London. In 1916 he went to France to convince the French Government of the necessity of disintegrating Austria-Hungary. Proceeding to Russia in 1917, he formed Czechoslovak legions from prisoners captured by the Allies. Soon they were fighting against the Central Powers, just as their sons fought Hitler's hordes on the side of the Allies in World War II. When Russia collapsed in 1917, a Czech army in Russia fought its way through Russia to Siberia and ultimately trekked back to Europe.

Masaryk ably exploited the feats of the Czechoslovak legions, with considerable financial help from American Czechoslovaks. In March, 1918, he went to the United States to persuade President Wilson, who had previously favored the preservation of the Austrian Empire on a federal basis, to acquiesce in the dissolution of the empire. As a result, the Czechoslovak National Council, headed by Beneš in Paris, was recognized by the Allied Powers as the Czechoslovak Government. The proclamation of Czechoslovak independence in Washington, D. C., on October 18, 1918, was the first legal step in the liberation of his country. The Czech National Council seized power in Prague on October 28, 1918, on the basis of the Washington Declaration. Delegates of all the

Slovak parties assembled on October 30, 1918, to organize a Slovak National Council which affirmed the right of self-determination, denied authority to the Hungarian Government "to speak and act in the name of the Czechoslovak nation living within the limits of Hungary," and declared that "the Slovaks form linguistically and historically a part of the Czechoslovak nation."

On November 14, 1918, the Revolutionary Assembly met in Prague, deposed the Habsburgs, proclaimed a Republic, elected Masaryk as President by acclamation, with Beneš as Foreign Minister, and enacted a provisional constitution. In December, 1918, Masaryk moved into the Hradčany Castle of Prague. With this a fairy tale came true: the tale of the working lad who starts off as a child in quest of truth and arrives home as the lord of the manor in the palace where his father had served the emperor as coachman. An ancient nation, possessing beautiful traditions, appeared on the world stage in modern attire, with progressive ideas and high ideals.

Bibliography

(At the end of Chapter XVII)

Chapter IV

POLAND (UP TO 1918)

Polish Origins

BETWEEN the Baltic Sea and the Carpathian mountains, on a vast plain cut by the Oder, Warta, and Vistula Rivers, Slavonic tribes called Polanians, Vistulians, Mazovians, Silesians, Pomeranians, and many others have dwelt since time immemorial. Those tribes united to form the Polish nation.

It would be difficult to understand the history and the present problems of modern Poland without some knowledge of her remote past. Since these pages are addressed primarily to the general reader, we shall limit our presentation to the most essential facts, the effects of which have a bearing on what is happening today.

Poland Under the Piasts (962-1370)

Poland's recorded history begins in 963 A. D., the year of the first recorded conflict between Poles and Germans. (Some historians prefer to set the opening date at 966 A. D.—the year of Poland's conversion to Christianity.) At that time, the Slavs who inhabited Central Europe were little differentiated racially, linguistically, economically, or socially although some tribes had already begun to coalesce into separate states, such as the Czech state. Poland was also beginning to take shape. The tribes which inhabited the area of present-day western Poland, Silesia, and certain adjacent parts of present-day Germany had gradually come under the domination of one central prince, who now applied the name of his tribe, the "Polans," to all the inhabitants of his loosely united domain.

The ecclesiastical organization established in Poland after its conversion to Christianity also contributed to the process of consolidation. Poland was first set up as an independent bishopric; later it was elevated to an archbishopric.

Although Poland, under the Piast dynasty, occasionally rose to a place of importance in history, it was subdivided during most of that period, like the rest of Europe, into numerous duchies and principalities jealous of and fighting for their independence. But, while the feudal system in Western Europe was strong enough to hold the subdivisions together in larger units, Polish feudalism was weak and backward. Cohesion was provided rather by the ecclesiastical organization and tradition.

In the thirteenth century, toward the end of the Piast period, the constant threat of Tartar invasions which menaced all of Europe for a time, was an important factor. The major Tartar defeat at Lignica, capital of a Polish principality in Silesia, contributed to the elimination of the Tartar threat to Western Europe, but Poland continued to face it and Russia was actually overrun by overwhelming Tartar hordes for centuries.

Another important event was the settlement of what is today Eastern Prussia by the Teutonic Knights, who conquered the native "Prus" (a Baltic people akin to the Latvians and the Lithuanians) and established their own state.

Furthermore, the disappearance of the broad belt of Slavonic nations west of Poland, as a result of German conquest late in the twelfth century, had disastrous effects. Germany became Poland's neighbor along her entire western frontier and Poland lost Pomerania to the German Empire and the Teutonic Knights.

Toward the end of the thirteenth century, centripetal tendencies again came to the fore in Poland. After numerous efforts at unification, a Polish prince, Wladyslaw II, finally re-established the Kingdom of Poland. Despite the loss of Silesia and Pomerania, Poland was now a recognized kingdom with a policy of its own, both at home and abroad.

The new foreign policy was instituted by Casimir the Great, last of the Piasts and Wladyslaw's successor. Realizing that his western neighbors were too strong for him to cope with, he deliberately turned Poland's face to the east. Russia was divided into numerous petty duchies, most of them still subject to Tartar rule, and Poland was able to secure a sizable slice of Russian territory, the so-called "Red Russia" (approximately the area of Eastern Galicia), which had already once belonged to her. Casimir also consolidated his father's policy of friendship with Lithuania for mutual protection against the Teutonic Order, a friendship that contravened the accepted custom in fourteenth-century Europe, for Lithuania was still pagan.

Casimir left his mark on Poland's internal organization, too. He re-established a unified administration and promulgated the "Statutes of Wislica," codifying Polish common law and introducing some elements of Western common law. Casimir's reign was one of unaccustomed peace and prosperity, attested by the many splendid mediaeval buildings in Polish cities which were built at that time. His major achievement, however, was the establishment of the University of Cracow (1364 A. D.), the first Polish university and second only to Prague in its antiquity among Central European seats of higher learning. The first German university (Vienna) was established in 1365.

Transition and the Jagellonian Period (1370-1572)

Casimir the Great was succeeded by his nephew, Louis of Anjou, also known as Louis the Great, King of Hungary. In order to guarantee the right of succession to one of his daughters (he had no sons), Louis not only had to confirm all the privileges enjoyed by the nobles before he became king,[1] but also to free the nobles from most of the taxes they had previously paid to the royal treasury. This novel concession was an important point in Polish history, for it marked the first grant of a general economic privilege to the nobility.

After Louis' death, Jadwiga, his youngest daughter, succeeded to the Polish throne. Being a young girl, she could not rule the country personally. The selection of her husband therefore became an important political problem. In the meantime, Poland was governed by the dignitaries of the crown, most of them appointees of Casimir the Great. These rulers of Poland were eager to cement the friendship with Lithuania into an alliance directed against the Teutonic Order, Poland's chief enemy. Such an alliance, they felt, could best be furthered by a marriage between Jagiello, the ruling prince of Lithuania, and Queen Jadwiga.

Both Jagiello and Jadwiga accepted this proposal, which was also supported by the Catholic Church. In order to marry Jadwiga, Jagiello had to embrace Catholicism (he was a pagan), automatically bringing his pagan subjects[2] into the Church as well. It was also agreed that, upon his marriage, Jagiello would become King of Poland in his own right and that Lithuania would become a part of Poland (Treaty of Krewo, 1385). Despite this agreement, however, the Lithuanians were able to preserve their separate political existence. For some time, Jagiello's person was the only link between the two countries.

---

[1] It was a mediaeval custom for a new king always to confirm the privileges granted by his predecessors.

[2] A considerable proportion of Jagiello's subjects were already Christians but belonged to the Orthodox Church, especially in the former Russian lands.

Although the Jagellonians consolidated the Polish tendency to face east instead of west into a permanent policy, Poland still retained considerable interest in Western affairs. The question of Poland's relations with the Teutonic Order also continued to loom large in the calculations of Polish statesmen, although its importance was substantially reduced after 1415, when the Order was decisively defeated near Grunwald and Tannenberg (East Prussia) by the Poles and Lithuanians assisted by the Czechs and Russians.[3]

Poland's association with Lithuania, originally a safeguard against the growing power of the Teutonic Order, soon involved Poland in all the difficulties troubling the overextended Lithuanian state. Lithuania's deep involvement in Russian affairs (most of her territory had previously been Russian) diverted much of her energy and strength into struggles with the Tartars and Mongols who controlled most of Russia. Furthermore, after northeastern Russia had freed itself from Mongol rule and the new Russian state was created,[4] it strove not only to liberate the Russian areas still under Mongol or Tartar domination, but also to secure control over autonomous Russian areas[5] and those subject to other foreign rulers. Poland, whose kings were also Grand Dukes of Lithuania, was thus inevitably drawn into the Lithuanian-Russian disputes.[6]

During the Jagellonian period, Poland's internal organization underwent many important changes. It was then that the essential elements of the constitutional system which was to last well into the eighteenth century were created. In western Europe the role of the nobles, so important in the thirteenth and fourteenth centuries, was visibly declining, with a corresponding increase in the power of the Crown, but the contrary was happening in Poland. Jagiello and his successors, although elected kings, were never the absolute rulers of Poland,[7] and their ambitious plans in the field of foreign politics

---

[3] Jagiello's wars against the Teutonic Order profited Poland little in terms of territorial changes. It remained for his sons to recover the territory taken by the Order from Poland in the thirteenth and fourteenth centuries, including Danzig and present-day Polish Pomerania (Treaty of Torun, 1466). The remainder of the Order's territory (present-day East Prussia) was left to it as a Polish fief. The problem of the Teutonic Order was finally settled in 1525, when its Grand Master, Albrecht Hohenzollern, became a Lutheran, and its lands were changed into the secular Duchy of Prussia, a Polish fief.

[4] This new Russian state was often called the "Muscovite" state (drawing its name from Moscow, its capital) to distinguish it from the old Russian state centered around Kiev, Russia's capital before the Tartar invasion.

[5] Such as the autonomous Republics of Novgorod and Pskov, which were brought into the new Russian state despite the desperate resistance of their Western-minded populations.

[6] This became increasingly important in the second half of the Jagellonian period in Poland.

[7] The situation was different in Lithuania, which was Jagiello's patrimony.

forced them to make repeated concessions to the nobles in exchange for their support.

The group of courtiers, mostly appointees of Casimir the Great and their descendants, who served in the most important Polish offices during Jagiello's reign, soon consolidated their position by increasing their ranks. Together with the descendants of old, powerful Polish families, as well as certain newcomers, they welded themselves into a closely knit oligarchy, commonly known as "the Magnates," which was very influential throughout the reign of Jagiello's sons. The officials recruited from this powerful group met regularly as the Royal Council and soon ·thereafter began to call themselves the Senate.

The tax problem, as well as the fact that all male members of the Polish gentry were obligated to render military service in times of war, created the basis for the rapid development of that group's political power. As early as during Jagiello's reign, the crown had to grant personal immunity to the members of the nobility.[8] Later King Casimir granted the gentry another important privilege, known as the "Privilege of Nieszawa," by which he promised to convene a congress of deputies of the various provincial nobles' conventions and to accept its advice on all important matters. Thus the Polish Diet was born.[9]

The Diet, and especially the House of Deputies, began to play an ever-increasing role in the nation's government. The House gradually assumed the right to impose taxes, greatly augmenting the power of the nobility over the rest of the nation. This increase in the gentry's power soon made itself felt in legislation profitable to that class but detrimental to the interests of other groups within the nation.

The Diet's legislative powers were confirmed in the so-called "Nihil Novi" Act of 1505, which stipulated that no new legislation could be adopted in Poland without the consent of the Diet. The House of Deputies, far more powerful than the Senate, transacted business under the chairmanship of a Speaker (called a *Marshal*) who was elected for the duration of the session.[8] The voting procedure was based on the principle of unanimity, every bill requiring the approval of all the deputies. Each individual deputy therefore possessed a theoretical veto power over any bill he opposed. This "liberum veto" could be especially hampering to the legislative process, because all the bills voted at any session were frequently embodied in a single act. Consequently, the veto of any bill was, in effect, a veto of all the bills in the act under

[8] The so-called "Neminem captivabimus" privilege of 1430 reads: "We shall not imprison anyone without lawful verdict."

[9] Regular Diets were held for six weeks every two years; extraordinary sessions were convened by the King whenever necessary.

consideration. These dangers, however, were merely theoretical during the Jagellonian period, for at that time small minorities opposed to any given legislation refrained from using their veto power and contented themselves with compromise concessions obtained from the majority under the implicit threat of the veto.

The Diet, dominated by the gentry-controlled House of Deputies, soon began to use its power to impose its will in questions concerning the properties of the crown and the treasury's income.

Sixteenth-century Poland was closely connected, both politically and culturally, with Western and Central Europe. Most of the conditions which gave rise to the Reformation movement in other European countries existed in Poland as well, and the intellectual and religious trends which permeated those countries were equally potent in Poland. All the major Protestant denominations found enthusiastic supporters in Poland, sometimes motivated not so much by religious conviction as by reluctance to pay tithes and St. Peter's penny, as well as the desire to appropriate Church estates.

Lutheranism preceded the other Protestant denominations in Poland. Perhaps because it first took root among the German-speaking burghers of the Polish-Pomeranian cities, which frequently regarded themselves as free cities under Poland's protection rather than as constituent parts of Poland, the Polish Government reacted with severe edicts against the "heretics." But these edicts were difficult to carry out, especially since Polish Pomerania was the immediate neighbor of East Prussia, which was ruled by a Lutheran prince, a vassal of Poland and, by virtue of his position, a ranking Polish senator. Moreover, as subsequent waves of Protestant ideas gained wide influence among the gentry and officialdom, the anti-Protestant laws lapsed because the temporal powers generally did not carry out the sentences imposed by ecclesiastical courts. A number of sects which were persecuted in all other countries (including Protestant states) found refuge and followers in Poland.

The most important permanent effect of the Reformation in Poland was the development of a national Polish literature, resulting from the attempt of both Protestants and Catholics to reach the laity and the less educated classes.

Poland and Lithuania

Although the original effort to achieve Polish-Lithuanian unification by the absorption of Lithuania into Poland had failed, the two countries continued to collaborate very closely as long as they were threatened by the Teutonic Order. During most of the Jagellonian period both countries had common rulers. At times this link was discarded and Lithuania had a Grand Duke of its own[10] (usually a younger brother of the King of Poland), or a separate Administrator, the common monarch retaining the Grand-Ducal title but delegating authority to a member of his family. On the whole, Polish-Lithuanian relations at that time amounted rather to a close alliance than to an actual union.

Lithuania was always eager to maintain her bonds with Poland. The Lithuanian nobility emulated the Polish nobility culturally and socially, gradually even adopting the Polish language. Resenting their lack of political power, they demanded that parliamentary institutions similar to those of Poland be established in Lithuania or that the scope of the Polish institutions be extended to include their country. This demand was strongly opposed by the Lithuanian aristocracy, descendants of the junior members of the Grand-Ducal family, who were jealous of their exclusive privilege of advising and influencing the Grand Duke.

While the Jagellonian succession in Lithuania was assured, the Poles felt secure in the stability of their relations. When the Jagellonian dynasty threatened to become extinct, it became necessary to evolve another tie. At the Diet of Lublin, in 1569, (three years before the death of the last Jagellonian king), a solution was adopted which provided for the joint election of a common monarch, to bear the dual title of King of Poland and Grand Duke of Lithuania. The two countries were also to have a common Diet. Lithuania, however, was to retain her autonomy and be governed by her own ministers. Thus the constitutional basis was laid for what was subsequently known as the "Commonwealth of the Two Nations," which lasted almost until the Partition of Poland.

Poland Under Elected Kings (1572-1764)

The kings of Poland were elected during the Jagellonian period, but it had been an established practice that a son or a brother of the king was invariably chosen to succeed him. Later elections were no longer subject to this restriction. In fact, kinship to the preceding king be-

---

[10] The Act of Horodlo (1413, known as the Union of Horodlo) provided that Lithuania was to have a Grand Duke of its own, appointed by the King of Poland by virtue of his hereditary rights over Lithuania, but subject to the consent of the Grand Ducal Council. Moreover, the approval of the Grand Duke was necessary to validate the election of a King of Poland. (The Grand Duke had to be a descendant of Jagiello.) Whenever the Poles felt that common interests would best be served by both countries having a common ruler, they simply elected the Grand Duke of Lithuania as King of Poland.

came a handicap because the Polish gentry carefully avoided anything resembling dynastic continuity. They feared the creation of conditions favorable to the establishment of absolutism along the pattern prevailing in much of Europe at that time.

Under her freely elected kings, Poland was continually troubled by internal weakness and wars—most of them fought on Polish soil. Although the last years of that period saw the introduction of far-reaching reforms, these were unable to counteract the effects of the long years of decay caused by unstable foreign and domestic relations, or to prevent the partitions which finally led to the disappearance of the Polish state. Research into the causes of that decay is one of the principal preoccupations of Polish historical science.

Meanwhile, after the fall of the Byzantine Empire in 1453, Poland was predestined to be always the first to meet the shock of Turkish invasions. During the fifteenth, sixteenth, and seventeenth centuries, Poland constantly shed blood in repulsing the onslaughts of the Turks, in those days the greatest military power in Europe. King John Sobieski's defeat of the Turks under the walls of Vienna in 1683 made him a European hero.[11]

Poland's relations with Russia during the period of elected kings were decisive for her future. Frequent conflicts took place between Poland and Russia over boundary questions and Poland often interfered in Russian affairs. The new Russian dynasty (the Romanov) retaliated. The Russians posed as protectors of their Orthodox co-religionists in Poland and repeatedly intervened in Poland's elections, including the elections of kings.

Internally, the most important constitutional innovation of the period was the changed conception of the king's position. Although he was still said to rule "by the grace of God," he was usually elected[12] on the basis of what closely resembled a modern political platform. The candidate for the throne promised not only to maintain existing laws and recognize the privileges granted by earlier kings,[13] but also pledged himself to a definite program, such as the pursuit of specific policies, maintenance of a certain financial relationship with the State, and promulgation of specific legislation. The king's promises were

---

[11] For additional information on Poland's role in European politics, including Polish-Swedish relations, see note on page 130.

[12] After 1573, kings were elected by a special meeting of all Polish nobles. The election was usually by a voice vote and no proper polling procedure ever existed. Hence there were many contested elections.

[13] The promise to maintain existing laws and to uphold privileges granted by predecessors was usually a part of the coronation oath in every constitutional monarchy. It is the other elements of the "pacta conventa" which gave that institution its special significance.

put into contractual form, called "pacta conventa," and confirmed by him under oath. The ambition to become king often prompted aspirants to make promises considerably limiting the royal power and it was difficult for them subsequently to evade the provisions of the "pacta conventa," which usually contained a clause authorizing the nation to withhold obedience from the king if he broke his pledges.

The *"Confederations"* were another important constitutional innovation. Originally formed for the purpose of pursuing the common aims of the membership, they soon assumed an important function in public life. The crisis that arose after the death of the last Jagellonian was overcome by the formation of a confederation of the gentry, representing the entire Polish body politic. Once it was accepted that a confederation could take the place of royal authority during an "interregnum," it soon was taken for granted that a confederation could replace royal authority during the king's absence from the country, or whenever the nobility wished to force the king into a course of action he was reluctant to follow. Thus the confederations became an instrument for circumventing constitutional processes which involved royal assent.

The so-called General Confederation was regarded as representing the entire Polish gentry and, therefore, as superior to the king and vested with the power to bring the king to judgment. It is interesting to note that in the confederations, as well as in their specific bodies, including the General Council (organized along the model of the Diet), all decisions were reached by a majority vote, while the regular Diets required the unanimous vote of the Deputies for the adoption of bills. As a result, the confederations lent themselves widely to irregular and unconstitutional procedures. Powerful individuals could always organize a confederation and use it as a pressure group against the king or the Diet. Despite consistent abuses, however, the Polish gentry considered the confederations a safeguard of their constitutional liberties and could not be persuaded to limit their power.

The most important change in Poland's constitutional life during this period was brought about not by legislation, but by custom. We have seen how the "liberum veto" of each member of the House of Deputies was interpreted in the Jagellonian period and why it did not cause difficulties at that time. Later, however, there was less restraint. After the middle of the seventeenth century, the right of the "liberum veto" was frequently invoked against legislation opposed only by small minorities or even by individuals. Its frequent use was especially disastrous because the "liberum veto" of any bill invalidated all other bills adopted at the same session of the Diet and thus often brought all legislative activity to a standstill, gravely hampering Poland's development. The certainty of a "liberum veto" of any measure which, while aiming to modernize Poland's governmental, social, or legal structure, interfered with the privileges of the nobility lowered the level of political thinking. In order to circumvent this threat and to enact the most essential legislation, the members of the Diet often constituted themselves a "confederation," which enabled them to reach a decision by a majority vote. Although great doubts existed as to the constitutionality of this expedient, it should be remembered that most of the reform bills of the second half of the eighteenth century were adopted in this way.

Under the elected kings, Poland was almost continuously engaged in war. It was only during the last years of that period that Poland enjoyed peace, which permitted the development of the intellectual basis for a movement of reform that was soon to play an important role. Two questions of internal policy constantly agitated the minds of the Polish gentry and repeatedly cropped up in Polish political debates under various forms: the dread of absolute royal power and the question of the treatment of Dissidents.

Absolute royal power became the most abhorred of political institutions. Poland's constitutional organization at the close of the Jagellonian period contained provisions which enabled the king to exercise his power within the limits of existing legislation but prevented him from extending his authority beyond those limits. The Polish nobility, however, often considered these provisions inadequate, hence the introduction of additional limitations upon royal prerogatives by means of the "pacta conventa," frequent use of the veto power, and the confederations. The fear that the king might use a standing army to strengthen his power led the Diet to refuse repeatedly to authorize taxes for the upkeep of a larger regular army, with the result that Poland almost invariably lost the first battles in every war. Furthermore, whatever the final outcome, most of the wars were fought on Polish territory because of Poland's initial military weakness.

The other question which preoccupied the Polish nobles was that of the Dissidents, including both Protestants and adherents of the Greek-Orthodox Church. We have seen how conditions in Poland under the last Jagellonian king favored the spread of Protestant creeds. Although the Catholics rapidly regained ground after the Council of Trent had drawn a clear dividing line between Catholicism and Protestantism, and after the newly created Jesuit Order began its work, the spirit of tolerance was still strong in Poland.

Shortly after the death of the last Jagellonian king, Catholics and

Protestants formed the Confederation of Warsaw (1573) for the purpose of establishing the principles upon which their relations would subsequently rest. The Act of the Confederation of Warsaw proclaimed full equality between Catholics and Protestants in public and private rights and expressly condemned religious persecution. For nearly a century these principles were honored, although the Protestants were a gradually diminishing group in Poland. The decline of Protestantism was a result both of intensive proselyting work on the part of the Jesuits and other Catholic Orders and of the policy of some of the kings who respected the equal rights of the Protestants but in effect encouraged conversion to Catholicism by rewarding it with public favors.

Poland's continuous wars with Turkey and Sweden—which had important religious aspects—tended to strengthen Catholic sentiment and the Catholic hierarchy worked tirelessly to tie up Polish national devotion with devotion to the Catholic Church. In this connection, the collaboration of Polish Protestants with the Swedes during the war of 1654-1660 was very detrimental to Protestantism in Poland. During that war and, to an even greater extent, after the war, thousands of Protestants adopted Catholicism in order to dissociate themselves from the pro-Swedish policy of their leaders and to escape the suspicion of disloyalty. However, except for the banishment of Anti-Trinitarians (known in Poland as Aryans), the legal rights of the Protestants remained unimpaired. It was not until early in the eighteenth century that, under the influence of religious bigotry, legal discrimination began to be applied to the small remnants of Polish Protestantism.

The adherents of the Greek-Orthodox Church always enjoyed full civil rights. Until the end of the sixteenth century, they also enjoyed full public rights and occupied many prominent offices, particularly in Lithuania. However, when a Union was concluded between the Orthodox and the Catholic Churches in Poland in 1595, creating the Greek-Catholic Church, the privileges theretofore enjoyed by the adherents of the former passed to the Greek-Catholics. Thenceforth the Greek-Orthodox Church no longer had any official status. Moreover, since most of the Orthodox nobles had adopted Catholicism, there were now few members of the Orthodox Church eligible for public office. About the middle of the eighteenth century, Protestants and members of the Greek-Orthodox Church sought jointly to re-establish religious equality in Poland. They encountered strong opposition, but it was finally overcome by the open intervention of Russia and Prussia in their favor some time later.

Meanwhile, the loss of status by the Greek-Orthodox Church was greatly resented by the Cossacks, most of whom were Greek-Orthodox, and was one of the reasons for the repeated Cossack rebellions, the most important of which (from the standpoint of long-range effects) began in 1648. To an even greater extent, the Cossack rebellions were caused by the efforts of the Polish land-owners in the Ruthenian provinces to reduce the Cossacks to the level of peasants.

The Cossacks had always enjoyed the status of freemen; those under Polish sovereignty lived on free land along the shores of the lower Dnieper. Agriculture was one of their chief occupations, but a considerable number of them were professional soldiers who served Poland as mercenaries in her wars against Russia and Turkey. When Poland was not at war with Russia or Turkey, the Cossacks frequently organized independent expeditions into the Turkish borderlands or even against Turkish cities on the Black Sea coast. These ventures, like those of the Tartars, who, while nominally subject to Turkey, often engaged in unofficial attacks on Poland, created considerable tension between Poland and Turkey. The decision of the Polish Government to put an end to this problem by exercising stricter control over the Cossacks was still another reason for the great Cossack insurrection. However, the threat of reduction to peasant status, involving the obligation to render part-time free labor service on the estates of the Polish landlords, was undoubtedly the main reason for the uprising.

The great Cossack rebellion, coupled with the war against the Tartars, who coöperated for a time with the Cossacks, and the war with Russia which broke out in connection with it some years later, was one of the bloodiest and most cruel conflicts ever fought on Polish soil. All of Poland's Ruthenian provinces were laid waste. The Cossacks finally placed themselves under Russian protection, and the Ukraine was ultimately divided between Poland and Russia. Fought between 1648 and 1660, these wars wrought irreparable damage in Poland, leaving in their wake immense material and cultural destruction and laying the foundation for Poland's subsequent downfall.

The Economic and Social Structure of Pre-Partition Poland

Poland's economic and social history up to the end of the eighteenth century falls into two main periods. During the first, Poland was divided into numerous self-contained economic units with a minimum of trade between them, while in the later period economic life became increasingly dependent upon a market for the goods produced by the country. In both periods, agriculture was the mainstay of Poland's economy.

The economic units of the first period may be divided into two categories. On the one hand, there were the fair-sized estates, consisting partly of arable land but mostly of wooded areas. They were either inhabited by nobles who had inherited them or received them from the king as a reward for services, and by peasants, or they belonged to monasteries. On the other hand, there were the towns, surrounded within an easily accessible radius by a limited number of estates of varying size and similarly inhabited by nobles and peasants.

The isolated estate was by far the predominant form. Its owner, in accordance with feudal custom, was obliged to render military service at the behest of his overlord—the king or the regional duke. His chief occupation in peacetime was hunting, which at that time was not just a pleasant sport but a highly important economic function. In most cases, the landlord did not take part in agricultural production. This was the main occupation of the peasants, who paid their rent in agricultural produce which provided sustenance for the landlord, his family, and his servants. The peasants were free at first to move from one estate to another, but gradually limitations were imposed which restricted their right of movement. The villages were usually autonomous, although the elders were not always chosen by free election. In making grants to deserving knights, the kings often bestowed upon them the right to appoint village elders.

Taxes at the time were extremely light. Whenever the king or the regional duke needed supplies for his wars, he usually found it more practical to obtain them by raising the rent of the peasants on his own estates than by general taxation. It was only in the fourteenth century, when the use of money became more frequent, that the kings were able to levy taxes in money. The gentry strenuously resisted this innovation and finally succeeded in manipulating King Louis (1370-1382) into granting them almost total tax exemption.

The second type of economic unit in that early period was the town, with its fringe of estates of varying size. The essential difference between the economic life of isolated estates and those near towns consisted in the fact that the towns provided small but ready markets for agricultural produce. The chief importance of the towns, however, was that they served as channels through which limited quantities of foreign goods penetrated into the country, thus improving the living standard in the neighboring areas. Such improvement, of course, was usually limited to the gentry.

The handicraftsmen who settled in the towns also produced various goods, often in competition with the peasants' home industries, and since the city products were superior in quality, they contributed to the gradual decline of home industry in the countryside. Instead of collecting part of their rents in the form of peasant-handicraft products, the landlords preferred to buy city goods and increased the rents in agricultural produce instead.

During the thirteenth century, several large-scale Tartar invasions destroyed practically all Polish towns. The dukes turned to foreign countries, especially to Germany, Poland's nearest neighbor, in quest of prospective settlers. The promise of various privileges brought a considerable number of immigrants into Poland.

Although not all the Germans settled in towns (many settled on farms), it was the German colonization of Polish towns that became the paramount feature of the German migration to Poland. In accordance with the mediaeval principle of personal law, the Germans were permitted to establish their own administrative and juridical systems in the towns where they settled. These towns—"German-law towns," as they were called—were administered by officials elected by the original settlers and their descendants. However, the right to appoint the highest officials was often reserved by the king or duke who granted the original charter of settlement. The fact that Poland's towns were ruled by German law and the fact that most of their inhabitants were German influenced their future, for a feeling soon developed among the gentry that the towns were not really part of Polish national life. As a result, the towns never acquired any influence in national affairs.

The second part of the fifteenth century is known in history as a period of great discoveries. Poland did not take any direct part in the treasure-hunting overseas expeditions which resulted in the discovery of new lands and their subsequent colonization,[14] but it felt the influence of the new trends which followed these developments. One of the most important results of the great discoveries was the growth of many western European towns (mostly Dutch and British seaports) into thriving trading communities, with populations too great to be fed by the immediate countryside. Poland soon came into the picture as the most reliable source of additional foodstuffs, mostly grain. Of course the process of converting the heretofore self-contained Polish landed estates into large-scale suppliers of grain took some time. The Polish grain trade was conducted chiefly by wholesale merchants who resided

---

[14] Individual Poles took part in various overseas expeditions, but did it under foreign auspices. Small groups of Poles were among the original settlers of Virginia.

almost exclusively in the city of Danzig, which enjoyed an autonomous status under Polish sovereignty. The Danzig wholesalers offered ever higher prices for grain in order to induce the Polish landlords to increase production beyond their own needs, thus creating a marketable surplus.

Decisive changes then began to take place in the position of the Polish peasantry. The gentry gradually began to demand that the peasants render part-time unpaid service on the fields of their landlords. Such labor was levied either in lieu of a part of the existing rents, or as an outright additional obligation. The peasants attempted to escape this new burden by moving to other areas, but the gentry soon adopted legislation depriving them of the freedom of movement and subjecting them to the jurisdiction of their landlords.

The amount of work (socage) to be done by the peasants for their landlords was expressed in terms of work days per week and fixed by custom or by law. It varied in different regions. The demands of the landlords increased with the improvement of the market for Polish grain, but the peasants had no legal recourse. According to the law, the landlords were sole judges in all criminal and civil cases involving the peasants. Despite frequent criticism by progressive thinkers, these conditions persisted in most of Poland, with only minor changes, until the nineteenth century. Peasant living conditions were better on estates belonging to the crown or to the Church, where their obligation to work for the landlord was either kept within reasonable limits or replaced entirely by the payment of rent in produce or money. Peasants on private estates, however, could escape servitude only by running away. Those in the Ruthenian provinces often fled to the Cossacks, who therefore had exact knowledge of the treatment of peasants in Poland and resented all the more the proposal to reduce them to peasant status.

The large exports of grain and timber brought considerable wealth to the Polish gentry. A large part of the money received by the Polish nobles was spent for foreign products purchased abroad and the political power of the gentry was so great that a law was soon passed exempting them from payment of customs duties. The Polish towns were thus placed at a great disadvantage. On the one hand, they could not continue to function as importers of foreign goods. Their only possible customers, the nobles, were able to purchase them more cheaply direct from foreign merchants, thus eliminating both the profit margin of the Polish importer and the customs duties which Polish burghers still had to pay. On the other hand, the fact that the nobles could purchase cheaply the finished products of skilled foreign artisans discouraged domestic handicrafts. At the same time, the burghers and the Jews in the Polish towns had to pay most of the taxes, for the gentry paid almost no taxes at all and the clergy paid only such taxes as they chose.

The development of the Polish towns—with several exceptions in Poland proper and with the exception of Pomeranian towns, which enjoyed special status—lagged far behind that of the towns of Western Europe. Both the economic handicaps outlined above and the persistent feeling among the gentry that the towns, because of their originally predominant German population, did not belong to the Polish body politic, prevented them from acquiring political importance. The occasional representation they were permitted at first in the Chamber of Deputies soon disappeared altogether.

In internal administration, only so-called royal towns, that is, towns established on the basis of a royal charter, preserved their autonomy. It was therefore mainly in royal towns that the descendants of later settlers, deprived of the franchise, vigorously pressed their demands for the right to vote. In many cases the crown finally had to intervene to break the deadlock created by the outright refusal of the "old" families to accede to these demands.

In the fifteenth century, the Jews began to play a considerable part in the economic life of Poland. Jews had probably lived in Poland from its earliest recorded history, but it was not until the thirteenth century that the first official charter was issued permitting them to live in that part of Poland which was ruled by the duke who granted the charter. During the next hundred years a large number of Jews, expelled from many western European countries, where they were severely persecuted, migrated to Poland. In the fourteenth century, King Casimir the Great extended the regional charter to include all of Poland and also broadened its scope. In this early period, the Jews usually engaged in occupations which at that time were forbidden to Christians, such as money-lending and pawnbroking. Other Jews were employed at various trades and some of them owned farms. There is also evidence that Jews held various offices under the kings of Poland, mostly taking charge of their financial affairs, supervising mints, exchanging foreign coins, and so forth.

The position of the Jews changed for the worse in the fifteenth century. Although Jews had always lived in special districts in the towns, a rigorous ghetto system was now introduced. At the same time the number of Jews increased greatly, forcing them to venture outside the traditional Jewish trades, and certain trades thenceforth assumed a predominantly Jewish character in Poland.

Jews were widely and genuinely tolerated in Poland, and while there were isolated cases of cruel persecution of individuals—mostly of learned Jews whose intellectual contact with Christians was greatly resented in some circles—there were never any mass pogroms or mass expulsions of Jews from their homes. One other fact is worth noting. Converted Jews were granted the status of nobility, for some time automatically, later by authorization of the Diet.

Culture and Literature in Pre-Partition Poland[15]

Three elements are characteristic of Polish culture as a whole. First, it is a Western culture with a Latin basis, Poland being the easternmost area of Latin culture in Europe. Second, its development has been uneven and frequently checked by a variety of factors, such as internal misrule in the latter half of the seventeenth and the first half of the eighteenth centuries, and the effects of partition. Third, the peak of its development in all fields—literature, art, and science—came at a time when there was no independent Polish state.

In the pre-Partition period, Polish culture was characterized by its decentralization and its essentially rural pattern, in contrast to the urban culture of the West, and the fact that, in the main, it was limited to the gentry.

There is no record of Polish culture in pre-Christian Poland. We can, however, assume that it was similar to that of other Slav tribes, based on tribal traditions, limited local self-rule, and a primitive paganism. Available records reach back to the tenth century, when Poland emerged as a national identity. These show that Polish culture lagged behind that of other Western European nations, probably because of Poland's later entry into recorded history.

As in the rest of Europe, the Roman Catholic Church was the first to spread spiritual and to some extent also material culture. It was in monasteries that monks created the first monuments of Polish literature: annals, written in Latin, the earliest of which date back to the late tenth century. Polish chronicles, which emerged from these annals, were represented by Gallus, Kadlubek, and Janko of Czarnkow, who wrote in the twelfth, thirteenth, and fourteenth centuries respectively. The first writings in Polish appeared in the thirteenth and fourteenth centuries. They were collections of sermons, the so-called Flo-

---

[15] This section was contributed by Professor Manfred Kridl, Smith College.

rian psalter, and, above all, the well-known hymn to the Virgin Mary (the "Bogurodzica" hymn). All that early literature was of a purely religious character. Lay literature, such as ballads, legends, and folk-songs, existed, but no written versions have been found.

In the field of architecture, the thirteenth and fourteenth centuries saw the gradual substitution of brick and stone buildings, adorned by sculpture and painting, for the earlier wooden buildings which disappeared almost without a trace. Few monuments of the early Romanesque style have survived. Foremost among them are the Churches of the Holy Cross and St. Adalbert in Cracow, and the first brick church, that of St. James, in Sandomierz. The monuments of early Polish sculpture, painting (mostly illuminated missals), and music are few. The first Polish schools were established in connection with cathedrals, collegiates, and parish churches.

With the increase of Poland's political power in the fourteenth and fifteenth centuries, the cultural level rose as well. King Casimir the Great stimulated this development. He built many walled cities and castles and established Cracow University in 1364. Reorganized in 1400, it was subsequently called the Jagellonian University. The fifteenth century witnessed its greatest development, when almost half of its enrollment consisted of foreigners (Hungarians, Germans, and even Swiss). The famous astronomers, Adalbertus of Brudzew and Nicolaus Copernicus, were alumni of the Jagellonian University. The level of other schools also improved, and, for the first time, educated laymen began to appear. The Polish delegations at the councils of Constance and Basle were notable for the education and eloquence of their members. Some towns developed rapidly, and by the end of the fifteenth century the capital city of Cracow compared favorably with Western European cities in the cultural level of its burghers, the splendor of its royal, episcopal, and lords' courts, and its scientific and artistic achievements.

Latin was still predominant in literature. Notable advances were achieved in learning, theology, rhetoric, and Latin poetry. John Dlugosz, Polish historian of the fifteenth century, could well be compared with outstanding contemporary historians of other countries. He made extensive use of source material in his *Polish Chronicle.* Another contemporary, John Ostrorog, usually considered Poland's first political writer, wrote the Latin treatise, *Monumentum pro Reipublicae Ordinatione,* assailing the ties between State and Church and the payment of St. Peter's penny. He also protested against the appointment of Bishops by the Pope and demanded the unification of Polish laws.

Humanism found a ready response in Poland and was spread both by foreigners—among whom Philip Buonacorsi Callimachus is the best known—and by Poles who had studied abroad. The number of writings in Polish increased. While the prose of the period was all of a religious nature, comprising translations of psalms and sections of the Bible, the poetry was not exclusively religious and the earliest known Polish lyric verse was produced at that time. First attempts to fix Polish spelling were made in the fifteenth century.

Gothic architecture made its appearance in Poland in the fourteenth century. The Polish form of the Gothic style was characterized by the use of brick instead of the stone which is dominant in Western European Gothic. The best-known monuments of Polish Gothic architecture are St. Mary's Church in Cracow, part of the Cracow Cathedral, and the old building of the Jagellonian University. Polish Gothic sculpture is best represented by Wit Stwosz's famous carved wooden altar in St. Mary's Church in Cracow. Few relics of Polish painting survive from that period, and its music had an almost exclusively liturgical character.

In the sixteenth century, Poland was the only great Slav power in Europe. Russia was still under the spell of Mongolian influence, Bohemia had passed the peak of its power, and the Balkan states were under Turkish rule. Poland was highly esteemed by her neighbors, politically and culturally, hence the election of Polish princes to the thrones of Bohemia and Hungary as well as Prussia's decision to become Poland's fief. Germans living in Poland gradually became assimilated, while Lithuanians and Ruthenians accepted Polish culture as their own.

Thanks to the high development of Polish culture, the sixteenth century has been called Poland's "Golden Age." This development was partly an outgrowth of the Polish gentry's struggle against royal supremacy and the influence of the magnates, which gave rise to an abundant political literature. Humanistic influences account for the development of poetry, while the religious discussion which attended the spread of the Reformation led to an increase of writings in the Polish language, which gradually assumed the place theretofore occupied by Latin. The most outstanding political writer of the period was Andrew Modrzewski, author of the Latin treatise *De Republica Emendanda*, which demanded admission of the burghers to certain privileges of the gentry, equality before the law for all Poles, and personal liberty for the peasants. In the sphere of international politics, Modrzewski advocated a system which would make war impossible and devised plans for the reconciliation of the Catholic and Protestant

Churches. Most of Modrzewski's ideas were centuries in advance of his time, hence his notoriety.

The basis for a literature in the Polish language was created by Nicolaus Rey, a Protestant noble of the sixteenth century, who was an extremely prolific writer. While a considerable part of his work was devoted to religious polemics, he also wrote much prose and verse of general interest, thereby demonstrating that the Polish language was suited to a variety of literary forms. Rey's writings are of great interest even today, not only because they are an excellent example of sixteenth century Polish, but also because of their intrinsic value. Genuine poetry was written by John Kochanowski, admittedly the greatest Slav poet of his time. Having studied in Italy and France, he decided to follow Ronsard's ideas by creating national Polish poetry, patterned on classic models. His genius, however, transcended the pattern set by Ronsard, and he is still read today for the excellence of his style and his profound expression of universal human emotions. His "Threnodies" and his paraphrases of David's Psalter are masterpieces. Public speaking was represented by Father Peter Skarga, a Jesuit who was chaplain to King Sigismund III. In his "Parliamentary Sermons," Father Skarga advocated strengthening of the royal power and curbs on Protestantism, but he also demanded justice for the peasants, whose oppression by the landlords had become increasingly disturbing. Skarga's sermons are models of eloquence and piety.

While Kochanowski, Modrzewski, Rey, and Skarga were the outstanding protagonists of Polish literature in the "Golden Age," they were followed by a large number of gifted poets, political writers, and historians, many of whom had a wide European background as a result of education or diplomatic service abroad. The first book (a prayer-book) to be printed in Polish appeared in the early 16th century, but by the end of the century books in Polish were fairly common. Most of them were printed in Cracow, one of the most important printing centers in Europe at that time.

We have already seen how the development of the Protestant movement favored the development of Polish literature. It contributed also to the spreading of culture to provincial cities, due probably to the desire of each Protestant denomination to have its own academic and publication center. Many Polish Protestant theologians enjoyed high esteem among Protestants throughout Europe (John Laski, John Seklucjan, and others). In 1561, one of the Protestant denominations published the first complete Polish translation of the Bible.

Although Polish schools, notably Cracow University, lagged behind this splendid intellectual development, many prominent scientists lived and worked in Poland in the fields of medicine, classical philology, and law. Outstanding among them was Nicolaus Copernicus, the author of the treatise *De Revolutionibus Orbium Coelestium* (published in 1543). New universities were established in Zamosc (1595) and Wilno (1578), but only the latter survived.

In the field of architecture, the Renaissance style triumphed. The best examples of it are the Royal Castle in Cracow and Cracow Cathedral, in which new parts, in Renaissance style, were added or superimposed on earlier parts. Sculpture was strictly religious and limited to church decoration, while painting was done principally by Italian and German painters living in Poland. Church music was also under Italian influence.

The "Golden Age" continued through the early seventeenth century. At that time Polish poetry was represented by the humanist, Simon Szymonowicz, while Father Matthew Sarbiewski wrote excellent Latin poetry, widely read throughout Europe. But as the seventeenth century advanced, a decline became noticeable. The reasons are plain. The "Golden Age" grew out of three elements: the political situation, humanist contacts with foreign countries, and the Protestant movement. In the seventeenth century the gentry, having attained all their political aims, became a conservative class unable to bring forth new ideas. Humanist contacts with foreign countries became scarce, while political factors hastened the decline of Protestantism. Moreover, Poland was almost continually at war during the seventeenth century and many of the wars ravaged the cultural centers of Poland.

All of these factors combined to lower Poland's cultural level. Literature became baroque in style and "Sarmatian" (narrowly Polish) in outlook and interest, in contrast to the worldwide interest and outlook of the poets and writers of the preceding century. The best-known poet of the period is Waclaw Potocki, whose language is a fine specimen of seventeenth-century Polish. But the works of most contemporary writers were less pure linguistically and abundantly seasoned with Latin. An excellent example of the contemporary style is the "Memoirs" of John C. Pasek, a Polish noble who was active in the nation's affairs in the seventeenth century and left a rather noteworthy account of his experiences. A new and interesting literature came into being in the towns, among the burghers, but relatively little of it has survived. It was also at this time that the first Polish paper, "The Polish Mercury," was published. In architecture, baroque became predominant and left its imprint on many Polish cities, mostly in the form of imposing churches.

It is important to note that throughout the seventeenth century the influence of Polish culture was very strong among the Ruthenians and Lithuanians. The gentry of these nations adopted Polish as their language, leaving their own languages to the peasants. For a short time, Polish culture exercised a similar influence in Russia until political and religious factors intervened to end it.

While Polish culture continued to decline in the early eighteenth century, there were exceptions in the persons of Bishop Joseph A. Zaluski, founder of the first Polish public library consisting of about 200,000 volumes (a very large library for that time), Elizabeth Druzbacka, first Polish woman writer, and King Stanislaw Leszczynski. The latter wrote the political treatise, *The Free Voice, Safeguarding Freedom*, which advocated certain constitutional reforms. The activity of Father Stanislaus Konarski was especially noteworthy. A Piarist, he established modern schools under the auspices of his Order whose popularity forced the Jesuits and other orders to adopt more modern curricula in their own schools, including Polish instruction in classrooms where Latin had reigned supreme. He was also a political writer of consequence and is best known for his criticism of the "liberum veto."

Belated Reforms and the Partitions of Poland (1764-1795)

Toward the middle of the eighteenth century, criticism of some of Poland's institutions spread among the gentry, and a faction gradually emerged which advocated substantial changes in Poland's governmental apparatus. This group urged some strengthening of executive power, a more orderly process of legislation—mainly by elimination of the "liberum veto" system—and reorganization of the judiciary. The reform party, commonly called the "Family," [16] tried to obtain the king's support for its program. Augustus III, who was also Prince-Elector of Saxony, had his own aim, namely the establishment of a hereditary monarchy with his own family as the ruling dynasty. The two programs were combined and presented jointly for public discussion. The conservative faction which opposed these reforms was commonly called "Republican." In the name of Republicanism,[17] it defended the electoral method of determining royal succession and especially the

---

[16] Many of the original leaders of the reform party were members of the influential Czartoryski family. Hence the name "Family" was applied to that party.

[17] Since its kings were elected and the origin of their power thus lay with the Polish nation (at that time regarded as being fully represented by the gentry alone), Poland was considered a Republic, not a monarchy.

"liberum veto" as the only effective safeguards of individual rights against the preponderance of the state.[18]

The struggle between the Polish factions was complicated by the fact that they were used by rival foreign powers which sought to influence Poland for their own ends. As of old, therefore, conflicting views regarding Poland's domestic policy became intricately interwoven with conflicting orientations in foreign policy. The "Family" favored the maintenance of close ties with Russia and hoped to achieve their proposed constitutional reforms without antagonizing Russia. They believed their eastern neighbor could be persuaded to agree to them in exchange for assurances of a foreign policy conforming to Russian desires.

Russia, however, soon decided that it would be more profitable to have a weak Poland as a neighbor. Soon after the death of Augustus III and the election of the "Family" candidate to the throne in the person of Stanislaus Augustus (1764-1795), the last king of independent Poland, the influence of Catherine II, Empress of Russia, caused the reform program to be whittled down. A judicial reform bill was passed and a permanent council of state was established, the deputies' privilege of "liberum veto" was limited to bills concerning constitutional and political matters, and full equality of non-Catholic Christians was proclaimed. All other provisions of the old constitutional system were expressly upheld. A few years later, after the suppression of the Jesuit Order, a Ministry of Public Education was created with the power of establishing schools and supervising existing schools. The only reform, however, which was favored by all parties—the military strengthening of Poland—was thwarted by Russian influence.

Limited as they were, these reforms enraged the conservatives. Indignation was especially widespread among the bigoted gentry. The memory of the Republican struggle against the Russophile "Family" was still fresh, and since these measures had Russia's approval and conformed with the wishes of the king (who had been a "Family" candidate), the conservative gentry turned not only against the king, but also against Russia.

The signal for the uprising was given by a confederation which was formed in 1768, in the town of Bar, by the conservative Republicans. It was directed primarily against the king, whom the Republicans accused of violating the constitution of Poland by granting full equality

---

[18] The supporters of the *liberum veto* considered the principle of unanimous consent the essence of republicanism. They regarded majority rule as abject a tyranny as rule by an absolute king.

to Dissidents. The Confederation of Bar is often described as Poland's first uprising against foreign oppression, but it must be remembered that it was originally directed against progressive reform. When the rebellion was finally put down[19] by Polish and Russian troops, Poland had to pay dearly for it. The First Partition of Poland (1772) was the direct result of the civil war started by the Bar Confederation.

Russia, whose influence was dominant in Poland, was opposed to the Partition at first, while Prussia was its driving motor. As a result of complicated developments in European politics, however, Russia finally had to accept the principle of partition, with Russia and Prussia getting parts of Poland and Austria also being admitted to the partnership.

Russia received a slice of Lithuania, an area mostly Russian and White Russian in population and of minor importance; Prussia took Polish Pomerania and some adjacent areas; Austria received what came to be known as Galicia (Southern Poland). The areas taken by Prussia and Austria were almost purely Polish in population and culture and enjoyed a higher level of economic development than the rest of Poland. Their loss was highly detrimental to Poland. The three "Partition Powers" later submitted a treaty sanctioning the Partition for Poland's signature. It was ratified by the Polish Diet under the pressure of Russian troops and Russian bribes to the deputies.

The years which followed the First Partition were notable for a higher level of political thought, due partly to improvements in public education brought about by the activities of the Educational Commission and partly to intelligent public discussion led by two progressive Catholic priests, Stanislaw Staszic, a burgher, and Hugo Kollatay, a nobleman. Additional judicial bills were passed, abolishing mediaeval practices in the Polish judiciary. The demands for the extension of political rights, including the franchise, to the burghers, and for the restoration of efficient military organization gained wide popularity and were finally embodied in bills voted by the Diet elected in 1788.

Full civil rights, including the "neminem captivabimus" privilege (see footnote 10) and representation in the House of Deputies, were granted to the burghers, and the autonomous city governments were modernized. A bill modernizing Poland's constitutional structure was passed by the House of Deputies on May 3, 1791, over a small but vocal opposition. The Act of May 3 provided Poland with a constitutional

---

[19] Many Confederates fled abroad, among them Casimir Pulaski, son of one of the leaders and himself an officer of the Confederate troops. He later came to America to fight and die in the Revolutionary War.

structure patterned in part after the British parliamentary system and influenced by the Constitution of the United States and the debates in the French Constitutional Assembly. Fortunately, since Poland's political institutions had even previously been similar to those of England (although functioning differently), the reforms were acceptable to moderate conservatives, for they made no clear-cut break with the past.

According to the new Constitution, legislative power was vested in a bicameral Diet, the houses of which retained the traditional names of Senate and House of Deputies. All bills had to pass both Houses and were subject to majority approval, thus conclusively abolishing the "liberum veto." Executive power was vested in the king and a Cabinet responsible to the Diet. It was also established that, upon the death of Stanislaus Augustus, Poland was to become a hereditary monarchy with the Saxon ruling family as the national dynasty.[20]

In social matters, the Constitution was much more conservative. It upheld the existing system of landed estates and the recent law concerning towns and burghers, but the peasants received no more than a general promise of legal protection. On the whole, however, this Constitution established the mechanism for further free political development.

Having failed to prevent the adoption of the constitutional reform, the Conservatives now turned to Russia for aid. Catherine the Great made it very plain that she disapproved of the Constitution of May 3. The responsible system of government which it established in Poland rendered it difficult for irresponsible individuals who might be in Russia's service to gain positions of influence and thus endangered the future of Russia's dominance in Poland.

As soon as Russia's wars against Sweden and Turkey were ended, she was free to intervene in Poland. The Conservative magnates, deprived of their old power by the introduction of responsible government, organized the Confederation of 1792 with the aid of a considerable section of the gentry. Their avowed aim was to overthrow the Constitution. Significantly, the Confederation was organized in the town of Targowica, near the Russian border, and most of its leaders came there from Russia, where they had fled after the adoption of the Constitution.

The Conservatives invoked a previous treaty by which Russia had guaranteed Polish institutions, asking Russia to enforce it, and the Russian government proclaimed that Poland had violated that treaty by adopting the new Constitution. Russian troops crossed the Polish border and soon pushed back the much weaker Polish troops led by

---

[20] Two members of the Saxon ruling family had been kings of Poland prior to the reign of childless Stanislaus Augustus.

Prince Joseph Poniatowski, the king's nephew and Commander-in-Chief, and by Generals Kosciuszko (of American Revolutionary fame) and Dabrowski, three men who were destined to play a prominent role in Polish history.

The Russian successes frightened the king into joining the Confederation of Targowica and thus abolishing the recently adopted Constitution. Several of the most prominent advocates of the Constitution and some of the generals of the defeated army fled abroad. The Russians once more occupied Poland and many of the Polish troop units were either disbanded or impressed into Russian service. By that time, anti-Russian feeling—strengthened by the news of the progress of the victorious army of the French Revolution—became so strong that the Russians decided to reduce Poland to total impotence. Accordingly, Russia and Prussia arranged for the Second Partition, appropriating more than one half of the territory left to Poland after the First Partition. Following the earlier pattern, a treaty sanctioning the Second Partition was also submitted to Poland and the helpless Polish Diet was forced to ratify it.

In the meantime, the ideas of the French Revolution gained considerable influence among the Polish middle classes and the poorer gentry, and the victories of French revolutionary troops stirred the imagination of many Polish military leaders. A plan was conceived for an armed uprising, in alliance with France, against Russia and Prussia, and its realization was precipitated by the impending dissolution of the remnants of the Polish Army. Early in 1794, the insurrection broke out under the leadership of Kosciuszko. For over half a year Polish troops, reinforced by inadequately armed but enthusiastic peasant volunteers, fought against numerically superior Russian and Prussian troops. In the end, the Poles were defeated. Kosciuszko was taken prisoner and the remaining Polish troops capitulated.

Kosciuszko and the men who surrounded him were progressives who advocated complete freedom for peasants in the social field and the establishment of a democratic republic in the political field. However, the need to enlist the support of the gentry forced them to modify their program. They therefore promised the peasants only personal freedom and a reduction in the amount of serf labor (socage), with special privileges to peasants who had taken an active part in the insurrection. Kosciuszko also had to compromise on the political program and promise to leave the king in office, although without power.

After the collapse of the insurrection, all of Poland was occupied by Russian and Prussian troops, with Austrians joining them soon afterwards. It was then decided that it was unsafe for the partitioning Powers to leave any part of Poland independent. Accordingly, in 1795, what remained of Poland after the Second Partition was divided among Russia, Prussia, and Austria. That year marked the end of the old Polish state.

Polish Culture in the Time of Stanislaus Augustus [21]

The reign of Stanislaus Augustus, last king of independent Poland, produced new and vigorous cultural development. The quality of the schools improved markedly, particularly after the establishment of the Educational Commission. Links with Western Europe were renewed, but this time it was in France that Polish intellectuals found inspiration. French rationalist philosophy and democratic political ideas influenced the more advanced Polish thinkers, most of whom were connected with the party which worked for political reform and the transformation of Poland into a modern nation. Best-known among them were Stanislaw Staszic and Hugo Kollatay.

Foremost among the poets was Bishop Ignatius Krasicki, who wrote fables and satires, and was also the author of the first modern Polish novel. Francis Karpinski is noteworthy for his religious poems and Dyonisius Kniaznin for his interesting erotic lyrics. The Polish theater also made great progress, thanks to the large number of plays written in Polish at that time. The playwright who is most memorable was Francis Zablocki. Kosciuszko's aide-de-camp, John U. Niemcewicz, was another widely read novelist and playwright. He also adapted much foreign (especially English) literature to Polish and is known as the first Polish writer to raise the Jewish question in a novel.

The Educational Commission reorganized the Universities of Cracow and Wilno and established a wide network of secondary schools, creating new opportunities for many scientists. Best-known among these were the historian Adam Naruszewicz, the botanist Stanislaus Jundzill and the Sniadecki brothers—Jan, a mathematician, and Andrew, a chemist. The establishment of Polish instruction in the schools led to intensive research in the Polish language and the writing of the first Polish grammar by Onufrius Kopczynski.

The generosity of King Stanislaus Augustus, who was a connoisseur, encouraged a new flowering of Polish art. The neo-classic style gradually gained favor in Poland, supplanting the baroque which had reigned supreme for nearly two centuries. The Lazienki Palace in Warsaw is probably the best monument of the Polish neo-classic style. In paint-

---

[21] This section was contributed by Professor Manfred Kridl, Smith College.

ing, the Poles made considerable progress. However, there were still well-known foreigners, notably Italians, many of whom came to Poland to paint for the king. Best-known among these latter were Canaletto and Bacciarelli. The king established an imposing art gallery which became one of the glories of the nation.

Poland and Napoleon (1795-1815)

Poland had lost her independence. And yet Poland, though dismembered, was not dead.[22] Napoleon wished to re-establish Poland. He was not interested in Poland for its own sake, but as a bitter foe of Prussia, Russia, and Austria. Following the Franco-Prussian war of 1806-1807, Prussia was forced to surrender a part of her Polish loot and the establishment of the Duchy of Warsaw, under the nominal sovereignty of the King of Saxony, soon followed. In 1809, Austria also had to yield her share in Poland's Third Partition, which was added to the Duchy of Warsaw. The Duchy received a constitution patterned on the Napoleonic constitutions of France and the Code Napoleon was also introduced. But Napoleon's will was supreme in the Duchy and his chief interest lay in using Poland as a French stronghold in Eastern Europe and in Poland's contribution to his armies. The Army of the Duchy participated in Napoleon's campaign against Russia in 1812 as a part of the Grand Army.

After Napoleon's defeat, the Russians ruled the Duchy. Emperor Alexander I became Poland's King, although he had to cede the western part of the Duchy, the province of Poznan, to Prussia. The city of Cracow, with its surrounding territory, was proclaimed a free city under the joint protection of Russia, Prussia, and Austria.

The Struggle for Independence (1815-1865)

The Kingdom of Poland, organized in 1815 according to decisions of the Vienna Congress, is usually known as "Congress Poland." Alexander I granted it a constitution that was liberal for its time; it established ministerial responsibility and vested legislative power in a bicameral Diet. Although only the House of Deputies was elected (on the basis of a rather limited franchise) and the Senate was appointed by the king-emperor, the Diet legislated wisely and many of its laws proved extremely helpful to the future development of the country. The executive power was vested in Ministers, most of whom were good administrators. The judiciary was well organized and proved its inde-

---

[22] For additional information on Polish Legions, the Duchy of Warsaw, and the Polish question at the Congress of Vienna in 1815, see note on page 130.

pendence by repeated acquittals of Poles accused of contacts with early Russian revolutionaries.

The Polish troops which had fought under Napoleon were returned to Poland and reorganized into a new army, which was intelligently built up by a permanent recruiting system. Alexander's brother, the Grand Duke Constantine, was appointed Commander-in-Chief of the Polish Army and his high-handed manner caused the first friction between Poles and Russians in the Congress Kingdom. Later Constantine became friendlier towards the Poles, but much of the tension generated by his earlier attitude persisted and was further intensified by the attitude of Senator Novosiltsov, Russian Commissioner in Poland, who undertook the task of supervising Poland after Constantine had become more lenient.

The greatest progress in Congress Poland was made in the economic field. Poland was far ahead of Russia in economic development, and the products of Polish industry, notably textiles, found a ready market in Russia despite the still existing customs barrier between the two countries.

When Nikolai tried to weaken the Polish constitution, the opposition eventually culminated in the revolution of 1830. It was defeated. A second revolution occurred in 1863. The Tsar suppressed it with great effort and bloody reprisals followed. From then until World War I, Poland was treated as a conquered province, no efforts being spared to Russianize the Polish population. Congress Poland was incorporated into Russia, all of its institutions were abolished, and Polish was prohibited in administration and education.[23]

A similar situation existed in Austria and Prussia. At the Congress of Vienna, both Prussia and Austria pledged themselves to grant their Polish lands a measure of self-government. Both pretended to observe their pledges at first. But after the abolition of the constitution of Congress Poland, all vestiges of Polish administration were gradually abolished; the use of the Polish language in public life and in the schools was steadily restricted in favor of German. However, as a result of differences in the social policies of the two governments, the social structure of the Polish provinces under their rule developed differently.

The Prussian Government fully liberated the peasant, making him an independent owner of the land he tilled. The Austrian Government left the economic relationship between peasant and landlord unchanged (until 1848), and even gave the latter additional power over

---

[23] For additional information concerning the "November Insurrection" (1830), the "January Insurrection" (1863), and Polish-Russian relations in the 19th century, see note on page 130.

the peasants. Accordingly, the reaction of the two parts of the country to their respective governments' attempts at Germanization was different. In Prussian Poland the peasants, who enjoyed a better economic and social status, clearly saw their government's attempts to revive a policy of national oppression, and it was on them and on the Polish townsfolk that resistance was built. It took the form of organizational work to improve economic and cultural standards, with political factors in the background. In Austrian Poland (Galicia), peasant resentment was directed not against Austria, but against the Polish landlords. The latter, for their part, maintained friendly relations with the Austrian Government which protected them from peasant vengeance. Galicia, therefore, had only a small opposition group, consisting mainly of intellectuals and poor noblemen. As a result of their weakness, their activities assumed a conspiratorial character.

After 1840, the conspiratorial groups in Galicia began to prepare an uprising against Austria. They persuaded radical groups in Prussian Poland to do likewise, but the attempts at insurrection in Prussia proved abortive. In Galicia, an uncommonly bloody uprising of the peasants against the landlords broke out before the scheduled national insurrection, set for 1846. It is generally suspected that the Austrian authorities encouraged the peasants in order to frighten the gentry into withholding aid from the impending national insurrection. In Cracow, the proposed headquarters for the national insurrection, power was seized by radical Polish revolutionaries with socialist tendencies, but the movement was rapidly suppressed and Cracow was annexed by Austria.

The European revolutions of 1848 had wide repercussions in Austrian and Prussian Poland, but the revolutionary freedom attained by these provinces was brief and alien rule was soon re-established. Soon, however, both Prussia and Austria began to move toward constitutional rule and the Poles, especially in Austrian Poland, were granted their share of constitutional rights, by means of which they were able to protect their national rights.

Contemporary Poland in the Making (1865-1914)

After 1865, the fundamental economic changes which determined the character of the new Poland were, on the one hand, the emergence of capitalism, and, on the other, the economic integration of the Polish lands into the three powers which had absorbed them. These changes were to be seen most clearly in Russian Poland. Since 1815 the changing administrations of Congress Poland had consistently endeavored to foster the development of industry, railways, and banks, the indispensable attributes of modern capitalism. The rise in Russia's standard of living and her Asiatic expansion created an enormous market, separated from all foreign countries by a customs barrier. This gave Congress Poland an extraordinary opportunity, which was fully utilized to the vast benefit of Polish industries.

In Prussian Poland the situation was different. Here a predominantly agricultural region was annexed by a nation which was rapidly becoming industrialized. Therefore Prussian Poland became, in a sense, Germany's granary. Germany's customs frontier protected her Polish subjects, who thus enjoyed considerable prosperity. Austrian Poland (Galicia), on the other hand, lagged behind economically, mainly because the Austrian Government gave preferential treatment in encouraging economic development to Austria proper and the Sudeten section of the Czechs.

Poland's social structure also underwent rapid changes. These were due principally to the final liberation of the peasants, completed in 1864, when the Russian Government, following the example set by Prussia in 1817 and by Austria in 1848, established peasant ownership of land and abolished socage. The results of this reform, however, were also different in the various parts of Poland. In Congress Poland the rule prohibiting the subdivision of the peasants' holdings created a large supply of manpower for growing industry. Similarly, the Prussian policy of creating medium-sized farms for peasants left many peasants landless; these went to work as farmhands on the great estates producing grain for Germany's industrial west. In Galicia, however, the emancipation led to a grave overcrowding of the countryside, for the Austrian law of inheritance had no provision against the subdivision of farms. Since there were no other economic outlets for the peasant masses (except emigration to America), great misery ensued.

But the peasants' status was not the only area of social change. A new middle class developed. Owners of marginal landed estates, unable to survive competition when the source of cheap manpower disappeared with the abolition of socage, flocked to the towns to take up trading or the professions and soon merged with the old burghers. Educated peasants' sons were also gradually absorbed into the new middle class. However, since many members of the middle class were Jews, who rarely became assimilated, the middle class was never fully unified.

In Galicia, where the Jews enjoyed full legal equality and where they came closest to social equality with Gentile Poles, many Jews took an active part in Polish public life, and became, for all practical purposes, full-fledged members of the Polish community. But in the Russian-dominated part of Poland, the Jews were hampered by various legal restrictions imposed by the Tsarist Government which prevented their assimilation with the Gentile Poles. In Prussian Poland, the Jews took the German side in the struggle against the Poles and this served to estrange them from the Poles. Within a short time most of the Jews who had lived in Prussian Poland moved to Germany proper, where they actively participated in the development of that nation's economic life.

All these economic changes inevitably resulted in full legal equality, although division into social classes persisted and the aristocracy retained its social dominance.

During the years of extreme Russian oppression which followed the 1863-1865 uprising, the Poles generally felt that only a great European conflict that ranged the partition Powers in opposite camps could create favorable conditions for another struggle for Poland's independence. In the meantime, they argued, Poles should devote themselves to business and professional activities, commonly called "organic work" (a counterpart of the French slogan—"*enrichissez-vous*"). The flourishing state of business made it easy to adopt this attitude—called "positivism" because it employed the philosophical argument of Auguste Comte, the French positivist. Despite national oppression, the increasing dependence of Polish industry upon Russian markets led to pro-Russian feeling among the Polish middle class and the emerging Polish capitalists. Some Poles began to doubt the advisability of re-establishing an independent Poland even if an opportunity should arise, fearing that Poland could not exist if it was severed from Russia. Many Poles argued that the best thing for Poland would be autonomy within the framework of the Russian Empire.

But as the wealthier classes became increasingly more loyal to the Tsar's rule, a new class emerged which soon became the strongest opposition. That was the Polish working class. Within a generation after the emergence of capitalism in Poland, the Polish workers became class conscious and formed socialist and trade union organizations similar to those of other European countries. Because of the prevailing political system, however, these groups had to work underground. Before 1900 there were many competing organizations, but when the Polish Socialist Party (P.P.S.) was formed in 1892, it rapidly assumed a position of leadership.

Like other Socialist Parties, the P.P.S. advocated a new economic and social order, but it also taught that the building of a Socialist society in Poland would have to be preceded by the establishment of an independent democratic Polish Republic, for Tsarist rule made the struggle for Socialism more difficult and raised national problems which tended to confuse the basic economic and social issues. Despite continual persecution by Tsarist police, the Polish Socialist Party, which enjoyed a brilliant leadership (including among its leaders Pilsudski, the future Polish dictator), organized the Polish workers into a vanguard of national resistance against Russia. Seeking to counteract the Socialist activities, Polish capitalists and landowners took over the originally progressive National Democratic Party and converted it into an instrument of their reactionary pro-Tsarist policy. The National Democrats (the so-called "Endeks"), under the leadership of Roman Dmowski, made use of a contemporary equivalent of the "Red scare" and anti-Semitism to gain influence among the Polish middle class.

The struggles between Socialists and National Democrats were especially bitter in 1905, when, concurrently with the Russian Revolution, a violent revolutionary wave swept Poland, encouraging the Socialist movement to believe that this upsurge meant the beginning of a new struggle for national independence. Tsardom, however, survived the crisis, and brutal repressions forced the P.P.S. to go underground once more. But during the revolutionary years many concessions had been wrung from the Tsarist Government, including the right to establish private Polish schools. Other concessions were embodied in the Russian constitution which was granted after the revolution. They enabled Poles to publish newspapers under a moderate censorship, to organize public meetings, and to send deputies to the Russian Duma (parliament).

Since the Socialists boycotted the Duma, most of the seats were taken by the Endeks, who used them to ingratiate themselves with the Russian Government by voting for military credits and supporting its expansionist tendencies. The last years before 1914 also saw the emergence of a separate political movement of the peasants and of a strong coöperative movement. The latter sprang from the desire to create a framework within which Poles could live freely among themselves, without the interference of Russian authorities.

After the suppression of the revolution of 1848, Austria was unable to return to her former ruthless methods in governing Galicia. Despite the revival of absolutist rule, the administration of Galicia had to be entrusted to a Polish Governor, Count Goluchowski. Although he was constantly hindered in his work by the central government, he was able to prevent the further Germanization of schools, to introduce a series of administrative reforms, and to encourage the employment of Poles in government service. Goluchowski's greatest achievement, however, was his prevention of the separation of Galicia into western and eastern sections. Such a division would have been disastrous for Polish national aspirations because the Ruthenians, who were then in a majority in Eastern Galicia, would have been able to liquidate Polish influence there.

The collapse of the insurrection of 1863 made it plain to Galician Poles, as it did to those under Russian rule, that the period of the direct struggle for independence was over. At the same time, Austria's defeats in the wars of 1859 and 1866 compelled her to establish complete constitutional rule. One of the basic elements of Austrian constitutionalism was the autonomy of the component parts of the empire, including Galicia. The fact that Goluchowski served as Austrian Premier during a part of the crucial period in which the changes in Austria's constitutional organization were being decided certainly contributed to progress toward Galician autonomy, which became effective in 1866. This important success, coupled with the violent repressions then taking place in Russian Poland, caused a genuine change of attitude among the Polish Galician population, who decided to remain with Austria until a better opportunity developed.

The policy of coöperation with Austria was carried out chiefly by the landowning class, organized into the Conservative Party, which had a clear majority both in the Galician Diet (legislature) and in the Galician delegation to the Austrian Parliament. The middle-class Democratic Party differed from the Conservatives mainly in that it urged progressive reforms, but within the framework of existing institutions. The peasants had little political consciousness at first, and usually elected the most conservative deputies. It was only toward the turn of the century that the powerful Peasant Party emerged which was soon to sweep entrenched Conservative constituencies.

Galician autonomy meant, above all, complete Polonization of public life, including administration and education. In Eastern Galicia, however, the Ruthenian language enjoyed equal rights with the Polish. The Poles took over the complex Austrian administrative apparatus and instituted an equally elaborate system of local self-government, employing a large group of civil servants (including teachers) and providing welcome opportunities for employment in a poor country with few openings in trade. Hence the Galician middle class included a large proportion of civil servants. This was in contrast with the middle class of Russian Poland, which consisted largely of businessmen.

Industry developed slowly in Galicia, mainly in connection with such existing natural resources as salt, petrol, and coal rather than with manufacturing activities. The Galician workers, although they were few in numbers, proved very responsive to Socialist ideas, and it was in Galicia that the first modern Polish labor movement arose. The Socialist Party and the trade unions were not forced to go underground in constitutional Austria, as they were in absolutist Russia, and their dynamic energy soon attracted considerable groups of professional people and landless peasants. The Socialist Party in Galicia therefore wielded an influence far greater than the number of industrial workers might have warranted. Led by Ignacy Daszynski, it coöperated with the Polish Socialist Party of Russian Poland. Sharing the latter's views and hopes about Poland's future, it used available constitutional means to further them.

The emergence of the Socialist and Peasant parties meant a complete change in Galicia's political picture. The process of change, which began about 1890, was subsequently interrupted by the First World War. The Ukrainian Party which emerged in Eastern Galicia maintained that the Ruthenians were not a branch of the Russian nation (a view held by earlier Ruthenian leaders), but a separate nation which must struggle for its national rights against Russians and Poles alike. The success of the Ukrainian Party was so overwhelming that the name "Ukrainian" was soon adopted to designate the Ruthenian nation.

The main importance of Galicia's constitutional period to Polish national life lay in the fact that, while Polish national and cultural life was stifled and repressed in Russian and Prussian Poland, Galicia built a complete network of Polish schools, including two universities, one polytechnical institute and an academy of sciences. Thousands of pupils were taught yearly to become good Poles in these schools. It was also in Galicia that Polish literature took refuge, for magazines and books were published there without censorship. Thus Galicia, and especially the city of Cracow, became for many years the center of Polish national life, taking the place of Warsaw, which had held that position until 1831, and Paris, which had held it during the period which followed the failure of the November insurrection.

Throughout these years, Prussian Poland was the scene of ever-increasing German efforts to suppress Polish national life. The prohibition upon the use of the Polish language in public life was followed by the mass settlement of German peasants on land forcibly purchased from Poles. At one time, the Poles were even forbidden to build houses on their own land. Material prosperity, however, enabled the Poles to resist in the economic sphere. A large trading middle class arose, making the Poles largely independent of German business, and the extraordinary development of Polish coöperatives had a similar effect.

The ability of the Poles to resist German attempts at suppression had not only saved the Duchy of Poznan for Polish national life, but also revived Polish feeling in Pomerania, which had been severed from Poland in the first partition; in Silesia, which had been detached from Poland in the fourteenth century; and in southern East Prussia (Masuria), which had never directly belonged to Poland at all. In these provinces, the Polish language had been reduced to the level of a peasant dialect but, despite administrative reprisals, it again became the national tongue.

Politically, the Prussian Poles were very conservative. They followed the National Democrats and disapproved of the strongly developed Socialist movement in the other parts of Poland. Because of the intense national oppression, however, the Conservatives in Prussian Poland did not follow the other Polish Conservatives in developing complete loyalty to the empire of which they had become a part, although there were occasional advocates of such loyalty.

Culture and Literature in Post-Partition Poland [24]

The Partitions of Poland and the subsequent downfall of the Polish state came at a time when the Polish nation was in the midst of a process of political and moral regeneration. The Poles continued their cultural development after the Polish state had ceased to exist. The course of this development, however, could not proceed normally, for each of the parts into which Poland had been divided became subject to different political conditions.

The period between the Third Partition and the collapse of the November insurrection (1795-1831) was of a somewhat transitional character culturally. Three main centers of Polish cultural life developed under Russian rule: Wilno, where an active intellectual life was centered around the university, reorganized by the Educational Commission; Krzemieniec, with its recently organized Lyceum; and Pulawy, the principal seat of the Czartoryski family, who used their influence to secure refuge for Polish patriotic writers and thinkers and established a magnificent library. Warsaw, under Prussian rule, declined to the level of a provincial town, but some intellectual activity continued there as well. A Society of Friends of Scientific Development was organized and many important Polish books were published,

---

[24] This section was contributed by Professor Manfred Kridl, Smith College.

including the first full Polish dictionary by Linde, and works by such writers as Kollatay, Sniadecki, and Czacki. After the establishment of the Duchy of Warsaw, there was a considerable gain in the number and quality of schools.

In the Congress Kingdom, created in Vienna in 1815, Polish cultural and intellectual life was able to develop freely for some time. A University and a Polytechnical Institute were established in Warsaw, but Wilno University remained foremost among Polish educational institutions, principally because of its excellent faculty which included the famous historian Lelewel.

In Warsaw, many newspapers and literary journals were launched. A struggle was waged between adherents of two literary trends: classicism and pre-romanticism. The first emulated the writings of the classic Greeks and Romans, as well as the French, while the second favored English writers of the late eighteenth century and modern German writers. Considerable development also took place in Polish music. Many Polish musicians toured Europe, drawing large and enthusiastic audiences and winning the recognition of many eminent Europeans, including Goethe. Frederic Chopin, who was soon to become a world-famous composer, was then studying at the Warsaw Conservatory.

Polish romanticism shared the general elements of European romanticism, but it also contained specifically Polish features especially after the failure of the November insurrection, when it became ardently patriotic. The leader of Polish romanticism and the greatest Polish poet of all time was Adam Mickiewicz (1798-1855), best known for his unique modern epic, *Pan Tadeusz*, his romantic drama, *Dziady* (The Forefathers), and his Crimean and love sonnets. Mickiewicz won for Poland a place in world literature. But in addition to being a great poet, he was also an ardent patriot. He worked consistently to link the cause of Poland's freedom with the cause of freedom and democracy throughout the world. He was also a great scholar, and for years was Professor of Slavic literatures at the College de France.

Next to Mickiewicz, the most important Polish romantic writer was Julius Slowacki (1809-1849), best-known for his numerous plays. Their excellence and variety mark him as the originator of modern Polish drama. Another important romantic writer was Zygmunt Krasinski, who will be remembered chiefly for his *Un-Divine Comedy* in which, as early as 1833, he foresaw and discussed the modern class struggle. In a class by himself is the lyric poet, Cyprian Norwid.

Most of these poets did not write in Poland, but abroad, chiefly in

France, which had become the center of the "Great Emigration" and of Polish cultural life after the collapse of the November insurrection of 1830-1831. France at that time was also the home of Polish science, politics, and literature. The historian Joachim Lelewel, formerly Professor of Wilno University and member of the National Government during the November uprising, and the writer Maurycy Mochnacki, former deputy to the Polish Diet, analyzed the causes which led to the failure of the uprising and laid them to its timidity in social questions. The Democratic Society, a radical group, which published its Manifesto in 1836, drew heavily on their ideas. The first Polish Socialist organization, known as "Polish People" and headed by Gabriel Worcell, was partly an offshoot of the Democratic Society. A religious movement, paralleling in intensity the radical social and political movement in the Great Emigration, led to the creation of a new religious order, the Resurrectionists.

In Poland, meanwhile, intellectual life continued, although under severe handicaps. The literary form which had its best development inside Poland was the novel, represented by Henryk Rzewuski, Joseph Korzeniowski, and Joseph I. Kraszewski, who wrote in the manner current at that time and practiced by such writers as Stendhal, Balzac, Dickens, and Thackeray. Kraszewski was an extremely prolific writer. He produced about 700 books, more than half of them novels, many historical. Rzewuski is best known for his *Memoirs of Soplica,* an excellent description of Polish country life in the eighteenth century, while Korzeniowski concentrated on novels dealing with the nineteenth-century Polish gentry among whom he lived. The field of comedy was represented by Alexander Fredro, whose pieces are even today the mainstay of the Polish theatrical repertory. Fredro, noteworthy for his wit and excellence of form, developed completely apart from the Polish literature of his time and is therefore a very interesting literary phenomenon.

The downfall of the Polish state adversely affected Polish architecture, for this branch of art develops best when supported by large state expenditures for public buildings and monuments. The partitioning Powers did little in this field. However, during the brief period of the Congress Kingdom's autonomy, considerable construction was undertaken and the "Empire" style found its way into Poland. Sculpture was backward, and the best Polish monuments of the time, those of Copernicus and Prince Joseph Poniatowski (which stood in Warsaw before the German occupation), were both creations of the Danish artist, Thorwaldsen. Polish music of the period is represented by the famous composer Frederic Chopin (1810-1849) and by the opera composer, Stanislaw Moniuszko.

The failure of the 1863-1865 insurrection against Russia led to a change of orientation among the Poles. Thoughts of armed resistance and political action were abandoned and replaced by the slogan of "organic work." In the cultural field, these years are known as the "positivist" period; it lasted almost until the end of the nineteenth century. Started in Russian Poland, where it was predominant for a time as a reaction against romanticism, positivism was also partly accepted in Prussian and Austrian Poland. It advocated economic and educational activities and struggle against social and economic backwardness. The leader of the Warsaw positivists was Alexander Swietochowski (1849-1938), a prolific writer on social and economic questions who was also a critic and a writer of novels and dramas. He was surrounded by many others. They published a number of books despite the rigorous censorship policy of the Russian Government.

Polish realist novels of the period compare favorably with contemporary Russian and Western European novels. The most famous Polish novelist of that time was Boleslaw Prus (1847-1912), the author of *Lalka* ("The Doll"), an excellent picture of contemporary Polish society, and of *The Pharaoh,* a historical novel inspired by ancient Egypt and equalled only by Flaubert's *Salammbo.* Prus wrote extensively in newspapers and periodicals and was an uncompromising fighter for progress and humanity. The same spirit infused the work of Mrs. Eliza Orzeszkowa, who wrote many novels dealing with peasant and Jewish problems.

Outside of Poland, the best-known Polish writer of the period was Henryk Sienkiewicz, the first Pole to receive the Nobel Prize in literature. In Poland he is best known for his novels which dealt with events in Polish history, such as *By Fire and Sword, The Deluge, Pan Wolodyjowski, The Teutonic Knights,* and for his short tales. They treated historic facts in the light of adventure, much like the works of the elder Dumas, but their language and style were far more faithful to the periods described than were those of Dumas' novels. Abroad, Sienkiewicz is best known for his book *Quo Vadis,* describing the persecutions of Christians in ancient Rome under Emperor Nero. Poetry was represented by A. Asnyk and M. Konopnicka.

Polish science made great progress, both in Galicia, where it was centered in the two universities and the Polytechnical Institute, and in Russian Poland, where Polish scientists had to rely on organized self-help, as the universities were Russified. Among the sciences, history and the history of literature were the most advanced. In the latter field, the principal achievement was the compilation, by Karol Estreicher, of the *Polish Bibliography,* an almost complete catalogue of all books published in Polish, in Poland, or about Poland, which has since become an indispensable aid to all students of the Polish past. Philology also developed, represented by such scholars as J. Baudouin de Courtenay and J. Rozwadowski. Lexicology was enriched by Karlowicz's *Dictionary of the Polish Language* and *Dictionary of Polish Idioms,* as well as by the *Old Polish Encyclopedia* by Gloger. Sociology is represented by Ludwik Krzywicki, geography by Waclaw Nalkowski, philosophy by Adam Mahrburg. In the field of exact science, it is sufficient to mention the names of Zygmunt Wroblewski and Karol Olszewski, whose work with low temperatures and liquefaction of the air is universally known.

Polish painting also entered a period of intensified development. It concentrated upon historical or realistic subjects, in general. Its principal representative was Jan Matejko, who painted many huge canvasses of scenes from Polish history. Another Polish painter, Artur Grotger, produced many paintings depicting scenes of the 1863 insurrection. Realism was represented by the brothers Gierymski and J. Chelmonski.

The reaction against positivism and realism, known in Western Europe as "symbolism" and "modernism," appeared in Poland as the "Young Poland" movement. It influenced poetry, the novel, and the theater, all of which had followed a parallel development. The main organ of the new current was the Cracow literary periodical *Zycie* ("Life"), edited by St. Przybyszewski, a writer highly regarded not only in Poland but also among German and Scandinavian modernists. He was surrounded by a group of poets, among whom Kazimierz Tetmajer, Jan Kasprowicz, and Leopold Staff were the most outstanding.

The most representative of the Polish novelists of the time was Stefan Zeromski (1864-1925), a prolific writer of novels which combined realism of style with lyricism in the treatment of the topics. Zeromski is best known for his sharp criticism of existing social conditions, and his writings, largely devoted to social topics, stimulated social consciousness on the part of the Polish public. He discussed Russian educational methods in the novel *Sisyphus' Works,* the attitudes of social workers in *Homeless People,* sin and crime in *History of Sin,* the tragedy of the 1863 insurrection in *The Faithful River,* and the story of the Polish soldiers under Napoleon in *Ashes.*

Another important novelist of the time is Wladyslaw S. Reymont (1868-1925), who wrote many novels about contemporary life and Poland's past. His best-known novel, which brought him the Nobel Prize, is *The Peasants,* hailed by European critics as the best study of modern peasant life. Andrew Strug, a Socialist leader and an outstanding novelist, devoted much of his writing to the artistic depiction of the Polish workers' fight for independence. Wladyslaw Orkan and the poet Tetmajer wrote much about the fate of the peasants, with especial attention to the mountain people of Southern Poland. A new type of drama was created by St. Wyspianski, a painter and poet, combining Greek, Shakespearian, romantic and folklore elements. He wrote tragedies and other plays devoted to the Polish past and present (*The Wedding, The November Night*).

In painting, realism was followed by impressionism, represented by such painters as Wyczolkowski, Stanislawski, Falat, Mehoffer, and others, most of whom were well known in Western Europe. Polish music was noteworthy for the excellence of Polish virtuosos, such as Wieniawski and Paderewski, rather than for its composers; among the latter W. Zelenski and Z. Noskowski were prominent. The Polish theater attained a high level of dramatic art, especially in Cracow and Lwow and later in Warsaw.

Poland and World War I (1914-1918)

The outbreak of World War I—a historical event upon which, as all Poles agreed, the re-establishment of their country's freedom depended —found the Poles unprepared for the re-establishment of their country's freedom. The nation was divided in its aims, mostly on geographical lines. The Galician Poles generally hoped for a victory of the Central Powers, whom they expected to extend the Galician autonomous system to Congress Poland. Most of the inhabitants of Congress Poland, on the other hand, hoped for a Russian victory, in the expectation that it would bring about Russian annexation of the Austrian- and Prussian-held parts of Poland, which, in turn, would so reinforce the Polish element within Russia that the Tsarist Government would be compelled to grant Poland autonomy. This line of reasoning was encouraged by a manifesto issued a few days after the beginning of the war by the Grand Duke Nicolai, Commander-in-Chief of the Russian Army, who promised the Poles "reunion of their country under the sceptre of the Emperor of Russia."

The Polish Socialists and a few minor progressive groups associated with them had another view of coming events. They foresaw a temporary victory of the Central Powers over Russia, followed by a victory of the Western Allies over Germany. From this defeat of all the partition Powers, they argued, an independent Poland was bound to arise. In order, however, to make Poland's aims clear, the Polish Socialists urged that Poles take an active part in the war, not just as soldiers of the Russian, Austrian, and German Armies, but as Poles fighting under their own national flag. Since it was impossible to fight simultaneously against Russia, Germany, and Austria and since they regarded Tsarist Russia as Poland's most dangerous enemy, they decided for the time being to assist Austria.

Joseph Pilsudski, at that time one of the leaders of the Polish Socialists, worked energetically to train Polish military cadres. He was assisted by political friends who, like himself, had taken refuge in Galicia from Tsarist persecution after the failure of the revolutionary movement of 1905-1906, and by many members and sympathizers of the progressive parties of Galicia—Socialists, Peasants, and Democrats. They organized the "Riflemen's Union," a semi-military organization preparing for war against Russia. Similar organizations were soon formed by others who began to share their views regarding Poland's future, but were unwilling to submit to the ideological leadership of the Socialists or the personal leadership of Pilsudski. All these organizations began to coöperate shortly before the war, and their joint forces supplied the cadres for the Polish military organization (named after the Polish Legions which had fought for the French Republic and Napoleon more than a hundred years earlier) which was launched when the war finally broke out. In the very first days of the war some of the Legions, which fought in Polish uniforms and under Polish command, were able to take the field against the Russians.

The participation of the Legions in the war on the side of Austria brought them recognition and popularity in Galicia, extending beyond the ranks of the progressive groups which had backed them from the very first. A Supreme National Committee (N.K.N.) was formed by all Polish political parties in Galicia in order to supply political leadership for the Legions and to administer the parts of Congress Poland liberated from Russian rule. The original aims of the N.K.N. were never realized, for the Legions were jealous of their independence and resented the attempt of the N.K.N., which included many conservative politicians (including even some "Endeks" at first), to dominate them. The administration of formerly Russian-Polish territory was placed in the hands of German and Austrian military governors. But despite these difficulties, the N.K.N. assumed the character of a political representation of the Austrian Poles, dealing with the Austrian and German Governments in matters concerning Polish affairs. In the

Allied camp, meanwhile, the Polish cause made no progress, for the
Tsarist Government confined itself to vague promises and dismissed all
attempts at mediation by Great Britain, France, and Italy as interference
in a purely internal Russian question.

By the end of 1915, Russian troops were driven out of most of Congress Poland and the country was divided into an Austrian and a German zone of administration. The Austrians, while technically in-
stituting military rule, exercised it through Polish officers and officials
in their service. But German military rule was unusually harsh, and
the only concessions wrung from the Germans were the re-establishment of limited municipal self-government and the reopening of Warsaw University, this time with Polish as the language of instruction.
Germans and Austrians were unable to agree concerning the future of
the Kingdom of Poland. Austria planned to unite Congress Poland
with Galicia and thus add a third section to the Austro-Hungarian
monarchy. Germany, on the other hand, rejected all proposed changes
in Galicia, wishing to annex considerable parts of Congress Poland outright and make of the rest a puppet state under German influence.

When the Central Powers began to feel a manpower shortage in
their armies, they became eager to enlist young Poles to fight for them.
The Russians had not succeeded in mobilizing the Poles before they
were driven out. The Central Powers therefore evolved a plan to proclaim the independence of the Kingdom of Poland, without as yet fixing its borders or selecting the future King. Their plan was then to
conclude an alliance with it and use its army, which was then to be organized, for their own military purposes. Accordingly a manifesto was
issued on November 5, 1916, establishing Poland's independence. This
was soon followed by the organization of a Council of State and the
first Polish administrative departments. While there is no doubt of the
real purpose of these steps, the manifesto nevertheless again raised the
Polish problem to international status.

Early in 1917, the Germans began to organize the new Polish army,
which they called "The Polish Armed Forces." It was planned to use
the Polish Legions, which had grown to a nearly complete Army
Corps through voluntary enlistments and which had fought with
distinction against the Tsar's troops, as a nucleus for the new army.
In the meantime, however, the international situation had changed
substantially. The Democratic Revolution which broke out in Russia
in February-March, 1917, had already destroyed the hated Tsarist
regime and proclaimed Poland's independence. A month later, the
United States of America declared war on Germany. The Russian
Revolution and America's participation in the war greatly changed the

relation of forces in the Allied camp, and it was plain that the Polish question would no longer be considered a purely Russian affair. The political leadership of the Polish Legions decided to resist the German efforts to use the Legions in building "The Polish Armed Forces," and to prevent, as far as they could, the formation of the latter. When the soldiers of the Polish Legions were ordered to take a new oath, pledging "brotherhood in arms with the German and Austrian Armies," Pilsudski and most of the Legionnaires refused to take it. Thereupon the refractory units were disbanded. All formerly Russian subjects were interned and the Galicians were impressed into the Austrian Army. Pilsudski himself was imprisoned in Magdeburg. Only a few units took the oath and were continued as the "Legion," but they had none of the prestige enjoyed by the Legions while they were under Pilsudski's command.

The "oath crisis" brought about a definite change in the attitude of the Poles toward the Germans and resulted in new forms of Polish military effort. A secret organization (generally known as the P.O.W.), which had been used for sabotage activities behind the Russian lines before the Russian troops were evicted from Poland, was revived by elements in sympathy with Pilsudski's stand in the "oath crisis". It prepared a new, genuinely Polish underground army, which was to strike at the decisive hour of the struggle for independence in coöperation with the military units of the Polish Socialist Party. The Germans tried to woo the Poles by establishing a Regency Council, calling elections for a new Council of State (to take the place of the original one, the members of which had resigned during the "oath crisis"), and enlarging the scope of authority of the Polish administrative departments. These measures, however, failed to change the temper of the Poles, who had decisively turned against the Germans. The strongest opposition to the Germans at that time was offered by the Socialists and the progressive groups coöperating with them.

Changes favoring the Poles had meanwhile taken place in the countries of the Western Allies. France authorized the formation of a Polish army on her soil from among Poles living in France, Polish volunteers from the United States, and German and Austrian prisoners of war of Polish origin. President Wilson proclaimed Poland's right to full independence and access to the sea as one of his fourteen points, and the Polish cause was given representation among the Western Allies through the Polish National Committee. This Committee was organized by the National Democratic leader, Roman Dmowski, who left Russia after the revolution had destroyed the Tsarist regime in which he had placed so much confidence. In Russia, especially after the October Revolution, Polish soldiers began to leave the Russian units and form separate corps for future service in Poland.

When Germany and Austria concluded the Brest-Litovsk peace treaty with Soviet Russia and the Ukraine, early in 1918, the shift in the Polish attitude toward the belligerents was confirmed. Not only did that treaty make no provision for the reunion of formerly Russian-Polish areas with Congress Poland, but it also ceded to the Ukraine the Chelm region of Congress Poland, which contained an infinitesimal Ukrainian minority.

Following the treaty, the remnants of the Polish Legion crossed the front line to march into Russia for reunion with the Polish corps recently organized there, and a wave of protest strikes and demonstrations swept Poland. Polish officers and civilian employees in the Austrian service, including the Military Governor General of the Austrian zone in occupied Poland, resigned en masse, and the Polish deputies to the Austrian Parliament issued repeated manifestoes calling for the reestablishment of a genuinely independent Poland and finally even repudiating Austria's claim to their allegiance.

The Habsburg monarchy, on the threshold of defeat and revolution, was helpless. In October, 1918, a temporary Polish administration was set up in western Galicia. On October 31, 1918, it took over authority in Cracow, which thus became the first Polish city to enjoy complete freedom. Austrian-occupied Congress Poland followed suit within a few days. The German-occupied zone, including Warsaw, became free on November 11, after the German revolution. The Germans were disarmed and withdrew. Considerable parts of Poland were thus liberated, forming the nucleus of the modern Polish Republic.

Bibliography

(At the end of Chapter XVIII)

Note by the Editor

Extensive sections of Dr. Ehrenpreis' manuscript, dealing with: the general aspects of Jagellonian foreign policy; Poland's role in European politics in the period of Elected Kings (1572-1764), including Polish-Swedish relations; the organization and development of the Polish Legions; the Duchy of Warsaw and the Polish question at the Congress of Vienna in 1815; the Polish insurrections of 1830-1831 (the "November Insurrection"), and of 1863 (the "January Insurrection"); as well as with Polish-Russian relations during the 19th century in general, have been eliminated by the Editor for lack of space and in order to avoid duplication with material contained in other chapters. Moreover, Dr. Ehrenpreis' original sections dealing with the Reformation and Counter Reformation movements and the Partitions of Poland have been condensed for similar reasons. For this information the reader is referred to the bibliography.

CHAPTER V

RUSSIA (UP TO 1918)

The Land and the People

ONE thousand years of Russian history have unfolded on a wide stage of endless forests in the north and broad steppes in the south, a uniform and melancholy land stretching without border or shape to the farthest limits of the horizon. Almost all of its mighty rivers flow north and south. They empty either into the Black and Baltic Seas, connected only by narrow straits with the maritime routes of world trade and civilization, or into the Caspian Sea and the Arctic Ocean, inaccessible to outside contacts. The most western of these river connections formed an ancient trade route from the Baltic to the Black Sea. Along it, in the sixth and seventh centuries, the first Slav settlements developed out of which Russia grew later: Novgorod in the north, Smolensk in the center, and Kiev in the south. Their peaceful life was threatened by ravaging expeditions of warlike tribes from the north and east.

From Scandinavia came the warlike Varangers or Vikings. The head of one of their bands, Rurik, was invited, according to tradition, to become prince of Novgorod (862). His successor, Oleg, conquered Kiev (882) and Smolensk. These princes founded the dynasty which ruled Russia for centuries with Kiev on the Dnieper River as its center and capital and later split in several branches, among which the Moscow division assumed leadership. The western river towns and routes were endangered, however, by the ever-present menace of invasions from the east. Asiatic peoples in a long succession, among them the Khazars, Pechenegs, Polovtsy, and finally the Tartars, pressed forward across the steppes toward the wealth of the Byzantine Empire. For these Asiatic tribes and for the eastern Slavs, Constantinople was a center of attraction like Rome for the Germans; an eternal goal of conquest and an ever-flowing source of civilization. From Byzantium, Christianity spread to the eastern Slavs. In the reign of Vladimir I

(978-1015), the Russians accepted Christianity under the patriarchs of Constantinople. The new civilization was consolidated under Yaroslav (1019-1054), when the first Russian chronicles were written and Russian law, the *Russkaya Pravda,* was codified.

This period of progress and prosperity based on trade did not last long. In addition to the almost yearly invasions from the east, internal feuds within the ruling groups hastened the disintegration of the realm of Kiev. Trade declined and life became difficult. As a result, the great expansionist movement which has been characteristic of Russian history began. As in America, Russian history was the epic of building a vast empire by penetrating into thinly settled regions and destroying or mingling with the sparse native populations. The road of American empire building moved westward, over prairies, rivers, and mountains, until it finally reached the Pacific Ocean. The Russian imperial march moved generally eastward until it too reached the Pacific and even at one time overflowed onto the American continent. Colonists from England who had crossed the Atlantic from the western rim of Europe and Slavs who had been the eastern outpost of Europe and had crossed the immense land areas of northern Asia finally met around the Pacific shore.

Except for China, the Russian Empire is the only example of a purely continental empire in modern history, a continent of itself covering the eastern half of Europe and the northern half of Asia. Like all empires, it includes many peoples, races, and climates. Such a vast edifice, growing through many centuries in a spirit of vigorous expansion and conquest, would not have been possible without the pioneer stamina of the people, in spite of governmental inefficiency and oppression.[1] For unlike the British and American Empires, the Russian Empire was not built on the principles of local self-government and individual liberty. It has resembled rather a military camp ever ready for defense or conquest, always feeling threatened by powerful enemies from without and disintegrating tendencies from within. Its organization and spirit have always stood at the opposite pole from Western tradition. The Russia of Kiev, although shaped by the influence of Byzantium, remained in contact with Europe. But later events erected an almost insurmountable barrier between Europe and Russia which caused the vast Empire to develop for centuries in its own way, a world in itself, turned more toward Asia than toward Europe, until vigorous efforts were

---

[1] "Russian history is a history of the expansion over a vast continent of a vigorous people imbued with the pioneer spirit," George Vernadsky, *Political and Diplomatic History of Russia,* p. 4. See on that expansion especially Robert J. Kerner, *The Urge to the Sea* (Berkeley: University of California Press, 1942) and *The Russian Adventure* (1943).

made for a new rapprochement between Russia and Europe in the eighteenth century.

The migrations from Kiev proceeded in three directions. Some turned westward, back in the direction of the Carpathian mountains where the Slavs had probably originated and founded there the principalities of Galicia and Volynia in the territory which is at present known as the western Ukraine. These principalities, in which the nobility or *boyars* occupied a strong position, fell under Polish and Lithuanian rule in the fourteenth century. Another stream of migrants turned northward and settled in Novgorod the Great on the river Volkhov, where a free urban constitution found its expression in the town meeting, the *veche,* attended by all free citizens. But by far the most important venture was the expansion toward the basin of the upper Volga, where the new Principality of Suzdal-Vladimir arose and the new town of Moscow was mentioned for the first time in 1147. In the vast expanses to the north and northeast (the whole of northern Russia to the Arctic Sea and to the Ural mountains was colonized by Novgorod), the Slavs met primitive Finnish tribes and intermingled freely with them, thus laying the foundation for the growth of a new nationality, so that the migrations brought about a split among the eastern Slavs.

The Russians of the east and north, oriented towards Asia and mixing with many of the semi-nomadic tribes of the Eurasian continent, developed into the Great Russians ultimately centered in Moscow. The eastern Slavs remaining along the Dnieper and spreading westward from there, called the Little Russians, developed into a separate nationality with their own language and culture, the Ukrainians or Ruthenians, with Kiev as their center. They did not succeed in forming an independent state of their own for any considerable period and their fertile land became a battle-ground between the Russians on the one hand and the Poles and Lithuanians on the other.[2] North of the Ukrainians a third eastern Slav people, the White Russians, who came under the domination of Lithuania in the fourteenth century, separated from the rest of the eastern Slav family. These two western branches remained in closer contact with Europe, but in the thirteenth

[2] On the history of the Ukraine and on the Ukrainian national movement, see Michael Hrushevsky, *A History of the Ukraine,* ed. by O. J. Frederiksen, Preface by George Vernadsky (New Haven: Yale University Press, 1941). Hrushevsky was the foremost Ukrainian historian. W.E.D. Allen, *The Ukraine, a History,* (Cambridge University Press, 1940) inclines less to the Ukrainian national point of view. Both books contain full bibliographies. See also D. Doroshenko, *History of the Ukraine* (Edmonton, Canada: Institute Press, 1939), and Clarence A. Manning, *Ukrainian Literature, Studies of the Leading Authors,* (Jersey City, N. J.: Ukrainian National Association, 1944).

century the center of gravity of eastern Slavonic life shifted definitely from the west and southwest to the east and northeast. New enemy forces pressing upon the disunited Slavs from west and east were responsible for this development.

In the northwest, German invaders, first the Livonian Order of Swordbearers, a little later the Teutonic Knights, conquered the southeastern shores of the Baltic Sea. Riga was founded as a center of German commercial and cultural influence. Alexander Nevsky, Prince of Novgorod, defeated the Teutonic Knights in the battle of Lake Peipus (1242), but he had to accept the overlordship of the Tartars or Mongols who swept into Russia in 1223 and by 1240 had overrun southern and central Russia and seized Kiev. They established their empire, the Golden Horde, on the lower Volga with Sarai, near present-day Stalingrad, as their capital. Russia was under Mongol domination for almost 300 years. Though the Asiatic Khans did not interfere much with the administration of the Russian principalities, the Russian nobility accepted the customs and ways of life of the Tartars and freely intermarried with them.

For centuries Russia lost all touch with Europe, from which it was separated by the rise of a powerful Polish and Lithuanian state in the west, and succumbed to the cultural and social influences of Asia while preserving the Greek Orthodox faith. The grand princes of Moscow curried the favor of the Tartar Khans and were entrusted by them with the collection of tribute from other Russian princes. Moscow, situated on a tributary of the Oka which emptied into the upper Volga, was most favorably situated for intercourse with the Golden Horde. Nizhni Novgorod (now called Gorky) at the confluence of the Oka and Volga, an important trade and communication center, was annexed by Moscow at the beginning of the fifteenth century. By then Moscow was well on the road to becoming the dominant power of Russia.

The Empire of Moscow

Several circumstances made Moscow the center of Russia, chief among them its geographic position and a succession of great princes who combined ruthless energy, astute intelligence, and far-reaching ambition. After Dmitri Donskoi had inflicted a defeat upon the Tartars for the first time at Kulikovo (1380), Ivan III (1462-1505) was able to shake off the Tartar yoke a century later. The Tartars were weakened by endless dissensions at the very time that Moscow unified Russia. Ivan conquered Moscow's chief rivals among the eastern Slavs, Novgorod with its vast lands, and Tver, and invaded Lithuania which had sided with Tver and had several times threatened Moscow itself in the fourteenth century. The Lithuanians, one of the last European peoples to be converted to Christianity, created a powerful state with Vilna as its capital under Gedymin (1316-1341), and widened it under Olgerd (1341-1377) to include the whole of White Russia and the central Ukraine down to the Black Sea. Olgerd's son, Jagiello (1377-1434), became King of Poland, established the personal union between the two countries, converted the Lithuanians to Roman Catholicism, and defeated the Teutonic Knights in the battle of Tannenberg (1415). His descendants ruled for almost two centuries in Poland and Lithuania. The dynasty came to an end with Sigismund II (1548-1572), under whom Poland and Lithuania were united in the Union of Lublin (1569), which resulted in the absorption of the Lithuanian nobility by the superior Polish civilization.[3]

Ivan III married the niece of the last Byzantine emperor, Sophia Paleologa, in 1472. As a result of this connection and of their growing power, the grand princes of Moscow began to regard themselves as the heirs to the imperial dignity and claims of Constantinople and the eastern Roman Empire. Ivan III and his successors, Basil III (1505-1533) and Ivan IV (1533-1584), proclaimed Moscow as the third Rome, the champion of the faith, and the center of the universe, and at the same time declared themselves the sovereigns over all Russian lands.[4] They accepted the title of Tsar-Autocrat, a translation from the Greek, broke the power of the *boyars,* and combined a Byzantine ceremonial with the continuing cultural and social influence of the Tartar East. At the same time new ties were sought with the West: Italian architects rebuilt and enlarged the Kremlin and English merchants settled in Moscow with special privileges and carried on trade through Archangel. But the Polish-Lithuanian commonwealth and Sweden—then rising to become the great imperial power in the Baltic—cut Russia off from the west except for the tenuous link with England across the Arctic. Naturally Eastern influences prevailed over those of the West. In many ways, the reign of Ivan IV and his successors witnessed the

---

[3] On Lithuania, see E. J. Harrison, *Lithuania Past and Present* (New York: Robert M. McBrite & Co., 1923) and Owen J. C. Norem, *Timeless Lithuania* (Chicago: Amerlith Press, 1943).

[4] The Russian title *tsar samoderzhets,* emperor-autocrat, is the translation of the Greek title of the Roman emperors Βασιλεύς Αὐτοκράτωρ. When the patriarch of Moscow was installed in 1589 the charter affirmed that "because the old Rome has collapsed on account of the heresy of Apollinarius, and the second Rome, which is Constantinople, is now in possession of the godless Tures, Thy great kingdom, O pious Tsar, is the third Rome. It surpasses with its devotion everyone else and all other Christian kingdoms are now merged in Thy kingdom. Thou art the only Christian sovereign in the whole world, the master of all the Christians." See Nicolas Zernov, *Moscow, the Third Rome* (London: S.C.M. Press, 1937).

confirmation of an Asiatic despotism in Russia which overrode all law and individual rights.

The half century of Ivan's reign was filled with incessant warfare. The Tartar principalities of Kazan on the middle Volga and Astrakhan on the lower Volga were conquered, and the Russian Empire now stretched from the Arctic Ocean to the Caspian Sea, from Novgorod to the Ural mountains. However, it remained vulnerable in the west and in the south, and the unending wars against Poland, Sweden, and the Crimean Tartars sapped Moscow's resources.

In his earlier years, Ivan tried a number of promising governmental reforms to win the support of the middle classes. The nobility was represented in the Duma (Council) of Boyars, while the *Zemsky Sobor,* a national assembly meeting in 1550, was to be the spokesman of all classes. But Ivan soon turned from this attempt at a progressive reign of law to a period of frightful lawlessness which characterized the last twenty years of his regime. It was marked "by incredible excesses and fantastic self-debasement" and earned him the title of Ivan the Dread. The devastations of war and the unbearable burden of recruitment and taxes produced a new migration of the peasants, largely to the open vastness of the east and the fertile lands of the south. The peasants tried to escape the compulsory labor or *barshchina* and the rent or *obrok* which became heavier and heavier as the state was organized more and more for permanent warfare and the land and its inhabitants were more and more regarded as the personal property of the Tsar.

Many of the peasants who escaped to the thinly populated frontier districts became military colonists used for the defense of the frontier and settled along the rivers in the south and the east. Thus arose the Cossack communities with their military organization and their spirit of enterprise. In 1581, Cossacks under Ermak and traders under Strogonov began the conquest of Siberia. In the next year they reached the great rivers Irtysh and Obi, and sixty years later (1643), Russians stood at the shores of the Pacific and entered into diplomatic negotiations with China. Meanwhile they had explored the course of the great Siberian rivers, the Yenisei and Lena, down to their mouths on the Arctic Ocean, and from then on the wealth of furs and minerals in Siberia and the Arctic region never ceased to interest the Russians.

But the Russian monarchy of the period was too weak to support colonizing ventures actively. The House of Rurik ended with Ivan's son, Feodor (1584-1598), an insignificant ruler. For fifteen years Russia was in the throes of a violent struggle for the succession among the leading *boyar* families and some pretenders who claimed to be Dmitri,

Ivan's son. Feodor was followed first by Boris Godunov (1598-1605), a *boyar* of Tartar descent and a brother-in-law of the preceding Tsar. He was a man of great intelligence who tried to reform Russia by Westernization, but was too weak to stem the rising chaos which had its roots in social discontent. During the ensuing "time of troubles" the whole of Russia was torn by a civil war which gave the Poles an opportunity, in collaboration with the Cossacks and other Russian factions, to gain a foothold in Moscow itself and to occupy the Kremlin. This aroused Russian religious patriotism, and Moscow was recaptured in 1612 under the leadership of Kuzma Minin, a merchant of Nizhni Novgorod, and Prince Dmitri Bozharsky. The *Zemsky Sobor* was called and elected a new tsar, the young Michael Romanov (1613-1645), founder of the Romanov dynasty (1613-1917).

His reign was not fortunate. The treaty of 1634 which established peace with Poland left the latter in control of Smolensk. Worse than that, however, was the growth of the omnipotence of the state and its ever-increasing demands on the national resources. Serfdom became a state institution, the peasants mere chattels subject to the absolute power of their master. The *Ulozhenie* or statute of 1649 embellished serfdom with some of the worst features of slavery. Peasants who fled and those who sheltered fugitives were severely punished. A large majority of the population thus became subject to arbitrary masters. All seeds of liberty under law and of rational progress were destroyed, and for over two hundred and fifty years Russia became the scene of social disorder and peasant uprisings which kept the nation from an integration and activization of its classes and forces.

More and more Russia became identified with autocracy. "In Moscow the sovereign was everything; hence the extraordinary persistence with which the popular imagination fastened itself to the idea of a tsar. Under the new dynasty we are to have a history more and more restricted to the state alone; the life of the people is entirely suppressed." [5] In the omnipotent and autocratic state there were no true citizens with rights of their own, only subjects serving the state in complete submission except for occasional revolts and riots which only increased the general lawlessness. [6] Human rights and legally protected liberties of

---

[5] Pares, Bernard, *History of Russia,* pp. 127, 147.

[6] The most important peasant risings were those of the Don Cossack Stephen Rasin (1667-1671), which swept the whole Volga region, and the even more formidable revolt led by Emelian Pugachev, a Don Cossack whose army made up of Cossacks, peasants, and many non-Russian Tartar and Finnish tribes, represented a serious threat from 1773 to 1775. He made himself master of many cities on the Volga and in the Urals and many peasants flocked to his standards. He was finally defeated by the great Russian general Alexander Suvorov.

the individual remained unknown in Russia. The vitalizing intellectual and social revolutions which have shaped modern Europe, the reception of Aristotelian philosophy and of Roman law, Renaissance and Reformation, did not reach and fertilize Russia. In seventeenth century England, these forces grew into the mighty tree of modern liberty, the seeds of which spread from there to America and western Europe, but in Russia the roots of law and freedom withered away. Thus the gulf between Russia and Europe created by the Mongol invasion remained after the Mongols had been driven out.

The Church also decayed and lost its moral authority in the seventeenth century. In 1654, the patriarch Nikon wished to introduce certain external church reforms in accordance with the Greek tradition, such as the right spelling of the word Jesus and the making of the sign of the cross with two fingers instead of three. But the Old Believers revolted and prolonged troubles and persecutions began.[7] Nikon was finally deposed but his reforms were retained. The dissidents (*raskolniki*) split into many sects. Among them were to be found some of the most enterprising, industrious, and progressive elements of modern Russia, as well as some of the strangest mystical sects. These groups managed to retain some vitality, but the Church as a whole submitted entirely to the state and became its instrument. During that period the only progressive leadership in the Russian Church was provided by the Ukrainian clergy who had received a higher education in the Academy of Kiev under Western and Greek influences.

In the seventeenth century the Ukraine, which had fallen under Polish-Lithuanian domination, experienced a national revival. It was not centered this time in the cities but in the steppes, in the Cossack Host of the Zaporozhe, the Dnieper region "below the rapids" around the fortress Sich. A frontier land situated where Russian, Polish, Turkish, and Swedish influences met and conflicted, the Ukraine became the battleground of imperial ambitions pressing from all sides. In 1648 Bohdan Khmelnitsky, Hetman or Elder of the Cossack Host, led an uprising against the Poles, and in 1654 the General Assembly or Rada of the Cossacks accepted a Russian protectorate at Pereyaslavl.[8] Ukrainian culture revived in this new Cossack state and Kiev soon took intellectual precedence over Moscow.

---

[7] The most interesting personality among the Old Believers was the Arch-Priest Avvakum. See his *The Life of Arch-priest Avvakum by Himself*, tr. by Jane Harrison and Hope Mirrles (London: Hogarth Press, s. a.).

[8] It was then that the Tsar adopted the title "Tsar of all the Great Russia, the Little Russia and the White Russia". See also George Vernadsky, *Bochdan, Hetman of Ukraine* (New Haven: Yale University Press, 1941).

The Ukraine was partitioned as a result of a Russian-Polish war. Its western part remained with Poland, the eastern part with Kiev became an autonomous state under Russian protection. Through that newly acquired territory, Moscow came into contact and soon into conflict with the Ottoman Empire, for Kiev and the Dnieper were still the ancient route to Constantinople. Moscow's protection was no unmixed blessing for the Ukraine, the autonomy of which was more and more curtailed. Hetman Ivan Mazepa's attempt "to defend the Ukraine from the tyranny of Muscovy" with the help of the Swedes failed in 1709. The Hetman's power was whittled away and finally abolished. In 1780, the Ukraine became an integral part of the Russian Empire and the history of the Cossack state and Ukrainian freedom came to an end. The re-awakening of Ukrainian national consciousness in the nineteenth century, however, regarded the Kiev State which had lasted until 1240 and the Ukraine of the Hetmans as a legitimization of the Ukraine's claims to national independence and as an inspiration for its cultural revival.

The Empire of St. Petersburg

So far Poland had been the bridge between Russia and Europe, and small numbers of foreign colonists who settled in Moscow, especially Germans, provided a tenuous contact with the West. The turning point in Russian history came when Peter I (1689-1725) decided to break a wide window through the wall separating Russia from Europe, to force a direct contact with the West, and to lay the foundation for Russian growth by a Europeanization of the administration and army. In the west the wall surrounding Russia was formed by three powerful states, Sweden in the north, Poland in the center, Turkey in the south. Peter and his successors waged a bitter struggle with all of them until Russia emerged the undisputed master, broke down the barrier and pushed her frontiers far into Europe.

Peter understood clearly that without modernization the Russian state could not hold its own against Europe, much less expand and impose its will. He therefore wished to import from Europe, which he distrusted and feared, not the spiritual ideals of liberty and human dignity but the practical efficiency and technical skill needed to strengthen his country for war. War filled practically all the years of Peter's reign, so his reforms had to be hasty, undertaken with an enormous wastage of wealth, labor, and human lives. The costs were not counted, yet the reforms remained superficial, imposed by the ruthless and tyrannical will of the autocrat without any real support or active collaboration by the people. Thus a state was created which reared its subjects "to an atmosphere of arbitrary rule, general contempt for legality and the person, and to a blunted sense of morality." Although Peter's immense efforts produced only a thin veneer over the primitivity of Russian life, they left a deep ferment in it. His reforms were discussed and disputed for two centuries. Many saw in him the anti-Christ who had undermined the Christian foundation of the true Russian order and exposed it to the destructive influences of un-Christian Europe. Others idolized him as the father of a better Russia. Some among them accepted his methods of brute force and regimentation and found themselves opposed at every turn, as he had been, by the inertia of the people.[9]

Peter had to fight on all the frontiers of his immense realm. In 1689 Russia faced her first armed conflict with China when Russian pioneers penetrated the Amur region of Manchuria. In the southwest, Peter occupied the Turkish fortress of Azov on the Black Sea for some time in the first of the two wars he fought against the Turks. But his most important struggle took place in the northwest against Charles XII of Sweden, whom he defeated in the battle of Poltava (1709). From Sweden he finally gained, in 1721, the Baltic provinces and islands which enabled him to establish direct connections with western Europe. Peter made Great Russia a European power, turning her face resolutely away from Asia towards the West. The transfer of the capital from historic Moscow, which represented traditional Holy Russia, to an entirely new city without any roots in Russian soil or history, symbolized the modernization and secularization of Russia. St. Petersburg was built in 1703 on newly conquered marshy land on Russia's border nearest to Europe. Peter was the first Russian sovereign to visit Europe and to grow enthusiastic about the mechanical civilization of the industrialized West. Under its influence, he laid the foundations of the modern Russian nation.

The religious oriental civilization of Russia gave way slowly to a modern secular civilization. Peter reformed the calendar, introduced a simplified alphabet, substituted a simpler language nearer to every-

---

[9] On Peter the Great, his reforms, and their consequences, see V. O. Kluchevsky, *A History of Russia,* tr. by C. J. Hogarth (London: Dent, 1926) vol. IV; Hans Kohn, *The Idea of Nationalism* (New York: Macmillan, 1944) p. 560-572; E. Schuyler, *Peter the Great,* 2 vols. (New York, 1884); Kasimierz Waliszewski, *Peter the Great,* 2 vols. (London & New York, 1897.) Peter abolished the patriarchate (1721) and replaced it by the Holy Synod, a council of bishops of the Orthodox Church, presided over by a layman (procurator) appointed by the Tsar. This measure did not secularize or reform Russian life, but completely subordinated the Church to the Tsar, who now became, in a way unknown anywhere in the West, the undisputed secular and ecclesiastical head of the totality of Russian life.

day speech for the archaic religious literary style, began to publish the first newspaper in Russian and to print the first secular books: manuals of science and of the new ways of life. The administration and the army were largely patterned on the German example. In the Kiev period, Byzantine influences had predominated, chiefly through the Church; in the Moscow period, Tartar influences had prevailed. The St. Petersburg period was shaped by Germany as a teacher, working through the court and the bureaucracy. German scholars helped to found the first Russian University in Moscow (1755). The Imperial Academy of Science of Petersburg (1726) consisted largely of foreigners. Literary life in Russia, however, developed under French influence, as did German literature itself in the first half of the eighteenth century, and Catherine II (1762-1796), herself a prolific writer, established the court as a model of Westernized cultural life.

Soon, however, native forces began to play a more active role. Michael Lomonosov (1712-1765), the son of a peasant from Archangel, showed the immense abilities and adaptability of the Russian people emerging from seclusion and backwardness. This self-made man not only became a scientist of the first rank, but helped through his Russian grammar to transform the language into an instrument for the expression of modern thought. He wrote a Russian history to "reveal the glorious deeds of our rulers," so that everyone "might find in the Slavic sagas deeds as magnificent as those of ancient Greece and Rome, and Russia need never again be humiliated." He appealed to Russian youth to enrich Russian literature and to study diligently, so that Russia would have her own Platos and Newtons, become glorious, and utilize her immense idle natural resources. By the end of the eighteenth century a modern Russian literature began to develop in many fields. A new self-confidence animated the Russian educated class, which viewed Russia as the equal and soon as the superior of Europe. This new pride was strengthened by Russian achievements in the field of foreign policy. During the eighteenth century Russia became an active and full-fledged member of the concert of European great powers.

A rapid decline in the moral and material position of the formerly powerful Polish and Turkish states went hand in hand with the rise of Russian might and the progress of Russian civilization. Sweden had been eliminated as a great power in 1721 and two Swedish attempts to regain Karelia and parts of Finland failed. Several wars with the Turks brought important successes: the treaty of Kutchuk Kainarji (1774), by which Russia acquired the right to intervene on behalf of the Danubian Turkish provinces of Moldavia and Wallachia and in the affairs of Greek Orthodox Christians in the Ottoman Empire; and the annexation of the Crimea (1783). Russia participated actively in the Seven Years' War, in which her armies reached Central Europe, and occupied Berlin for a short time in 1760. But the most important Russian successes were achieved against Poland, where Russia's influence was paramount after 1733. By the three partitions of Poland (1772, 1793, 1795), Russia acquired the whole of Lithuania, White Russia, and the Ukraine (except for Galicia, which went to Austria) and thus became a direct neighbor of Prussia and Austria. Poland was extinguished as an independent nation for one hundred and twenty-three years.[10]

In its internal development, Russia changed from an unlimited autocracy into a state in which the tsar recognized certain rights of the nobility. Under Catherine II the aristocracy was freed from its obligations of service to the state, received legal rights and soon a number of important privileges at the expense of the peasant masses. Catherine also modernized the provincial administration and a free public opinion began to develop under the influence of French rationalism. Yet serfdom remained the foundation of the state and all attempts at more thoroughgoing reforms collapsed because of the great fear of the French Revolution.

The Napoleonic Period

The war against the French Revolution completed Russia's rise to a dominant position in the councils of Europe. Paul I (1796-1801) participated in the war of the second coalition against the French Republic. In 1799 Alexander Suvorov, the greatest Russian general of all time, led victorious Russian armies deep into Italy and defeated the French in the battles of the Trebbia and Novi. Paul's successor, Alexander I (1801-1825), participated in the war of the third coalition which ended in the alliance between Alexander and Napoleon at Tilsit in 1807, an alliance broken in 1812 by Napoleon's invasion of Russia. In the ensuing "Great Patriotic War," as the war is known in Russian history, the Russians under General Michael Kutusov abandoned Moscow after the battle of Borodino (September, 1812), but forced Napoleon to retreat from the city by burning Moscow. Retreating toward Smolensk, Na-

---

[10] On the partitions of Poland, see R. Nisbet Bain, *Slavonic Europe, a Political History of Poland and Russia from 1447-1796* (Cambridge University Press, 1908); R. H. Lord, *The Second Partition of Poland* (Cambridge: Harvard University Press, 1915); on Poland in general, *The Cambridge History of Poland*, Vol. II (Cambridge University Press, 1941); O. Halecki, *History of Poland* (New York: Roy, 1943); Waclaw Lednicki, *Life and Culture of Poland as reflected in Polish Literature* (New York: Roy, 1944).

poleon escaped from Russia harassed by the severe winter and by enemy forces (crossing the Beresina river). The Russians were not satisfied with driving the invader from their soil, but defeated Napoleon in Germany and France in an alliance with Prussia, Britain, and Austria. In March, 1814, Russian troops under Alexander I set foot in Paris.

At the Congress of Vienna (1814-1815), Alexander I was one of the dominant figures, the father of the Holy Alliance (September, 1815). Like that of all important Russian rulers, Alexander's career was one of wars and conquests. His grandmother Catherine had named him in memory of the imperial example of Alexander the Great and had called her second grandson Constantine, with similar historic implications. Under Alexander, Russia fought with Persia and annexed Georgia and Daghestan in the Caucasus, built frontier fortifications in Alaska and northern California, and acquired the whole of Finland in a war with Sweden. Finland, however, retained an autonomous constitution as a Grand Duchy. Poland likewise was joined with Russia by the Congress of Vienna as an autonomous kingdom with its own constitution and administration.

The period of the Napoleonic Wars saw the rise of Russia as the leading military power in Europe and also sharpened the discussion about Russia's position in the world. Alexander I started his life with liberal ideas, and Count Michael Speransky prepared detailed plans for internal reform and the reorganization of national life. But reactionary tendencies soon prevailed. Nikolai Karamzin (1765-1826), who in his younger years created the modern Russian literary style under French influence and who later turned to writing the first widely read *History of the Russian State*, glorified autocracy, orthodoxy, and the Russian past. He saw the greatness of Russia not in Peter but in Ivan the Dread. He aroused a great pride in Russia in the hearts of his readers. "Looking on the immensity of that monarchy which is unique in the world, our mind feels overwhelmed. Never did Rome equal it in greatness." He regarded obedience to the autocrat as the basic strength of the nation and advised isolation and reliance upon Russia's native forces. Karamzin's philosophy of history became the official attitude of Russia in the nineteenth century.

But contact with Europe, through the Napoleonic Wars, had become too close to allow the glorification of the past to remain unchallenged. As a result, members of the nobility and the officer class, organized in secret societies, staged an uprising at the death of Alexander I in December, 1825, to overthrow autocracy, to abolish serfdom, and to introduce constitutional government. They failed because they were completely unsupported by the people. But they left a deep impression upon all subsequent revolutionary movements in Russia. The struggle between autocracy and constitutionalism which began in 1825 was to fill the history of nineteenth-century Russia. It is not yet decided. Even when autocracy crashed in 1917, constitutionalism was not victorious. The forces of liberty and law in Russia were too weak to triumph. Nineteenth-century autocracy caused Russia to lag far behind Europe.[11]

Nineteenth-Century Russia

Russia's problem in the nineteenth century can be simply stated. It remained an eighteenth-century state based on autocracy and nobility at a time when these forces were no longer sufficient to insure Russia's vitality in altered social circumstances. In western Europe, state and society worked harmoniously under the guidance of an awakened public opinion. Even in central Europe, modern nations grew up by the integration of the people into the nation. But in Russia the gulf between the state and the people widened and public opinion, growing slowly through literature as its only available outlet, was forced into opposition. Yet it lacked the social strength to overcome the lawlessness of autocracy by imposing a rule of law.

In spite of these internal tensions and Russia's general backwardness, imperial expansion did not slacken. The western frontiers of the empire were well established by 1815. Finland, the Baltic provinces, Poland, and Bessarabia formed Russia's vanguard on its western approaches and secured its access to the Baltic and Black Seas. Efforts to control the Balkan peninsula and the Straits of Constantinople and thus to secure the road to the Mediterranean failed, in spite of the fact that Russia waged a number of wars against Turkey (1806-1812, 1828-29, 1853-56, 1877-78). These wars were officially undertaken for the "liberation" of the people of orthodox faith in the Ottoman Empire or of the Balkan Slavs, and were supported by the religious and pan-Slav nationalist currents in Russia.

---

[11] Mazour, Anatole G., *The First Russian Revolution, 1825* (Berkeley: University of California Press, 1937). The great revolutionary thinker, Alexander Herzen, wrote of the Decembrists: "The heritage we received from the Decembrists was an awakened feeling of human dignity, the striving for independence, the hatred for slavery, the respect for Western Europe and for the Revolution, the faith in the possibility of an upheaval in Russia, the passionate desire to take part in it, the youth and freshness of our energies." (*My Past and Thoughts, The Memoirs of Alexander Herzen,* tr. by Constance Garnett. (London: Chatto and Windus, 1927). Vol. VI, p. 204. Pushkin, the greatest Russian poet, characterized on the other hand Karamzin's famous history in the following lines: "In his *History,* beauty and simplicity prove without bias the necessity of autocracy and the charm of the whip."

Nineteenth-century Russia was more successful in its vast empire building in Asia, where it pressed relentlessly forward towards the Persian Gulf, the Indian Ocean, and the ice-free ports of the Pacific. From Persia, Russia acquired Armenia and possessions south of the Caucasus Mountains. In central Asia, the Russians conquered the Mohammedan khanats of Kokand, Bokhara, and Khiva (1865-1881) and advanced their frontier to Afghanistan and the Pamir plateau, only a short distance from British India. Throughout the nineteenth century, Britain felt that her Asiatic possessions were threatened by Russia. In the Far East, Russia acquired from China the left bank of the Amur River in Manchuria and the coastal region of eastern Manchuria where Vladivostok, the "Ruler of the East," was founded in 1860. By the end of the century, the Russians had penetrated into Manchuria, interfered in Korea, and established an ice-free port in Port Arthur (1898) on the Liaotung Peninsula. These advances brought about the war with Japan (1904-05). The defeat in that war turned Russia's attention from the Far East back to the Balkans, where Russian aspirations clashed with German and resulted in the outbreak of World War I.

All through the nineteenth century, the Russian Government had felt a deep affinity and community of interest with the German monarchies, especially with Prussia. From the Holy Alliance (an alliance of the Romanovs with the Habsburgs and Hohenzollerns) until Bismarck's dismissal (1890), the Russian and Prussian rulers saw in close collaboration a bulwark against the penetration of Western democratic ideals into their domains. Only the growing fear of Germany's limitless aspirations, as openly expressed under William II, drove the Russian autocrat, very much against his inclinations, into an alliance with republican France (1891-1894). Fear and distrust of Germany also brought about an entente between Russia and Britain (1907). In World War I, Russia thus found herself fighting on the same side as the Western democracies against the common threat of Germany. Strategic necessity and the will to survive brought them together rather than any similarity of political ideas.

The political ideas of official Russia were set for the nineteenth century under Nikolai I (1825-1855). He came to the throne as a suppressor of the Decembrist revolution and in 1830-31 defeated the revolution of Poland which ended in the abrogation of the Polish constitution and the forcible Russification of the country.

Nikolai thus became a determined opponent of all liberal and progressive ideas. He firmly believed that Russia was the Ark of Salvation in the general flood of liberalism which swept over Europe. Russia became the most reactionary country, ruled with extreme brutality, in which every attempt at independent thinking or individual action was ruthlessly suppressed. All intellectual life was strictly controlled, all liberal manifestations were drastically repressed. The whole state was nothing but an immense police barracks, a bureaucratic machine deadening all spontaneous life and tempered only by inefficiency and corruption. The famous secret police (the "third section of His Majesty's own chancery") was in control of all Russian life from 1826 to 1880. Count Uvarov, Minister of Education from 1833 to 1849, proclaimed orthodoxy, autocracy, and Russian nationality as the foundation of national education. "The emperor of all Russia is an autocratic and unlimited monarch. God himself commands to obey the Tsar's supreme command not only out of fear, but for conscience's sake." Throughout the empire unquestioning discipline was enforced in the spirit of absolute authority.

Under these conditions, Russian creative life found its refuge in literature which mirrored and analyzed the existing situation. It speaks well for the vitality of the Russian people that a flowering of literature set in under the regime of Nikolai I which almost at one stroke made this young literature equal to its older European sisters.[12] Western influences could not be entirely kept out by the autocracy. The romantic poets of England and France, especially Lord Byron, influenced artistic youth. The German philosophers Hegel, Schelling, and Feuerbach, and the French socialists, especially Saint Simon, were eagerly read by the intellectuals in Moscow and St. Petersburg. Russian literature found its greatest poet in Alexander Pushkin (1799-1837), whose novel in verse *Eugene Onegin* (1823-31) introduced two model types for nineteenth-century Russian literature. One was the male hero, highly gifted, full of pride, plans, and intentions, but unable to realize them, a Hamlet-like figure of a "superfluous man," fundamentally an egoist inspired by many beautiful words.[13] The other was Tatyana, the noble

---

[12] This flowering of literature was really remarkable in a society of which Bernard Pares, *A History of Russia,* p. 328f writes: "While the censorship crippled thought and the bureaucracy pounded out its innumerable regulations, the public lay in a state of torpor. Nothing is more striking than the abasement of so many even of the most independent minds before the authority of the supreme drill master. Servility was the rule everywhere, the very qualities of loyalty and service took a character of degradation."

[13] The character of Onegin is indicated by the brief characterization in French by which Pushkin prefaces his novel: "Pétri de vanité il avait avouer encore plus de cette espèce d'orgueil qui fait avouer avec la même indifférence les bonnes comme les mauvaises actions, suite d'un sentiment de supériorité, peut-être imaginaire." Pushkin, who was killed in a duel, foresaw in one of his last poems, *Unto myself I rear a monument,* his future fame. Much of his work was set to music by famous Russian composers. Michael Glinka (1803-1857), the first modern Russian composer, who wrote the famous patriotic opera, *The Life for the Tsar* (1836),

Russian girl of whose many sisters Turgenyev said, "Russian women, you are all more lofty than we men."[14]

The other great poet of the period, Michael Lermontov (1814-1841), created a similar hero in his novel, *A Hero of Our Time* (1840): Petchorin, who ends as a disillusioned man and regards his own frustration with an aloof irony, but is in reality a suppressed idealist who has become skeptical of all ideas because the hostile environment was too strong and too repellent. What this environment was is revealed to us in bitter satires, like the famous play *The Misfortune of Being Clever* by Alexander Griboyedov (1795-1829) and the *Inspector General* by Nikolai Gogol (1809-1852), who unfolds a Dickensian panorama of contemporary life among Russian landowners in his novel *Dead Souls* (1842). Everywhere servility, intellectual stagnation, and vulgarity are encountered. Russian literature thus easily becomes an indictment of Russian life. Most of the authors belonged to the aristocracy, even to court circles; they grew up in the atmosphere of serfdom and idleness; some of them became a characteristic Russian type, the "repentant aristocrat" who confesses his sins and those of his society. The general apathy of the life of the gentry has been masterfully depicted by Ivan Goncharov (1812-1891) in his famous novel *Oblomov* (1857), the story of a young man whose good will and charm are entirely wasted through indecision and passivity. The oppressive atmosphere of Russian autocracy sentenced its best sons to a parasitic existence.

Condemned to inactivity, Russian intellectuals spent most of their time needlessly discussing the future of Russia, the meaning of her history, and her place in the world. Deeply aware of the almost unbridgeable differences between Russia and Europe, all their thoughts revolved around the relations of these two worlds. One school, the Westerners, believed in the need for the Europeanization of Russia, of the broadening and deepening of Peter's work. They were appalled by the primitivity and backwardness of Russian life, and saw the cause of Russia's stagnation in the separation from the West.[15] On the other hand, the

---

composed Pushkin's poem, *Russlan and Lyudmilla*. Modest Moussorgsky (1835-1881) based his opera *Boris Godunov* on Pushkin's drama of the same name, and Peter Tschaikovsky (1840-93) owed much of his early popularity to his *Eugene Onegin* (1879).

[14] In Turgenyev's *Virgin Soil*. In Turgenyev's novels, as in most Russian novels of the nineteenth century, men are often vacillating and weak, women generous and self-reliant.

[15] One of the most interesting early thinkers appalled by Russia's time-lag was Peter Chaadayev (1794-1856). In his first Letter, published in 1836, he wrote: "We are neither part of the West nor of the East. We have lived as it were outside of history and have remained untouched by the universal education of the human race . . . Lonely in the world, we have given nothing at all to the world . . . Not one useful thought grew on the barren soil of our land, we made no effort to think for ourselves and of what others thought we accepted only the surface and frill." But even many of the Westerners were convinced of Russia's superiority

Slavophiles looked back to Russia before Peter, which they idealized in a romantic way and in which they found a national unity firmly established on the rock of orthodox faith. They saw in the West a civilization decaying as a result of rationalism and materialism, and a society disintegrating as a result of class war and greed. Only in Russia did they find harmony and wholeness; from Russia alone, therefore, would come the salvation of Europe. Out of the narrow and miserable reality of Russian life grew fantastic dreams of Russia as a savior of mankind from social and moral chaos, as the founder of a universal and harmonious civilization. This Russian messianism often expressed itself in an unbridled glorification of reaction, a nostalgia for the past, sometimes however as the hope of a typically Russian socialism which would not have to pass through the ugliness and degradation of Western capitalistic society but would spring straight out of the deep resources of the Russian masses with their communal traditions of *mir* and *artel*.[16] In any case Russia was regarded as fundamentally different from the West, which was old and spent, while Russia, young and yet unfulfilled, could confidently expect the dawn of her day if she would only keep herself uncontaminated by Europe's poison.[17] But all these dreams of Russia's superiority and of the West's decay were shattered for the time being when the much-vaunted power of Russia collapsed miserably in the Crimean War as a result of general inefficiency and corruption. The need for reform became manifest to everybody.

The new Tsar Alexander II (1855-1881) set out as the reforming

---

or at least potential superiority. Alexander Herzen (1812-1870), who lived abroad after 1847 and published *Kolokol* (The Bell), the first revolutionary periodical of importance, developed more and more faith in Russia. "Russia," he wrote, "is not bound like Europe by the past or by scruples. She is too unhappy to be satisfied with anything less than full freedom. Once Russia will have gained strength, she will lead mankind to the destruction of decaying civilization."

[16] The *artel* was a coöperative craft society, reminiscent in some ways of the mediaeval guild; the *mir* was a village community considering the land as common property. Slavophiles regarded the *mir* as ancient and exclusively Russian. In reality the *mir* was discovered for them by a German traveler and student of Russia, August von Haxthausen, in the nineteenth century. It is in no way confined to Russians or Slavs, and the Russian *mir*, far from being an expression of basic national ideals, is a fairly recent growth due to considerations of tax collection or to growing population pressure.

[17] The Slavophiles owed their theory not to any original Russian thought but to the influence and imitation of German romanticism and its anti-Western attitude. See Hans Kohn, *Not By Arms Alone* (Cambridge: Harvard University Press, 1940), pp. 105ff. The extravagant claims of Russian messianism were rebuked by the great Russian thinker, Vladimir Soloviev (1853-1900): "The Slavophiles did not feel and recognize the common root of evil in Russian life, of that evil that caused the violence done to the serfs, the injustice of the officials and many other things, the general lawlessness which could arise because the concepts of honor and dignity of human personality were still very weak." The principle of human rights and of the absolute value of the free personality should have been opposed, historically, to this lawlessness. These are Western European principles which had no connection with anything peculiarly Russian. He regarded Russia's isolation as Russia's misfortune.

Tsar, but his good intentions were largely frustrated by the half-heartedness of his attempts and the inertia of the administration. Even so, the foundations were laid for the transformation of Russian society during his regime. On March 3, 1861, serfdom was abolished, after a relative freedom of press had allowed a discussion of the urgency and methods of the proposed measure. The former serfs received land allotted to them as communal village property—*mir*—with periodic redistribution of plots which were not consolidated enough to allow any progressive intensification of agriculture. The landlords were reimbursed by government bonds for which the peasants had to pay in forty-nine annuities guaranteed by the *mir*. The emancipation of the serfs weakened the landowners economically without fully satisfying the land hunger of the peasantry, but it freed almost 70 per cent of the population from its bonds, mobilized new social forces, made industrialization possible, and necessitated a complete overhauling of the administration. In 1864 thorough reforms improved the judiciary and the foundations for provincial self-government were laid in the *zemstvo*. In 1870 municipal self-government was granted. In 1874 universal army service was modernized and humanized, and a number of educational reforms expanded scholastic opportunities, especially for women who were admitted to the universities in 1876.[18]

The freer life under Alexander II witnessed the second great flowering of Russian literature, no longer an age in which poets dominated, but novelists who analyzed society and dug deep into the heart of Russia. Ivan Turgenyev (1818-1883), Fedor Dostoyevsky (1821-1881), and Count Leo Tolstoi (1828-1910) established the world fame of Russian letters. Turgenyev was a Westerner of aristocratic birth whose novels represent stylistic masterpieces. Dostoyevsky, who came from the lower urban middle class, hated Europe and joined the Slavophiles. No writer has ever shown a deeper psychological insight into the innermost recesses of the human heart. All his characters are typically Russians, sinners and criminals and little men who suffer and talk and reveal. Tolstoi, like Turgenyev a scion of the landowning nobility, did not migrate to Europe; from his country estate at Yasnaya Polyana he gave to the world the great panorama of *War and Peace*, a glorification of the Russian masses as the real hero of the patriotic War of

---

[18] On Russian life before the emancipation, see the famous memoirs of Alexander Herzen (see note 11), of Prince Peter Kropotkin, *Memoirs of a Revolutionist* (Boston: 1899), and of Sergey Aksakov, *Chronicles of a Russian Family* (for the end of the eighteenth century) tr. by M. C. Beverley (New York: Dutton, n.d.); on the revolutionary activity under Alexander II the works by Stepniak (S. M. Kravchinski), among them *Underground Russia, Revolutionary Profiles and Sketches from Life* (New York: Scribner, 1883).

1812, and turned later from artistic creation to the problems of social ethics and religious quest which underlie so much of Russian thinking. Like Dostoyevsky, Tolstoi was a God-seeker, but he had none of the former's darkness and depth; he was much more a universal figure with a Rousseau-like confidence in the goodness of the common man and an eighteenth-century faith in the light of reason. But it is Dostoyevsky whose novels and journalistic writings hold the key to an understanding of many sides of the Russian of the nineteenth century, a man in many ways alien to Europe.

Forces of Transformation

At the same time, forces were at work transforming Russia under the impact of Western civilization and of modern industrial society. Alexander's reforms held out new vistas but did not fulfill their promise. But Russia's energies had been liberated; after the long winter of Nikolai's oppression the earth began to thaw. The young revolutionary movement which began in the '60's was a movement of the intelligentsia, the product of discussions and dreams, without any close contact with reality and therefore doomed to sterility, but it filled the hearts of Russian youth with fervent ideals and broke the intellectual and moral stagnation. People of the generation of the '60's are known as nihilists and have been portrayed in the famous figure of the student Bazarov in Turgenyev's *Fathers and Sons*. They rejected the romantic sentimentality and the aristocratic boredom of the older generation, they dreamt of uprooting all the rotten past and of building an entirely new society based upon science. What Russia needed, in their opinion, were factories and laboratories, not poetry or religion.

But in reality they also remained dreamers who did not take any practical steps towards the realization of their programs. They developed, in their rejection of traditional morality and in their helplessness against the power of governmental terror, the mysticism of revolutionary activity. Secret organizations carried on the fight with the police and with the oppressive state machine which stifled all individuality and condemned it to passivity, but these exciting conspiracies with their inherent danger sometimes created an amoral attitude in which the revolution became an aim in itself and all means to that end seemed permissible. The extreme case of Sergei Nechayev, who was tried in 1871, served as a model for Dostoyevsky's novel *The Possessed*, in which he drew a hateful picture of the nihilists.

The longing of the intelligentsia to end their isolation and to bridge the gulf separating them from the masses brought about in the '70's the movement known as "going to the people", the *narodnichestvo*. The effort to enlighten the peasants foundered on the lethargy of the masses; the ethical duty of devotion to them, as preached by Peter Lavrov (1823-1900), proved a quixotic enterprise.

So revolutionary youth turned to another quixotic quest: an effort to break the power of government reaction by organized terror which would liberate the masses. In 1876 an organization known as *zemlya i volya* (land and liberty) was founded and in 1879 another called *narodnaya volya* (will of the people). Terrorist acts followed in quick succession. In 1878 Vyera Zasulich attempted to assassinate General Trepov and was acquitted by a jury; in the same year Stepnyak killed the chief of the gendarmerie. Only three years later the last of a long line of attempts on the life of the Tsar succeeded. On March 13, 1881, the Tsar liberator perished by bombs thrown by the terrorists. Many of them had no clear political program. They lived by a mystical faith in the Russian masses and the traditional communal forms of their life in which they saw a bulwark against Western capitalism and a basis for a future socialist organization on the land. "Land and liberty" meant to them the socialization of the land and the convocation of a constituent assembly, the demands of the later Socialist Revolutionary Party which united the overwhelming majority of the Russian masses behind its program in 1917.

Alexander III (1881-1894) ascended the throne determined to avenge his father and to stamp out revolution. He succeeded and a new dark age descended upon Russia: the stifling "Gray Days" with their total absence of any sense of social purpose and creative labor. The populism of the '70's had failed to take root. Turgenyev in his last novel *Virgin Soil* has left us a picture of the verbose utopianism of the idealistic youth movement; but in his novel there is also a lonely figure, the engineer and factory executive Solomin, a silent man of peasant origin who knows the masses, who does not talk, who has no great dreams, who has learned from the West the need of concrete constructive action in daily life to clean up the Augean Stables of Russia. But Solomin's time had not yet come. Under Alexander III, Russia followed the road of the most reactionary Slavophilism. Constantine Pobyedonostsev (1827-1907), the former tutor of the Tsar, became procurator of the Holy Synod and Russia's intellectual mentor until 1905; the chauvinistic journalism of Michael Katkov (1818-1887) set the official tone. In this atmosphere of reaction and oppression, Anton Chekhov (1860-1904) wrote his plays and short stories portraying the hopeless sadness of middle-class life, especially in the provinces, the bankruptcy of the intellectuals, and the inertia which spent itself in beautiful words and dreams without strength.

Yet it was under Alexander III and his son Nikolai II (1894-1917) that the irresistible march of capitalistic penetration transformed Russia. For military purposes railroads had to be built, industries established, the mineral wealth of the country tapped. Foreign capital flowed into Russia and brought a wave of prosperity. The cities began to grow; the urban population in Russia had amounted to only 4.4 per cent in 1812. By 1897 it had reached 13.25 per cent, still a very low proportion compared with Western Europe. Agricultural output still remained much too low; industrialization was spotty and topheavy. Yet it changed Russia. Sergei Witte (1849-1915), Minister of Communications and later of Finance, promoted the penetration of capitalism, but this industrial advance made the discrepancy between a halfway modernized façade and the backward governmental reality even more glaring.[19]

Nor was Russia strengthened when Alexander III began a ruthless policy of oppression of all the national and religious minorities of the vast Russian Empire, within which the Great Russians formed only 43 per cent of the population. A definite attempt was made to Russify the non-Russian peoples and the schools were devoted to that purpose. Many peoples like the Ukrainians and the Lithuanians were not permitted to use their own tongues. The Russian language was the only official language, the Russian element was favored in every possible way. Nothing was done for the cultural and economic progress of the non-Russian populations, least of all for the *inorodtsi* ("of alien origin", mostly Asiatics). State and Church rivaled one another in their ruthless policy of colonization at the expense of the people of non-Orthodox faith, especially the Mohammedans. The Jews were singled out and openly persecuted, partly through pogroms, often organized by the government police, partly through the denial of legal equality. As a result, the nationalist movements among the more progressive of these peoples began to work hand-in-hand with the Russian revolutionaries for a change in the Russian system of government. Russian chauvinism continually fed the flame of nationalism among the oppressed minorities.

The industrialization of Russia brought to the fore new classes, a

---

[19] On that period, see K. P. Pobyedonostsev, *Reflections of a Russian Statesman* (London, 1898) and *Memoirs of Count Witte* (New York: Doubleday Doran, 1921). On the Russian nationalism of the period, see Hans Kohn, *Prophets and Peoples* (New York: Macmillan, 1946) Ch. V.

strengthened bourgeoisie and a proletariat. The middle class demanded reforms which would free their economic activities from obsolete fetters and would guarantee legal security; the proletariat began to show signs of industrial unrest. The ideas of Karl Marx had penetrated into Russia through George Plekhanov (1857-1918), and in 1898 the Social Democratic Labor Party of Russia was founded. At its second party congress in 1903 it split into a minority group (Mensheviks), who favored a loosely organized mass party, and a majority group (Bolsheviks) under Vladimir Ulyanov (Nikolai Lenin, 1870-1924), who demanded a highly centralized and disciplined party with a small membership of picked revolutionaries ready for action at the decisive moment. The new economic activities and growing prosperity rekindled a new revolutionary spirit.

By the beginning of the twentieth century a wave of strikes spread over Russia. Terrorist activity was resumed and culminated in the assassination of Viacheslav Plehve, the energetic Minister of the Interior, in 1904. A new spirit of self-confidence filled the masses and spread to the intelligentsia. The Russian writer Maxim Gorky (Alexei Peshkov, 1868-1936) portrayed in his short stories the new Russian, a rebel and no longer a captive of life, showing no self-pity or self-accusation, but aggressive energy and hard courage. A new Russia was emerging. The Russian masses from which Gorky himself had come began to stir and to demand, still vaguely, not individual liberties but free scope for a release of their energies. Russia's defeat in the War of 1904-05 against Japan again revealed the incompetence of the government. In 1905 the Russian Revolution began.

Revolution

The Revolution of 1905 was an unorganized movement. It began on the "Bloody Sunday" in January when a demonstration of unarmed workers marching to present a petition to the Tsar were fired upon in the typically cruel Russian way. Peasant uprisings, workers' strikes, unrest of the non-Russian nationalities spread throughout the empire. But the autocracy did not yield until October, when a general strike, directed by councils of workmen (soviets) formed for that purpose in St. Petersburg and other cities, paralyzed the country. At the end of October the Tsar found himself forced to promise a constitution with legislative powers for an elected Duma and the granting of civil liberties. This concession split the revolutionaries. The middle classes were ready to accept the constitution as a first step, but the workers rejected it.   Their armed insurrection in Moscow at the end of December was crushed.   Reaction triumphed.   With the support of the extreme nationalists and of the dregs of the masses, it organized pogroms against the intelligentsia and the Jews.   Prime Minister Witte, appointed in October, 1905, was dismissed as too liberal in May, 1906, and replaced by Goremykin, an old arch-reactionary.

The first two Dumas, elected in May, 1906, and in March, 1907, were dismissed after a few months because the liberal opposition in them was too strong.   It was represented by the Socialists and by the progressive bourgeoisie which, under the leadership of Professor Paul Milyukov, formed the Constitutional Democratic Party (*kadets*).   The government imposed an electoral reform in 1907 which deprived the non-Russian nationalities and the masses of a large share of their representation.   As a result, the third Duma (1907-1912) and the fourth Duma (1912-1917) were in more of a mood to coöperate with the reactionary government.   The autocracy found in Peter Stolypin (1862-1911) an energetic Minister of the Interior.   His agrarian reforms in 1906 tried to gain a broader base of support for the government in a prosperous peasant class.   They favored the dissolution of the *mir* and the consolidation of scattered peasant holdings.   Better credit facilities were provided and agriculture reaped rapid benefits.   The more energetic peasants were able to buy more land and to develop it.   This growing class of prosperous peasants (*kulaks*) contrasted the more sharply with the poorer peasants of the villages who lacked the intelligence and industry to take advantage of Stolypin's progressive reforms.[20]

The revolution of 1905 failed to break the hold of autocracy on Russia.   There had been no coöperation between the four different groups which found themselves in a revolutionary situation: the peasants, the workers, the middle class, and the non-Russian nationalities.   They were united only in a negative aim and had no concerted plan of action. The year of struggle and hopes was followed by a period of disillusion and soul-searching on the part of the intelligentsia.   Yet the 1905 revolution was not wholly unsuccessful: it had aroused the peasants and the non-Russian nationalities from their lethargy and taught them lessons not easily forgotten.

By 1910 the revolutionary spirit was again revived in Russia.   Coöperative societies and trade unions slowly trained new revolutionary

---

[20] Milyukov, Paul N., *Russia and its Crisis* (Chicago, 1905) and Maurice Baring, *A Year in Russia* (London, 1908).   On the Russian revolution and its background, see Hans Kohn, *Revolutions and Dictatorships,* 3rd ed., (Cambridge: Harvard University Press, 1943) pp. 84-144.

forces. In a patriotic fervor to reassert Russia's position as a great power, the government and the Duma collaborated to expand industrialization, to improve communications, and to modernize the army. Strikes involved a growing number of workers and were sometimes suppressed with the utmost brutality, like the strike in the Lena goldfields in 1912. Terrorism again made its appearance and demanded its victims, one of whom was Stolypin. He was the last able pillar of court reaction. Thereafter the court, more and more under the influence of Gregory Rasputin, grew completely out of touch with the times and with the nation. It regarded even the overwhelmingly reactionary Duma as a radical body. It appointed ministers without the slightest qualifications for their tasks for reasons of intrigue and favoritism. Russia entered World War I under these conditions, before the necessary reforms of army and administration made her strong enough to face the immense strain of a modern war against a powerful enemy in which the existence of the nation itself was at stake.[21]

The inefficiency and corruption of the government soon chilled the patriotic zeal which had swept over Russia in 1914 and had united the nation in unprecedented enthusiasm. The war demanded ever-growing sacrifices; the armies lacked sufficient supplies and competent leadership. Economic chaos grew rapidly. The breakdown of transportation subjected the populations in the industrial centers to increasing hardships. The confidence of the upper classes in the government was definitely shaken—the fatherland seemed endangered by inefficiency and perhaps by outright treason. Under these circumstances, the patriotism of the educated classes and the longing of the masses for peace and bread combined. As a result, the Tsarist autocracy collapsed in March, 1917.

With no preconceived plan or concerted action, the revolution grew out of hunger demonstrations of Petrograd workers.[22] Tsarism fell without any show of resistance and simply disintegrated. The Duma found itself forced to appoint a provisional government headed by Prince Lvov, which included as its outstanding personalities Paul Milyukov and Alexander Kerensky, a young labor lawyer. Soon the authority of the new government was paralleled by that of the soviets

---

[21] On the disintegration of Tsarism, see Sir Bernard Pares, *The Fall of the Russian Monarchy* (London: Cape, 1939); Michael T. Florinsky, *The End of the Russian Empire* (New Haven: Yale University Press, 1931); *Letters of the Tsaritsa to the Tsar, 1914-1916* (London: Duckworth, 1924).

[22] Golder, F. A., *Documents of Russian History, 1914-1917* (New York: Century, 1927) and Michael Karpovich, "The Russian Revolution of 1917", *Journal of Modern History*, Vol. II (1930), pp. 258-280.

of workers, peasants, and soldiers who acted as the representatives of the masses. But the situation was fundamentally unstable, partly as a result of this dual government. The national consciousness of the masses was not strong enough to rouse them to a recognition of the danger to the fatherland. The industrial equipment of the country was too backward to allow a successful prosecution of the war. The masses demanded peace and land above all; the intellectual classes gave precedence to the war in alliance with the Western democracies and hoped for the establishment of liberty under law and an ordered civilization in Russia. They underestimated the backwardness of the masses and the strength of the autocratic tradition.

The Bolsheviks understood the situation better. Their leader Lenin had returned from exile with the help of the German General Staff, who hoped to find in him an instrument for the final dissolution of the Russian army. Unhampered by any scruples, the Bolsheviks put themselves ahead of the popular demand, and accepted the dynamics of the revolution. They represented in a mounting chaos of conflicting aspirations and currents the only well-disciplined group with clear-cut directives. Thus they succeeded in overthrowing the provisional government, which itself had moved steadily to the left and was then headed by Kerensky, in November, 1917. The Constituent Assembly had been elected by general democratic votes throughout Russia to realize the dream of Russian liberty and the promises of human dignity which had inspired the progressive movement in the nineteenth century. It met in January, 1918, and was dispersed by the Bolsheviks without any great resistance. Western liberty had not found the soil prepared by Russian history propitious for its growth in the revolutionary storm of 1917. The government of Russia and its vast empire were seized by a new autocracy which continued the work of Peter with ruthless energy, broadening and deepening it beyond expectation, releasing the creative energies of the masses in a new pioneering venture, and providing the Russian empire with a foundation of unprecedented strength.

Bibliography

Pares, Sir Bernard, History of Russia (New York: Knopf, 1937).
Tompkins, Stuart Ramsay, Russia Through the Ages (New York: Prentice-Hall, 1940).
Vernadsky, George, Political and Diplomatic History of Russia (Boston: Little, Brown, 1936).
    These are the standard texts on Russian history, all three well organized and providing the background for a more detailed study of the modern period of Russian history which forms the theme of

Kornilov, Alexander, *Modern Russian History* (New York: Knopf, 1943). This deals with the period from the age of Catherine the Great to the end of the nineteenth century. Kornilov's book is the best Russian textbook which has been translated into English. The greatest Russian historians of the nineteenth century were Sergey M. Solovyev (1820-1879); Vasily O. Klyuchevsky (1841-1911), whose masterful work is available in an English translation, but only in a very poor one; Sergey F. Platonov (1861-1933); and Paul N. Milyukov (1869-1941), whose special field, in which he became an authority, was the intellectual history of Russia. See about Russian historians:

Mazour, Anatole G., *An Outline of Modern Russian Historiography* (Berkeley: U. of Calif. Press, 1939).

Von Eckardt, Hans, *Russia* (New York: Knopf, 1932).

Sumner, B. H., *A Short History of Russia* (New York: Reynal & Hitchcock, 1944).
    Both these books offer a synthesis of Russian history and can be used with much interest by the student who is familiar with the facts. Sumner replaces a chronological arrangement by a topical one, starting in every case with the present situation and supplying the historical background.

Curzon, Lord George N., *Russia in Central Asia* (London: Longmans, Green, 1889).

Lobanov-Rostovsky, Prince A., *Russia and Asia* (New York: Macmillan, 1933).

Skrine, F. H., *Expansion of Russia, 1815-1910* (Cambridge University Press, 1915).

Vambéry, Arminius, *Western Culture in Eastern Lands* (London: John Murray, 1906).
    These books deal especially with Russia and Asia. The book by Prince Lobanov-Rostovsky is by far the most comprehensive. Vambéry, a Hungarian scholar, one of the first Europeans to travel through central Asia and to describe those countries, compares Russian and British methods of colonization in his book.

Mavor, J., *An Economic History of Russia* (2 vols., new ed. London: Allen & Unwin, 1925).

Mirsky, Prince D. S., *Russia: A Social History* (London: The Cresset Press, 1931).

Robinson, Geroid T., *Rural Russia Under the Old Regime* (New York: Longmans, Green, 1932).
    These are three standard works on the economic and social history of Russia.

Maynard, John, *Russia in Flux, Before October* (London: Gollancz, 1941). One of the most thoughtful and interesting volumes on Russia before the October Revolution. Deals in detail with the revolutionary movement, with the religious development and agrarian problems of modern Russia, and with the revolution of 1905.

Milyukov, Paul, *Outlines of Russian Culture* (ed. by Michael Karpovich, 3 vols. Philadelphia: U. of Penna. Press, 1942). Of the three volumes, one deals with the Church and religious life, the second with literature, the third with architecture, painting, and music.

Hecker, Julius F., *Russian Sociology* (New York: Columbia University Press, 1915). A history of social thought and theory in Russia. An important study, yet on the whole less important than the famous standard work by

Masaryk, T. G., *The Spirit of Russia,* 2 vols. (London: Allen & Unwin, 1919). Penetrating studies of the leading thinkers of Russia in the nineteenth century with a critical evaluation of Russian religious and social philosophy. The original title of the book which appeared in German in 1913 and in Czech in 1921 (2nd revised edition 1930, 1933) was "Russia and Europe, Studies of the Intellectual Trends in Russia." The Russian philosophy of history and religion is regarded as the key to the understanding of Russia as contrasted with Europe. A third volume was to deal with Dostoyevsky as a typical Russian philosopher.

Bulgakov, Sergius, *The Orthodox Church* (London: Centenary Press, 1935). Bulgakov is one of the leading contemporary theologians of the Orthodox Church who had originally belonged in his youth to the Marxist school, as had also Nicolai Berdyaev.

Conybeare, Frederick C., *Russian Dissenters* (Cambridge: Harvard University Press, 1921). The Russian dissent has been one of the most characteristic movements of Russian religious and social life in the last three centuries. This is an authoritative and comprehensive study in English.

Curtiss, John S., *Church and State in Russia* (New York: Columbia University Press, 1940). A highly competent and exhaustive study on the relations of State and Church in Russia during the last period of the empire: 1900-1917.

Wiener, Leo, *Anthology of Russian Literature from the Earliest Period to the Present Time,* 2 vols. (New York: Putnam, 1902, 1903). The standard work and at the same time a pioneer in the field. The first volume deals with the literature to the end of the eighteenth century; the second with the nineteenth century. The extracts are well chosen, but unfortunately too short.

Kropotkin, Prince Peter, *Ideals and Realities in Russian Literature* (New York: Knopf, 1916).

Mirsky, Prince D. S., *A History of Russian Literature from the Earliest Times to the Death of Dostoyevsky* (New York: Knopf, 1934).

Mirsky, Prince D. S., *Contemporary Russian Literature 1881-1925* (New York: Knopf, 1926).

Baring, M., *An Outline of Russian Literature* (New York: Holt, 1915).

Prince Kropotkin, the famous Russian anarchist leader, stresses in his history especially the social implications and teachings of the great Russian writers. Written in a simple and straightforward style, the book reflects a nineteenth-century interpretation. More modern in his approach is Prince Mirsky, a Russian aristocrat favorable to the Marxist revolution. Baring is one of the keenest English observers of Russian

civilization. All of his writings show an extremely fine understanding
of Russian literature and the Russian mind.

Wallace, Donald Mackenzie, *Russia* (rev. ed., London: Cassell, 1912). The
standard work on nineteenth-century Russia by a foreign observer, it
offers an encyclopedic view of Russian life in the second half of the
nineteenth century. Comparable in scope is the standard work for the
same period in French:

Leroy-Beaulieu, Anatole, *L'Empire des Tsars*, 3 vols. (Paris: Hachette, 1890).

Williams, H. W., *Russia of the Russians*, 2nd ed. (New York: Scribner's,
1915). An excellent introduction to all aspects of Russian life and civilization at the beginning of the twentieth century.

CHAPTER VI

THE BALTIC STATES (FINLAND)
(UP TO 1918)

THE Baltic states include Lithuania, Latvia, Estonia, and Finland. They were formerly Russian provinces, but became independent in 1918 and existed in the years after World War I as buffer states between Soviet Russia and the West. The region has played a role in history quite out of proportion to the size of the countries and their relatively small populations. The life of these peoples was linked up with the Baltic Sea, with the Vistula, and the Daugava (Dvina), with the trade routes going up these rivers and continuing southeast down the Dniester and the Dnieper. Thus the Baltic area formed a northern outlet for the Ukraine and for Asia beyond it, linking them up with the Baltic Sea, the Scandinavian countries, Britain, and the open ocean.

The Baltic Sea, surrounded by Sweden, Denmark, Germany, Poland, Lithuania, Latvia, Estonia, Soviet Russia, and Finland, is named for the Baltic peoples—the Latvians and Lithuanians (and the forcibly Germanized Old-Prussians)—the autochthonous inhabitants of the eastern shores of the Baltic ("Balts" in Latvian means white or shining). The name "Baltic Sea" appeared for the first time in 1070 in the works of Bishop Adam of Bremer.

The Lithuanians, Estonians, and Latvians, hemmed in by the Germans, the Poles, and the Russians, and watched from overseas by the Danes and the Swedes, were invaded by all of them at various times and provided both battlefields and colonies for half a dozen neighbors. But they were nonetheless able to preserve their own distinctive features and emerged in 1917 as clearly formed nations.

The Finns belong to a different family. Having been a part of Sweden for centuries (until 1809) as a Grand Duchy under Swedish suzerainty, they prefer to be considered members of the Scandinavia group. The Estonians, of the same racial stock as the Finns, once also belonged to the Swedish realm for nearly two centuries (1560-1721). The Letts and Lithuanians are the sole representatives of a distinct Aestian or Baltic branch of the Indo-Germanic language. Lithuanian is the closest to ancient Sanskrit of any language spoken today. In Latvia there was a tiny remnant of the Livonians (Livs), with whom the German merchants first came in contact and for whom they named Livonia, the modern Latvia. The Livs became assimilated by the Latvians in the course of time, but they are racially akin to the Estonians. The latter are probably of Mongolian origin and belong to the Fenno-Ugrian group (like the Finns and Magyars). Livonia proper (a Latvian province north of the Daugava River) was also Swedish for more than a hundred years (1600-1721). All these peoples shared Russian domination after the beginning of the nineteenth century.

The role played by the Baltic Germans in the region is especially interesting. They maintained the position of a ruling class, socially exclusive and nationally distinct, even under the Tsars. Their domination was an expression of the fundamental Baltic problem—the struggle for dominance, latent or active, between Russia and Germany. In the nineteenth century, the Baltic provinces unquestionably profited from their connection with a vast hinterland as Russia's famous "window" to the West. After serving their historic role as a battleground again in World War I, they enjoyed two decades of independence.

The Land and the People

Finland is located in the northeastern corner of Europe. Known as the "land of a thousand lakes" and mighty forests, its western and southern shores lie on the Baltic Sea and its northern shores on the Arctic Ocean. Its border neighbors are Russia and Sweden, and it is ordinarily classified as a Scandinavian state. The population is just under 4,000,000 people, most of whom earn their living by agriculture, lumbering, fishing, and manufacturing. The climate compares with that of Minnesota and northern New England, although the winters are much colder, for the northern part lies within the Arctic Circle and is served by an Arctic highway. Helsinki (Helsingfors), the capital, lies on the northern shore of the Gulf of Finland, an eastern arm of the Baltic Sea.[1]

The country is low-lying and hilly. At one time it was the bed of the Arctic Ocean. Pines and firs are the commonest trees, but the vegetation of Central Europe and the birches of the sub-Alpine zone are found in considerable profusion. Animal life is like that of the rest of

[1] *Die Nordischen Länder in der Weltwirtschaft* (Copenhagen: Einar Munksgaard, 1938) pp. 1ff.

Scandinavia, although animals such as the elk and the deer, which once abounded, have been largely killed off.

The most densely populated area is the province of Nyland and the greatest concentration of people is to be found along the coast, where agriculture is most profitable because of the fertility of the soil. The country is inhabited by two races speaking different languages: Finnish and Swedish. Eighty-eight per cent of the people are Finnish and approximately 11 per cent are Swedish. The Swedes live on the Åland Islands, the coast of Nyland, and part of the coast of Ostrobothnia. The two races are closely intermingled in some places. In general, the Swedes are taller and have longer skulls. The Finns are subdivided into the Karelians, who extend far into Russia, and the Tavasts, living in the west. There are a few Lapps in the north, a few Jews, Russians, Germans, and Gypsies scattered through the country.

Geopolitical Significance of Finland

Finland is a poor country in many respects, and is one of the most remote outposts of Western civilization. For centuries it was a battleground for Sweden and Russia (or Novgorod). With its neighbors, the Baltic States, it has been a buffer state during constant warfare. The two Russian wars of the present generation are but recent continuations of a long series of conflicts between Russia and Finland which have generally left the latter stripped of manpower, exhausted, and impoverished. The Russian demands on Finland in 1939 were strategic and looked to the ultimate absorption of that country.[2]

The geopolitical significance of Finland can be seen in the fact that Germany asked for the use of Finnish transportation facilities in order to set her northern anchor firmly before attacking Russia in the summer of 1941. To Sweden and the rest of Scandinavia, Finnish independence means security against Russia, but Finnish subservience to any other power robs Sweden and Norway of a vital buffer.

Early History

Opinions differ about the early settlers of Finland. One of them holds that two influences from different directions, one from the west and one from the east, met in Finland in prehistoric times. The first real settlement of the country was in progress about 100 A.D. and there is reason to believe, from the bronze and iron artifacts, that a population similar to that of Sweden settled on the western coast of Finland.

---

[2] Kalijarvi, Thorsten V., "Finland," Chapter XXIII, pp. 478-489, in *Contemporary Europe*, Joseph S. Roucek, ed. (New York: D. Van Nostrand, 1941).

Evidently there were also a few migratory Lapps. Some time between 400 and 700 A.D. two waves of migration moved into Finland: the Tavasts from Estonia and Ösel came to the west coast of Finland, while at the same time the Karelians flowed northward over the Karelian Isthmus as far as the White Sea in the eastern section. The existing Scandinavian population and the Lapps mingled with the newcomers. The Karelian migrants came from the neighborhood of the Düna River, where they are mentioned by Tacitus. They had been in contact with the Lithuanians and the Goths, from whom they received important knowledge about cattle breeding, agriculture, dwellings, dress, food, weapons, navigation, and social and religious customs. By 700 A.D. the Finnish inhabitants could be divided into three groups: those who lived in Suomi, or the Finns who ultimately gave Finland its name; those who lived in Tavastland (called Hämälaiset by the modern Finnish nationalists); and the Karelians whose numbers were constantly increased by migrations from the east. Commercial centers developed at Turku, Tavastland, and Björkö.

These early settlers were hunters and fishers in the eastern and northern sections, but traders and tillers of the soil in the west and south. One interesting practice was the burning of forests in order to clear the land because of the dense woods.[3] The eastern and central parts of the country were very sparsely populated.

The Karelians came under the influence of the Greek Orthodox Church and in the latter part of this early period the Novgorod government sought to gain possession of the whole of Finland. The records are obscure, but it is definitely known that the other two groups of Finns came under the influence of the Roman Catholic Church, sought the aid of the Swedes after they had organized themselves into a defensive league, and then attempted to conquer Karelia. Meanwhile, the Frisian trade dominated this section in the ninth century and there are records of battles with the Germanic peoples who lived in Ostrobothnia during the great migration.

In the early years, three bishops of English origin exercised great influence on Finnish religion. An expedition under Eric IX, the Bishop of Upsala, then named Henry and later Sir Henry, started the Finns on the road to Christianity. This first crusade in 1165 had little lasting value, but a second effort in 1172 by Cardinal Nicolaus Albanus (also an Englishman) was more effective. In 1220 the first Finnish bishop (Bishop Thomas), aggressively spreading Christianity to Häme,

---

[3] This practice of the Finns continued even to the time when they shared in the colonizing of this country.

succeeded in securing Papal protection for Finland against the Novgorod attacks.[4]

Early Connections with Sweden (1249-1599)

The second crusade directed against Tavastland or Häme by Earl Birger in 1249 established Swedish control in this area and synchronized with the appointment of a Swedish bishop, all of which had been anticipated by a Papal award of suzerainty over Finland to Sweden as far back as 1216. In 1293, Torgils Knutson led a third crusade into Karelia and fortified Viborg (Viipuri) in eastern Finland. Sweden thus definitely entered upon a program of acquisition that brought her into conflict with the Novgorod Russians over the possession of Karelia. Not until 1323, in the peace of Schlüsselburg, was this conquest completed. The treaty awarded three sections of Karelia to Sweden (Savolaks, Jääski, and Äyräpää); the remainder of the Karelian area was recognized as belonging to Russia.

During this period, trade went on in the northern section with its vague boundaries, boundless forests, well-stocked salmon streams, and fur-bearing animals. The whole area as far as the territory of the Lapps became Swedish and control of it was given to the Birka (a trading organization). Conflicts between Finland and Sweden occurred until a rough boundary was established in 1374. Meanwhile Swedish control over Finland grew stronger and stronger, and in 1362 the inhabitants of Finland were accorded full rights of Swedish citizenship and the right to participate in the election of the king of Sweden. As for religion, the Catholic Church was accorded the same rights in temporal affairs as in other parts of Europe, and the Bishop of Åbo became *ex-officio* a member of the Council of the Kingdom of Sweden. This bishopric was presided over by a number of Finns.

A governmental reorganization resulted in a judicial and administrative system for Finland differing substantially from that of Sweden. There seems to have been little effort on the part of Sweden to control Finland except through her nobles, although a competing Finnish nobility arose during the fourteenth century. The Kalmar Union among the Scandinavian states made it possible for Finland to maintain her autonomy, and under Eric of Pomerania, at the turn of the fifteenth century, she received her own currency, a supreme court, and her own system of law. Finland was therefore not a colony of Sweden, but rather a province participating in the election of the king, with the

---

[4] Blomstedt, Kaarlo, *Finland, Its Country and People, A Short Survey*. (Helsingfors: Government Printing Office, 1919), pp. 13 and 14.

right of the clergy and the peasantry to be represented in the election. Furthermore, when later Swedish governmental institutions were established, such as the Diet, the equality of Finland was plainly recognized.[5]

The Mongol domination of Russia had diverted the Novgorod attacks on Finland, but when Tsar Ivan Vasilyevitch II broke away from Mongol control he returned to conflicts with Sweden. It was he who inaugurated the great Russian war against Finland in 1473, which ended in the Treaty of Novgorod in 1497, after Finland was completely overrun.

The Reformation reached Finland about 1527 during the reign of Gustav Vasa. Bishop Mikael Agricola, father of the Finnish literary language and a translator of the New Testament into Finnish, was its chief protagonist. Although he had been anticipated by Pietari Sarkilahti in the 1520's, it was the Diet of Vesterås in 1527 which broke relations with Rome for the whole Swedish state (including Finland). The property of the Church reverted to the Crown. This, however, was not the end of the matter, for King Sigismund (1592-1599) adhered to the Catholic Church. Thereupon the Council of Upsala (1593) made the final break and adopted the Lutheran Augsburg Confession as the foundation for the Church of Sweden and Finland. The same religious arrangement remains in effect today.

At the same time Gustav Vasa, during whose reign the Reformation took place, strengthened the government of Finland, established its independence of the Hanseatic League, and stimulated the settlement of the interior regions until Finland had a permanent population spread over its entire area for the first time in its history. He also attempted to drive out the Russians (1555-1557), but the conflict was inconclusive.

In 1556, while this war was going on, the King visited Finland and established the first Duchy of Finland for his favorite son Johann, including in it the most desirable parts of the country. This Duchy had only a short life because Johann was seized and imprisoned by his brother Eric XIV. However, after another brief and inconclusive war between Sweden and Russia, King Johann III raised Finland to the status of a Grand Duchy when Pontus de la Gardie took Kexholm and other similar fortified places in Estonia. Peace followed in 1595, and Russia acknowledged that Finland was a part of the Swedish state and that its northern frontier was the Arctic Ocean and the Varanger Fjord.[6]

---

[5] Kalijarvi, *op. cit.*

[6] For a cursory survey, see John Saari, "Finnish Nationalism Justifying Independence," *The Annals*, CCXXXII (March, 1944), pp. 33 to 35.

During this century, Sweden became a hereditary instead of an elective monarchy. With the centralization of the Swedish government, Finland gradually lost her autonomy. Toward the end of the sixteenth century, Finnish peasants rebelled against Sigismund in the Mallet War of 1596 and 1597. He was succeeded by Charles IX, who brought the whole country under complete Swedish control, defeating the Finnish nobles and ending their power permanently.

Meanwhile the struggle with Russia continued. De la Gardie and Everet Horn won victory after victory under Gustavus Adolphus II, bringing Kexholm and Ingria under Swedish domination in the Peace of Stolbova (1617). This peace marked the beginning of Swedish greatness and was highly significant to Finland, for it added large areas which belonged to her geographically and ethnographically and also placed a buffer fringe around the main Finnish area which would have to bear the brunt of fighting in the future. Thus it was possible, during the next century, to reorganize the Finnish commercial and judicial system, educational institutions, and the government in general in comparative peace. The most noteworthy leader and governor in this period was Per Brahe, who established the University of Åbo and carried through many local reforms during Queen Christina's regime.

The Thirty Years' War, in which Sweden played the leading role for many years, saw Finnish soldiers fighting on the continent of Europe and made them known to the rest of Europe for the first time in history. Unfortunately, during this period, the land was placed under the feudalistic control of earls, barons, victorious generals, and lesser nobles, most of whom were Swedish. Consequently a wider gulf than ever developed between the Swedish nobles and intellectuals and the Finnish masses. Later the Finns were to work assiduously to reduce these feudal holdings, especially under Charles X, Gustav X, and Charles XI.

Sweden's greatness tended to curtail the use of Finnish, making it the language of the peasantry and Swedish the language of the educated classes, the officials, and the nobility. Even the famous elementary education reforms of the bishops of Åbo (Isak Rothovius, Johannes Gezelius, Sr., and Johannes Gezelius, Jr.) made little difference in this situation.[7] However, there is no gainsaying that Finland was safe during this period, especially after 1561, when Sweden took Livonia from Poland after having previously secured Estonia. For the time being, Finland and the Finns were free from Russian wars.

---

[7] Blomstedt, *op. cit.*, p. 15.

From King Charles XII to King Gustav Adolph IV
(1599-1778)

As already mentioned, Sweden entered the ranks of great powers early in the seventeenth century, under Gustavus Adolphus II. Her policy carried her eastward and southward into Russian areas. The country expanded at the expense of all her neighbors. This greatness carried Finland with it and exhausted her in the ruinous wars of Charles XII. But that was not the end of Finland's woes. In 1658, another bitter and inconclusive war broke out with Russia in the reign of Carl Gustav. Sweden spent the whole seventeenth century in constant warfare, conscripting recruits from Finland, taxing the Finns heavily, and giving them little or no benefit or respite even in the heyday of victory. Almost all of Sweden's measures as a great power were definitely harmful to Finland.[8]

During this time the government became more highly centralized than ever. The provincial governors were replaced by special governors-general, who only occasionally appeared in Finland. Provincial meetings were abolished after 1677. Local government was seriously weakened and most officials were appointed by the Crown. These centralizing efforts were intensified as time went on, particularly in the reign of Charles XI (1660-1697). By 1654, when three-fourths of the land of Finland had been bestowed on the nobles, most of them lived in Sweden. They regarded their Finnish possessions as a convenient source of income, not as a place to live. Large estates expanded, the farmer class was weakened by overtaxation, agriculture remained poor, epidemics swept the land, famine marched on the heels of disease. In the reign of Charles XII, the Great Death (1695-1697) killed off over 130,000 people—more than a quarter of the whole Finnish population. Yet the Finns remained loyal to Sweden through all these vicissitudes.

Then the eighteenth century dawned and the Great Northern War broke out. The glorious victories of Charles at Narva in 1700 and his magnificent crossing of the Düna River became, through his own obstinacy, only preludes to final defeat. Ten years later Viborg was lost, and after the disastrous battles at Pelkane in 1713 and Storkyro in 1714, the whole of Finland fell under Russian rule. In the Peace of Nystad (1721), Sweden surrendered to Russia Kexholm, all the provinces of Ingria, and the part of Finland including Viborg. There were grave doubts as to whether Sweden would ever be able to defend Finland against Russia in the future.

---

[8] *The Finland Yearbook, 1939-40,* (Helsinki: Oy, Suomen Kirja, Ltd., 1939) p. 45.

Twenty years later, the Swedes fought another rash war against Russia (1741-1743). While it was going on, Empress Elizabeth of Russia notified the Finnish people that she intended to make Finland a separate state under Russian suzerainty. In this so-called War of the Hats, Sweden lost another section of Finland as far as the River Kymmene. It looked as if she were destined to lose all of Finland piece by piece. Meanwhile bitterness had grown up in Finland against the autocracy of Charles. After his death, a new constitution was adopted in 1719-1720. It gave Finland, although ruled by a king, an essentially republican form of government with a Diet composed of Four Estates and a governing council responsible to the Diet. Great strides forward were made in Finnish economic life under the leadership of Anders Chydenius, and social advances were also scored under the leadership of Anders Kepplerus. The years 1765 and 1766 saw rapid gains in commerce, freedom of the press, party politics, and political literature. In the same period the so-called "Cap" party, blindly subservient to Russia, endangered the independence of the Finnish state.

Gustav III ascended the Swedish throne in 1772 and held it until 1792. The position of the Finnish people definitely improved during his reign, and an independent Finnish party under George Magnus Sprengtporten was organized. But war broke out with Russia again in 1788 and the Finnish party was dispersed by the king. Great harm was done to the Finnish cause because Finnish officers opened negotiations prematurely with the enemy. The war ended with the Peace of Verälä, which did not alter the boundaries of Finland. But Finnish independence and the Finnish national spirit were developing, as indicated in Professor H. C. Porthan's Swedish philological and historical works.[9]

Gustav Adolph IV, Napoleon, and the Peace of Frederikshamn (1778-1809)

Toward the end of the eighteenth century, Finland still remained basically an agricultural country, possessed of an excellent commerce and owning a wealth of forests and land. Industry had made little progress.[10] Finnish culture was centered at Turku University. A romantic movement aroused interest in the nation's history, language, and folklore, although it was led and fostered by the Swedish-speaking educated class.

King Gustav Adolph IV's anti-Napoleonic policy doomed Finland to 108 years of Russian rule. Sweden refused to join France in the

[9] Kalijarvi, op. cit.
[10] Die Nordischen, et cetera, op. cit., Chs. I and II.

continental blockade and Napoleon, in retaliation, granted Finland to
the tsar. War broke out, but the result was a foregone conclusion.
When the supposedly impregnable fortress of Sveaborg, outside the
walls of Helsingfors, capitulated in May, 1809, Russian victory was assured. The Peace of Frederikshamn, signed on September 17, 1809,
compelled Sweden to cede all of Finland to Russia, including the Åland
Islands and the eastern part of Vestrobothnia as far as the Torneå River.
That ended an affiliation of centuries between Finland and Sweden.[11]
The change corresponded roughly with the first stirrings of a new Finnish nationalism, which grew steadily stronger and more outspoken.

However, as early as October, 1808, eight months after his army
under Buxhoevden had crossed the Finnish frontier, the relatively
liberal-minded Tsar Alexander I invited a Finnish deputation to St.
Petersburg. Its spokesman was Baron K. Mannerheim. At the request of this group, a Diet was convened at Bårgo (now known as
Porvoo). Here a formal Finnish constitution was ratified by the Tsar,
who recognized Finland as a Grand Duchy. A separate governing
Council was set up, known a few years later as the Senate. This Council consisted of Finns and had control over finance, military affairs, and
other governmental matters. A Russian governor-general was appointed to oversee Russian interests in Finland. In closing the Diet,
Tsar Alexander announced that the Finnish people were henceforth
raised to nationhood. Thus, even before the Peace of Frederikshamn,
the Finnish people and Alexander I had thus reached an agreement
governing their relations with each other whereby Finland was granted
a substantial degree of autonomy.

Finland as a Part of Russia (1809-1917)

Alexander I, while he lived, tried to preserve the political autonomy
of Finland by recognizing its central government. The first President
of Finland was Gustav Magnus Armfelt. During this time, too, the
territories which had formerly been taken from Finland by Russia back
in 1721 and 1743, including the province of Viborg, were united with
the rest of the country. The inhabitants of these districts were given
equal rights with other Finnish citizens. The capital was located at
Helsingfors in 1816.[12]

In 1825, Nikolai I succeeded Alexander. The new Tsar was a reactionary. The rights of Finland were progressively restricted by his
governor-general, Zakrevski. The Russian nobles were granted free-

---

[11] *The Finland Yearbook, op. cit.,* p. 51.
[12] Kalijarvi, *op. cit.*

holds in the province of Viborg in 1826. A strict censorship was established in 1829, and nothing could be printed in Finnish except religious and economic works.

Soon afterward a strong new nationalistic movement made its appearance. Building on the foundations already laid down by A. R. Arvidson, J. W. Snellman began a defense of Finnish patriotism in his newspaper, *Saima*. There were others of similar mind, among them the famous E. Lönnrot, J. L. Runeberg, S. R. Cygnaeus, and Z. Topelius. Financial changes, the improvement in the economic condition of Finland, and the growth of trade schools and agricultural schools led to better conditions. Tsar Alexander II (1855-1881) assisted Finnish nationalism, especially through his imperial Edict of 1863 by which the Finnish language was raised to equality with Swedish. The Diet was also re-convened in that year, and political discussions became very active. The Finnish party followed Snellman. The Liberal party and the Swedish party divided on questions of program and policy.[13]

The Crimean War broke out just before Alexander II ascended the throne. Sveaborg was bombarded in August, 1855. Hopes actually arose that Finland might possibly break away from Russia. But the summoning of the Diet and the new ordinances of 1869 helped to allay unrest. Through all these events the use of the Finnish language increased. Finally, in 1877-1878, Finland secured her own army, her own elementary schools, and generally improved conditions.

The situation changed, however, when the next Tsar, Alexander III, attacked Finnish autonomy. During the reign of Nikolai II (1894-1917), Russian newspapers promoted a systematic Russian oppression of Finland. The famous February Manifesto of 1899 cut down the powers of the Diet and decrees restricting Finnish liberties were issued. Governor-General N. Bobrikov used restrictive measures which aroused passive resistance among the population. A Russian was appointed Secretary of State for Finland. Conditions went from bad to worse. Bobrikov was assassinated in 1904 and thereafter events moved rapidly. The general strike in Russia in 1905 had repercussions in Finland. The Tsar restored Finnish constitutional rights and convened the Diet. But in 1908 a new period of oppression began, worse than the earlier one, and in 1910 an imperial edict deprived Finland of most of its remaining rights.

The outbreak of the First World War in 1914 brought no relief to Finnish suffering. Russia announced her intention of terminating Diet

---

[13] For the most useful work in English on this phase, see J. H. Wuorinen, *Nationalism in Modern Finland* (New York: Columbia University Press, 1931).

sessions for the duration of the war. The so-called "Activist" movement, advocating independence for Finland, came to the fore. Its leaders arranged with Germany to train Finnish troops and officers in that country to aid in the fight for Finnish liberation from Russia. These trainees were the famous Jäger battalion, which stood the country in good stead in the war for independence in 1918. There was much bitter feeling against Russia in Finland, accompanied by the hope that Russia would be defeated and that Finland would secure her independence thereby. The Russians did their best to punish hostile Finns, including the president of the Diet, P. E. Svinhufvud, who was ousted and sent to Siberia.

Then came the Russian Revolution of 1917. Confusion broke out in Finland. Even though the new Russian Government acknowledged Finnish autonomy and the Diet was re-convened, violent riots occurred when the Red Guards were established in Finland to support Russian troops after the October Revolution. Efforts to reach an understanding with the Russian Government were unsuccessful and Bolshevists overran the country. On the 6th of December, 1917, the Diet proclaimed Finland a sovereign state. In January, 1918, Russia, France, Germany, and the Scandinavian countries recognized Finland's independence.

But despite the Russian acknowledgment of Finnish independence, Russian soldiers still remained in the country. Finnish civil war broke out, instigated by extreme Leftists and supported by Russian soldiers known as the Finnish Red Guards. The rebels seized control of the capital. Then General Gustav Mannerheim, at the head of the civic guard of Pohjanmaa and Karelia, led the White forces to end the Red rebellion. Finnish independence and order were thus finally established.[14] But it was not until the Treaty of Dorpat or Tartu in 1920 that the boundaries were defined and Russia ceded the Petsamo area and the Arctic coast to Finland.

There was some question about the form the new government should take. The monarchists were in control and an effort was made to secure Prince Frederick Carl of Hesse as the new king of Finland, but he refused the invitation. P. Svinhufvud, who had been acting as the regent, was followed on September 12, 1918, by Baron Gustav Mannerheim as the new regent. Finally a new republican constitution was adopted for the country in June, 1919.

---

[14] Söderhjelm, Henning, *The Red Insurrection in Finland in 1918* (London: Harrison and Sons, 1919).

Finnish Nationalism

As noted above, the Swedish influence on Finland was tremendous. Today, in consequence, Finland considers herself a Scandinavian country. But this does not mean that she is Swedish. During the nineteenth century, Finnish nationalism found its most vigorous early roots in the work of A. I. Arvidson. In the generation after 1820, Finnish education, Finnish folk studies, and the Finnish press gave strong impetus to the movement in the quarrels with the Russian rulers. In the next twenty years, party differences and the work of Johann Wilhelm Snellman, already mentioned, gave Finnish nationalism its present form and purpose. It has two chief objectives: (1) freedom and independence from Russia; (2) supremacy of the Finnish language and customs over Swedish. Complete success seemed to have been attained on the first objective up to a short time ago. The struggle continues on the second.[15]

Finnish Culture and Social Progress

The high degree of literacy in Finland may be traced in part to the influence of the Church, which insisted that people must be able to read in order to marry, and in part to the elementary and other schools which grew up in the past century. In 1866, under the direction of Uno Cygnaeus, a number of secondary schools, one state university, and several so-called "technical" high schools were established. This progress was accompanied by a number of excellent literary works.

Finnish scientific societies, the Finnish Literary Society, and the Fenno-Ugrian Society flourished until the outbreak of the recent wars. Finnish scientists and research workers have carried their studies into many different fields. Their activities are of far-reaching importance.

Land reform has been extensive and every effort has been made to divide the land among the tenant farmers. Social legislation is advanced, particularly in the care of children, health institutes, and coöperative effort. Labor has profited by an eight-hour day, compulsory accident insurance, old-age pensions, disability insurance, and other similar measures. The place of woman, both in labor and in welfare, has been one of the most enlightened contributions which Finland has made to the modern world. More will be said of these in Chapter 19.

Like the other Scandinavian countries, Finland has made long strides

---

[15] Wuorinen, *op. cit.*

forward in developing her coöperative enterprises and stands shoulder to shoulder with Sweden and Denmark in this respect.[16]

Conclusion

The music of Finland is written largely in the minor key and so is her history. Through the centuries before the Russian acquisition, Finland had been thrown into one war after another between Russia and Sweden. By 1917, she had declared her independence in the midst of Russian revolutions. As an independent state she is destined to look forward to further complications with Russia, regardless of the rulers or the form of government of that country.[17]

Bibliography

Blomstedt, Kaarlo, *Finland, Its Country and People, A Short Survey* (Helsingfors: Government Printing Office, 1919). Very useful.

Hannula, J. O., *Finland's War of Independence* (London: Faber and Faber, 1939). A clarifying account of a confused period in Finnish history.

Hook, Frank E., *The Finns in American Colonial History* (Washington: U. S. Government Printing Office, 1937). Remarks on the occasion of the tercentennary. A perspective.

Kalijarvi, Thorsten V., "Finland," Chapter XXIII of Joseph Roucek, *Contemporary Europe* (New York: D. Van Nostrand, 1941). A brief account of contemporary Finnish history.

Kalijarvi, Thorsten V., "The Question of East Karelia," *American Journal of International Law*, XVIII:1 (1924), pp. 93 ff. A general background.

Sanberg, Börje, and Vihejunri, H. J., *Finlandia* (Helsinki: Kustonnuso Sakeyhtiö Otava, 1934). Excellent views of land and people.

Sketches of Finland (Helsinki: Oy. F. Tilgmann, 1939). General background for anyone not acquainted with the country.

Stenberg, Herman, *The Greater Finland* (Helsinki: The Karelian Citizens League, 1919). A blast for a greater Finland.

The Treaty of Peace Between Finland and the Russian Soviet Republic (Helsingfors: Government Printing Office, 1921). Peace of Dorpat or Tartu, October 14, 1920. Basic reading.

Wuorinen, John H., *Nationalism in Modern Finland* (New York: Columbia University Press, 1931). The best work in English on the subject; especially useful for the period since 1808.

---

[16] Bakken, Henry H., *Coöperation to the Finnish* (Madison, Wis., 1939).

[17] *Sketches of Finland* (Helsinki: Oy. F. Tilgmann, Ltd., 1939).

CHAPTER VII

THE BALTIC STATES (LATVIA, LITHUANIA, ESTONIA) (UP TO 1918)

Geography of the Baltic Area

BEFORE discussing Latvia, Lithuania, and Estonia specifically, it is necessary to consider the region in which they are located. The three states occupy much of the eastern shore of the Baltic Sea and have always shared in its history.

Taking the Baltic region as a whole, and including therein Norway, Denmark, Sweden, Finland, Poland, Latvia, Lithuania, Estonia, Russia, and Germany, one finds that these countries are bound together by the Baltic Sea, which includes the Gulf of Finland and the Gulf of Bothnia. This sea possesses especial strategic importance. Along its shores are a number of key military points, particularly the islands of Åland, Dagö, Ösel, Gotland, Bornholm, Seeland, Lolland, and Fünen. Most of this area has been under German influence in the past and only a relatively small part of the eastern shore has come under Slavic domination. The chief channels of commerce have been with Germany and Sweden, and the chief ports have been Leningrad, St. Petersburg, Helsinki, Reval, Libau, Memel, Windau, Stockholm, and Riga.[1]

At no time in history has the whole area surrounding this sea fallen under the rule of a single state. All of its sea-borne traffic with the outside world necessarily passes through the Skagerrak and Kattegatt, which have usually been dominated, in the last analysis, by British sea power. Non-sea contacts by land, canal, rail, and air with the rest of the world are varied and numerous.[2]

Historically, German influence has been strong from the seaward side but not from the land side. Thus, Denmark and Sweden have been influenced by England, while Finland, Latvia, Lithuania, and

---

[1] Vogel, Walther, *Das Neue Europa*, 3rd ed. (Bonn & Leipzig: Kurt Schroeder, 1923), pp. 397-404.

[2] Vogel, *op. cit.*

Estonia have recently been equally affected by Russia. As far as the three states under consideration in this chapter are concerned, they are and always have been subject to constant German pressure from the west and to Russian pressure from the east.[3]

With the exception of Germany and Russia, all of the Baltic states are comparatively small, with populations ranging from a little over a million in Estonia to approximately seven million in Sweden. They have tried unions and neutralization of such areas as the Åland Islands as solutions for their defense problems, without success. At best, these states live a precarious existence subject to the programs and objectives of their more powerful neighbors.[4]

Except for Russia, Germany, and Sweden, the Baltic states have few resources. Forests abound in Finland, which also possesses waterpower. Phosphorus is found in Estonia, and nickel in Finland. Of course, these do not exhaust the list, but they do give some idea of the limited economic power of these countries. All Baltic lands depend upon overseas communications and business for their existence and therefore need strong naval and military protection under normal conditions. But they do not have it and are therefore subject to the dominant naval power in the region, generally England.

Latvia, Lithuania, and Estonia as a Unit

Before considering the history of each of these countries by itself, it is again necessary to treat them as a unit. Latvia, Lithuania, and Estonia cover a combined area of approximately 65,000 square miles. They comprise a belt of territory the size of England, stretching from the Gulf of Finland in the north to the Niemen River in the south, and from the Baltic Sea on the west to the swampy Russian plain on the east. The people who live in these countries are Estonians, Latvians, Lithuanians, Germans, Russians, Poles, Swedes, Livonians, and Jews. They practice three principal forms of religion: (1) Lutheran in Latvia and Estonia; (2) Roman Catholic in Lithuania; and (3) Orthodox Catholic in all three.

Little is known of the aboriginal inhabitants of this region. From the ninth to the twelfth centuries, Vikings ravaged the area, opening trade routes to Russia and finally establishing Danish control over northern Livonia (now Estonia). In 1200, the crusades of the German Knights of the Order of the Sword (*Schwertritter Orden*), began from

---

[3] Bowman, Isaiah, *The New World*, 4th ed. (New York: World Book Co., 1928), pp. 436-449.

[4] *Aufsätze in Geopolitic*, 7 (1928).

the south. They reached Estonia, captured Riga, and set up a regime there from which the Order ruled both Courland and Livonia, the present Latvia and Estonia. Thus, a German nobility or Baltic Baron group was established to govern the whole Baltic coast and retained fundamental control over this area until Hitler recalled it to Germany at the start of the Second World War.

Lithuania, except for the small strip of Memel, which she lost in 1410, never succumbed to the Knights, but fell under Polish influence.[5]

In the sixteenth century, Sweden conquered both Estonia and Latvia, only to lose them to Peter the Great of Russia in 1710. Meanwhile Lithuania remained with Poland, as did a segment of Latvia. When Poland was divided at the end of the eighteenth century, Russia absorbed Lithuania in the process.[6] At the end of the eighteenth century, Russia had therefore conquered all of the Baltic coast, and continued to rule it until the end of the First World War. In many respects, however, the Baltic Barons remained the real rulers of Latvia and Estonia.

During the second half of the nineteenth century Russia set out systematically to russify these countries.[7] The most notable act of this nature was the press prohibition of 1864 imposed upon Lithuania. The people of Latvia, Lithuania, and Estonia did not consider themselves Slavic and none of them practiced Orthodox Catholicism; yet the Russian language was fostered and the Orthodox Church was promoted. The whole area was tied more and more closely to Russia in culture, religion, and economics. The German, Russian, and Polish nobility abetted russification because it meant their self-perpetuation in office. Consequently they were hated. It was not hard for leaders in all three countries to arouse a nationalistic feeling in each racial group under such conditions. Native schools, banks, coöperatives, press, and literature fed and fanned the rising flame of nationalism. This was the background for the independence movement in all three states.

Lithuania

The only one of the three states to have led an independent existence prior to 1918 was Lithuania. Its people are usually but not invariably blond, long-headed, blue-eyed, tall of frame, and massive of physique. They are distinct from both Slavs and Germans, belonging to the Baltic

---

[5] Helmreich, Ernest C., "The Baltic States," Chapter XX in *Contemporary Europe*, Joseph S. Roucek, ed. (New York: D. Van Nostrand, 1941), pp. 433-435.

[6] *Ibid.*, pp. 435-436.

[7] *Ibid.*, p. 436.

group of the eastern branch of the Indo-European peoples. Their language is not Slavic, but the purest remnant of spoken Sanskrit extant. There are numbers of Germans, Russians, and Poles among the population of less than 2,500,000.

The country itself covered an area of 21,482 square miles before the Second World War.[8] It is low-lying moraine for the most part, rich in rivers, particularly the Niemen and the Dvina, and in lakes. Amber, gypsum, and lime are the richest natural resources after forests and timber. The chief city is Kaunas, the capital.[9]

History.[10] Heavy forests, swampy lands, and rivers separated the early Lithuanian tribes from the rest of the Baltic area. These tribes occupied a region extending inland to Kaunas. Since the country is level, it became an object of attack by covetous neighbors as soon as it was cleared. In 1226 the Poles, unable to conquer the early Prussians (kinsmen of the Lithuanians), invited the Teutonic Knights to aid them. The territory was taken from the Prussians and was then completely germanized. This included the territory between the Pregel and Niemen Rivers, now known as Memelland.

In about the twelfth century, the Greek Orthodox Russians to the east and the Roman Catholic Poles to the south undertook to Christianize the Lithuanians. The Poles were aided by the Teutonic Order and the Knights of the Sword. Under this pressure, the Lithuanians were organized into a Grand Duchy by Rimgaudas and then into a Kingdom by Mindaugas, who was crowned King of Lithuania by Pope Innocent IV in 1252. War with the Germanic Orders, however, continued until 1386, when Lithuania accepted Christianity officially.

When the Tartars under Genghis Khan invaded Europe, Lithuania met them and confined their hordes to the Volga and the Sea of Azov. Lithuania grew from the thirteenth into the fifteenth centuries until, between 1392 and 1410, it stretched from the Baltic to the Black Sea, from the Ugra River in the east to the Narva and Bug Rivers in the west.

In 1386 Jadwiga, the Queen of Poland, was married to Jagiello, the Grand Duke of Lithuania. Jagiello thereupon became the King of Poland. This is supposed to have begun the union of the two countries. But they did not actually unite, and Vytautas, a Lithuanian statesman, was elected Grand Duke in place of Jagiello. Under the latter's leader-

---

[8] Including Memel and excluding Vilna.

[9] Vogel, *op. cit.*

[10] Hertmanowicz, Joseph J., *Historical Outlines on Lithuania* (Chicago: Edgar A. Russell, 1921); also Age Meyer Benedictsen, *Lithuania* (Copenhagen: Egmont H. Petersens Kgl. Haf-Bogtrykkeri, 1925).

ship, Poland and Lithuania undertook a joint campaign against the Teutonic Knights and defeated them in the Battle of Tannenberg Forest. Although Emperor Sigismund (*in absentia*) crowned Vytautas King of Lithuania, the crown was spirited away at the border by the Polish nobility. After that, although Grand Dukes of Lithuania were often elected Kings of Poland, Lithuania struggled vainly to break away from Polish control. At last, in the Union of Lublin (1569), the two countries were formally welded into a single state. It was a confused union, somewhat after the pattern of the Austria-Hungary of 1914.

The Union of Lublin was followed by a polonization of Lithuania. Power gravitated into the hands of the nobility. Polish nobles took over partial control of Lithuania, whereas Lithuanian nobles merely copied the Polish nobility. Wars with Russia only served to increase polonizing tendencies and to end the last vestiges of Russian and Greek Orthodox influence. The polonization program reached into education, including the University of Vilna, to the detriment of the Lithuanian language.

Then came the eighteenth century partitions of Poland (and of Lithuania). In 1772, Russia took the contiguous Lithuanian provinces as part of her share. In 1793, the so-called older-Russian-Lithuania was gathered up by Russia in the Second Partition. This included Vilna, the old Lithuanian capital, which by now had a substantial Polish population. In the Third Partition (1795), Russia absorbed all the rest of Lithuania (Lithuania proper) except for the Suwalki region, which went to Prussia. Later this region was taken away from Prussia by Napoleon and was subsequently given to Russia by the Congress of Vienna.[11]

Russian rule was fairly reasonable at first, but it gradually deteriorated and the russification of the Lithuanian people began. Russians colonized Lithuanian lands. The University of Vilna was closed in 1832. In 1840, the Lithuanian Statute was abolished and Russian law substituted for it. Lithuanian newspapers were suppressed in 1864. Russian schools were opened in 1867. Religious persecutions were intense. But even this severe oppression did not kill the spark of national identity. From 1795 to 1915 the yoke was heavy. In 1904 and 1905 the renaissance of Lithuanian independence began, thus coinciding with the Russo-Japanese War and the Great Strike. Religious and intellectual leaders and even the polonized nobility began to

---

[11] On this whole section, see P. Zadeikis, *Introducing Lithuania* (New York: Lithuanian Government, 1933). Very helpful.

promote the Lithuanian language, literature, pride, spirit, and nationalism.

The chance for independence did not come until 1918, but it was preceded by a long train of events. In 1915, a Congress of Vilna established a committee to protect Lithuanian interests against German inroads. It was headed by the hard-fighting Antanas Smetona. In the fall of 1917, with German encouragement, the *Taryba* (National Council) of 20 members was called. On February 16, 1918, the *Taryba* proclaimed Lithuania an independent state. Its independence was recognized by Germany in March. A provisional constitution was adopted. On October 18, 1918, Smetona became president and Augustinas Voldemaras was designated premier.[12]

Politics. A strong movement for a democratic form of government was reflected in the political parties in 1918: the Social Democrats, the Peoples Socialist Party, the Democratic Party, the Christian Democrats, and the Catholic Union. Years of effort to break away from the Polish Union had at last been successful. The masses who had suffered under the Polish or polophile nobility were all for democracy. Space does not permit a detailed tracing of the evolution of this idea from 1905 to 1918, but in the latter year it had become an unanswerable demand. Centuries of oppression and disadvantageous union with other nations were brought to an end with independence.[13]

Culture. The Lithuanians are a peasant folk, solid, substantial, and courageous. Their folklore is rich in song and story, marked by grace, variety, deep poetic feeling, and novelty. The Latin language was adopted at the same time as Christianity, as shown by some of the letters of Gediminas and Vytautas. During the period of polonization, the Polish language crept into literary use.

Lithuanian literature was spurred in the sixteenth, seventeenth, and eighteenth centuries by the invention of printing. Higher education was concentrated in the Universities of Vilna and Königsberg. The first Lithuanian authors of note were Martin Mosvidius, John Bretkunas (1535-1602), and Reverend Dauksha. K. Shirvydas was outstanding as a lexicographer, Daniel Klein as a grammarian, and Morkunas as a translator. Christian Donelaitis was the first major Lithuanian poet: his most famous work was *Seasons of the Year*.

History and religious writings were stimulated at the beginning of

---

[12] *Lithuanian Recognition* (Washington, D. C.: Lithuanian Information Bureau, 1921).

[13] T. Norus and J. Zilius, *Lithuania's Case for Independence* (Washington: B. F. Johnson, 1918), pp. 53-64.

the nineteenth century, especially by D. Poshka, Bishop Baronas, and Ivinskas. Folklore was gathered by the Juskevichius brothers. Much of the literature was Polish, coming from the pens of polonized nobles trained at the University of Vilna.

The press restrictions for forty years after 1864 blighted these literary efforts, although a new movement began in 1883 in the Lithuanian press abroad. It was stimulated by Dr. John Basanavichius and especially by the *Auszra* (Dawn) published in Tilsit, Prussia. In 1891 the movement became stronger and new societies appeared, such as the Lithuanian Scientific Society and the Society of Fine Arts. This literary and cultural movement gained in strength, especially among the Lithuanians in the United States.[14]

Economics. Lithuanian soil is favorable to agriculture and the economic life of the country depends upon it. At the moment of independence, about 40 per cent of the land belonged to the *Boyars* (large landholders), 43 per cent to the small peasants, 5 per cent to urban holders, and 12 per cent to the state. Eighteen per cent of the people owned no land. Farm products consisted chiefly of oats, barley, potatoes, wheat, peas, and flax. Fruits, vegetables, and livestock were also raised.

The chief products, however, came from Lithuania's forests: pine, oak, birch, maple, and linden of the best quality. Timber was exported. Fishing was a source of food. Peat, amber, mineral springs, and small manufacturing industries rounded out the economic resources of the country. Opportunities beckoned in industry, agriculture, textiles, and forestry.[15]

Latvia

Before treating Latvia and Estonia separately, it is well to note a few facts which pertain to them both. When these two new states came into existence after the First World War, they were established chiefly because they were inhabited by two entirely different peoples, the Estonians and the Latvians. These people lived in the land which at one time had been three provinces on the Baltic: Estonia, Livonia, and Courland.[16]

The new Estonia was made up of the old province of Estonia and

---

[14] Ibid.

[15] Lyde, Lionel W., *The Continent of Europe* (London: The Macmillan Co., 1924), pp. 403, 412, 413.

[16] Before the First World War these were known in Russia as the "Eastern German provinces" and in Germany as "Livland." Elsewhere they were looked upon as part of the Baltic coast of Russia.

part of Livonia. The new Latvia was made up of the rest of Livonia and the old province of Courland. Both countries had been the scene of many bitter racial and political struggles. A strong class of German Barons, augmented by powerful German traders, had ruled the region for hundreds of years. The peasants had been exploited since the twelfth century. The common people had been subjected to intense russification after 1884. Socialism took root prior to 1905, with the result that both Latvia and Estonia joined the other subject peoples of Russia in that year in an attempt to overthrow the Russian government and seize the estates of the landlords, who in their case were Germans.[17]

Area and population. Latvia has an area of 25,402 square miles. Like Lithuania, its territory is mostly moraine dotted with hundreds of lakes and over five hundred rivers. The climate is mild. The resources of the state are chiefly forest and agricultural products.

The Latvians are related to the Lithuanians and are therefore neither Slavic nor Teutonic. They are divided from the Estonians by a language frontier which extends from Hainasch on the Baltic coast in a huge bow to Salis, thence to Walk, and thence eastward. The Latvians have their own racial characteristics and more nearly resemble the Swedes than they do the Russians or perhaps even the Lithuanians. It is not certain whether this is due to natural developments or the historical accident of Swedish occupation. When freedom was attained, the population was 1,596,131, of which 75 per cent were of the Latvian race belonging to the Baltic branch of the Indo-European family already mentioned. The rest of the people were Jews, Germans, White Russians, Great Russians, and Poles.

History.[18] Although the state of Latvia does not appear on any map of Europe prior to 1917-1920, the Latvian people had had an existence of their own from prehistoric times. When Finland and Lithuania were being Christianized, these people were known to the world by their tribal names: Selonians, Latgallians, Couronians, Talavians, and Semigallians.

At the beginning of the thirteenth century (1207), several of these tribes were combined into the Bishopric of Terra Mariana, which remained a principality of the Holy Roman Empire until 1561. In the latter year Courland and Semigallia were combined into a separate independent duchy, Livonia became the Transdüna Duchy, Latgallia became a Polish fief, and Estonia became Swedish. In the 1795 Parti-

---

[17] Bowman, *op. cit.,* Chapter 22.
[18] Bilmanis, Alfred, "Free Latvia in Free Europe," *Annals,* CCXXXII (March, 1944), pp. 39-42.

tion of Poland, Russia took over Courland with the aid of the German barons. Napoleon gave Courland its independence, but Russia regained control of the province in 1813.

Russia had thus established control over all of present-day Latvia by 1813. During the Russian domination, conditions in Latvia grew progressively worse. By the beginning of the twentieth century, russification was meeting the same response in Latvia as elsewhere in the Baltic regions—passive resistence accompanied by rising nationalism. In 1903, the first demand for Latvian independence from Russia was made by a conference of revolutionaries in Berne, Switzerland. When the Russian revolution of 1905 broke out, the Latvians took an active part through their Revolutionary Federative Committee.

This revolt was put down with the aid of firing squads but the Latvians took a page from the book of the Poles, Finns, and other subject peoples of Russia. They organized rifle regiments and took an active part in the First World War. On July 5, 1917, the Kerensky government of Russia gave the Latvians restricted rights of self-government. But this did not satisfy the Latvian people, who demanded, at the Riga Conference of July 30, 1917, autonomy for Latvia with the right of self-determination as to what their future form of government was to be. When the Bolshevik Revolution took place in Russia, the Latvians sought further freedom and the Latvian Provisional Committee declared the independence of Latvia on November 17-18, 1917. Great Britain recognized Latvian independence on Armistice Day of the First World War. Peace treaties with Germany and Russia in 1920 confirmed this independence, and in January, 1921, Latvia was recognized by the major victorious powers. Later she became a member of the League of Nations.[19]

Politics. This new state was faced with the shaping of a government and the establishment of control over its people and their activities. The election of President K. Ulmanis in 1918 was followed by the establishment of a constitution and a democratic form of government. The subsequent operation of that government will be described in another chapter. The long historical background, which gave immediate life to Lithuanian politics, was lacking in the case of Latvia.

Economic and social factors. The Latvian economy is chiefly agricultural, depending upon cattle-breeding, grain-growing, flax-growing, and fishing, for the livelihood of the inhabitants. Latvia is also an important gateway for Russian trade, having easy access by canal to the Volga and Dnieper Rivers. The deep cellars and grain storage

---

[19] Ibid.

facilities of Riga give evidence not only of its importance as one of the old Hansa towns, but also of its present significance. Libau and Windau are important ports kept open all year by ice-breakers. While more than 70 per cent of the people are employed in agriculture at present, only a comparative few are engaged in commerce and transportation. A new industrialization began with independence and was well on its way early in the nineteen twenties.[20] The Latvians build their whole social structure around the family. They are religious, moral, and democratic.

Estonia

Estonia covers an area of 18,370 square miles (a little more than Denmark or Switzerland) and lies across the Gulf of Finland from Finland. It is part of the moraine already described in reference to Latvia and Lithuania, and has many lakes and rivers. Its natural resources are about the same as those of the other Baltic states. It is bordered on the south by Latvia and on the east by the Soviet Union.

The population at the time of independence was 1,126,413. Of these, over 88 per cent were Estonians, the rest were Swedes, Germans, Russians, and Latvians. The Estonians are a branch of the Fenno-Ugrian group. They are tall, fair-haired, blue- or grey-eyed, with rosy complexions, and are not distinguishable from the Swedes and the Germans who live among them.

Like the other two Baltic states described above, Estonia is agricultural, although it does possess harbor facilities at Tallinn (the capital) and Baltiski. Sixty per cent of its people are engaged in agriculture, 17 per cent in industry, and a small number in commerce, transportation, communication, and the professions.[21]

History.[22] The present inhabitants of Estonia have lived there since the beginning of history. Hostile tribes seem to have struck at the aborigines, who were able to maintain their independence and freedom in spite of attacks from the southeast and west. Gothic influence was pronounced in the early days. Like the Latvians, the Estonians were divided into tribes and the country was ruled by chieftains.

In the section on Latvia, it was noted that Sweden took possession of Estonia in 1561, after the Teutonic Order had held it since the thirteenth century, only to lose it to Russia in 1710. It should be noted further that the Danes held part of Estonia during the thirteenth and

---

[20] Vogel, *op. cit.*

[21] Bowman, *op. cit.*, for both Latvia and Estonia; also Vogel, *op. cit.*

[22] Kaiv, Johannes, "Estonian Nationalism." *Annals*, CCXXXII (March, 1944), pp. 39-42.

fourteenth centuries. Denmark sold her share of Estonia to the Teutonic Order in 1346. Prior to the Swedish acquisition, the natives had been brought to a state of serfdom. When the Swedes attempted to ameliorate these conditions, they met with the opposition of the Baltic Barons, who aided Russia in seizing the land from Sweden. Tsar Peter restored the mediaeval rights of the Baltic Barons. The last revolt of the Estonians in their search for freedom until the twentieth century took place in 1343 and was violently crushed. Swedish rule gave Lutheranism to the Estonians.

During the early nineteenth century, the relatively liberal Russian government which had accorded autonomy to Finland and greater freedom to the other subject states also accorded greater rights to Estonia. Like the other peoples subject to Russia, the Estonians experienced the late nineteenth-century efforts at russification and shared in the revolution of 1905. The Lithuanian and Latvian movements for independence made a strong impression on the Estonians. When the revolution of 1917 occurred in Russia, Estonia, like the other border peoples, had developed groups of intellectuals and revolutionaries who were anxious to strike for freedom. On March 11-13, 1917, a meeting of many of the leaders in this movement gathered at Tartu (Dorpat) and voted to draw up a petition for autonomy to be presented to the Provisional Russian government. This was done, and on March 30, 1917, the petition was reluctantly granted. Succeeding events followed the pattern already discussed in the cases of Estonia's neighbors. The newly established Estonian National Council (*Maanoukogu*) voted on November 15, 1917, to take advantage of the Soviet decree of November 2, and declared Estonia an independent state. On February 2, 1920, the Treaty of Tartu with Russia recognized Estonia's independence.

Politics. Freedom had been won after centuries of foreign rule, during which the Estonians had succeeded in rising from serfdom to independent nationhood. The setting was ripe for a democratic form of government, but, as will be seen in Chapter 19, the Estonians immediately experienced difficulties.

Culture.[23] Centuries of domination inevitably left a lasting impression on the culture of Estonia. German and Swedish influences were especially in evidence: the first because of the long rule of the Baltic Barons; the second because of its enlightened character.

The Estonian himself is usually an individualist governed by realism and a respect for traditionalism. His actions are often marked by ex-

---

[23] For material on culture, economics, welfare, and other subjects, see Albert Pullerits, *Estonia* (Tallinn: Tallinna Eesti Kirjastus-Ühisuse Trükikoda, 1935).

treme reserve and deliberation. He has developed a strong feeling of nationalism during the last few generations and reflects it in his thoughts and deeds.

Estonian literature is rich and interesting. Corresponding to the Finnish *Kalevala,* Estonia has her *Kalevipoeg* written by Dr. F. R. Kreuzwald (1803-1822), which led to an extensive collection of Estonian folklore archives at Tartu. These consist of rhymes, nursery songs, proverbs, riddles, imitations of the voices of nature, traditions, stories, and superstitions. Prose literature became a subject of great interest about 1890, although the first printed book appeared in 1535. During the last three generations a number of able writers have appeared, among them the short story writer Ernst Peterson, the "Young Estonia" novelist Fridebert Tuglas, the neo-romanticist Ernst Enno, the lyrical writer of the "Siruru" group, Marie Under, and the dramatist A. H. Tammsaare. One of the finest achievements of these writers has been the creation of a literary professional society which publishes its own monthly, *The Creation.* Literary contacts abroad are excellent.

In other ways, too, Estonian culture is of interest. Theatrical and operatic performances have wide public support. Estonia has developed stars of her own, such as Paul Pinna, Theodor Altermann, and Erna Villmer. There is no state theater, but theaters are owned and successfully promoted by private societies.

Estonia's people also love music, and singing festivals are very popular. Sometimes as many as 14,000 people participate in the chorus and 2,000 in the orchestra. Estonian composers who have made their mark include Alexander Sablemann, Alexander Tomson, Dr. K. A. Herman, Johannes Kapel, Rudolf Tobias, and Mart Saar. Fine arts are varied and well-supported. A rich peasant culture reaching back to the Middle Ages is to be seen in the museum in Tartu. The Finnish influence has been strong in architecture. Painting goes back as far as the church frescoes of Ridala and Muhu, which are fourteenth-century products. Selecting at random from a long list of distinguished painters, some of the more recent names include the portraitist and landscapist J. Köler, the Baltic-German K. F. E. Gebhardt, the illustrator of national epics Tonis Grenstein, the pastellist Ants Laipman, the modernist Konrad Mägi, and A. Vabbe of the influential Pallas School of Arts at Tartu. Sculpture is perhaps best represented by Jaan Koort. A lively press follows the pattern of Finland and the Scandinavian countries.

Economic and Social Factors. Estonia's economic life is much the same as that of the other two countries dealt with in this chapter.

Trading has been influenced chiefly by Russia and England, which have considered the Baltic their special trading sphere. Forestry products, cattle-breeding, poultry-raising, dairying, potato-farming, growing of flax and linseed, fishing, extraction of oil from shale, digging of peat, and the working of a few mineral deposits constitute the chief economic activities of the Estonians. Industrial life dates back to Russian rule, and manufacturing is represented chiefly in the engineering and textile works located at Tallinn. Industry in general is restricted to the working of chemicals, leather, textiles, paper, pulp, timber, foods, beverages, and power resources. Coöperatives have reached Estonia, which has begun to develop them to an effective degree.[24]

Social conditions were much the same in Estonia at the beginning of independence as they were in the neighboring lands. Landholding had to be rectified, pension regulations changed, and a whole new structure of social welfare erected. Relief and help to the needy, which had made great progress in small independent states, had not had an opportunity to develop in Estonia under Russian rule. Religion was the very center of life, the family was a strong social unit, and markets were the meeting-places for the majority of people. Minority groups were generously treated.

Bibliography

Bashford, Major Lindsay, "In the Little New Countries," *Blackwoods Magazine,* CCIX: 1265 (March, 1921), pp. 363-377; CCIX: 1266 (April, 1921), pp. 471-486. Helpful background material.

Carpenter, Frank G., and Harmon, Dudley, in "Carpenter's World Travels," *The British Isles and the Baltic States* (Garden City and New York: Doubleday, Doran and Co., Inc., 1930), Chapters 24 and 26. A short general account of Latvia and Estonia.

Education: See the three articles in *School Life,* XXIV (October, 1938-July, 1939): Kronlins, Janis, "The Latvian Schools and Their Attainments," XXIV: 9 (June, 1939), pp. 266-268.

Masiliunas, K., "Education in Lithuania," XXIV:6 (March, 1939), pp. 171-173, 184.

Speek, Peter Alexander, "Education in Estonia," XXIV:7 (April, 1939), pp. 206-208.

Harrison, E. G., *Lithuania, 1928* (London: Hazell, Watson, and Viney, Ltd., 1928). Parts II and III give fine geographical, topographical, and historical sketches. Part V deals with culture and Part VI with economics.

Independence for Lithuania, Statement by the Lithuanian National Council in the United States (Washington, D. C.: Government Printing Office, 1918). Balanced.

---

[24] Bowman, *op. cit.,* and Vogel, *op. cit.*

Meiksins, Gregory, *The Baltic Riddle* (New York: Fischer, 1943). Part I is reasonably helpful in this Russophile work.

"The Races of the Baltic," *National Geographic Magazine,* XXXIV:5 (November, 1918), pp. 463-466. The best short account of its kind.

Pullerits, Albert, *Estonia* (Tallinn: Tallinna Eesti Kirjastus-Ühisuse Trüki-koda, 1935). Authoritative, scholarly.

Ruhl, Arthur, *New Masters of the Baltic* (New York: E. P. Dutton, 1921). An interesting travelogue combined with history and factual material.

Ungern-Sternberg, Baroness Irina, "Estonia at Russia's Baltic Gate," *National Geographic,* LXXVI:6 (December, 1939), pp. 803-834. Helpful for orientation.

Williams, Maynard Owen, "Latvia, Home of the Letts," *National Geographic,* XLVI:4 (October, 1924), pp. 401-443. Much useful material.

THE BALKANS

To MOST Americans, the Balkans are a vague spot on the map, a mountainous region split up into small states that bicker with one another, sprinkled with Graustark castles, and peopled with half-barbaric nobles, bandits, and picturesque peasants. For many centuries the word "Balkans" has been used derogatorily with the implication of corruption, disorder, and anarchy, although in reality the Balkan peoples have set amazing examples of heroic struggles for the principles of freedom and independence.

The essential fact is that the Balkans have been a military highway for more than two thousand years. The peninsula, a traditional region of conflict, is the arm of Europe which winds down toward the Dardanelles. The Roman legions passed through it on their campaigns; centuries later Frederick Barbarossa crossed it with his armies on the Third Crusade. Countless hordes from Asia have swarmed across it into the fertile lands and rich cities of the West, and the armies of the West have swept back over it for conquest or crusade. The Balkan countries, at the crossing of the strategic sea and land routes of southeastern Europe, have been cast by geography in a "doormat" role.

The numerous fingerlike peninsulas jutting from Greece into the Aegean and Mediterranean seas are an index of the northwest-southeast trend of most of the Balkan mountain ranges. Rivers, main roads, and railways follow this "grain" of the land, which in early days laid the region open to the ebb and flow of tides of conquest and migration. The Danube River has always been the great corridor between Central and southeastern Europe. Travel across the Balkans is impeded by the successive, rugged ranges of the Dinaric Alps in Yugoslavia, the Pindus Mountains of western Greece, and the Rhodope Mountains of Bulgaria. North of the Rhodopes, the Balkan Mountains—a minor range from which the peninsula's name is derived—curve from the Black Sea to the Iron Gate of the Danube.

History has never been kind to the Balkans. Wave after wave of invaders have overrun the region, destroying political and social institutions, imposing an alien culture upon the resentful victims, and adding new racial groups to the existing intermixture.

Roughly speaking, the Balkans were in the process of transformation from the supernational order of the Byzantine Empire to that of national states when the Turks invaded them in the fourteenth century. In spite of much intermingling and many cases of doubtful nationality, five recognizable nations had emerged: the Bulgars in the northeast; the Serbs in what was later known as Old Serbia, Novi-Bazar, Montenegro, and northern Macedonia; the Croats in what later became Croatia and western Bosnia; the Greeks in Thrace, the Constantinople area, the islands, and the Hellenic peninsula; and the Albanians in Albania. Each of them (except the Albanians) possessed their own state or states. All of them had achieved a marked degree of moral and material civilization. All were primarily peasant states, but all boasted of cities, art, literature, some industries, and trade. Their courts were sometimes characterized by great splendor and they had a nobility and a clergy drawn from their own ranks.

Then came the Turkish invasion, which spread from Constantinople (1453) to the Balkans and eventually reached Vienna (1529). The old frontiers (with the exception of those of the Romanian principalities) were abolished, together with the old political organizations. The national social order vanished with political independence. The Serbs and Bulgars were reduced to a uniform peasant level. In fact, in the case of Bulgaria there was not even a native clergy. In Bosnia and Albania the native aristocrats embraced Islam and lost their nationality. Greece was more fortunate in being able to keep a middle class alive. In Romania, a landowning aristocracy of mixed Romano-Greek origin survived and goes down in history as a merciless exploiter of the Romanian peasantry. In general, the vast majority of the peoples who passed under Turkish rule were reduced to a primitive peasant mass.

The key to the psychology of the Balkan peoples is found in this centuries-old struggle with the Turks. To begin with their most striking feature, the obsessive nationalism of the Balkans is a direct and obvious product of the past. As subject nations, they survived the long period of Turkish control only by extreme devotion to their national character. Long training in obstruction has resulted in an immeasurable stolidity.

The impositions of foreign imperialism on the Balkans were manifold. In Macedonia and Old Serbia, the Turks despoiled the native population systematically for 550 years, until they reached a point beyond which the process could not be carried without danger of leaving no victims to be robbed in the future. The poverty of all Bosnians and Herzegovinians, except the Moslems and the Jews, is as ghastly an indictment of the Turks as of their successors, the Austrians. Dalmatia was picked clean by Venice. Croatia was held back from prosperity by Hungarian control in countless ways that have left it far behind its western neighbors in material progress. Empire has never meant trusteeship in the Balkans.

The circumstances of Balkan life have prevented any intertwining of religious and pacifist sentiment. The *comitadji,* those Robin Hoods of the Balkans who waged guerrilla warfare against the Turks, displayed a wide range of character. Some were highly disciplined, courageous, and ascetic men, often from good families. They harried the Turkish troops, particularly those sent to punish Christian families, and held unofficial courts to correct the collapse of the legal system in the Turkish provinces. Others were fanatics who were happy to massacre the Turks but even happier when they were purging their movement of suspected traitors. Still others were robust nationalists, to whom the raiding seemed a natural way of spirited living. And then there were blackguards who were in the business simply because they enjoyed murder and banditry.

The term *Exarch* shows the curious persistence of the Byzantine tradition in the Balkans. It was originally used by the Eastern emperors to denote a viceroy; the Exarch of Ravenna was the governor who represented their power in Italy. But later it exemplified the degradation which the Byzantine tradition had suffered in Turkish hands. It came to mean the Patriarch of a province, appointed to fulfill a political mission but with uncertain guarantees of support against the opponents of his mission.

In the eighteenth century, the Greek Orthodox Church fell into the power of the Phanariotes, the wealthy Greeks, who established themselves in Constantinople and worked hand-in-glove with the Turks. They did not object when their Moslem masters set them on the Slavs, although they themselves retained their Christianity. They persuaded the Sultan to put the whole of the Balkan Church under the power of the Patriarchate of Constantinople. Then they turned the Church into an elaborate fiscal system for fleecing the Slavs, by exacting numerous fees for the performance of all religious functions, even stripping the peasants of their last farthing as a charge for saying prayers for the dead. They also strove to deprive congregations of their racial identity. Slavs who wanted to become priests had to play traitors to their own blood. There was also a ruthless campaign against the use of the Serbian and Bulgarian languages. Hence the violent reaction of the

Balkan nations against the Exarchate and their persistent demands, in the nineteenth century, to have their own Exarchs.

As the Turks were gradually pushed back in the nineteenth century, the Balkan nations began to arise. The non-Moslem elements, the *rayahs* (a word denoting the inferiority of cattle or sheep), started a series of revolutions and gradually and painfully transformed the map of the Balkans into one of nominally sovereign states: Serbia, Greece, Montenegro, Romania, Bulgaria, and finally Albania (in 1913). The Balkan movements had three characteristic peculiarities. First, they were mass movements fomented by Turkish exploitation. Second, their leading elements came from the peasant class, since Turkish domination had annihilated nearly all other classes. Third, they aimed at freedom from the domination of Turkey (and later of Austria-Hungary, which started to occupy the territory evacuated by Turkey). The Western powers, on the whole, hampered rather than helped these movements. In fact, the Balkan nations had to fight on two fronts at the same time—militarily against the Turks and diplomatically against the Western powers. By 1914, the rivalry of the Great Powers—Germany, Russia, Austria-Hungary, Italy, France, and Great Britain—had caused the Balkans to be known as the "powder keg of Europe"—although the powder had been placed there by the Great Powers themselves.

European international relations in the fifty years preceding the outbreak of the First World War were closely bound up with Balkan problems—the disruption of the Turkish Empire, the rise of the Balkan states, and the ensuing clash of interests among the Balkan powers. Since Turkey controlled the Dardanelles and the eastern Mediterranean, the onslaughts weakening the Porte were of pivotal significance for Russia, which posed as the natural protector of the Slavs as well as of Orthodox Christians in the Balkans. Austria, anxious to control the Danube to its mouth and the Dardanelles as the outlet for the Danube, was deeply agitated by the possibility of having strong Slavic states under Russian leadership at her back door. German jingoes, envisaging a great empire along the "transversal Eurasian axis," devoted themselves to fostering the Berlin-Baghdad dream. England, eager to keep Russia out of Constantinople, doggedly worked for the safety of her gateway to India. France, accustomed to regard herself as the defender of Christianity in the Mediterranean orbit, found her claims contested by upstart Italy.

Each of the Great Powers had its own protégés among the Balkan

nations, and each in turn sought to obtain territorial and other gains
without regard to the problems of national minorities.   Directly and
indirectly, the Balkan Wars of 1912 and 1913 led to World War I.
Enlarged and confident, Serbia was attracted by the idea of freeing all
fellow-Slavs from Austria-Hungary.   Her hatred for Austria was the
spark that started the conflagration.

During the First World War, true to the ancient formula, the Balkans
were overrun by various armies.   At the end of the war, the map of the
Balkans was redrawn to correspond more definitely with the aspirations
of the Balkan nationalities.

CHAPTER VIII

ROMANIA (UP TO 1918)

The Roman Era

ROMANIA traces her history back to 101 A.D. At that time the Roman emperor Trajan defeated King Decebal of the Dacians, a tribe of the Thracians, and colonized the province. The capital, Sarmisegetuza, a lovely spot in Transylvania, was taken by assault. In eastern Banat, Dacia, Oltenia, and Transylvania, gold and other valuable mineral deposits soon attracted large numbers of Roman colonists to the new provinces. By 271 A.D., however, the Roman emperor Aurelian abandoned the Dacian colony. He removed his troops and government officials, but the Roman colonists remained.

Following the era of Roman domination, the country was transformed into a battleground for invading tribal armies until the seventh century. During these invasions, the remnants of the early Roman colonists and their descendants fled for refuge to the Carpathian Mountains or to the region south of the Danube. The inrushing armies of Slavs succeeded in dividing the Romanians from the Romans. It was to the Romanized Gauls that Byzantine writers applied the Slavonic word "Vlachs."

The Romans living in the secluded Carpathians were unmolested by the waves of barbaric invasion. The Slavs were about the only important group to penetrate the area and leave an impression on the people's language. Even in the twentieth century, traces of Dacian tastes and customs have been found to predominate in this Carpathian stronghold. But the invading armies left their imprint on the Dacians. The resulting conglomeration of traits produced a mixed group of inhabitants who were converted to Christianity, in the eleventh century, under the guidance of the Hellenic Orthodox Church at Constantinople.

The Transylvania Issue

The arrival of the Magyars in Transylvania in 1003 led to the subjugation of the Transylvanian Romanians by a barbarous Asiatic tribe,

but the majority of the Transylvanians have preserved their racial and
linguistic characteristics despite centuries of Magyar domination.

Transylvania remained under the rule of the Hungarians up to 1918
and has always been a subject of lively historical controversy. While
the Romanians claim to have settled Transylvania before the arrival of
the Hungarians, Hungarian philologists and historians claim that the
Romanians descended from Vlach herdsmen who had filtered into
Transylvania during mediaeval times—hence *after* its effective occupation by the Magyar warriors.[1]

The Roots of Modern Romania

The two Principalities of Wallachia and Moldavia, the nucleus of the
present Romanian nation, were founded in the fourteenth century by
the princes of a powerful feudal family—the Besarab. About a century later both were riven by internal strife. Both resorted to foreign
aid from Hungary, Poland, and Turkey to quell the disturbances. It
was then that two outstanding individuals rose to prominence: Vlad
the Impaler (1456-1462) in Wallachia, and Ştefan the Great (1457-
1504) in Moldavia.

In 1393 Wallachia acknowledged the suzerainty of the Sultan. The
countries were forced to pay increasing tribute to the Turks in 1411.
Vlad the Impaler came to the throne in 1456, three years after the fall
of Constantinople. He was able to hold back the Turks for a time, but
soon afterward Wallachia was forced to submit to Turkish domination.

Ştefan the Great fought for Moldavia's independence from Turks,
Poles, and Hungarians for many years. He is credited with having
crushed numerous Turkish onslaughts against Christianity. Nevertheless, he was a disappointed man when he died and urged his son Bogdan in his last breath, to submit to Turkish rule.

Toward the end of the sixteenth century, the Besarab dynasty contributed one of the most epic figures to Romanian history, Michael
(Mihaiu) the Brave (1593-1601). He succeeded for a brief time in
uniting Wallachia, Moldavia, Bessarabia, the Bukovina, and Transylvania—a united Romania unknown again until 1918. Down through
the centuries he has remained a symbol of unification.

Unfortunately Michael lost Transylvania to the Magyars before his
death. An era of decadence and corruption followed. Nobles ruling
the territories courted the good will of influential officials in Constan-

---

[1] For a review of the controversy, see Joseph S. Roucek, *Contemporary Roumania and Her
Problems* (Stanford University, Cal.: Stanford University Press, 1932), pp. 3-5; for the Hungarian claims, see Eugene Horvath, *Transylvania and the History of the Roumanians* (Budapest: 1935).

tinople. Several Wallachian and Moldavian princes attempted to follow in Michael's footsteps, but their efforts were futile because of this
political deterioration. By the end of the seventeenth century, the
Porte intervened more and more in the administration of the principalities. Although the provinces became mere Turkish dependencies,
they still enjoyed greater privileges than Serbia and other Turkish
provinces. Local administration, law courts, and law codes were permitted. In the following period the predominating influence was
Greek. Such names as Constantin Mavrocordat, who attempted to
provide reforms to benefit the peasant, and Basil Lupulo, who stimulated learning, are linked with these times.

National Regeneration

After the Treaty of Kutchuk-Kainardji (1774), Turkey regained
Wallachia and Moldavia after losing them first to Austria, then to Russia. Austria received the Bukovina, which she retained until the treaty
following World War I. Russia's powerful position at this time forced
recognition of a sort of Russian protectorate over the principalities.
She compelled the Porte to promise protection for the Christian faith.
National minorities looked to Russia as their champion thereafter. In
1821, Russia forced the Sultan to restore the Romanian princes to their
principalities. This marked the end of the oppressive rule of the
Phanariotes. A period of national regeneration led by Transylvanian
teachers followed.

While the principalities were under Turkish dominance, the Porte
had farmed out their administration to rich Greek merchants and bankers who lived in the Phanar (lighthouse) quarter of Constantinople,
the so-called "Phanariotes." The Phanariote period (1711-1821) was a
heavy economic drain upon the provinces. The anti-Greek hatred en-
gendered by Phanariote financial exactions is still strong in Romania
today. But the Phanariotes did bring with them the leavening influence of French literature and culture. This contact with French
civilization roused the sleeping Latin spirit in the Romanians. The
younger generation flocked to Paris, drawn there by liberal ideas.

The two Romanian provinces of Wallachia and Moldavia were in a
different position from other parts of the Balkan Peninsula in two important respects. They were not directly incorporated into the Turkish
Empire, and they preserved their aristocracy. They therefore resembled Russia, Hungary, and Poland in their social structure rather than
Serbia and Bulgaria, whose people had become purely peasants. In
the eighteenth century, the princes accepted French cultural ideas.

Later, French revolutionary ideas penetrated to the Romanian aristocracy through the Greek merchants established in Vienna. In 1791, as a result, some of the *boyars* in Wallachia demanded the right to form a nation and to elect a native prince.

However, a modern Romanian national consciousness really began only when Gheorghe Lazar, coming from Transylvania to Bucharest in 1816 as director of the school of St. Sava, propagated the theories of Bishop Micu and substituted the native vernacular for Greek as the language of instruction. But years of patient effort were required before any substantial number of provincial Romanians understood Lazar's efforts and began to found schools with teachers imported from Transylvania. The Romanian language, which so far had been the language of the lower-class peasants, became more appreciated and more widely used.

In the nineteenth century, Greek influence declined as Russian influence grew. The Romanians did not like the Russians, but welcomed them in 1828 when war broke out between Russia and Turkey. The Treaty of Adrianople (1829) granted virtual autonomy to the principalities, although the Russians occupied the country for a number of years. The revolutionary wave of 1848 also touched the Romanian provinces. It was Romanian good fortune that the views of Napoleon III of France coincided with the nationalistic principles propounded by Romanian agitators abroad. At the Paris Congress of 1856, the union of the principalities was suggested as a barrier against Russian expansion. The treaty of March 30, 1856, gave back to Moldavia three of the districts of southern Bessarabia which had been annexed by Russia in 1812.

The National Party, determined to overcome all obstacles to a complete union, elected Colonel Alexandre Ion I. Cuza as the prince of both principalities in 1859, and this act was grudgingly recognized by the Great Powers in 1861. Cuza's reign lasted seven years. Some of his drastic reforms aroused serious opposition, but he put through two outstanding measures: the secularization of the great estates of the monasteries in 1863, and the Rural Law of 1864 which acknowledged the peasants as the legitimate owners of the land they tilled. The personal vices of the prince, the unconstitutionality of many of his acts, and the prevailing financial distress forced Cuza to abdicate in 1866.

Charles of Hohenzollern-Sigmaringen was placed on the throne in the same year as the new prince, Carol I. He declared his country independent on May 10, 1877, and saw it expand considerably during his reign of 48 years. The Peace of Berlin in 1878 gave southern Bessarabia to Russia, but Romania got most of Dobrudja. In 1913, after the Second Balkan War, Romania received an additional section of this area, known as the "Quadrilateral." By deciding to fight on the side of the Allies in 1916, the Romanians eventually realized their national ambition. The peace treaties gave them Transylvania from Hungary, Bessarabia from Russia, and the Bukovina from Austria—triumphs that did much to strengthen the reign of Ferdinand I, at the helm since 1914.

Party Rule

On the eve of Romanian independence, a downtrodden peasantry left the government to a small minority of privileged landowners, professional people, and urban merchants. Up to World War I, power was held alternately by two political parties, the Conservatives and the Liberals.

The Liberal Party, relatively progressive at that time, was also emphatically nationalistic and was favored by the throne. Its great leader, Ion C. Bratianu (1821-1891), is justly regarded, with King Carol I, as the founder of modern Romania. Indeed, the Bratianu "dynasty" practically ruled the country from the establishment of the Hohenzollerns up to 1930.

The Conservatives, representing the landowners almost exclusively, were in the saddle less often than the Liberals. The Germanophile inclinations of Marghiloman's war government, which signed a humiliating peace with the Central Powers in 1918, and the effects of the agrarian reform proclaimed in 1919 terminated the party's existence.

Romania and World War I

Before the war began, Romania was approached by both hostile camps. Public opinion in Romania had been estranged by the repressive Hungarian policies in Transylvania and by the Bulgarophile leanings of Austria-Hungary after the Second Balkan War. But King Carol I, who wanted to switch his country to the side of the German cause, called a crown council on August 3, 1914, at 5:30 P.M. He was overruled and was "so overcome by spiritual and bodily anguish that he could no longer think." [2] He died on October 10 and was succeeded by Ferdinand, who was inclined to favor the Allies, especially since

---

[2] Schmitt, B. E., *The Coming of the War* (New York: Charles Scribner's Sons, 1930), Vol. II, p. 429.

Queen Marie was all out for the Allied cause. After signing secret treaties with Russia, France, England, and Italy on August 18, 1916, war was declared.

However, Romania's entry into the war was untimely. The Romanians failed to receive expected aid from their Allies, and Austrian and German armies invaded the country. It became a virtual colony of the Central Powers, especially in the economic sphere. The Peace of Bucharest, signed by Marghiloman on May 7, 1918, is worth studying as an example of what the Germans had in mind for those whom they had defeated. Fortunately, in November, 1918, as a result of events in the western theater of war, the German domination of Romania collapsed. On December 1, the king formally entered liberated Bucharest by the side of Bratianu, who was appointed head of the government.

As noted above, the peace treaties fulfilled Romania's nationalistic ambitions. She became a country equal in area to the combined states of New York, New Jersey, Pennsylvania, Delaware, Maryland, and Connecticut, or about equal to Norway or Italy. Thus the Romanian nation, split up for over one thousand years, became a political unit. The former Roman Dacia, built up by Emperor Trajan, was resurrected from its historical grave.

Bibliography

(At the end of Chapter XXII)

CHAPTER IX

YUGOSLAVIA (UP TO 1918)

Historic Background

YUGOSLAVIA'S historical importance lies largely in its geographic location. It is a highway between Central Europe and the Middle East. It is significant that the railroad lines between Vienna and the Adriatic ports and the line from the Middle East to Western Europe intersect in Yugoslavia, that World War I started because of a shot fired by a Serbian nationalist student, that great Allied armies met again on Yugoslav territory in World War II, and that the internal and external problems of Yugoslavia kept agitating international diplomacy in the months immediately following its conclusion.

The internal dissension which divides Yugoslavia today is nothing new to that unhappy land. Although the country as we know it now was a creation of the peace treaties following the First World War, the regions lying within its present boundaries have been torn for centuries by strife from within and without. Like the other Balkan countries, Yugoslavia has long been a pawn in the hands of the major powers of Europe, and has figured prominently in the wars of the past. The inhabitants of present-day Yugoslavia lived under six different governments before the First World War—a fact which makes it difficult to trace the country's history, but a fact which also accounts in large part for the constant friction and strife.

The name "Yugoslavia" means a country uniting the Southern Slavs within its boundary. It consists of the former independent Kingdoms of Serbia and Montenegro and the Yugoslav districts of the former Austro-Hungarian Empire. The latter include Croatia and Slavonia, formerly united with Hungary; Dalmatia, formerly an Austrian crown land; Bosnia and Herzegovina, formerly under common Austro-Hungarian government; the Slovenian parts of Austria (Krain and a part of Styria); and the Voivodina, which was formerly under Hungarian rule.

The Slavs

The cradle of the Slav race was on the northern slopes of the Carpathians—what is now eastern Poland and southwestern Russia—where they lived as an essentially agricultural people. The vacuum created by the breaking-up of the Roman Empire in central and southern Europe induced the migration of the Slavs to the south and west, during the sixth and seventh centuries, in the footsteps of the Teutonic tribes. At the end of this period the Slavs were in possession of all of southeastern and central Europe. The subsequent invasion by the Magyars and the expansion of the Germanic tribes from the west deprived the Slavs of some of their territories and have definitely separated the Southern Slavs from their northern brethren.[1]

Historical Divisions

The land of the Serbs, Croats, and Slovenes lies at the crossroads of the European Western world and the Eastern world, where Asia begins. The Roman Empire was divided in the middle of the land. Rome and Byzantium fought one another at the moral and political expense of the Southern Slavs. Because of their geographical position, they became separated not only politically but religiously. At that time, the acceptance of a religion had deeper implications than a simple act of faith. It was also a philosophical and political commitment which dominated the whole life of a nation.

The Serbs built their state upon an absolute union between the King, the Church, and the military class. The Croats and later the Slovenes entered into the whole mediaeval, feudal Western European world where the tendency from the beginning has been to separate the temporal power from the spiritual. That explains why the Serbs can easily accept federalism as a political philosophy and why they are always striving for the centralization of the state.

The mediaeval Balkan states were overthrown by the Turkish invasion of southeastern Europe. The Turkish domination still further separated the Serbs from the Croats, since the latter remained in the Austro-Hungarian sphere of influence. Until the twentieth century, the land of the Southern Slavs was shared between the Austro-Hungarian and the Turkish Empires.

The conflict with the Asiatic Turks created a national philosophy among the Southern Slavs known as "the spirit of Kossovo." The

[1] Radosavljevich, P. A., *Who Are the Slavs?* (Boston: Badger, 1919), 2 vols., contains a mass of valuable material.

plain of Kossovo (plain of the blackbirds) had been the scene of an epic battle in 1389, in which the Serbs (with some Croats and Slovenes) were crushed by the Turks. The national poetry (*Pijesma*) sung in Serbia, Bosnia, Herzegovina, Dalmatia, and Montenegro conveyed the "spirit of Kossovo" through the centuries. Unlike the Nazi *Weltanschauung,* "Kossovo" is not a form of national suicide, but a sacrifice by a nation for its resurrection through resistance.

All the Southern Slavs accepted this philosophy and applied it to their different historical positions. In Croatia, for instance, the struggle was analogous to the political and social development of western Europe. Matija Gupets, the Croatian peasant who led a sixteenth-century revolution against the landowners, is an exciting precursor of the Partisans in the Second World War. Dalmatia's intellectual independence of Venice and its great Croatian literature are miracles of national self-expression.

Throughout the Turkish domination, two small sections of the Yugoslav lands retained their independence. One was Montenegro which in its barren mountains developed a heroic tradition; the other was the Republic of Dubrovnik (Ragusa) which became rich by trade and was the center of a flourishing Yugoslav art and literature. Montenegro remained independent until it was merged with Yugoslavia by popular plebiscite in 1919. Dubrovnik lost its freedom in 1804, when it was taken by Napoleon's Marshal Marmont.

The nationalistic consciousness of the Serbs, who were less advanced than the Croats, was preserved through the centuries with folksongs (*pesme*), traditionally recited to the accompaniment of the one-stringed fiddle (*gusla*). The songs commemorated famous forebears and the struggle against the Turks, the legendary hero Prince Marko and the *Haiduks* (Robin Hood guerrillas), who went on fighting "the terrible Turk" in the mountains. By the end of the eighteenth century, many village notables (*knez*) began to come into contact with foreign lands as hog exporters. They led an uprising against the oppression of the Janissaries in 1804. This was the start of the movement for Serbian independence and eventually for Southern Slav unification. The result was the first Serbian autonomous state. It lasted for nine years under George Petrovich, better known as Kara George (Black George, 1766-1817). But the center of Southern Slav cultural life was in Hungary and Vienna.[2]

After two insurrections, the little Principality of Serbia was formed in 1830. Unable to expand northward into the rich plains inhabited

---

[2] Kohn, Hans, *The Idea of Nationalism* (New York: The Macmillan Co., 1944), p. 549.

by the Croats and Slovenes under Austrian rule, it continued its expansion southward at the expense of the Turks. The Balkan wars of 1912-1913 established the southern frontier much as it was after 1918.

Trend Toward a Yugoslav Union

The union of the various branches of Yugoslavs in 1918 was not such a haphazard act as the present friction between these groups would indicate. We have seen that, historically, the Croats, Slovenes, and Serbs were at least partly united at various times. Following the French revolution, the nationalistic aspirations of the Southern Slavs tended to focus on the ideal of a possible unification of all Yugoslavs. It is worth noting that this feeling was stronger among those living in Austria-Hungary than it was among the Serbians and Bulgarians. Several great names in Serbian literature—Dositeje Obradovitch, Vuk Karadchich, and the Montenegrin Bishop Peter II—were inspired by the movement known as "Illyrism" (*Illrski pokret*—from the name "Illyria" which the Romans applied to all provinces on the eastern Adriatic coast).

In the second half of the nineteenth century, the entire Croat intelligentsia gathered around Bishop Josip Juraj Strossmayer and enthusiastically promoted contacts with other Slavs. At the same time, the movement took on the aspect of "Yugoslavism" (*Jugoslvaenstvo*). On the eve of the First World War, a great majority of the Southern Slavs, particularly those in the Austro-Hungarian Empire, had accepted the idea as the only solution for their nationalistic ambitions. In this spirit the so-called "Resolution of Fiume" in 1905 made a declaration according to which "Croats and Serbs are the same nation, both by blood and language," which had the right "to decide freely and independently concerning their existence and future."[3]

The events which brought the Yugoslav question to the attention of the whole world by progressive stages were the annexation of Bosnia-Herzegovina by Austria-Hungary in 1908, the Balkan wars of 1912-1913, and the opening of World War I.[4]

The Serbian victories of 1912 and 1913 greatly strengthened the Yugoslav ideal. The murder of Archduke Francis Ferdinand in Sarajevo (June 28, 1914) led to World War I. The heir of the Austro-Hungarian throne was a marked man. Many Serbs feared that his

---

[3] Jászi, Oskar, *The Dissolution of the Habsburg Monarchy* (Chicago: Chicago University Press, 1929), Vol. V, Chapter VI, "Croatia Versus Hungary," pp. 366-378; Part IV, Chapter IV, "The Jugo-Slav Irredenta and the Road Toward the War," pp. 403-432.

[4] Fa, Sidney B., *The Origins of the World War* (New York: The Macmillan Co., 1931), second rev. ed., 2 vols.

scheme for transforming the Dual Monarchy into a Triple Monarchy with autonomy for the Slavs might wean their kinsmen in the Monarchy away from the "greater Serbia" movement.[5]

During World War I, Austrian armies occupied Serbia and Montenegro, as well as the Austrian provinces of Slovenia, Croatia, Voivodina, Dalmatia, and Bosnia-Herzegovina. Each of these countries had a different history during the war. Slovenians and Croatians fought in the Austrian army, not against the Serbs and not well against the Russians, but excellently against the Italians (especially after Austria published the London Secret Treaty). In the meantime, opposition to Francis Joseph's monarchy grew, and Serbs, Croats, and Slovenes formed their own legions in the Russian army.

At the beginning of the war, the Serbian Parliament proclaimed that its aim was the liberation and union of all Serbs, Croats, and Slovenes. Several Yugoslav leaders from Austria-Hungary fled to Rome, Paris, and London, and eventually formed the Yugoslav Committee in London, under Trumbitch, with a program for a united and independent Yugoslavia.[6] In July, 1917, Pashitch and Trumbitch signed a joint manifesto at Corfu, which laid the foundation for a future "Kingdom of the Serbs, Croats, and Slovenes." It was really a compromise between Pashitch's idea of a "Greater Serbia" and Trumbitch's hopes for a federal Yugoslavia in which the various peoples and provinces would enjoy home rule. It provided that the future State was to be a democratic monarchy under the House of Karageorgovich, that both alphabets and all three religions should enjoy equality, and that local autonomies should be established in accordance with social and economic conditions.[7]

The Formation of the New Kingdom

When the Austro-Hungarian Empire began to fall apart in 1918, the Slovenes under Dr. Korochets, a Catholic priest, convened a National Council in Ljubljana, attended by delegates from Bosnia-Herzegovina. It soon took on the character of an unofficial government in the Yugo-

---

[5] *Ibid.* The literature on the causes of World War I is enormous and cannot be enumerated here. But its influence on the interpretation of the historical role of Central-Eastern Europe is quite obvious. See Joseph S. Roucek, *Misapprehensions About Central-Eastern Europe in Anglo-Saxon Historiography* (New York: Polish Institute of Arts and Sciences in America, 1944); and B. E. Schmitt, "July, 1914: Thirty Years After." *Journal of Modern History,* XVI (September, 1944), pp. 169-204.

[6] Temperley, H. W., *A History of the Peace Conference of Paris* (London: 1920-1924), Vol. IV, pp. 171ff., gives a full account of the Yugoslav movement during World War I.

[7] The third ambiguous point became one of the most disputed points thereafter, the Croats maintaining that it meant federation, while the Serbs replied that it only covered local county councils.

slav districts of the Monarchy. This National Council of Slovenes, Croats, and Serbs desired union with Serbia, but wanted to discuss satisfactory terms of self-government. The advance of the Italians in the west forced the Council to appeal for Serbian help. Under pressure of the foreign danger, Pashitch met the leaders of the Yugoslav Committee and of the National Council in Geneva in the first week of November, 1918. It was agreed that a joint Serbo-Yugoslav Government should be set up at once, but that the existing governments should continue to function pending the drafting of a constitution by a Constituent Assembly. The Council sent a deputation to Prince Regent Alexander, offering him the Regency. Meanwhile, the Great Montenegrin National Assembly deposed King Nicholas on November 26, 1918, and proclaimed its union with Serbia. On December 1, 1918, the Regent proclaimed the Union of the Serbs, Croats, and Slovenes in a united Kingdom.[8]

Bibliography
(At the end of Chapter XXIII)

[8] When Serbia freed herself from the Turks, the Karageorgevichs and Obrenovichs, both swineherds by honorable profession and both desiring the throne, agreed on alternation on the throne until 1903, when ten revolver bullets and five saber cuts ended the career of Alexander Obrenovich. (B. Hardin, *Royal Purple* (Indianapolis: Bobbs-Merrill, 1935) gives a forceful story of this period.) Peter Karageorgevich, who returned from exile, became king and established the present line of Yugoslavian monarchs.

CHAPTER X

BULGARIA (UP TO 1918)

Stages of History

BULGARIA has passed through five well-defined stages of history. First it was a Roman province, or rather a part of the Roman provinces of Moesia and Thracia. In the next stage it was a contested area, fought for by the Byzantine Greeks and the barbarians who invaded it from the north. In the third stage it was a national Bulgarian Empire; in the fourth a Turkish province. Finally the Turkish power was ejected and the modern Kingdom of Bulgaria was established.

In Roman times, present-day Bulgaria was occupied by a population of Thraco-Illyrian descent. These people were expelled or absorbed by the great Slavonic migration which took place at various intervals between the second century and the beginning of the sixth century. Then the scattered Slavonic tribes were subjugated by the arrival, during the seventh century, of a horde of Tartar origin called "Bolgar" or "Bol-Agalar," under the leadership of Asparouh. These wild horsemen, despotically governed by their *khans* (chiefs) and *boyars* (nobles), were a Turanian tribe akin to the Huns, Tartars, Avars, Petchenugs, and Finns. The Bulgars made a gift of their name and political organization to the race they conquered, receiving in return the Slavic language, customs, and local institutions.

Christianity was adopted during the reign of Tsar Boris I (852-888), probably for political motives. During that period, two famous Slavonic missionaries, Cyril and Methodius,[1] invented the alphabet known as *Cirilitza* (*Girilitza*), which is now used by the Russians, the Serbs, and (until the beginning of the nineteenth century) by the Romanians. The adoption of the Slavonic or "Old Bulgarian" language as that of the official liturgy was the final stage in the assimilation of the original Bulgarian race with the Slavonic tribes.

---

[1] Actually most of the work was done among the Slavs of Moravia (present Czechoslovakia) by these two apostles, and the Bulgars were evangelized by their disciples.

In the schism between the churches of the East and West, Boris chose the Eastern Church in 1870. Bulgarian primates subsequently received the title of Patriarchs.

The Zenith of National Power

Under Simeon (893-927), Bulgarian national power reached its zenith. The Bulgarians conquered not only the Slavonic tribes along the Danube, but also those in Thrace and Macedonia. In the west and north, Thessalonica, Epirus, Albania, Sermium, Wallachia, and part of Hungary were incorporated in Simeon's dominions. Being the most powerful monarch in that section of Europe, Simeon assumed the title of "Emperor and Autocrat of all the Bulgars and Greeks," a title recognized by Pope Formosus. After Simeon's death, internal dissension broke up the Kingdom. In 967 the Russians made their first appearance in Bulgaria. In 971 Eastern Bulgaria was recovered for the Roman Empire, and in 1014 Basilius II brought it back under Byzantine dominion. The dynasty was extinguished and for more than a century and a half (1018-1186), all Bulgarian territories remained subject to Byzantine emperors.

The creation of the second Bulgarian Kingdom was another glorious chapter in Bulgarian history. In 1186, the brothers Ivan and Peter Asen of Tirnovo led a revolt of the Vlachs and Bulgars, and Ivan Asen assumed the title of "Tsar of the Bulgars and Greeks." He moved the capital from Preslav to Tirnovo, which the Bulgarians regard as the historic and sacred capital of their race. Ivan succeeded in regaining for his country its lost dominions and prestige. The greatest of the Bulgarian rulers was Ivan Asen II (1218-1241), whose power extended over Albania, Epirus, Macedonia, and Thrace. With the passing of the dynasty in 1257, a period of decadence began. On June 28, 1330, Tsar Michael Shishman was slain by the Serbians under Stephen Urosh III in the Battle of Kustendil. Though Bulgaria still retained its native rulers, it formed part of the short-lived empire of Stephen Dushan (1331-1355).

Turkish Rule

Then the Turks came. At first they invaded the entire valley of the Maritsa, and in 1382 they seized Sofia. Ivan Shishman III, the last Bulgarian tsar, was compelled to declare himself the vassal of Sultan Murad I in 1366 and had to send his sister to the harem of the conqueror.

The five centuries of Turkish rule (1396-1878) form a dark period in

Bulgarian history. Even so, the condition of the peasantry during the first three centuries of Turkish dominion was better than it had been under the tyrannical rule of the *boyars*. Many districts and classes enjoyed special privileges. Chief among them were merchants, miners, and the inhabitants of the "warrior villages," who received self-government and exemption from taxation in return for military service. Up to the end of the seventeenth century there was only one serious attempt at revolt, as distinguished from the guerrilla warfare maintained in the mountains by the outlaws (*haidouks*), whose exploits, like those of the Greek *klephts,* have been highly idealized in popular folklore. The revolt of 1595 and an equally unsuccessful uprising in 1688 were fostered by Austrian troops, but after the Peace of Belgrade (1739), Austria abandoned her active Balkan policy and Russia then assumed the role of protector of the Orthodox Christians in the Balkans.

The Bulgarians, in addition, suffered from the religious and nationalistic policy of the Greek Patriarch at Constantinople, who had been placed over the Patriarchate of Tirnovo. He forbade services to be held in the Bulgarian language, closed the schools, and ordered all libraries to be burned. A new kind of feudal system replaced that of the *boyars,* and fiefs or *spahiliks* were conferred on Ottoman chiefs and renegade Bulgarian nobles. But the Christians still enjoyed certain advantages. They were not subject to military service, the Turks made no systematic effort to exterminate their religion or language, and within certain limits they were allowed to retain their ancient local administration and the jurisdiction of their clergy in regard to inheritance and family affairs.

The Rise of Bulgarian Nationalism

At the beginning of the nineteenth century, the Bulgars were hardly known to Europe, or even to the students of Slavonic affairs. The Russian invasions of 1810 and 1828 only added to their suffering. But the national spirit was beginning to reassert itself.

In 1762 there arose from a cell in the monastery of Mount Athos the voice of the monk Paissy, calling upon the people not to be ashamed of their name and reminding them of their glorious past. He wrote a history of the Bulgarian tsars and saints. His call was heard and taken up by the priest Stoiko, later Bishop Sofrohi, who labored for fifty years to educate his people by his preaching and writing. He is the author of the first book printed in Bulgarian, in 1806. In 1814 the first reading book was published, which led to a new method of teaching.

The monk Neofit Bozveli inspired and led the struggle of the Bulgarian people to free themselves from the Greek Patriarchate's spiritual tyranny.

The Bulgar-Greek controversy over the affairs of the Bulgarian dioceses began in 1835. This was the first struggle in which the Bulgarian nation engaged as a whole. The root of the controversy can be found in the Turkish practice of recognizing only one clergy—since all the conquered nationalities in the Ottoman Empire had the same religion —as representative of the subject races. The Phanar (where the Greek Patriarchate was situated in Constantinople) became the sole Orthodox Church in Turkey. The Greek clergy used their power to spread Hellenic culture and civilization.

In 1860 the Bulgarians refused to recognize the Greek bishops as heads of the Bulgarian dioceses, and their demands were supported by the Russian representative in Constantinople. This forced the Porte to issue a *firman* (March 11, 1870), whereby the "Exarchate of all Bulgaria" was founded, thus placing the spiritual leadership of the Bulgarian people under the control of Bulgarian ecclesiastics. The Greek Patriarch excommunicated his Bulgarian prototype—which only strengthened the nationalistic tendencies of the Bulgarians.

The Bulgarians got international publicity in 1876, when their revolt was suppressed with the utmost ferocity by the Turks. But their cause was taken up by Gladstone in a celebrated pamphlet which aroused the indignation of Europe against the "terrible Turk."

Independent Bulgaria

As a result of the Russo-Turkish war, Russia dictated the Treaty of San Stefano (March 3, 1878), which gave Bulgaria nearly all she wanted territorially. But fear of growing Russian influence caused Lord Beaconsfield to call another European Conference in Berlin. By the Treaty of Berlin (July 13, 1878), the territory lying north of the Balkan range became an autonomous principality under the suzerainty of Turkey, but the territory lying south of the range—Eastern Rumelia —became a Turkish province. (Bulgaria wanted Thrace and Macedonia.) By a coup d'etat of 1885, which Turkey was too weak to oppose, Bulgaria effected the fusion of the principality and Eastern Rumelia under one prince, although the territory remained under Turkish overlordship. It was not until 1908, at the time of the "Young Turk" revolution, that Bulgaria finally declared her complete independence and was transformed from a tributary principality into an independent Kingdom. Prince Ferdinand became "Tsar of the Bulgarians" and started entertaining dreams of a "Greater Bulgaria."

Since 1878, Bulgaria's boundaries have expanded and contracted like an accordion in action. In 1885, as noted above, union with Eastern Rumelia (Thrace) extended her boundaries far south toward the Aegean Sea; the following year the border retreated with territories relinquished to Turkey. After the First Balkan War in 1912, when Bulgarians fought with Serbs, Greeks, and Montenegrins against the Turks, Bulgaria's acquisitions again expanded her boundaries westward and also southward all the way to the Aegean, opening up a direct sea route to the Mediterranean. Almost immediately, however, this was followed by another war in 1913, in which Greece, Serbia, Montenegro, and Romania joined with Turkey against Bulgaria, after Bulgaria struck the first blow. Their combined effort forced the latter country to give up many of her gains. By the Bucharest Peace Treaty, Bulgaria had to give up the Dobrudja Quadrilateral to Romania and lost practically all of Macedonia to Serbia and Greece, although it retained Western Thrace. The peace concluded with Bulgaria giving Eastern Thrace to Turkey.

To recoup her lost fortunes, Bulgaria entered World War I on the side of the Central Powers in October, 1915. Turkey ceded an additional strip of territory in Thrace to Bulgaria. But the Central Powers lost the war and the Peace Treaty of Neuilly (November 27, 1919) deprived Bulgaria of access to the Aegean Sea by giving Thrace to Greece. Some territory was also transferred to Yugoslavia.

Finally, to make the story more up-to-date, Romania ceded Dobrudja (acquired in 1913) to Bulgaria in 1940. After the conquest of Greece by the Axis, Bulgaria annexed Eastern Macedonia and Thrace.

The Macedonian Question

Bulgaria's modern history has been intimately associated with the eternal problem of Macedonia. The possession of Macedonia has been the common objective of the nationalistic ambitions of the three Balkan powers: Bulgaria, Serbia (now Yugoslavia), and Greece. Each of them regards it as vital to their national and other ambitions.

Macedonia's unique importance lies in the fact that it is located in the heart of the Balkan peninsula; whoever dominates the Vardar Valley is master of the peninsula. Since it is the geographical center of that part of the world, each group of people which settled within the peninsula's boundaries tended at one time or another to drift into the Vardar area. In addition, because of its position as the meeting place of the three Balkan states—Bulgaria, Greece, and Yugoslavia—it has been only natural that each of these peoples has tried to impose their own nationalistic sentiments and culture in the area. The inhabitants of the Vardar Valley and the surrounding region have been subjected to a constant barrage of propaganda intended to convince them that they are Bulgars—or Serbs—or Greeks. Jurisdiction over the territory has shifted back and forth as one or the other of the claimants won a move in the complicated game of national fortunes, or the even more intricate game of Europe's diplomatic balance of power. Nor has the struggle ceased at the present time.

Small wonder that out of this cockpit has arisen a constant threat to the peace and stability of Europe. Apart from the three contestants already mentioned, Turkey and Romania have occasionally participated in the scramble, as well as the Macedonians themselves. One consequence has been an excessive Macedonian nationalism, professedly autonomous in purpose, whose accepted program is revolution, insurrection, and extreme violence. Periodically the Macedonian organization directing the movement for autonomy lights a flare in the tinderbox of the Balkans with a well-placed assassination. When one remembers that the First World War resulted from a similar flare in this very region, it is easy to realize the importance of an understanding of the problem and its significance.

It must be emphasized that Macedonia has always been a loosely defined area, though the claimants are fond of appealing to their historic rights as far back as the ninth, tenth, and eleventh centuries. The fact is that Macedonia is more of a political problem than a geographical entity. Today its vague boundaries extend from the region of Salonica along the river Vardar to Skoplje (Uskub), westward to the Albanian frontier, and eastward to Strumnitsa on the Bulgarian border. Its territorial importance centers in the Vardar Valley, which now lies within the territories of Yugoslavia and Greece; but the third claimant, Bulgaria, still regards an outlet to the sea as important.

The name "Macedonia" came into use about the middle of the nineteenth century, when the Balkan nations were engaged in their struggle for liberation from Turkish rule. European Turkey was officially divided into "vilayets," and the territory now currently known as Macedonia comprised the vilayets of Kossovo, Monastir (Bitolia), and Salonica.

The widest definition of Macedonia can be found in the Bulgarian claims. Pro-Bulgarian writers generally give the boundaries of Macedonia as the river Mesta and the Rhodope Mountains in the east; the Aegean Sea and the Chalcidice Peninsula, the river Bistritsa (from the mouth up to its upper course) and Mount Grammos in the south; a line from Mount Grammos to the crest of the Shar in the west; the mountain chain from the Shar to the Rila in the north.

As far as Yugoslav claims are concerned, numerous Serbian authorities maintain that Macedonia comprises only the regions around Ochrida, Bitolia, Voden, Salonica, Dojran, Strumitsa, Seres, and Kavala. The region north of this part of the Balkans is, according to Serb sources, ethnically and historically Serbian country.

Greek writers usually identify their claims with the boundaries of the ancient Kingdom of Macedonia, with the reservation that the definition can now be rightly applied only to Southern Macedonia, which is largely within the boundaries of Greece.

If it had not been for Alexander the Great, possibly no one would ever have heard of Macedonia again after it was wiped from the map in 148 B.C. But it took only a few years for Alexander, who died in 324 B.C., to make the name of his homeland famous forever.

In the nineteenth century, the agitation of the Christian subjects of the Porte in this portion of the Turkish Empire and the ambitions of Greece, Serbia, and Bulgaria to annex part of the territory combined to create the so-called "Macedonian question." In 1878 and 1880 numerous outbreaks occurred in Macedonian districts. In 1893 the powerful Internal Macedonian Revolutionary Organization (*IMRO*) was created and proclaimed the ideal of "Macedonia for Macedonians." This organization rapidly extended its network. Soon its symbol—a piece of black cloth, signifying serfdom and oppression, with the words "Liberty or Death" embroidered across it—became widely known. Local branches were founded, usually led by schoolteachers, and monetary contributions were collected. The country was divided into revolutionary regions, districts, and communes, with officers at the head of each. The local committees, elected by universal suffrage, each sent a delegate to the *rayon* committee, geared into the *okrug* committee, the latter sending 47 delegates to the general congress which elected and granted executive authority to the central committee of three members of Salonica. (Hence the significance of the word *comitadji,* literally meaning committee.) The *chetas,* under the authority of the *rayon* committees, enforced the decisions of the *IMRO* and of its courts, as well as the collection of taxes. Supporting them, in case of emergency, were the secret village militia bodies with hidden arms.

The *IMRO* soon became a state within the state throughout Macedonia. Matters came to a climax in 1902, when bands of Sofia-inspired Young Macedonians, led by Bulgarian officers of Macedonian origin, invaded Macedonia. At the same time there were violent disagreements between the forces supported by Sofia, which utilized the Macedonian movement for nationalistic aims, and within the membership of the *IMRO* itself. The essential problem was whether Macedonia should become autonomous or should unite with Bulgaria in a federal arrangement. The problem was never solved, although submerged in blood. A chain of murders and executions characterized the whole history of the Macedonian movement.

In World War I, the *IMRO* supported Bulgaria, hoping to gain Macedonia's freedom as a reward for its support. It terrorized the Serbian element in the occupied Macedonia. The end of the war found the Bulgarian nation distraught and critical of all those associated with the national disaster. The *IMRO* incurred its share of the blame and nearly ceased to exist in the next few years.

Ferdinand's Rule

The pre-war political life of Bulgaria was characterized by the overwhelming influence of Prince (later Tsar) Ferdinand. The Constitution of 1879 vested the sovereignty of Bulgaria in the Bulgarian people. In the Bulgarian Constituent Assembly, political parties were promptly formed. The Liberal Party embraced the former rebels against Turkish rule, protagonists of absolute freedom, believers in the wisdom of the people. On the other hand, the Conservative Party was formed by intellectuals who profoundly mistrusted the people. The struggle between these two political factions was very bitter. The Liberals constantly repeated the charge that the Conservatives had been loyal to the Turkish Sultan. The Conservatives, on the other hand, called the Liberals "Communists." [2]

But eventually programmatic differences were forgotten and, at the turn of the century, Bulgaria was blessed with numerous party groups and smaller factions. But party names—with the exception of the Agrarian and Socialist Parties—denoted no particular political, social, or economic tendencies. All they indicated was a preoccupation with the interests of the most articulate classes of the nation—the urban, professional, and military classes. The town, parading as progressive,

---

[2] While most of the Liberals had no idea what a Communist was, the Conservatives knew well enough that the horrors of the alleged excesses of the Paris Commune were still fresh in the minds of the rulers of the European Powers.. They also knew that the only way to insure their dominant position in the government was to discredit the Liberals as Communists and thus secure the favor of the Bulgarian prince.

ruled the village. No party was so crudely obvious as to call itself conservative.[3]

Suspended by Prince Alexander of Battenberg in May, 1881, and reinstated in September, 1883, amended twice, in 1893 and 1911, and utterly disregarded by the Bulgarian rulers during most of half a century, the Bulgarian Constitution was effective only on paper. Under Ferdinand's rule, the tsar's power to dissolve the Bulgarian legislative body was widely misused. Out of 21 National Assemblies, 16 were dissolved. In nearly half a century Bulgaria had 37 Ministries, of which only 4 were formed from the majority party in the National Assembly. It was Ferdinand I who brought Bulgaria into World War I on the side of the Central Powers. As a result, he had to abdicate in favor of his son, Boris.

Bibliography
(At the end of chapter XXIV)

[3] Tchitchovsky, T., "Political and Social Aspects of Modern Bulgaria," *Slavonic Review*, VIII (1929-1930), pp. 176-187; R. H. Markham, *Meet Bulgaria* (Sofia: The Author, 1931), pp. 293-312.

CHAPTER XI

ALBANIA (UP TO 1918)

History

ALBANIA'S history has been almost invariably shaped by outside influences. It was in the direct path of Roman penetration toward the east. In the late Middle Ages, when Venice extended its power along the Dalmatian coast, Albania became the natural adjunct of its Adriatic domain. The Balkans were the spearhead of Turkish penetration to the west and Albania, wrested from the Venetians, fell under a long spell of Ottoman rule, only temporarily broken by the patriotic episode of the great Albanian leader Skanderbeg. During the latter part of the nineteenth century, with the decline of the Ottoman Empire, Albania was partitioned and repartitioned among her wrangling Balkan neighbors. During the first decade of the twentieth century, the Albanian situation became such a disturbing element in Balkan and European affairs that a Conference of Ambassadors (London, 1913) was called to define the frontiers of an independent Albanian state. This country, as big (or little) as Maryland, has known for centuries what it means to be invaded and occupied by stronger powers.

One of the oldest races in southeastern Europe and tracing their descent from the earliest Aryan immigrants to the Balkans, the Albanians have stubbornly preserved their racial traits and language despite the almost continuous political subjugation of their country. In the earliest days of its recorded history, as noted above, the territory that is now Albania was partitioned between the ancient Grecian Kingdom of Illyria in the north and Epirus in the south. Aristotle named Epirus as the original home of the Hellenes. Dodona, then in Albanian-inhabited territory, had the earliest of several famous ancient oracles and exerted considerable influence through the oracle's responses to the queries of Greek statesmen.

The Molossina chieftains of Epirus claimed direct descent from Pyrrhus, son of Achilles, who supposedly settled in Epirus after the sack of Troy. Proud and domineering Olympias, sister of King Alexander of Epirus, married Philip of Macedon and became the mother of Alexander the Great. After 146 B.C., Epirus became part of the Roman province of Macedonia.

A colorful figure of Illyria was the pirate queen Teuta (the "Catherine the Great" of Illyria), whose navy raised such havoc with Adriatic shipping that Rome took to arms for revenge and Teuta had to sue for peace in 227 B.C.

The Battle of Actium between the fleets of Antony and Cleopatra and of Octavian was fought off shores that were then Albanian. The *Via Egnatia,* great military highway from Rome to Constantinople, crossed Illyria (Rome's province of Illyricum) from Dyracchium (modern Durazzo) to Thessalonike (now in Greece). Through the succeeding Byzantine era, the time of the Crusades, and during the long period of Turkish domination, the *Via Egnatia* remained the only land thoroughfare between Asia and the Adriatic.

In 330 A.D., when the capital of the Roman Empire was transferred from Rome to Constantinople, Albania became a province of the Eastern (Byzantine) Empire. From the fifth century on, however, the country suffered invasions by Huns, Gauls, Goths, Slavs, Bulgars, Normans, Venetians, Sicilians, and Turks. Until the fourteenth century, the Albanians remained mostly under nominal Serbian rule. Upper Albania and part of southern Albania were ruled by the Montenegrin princely family of Balsa (Balsici), of Provençal origin. In 1360, after the death of the Serbian Emperor Dushan, it regained complete independence under native chiefs until 1431, when the Turks captured Yanina.

Under George Kastriota, nicknamed "Skanderbeg" (1403-1468), the Albanian national hero, the country became united and fought off the Turks for a generation. But after his death, Albania passed definitely under Turkish control. The Sultans maintained their suzerainty until 1912.

Albanian Nationalism

Despite their vague national tradition and their long submergence in the Turkish Empire, the Albanians have always considered themselves a separate ethnic group.[1] They have clung to age-long customs and have suffered only slight infusions into their language. This resistance to outside influence through centuries of constantly changing

[1] Roucek, Joseph S., "Albania as a Nation," *The Annals* of The American Academy of Political and Social Science, CCXXXII (March, 1944), pp. 107-109.

foreign domination is chiefly due to the nature of the land. Enclosed in their inaccessible mountain fastnesses, the Albanians have developed a highly static tribal civilization that could never be penetrated by those who overran the country. In general, Albanians became divided into two groups—the Ghegs, who lived mostly north of the Shkumin River, and the Tosks, living in the south. The Ghegs, living in greater isolation, are usually described as fierce, superstitious, and predatory, but also as brave, simple, and faithful. They are renowned as soldiers and as rebels. The Tosks, on the other hand, broadened by intercourse with the Greeks and the Vlachs, have turned to commercial and agricultural occupations in contrast to the pastoral pursuits of the Ghegs. The predominant religion is Mohammedan. However, a minority in the south belongs to the Greek Orthodox Church; and in the north to the Roman Catholic Church.

The Albanians possess a spirit of independence which is probably as strong as that of other European peoples. But they are more concerned with their own individual freedom and that of the immediate circle in which they live rather than with self-government for the entire country. Living in a compact tribal existence, bound and guided by time-honored traditions, they never felt the need and seldom the desire for central, unified home rule. This does not mean, however, that Albanian history has not had its periods of national resurgency. The spirit of independence was reawakened by the great Skanderbeg or by small nationalistic groups like the League for the Vindication of Albanian Territory.

Most nationalist movements of the Balkans derive their moral sustenance from the revival of their ancient dialects as written tools in the hands of poets and scholars. In emulation of the successful "nationalisms," a group of Albanian educators prepared the first Albanian *Abetare* (a book of ABC's) in Constantinople in 1879. Then books, magazines, and periodicals appeared in that "strange and accursed Albanian tongue." As a result of the San Stefano Treaty, which left territories inhabited exclusively by Albanians in Montenegro, Serbia, Bulgaria, and Greece, the Albanian nationalist leaders, suppressed in their own country, had to operate from Bucharest, Sofia, Cairo, and eventually the United States.[2] They cultivated especially Albania's historic epic of Skanderbeg, a military genius whose exploits were occasionally retold by romantic poets like Longfellow (in *Tales of a Wayside Inn*).

---

[2] Roucek, Joseph S., "Albanian Americans," in F. J. Brown and J. S. Roucek, *Our Racial and National Minorities* (New York: Prentice-Hall, Inc., 1937), pp. 331-339.

Albania and World War I

In 1912 a general uprising compelled the Turks to grant autonomy to the Albanians. European diplomacy forced Prince William of Wied onto the throne, but in a few months he was forced to leave the country because of World War I. During the war, the Serbs, Greeks, Italians, Austrians, Hungarians, and French occupied the country. On June 3, 1917, the commander of the Italian forces proclaimed Albania an independent country and set up a provisional government at Durazzo. The Treaty of London of April 26, 1915, promised, in Articles 6-7, that "Italy shall receive full sovereignty over Valona, the Island of Saseno and surrounding territory of sufficient extent to assure the defense of these points," and that "Italy shall be charged with the representation of the State of Albania in its relations with foreign powers."

When the Peace Conference opened in Paris in 1919, it appeared that Albania would be assigned to Italy as a mandate or protectorate. But any form of Italian mandate was overruled by President Wilson, who insisted on establishing an independent Albania.[3]

In 1920, despite the desire of Greece and Yugoslavia to partition the country, Albania joined the League of Nations and enjoyed national independence for the next two decades under the dapper, ambitious, wary-eyed Ahmed Bey Zog I, *Mbreti Shqiptarvet* ("Bird the First, King of All the Sons of the Eagle").

Bibliography

(At the end of Chapter XXV)

[3] For the United States' attitude in regard to Albania's independence, see Charles Seymour, *The Intimate Papers of Colonel House* (Cambridge: Riverside Press, 1920), Vol. IV, pp. 152-153, and Vol. III, p. 334.

CHAPTER XII

GREECE (UP TO 1920)

The Classical Period

CONTEMPORARY Greece traces her history back to the classical period of ancient Hellas, which gave rise to a political grouping of great weight and significance. It furnished the Greeks with a language, a culture, and an unbroken past. Despite the exposed geographical position of the Greeks, their language has survived not only the vicissitudes of political domination by both Romans and Ottomans, but also the graver peril of the Slavic migrations. The other aspects of the classical period have likewise survived in unbroken memory on Greek soil or abroad. It remained for the Greek renaissance of the nineteenth century to revive in the Greek mind the ancient glory that was Greece and to continue the culture that had already claimed the enthusiasm and admiration of the western world.

The third element of Greek nationalism, which postdates the classical period, is Christianity. Especially during the Ottoman period, religion became a sharp line of demarcation between conquerors and subject people. But the Greek Orthodox Church was even less successful as a unifying force among Christians in the East than the Roman Church was in the West. Two factors were responsible for this: the bitter rivalry between Catholicism and Orthodoxy, and the early tendency for the latter to organize into autonomous units parallel with local languages. This division, in combination with the pattern (established in the reign of Justinian) of subordinating the Church to political authority, has made the Church an ally of nationalism rather than a unifying force of internationalism. It is still exemplified by the rivalry between the Greek and Bulgarian Churches in Macedonia.

In 197 B.C., Macedonia fell to the Romans and within a few decades the Greek city-states to the south were likewise brought under direct Roman rule. By that time, however, classical civilization had blossomed forth in all its majesty. Poets, philosophers, sculptors, archi-

tects, administrators, military, and naval leaders all left behind them a
heritage of grandeur for all civilized people to cherish and emulate.
The story is too well-known to require elaboration.

The Byzantine Era

To complete the account of Greek nationalism and renaissance, another post-classical influence must be included—that of Byzantium.
With considerable justification, the Greeks have always looked upon it
as a Greek Empire and have used it as the goal of their contemporary
national aspirations. As recently as World War I, they have sought
repossession of their former capital, the eternal city of Constantinople.
The debacle in their Asia Minor campaign of 1920-22, however, followed by such a decisive act as the compulsory exchange of populations
between Greece and Turkey in 1923, forced the Greeks to resign themselves to the future of a small nation.

The Byzantine or Eastern Empire lasted for almost one thousand
years. During that long period, it waxed and waned between glory
under strong and intelligent leadership and humiliation at the hands of
ruthless enemies; between power generating additional power and impotence resulting in territorial and other losses; between Spartan discipline which led its people to victories and venal corruptness which
corroded everything in sight. The events of this "millennium" have
left a deep imprint on the Balkan peninsula and its peoples. They all
emanated from a renowned city—Byzantium—which was originally built about 657 B.C. on the shores of the Bosporus by Greek colonists and was renamed Constantinople by Emperor Constantine in 330
A.D. To indicate its political dignity, the new city was styled New
Rome; to perpetuate the fame of its founder, it was given the name of
Constantinople; to emphasize its religious authority, the Greek Patriarch signed himself as "Archbishop of Constantinople, New Rome."
The city served without interruption as the capital of the Eastern Empire until 1453, when it fell to the might of the Ottomans attacking
from the east. It continued as their capital until 1923, when it was
superseded by Ankara, the newly-built capital of the Republic of Turkey. At that time, its name was changed to Istanbul, which in Greek
simply means "to the city." It has never ceased to exert a tremendous
influence on human affairs because of its inherent commercial and
strategic importance.

Byzantine civilization, aside from other factors, was strongly influenced by two historical migrations. The first occurred in 544 B.C.,
when Byzantium was an obscure colonial town, as a result of the Per-

sian conquest of Ionia. The Persians drove great numbers of Greeks
away, among them merchants, mariners, artisans, and intellectuals.
Rather than submit to the Persian yoke, these inhabitants of flourishing
Ionian cities fled and carried their higher culture to Greece proper,
where civilization was dawning again after the Dorian invasion. The
result was an intermingling of eastern and western traditions and ideas
and the development of a new Greek civilization. The second migration occurred over a thousand years later, in the first centuries of the
Byzantine empire, when the Greeks of the post-Alexandrian colonization retreated towards the center of the empire under pressure from
Persians and Saracens to Constantinople and its surrounding provinces.
They formed the ruling class, the aristocracy of the Eastern Empire, to
which they gave their language—Greek—and their culture—formed
from Greek and Asiatic elements.

The checkered career of the great Byzantine empire was brought to
an end by Mohammed II, named "the Conqueror" because he carried
the renowned city of Constantinople by storm on May 29, 1453.

The Rise of Greek Nationalism

Between 1466, when the conquest of Greece was completed, and 1821,
when Bishop Germanos unfurled the standard of revolt against the
Turks, Greece was able to preserve contact with Western Europe. The
preservation of a distinctly national sentiment through dark ages of
Turkish rule is one of the most remarkable phenomena of modern history. It is true that the conquering Turk had found Greece an easy
prey. The gradual decline of the Byzantine Empire had led to decay
and stagnation in its outlying territories. Since the time of the Fourth
Crusade, there had been Frankish feudal principalities whose misrule
and incessant quarrels had reduced the Greek inhabitants to a state of
miserable servitude.

After deliberately exterminating the Frankish lords, Mohammed
handed over their lands to his own veterans for life as a reward for distinguished military service. He also compelled every unbeliever to pay
a poll tax, which no Moslem paid, and imposed a blood-tribute of Christian children by which one-fifth of the males were collected every four
years and educated as Mohammedans. This measure provided the
Sultan with a standing army and a devoted body of household slaves.

The only Christian administrative authority left was the Greek
Church. Its head, the Patriarch of Constantinople, remained the highest authority not only of the ecclesiastical body but also of the Greek
community, and acted as the representative of the Greek nation in its

dealings with the Ottoman Government. In isolated communities, the parish priest and the head-man of the village, together with the notables and the schoolmaster, preserved a semi-ecclesiastical communal system that did much to keep alive the sentiment of nationality. More than anyone else, these men kept alive the flame of Hellenism and national patriotism during the long centuries of Ottoman rule. Eventually an improved economic position, coupled with intellectual superiority, helped the Greeks to assert themselves officially and commercially. The Phanariotes, so-called from the quarter of the capital where the Patriarchate is still situated, constituted an important class of Greek officials in the service of Turkey. They were first employed in secretarial duties and finally emerged in more important posts, such as the Dragoman of the Porte, the Dragoman of the Fleet, and the Voivodes or Christian rulers of Moldavia and Wallachia.

Just as the declining vigor of the Ottomans gave a fresh scope to the Greeks in the sphere of official life and diplomacy, so in another field the indifference and contempt which Turks always felt for trade and commerce gave Greek genius an opening for far-flung commercial activities. The growing importance of the Greek element in the Ottoman Empire attracted the interest of neighboring states, particularly of Russia, to which the Greeks were bound by the tie of a common religion and in which they hoped to find a mighty ally in their aspirations for freedom.

In 1770 a project promoted by one Orloff (in the service of Catherine the Great) to establish an independent principality in Greece miscarried. Albanian troops, sent to suppress the revolt, remained to become a terror to both Christians and Moslems. In 1803 Koraes issued a spirited appeal to revolution, Rhigas was contributing stirring national songs, and Greek merchants in Odessa founded the National Hetairia, a literary and political union seeking the liberation of Greece.

The Bulgarian Exarchate and Greek Nationalism

Reference has already been made to the rivalry between the Greek and Bulgarian Churches. It began after the Turkish conquest, when the Greek Patriarch was recognized as the head and representative of all the Christian subjects of the empire. Fostered by Russian propaganda and encouraged by the Turks themselves, with a view to fomenting quarrels between their subject peoples, the growing sentiment of nationality among the Bulgarians chafed against a system that subjected them to Greek authority.

When the Greek Patriarch refused to sanction a separate Bulgarian

Church, an appeal to the Sultan resulted in a *firman* (February 28, 1870), by which a Bulgarian Exarchate was set up with headquarters in Constantinople, later transferred to Bulgaria. This rival ecclesiastical system and instrument was soon perverted by the Bulgarians to political purposes under the guise of religious enthusiasm. During the ensuing years, nothing so much tended to perpetuate Turkish misrule in Macedonia and render reform impossible as the dissensions between the Greek Patriarchate and the Bulgarian Exarchate. The political propaganda carried on by Bulgaria was largely responsible for the lack of understanding between that country, on the one hand, and Greece and Serbia on the other. The Second Balkan War, World War I, and World War II, involving all three countries, followed almost inevitably.

The Greek War of Independence

The first attempt at revolt was made in 1821, when the Hetairia appointed as its leader Alexander Ypsilanti, a Phanariote and an officer in the Russian army. His failure did not discourage the Greeks, who went ahead with the movement in the islands and in central and northern Greece. Their courage attracted a large number of Philhellenes to their ranks. Lovers of liberty were fired by Byron's passionate poetry; President Monroe voiced American sympathies in his message to Congress on December 4, 1822; the United States Senate, moved by the eloquence of Daniel Webster, passed resolutions of encouragement. The revival of Greek trade and commerce in the Mediterranean, a linguistic and cultural resurgence, the lofty principles of the French Revolution, and the organization of patriotic societies all combined to make the final steps for independence possible.

An offer of joint mediation between the warring Turks and Greeks submitted by the Great Powers on April 4, 1826, which recognized Greece as a tribute-paying dependency, was rejected by the Porte. It was followed by the Treaty of London of July 26, 1827, under which the "Greeks could hold under the Sultan as under a Lord Paramount." This was also rejected. After the Battle of Navarino of October 20, 1827, when the combined fleets of the Powers annihilated the Egyptian fleet, Turkey accepted the Protocol of 1827 as embodied in the new Treaty of Adrianople of September 14, 1829. Within a few months, however, a new Protocol was signed (February 3, 1830), which declared Greece to be an independent state with a monarchical government. Three years of internal confusion and unrest followed until February, 1833, when Prince Othon of Bavaria arrived as the first king.

Between Two Dynasties

Greek independence has been characterized by diplomatic complications and national problems lasting for more than one hundred years. These have included boundary disputes, loan settlements, changes of dynasty, political strife, and complications of international guarantees by the Great Powers. The revolution of 1862 forced Othon to leave the country. It was followed by political turmoil and civil strife until Prince William George of Glucksburg was crowned two years later as George I, King of the Hellenes. Territorial concessions, mainly by the Treaty of Berlin of 1878, extended the realm. Crete, southern Macedonia, Salonica, and the Chalcidice peninsula were assigned to Greece in 1913 as a result of the two Balkan wars. In March, 1913, the monarch was assassinated. His heir, Constantine, ascended the throne and occupied it until 1917, when he abdicated in favor of his second son Alexander. Alexander's death brought Constantine back until 1922, when he was banished in favor of his eldest son George II. The latter remained until 1924, when the monarchical system was eliminated by a plebiscite in favor of a republic.

Party Rule

The first constitution of 1844 was superseded by that of 1864, which set up a representative Assembly with members elected by direct, secret, and universal male suffrage; strictly limited the royal prerogatives by making the king's rule subject to the will of the people; and established local self-government on a system resembling that of the *Code Napoléon*. Under this constitution, revised in 1911, two statesmen left their official imprints on all the official acts of the young nation during its independent life of a little over one hundred years: Charilaos Tricoupis and Eleutherios Venizelos.

Tricoupis was associated with the events flowing from the Crimean War and subsequently with the two treaties signed in 1878: the Treaty of San Stefano and the Treaty of Berlin. The first treaty, between Russia and Turkey, sought to create a "Greater Bulgaria" by completely ignoring the territorial claims of Greece based on nationality and self-determination. The Treaty of Berlin, while recognizing the independence of Romania, Serbia, and Montenegro, likewise failed to grant the territorial expansion of Greece to the north. Internally, Tricoupis did his utmost to restore the financial position of Greece, to inaugurate road and rail construction, to attract foreign capital for the development of the mineral resources of the country, and to consolidate a constitutional and parliamentary government in Greece at a time when such a government was unknown in many other European states.

Venizelos came on the scene at the turn of the century, at the invitation of the Military League set up by young officers in 1909 as a rallying point against the politicians who had repeatedly humiliated the nation both at home and abroad. From 1911 until his death in 1936, Venizelos personified the claims and aspirations, the hopes and dreams, the forward march of the young nation. He succeeded in incorporating in it the coveted island of Crete, part of northern Epirus, Greek Macedonia, and eastern Thrace. Except for the phenomenal resurgence by the Turks following World War I and the desertion by their former allies, France and Italy, the Greeks might have emerged victorious from their war against Turkey in 1919-22, both in Asia Minor and in Thrace.

Following the revision of the constitution in 1911 and the return of law and order, Venizelos turned his attention to strengthening the nation's ties abroad, especially with neighboring countries. The Balkan League of Greece, Bulgaria, and Serbia successfully waged a war for the liberation of their nationals still under Turkish rule and might have achieved greater results except for the duplicity of the Bulgars, who demanded the lion's share of the spoils. The only "unredeemed" Greeks were those of Turkish Thrace and the mainland of Asia Minor, for whom the Greeks gambled at the end of the First World War and lost.

Bibliography
(At the end of Chapter XXVI)

CHAPTER XIII

TURKEY (UP TO 1920)

Origins of the Ottoman Empire

THE bulk of modern Turkey is in Asia, where this nation shares a common boundary with Soviet Russia, Iran (Persia), Iraq (Mesopotamia), and the Levant States. In Europe, across the narrow waters of the Bosporus and the Dardanelles, a small northwestern patch of Turkish territory touches the borders of Bulgaria and Greece. Even Romania, fronting on the almost landlocked Black Sea, is affected by Turkey's control of its water gates to the outside world.

Historic centers of once powerful empires, such as Ur, Sumeria, Babylon, Assyria, Phoenicia, and the ancient Hittite capital of Bogazköy, were situated in or near what is now Turkey. In its prime, the vast Ottoman Empire of the Turks spread into three continents, covering nearly three million square miles. After the First World War, the young Turkish republic still covered more than 297,000 square miles. Superimposed on a map of the United States, this territory would extend from New Jersey and southeastern New York to the Mississippi River and from the Great Lakes southward to include most of Tennessee and North Carolina.

Few Americans realize that old "Turkey," the pre-1914 Turkey out of whose chrysalis present-day Turkey has emerged, was not properly Turkey at all. Few Americans realize that less than sixty years ago it was a deadly insult, worse than the epithet "dog," to call any member of the state which we called Turkey a "Turk." In the language of Constantinople, Turkish though it was, the name "Turk" designated dirty and ill-smelling nomads who ranged from the wild wastes of inner Asia Minor to Turkestan, which means "Turkland," east of the Caspian Sea. In their own mind and their own speech the proud effendis, beys, and pashas of Constantinople were not Turks.

What were they? Osmanlis, anglicized from the Arabic into "Ottomans." The adjective Osmanli designates a dynasty rather than a people, a royal house developed from a family of chiefs of a small and originally unimportant tribe which came to settle in the northwestern corner of Asia Minor in the troubled times that marked the end of the Crusades. Osman, founder and namesake of the dynasty, was just a minor chief of an apparently still partly nomadic tribe of a type that still exists in Asia Minor. A descendant of a Mongol race in Central Asia, of which the Huns were also an offshoot, Osman began to rule in 1288.

The Osmanlis gradually conquered all of Asia Minor. In 1361 they captured Adrianople and thus came into contact with other Christian nations in the Balkans besides the Greeks, namely the Serbs and Hungarians. They were invited by the Greeks to help them against the menace of Tsar Dushan of Serbia, and won the battle of Kossovo in 1389.

Except for a short decade (1402-11), when Timur (Tamerlane) checked the Turks and plundered their cities, the Osmanli advance from the East across the length and breadth of the Byzantine Empire was constant and relentless. It continued westward to the door of Vienna long after the conquest of Constantinople in 1453, which signalled the final elimination of the Eastern Empire. Yet, while the latter lasted a "millennium," its conqueror and successor showed signs of decay and corruption within two hundred years after the "conquest." As early as the turn of the eighteenth century, the Turk was spoken of in European chancelleries as the "sick man of Europe." Sultans were enthroned, dethroned, or killed by the famous corps of Janissaries, a small force of infantry recruited from among converted Christians and trained to form a privileged caste of professional soldiers and religious fanatics. In their early appearance and before corruption had set in, these troops had greatly contributed to the glory and grandeur of the Empire. When Russia imposed the Treaty of Kutchuk-Kainardji, in 1774, the Turks met their first major humiliation. Turkey was forced to grant the Tsar the right to intervene at his discretion in the internal affairs of the Empire on the pretext of according protection to subject Christians.

Islam

For a Moslem, the faith of Islam proclaimed by Mohammed (570-632) is a revaluation of the religion and ethics of Judaism and Christianity. Guided by his Arab, Jewish, and Christian neighbors, the prophet considered himself the last of the tribe and maintained that he came to fulfill the law of Moses and to perfect the gospel of Jesus. In the Koran he completed the revelation of truth contained in the Old and New Testaments. In the eyes of a Moslem there is only one true Allah. He has the faith of perfect submission to God's will; he belongs to the chosen people and shares in their common fate.

The Arab caliphs, as successors to the prophet and vice-regents of God, ruled first at Medina until 661, then at Damascus until 750 and at Baghdad until 1258. When the Ottoman Sultan displaced them, they fled to Cairo. There they continued to exercise titular authority until 1517, when Selim I captured the last of them and took over the title. Kemal Ataturk not only deposed the last Ottoman Sultan, but also abolished the Moslem caliphate.

When Mohammed II, the "conqueror," took Constantinople in 1453, he granted special privileges to the Christians of the defunct Byzantine Empire; he made them subjects of his new Empire but not subject to Moslem faith and law. In addition to freedom of worship, he also granted them considerable freedom in matters of administrative and political jurisdiction. The Greek Patriarch of Constantinople, as the head of the Greek Orthodox Church, was represented at the Ottoman court as if he were the ambassador of a foreign power. The same applied to the heads of the Jewish, Serbian, Romanian, and Armenian Churches within the Ottoman Empire, but the Bulgarians were not granted this privilege until the Exarchate was created in 1870.

The System of Capitulations

Originally the term "capitulation" derived from the Latin *capitula* or stipulation and was used in 1275 by the Byzantine Emperor in an agreement with the Genoese. When the Ottomans occupied Constantinople, they found a well-established capitulatory system under which foreigners forming colonies within the Empire were amenable to their own consuls in accordance with the laws of their own countries. The Ottomans continued the system, regardless of the fact that their judicial system did not provide for the protection of the legal rights of foreigners. At the time, the system had little to do with race, creed, or nationality. It meant no derogation from the concept of sovereignty, nor did it reflect any reservation to the independent existence of a nation.

Extraterritorial rights were for the first time formally conferred on the French by Selim I in 1516, were renewed in 1522, and were then incorporated in a formal treaty of amity and commerce between the Sultan and Henry I of France in 1535. It was this treaty which gave rise to the system of capitulations in its later and more significant phases. Rather than a treaty of alliance, it amounted to a grand gesture, an exhibition of contemptuous magnanimity on the part of the Sultan toward a Christian underdog. The next to obtain these privileges were the British in 1579, followed by the other Western Powers. Their people, while sojourning in Turkey, were exempt from taxation, judicial administration, and other restrictions enforced on Ottoman subjects.

Many attempts were made to abolish this anomalous *imperium in imperio* but without success until after World War I, when the Nationalists under Kemal made the eradication of all capitulations a major feature of their program. Abolition of the system was decreed by Article 27 of the Treaty of Lausanne (July 24, 1923).

The Period of Decline and Liberation

The beginning of the decline of the Ottoman Empire can be traced to the failure of the Turks under Mohammed IV (1648-87) to capture Vienna in 1681, and the subsequent loss of territories suffered as a result of a general alliance by the Western Powers. It was aggravated when the Sultan was forced to sign the Peace of Karlowitz in 1699, justly called "the first dismemberment of the Ottoman Empire." This treaty was the initial step in the historical process which continued slowly but surely thereafter.

Toward the end of the eighteenth century, a new and powerful foe —the Russians—was added to the growing list of the enemies of the Sultan. The Treaty of Kutchuk-Kainardji (1774) marked the decisive turning point in the decline of the Empire. The guarantee of the territorial integrity of the Ottoman Empire, initiated at the Congress of Vienna of 1815 and re-emphasized at the Congress of Paris of 1856, was not due to any inherent Turkish strength but was rather the result of the conflicting interests of the Western Powers in that part of the world. Russia and Austria wanted to reach into the Mediterranean; Britain sought to block the route of both to India; non-Moslem Turkish subjects warred against the Empire for independence under the cloak of demands for reform. Despite these conflicts of interest, the nineteenth century witnessed the progressive disintegration of Turkey.

Greece was declared independent in 1829; France took Algiers in 1830; in the same year Egypt, aided and abetted by Britain, revolted against the rule of the Sultan; Russia exacted special privileges concerning freedom of passage for her warships through the Straits by the Treaty of Unkiar-Skelessi (1833). Almost half a century later, Turkey was forced: (a) to grant independence to Serbia, Montenegro, and Romania and to create a tributary state of Bulgaria, under the Treaty of

Berlin (1878); (b) to accept British occupation of Egypt, the key to the East and to India (1883); and (c) to recognize the independence of Bulgaria (1908). A general uprising of the Albanians in 1910 resulted in the proclaiming of Albanian independence by Austria and Italy, an act which was ratified by the Conference of Ambassadors in London on July 29, 1913. The preceding Italo-Turkish War of 1911 and the subsequent First World War forced Turkey to cede more territories and to grant additional privileges to foreign interests until she was left with a mere shell of her former power and glory.

Party Strife

The first appearance of party politics in Turkey dates from the time of the so-called "Young Ottomans" in the reign of Abdul-Aziz (1861-76). They banded together in a secret revolutionary society to depose the Sultan, who had reaffirmed the Treaty of Paris (1856), and to introduce constitutional reforms. Though both aims were speedily accomplished, Turkey in the ensuing years experienced defeats on both her diplomatic and internal fronts, lost considerable territory, and saw her sovereignty curbed by the Great Powers.

Events that followed made matters worse. Students of military and other schools, affiliated with revolutionary societies in Europe, were organized as the "Secret Society of Union and Progress" to agitate for constitutional reforms by revolutionary methods. Among the leaders of this Society were Talaat Bey, chief clerk in Salonica's post office, Enver Bey, and Mustapha Kemal, both officers in Turkey's Macedonian army. After their demand for the restoration of the constitution of July 23, 1908, was submitted to the Porte, the reaction was swift and bloody. Their officers and other adherents were massacred, Parliament was raided, deputies were murdered, and a new reactionary cabinet was formed. In retaliation, the "Young Turks" marched on Constantinople, deposed Sultan Abdul-Hamid II, and restored the constitution. Thereafter they became a regular political party until the birth of the new Republic of Turkey.

The Young Turk revolt was followed by six events of great significance for the decaying Empire: (a) Bulgaria proclaimed her independence on October 5, 1908; (b) Austria annexed Bosnia and Herzegovina the very next day; (c) the Armenians in eastern Anatolia rioted for reforms in 1909; (d) the Albanians revolted against the Sultan in 1910; (e) the Italo-Turkish war broke out in Africa in 1911 and the Italians took the entire Ottoman domain in Africa and the Dodecanese Islands in 1912; and (f) the two Balkan wars of 1912-13 followed. The first of these involved Turkey against a united Balkan coalition of Bulgaria, Greece, and Serbia-Montenegro. The second united the Young Turks with Greece, Serbia-Montenegro, and Romania against Greater Bulgaria. The paradox was that Turkey had lost these heterogeneous European possessions—two million Greeks and one million Serbs—but had actually gained strength and homogeneity.

World War I

Before casting their die with the Germans, the Young Turk cabinet made serious attempts to settle Turkish differences with England regarding the Persian Gulf controversy and the financial capitulations, and with France concerning the railroad controversy and the floating of a loan in Paris. But these attempts and the policy of "Ottomanism," which aimed to consolidate all racial and religious elements within the Empire, failed because the war faction (led by Enver, the War Minister, and Talaat, the Grand Vizier) had signed a secret alliance with Germany on August 2, 1914, and had mobilized the army. This faction argued that Turkey had lost her political isolation after the Crimean War and should join Germany to fight her hereditary enemy, Tsarist Russia.

The defeat of Turkey by the Allies had been anticipated by the signing of four secret agreements partitioning the Empire among themselves. The fact that they were not carried out was due to the Bolshevist revolution of 1917 and the Turkish Nationalist uprising rather than to any change of heart. The secret agreements provided that: (a) Russia was to get Constantinople and the Straits, with free port rights reserved to Britain and France; (b) Italy was to obtain a vast region in southwestern Anatolia, with a zone east of it carved out for the French; (c) the Arab states were to be turned over to Britain; and (d) Italy was to get Smyrna and its hinterland. The Treaty of Sèvres of 1920, which had incorporated all these provisions, was negated by the Treaty of Lausanne in 1923.

Bibliography

(At the end of Chapter XXVII)

PART III

PART III

CHAPTER XIV

CENTRAL-EASTERN EUROPE IN INTERNATIONAL RELATIONS (1914-1945)

Background and Summary

THE past and present international relations of the Baltic-Aegean area can be explained, in the simplest terms, by the question: "Who is to dominate Central-Eastern Europe?" In other words, the attempts of various powers to dominate the region, in the past as well as in the present, and the counter-action resulting from opposition to such imperialistic ambitions have been the essence of the international problems there. Whenever some great power, such as the Ottoman or the Habsburg or the Nazi Empire, succeeded in gaining temporary control of a part of this region, its domination was invariably challenged and eventually brought about the Empire's downfall.

From that standpoint, World War I ended with the defeat of Germany's ambition to control Central-Eastern Europe. The peace treaties changed the pressure on the Danubian Basin and the Balkans. The huge and unwieldy Austro-Hungarian Dual Monarchy, a satellite of Germany, was broken up. Austria and Hungary were made into separate countries, too small to play an important aggressive role. Poland was restored to the map of Europe. Czechoslovakia was created out of territory that had been part of the Dual Monarchy. Yugoslavia represented a synthesis of the former nations of Serbia and Montenegro plus a large slice of Austria-Hungary. Romania was given part of what had been Hungary and some of Bulgaria. The boundaries of Greece and Albania were not changed much, although the Greek frontiers were not finally settled until the end of the war with Turkey in 1922. Bulgaria, Germany's former ally, lost again its part of Dobrudja, Macedonia, and access to the Aegean Sea. Russia's losses resulted in the formation of four Baltic states—Lithuania, Latvia, Estonia, and Finland.

The first post-war decade was characterized by efforts at stabilization by all Central-Eastern European states. They were handicapped not only by economic and social difficulties, but also by the perpetual problem of minorities. The peace treaties tried to satisfy various racial and nationalistic ambitions by redrawing boundaries and creating new states. But the peoples were so mixed that racial and political lines could not be made to correspond. Consequently, every one of the Central-Eastern European countries contained "minorities." For example, the new boundaries left a good many Magyars in Czechoslovakia, Romania, and Yugoslavia. Most of the people in Hungary were resentful because so many Magyars had been taken from Hungary and because they believed that their kinsmen were badly treated in their new countries. On the other hand, Hungary's neighbors complained, not without justice, that non-Hungarians in Hungary were worse off than Hungarians living in the Little Entente states. The Bulgars thought that they should have southeastern Yugoslavia (Macedonia) because so many Bulgars lived there. The Macedonian problem and the resulting policy of terrorism agitated Europe, and the exchange of populations between Greece and Turkey was followed by serious internal and international repercussions.

With such a background, it is easy to understand why the Central-Eastern European states did not settle down peacefully after the war. Political upsets, frequently accompanied by assassinations, followed one another in rapid succession. Czechoslovakia, which had aptly been called "an island of democracy in a sea of dictatorships," was the only country that escaped such troubles up to 1938.

Back of the bickering of these small states appeared the more dangerous shadows of the great powers and their readiness to use their satellites as pawns in the larger game of European politics. After the war, the main trend of international relations in the region hinged on two major conflicts: the efforts of Italy and then of Germany to replace French and British influence in the region; and the struggle between the centripetal force of some form of Danubian or Balkan or Baltic coöperation, with Franco-British encouragement, and the centrifugal pull of the new German *Drang nach Osten*. Soviet Russia at first attempted little or no intervention in the region on national or Pan-Slavic lines.

For fifteen years after World War I the region was essentially an arena for clashing French and Italian interests. The second period began when a third rival, Germany, appeared on the scene and systematically developed her *Mitteleuropa* policy. The dismemberment of Czechoslovakia in September, 1938, by Hitler, in coöperation with Mussolini, Chamberlain, and Daladier—but without Stalin—marked the end of an epoch, the end of the whole system of collective security, the formal abdication by the western democracies of their influence in the region.

Munich, in short, meant that the system built up by the peace treaties was smashed by the revisionist powers, headed by Hitler's Germany. All attempts to block Germany's "Push to the East"—by the Little Entente, the Balkan Entente, or the Baltic Entente (all designed to uphold the provisions of the peace treaties)—went by the board.

France's hold on Central-Eastern Europe began to dissolve when Hitler became Chancellor of the Reich on January 30, 1933. Vain attempts had been made to substitute some form of "Danubian Confederation" for the hegemony of one dominant power. But the universal post-war tendency to seek self-sufficiency within even the smallest economic units prevented the realization of any far-reaching scheme of economic coöperation, including the Little Entente (originally designed to keep Hungary from regaining her territories lost to Czechoslovakia, Yugoslavia, and Romania). The division of Europe into victorious *status quo* powers and defeated revisionist states, plus the tendency of the great states to impose their own rivalries and dissensions on Central-Eastern Europe, checkmated all attempts at effective political or economic union.

While Italy was engaged in the Ethiopian venture, Germany took advantage of the situation to establish her hold on Central and Balkan Europe. Even the measures taken by Russia—which joined the League of Nations in 1934 and concluded alliances with France and Czechoslovakia in 1935—could not stop the growing pressure exerted by Germany. After the absorption of Austria, Munich was a long step in the plan to restore Germany's pre-war and wartime influence over Danubian and Balkan Europe, which stretches on both sides of the "transversal Eurasian axis." This axis contained most valuable resources—the oil fields of Romania and Mosul, and the granaries of Romania, Yugoslavia, and the Ukraine. Central-Eastern Europe was to the Nazis what the West once was to America, a sort of backdoor colony and source of supplies.

After the German seizure of Czechoslovakia, the war began in Poland. Russia had a pact with Germany, chiefly because she was not at all convinced that the western democracies really wanted to fight Hitler. During this maneuvering period, the Baltic states and Finland had to bow to Russian demands based on Moscow's decision not to allow them to become bases for coming German aggression.

But then came the first major step in Hitler's downfall. He signed his future death warrant when he attacked Russia. The course of the war, which was to become a world war in every sense of the word, was to allow him to conquer all the key points along the transversal Eurasian axis in Europe—only to lose them again as the United Nations, particularly Russia, began to push his hordes back into Germany. With the defeat of Germany in 1945, Russia became the dominant power between the Baltic and the Aegean. The coördination of Russia's foreign policies with those of Great Britain and the United States was the most important problem facing the Allies at the end of World War II. The decisions to be made in Central-Eastern Europe were to be the crucial test confronting the Allies after the defeat of Germany.*

*   *   *   *   *   *

Three factors merit analysis as a background for the study of international relations since the end of World War I. The first is the system of alliances which determined European political orientations before 1914. Friendships and alliances between nations are by no means eternal. History has often witnessed changes which transformed today's friends into tomorrow's enemies. Yet the diplomatic alignment of Europe before Sarajevo continued to exert its influence long after the alliances which were responsible for the famous division of Europe into two camps had been torn to shreds. Second, the secret treaties drawn up during the First World War need to be considered. They sketch the basis on which new friendships were to rest and present a picture of the future world as the leaders of that imperialistic era envisioned it. Failure to attain the goals which had been secretly promised angered imperialist-minded patriots and helped to undermine the Wilsonian idealism which had been advanced as a counterplan for a new order. Third, it is necessary to review the main provisions of the peace settlements. These were, in essence, an amalgam of the promises of the secret treaties, democratic international idealism, awakened nationalism, and the new social revolutionary ideology which had gripped Russia.

Pre-War Alliances

The Triple Alliance. In the nineteenth century, the great mass of Central Europe—the Germanies, the Danube Basin, and Italy—which had once had at least a titular unity under the Holy Roman Empire, was divided into three main units: Germany, Austria-Hungary, and

---

* The above summary paragraphs were written by the editor.

Italy. These three states made agreements which constituted what became known as the Triple Alliance. Romania, under the leadership of the Hohenzollern Carol I, threw in her lot with this group in 1883. Between 1881 and 1895, Serbia also was allied with Austria-Hungary, but afterward she gradually developed close ties with Russia. Plenty of differences existed among the Triple Alliance partners, but they were officially pledged to follow a common policy.

The Triple Entente. A counterbalance took shape soon after the Triple Alliance was created. In a series of military conventions negotiated from 1891 to 1894, Russia and France entered into what amounted to an alliance. Great Britain finally settled her outstanding disagreements with France in 1904 and with Russia in 1907. In these settlements, which came to be called "Ententes," England made no hard and fast promises of military aid. But, with the passage of time, conversations between military and naval leaders and coöperation in the various crises bound the three great powers of the Triple Entente quite as closely.

Certain other powers gravitated into the orbit of the Triple Entente. In 1902 Japan entered into a treaty of alliance with Great Britain, and Japanese relations with France and Russia were clarified in important agreements negotiated in 1907. France reached certain understandings with Italy (1900-1902) which virtually gave the Italians a foot in both camps. After many years of difficult negotiation, Russia was temporarily successful in fashioning a Balkan League consisting of Serbia, Bulgaria, Greece, and Montenegro (1912).

The Balkan Wars of 1912-1913 somewhat altered this situation.[1] In the first war, the Balkan League successfully drove the Turks out of most of the Balkan peninsula. Differences arose as to the division of the spoils, and in a second war Serbia, Greece, and Montenegro, with the help of Romania, defeated their former ally Bulgaria. The victorious group of powers favored the Triple Entente, while Bulgaria and Turkey were inclined toward the Triple Alliance. Romania, like Italy, was carrying water on both shoulders.

The Treaties of the First World War

Central Powers and their allies. With the outbreak of war in 1914, Italy and Romania declared their neutrality. They maintained that the

[1] On the various problems connected with the Balkan Wars, see Ernst C. Helmreich, *The Diplomacy of the Balkan Wars, 1912-1913* (Cambridge: Harvard University Press, 1938); E. C. Helmreich, "The Conflict Between Germany and Austria Over Balkan Policy, 1913-1914," *Essays in the History of Modern Europe,* ed. by Donald C. McKay (New York: Harpers, 1936), pp. 130-148.

Central Powers were engaged in an offensive war which they did not feel committed to support. Austria-Hungary offered territorial concessions to both Romania and Italy to entice them into the war on her side, or even as a reward for their continued neutrality. In each case, however, the Entente Powers outbid the Austrians.

Although Germany and Austria-Hungary lost the support of these two allies, they won the coöperation of Turkey by a treaty signed on August 2, 1914. Two months later Turkey entered the war. On August 6, 1914, Turkey and Bulgaria concluded a treaty which had long been on the fire. On September 6, 1915, Bulgaria signed a treaty which brought her into the war on the side of the Central Powers. Bulgaria was to receive the greater part of Macedonia and also the territory she had lost to Romania and Greece in 1913. These were much the same territorial prizes which Hitler was again to dangle before the Bulgarians several decades later. Beyond proclaiming an independent Poland in November, 1916, to be created out of former Russian territory, the Central Powers bound themselves to no further territorial distribution. They never drew up such definite treaties of partition as the Entente Powers.

Secret arrangements by the Entente Powers. Grand Duke Nikolai, in the early days of the war, promised to erect a reunited Poland out of German, Austrian, and Russian territories. It was to have a status of autonomy within the Russian Empire. Both sides thus tried to win Polish assistance. Romania, as we have seen, was formally bound to the Central Powers but inclining toward the Entente. In negotiations from 1914 to 1916, for the most part carried on from Petrograd, the Entente awarded to Romania the Austro-Hungarian territories which were largely inhabited by Romanians and also made arrangements to send them military supplies. On August 27, 1916, Romania came into the war on the Allied side.

When Turkey entered the war on October 31, 1914, the Entente Powers soon made plans for the partition of her territories. By the end of December, 1914, England had annexed Cyprus and Egypt, and France had annexed Morocco. On March 18, 1915, Great Britain, France, and Russia signed an agreement by which Russia was to obtain the territory Turkey still possessed in Europe: the city of Constantinople and additional lands which would have given Russia complete control of the Bosporus and one side of the Dardanelles. France and England received certain trade guarantees for the region of the Straits and the promise of certain territories to be defined later. Arabia was to be reorganized into independent Mohammedan states.

About a month after the entente allies had thus begun the liquidation of Turkey, they concluded the most famous secret treaty of all. This was the Treaty of London of April 26, 1915, by which Italy promised to enter the war within one month.[2] The Italians drove a good bargain. In Europe they were to obtain the Trentino, the German Tyrol to the Brenner frontier, Trieste, most of Istria, Dalmatia, various islands along the coast, and the Albanian port of Valona with the island of Saseno. Italian possession of the Dodecanese Islands, which had been seized from Turkey in the Tripolitan War of 1911-12, was also recognized. Russia did not like these territorial concessions, as they conflicted with the territorial grants which she had in mind for Serbia. Here then were planted the seeds of Italian-Yugoslav antagonism in the post-war period.

France and England did not find it difficult to hand over this territory along the Adriatic, which did not belong to them. They were vague about two areas where they had more direct interests—Asia Minor and the German colonies. In Asia Minor, Italy was to receive the region adjacent to the province of Adalia "which should be delimited at the proper time, due account being taken of the existing interests of France and Great Britain." Italy was never guaranteed a share in the German colonies but was promised compensation if France and Britain should seize them.

By the end of 1915, the Allies found it necessary to work out the partition of Turkey in more detail. Under the terms of the Sykes-Picot agreement of May, 1916, Russia was to obtain northeast Asia Minor; France was to get Syria, Adana, and a middle strip running northward to the future Russian and Persian frontiers; England was to obtain southern Mesopotamia, including Baghdad and Basra, and also the important Syrian ports of Haifa and Acre. The territory between the French and British zones was to be reserved for the creation of French- and British-dominated Arab states. Palestine and Alexandria were to be under international control.[3]

The Sykes-Picot agreement was contrary to pledges which Britain had made to the Sherif of Mecca, and also to the promises made to Italy in the Treaty of London. As soon as news of the agreement leaked to Rome, the Italians clamored for their additional pound of Turkish flesh. On April 17, 1917, the Prime Ministers of Great Britain, France, and Italy negotiated an agreement at St. Jean de Maurienne

---

[2] For text of the treaty, see H. W. V. Temperley, *A History of the Peace Conference of Paris,* 6 vols. (London: Henry Frowde and Hodder & Stoughton, 1920-1924), V, 384-393.

[3] See the map in Temperley, *History of the Peace Conference,* VI, 6.

whereby Italy's share of Asia Minor was expanded to include Smyrna. This agreement was to be ratified by Russia before it became valid, but the new revolutionary government never got around to it. Technically, therefore, France and England were not bound by these promises, but this was an argument which only irritated the Italians when it was advanced later. Nor were matters smoothed out at the peace table by the fact that Smyrna had at various times been held out as bait to the Greeks.[4]

Proposed partition of Germany and Austria-Hungary. While the Entente Powers were most explicit in their proposed liquidation of Turkey, Germany and Austria-Hungary were not ignored. After long discussions, France and Russia exchanged notes on February 14, 1917, defining their respective interests. France was to annex Alsace-Lorraine and the Saar Valley and was to dominate an autonomous neutral state to be created out of the remainder of German territory west of the Rhine. In return Russia was granted complete freedom to determine her western frontiers. This *carte blanche* of course meant that Russia expected to reap rich territorial gains at the expense of Germany and Austria-Hungary.

As already pointed out, Romania had been promised Transylvania and other portions of Hungary in September, 1916. As early as February of that same year, Masaryk had exacted from France a promise of help in establishing an independent Czechoslovak state. In July, 1917, England and France assured Pašić, the great leader of the Serbians, that a large South Slav state would be created after the war out of Serbia, Montenegro, Bosnia-Herzegovina, Croatia, and various other provinces of Austria-Hungary. In April, 1918, Italy welcomed representatives of the various nationalities of the Dual Monarchy and recognized the right of each nationality to independence in a solemn Pact of Rome. Clearly if the Habsburgs were to retain anything at all, it would be only a small rump Austria and Hungary.

Effects of the Russian revolution. All these agreements meant that Central-Eastern Europe was due for a radical reorganization. The difficulty was that very often the same territory was promised to and claimed by a number of states. Moreover, everything was predicated upon Russian participation in the Peace Conference. So the Russian revolution upset all these well-laid plans.

After this revolution, France and England went so far as to carry on the good work by dividing up the southern provinces of their former

---

[4] Howard, Harry N., *The Partition of Turkey. A Diplomatic History 1913-1923* (Norman: University of Oklahoma Press, 1931), pp. 148-152.

ally into spheres of influence. On December 23, 1917, they agreed that England was to be dominant in the section around the Caspian Sea, which would have given her control of the valuable oil deposits of the Caucasus. France in turn was to control the more westerly sections, which would have brought her the coal and iron deposits of the Donetz Basin. At that time it looked as if Russia was going to break up into small component parts, and it is always well to be prepared.

The publication by the Bolsheviks of the various secret agreements and Moscow's bitter denunciations of the imperialistic aims of the Entente did much to discredit all the secret treaties. In order to offset their bad influence on world opinion, President Wilson announced a new program in his Fourteen Points to which the Entente Powers were forced at least to pay lip service. But the fact that they never entirely surrendered the aims of the secret treaties is amply demonstrated by the peace treaties themselves.

The Peace Settlements

Treaty of Brest-Litovsk. The history of the peace treaties, particularly as they affect Central-Eastern Europe, must start with a consideration of the peace negotiations between Germany and Russia.[5] The overthrow of the Tsar in March, 1917, placed in control of Russian affairs a liberal government which was anxious to continue the war and obtain the territorial prizes that had been promised to the old regime. When Lenin took over the government in November, 1917, and organized the Bolshevik phase of the Russian revolution, he gained support by announcing a program of peace, bread, and distribution of land to the peasants. It is clear that Lenin, in inaugurating armistice negotiations with the Germans, hoped that all the powers would soon join and a general peace would be concluded.

The Western Powers, however, refused to listen to any such suggestions. The Soviet delegates met with German, Austro-Hungarian, Bulgarian, and Turkish negotiators at Brest-Litovsk. Delegates from the government of the Ukraine, which had assumed more and more independence ever since the overthrow of the Tsar, arrived a few days later. Much to the disgust of the Russians, these delegates were granted an official status. In fact, a treaty between the Central Powers and the Ukraine signed on February 9, 1918, was the first of the long series of peace treaties. The Austrians were particularly concerned

---

[5] The standard work on this settlement is John W. Wheeler-Bennett, *The Forgotten Peace, Brest-Litovsk, March 1918* (New York: William Morrow & Co., 1939).

with this settlement because they hoped to obtain immediate grain deliveries to alleviate the starvation which threatened Vienna and other large cities.

The Bolshevik leaders had hoped that a revolution would break out in Germany as well as in other countries and that a satisfactory and equitable peace could then be arranged by brother proletarians. But Lenin soon realized that the hour for the world revolution had not struck. Contrary to the wishes of Trotsky, he advocated the immediate signature of the treaty with Germany, even if the terms were drastic. After all, it was to be only an interlude, a step backward perhaps, but one that was necessary in order to take two steps forward. His primary objective was to save the Russian revolution. So the Peace of Brest-Litovsk was signed on March 3, 1918.

Strangely enough, both Germans and Russians were proclaiming the self-determination of nations at that time. The Germans had already officially established their version of an independent Poland and favored the creation of new Baltic states on the same model. Russia was forced to renounce her sovereignty in the territory west of a line running from the Gulf of Riga to a short distance above Dvinsk and then bending southwest to the border of the Ukraine at Pruzhany. In a supplementary treaty of August 27, 1918, Russia also gave up her last claims to Estonia and Livonia. In the south, Russia had to evacuate eastern Anatolia and the Russian-Turkish districts which had been annexed in 1878 (Ardahan, Kars, and Batum). Turkey eventually acquired the greater part of these districts.[6]

The Ukraine. The hardest blow of all to the Russians was the fact that they were compelled to conclude peace at once with the Ukrainian Republic and to recognize the treaty of peace between the Ukrainians and the Central Powers. The Ukraine was in turmoil. The Bolsheviks were sponsoring and supporting with arms a government in opposition to the one recognized by Germany and Austria. German troops were extending their zones of occupation. Ukrainian leaders hoped that Ukrainian nationalism would culminate in an independent state.[7]

Such a state met with German and Austrian approval. If they had not lost the war, a separatist Ukraine would no doubt have been maintained. On the other hand, it is worth noting that the Ukrainian leaders continued their fight for independence after the German collapse. Even after the Ukraine was controlled by the Bolsheviks, a separate

---

[6] Saucerman, Sophia, *International Transfers of Territory in Europe* (Washington: Government Printing Office, 1937), p. 100.

[7] Allen, W. E. D., *The Ukraine* (Cambridge: University Press, 1940), pp. 276ff.

status was maintained for some years. For example, the Treaty of Riga of March 18, 1921, expressly provided that Poland and Russia, "in accordance with the principles of national self-determination, recognize the independence of the Ukraine and of White Russia."[8] It was not until the formation of the Union of Socialist Soviet Republics (U.S.S.R.) in 1923 that the Ukraine lost its separate international position. Until then there had been Ukrainian ambassadors or ministers at Prague, Berlin, Moscow, and Vienna.

Brest-Litovsk in retrospect. The Treaty of Brest-Litovsk was a negotiated peace, especially the supplementary agreement of August 27, 1918, in the sense that its terms were drawn up at a conference and were discussed by the negotiators. Literally, however, the main terms were dictated by the Germans and the Russians had to sign. It was a hard peace, but no harder than other treaties which were to follow.

On November 13, 1918, the All-Russian Central Executive Committee of the Soviets unilaterally cancelled the treaty, and in Article 116 of the Treaty of Versailles Germany definitely recognized its abrogation. Yet when the final western boundary of Russia was drawn, more or less under Allied supervision, it was even more disadvantageous to the Russians than the Brest-Litovsk line. The one big difference was that an independent Ukraine had yielded to armed force. Substantial sections which the Germans had attributed to that state now went to Poland, and Romania acquired Bessarabia. Soviet Russia, at the expense of new wars, eventually regained the small states which had declared their independence in the Caucasus. The Entente Powers were not friendly to the Soviet regime and did nothing to help the new Russian Government regain control of old Russian territory.

Treaty of Bucharest. With the cessation of hostilities by Russia, Romania had to follow suit. On December 9, 1917, an armistice was arranged, followed on May 7, 1918, by the Treaty of Bucharest. Under its terms, Romania passed under the economic and political control of the Central Powers. The portion of the Dobrudja which Romania had acquired in 1913 had to be returned to Bulgaria and the portion from this boundary north to the Danube was ceded to the Central Powers jointly. Austria-Hungary was also to obtain boundary rectifications in the Carpathians. Although no definite provisions to that effect were inserted in the treaty, it was understood that the Central

---

[8] It is interesting to note that three texts of the treaty—Polish, Russian, Ukrainian—are published in the *Treaty Series of the League of Nations,* V., pp. 51ff. See also the note on "The Diplomatic Representation Abroad of the Ukrainian S.S.R." in Allen, *The Ukraine,* pp. 338-339. Some Ukrainian nationalists have continued their agitation for an independent Ukraine until the present day.

Powers would have no objection to Romanian acquisition of Bessarabia, a region which Romanian troops then occupied. Once this treaty was signed, the Entente Powers considered their promises to Romania no longer binding.

With the collapse of Bulgaria and Austria-Hungary, however, the Romanian Government denounced the Treaty of Bucharest and reentered the war on November 9, 1918. Romanian troops took possession of the Bukovina and Transylvania and began the advance which was ultimately to carry them beyond Budapest. Unlike Russia, Romania had a seat at the Peace Conference in Paris and was therefore able to confirm tremendous territorial gains.

The Peace Settlement in the Baltic Regions

By the terms of Brest-Litovsk, Russia had been forced to evacuate Finland, the Åland Islands, and those regions of Estonia and Livonia which were not already under German occupation. Finland had declared its independence on December 6, 1917, and by the time Germany collapsed on November 11, 1918, governments with varying degrees of autonomy or independence had been established in Poland, Lithuania, Latvia, and Estonia. Two days after the armistice on the Western Front, Russia denounced the Peace of Brest-Litovsk and began an offensive to regain the Baltic territories. The Red Army pushed forward even before the German forces withdrew. On December 8, 1918, Lenin signed a decree appointing a "Government of Soviet Estonia," followed on December 23 by similar proclamations for Latvia and Lithuania. Stalin was to follow similar tactics some decades later. But the peoples of these regions did not welcome deliverance by the Soviets. They raised armies and fought the Russians.

Under the terms of the Armistice Agreement of November 11, 1918, the German forces were to occupy Russian territories as long "as the Allies consider this desirable," a provision which was incorporated in Article 433 of the Treaty of Versailles. The Allies hoped to use the Germans as police units. This only added to the confusion of the political situation. At times, notably in Finland, the Germans helped to clear Russian forces from the land. At other times, the Germans came in conflict with national Lithuanian, Latvian, and Estonian forces. To complicate matters still further, an anti-Bolshevik White Russian force under General Yudenich, which received some assistance from the Allies, was formed on the Estonian-Russian border for a march on Petrograd. When this force was defeated in October, 1919, and retreated behind the Estonian defense lines, it was disarmed and interned.

The narrative of the warfare by which the Finns, Estonians, Latvians, and Lithuanians, largely through their own efforts, were able eventually to achieve their complete independence from Russia cannot be related in detail here. Again, as at Brest-Litovsk, Russia was forced to bide her time and conclude unfavorable peace treaties. She was particularly anxious to assure trade connections through the Baltic states and thus break the Entente blockade which was threatening to strangle Russia. The Soviet leaders also wanted peace along the shores of the Baltic so that they could center their attention on bigger game, the winning of Poland.[9] Had Poland fallen, it would have been an easy matter to rearrange the peace treaties which were signed with Estonia, Lithuania, Latvia, and Finland in 1920.

Conflict over Lithuania's borders. These treaties were all cut to the same pattern. The boundaries between the Baltic states and Russia were fixed. The Estonian-Latvian and Latvian-Lithuanian borders were left to direct negotiation between these states and were settled with little difficulty. The boundary between Poland and Lithuania, however, was another matter.

In the treaty with Russia, Lithuania had been promised possession of its ancient capital, the city and district of Vilna. In the course of history the city of Vilna had become largely populated by Poles, and Poland had taken possession of it by driving out the Russians in April, 1919. In their victorious advance against Poland in July, 1920, the Red Army in turn cleared Vilna, only to be forced out again a month later. The Russians had invited the Lithuanians into the city. Naturally skirmishes took place between Lithuanian and Polish units, and Poland appealed to the League of Nations.

The whole question of the eastern border of Poland was in flux at the time. In an effort to bring about some stability in the region, the Allied Supreme Council had recommended a certain frontier on July 11, 1920, "as the eastern boundary within which Poland was entitled to establish a Polish administration," the so-called Curzon line. It ran somewhat east of the frontier as defined at Brest-Litovsk.[10] This Curzon line, it should be emphasized, was never proposed as a final boundary but only as a limit which would mark the zone of Polish administration for the

[9] Pusta, Kaarel R., *The Soviet Union and the Baltic States* (New York: John Felsberg, 1943), p. 21.

[10] This demarcation line had been worked out by the Commission on Polish Affairs of the Peace Conference and was part of the Declaration of the Supreme Council of the Allied and Associated Powers of December 8, 1919. The Curzon note of July 11, 1920, took over this line but inadvertently made a mistake as to how it was to run in Eastern Galicia. See the carefully reasoned article by Witold Sivorakowski, "An Error in Curzon's Note," *Journal of Central European Affairs,* IV (April, 1944), pp. 1-26.

time being. According to the Curzon line, Vilna went to Lithuania but the neighboring territory to Poland.

In negotiations at Suwalki, on October 7, 1920, Poland and Lithuania accepted this demarcation. But before the agreement could be put into effect, General Zeligowski, ostensibly acting independently but actually under the orders of Marshal Pilsudski, entered Vilna and established a regime which later united with Poland. After much discussion the great powers recognized the Polish seizure, but Lithuania never did so. The frontier between the two countries remained closed until March, 1938, when Poland overawed the Lithuanians by threat of force.

Possession of Vilna gave Poland a thin strip of territory extending up to the Latvian border, thereby cutting off Lithuania from any direct contact with Russia. This very separation from Russia as well as rancor against Poland over Vilna and against Germany over Memel tended to improve Russo-Lithuanian relations in subsequent years. It should be noted here that in 1923 the Lithuanians, by a mild *coup d'état,* seized the important Memel territory which Germany had been forced to turn over to the Allies in 1919. By this stroke Lithuania obtained an excellent seaport with a total land area of 976 square miles and a population of 145,000, of whom about half were German-speaking and half Lithuanian-speaking. As they had acquiesced in the Polish seizure of Vilna, so did the Allies recognize Lithuania's action, but in this case they insisted that the Memel territory be given a large measure of local autonomy.

Establishment of Poland. As has been indicated, the fate of the Baltic states and of all Eastern Europe was to a great extent dependent upon what happened to Poland. During the First World War, a rather efficient Polish military organization outside of Russia had been recruited under the leadership of Pilsudski. When the Germans wanted to incorporate these forces into the German Army in April, 1917, by forcing them to take an oath of loyalty to the Kaiser as commander-in-chief, Pilsudski balked. He resigned his seat in the Council of State and was soon imprisoned. In November, 1918, when the Germans were preparing to retreat, Pilsudski was the logical man to organize a Polish Army. The Germans facilitated his return to Warsaw, where almost superhuman tasks awaited him.

Polish governments existed in Posen, in Lublin, in Cracow, and in Warsaw, and there was also a Polish National Committee installed in Paris which had been recognized by the Allies. This latter body was headed by Dmowski, an old political rival of Pilsudski. While seeking to establish a unified political leadership—which was achieved in a measure through the election of a Diet on January 20, 1919, and the subsequent appointment of Paderewski as Premier—Pilsudski undertook to organize an army and to occupy the territory which he hoped would constitute the future Polish state. Poland was created even more by this armed conflict, which lasted until 1921, than by the actions of diplomats at the Peace Conference of Paris.

The problem of Galicia. Galicia, which had been part of the Austrian Empire, was divided for judicial purposes into Western Galicia, with Cracow as its center, and Eastern Galicia, with its capital at Lemberg (Lwow). Western Galicia is almost solidly Polish and passed under Polish control immediately after the collapse of Austria. Eastern Galicia, on the other hand, especially in the easterly portions, is inhabited by many Ruthenians and Jews. There was never much of a dispute about the portions of Eastern Galicia west of the river San, which was almost entirely Polish in population, but there were serious disputes over the portions east of the San. Here the Ukrainians (Ruthenians) entered the lists against the Poles and besieged the city of Lemberg. This city and its immediate vicinity is largely Polish and was able to hold out until Pilsudski sent reinforcements.

The Allies were far from agreed as to what should be done with the territory. All of the delegations except the British favored Polish acquisition under special safeguards. The Ukrainians were not well represented at Paris or on the battlefield. In June, 1919, the Poles, with the blessing of the Allies, occupied all of Eastern Galicia as a safeguard against the spreading tide of Bolshevism. Finally on March 15, 1923, the Supreme Council awarded Poland full possession of this territory.

Polish-Russian conflict. This latter decision was largely influenced by continuing warfare in this part of the world. In the spring of 1919, the Poles not only fought the Ukrainians in Galicia, but also clashed with the Czechs over Teschen, Spiš (Szeps), and Orava (Árva), with the Germans in various districts (notably in Posen), and with the Russians. Tentative peace negotiations with Russia came to nothing and active warfare broke out in April, 1920. This time Pilsudski, in the hope of setting up a Ukrainian state which might eventually federate with Poland, entered into an agreement with the Ukrainian leader Petlura. Having been left at the mercy of the Red Army by the withdrawal of the Germans and the defeat of the White Russian Armies, Petlura in desperation decided to coöperate with the Poles.

After initial victories, which extended even to the capture of Kiev, the Poles were driven back to the gates of Warsaw. A soviet Polish government was set up at Bialystok, headed by Polish Communists. Poland meanwhile appealed frantically for aid. France sent General Weygand and an able corps of officers as well as supplies. Incidentally a strike of longshoremen in Danzig and their refusal at this critical time to unload a ship with Polish military supplies had important repercussions later. The need of building an all-Polish port at Gdynia, even at great financial sacrifice, was brought home to all Poles. By mid-August Pilsudski and Weygand were ready to strike. Their daring military strategy proved successful and the Russians were forced to a general retreat. Congress Poland, Galicia, and large sections of White Russia were soon under Polish occupation.

On October 12, 1920, Russia and Poland signed an armistice and preliminaries of peace at Riga. This peace was finally ratified and went into effect on April 30, 1921. Under its terms, Poland gained about 100,000 square miles of territory beyond the temporary boundary line proposed by Lord Curzon. Only 30 per cent of the 4,000,000 population were Polish, even according to Polish figures. White Russians and Ukrainians, each numbering about 22 per cent, were the next largest groups. Poland still had not obtained her historic eastern borders of 1772, but she had acquired more territory than current ethnographic frontiers justified.

Danzig and the Corridor. Poland's western frontiers were carefully determined by the Treaty of Versailles. Point thirteen of Wilson's program had provided: "An independent Polish state should be erected, which should include the territories inhabited by indisputably Polish populations which should be assured a free and secure access to the sea, and whose political and economic independence and territorial integrity should be guaranteed by international covenant." What territories were indisputably Polish? How was Poland to be assured free access to the sea? A plan was devised, largely under American leadership, to grant Poland a strip of territory along the Vistula extending to the Baltic.

Historically this province of West Prussia had been wrested from the control of Polish rulers by the Teutonic Knights about 1308, to be retaken in 1466. The province had always maintained a large measure of self-government. In 1772 it went to Prussia in the First Partition of Poland. The important city of Danzig had much the same history except that it was not awarded to Prussia until the Second Partition of Poland in 1793 and was a Free City during the period of Napoleonic domination (1807-14).

Since the city was overwhelmingly German in population, and also since Britain was interested in having an international trade center in this Baltic area, Danzig was again constituted a Free City, under the League of Nations, in 1919. The League was to be represented by a High Commissioner with certain supervisory rights and Danzig was to choose its own local governing officials. Poland was awarded certain special rights which were regulated by a treaty between Danzig and Poland on November 9, 1920, and subsequently modified at various times. Polish rights along the waterfront were carefully regulated. Danzig was incorporated into the Polish customs frontier and Poland was to conduct the city's foreign relations.

In addition to West Prussia—which in general practice has been labeled the "Corridor," since it separates East Prussia from the rest of Germany, but which the Poles call "Pomorze" and consider an integral part of Poland—Poland was granted outright the neighboring provinces of Posen (Posnania) and a small section of Middle Silesia.[11] Various other territories were also demanded by the Polish representatives at the Peace Conference. Largely because of the insistence of the British delegation, plebiscites were ordered for these regions. The Poles have sometimes maintained that the balloting would have turned out differently if it had not occurred at a moment when Polish fortunes were at a low ebb. The voting in the Marienwelder and Allenstein areas, however, was decisive in favor of remaining with Germany.

Upper Silesia. The plebiscite in Upper Silesia was a far more complicated affair and was not held until March 20, 1921. In this case 707,605 votes and 844 communes favored Germany, whereas 479,359 votes and 675 communes favored Poland. In the treaty specifying the conditions under which the plebiscite was to be held, it was provided that the vote should be taken by communes and that an International Commission should then determine the boundary.

The French members of the International Commission proposed a line very favorable to the Poles. The British demurred, but their line in turn was rejected, as was the compromise line suggested by the Italian member. Unable to reach a decision, the Commission dumped the problem into the lap of the League of Nations, agreeing in advance to approve its award. Meanwhile armed clashes between Poles and Germans had occurred.

The Council appointed a committee of representatives from Belgium, Spain, China, and Brazil to fix the frontier. Their decision pleased no

---

[11] For population figures, see Temperley, *History of the Peace Conference* (London: Frowde, 1921-24), II, 214. In regard to this whole eastern settlement, see Ian F. D. Morrow, *The Peace Settlement in the German-Polish Borderlands* (London: Oxford University Press, 1936).

one. Poland was given the greater share of the mineral wealth and industrial establishments of the region. The Germans, on the other hand, received about two-thirds of the total area. Each side received a substantial minority population, about 572,000 Poles remaining in Germany and 350,000 Germans being transferred to Poland. To provide protection for these minorities and to regulate many other matters, a detailed "Upper Silesian Convention" was concluded between Germany and Poland on May 15, 1922.

It was easy to point out that the boundary line was absurdly drawn. For example, "in some places coal mines had been divided so that the shafts are on one side and the pits on the other; a zinc mine has the mine proper on one side, the plant to wash the zinc on the other. Iron foundries are cut off from their sources of supply. Electrical systems, transportation systems, roads—all are cut by the new frontier. Even water works are divided—the water tower of the German city of Beuthen, for instance, being now in Poland." [12]   Details like these often arouse indignation and antagonism far beyond their real significance.

Polish-Czechoslovak boundary. From Austria, Poland claimed the territory of Teschen, a valuable industrial and communications center. Both Poles and Czechs inhabited this area and in January, 1919, while the Poles were busy fighting for Lemberg (Lwow), Czechoslovakia sent troops to occupy this territory, dispersing the small Polish garrison. Similar situations developed at Spiš and Orava, two small border districts which had formerly been part of Hungary. Finally the two contestants agreed to abide by the decision of a plebiscite. It was never held, as the Council of Ambassadors intervened and made an award in July, 1920, which was on the whole favorable to Czechoslovakia. At that time the Bolsheviks were at the gates of Warsaw and Poland was beseeching aid from the western powers. Ever since the Poles have felt that they were forced to accept this settlement under duress. It was the basic cause of Polish-Czech antagonism in the next two decades. Under cover of Hitler's action, Poland forced Czechoslovakia to yield these territories to her in 1938.

Poland had not only achieved her independence but, thanks to her aggressive policy, had obtained frontiers which aroused antagonism on all sides. The only neighbors with whom she had anything approximating peaceful frontier relations were Romania and Latvia, and in these cases the frontiers were relatively short. Poland, bitten by the

---

[12] "German-Polish Relations," *Foreign Policy Association Information Service*, III (August 17, 1927), 180; see also *The Cambridge History of Poland from Augustus II to Pilsudski, 1697-1935* (Cambridge: University Press, 1941), pp. 514-519.

desire to be a great power, aimed to make herself the decisive factor in the historic struggle to maintain a balance of power in Europe.

The Peace Settlement in the Danubian Basin

The tenth point of Wilson's famous fourteen as announced on January 8, 1918, proclaimed:

"The peoples of Austria-Hungary, whose place among the nations we wish to see safeguarded and assured, should be accorded the freest opportunity of autonomous development."

The phrase "autonomous development" was vague, but hardly went as far as the commitments which had already been made by Russia, France, and England.

As negotiations for the armistice got under way in September and October of 1918, Austrian leaders attempted to reorganize the state along national lines. An effort to create a cabinet from leaders of all the nationalities collapsed and in desperation the Emperor, on October 16, issued a manifesto establishing a federal state. Members from the various nations elected to the *Reichsrat* were to form National Councils. When news of the manifesto reached Budapest, the Hungarian Premier declared that in future the connection between Austria and Hungary would be reduced to a personal union. Henceforth Hungary would settle all political and economic questions independently.

The Manifesto of October 16 was never applied in practice. It was, however, useful in paving the way for a peaceful dissolution of the monarchy. National Committees met and proclaimed the establishment of independent Czech-Slovak, Serb-Croat-Slovene, and German-Austrian states. The Poles threw in their lot with Warsaw and the Ruthenians cast their eyes toward the Ukraine. The Austrian government did not think of using armed force to put down these national uprisings, as had been the policy in 1848.

By this time Wilson was no longer talking of autonomy but of independence for the subject nationalities. The Austrian Germans and the Hungarians also demanded their own independence from the Habsburgs and hoped that their states would be recognized as new entities. Unfortunately for them, they were called upon to negotiate an armistice with Italy on November 3, 1918, and with Serbia ten days later. The new Austria and the new Hungary, in spite of their demand to be treated like Czechoslovakia or Yugoslavia, were considered as the successor states of the old enemy—Habsburg Austria-Hungary. As such

they were summoned to the Conference at Paris to sign a peace treaty
with the victorious allied and associated powers.

General boundary problems. To a great extent the peace negotiators
were faced with a *fait accompli.* No sooner had the old monarchy collapsed than Czechs, Slovaks, Poles, Ruthenians, Romanians, Yugo-
Slavs, and Italians began to occupy the territories they expected to possess. Although the major territorial divisions were thus ordained in
advance, the various commissions of the Peace Conference had plenty
of work to do to settle disputed frontier zones.

Unfortunately ethnographic boundaries did not coincide with religious dioceses, with strategic frontiers, or with clearly marked economic units. Railroads and roads had been laid out to serve a large
mid-Danubian empire and tended to center in Vienna or Budapest.
Now these same lines of communication were expected to serve a number of jealous independent sovereignties. It did not seem wise to have
a railway repeatedly meander in and out of two neighboring states, and
boundaries were drawn accordingly. Political considerations, particularly the idea that since Austria and Hungary had lost the war they
should therefore expiate their past sins, were the constant background
of all decisions.

Plebiscites were denied except in two cases. In the Klagenfurt area,
the people voted to remain with Austria rather than join Yugoslavia.
The Burgenland (a German-populated region of Hungary close to
Vienna) went to the Austrian Republic without any plebiscite, but the
Hungarians were able to win back Sopron (Ödenburg), the provincial
capital, by means of a plebiscite held in 1921. In no other regions of
the Dual Monarchy were the people asked to express an opinion as to
what state they wished to join.

Treaty of St. Germain. On July 20 the Austrian delegation was
presented with the proposed treaty, which was signed with some modifications at St. Germain on September 10, 1919. In many ways it
was patterned on the Treaty of Versailles. Similar provisions dealing
with the League of Nations, labor, reparations, and disarmament were
included. The new Austrian Republic was forced to recognize cessions of old Austrian territory: Bukovina to Romania; Galicia and a
small part of Silesia to Poland; Bohemia and Moravia to Czechoslovakia; parts of Styria, Carinthia, Carniola, Istria, and Dalmatia to Yugoslavia; and Trieste, parts of Istria, Tyrol, and bits of other provinces to
Italy.

Appealing to the doctrine of self-determination, the Austrian Republic laid claim to some of the German sections of Bohemia. These

claims were denied, as were also Austrian protests against adding the
German-populated portions of Tyrol to Italy. Austria was likewise
forced to forego its desire to unite with the newly created Weimar Republic of Germany. Had the Allies not forbidden it, there can be little
doubt that *Anschluss* would have taken place at this time. Both Austria and Germany inserted statements in their first constitutions looking
toward this solution.

Treaty of Trianon. Although the Peace Conference had reached
most of its decisions much earlier, the peace terms were not submitted
to the Hungarians until January 15, 1920, and were not signed until
June 4, 1920, at Trianon. This delay is explained by events in Hungary
itself which are discussed in other chapters.

The conservative governing group headed by Admiral Horthy, who
finally signed the treaty, represented the same class that took their
country into the war in 1914. Yet they fared the same as the democrats and socialists in Germany and Austria. Slovakia and sub-Carpathian Ruthenia were ceded to Czechoslovakia; Croatia and Slavonia
and a goodly portion of the Banat of Temesvár to Yugoslavia; and the
rest of the Banat and Transylvania went to Romania. As already mentioned, Burgenland (except for the city of Sopron) went to Austria, and
the city and district of Fiume were eventually to be divided between
Italy and Yugoslavia. There is a good deal of evidence to support the
Hungarian claim that many of the people of these regions or parts of
the regions might well have voted to remain with Hungary even if they
were not Magyars racially. But no plebiscites were held. In all, about
three and a half million Magyars were destined to live in neighboring
countries, many of them in large blocs close to the frontier.

The Peace Settlement in the Balkans

The peace treaties just discussed show how unsatisfactory it is to
divide eastern Europe arbitrarily into a Danube Basin and a Balkan
Peninsula. Romania, Yugoslavia, and Bulgaria are Danubian states,
but they must also be considered as Balkan. The Turkish settlement
ties up the Balkans with the whole problem of the Near East in similar
fashion. National-political interests simply do not coincide with neatly
drawn geographic areas.

Bulgaria and the war. Bulgaria entered the war on October 14, 1915,
and soon won from Serbia much of the territory which had been promised her by the Central Powers. The French and English, with the
consent of Premier Venizelos but against the opposition of King Constantine and most of the Greek people, had landed troops at the Greek

port of Salonica in October, 1915. It was not until after the forced abdication of King Constantine in 1917, when Greece officially entered the war, that this allied Balkan front achieved any substantial gains. By the spring of 1918, war weariness had gripped the Bulgarian forces. When the Germans not only were unable to furnish reinforcements but withdrew regiments instead, the Bulgarian front collapsed. On September 29, 1918, an armistice was concluded which amounted to unconditional surrender. On October 5, Tsar Ferdinand abdicated and a short time later his eldest son was recognized as Boris III.

The Bulgarian peace delegation under Stambulisky shouldered the responsibility of signing the Treaty of Neuilly on November 27, 1919.[13] Bulgaria lost its coastline on the Aegean to Greece but was accorded certain rights of transit and port privileges. Four small but important areas centering in Strumitsa, Bosilgrad, Tsarbrod, and the river Timok went to Yugoslavia, while Romania regained the Dobrudja. Like all the other defeated states, Bulgaria's armament was limited, but the definite reparations bill of $450,000,000 was an improvement over the indefinite and more burdensome reparation charges of the other treaties.

The Turkish problem. On September 30, 1918, the day after Bulgaria signed an armistice, Turkey also laid down her arms. Negotiations with Turkey were even slower than with the other states. This was due to the Greek-Turkish conflict, which broke out in May, 1919, and to the rise of the revolutionary Ankara government of Mustapha Kemal Pasha which is discussed elsewhere. The Treaty of Sèvres, signed by the Allies and the Sultan's government at Constantinople on August 20, 1920, was never accepted by Kemal. This treaty marks the high point of British and Greek policy in the Near East. The other powers were not pleased with their handiwork and the Allies were soon working at cross-purposes. While Britain continued to support the Greeks in their campaign against Turkey, Italy and France made their peace with the Ankara government in 1921. At the same time, Kemal negotiated a treaty of friendship with Russia in which Turkish-Russian territorial differences were adjusted.

With Allied support of Greece split and with war supplies reaching his armies from Russia, Kemal was able to throw the Greeks out of Asia Minor in September, 1922. The nationalist Turkish armies threatened to seize Constantinople. While willing enough to have the Greeks fight the Turks, the British, who were occupying the Straits region,

---

[13] On the Treaty of Neuilly, see G. P. Genov, *Bulgaria and the Treaty of Neuilly* (Sofia: Hristo G. Danov, 1935).

were reluctant to become involved in active hostilities. An armistice was arranged under British auspices on October 11, 1922.

The Turkish National Assembly then clarified the situation by abolishing the Sultanate. The Sultan was evacuated from Constantinople on a British warship. Formation of the new National Government at Ankara not only prevented the total dismemberment of Turkey, but also laid the foundation for a modern Turkish state. The Turks were the first to demonstrate that fundamental revision of the peace treaties could be brought about only by force of arms.

The Treaty of Lausanne. The Ankara government was now the sole recognized government of Turkey. On November 20, 1922, a conference met at Lausanne to work out new peace terms, but the final treaty was not signed until July 24, 1923. Turkey regained Thrace up to the Maritsa River, the islands of Imbros and Tenedos, and Asia Minor from the Aegean to the Persian frontier. The former Turkish territories to the south were divided into Arab states with varying degrees of independence or into mandates under French and English supervision. Greece, which had expected so much, had to be content with the Aegean islands minus the Dodecanese, which were definitely awarded to Italy. The Straits were to be demilitarized and open to all ships in time of peace. In time of war the same was true if Turkey remained neutral; if Turkey was a belligerent, enemy ships but not neutrals could be excluded. Turkey cancelled the capitulations, the special privileges awarded to foreign nations dating back to 1535.

Greece and Turkey signed a separate agreement for the exchange of populations. It was a radical solution of the minority problem and entailed great human and financial cost. In the end, 189,916 Greeks were called back from Asia Minor and settled mostly in Macedonia and Thrace. At the same time, 355,635 Moslems were repatriated.[14] The League of Nations and the Near East Relief Commission rendered signal service in carrying out this difficult project.

Albania. Forced to curtail her vast claims against Turkey but receiving substantially what she wanted from Bulgaria, Greece was again denied her demand for an additional (Albanian) section of Epirus. Albania had first been recognized as an independent state, due to the insistence of Austria-Hungary and Italy, during the Balkan Wars of 1912-1913. After great effort the Powers had finally agreed upon the

---

[14] "The Exchange of Minorities and Transfers of Population in Europe Since 1919," *Bulletin of International News*, XXI (July 22, 1944), 586; see also S. P. Ladas, *The Exchange of Minorities: Bulgaria, Greece, and Turkey* (New York: Macmillan, 1935).

frontiers of the new state in 1913-1914.[15] The newly established government of Prince William of Wied collapsed with the outbreak of war, and eventually Albania came under Austrian occupation. With the end of the war, the Albanians convened a National Assembly and elected a President on December 25, 1918. They soon clashed with the Serbians, who attempted to occupy the northern sections of the country, and also with the Italians and Greeks who were active in the south. The bitter hostility between Italians and Greeks partly accounts for the fact that neither of them received their territorial demands here or in Asia Minor.

The Albanians slipped into the League of Nations on December 17, 1920, and thereby assured themselves an international standing. On November 9, 1921, pre-war diplomacy received a pat on the back when the Conference of Ambassadors decided that the frontiers of Albania should be those of 1913, except for slight concessions to Yugoslavia.

Yugoslavia. Cut shorter than they thought right in Albania, the Serbians, through the formation of the large Serb-Croat-Slovene State (officially known later as Yugoslavia), became the dominant element in the largest of the Balkan states. Montenegro, over the protests of the old ruling house but supposedly with popular approval, gave up its independent status. The Yugoslavs had repeated difficulties with Italy. The boundaries as finally drawn incorporated a large number of Slovenes into Italy. Difficulties also arose over Fiume, which Italy solved in her own favor through the use of force, although the final settlement was not negotiated until January 27, 1924. Yugoslavia obtained the neighboring Port Baros and certain facilities in the main harbor of Fiume.[16]

Romanian seizure of Bessarabia. A word remains to be said about one other important territorial settlement related to Balkan affairs. In March, 1917, immediately after the overthrow of the Tsar, a democratic Moldavian (Bessarabian) Republic declared itself an autonomous area within the Russian state. At the invitation of this government, protested by Russia, Romanian troops occupied the territory in January, 1918. In March of that year the Moldavian Diet, having previously declared itself independent, voted for union with Romania. Romanian troops continued in occupation and the Russians, busy elsewhere, never got around to throwing them out.

Finally, by a treaty of October 28, 1920, the principal allied powers—

---

[15] Helmreich, *Diplomacy of the Balkan Wars*, Chs. XIII, XIV, XX.

[16] Toynbee, Arnold J., *Survey of International Affairs* (London: Oxford Press, 1925), 1924, pp. 408-422.

Great Britain, France, Italy, and Japan—recognized Romania's right to annex Bessarabia. The treaty was indeed a unique document. "It authorized the transfer of an entire province from one state to another, yet it did not bear the signature of the state whose territory it alienated. It provided, moreover, that all questions which might be raised concerning its details by Russia, the despoiled party, should be submitted to the arbitration of the Council of the League of Nations, of which Russia was not a member and whose authority it consistently flouted." [17] Expanded Yugoslavia and Romania, through their great territorial acquisitions, acquired border problems which were to complicate their relations with their neighboring states in the years to follow.

The Minority Treaties

The idea of inserting certain clauses into treaties for the protection of minorities was not new to European diplomacy. [18]   A long list of precedents can be cited, especially in connection with guarantees of freedom of religion.   Such clauses were incorporated in the 1919 treaties largely because of a desire to protect the Jews and because of the influence of the powerful "Committee of Jewish Delegations."

Poland was the logical state with which to negotiate the initial minority treaty, on which all others were to be patterned.   She was involved directly in the German problem, which was the primary concern of the Peace Conference, and also had one of the largest Jewish populations.   Poland reluctantly signed the treaty with the allied and associated powers on June 28, 1919.

The pill was somewhat easier for Poland to swallow because Czechoslovakia, Romania, Yugoslavia, and Greece were also required to sign such treaties.   Similar provisions were incorporated into the minority articles of the Treaties of St. Germain, Trianon, Neuilly, and Lausanne. Later a scheme was devised under which, by a declaration on entering the League, Albania, Estonia, Latvia, and Lithuania should recognize similar obligations to their minorities.   Finland, out of consideration for its own historic constitution and practices, was not required to give a similar guarantee, but did make a far-reaching declaration to the League with respect to the Åland Islands.   In 1932, when Iraq was

---

[17] "Post-War Rumania," *Foreign Policy Association Information Service*, III (February 3, 1928), 385.
[18] Macartney, C. A., *National States and National Minorities* (London: Oxford Press, 1934), Ch. V; Temperley, *History of the Peace Conference* (London: Frowde, 1921-24), V, 112-119; Jacob Robinson *et al., Were the Minorities Treaties a Failure?* (New York: Institute of Jewish Affairs, 1943), Ch. I; see also Joseph S. Roucek, *The Working of the Minorities System Under the League of Nations* (Prague: Orbis, 1929).

admitted to the League, she made a minorities declaration modelled on that of Albania. Thus the minorities states constituted a vertical belt across Europe into Asia Minor.

Although humanitarian motives were a factor, the great powers were clearly more concerned with insuring the tranquillity of the states than in providing for the welfare of the minorities. None of the great powers was called upon to make any guarantees to its own minorities, which greatly irritated the small powers. Germany, it is true, entered into a special scheme with Poland in regard to Upper Silesia. Its operation, however, was different from that of the regular minority procedure of the League of Nations.

The minority rights guaranteed in the various treaties and declarations were placed under the protection of the League. A member of the Council of the League could request investigations, but this was seldom done. The other procedure was to submit petitions to the Secretary of the League. He examined the petition and if he found that the complaint had substance, it was submitted directly to the state concerned. If redress was not obtained, the petition went to the Council, which appointed a committee of three to investigate and attempt to work out a solution. These committees were usually able to get the respective states to give promises of reform.

Leaders in many of the minorities states did all they could from the first to sabotage these treaties, which had been forced upon them. When Russia joined the League in 1934 and received a seat in the Council, the Poles feared that the Russians might exercise their right as council members to bring many minority problems to the direct attention of the League. Such action was far more embarrassing than the involved system of petitions by the minorities themselves. Consequently the Poles denounced the Minority Treaties in 1934. The fact that the treaties did not bring adequate protection to minorities in all cases is a reflection rather on the limitations of man than on the provisions of the law.

From the Peace Treaties to the Pact of Locarno
(1920-1925)

The League of Nations. On January 10, 1920, the League of Nations began its official existence.[19] It would require a volume to chronicle its

---

[19] Of the states in Central-Eastern Europe, Greece, Romania, Yugoslavia, Czechoslovakia, and Poland were the only charter members. Albania, Austria, Bulgaria, and Finland were admitted to membership in December, 1920; Estonia, Latvia, and Lithuania in September, 1921; Hungary in September, 1922; Germany in September, 1926; Turkey in July, 1932; and Russia in September, 1934.

work in Central-Eastern Europe, even in the first five years. The Financial Committee of the League especially rendered great services in the reconstruction of Austria and Hungary, in providing money for the refugee settlement in Bulgaria and Greece, and in organizing the financial systems of Danzig and Estonia.

The services of the League in the adjustment of disputes are also worth noting. The League settled differences between Sweden and Finland over the Åland Islands (1920-21); dealt numerous times with the difficulties of Lithuania and Poland over Vilna (1920 and later); supervised the establishment of the Albanian frontier (1921); ended a dispute between Czechoslovakia and Poland over their frontier in the Janorzina region (1920); drew the boundary in Upper Silesia after the plebiscite (1921); settled a serious difficulty between Greece and Italy arising out of the murder of an Italian member of the commission establishing the Albanian-Greek frontier, whose death Mussolini had avenged by bombarding Corfu (1923); supervised the transfer of Memel to Lithuania (1924); conciliated Greece and Bulgaria after a border clash in 1925; and fixed the boundary between Iraq and Turkey in the vital Mosul oil district (1925). Because of British interests in this region, the Treaty of Lausanne had not settled the boundary here. Now Mosul went to Iraq, which was under mandate to Great Britain.[20]

As members of the League, the states in Central-Eastern Europe shared in its general activities as well as those of the International Labor Office and the World Court. They supported the League security provisions, but did not rely on them any more than did the great western powers. Always drafting their agreements so as not to violate the League Covenant, they developed a network of alliances. These were designed to further the participants' security, which meant specifically the maintenance of the peace treaties.

The Little Entente. One of the first and also one of the most stable alliance blocs to emerge in the post-war years was derisively dubbed the "Little Entente." This grouping was brought about by three bilateral treaties: one between Czechoslovakia and Yugoslavia on August 14, 1920; another between Czechoslovakia and Romania on April 23, 1921; and a third between Romania and Yugoslavia on June 7, 1921.

The main object of the treaties was to protect the three states against an unprovoked attack by Hungary, which meant any attempted revision by force of the Trianon Treaty or a restoration of the Habsburgs.

---

[20] Myers, Denys P., *Handbook of the League of Nations Since 1920* (Boston: World Peace Foundation, 1930), pp. 272-281; for a discussion of the work of the financial committee, see pp. 74-84.

Romania and Yugoslavia in addition mutually pledged themselves to aid each other if Bulgaria attacked either one. These treaties were limited in scope and did not pledge aid if one of the parties was attacked by a great power.

More important than the letter of the obligations was the fact that the alliances constituted a bond of friendship between the three states. This carried over into foreign policy beyond the sphere of thwarting Magyar revisionism. The Little Entente remained primarily a political bloc to the end, although attempts were made, especially after 1927, to give it an economic foundation through trade coöperation among the three states. In 1933, efforts were made to have the Little Entente powers speak with one voice at the League of Nations and in European councils. Actually such unanimity was seldom in evidence. Each country had too many problems of its own in which the others did not wish to become involved.

The Little Entente treaties did not prevent the members of the Entente from negotiating alliances with' other states. The treaty of alliance between Poland and Romania of March 3, 1921, brought into being by a common fear of Russia, was popular in both countries. Poland might be at cross-purposes with Russia, with Lithuania, with Germany, with Czechoslovakia, but she always had one friend— Romania.

French alliance policy. In pre-war Europe, France had sought Russian bayonets to prick Germany's eastern flank. After the war, French fear of Germany remained, but communist ideology, Russian civil war, and the Soviet cancellation of Tsarist bonds held by French voters destroyed Russia's alliance value in French eyes. Besides, Russia no longer bordered on Germany. Consequently the French did their best to create a strong Poland, favoring the Polish cause whenever questions arose at the Peace Conference.

Having already negotiated an alliance with Belgium, France extended her quest for security to Eastern Europe. She concluded a formal alliance with Poland on February 19, 1921. Each signatory promised to come to the aid of the other in case of attack by Germany. Backing was given to the treaty by a military convention of September, 1922. Although the Franco-Polish alliance remained in effect right down to 1939 and neither power thought seriously of breaking it, there were periods when Polish-French relations cooled perceptibly.

In 1924, France extended her eastern security system by negotiating a treaty of alliance with Czechoslovakia. Not only did both countries pledge mutual aid against Germany, but they also agreed to oppose

German-Austrian *Anschluss*. Neither Hohenzollerns nor Habsburgs were to be permitted to regain their thrones. This alliance treaty was definite and far-reaching; Germany now faced united enemies on her western and eastern frontier. One weak point, however, was that Poland and Czechoslovakia were both bound to France and to Romania but could come to no real agreement with each other. In 1921, Poland and Czechoslovakia did sign a broad treaty of friendship, but it was not ratified and relations between the two countries were never friendly. The Poles could not forget Teschen.

Italian policy. Italy in the 1920's was still concerned with the maintenance of the peace treaties and as yet had taken few steps to tie up with Hungary. Italian-Yugoslav relations were unfriendly because of the Italian seizure of Fiume and a host of other boundary difficulties. Finally, in January, 1924, Italy and Yugoslavia reached a settlement, but it did not bring about friendly relations. France had been able to obtain a formal alliance with Czechoslovakia, but the best Mussolini could do was a vague treaty of friendship.

Alliances in the Baltic region. The Baltic states, having achieved their independence through their coöperative efforts against Russia, quite naturally attempted to form a bloc designed to assure their future security. Various conferences were held, but it was soon clear that it would be impossible to tie Finland, Estonia, Latvia, Lithuania, and Poland together. Finland more and more preferred to orient herself with the Scandinavian nations, and Polish-Lithuanian antagonism over Vilna precluded any genuine coöperation between them.

The only real agreement that emerged from all the discussions was a treaty of alliance between Estonia and Latvia on November 1, 1923, whereby each promised the other military aid if attacked. A contemplated customs union in which Lithuania was to be a partner never materialized.

Russia of course was concerned with these negotiations among the Baltic States and attempted to take them in hand by calling a Baltic disarmament conference in Moscow for December, 1922.[21] The Baltic States pressed for non-aggression and arbitration pacts first and disarmament later, while the Russians wanted the procedure reversed. The conference failed, but it marked the beginning of Russia's policy of surrounding herself with a vast maze of treaties of friendship, of neutrality, of arbitration, of conciliation, or of mutual assistance. Clear-cut treaties of alliance were as a rule not a part of Russian policy,

---

[21] Graham, Malbone W., "Security in the Baltic States," *Foreign Policy Reports,* III (Feb. 17, 1932), 440.

although the same objects were sought through agreements bearing a more non-committal name.

Russian-German treaty. Russia was still considered an outsider in western European affairs. The Russian famine of 1921, together with less altruistic reasons of trade, demanded that something be done to restore Russia's economy. Certain internal economic changes described elsewhere made this seem more feasible. An economic and financial conference was called at Genoa, April 10-May 19, 1922. The conference itself produced no great results, but the Treaty of Rapallo signed by Russia and Germany during this meeting was of great importance. It called for the immediate resumption of full diplomatic and consular relations, mutual renunciation of claims for war damages and indemnities, and the promise of each government to help supply the other's economic needs. Specifically this meant that the German Government would help to finance the policy of trade expansion which German industrialists were eager to undertake. The old fear of a Russian-German coalition began to haunt European capitals. In 1923 Germany was declared in default on reparations payments and France, in an effort to force collection, occupied the Ruhr on January 11. When Poland offered her aid to France if an armed conflict developed, Russia let it be known that Russian forces would invade Poland in such an eventuality. The Treaty of Rapallo seemed to be paying dividends.

The occupation of the Ruhr hastened the disintegration of the German economy, which was brought to total collapse when inflation erased the German financial structure. The German cabinet resigned and Gustav Stresemann took charge of German foreign affairs in the new government, a post he was to hold, in spite of many cabinet changes, until his death in October, 1929. He inaugurated what was described as a policy of fulfillment. As an earnest of his good intentions, he ended passive resistance in the Ruhr on September 26, 1923.

This added fuel to the fire being nursed along by a group of German nationalists. On November 8-11, under the leadership of Hitler and Ludendorff, they attempted to seize power in what has since become famous as the Beer Hall *Putsch*. Sentenced to imprisonment, Hitler occupied himself by dictating his famous *Mein Kampf,* a book in which he outlined his fateful policy of German expansion into Eastern Europe.

The Locarno Pact. Stresemann's policy soon began to show results. A new *Rentenmark* gave Germany a sound currency system again. The French-dominated separatist states in the Rhineland collapsed and on November 18, 1924, France withdrew her troops from the Ruhr.

The Dawes Plan (1924) at least made an attempt to straighten out the reparations settlement, although it promised no great financial relief. Above all, investment capital began to flood into Germany. In April, 1925, Germany felt that some of her prestige and independence was restored when Hindenburg took over the office of President. Stresemann, continuing his policy of western rapprochement, proposed a Rhineland Mutual Guarantee Pact. English and French statesmen were responsive. Such a pact would not only settle the problem of the Rhine, but it might undermine the German-Russian friendship heralded by the distasteful Treaty of Rapallo. The result was the famous Locarno Pact of October, 1925.

By this agreement Germany accepted her western frontier, but refused to extend the same promise to her eastern borders. The most she would do in that connection was to renounce the use of force by signing arbitration treaties with Poland and Czechoslovakia. Stresemann was no more willing than any other important German statesman to accept the eastern frontiers as definitive. In this he unquestionably had the support of the overwhelming majority of Germans. Britain and Italy each guaranteed to come to the aid of the other if Belgium, France, or Germany tried to change their common frontiers by force, but undertook no obligations with respect to Eastern Europe. France contracted new mutual assistance treaties with Poland and Czechoslovakia against possible German aggression which extended the obligations already undertaken with these countries by previous agreements.

The Poles protested strongly against the differentiation between the Rhine and Vistula frontiers. Russia also was alarmed and felt more isolated than ever. But the latter received some consolation in the signing of a trade treaty with Germany four days before the actual signature of the Locarno Pact. The Russian press christened this the "Anti-Locarno Pact." [22] To show the world that their relations remained unaffected, Germany and Russia signed a non-aggression treaty at Berlin on April 24, 1926, which was considered an extension of the Treaty of Rapallo (1922).

From Locarno to Hitler (1925-1933)

More important than the actual terms of the Locarno Pact was the famed "Locarno Spirit" which supposedly began to hover over Europe. Tension was reduced. Europe and the world entered upon a fleeting moment of prosperity which only made the depths of the subsequent

[22] Dallin, David J., *Russia and Postwar Europe* (New Haven: Yale University Press, 1943), p. 77.

economic depression seem greater. As part of the Locarno settlement, Germany was to enter the League. Inability to come to an agreement on Council seats in February postponed Germany's entrance until September, 1926. Thereafter the German minorities scattered around Europe were to have a champion on the League Council.

The arbitration treaties which were a part of the Locarno Pact and the German-Russian treaty were only a few of the many concluded in an attempt to create an illusion of confidence in Eastern Europe. In part the epidemic of treaties was the result of the abortive Draft Treaty of Mutual Assistance, proposed to the League by Lord Robert Cecil in 1923, and of the Geneva Protocol. The Draft Treaty was designed to enforce the general guarantee of the League through the formation of regional mutual assistance pacts whose obligations would be limited to the same continent as the aggressor states. Limiting liability on continental lines was contrary to the organization and interests of the world empire of Great Britain, and a newly organized British Government under Ramsay MacDonald killed the Draft Treaty, although it had the warm support of France and her allies.

MacDonald then proposed a new scheme, to be known as the "Geneva Protocol." Drafted in 1924 by Beneš of Czechoslovakia and Politis of Greece, the Protocol provided for compulsory arbitration of disputes and defined an aggressor as the nation unwilling to submit its case to arbitration. The Protocol was meant to stop certain loopholes in League procedure which permitted war as an instrument of policy when a decision had not been reached through League instrumentalities. Seventeen countries accepted the Protocol, and then the whole thing collapsed. Great Britain, now under a conservative government, bowed to strenuous objections from the Dominions, who were afraid of becoming too easily involved in economic sanctions and refused to approve the Protocol in March, 1925.

What might have been accomplished by these multilateral agreements was now left to bilateral treaties. A glance through the Index volumes of the League of Nations Treaty Series will indicate how numerous these bilateral agreements were. No useful purpose would be served in trying to enumerate them here.

After Locarno, Germany and Russia busied themselves chiefly in building up their internal strength. France and Italy, however, began actively to challenge each other in the affairs of Central and Eastern Europe.

Widening of French alliance system. France, having strengthened her alliances with Poland and Czechoslovakia by the Locarno agreements, sought to establish direct ties with Czechoslovakia's allies of the Little Entente. On June 10, 1926, France concluded a treaty of friendship with Romania. All disputes between the two were to be submitted to arbitration. Furthermore they agreed to act together in the "event of any modification or attempted modification of the political status of the countries of Europe," or in case either was attacked without provocation. All action, however, was to be within the framework of the League. A year later a similar treaty was concluded between France and Yugoslavia (November 11, 1927). More important perhaps than the treaties was the fact that France now extended financial and military assistance to these countries.[23]

Italian policy. On the opposite side of the fence were of course the defeated powers who wanted to force a revision of the peace treaties. Italy, too, gradually began to shift over to this position, for she was far from pleased with the way she had been treated at the Peace Conference. She never was satisfied with the small bits of territory which France and England turned over to her as compensation for their seizure of the German colonies. Nor did France and Italy see eye to eye on naval disarmament in the Mediterranean. Italy's relations with Yugoslavia never became cordial in spite of several treaties and she particularly resented the rapprochement—which was often labeled an alliance—between Paris and Belgrade. In order to parry France's power and to avoid being excluded from the affairs of Central Europe and the Balkans, Italy undertook to build up her own bloc of states.

Mussolini began his alliance system by pushing Italy's old imperialistic interests in Albania. An Italian financial group gave aid to King Zog in 1925. A pact of friendship in 1926 was followed by a treaty of defensive alliance and a loan agreement in 1931. Italy now completely dominated Albania. The Albanian Government took Italian gold, but this created no love for Italy among the independence-loving Albanian people.

Common antagonism toward Yugoslavia also paved the way for a treaty of friendship with Hungary on April 5, 1927. Hungary by this treaty began to break through the encirclement of the Little Entente. By tying up with Budapest, Mussolini was willy-nilly forced to sponsor the cause of treaty revision and eventually to support German policy. Italy concluded a treaty of neutrality, conciliation, and judicial settlement with Turkey on May 30, 1928.

---

[23] For a list of French loans to Belgium, Poland, Czechoslovakia, Romania, and Yugoslavia, see John C. deWilde, "French Financial Policy," *Foreign Policy Reports,* VIII (Dec. 7, 1932), 236.

The frenzy of treaty-making continued with treaties of friendship with Ethiopia and Greece in the fall of 1928. Both were really smokescreens. More significant was the treaty of friendship with Austria of February 6, 1930, and the inauguration of a policy of friendliness toward Bulgaria. With the marriage of King Boris to Princess Giovanna on October 25, 1930, Bulgaria was supposed to come into the Italian orbit. By these newer alignments, Italy's older treaties of friendship with Czechoslovakia and Romania lost most of their significance, although they remained technically in force.

Kellogg-Briand Pact. While France and Italy were busy playing power politics by adding the friendship of one state after the other, the powers collectively agreed that they would outlaw war. In a solemn pact sponsored in 1927-28 by Secretary of State Kellogg of the United States and by Briand of France, the signatory states promised to seek a settlement of their disputes only by pacific means and renounced war as an instrument of national policy. Actually only wars of aggression were outlawed. No enforcement machinery was set up, but in subsequent years the pact became a point of departure for protests against the action of aggressive states. For example, the United States cited it both in respect to Japanese-Chinese and German-Polish difficulties.

Although at first skeptical about the worth of the Kellogg-Briand Pact, Litvinov, Commissar of Foreign Affairs at Moscow, decided it would be a good thing to bring the pact into operation locally without waiting for the United States and other powers to ratify it. In February, 1929, Russia and her neighbors to the west—Estonia, Latvia, Lithuania, Poland, and Romania—signed the so-called Litvinov Protocol putting the Kellogg-Briand Pact into effect at once. Its chief significance was to advertise Russia's "non-aggressive" policy.

The Balkan conferences. Collective action in the Baltic encouraged similar action in the Balkans. Actually an era of better if not yet really good feeling had struck this region with a genuine effort on the part of most of the governments to settle their minor border disputes amicably. Inter-Balkan relations were thus at a post-war peak when the twenty-seventh Universal Peace Conference met at Athens on October 6-10, 1929. Here a committee composed of representatives of all the Balkan states was appointed to study the possibility of forming a Balkan Union.

As a result of its efforts, the first Balkan Conference was held at Athens in October, 1930.[24] There were to be annual meetings and the

---

[24] Padelford, Norman J., *Peace in the Balkans* (New York: Oxford, 1935); Kerner, R. J., and Howard, H. N., *The Balkan Conferences and the Balkan Entente 1930-1935* (Berkeley: University of California Press, 1936).

main purpose of the conference was to encourage economic, political, social, and cultural coöperation.   Not content, however, with this general program, the first conference decided to study the possibilities of drafting a Balkan pact which would outlaw war.   This carried over the idea of the Litvinov Protocol to the Balkans.

Nothing demonstrated more conclusively the inherent weakness of the great international agreements, such as the League itself or the Kellogg Pact, than the feeling that they had to be strengthened by bilateral or regional agreements.   The attempt to implement outlawry of war in the Balkans by a mutual guarantee of existing frontiers eventually led to disbandment of the Balkan Conferences.   Again an institution which might have been of great service in laying a foundation for peace and friendship was ruined by forcing upon it the problem of dealing directly with the abolition of war.

The position of Austria.   France and Italy, of course, watched the Balkan Conferences closely.   Neither wanted an effective Balkan Union which might act independently, nor one which might destroy the centers of interest they had established there.   Although French and Italian blocs had shaped up in Central and Southeastern Europe by 1930, the region was not yet divided into hostile camps.   On the plane of high European politics, France and Italy still clung to a policy of coöperation, the very core of which was their common interest in the prevention of Austrian *Anschluss* with Germany.   Italian policy in this regard ran parallel with that of the Little Entente.   This policy cannot be characterized as Austrophile, for in this period, at least, the overwhelming sentiment in Austria was for closer coöperation with Germany.

When Germany and Austria signed the Vienna Protocol on March 19, 1931, providing for a customs union between the two countries, France and the Little Entente protested the loudest, but Italy shared their views.   The project for the customs union had to be abandoned when the Permanent Court of International Justice ruled that it was contrary to obligations Austria had assumed in accepting financial assistance from the League in 1922.

Italy sided with Germany, however, in opposing various French plans for a Danubian Union which would have tied Austria, Hungary, Czechoslovakia, Romania, and Yugoslavia together by a system of preferential tariffs and mutually favorable quota allotments.   Instead of attempting any basic solution of the economic paralysis of Austria, the powers applied another court-plaster in the shape of a second international loan.

The economic crisis and European coöperation. As a result of the general depression which hit Europe even before the 1929 crash in the United States, there were a whole series of conferences and discussions to revive trade. This was no new phenomenon. In the depression years immediately after the First World War, there had likewise been many attempts to revive trade. The peace treaties had sought to encourage the establishment of preferential customs regimes among the Austro-Hungarian succession states. This was one of the chief topics discussed by these powers at the conference held at Porto Rosa in October, 1921. Various protocols ameliorating trading conditions were adopted, notably in respect to rolling stock on the railroads, but the proposed general tariff union was rejected. Nor did the Genoa Conference of the following year bring multilateral economic agreements into being. Instead, each country was left to negotiate its own trade agreements and "the members of the Little Entente in particular proceeded to strengthen economic ties with one another." [25]

In 1927, and with renewed energy in 1934, the Little Entente powers attempted to push this economic collaboration further by establishing a central organ of direction. But the effort met with no great success because the economies of the three states were basically parallel rather than complementary. Peasants everywhere clamored for help and industrialists for protection. The same was true in the Baltic region, where, in spite of special agreements, Estonia, Latvia, and Lithuania did little trading among themselves.

In 1930 Poland took the lead in organizing what became known as the "Agrarian Bloc," consisting of Poland, Czechoslovakia, Romania, Yugoslavia, Bulgaria, Hungary, Estonia, and Latvia. From September to November no less than five conferences were held at different capitals to devise a way to combat the agricultural depression. It was decided to request the industrial countries of western Europe to grant these countries preferential tariff treatment for agricultural products. This was difficult to do, as such a request ran counter to the most-favored-nation clauses of existing trade treaties. The final act of the

[25] Vondracek, Felix John, *The Foreign Policy of Czechoslovakia 1918-1935* (New York: Columbia University Press, 1937), p. 191. For discussions of the attempts to reach economic agreements in Central Europe, see Gerhard Schacher, *Central Europe and the Western World* (London: George Allen & Unwin, 1936), Ch. III (The Economic Little Entente), Chs. XVIII-XXIV; Antonin Basch, *The Danube Basin and the German Economic Sphere* (New York: Columbia University Press, 1943), Chs. IV, X; Margaret S. Gordon, *Barriers to World Trade. A Study of Recent Commercial Policy* (New York: Macmillan, 1941), pp. 33-35, 444-454; see also particularly Josef Hanč, *Tornado Across Eastern Europe* (New York: Greystone Press, 1942), pp. 106-116.

Second Conference on Concerted Economic Action, held under League auspices in November, 1930, recognized such preferences, but with so many reservations that the scheme had little practical value. The general program of bringing relief through preferential tariffs continued to be discussed at the Stresa Conference of 1932 and at the London Economic Conference of 1933. Unfortunately this widely heralded meeting was a failure. The Central-Eastern European states were left to work out their own foreign trade problems with the western industrial states through numerous bilateral trade treaties, many of them containing preferential tariff, quota, and currency arrangements.

As early as 1930, Briand as Foreign Minister of France had advocated a Federation of Europe. In his plan, economic problems were subordinated to political considerations. A Commission of Inquiry on European Union was set up under League auspices but was unable to make much progress, although the discussion brought out the importance of the economic problems. The proposal for a German-Austrian customs union in 1931 roused the French to make another proposal intended to solve the economic problems of Central-Eastern Europe. In 1932, Premier Tardieu announced a plan for a Danubian Federation which was to be welded together by preferential reciprocal tariffs between Austria, Czechoslovakia, Hungary, Romania, and Yugoslavia. Not all these states themselves would agree to it, nor was the plan supported by Germany, Italy, or Great Britain. The general impression was that the scheme was secretly designed to extend French control over Central Europe.

Although Tardieu's hopes of creating a political Danubian Federation on an economic foundation were dashed, other economic agreements were negotiated. The Rome Protocols of 1934, which will be referred to later, were based on the idea of increasing Italian-Austrian-Hungarian mutual trade. The Balkan states also attempted to give substance to newly developed friendships by pushing economic collaboration as part of their program of Balkan Conferences (1930-1933). At the 1933 conference a "Draft of a Regional Economic Understanding," designed to increase intra-Balkan trade was adopted. The results were not significant because political obstacles stood in the way.

Reparations. Just as in the case of Germany, the reparations demands upon Austria, Hungary, and Bulgaria were gradually revised downward as a result of the depression years. Austria was freed entirely of reparations obligations, and Hungarian and Bulgarian payments were reduced by approximately one-third. A settlement was also reached of the long dispute over compensation for property of those citizens who had elected Hungarian nationality. This had been a particularly disturbing factor in Hungarian-Romanian relations. Obligations of Poland, Czechoslovakia, Romania, and Yugoslavia, arising from their assumption of part of the state debt of the old Dual Monarchy, from their acquisition of former state property, and from so-called liberation loans which had been advanced to them by the Allies, were also scaled down. Payments which were still to be made under these Hague agreements were stopped under the general moratorium of 1931.[26]

The settlement of these financial problems somewhat eased the political differences between the various states and was a factor in obliterating the old division of Europe into debtor and creditor nations. It therefore constituted in itself a major victory for the doctrine of revisionism.

Disarmament. The allies had disarmed the defeated states in 1919, which was to be the first step in a general disarmament program. In December, 1925, the Council of the League set up a Preparatory Commission to prepare the agenda for a disarmament conference. This conference did not meet until 1932 to discuss a draft proposal finally worked out by the Commission. Although the conference struggled on until 1934, it achieved no concrete results. Haunted by the specter of insecurity, in which fear of the spread of communism played a major role, the victorious powers would not disarm to the level of the defeated states, nor were they willing to permit the defeated states to build up to anything like parity.

In October, 1933, Hitler followed the example first set by the German Government under Von Papen in September, 1932, and withdrew the German delegation from the conference for the second time. Hitler emphasized his action by withdrawing from the League of Nations as well. He pushed the rearmament of Germany boldly and there was no one who dared to stop him. A new period had begun in European history.

Hitler in Europe (1933-1939)

When Hitler became Chancellor of Germany on January 30, 1933, he not only became the leader of Germany but he also seized the initiative in European affairs. It would, of course, be inaccurate to say that all events in European history were the result of his policies, yet his peri-

---

[26] For a compact sketch of the history of reparations and debt payments in Central Europe, see Toynbee, *Survey of International Relations,* 1932, pp. 137-172.

odic bold strokes can well serve as milestones to mark the course of international affairs in these years.

Fearful that the victory of National Socialism in Germany would soon lead to a concerted demand for treaty revision, the powers of the Little Entente concluded a pact of reorganization on February 16, 1933. Under it they established a permanent council, consisting of the three foreign ministers, and a permanent secretariat. The council was to present a common front in foreign affairs and closer economic coöperation within the Entente was foreseen.

France was pleased by this new agreement, but it was roundly denounced in Germany, Hungary, and Italy. Mussolini proposed a new peace formula whereby Great Britain, France, Germany, and Italy would conclude a Four Power Pact for coöperation in the solution of European problems. The small powers, left out in the cold, were seized with fear that they would be sacrificed to the cause of revisionism. Poland was especially disturbed by the proposal and joined with the Little Entente to bring pressure on France to sabotage Mussolini's plan. Eventually an emasculated Four Power Pact was signed on June 15, 1933, but as it never was ratified it remains only another landmark in a long series of futile projects to manage European affairs through the peaceful coöperation of the great powers.

France meanwhile turned her attention to cultivating good relations with Russia. On November 29, 1932, a Franco-Russian non-aggression pact was signed. It was ratified by the French Chamber of Deputies on February 15, 1933, fifteen days after Hitler came to power. This was followed by trade negotiations which were formulated into an agreement on January 11, 1934.

While Germany was giving the world a case of jitters in 1933, Russia ostentatiously displayed her peaceful intentions by signing a whole series of "definition-of-aggression" pacts with Poland, Estonia, Latvia, Lithuania, Czechoslovakia, Yugoslavia, Romania, Turkey, Persia, and Afghanistan.

When Hitler withdrew from the League of Nations and the Disarmament Conference on October 14, 1933, his action was approved by a large majority of the German electorate in a synthetic plebiscite. The withdrawal was of course accompanied by many professions of peaceful intent as well as demands for equality. He next engineered a major coup by concluding a ten-year non-aggression pact with Poland on January 26, 1934.

Polish-German treaty. For years Poland and Germany had been wrangling over their mutual frontiers, over the free city of Danzig, over the treatment of minorities, and over tariff questions.[27] To put an end to all this and inaugurate a policy of friendship was indeed an accomplishment. By doing so, Germany at one and the same time obtained a buffer against Russia, cast doubts on the French alliance system, and gained a respite to tackle the more immediate obectives of German policy. Poland made an express reservation that her previous obligations to the League, to France, and to Romania should not be impaired by the new agreement. Nevertheless the pact gave evidence of Poland's independent position and perhaps even elevated her a bit toward the status of a great power.

In effect, France was warned not to become too friendly with Russia, although Poland herself immediately tried to reassure Soviet leaders by renewing the non-aggression pact which was not due to expire until 1935. Poland felt that her earlier hope of creating a group of powers hostile to both Russia and Germany was no longer feasible. It was therefore necessary to tie up more closely with one or the other. Pilsudski chose Germany in 1934, not because he loved her more, but because he feared and hated her less.

The Balkan Pact. If the French had lost some face in Poland, they made up for it in the Balkans. The effort to come to some agreement to outlaw war and guarantee existing frontiers led to the conclusion of the Balkan Pact (February 9, 1934) which gave the *coup de grace* to the Balkan Conference. In the Balkan Pact, Turkey, Greece, Yugoslavia, and Romania mutually guaranteed their existing frontiers. Although drawn in general terms, the agreement was actually directed against Bulgaria. In a secret protocol, Turkey and Greece made a reservation that the obligations they assumed did not extend to involvement in a war with a major power. The pact was definitely antirevisionist, and thus fitted in with French ideas. It was hailed in some quarters as an extension of the Little Entente, since Romania and Yugoslavia were members of both groups.

The Baltic Entente. A weak point in the French wall around Germany was still the Baltic, but plans were also developed here. Having consulted with Russia and obtained the approval of Great Britain, Barthou of France proposed an Eastern Locarno in the early days of July, 1934. Poland, Russia, Germany, Czechoslovakia, Finland, Latvia,

---

[27] Kruszewski, Charles, "The German-Polish Tariff War (1925-1934) and Its Aftermath," *Journal of Central European Affairs,* III (October 1943), 294-315; Shepard Stone, "German-Polish Disputes. Danzig, the Polish Corridor and East Prussia," *Foreign Policy Reports,* IX (July 5, 1933); Morrow, *Peace Settlement in the German Polish Borderlands, passim.*

Estonia and Lithuania were to sign a mutual assistance pact which would be guaranteed by France.

The inclusion of Czechoslovakia, a member of the Little Entente, brought the Baltic powers into Danubian politics. It was not until September 8, 1934, that Hitler announced his refusal. He was willing to negotiate bilateral agreements, but refused to assume multilateral obligations. Poland also was cool to the pact, nor did she favor Russia's admission to the League, which was being sponsored by France. With Russia on the Council, Poland feared that her White Russian and Ruthenian minorities would have an all-too-willing spokesman. Instead of a grandiose Eastern Locarno as envisaged by Barthou, a far more modest Baltic Entente between Estonia, Latvia, and Lithuania was signed on September 12, 1934. Their ten-year "Treaty of Good Understanding and Coöperation" called for biennial conferences and greater unity on matters of foreign policy.

The Rome Protocols. Italy countered the extension of French influence in Central and Southeastern Europe by the Rome Protocols of March 17, 1934. Chancellor Dollfuss of Austria, with Mussolini's special blessing, had made war on social democracy and established his dictatorship in February. He and Premier Goemboes of Hungary now journeyed to the Italian capital, where a political and economic agreement was signed. The three countries were to pursue a common policy and to take steps to increase their mutual trade. Mussolini spoke of obtaining justice for Hungary, which was enough to evoke loud protests from the Little Entente. Beneš announced that an Italian solution of the Austrian problem could not be permitted and called for an international guarantee of Austrian independence.

Nazi Austrian Putsch. Hitler now believed that the time was ripe to back a Nazi revolution in Austria. Chancellor Dollfuss was murdered on July 25, 1934, but the *Putsch* failed. The Austrian Nazis were not as yet a match for the supporters of the Dollfuss dictatorship and Hitler did not dare to risk open intervention. Mussolini had mobilized some divisions and sent them to the Brenner, an action welcomed by France and the Little Entente. The World War victors spoke in unison for the last time. The "future of Austria" was not a solid keystone for their coalition.

French policy. For a time it seemed that the French security system was riding high. France now had anti-revisionist ties, directly or indirectly, with Poland, Czechoslovakia, Yugoslavia, Romania, Turkey, and Greece. Great Britain was friendly, Italy was still hostile to *Anschluss,* and relations with Russia had improved.

Such a group of friends, however, was really too diverse to make a sound structure. When France tried to top off her whole eastern security system by negotiating a firm Russian alliance, the base began to crumble. Poland and Romania definitely wanted protection against Russia, and Yugoslavia, influenced more than any other state by emigré Russian mentality, had not even recognized the Soviet Union diplomatically. Groups within France as well as in England looked askance at closer ties with the Soviets.[28]

In an effort to reassure Yugoslavia of France's friendship in spite of more intimate ties between Paris, Rome, and Moscow, Barthou arranged for King Alexander to make a state visit to France. Unfortunately, when the king landed in Marseilles on October 9, 1934, both he and Barthou were assassinated by members of a Balkan terrorist organization. There were intimations that the Italian Government was implicated, but no one pushed the matter. Yugoslav wrath was directed against Hungary, which at times had harbored the terrorists.

French-Italian friendship was confirmed on January 7, 1935, when the two reached an agreement about African affairs. Mussolini at least thought he was assuring himself a free hand in Ethiopia. He promised in return to coöperate with France in the event of a new threat to Austrian independence. The new friendship between Italy and France met with warm support in Great Britain and even among the powers of the Little Entente. Hungary felt herself forsaken and turned to Germany for aid and comfort.

German rearmament. Having won a tremendous vote of confidence in capturing the Saar Plebiscite in January, 1935, Hitler pressed on. Equality of armament had always been a German demand. Failure of the disarmament conference had led to new armament programs in all countries. On March 16, 1935—the very day that the French Chamber of Deputies voted for extension of the period of military service to two years—Hitler announced the reintroduction of compulsory military service in Germany. A week earlier he had announced the creation of an air force. Both actions represented unilateral denunciations of the disarmament clauses of the Treaty of Versailles.

The powers protested, France and Italy more sharply than Great Britain. England sent Sir John Simon to Berlin for a conference, while Anthony Eden hastened to Warsaw and Moscow in an effort to revive the defunct Eastern Locarno Plan. At Warsaw he found the Poles un-

---

[28] Micaud, Charles A., *The French Right and Nazi Germany 1938-1939* (Durham: Duke University Press, 1943), Ch. V.

willing to undertake what would be regarded as an anti-German move without positive assurance that Britain would guarantee the *status quo* in Eastern Europe against Germany.[29]   Britain was eager to do this in 1939, but rebuffed the suggestion in 1935.

To meet the new situation, Great Britain, France, and Italy conferred at Stresa in April.   Here they reaffirmed their determination to uphold the independence of Austria and to press for condemnation of Germany's action by the League.   But a more direct answer to Germany was the signing of the Franco-Russian mutual assistance pact of May 2.   This was followed by a similar pact between Russia and Czechoslovakia on May 16.   The latter, however, contained one very significant reservation, that the pledge of mutual assistance would become effective only if the victim of aggression received aid from France. Neither Russia nor Czechoslovakia was bound to aid the other until France acted.   These treaties were soon followed by military conversations for the coördination of defense plans.

While France worked against Hitler, Great Britain negotiated a naval agreement with him (June 18, 1935).   It was clear that the Germans would have arms and the British thought it realistic to tie the Germans to a promise not to exceed 35 per cent of the total British tonnage. Such a fleet could not successfully challenge the British, but it could control the Baltic Sea.   Britain was not opposed to that.   Fear of communism and hostility to Russian policy in China influenced the British attitude.   The agreement caused consternation in the capitals of Europe.   It particularly hindered the development of close Anglo-French-Russian relations, for which the French had hoped to lay the foundation in their treaty with the Soviet Union.

Italian attack on Ethiopia.   Meanwhile German rearmament increased the alliance value of Italy to France.   Mussolini decided to choose this advantageous moment to invade Ethiopia.   The League, to which Ethiopia appealed, endorsed a policy of economic sanctions against Italy.   All the states of Central and Eastern Europe except Albania, Austria, and Hungary participated in these sanctions.   The rupture of trade relations with Italy hit some of the countries very hard, especially Yugoslavia.   It added to economic distress in Central-Eastern Europe and offered an opportunity to Germany to pick up new markets.

The enforcement of economic sanctions led to a great wave of Italian indignation against France and England, considered responsible for the policy.   French and British statesmen saw the possibility of

---

[29] Dean, Vera Micheles, "Europe's Struggle for Security," *Foreign Policy Reports,* XI (June 19, 1935), 101.

counting on Italy to help check Germany vanishing. In the eyes of many rightist politicians in both countries, friendship with Italy was worth much more than an independent Ethiopia, a strong League, or an alliance with Russia. France and England soon did their best to appease Italy while trying to save face with the League.

Reoccupation of the Rhineland. Italian occupation of Ethiopia and the weak-kneed enforcement of sanctions indicated the difficulty of formulating a united European policy. Hitler seized the opportunity to put over his boldest stroke to date—military reoccupation of the Rhineland (March 7, 1936).

It seemed that France must act then or never if the peace treaties were not to be torn to shreds. France protested but refused to meet the challenge by sending her armies into the Rhineland. This has often been described as a great mistake. Perhaps it was, but the issue did not then seem a good one on which to risk a European war. After all, the Rhineland was part of Germany and it was hardly reasonable to expect that Germany in the long run would have an army in only part of her territory. Many hold that a real threat of force would have caused Hitler to draw back his armies. At the time Hitler was probably not ready for war, but in the light of subsequent history the theory that Hitler's moves were one big bluff after another is hardly tenable. However, the fact that France did nothing more than protest had a deleterious effect on her friendships in eastern Europe. Some statesmen in this section began to form the opinion that it would be safer to make a deal with Hitler than to rely on French support against Hitler.

Rome-Berlin Axis. The Spanish Civil War, which broke out on July 17, 1936, ranged Italy on the side of Nazi Germany against the Russians, who supported the Republican forces in Spain. Both England and France remained aloof, partly from a desire to retain Italian friendship. Nevertheless the foundation was laid for the Rome-Berlin Axis at Berchtesgaden on October 25-27, 1936. Here Italy and Germany promised mutual coöperation in foreign policy, especially in the matter of "saving European civilization from the grave dangers of communism." Germany recognized the Italian conquest of Ethiopia. Most important of all, Italy apparently withdrew her objections to the *Anschluss* between Austria and Germany. Henceforth Europe was supposed to revolve around this Central European-Mediterranean axis.

Germany further countered the Franco-Russian alliance by negotiating a pact with Japan. Taking advantage of the distinction which Soviet officials themselves always insisted on making between the Russian Government and the directing body of the Communist Party

(Comintern), this agreement was labeled the Anti-Comintern Pact. Officially therefore, it was not directed against Russia but only against the spread of communism.

German trade expansion. As the Spanish war dragged through 1937, Hitler not only continued to rebuild the German army, but also further expanded the basis for a wartime economy. Germany was to be made as self-sufficient as possible: first, by developing the German economy itself; second, by establishing trade relations with neighboring states that would not be subject to sea blockade in case of war. *Grossraumwirtschaft* was what the Germans called this idea of a regional economy centered in Berlin.

These were years of severe agricultural depression and the countries of Southeastern Europe, unable to sell their products elsewhere, had little alternative but to increase their trade with Germany. Germany was willing to pay high prices. Most of the transactions were on a barter basis and were transacted through clearing agreements involving mutually managed currencies. It is true that Germany held the upper hand in these transactions, but the allegation that the Germans were getting valuable products and giving only harmonicas and toothbrushes in exchange is absurd. The peoples of the Balkans are no fools, particularly when it comes to trading.

As was to be expected, trade connections were often made contingent on political concessions, friendships, and understandings. Even if this had not been the case, the very existence of the trade would have given Germany new standing in these countries. France and the United States had agricultural surpluses of their own, and Great Britain was pledged under the Ottawa agreements to buy most of her agricultural imports from the Dominions.

Alarmed by the trend of events, Delbos, the French Foreign Minister, made a tour of the capitals of Poland, Romania, Yugoslavia, and Czechoslovakia in December, 1937. His reception was correct enough everywhere, but only in Prague did he feel real warmth and an anxiety to maintain intimate ties of alliance. He discovered also that the independence of Austria had lost significance as an issue in European diplomacy.

German seizure of Austria. After the unsuccessful *Putsch* in 1934, Hitler's policy toward Austria had been circumspect on the surface, but the Austrian Nazi Party had been gradually developed into a strong organization. On July 11, 1936, Hitler had negotiated a treaty of friendship with Schuschnigg, who had taken over the dictatorship in Austria after the assassination of Dollfuss.

In line with this treaty, Schuschnigg was persuaded to go to Berchtesgaden for a conference in February, 1938. Hitler made far-reaching demands. After yielding, Schuschnigg decided to strengthen his position by calling for a national plebiscite on the question of independence for Austria. It was a spectacular stroke and the issue was formulated in such a way that the Nazis were almost certain to get a black eye out of the whole affair. Hitler's answer was to demand cancellation of the plebiscite, Schuschnigg's resignation, and appointment of a Nazi Austrian Government by President Miklas. By the evening of March 11, 1938, Austrian Nazis were in control of the government at Vienna. In the early morning hours of March 12, German troops crossed the frontier and quickly occupied the country.

Britain and France were upset, but did nothing. Czechoslovakia, greatly alarmed, limited herself to stating that she would defend herself if attacked. The treaties of the Little Entente did not bind Romania and Yugoslavia to aid Czechoslovakia against Germany, and they were not disposed to go to war to preserve Austrian independence.

Meanwhile Poland despatched an ultimatum to the Lithuanian Government demanding immediate opening of their common frontier and establishment of diplomatic and consular relations. With Polish forces mobilized on the border, the Lithuanians had no choice but to give in and end their tacit eighteen-year conflict with the "despoilers of Vilna." The Hitlerian technique of conducting foreign affairs was spreading!

German-Czech crisis. Whether Hitler really intended to force a solution of the German minority problem in Czechoslovakia at the end of March, 1938, is uncertain. He probably was only feeling out the ground. In any event the Czech Government mobilized 400,000 men and nothing happened. But the minority strife in Czechoslovakia continued. It was enhanced by Nazi policy, but it was not conjured up by the Nazis. This minority question had a long historical background.[30] Democratic Czechoslovakia had no more solved its minority problems than dictatorial Poland or Romania.

At the Nazi Party Congress in Nürnberg on September 12, 1938, Hitler demanded that the Sudeten Germans be given the right of self-determination. Disorders broke out in Czechoslovakia and martial law was proclaimed. A series of conferences took place between Prime Minister Chamberlain of Great Britain and Hitler, and between

---

[30] Wiskemann, Elizabeth, *Czechs and Germans. A Study of the Struggle in the Historic Provinces of Bohemia and Moravia* (London: Oxford, 1938); Thomson, S. Harrison, *Czechoslovakia in European History* (Princeton: University Press, 1943), Chs. VI-IX; Falk, Karl, "Strife in Czechoslovakia: The German Minority Question," *Foreign Policy Reports,* XIV (March 15, 1938).

Boundaries at the time of the Munich Agreement.

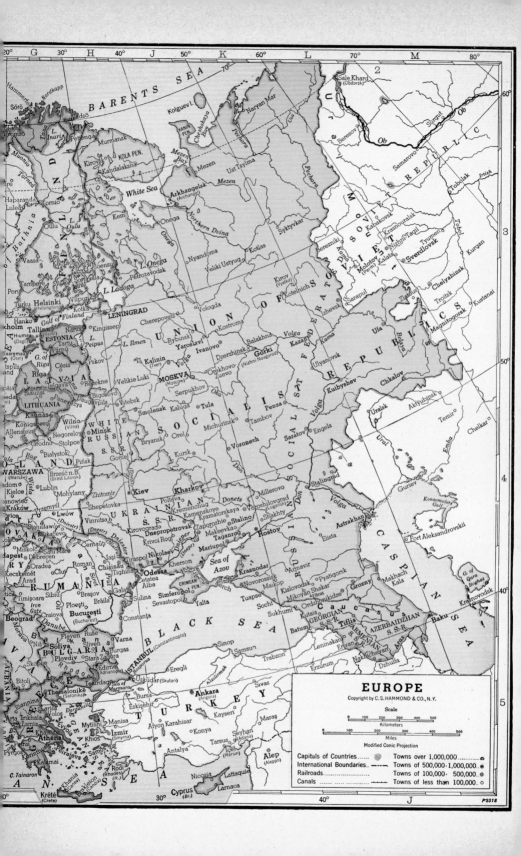

EUROPE

Copyright by C.S. HAMMOND & CO., N.Y.

Scale

Kilometers

Miles

Modified Conic Projection

Capitals of Countries......   Towns over 1,000,000.............
International Boundaries..- - - -   Towns of 500,000-1,000,000.
Railroads.....................   Towns of 100,000- 500,000..
Canals ....   Towns of less than 100,000..

Premier Daladier of France and Chamberlain. The Czech Government did not readily accept British and French advice to yield. Further conferences followed while tension grew with Hitler's increasing demands. The Czech Government ordered complete mobilization, the French Government partial mobilization, and the British issued a forthright statement that an unprovoked attack upon Czechoslovakia would mean a general war.[31]

At the last moment, like the climax of a movie thriller, Mussolini arranged for a conference of Hitler, Chamberlain, Daladier, and himself at Munich. Czechoslovakia's interests were sacrificed to appease Hitler. It was four-power diplomacy, for Russia was completely ignored throughout this crisis. The peoples of Europe breathed more easily and in most countries there was heartfelt thanks that they had been spared the horrors of war.

Czechoslovak statesmen were present in Munich but did not participate in the negotiations. The decisions were handed to them with the clear understanding that they had better be accepted. Under the terms of the Munich agreement, the predominantly German-Sudeten sections of Bohemia (according to the Austrian census of 1910) were to be transferred to Germany by October 10. An international commission was to settle the question of disputed areas. Its decisions ultimately proved favorable to Germany. France and England undertook to guarantee the new frontiers of Czechoslovakia against unprovoked aggression. Italy and Germany agreed to do the same as soon as Polish and Hungarian claims were settled. Germany acquired about 10,000 square miles of territory with a population of 3,500,000, of whom about 700,000 were Czechs.

When Hitler took Austria the Poles had cleared accounts with Lithuania. This time they laid claim to the long disputed Teschen area and the small districts of Spiš and Orava in Slovakia. All three of these territories had been partitioned to the advantage of Czechoslovakia in 1920. The Prague government had to accept what amounted to an ultimatum, and Poland acquired an area of about 400 square miles and a population of about 240,000. Scarcely 100,000 of these were Poles in 1939.

Hungary also demanded territories in Slovakia and Ruthenia. She was finally awarded about 4,800 square miles along the southern boundary of these provinces. German and Italian statesmen, meeting at Vienna on November 2, 1938, worked out the final boundary lines.

---

[31] The French were very skeptical of this declaration. See Alexander Werth, *The Twilight of France 1933-1940* (New York: Harpers, 1942), pp. 243-245.

The Germans saw to it that Poland and Hungary did not have a common frontier, much to the disgust of Warsaw. The Poles feared that an autonomous Carpatho-Ukraine (Ruthenia) might put ideas into the heads of their own obstreperous Ruthenian minority. The largest national group in the territory acquired by Hungary was Magyar, but there was a large minority made up of various nationalities.

As a result of these settlements, Czechoslovakia lost about 29 per cent of its territory and 34 per cent of its population. It had given up important manufacturing centers and its great fortification system directed against Germany. In a forecast of similar demands to be made on Poland, Germany obtained from Czechoslovakia on November 20, 1938, the right to build an extraterritorial German highway across Moravia to Vienna and a canal connecting the Oder and Danube rivers.

German-Polish relations. Before the details of the Munich agreement had all been settled, Foreign Minister Ribbentrop proposed a general settlement of issues between Poland and Germany. Danzig was to be reunited with Germany, but Poland was to be guaranteed railway and economic facilities there. Poland was also to permit the building of an extraterritorial motor road and railway line across the Polish Corridor (Pomorze). The German-Polish agreement of 1934 was to be extended for twenty-five years. Ribbentrop further sketched the possibility of future coöperation between Poland and Germany in colonial affairs, the emigration of Jews from Poland, and a joint policy toward Russia on the basis of the Anti-Comintern Pact.

This German offer was immediately refused with the warning that any attempt to incorporate Danzig into the Reich must lead to a conflict. The refusal was driven home by the sudden renewal of the Polish-Russian Pact on November 26. Poland did suggest the possibility of replacing the League of Nations guarantee of the independence of Danzig by a bilateral Polish-German Agreement.

Ribbentrop's program was discussed again when Foreign Minister Beck visited Hitler on January 5, 1939, and for a third time when the German foreign minister visited Poland at the end of that month. At this later meeting "Beck categorically rejected von Ribbentrop's postulate as to the extraterritoriality of a motor road across Pomorze." [32]

Seizure of Prague. How much the failure to reach a settlement with Poland influenced Hitler to seize Prague on March 15, 1939, and put an end to the remnants of Czechoslovakian independence is not known. Certainly this act did much to strengthen his military position vis-à-vis

---

[32] Ministry of Foreign Affairs, *Official Documents Concerning Polish-German and Polish-Soviet Relations 1933-1939* (London: Hutchinson, n.d.), Nos. 44, 45, 48, 49, 51, 52, 53.

the Polish state. Bohemia-Moravia now became a protectorate of the Reich, Slovakia an "independent" state under German protection, and the Carpatho-Ukraine (after one day of independence) was occupied by Hungary. Hungary also obtained a further bit of territory from Slovakia at this time.

Hitler followed through by demanding the return of Memel from the Lithuanian Government. On March 22, 1939, the two states signed an agreement. Lithuania in future had to be content with a free zone at Memel. To assure the friendly development of relations between their respective states, the two signatories rather ironically agreed not to use force in their mutual relations.[33]

On March 21 Ribbentrop, for a fourth time, inaugurated discussions in regard to a Danzig-Corridor settlement. He stressed the point that Germany had just demonstrated her good will toward Poland by permitting the establishment of a common Polish-Hungarian frontier. That same day the British ambassador at Warsaw proposed that Poland join with the French, British, and Soviet Governments in a declaration that when any action constituted a threat to the political independence of any European state they would "consult together as to what steps should be taken to offer joint resistance to any such action." [34]

Not liking a multilateral agreement when it included Russia, Polish Foreign Minister Beck countered on March 23 with the suggestion that it would be more expedient for Great Britain and Poland to enter into a bilateral agreement. Two days later he gave the same refusal to the German proposal that he had given in October and January.

The seizure of Prague had disillusioned Chamberlain and brought a complete reversal of British policy. Up to that time the British Government had always been chary about incurring written obligations, especially in Central and Eastern Europe. What Britain had refused to do for centuries, Chamberlain now could not do fast enough. Unable to wait for negotiations, he had his ambassador on March 30 "ask the Polish Government whether they had any objection to a British Government guarantee to meet any action which clearly threatened Polish independence, and which the Polish Government accordingly considered it vital to resist with their national forces?" [35] The Polish Government naturally did not object to such a generous offer and on March 31 Chamberlain made his famous declaration in the House of Commons.

[33] Estonia and Latvia also signed non-aggression pacts with Hitler on June 7, 1939.
[34] *Polish Documents*, No. 65.
[35] *Ibid.*, No. 68.

Events now moved swiftly. France supported the British declaration on Poland. Beck paid a visit to London, and on April 6 it was announced that Poland assumed the same obligation to aid Great Britain as Great Britain had assumed toward Poland. A formal mutual assistance treaty would follow. It was not actually signed until August 25, 1939.

Repercussions in Eastern Europe. Mussolini now decided it was time to enter the limelight and Italian troops occupied Albania on April 7. King Zog fled to Greece with his retinue, and King Victor Emmanuel III of Italy added the title "King of Albania" to an already impressive list. Four days later Hungary, whose appetite had only been whetted by its recent territorial acquisitions, withdrew from the League of Nations.

France and Great Britain, in a frantic effort to stop further territorial changes, guaranteed on April 13 the independence of Romania and Greece. Negotiations were at once initiated with Russia and Turkey to convince them that these guarantees were not directed against them and to win their support. An Anglo-Turkish mutual assistance accord was signed on May 12, and a similar French-Turkish agreement on June 23, by which Turkey acquired some land in Syria. In its permanent form the Anglo-Turkish alliance treaty of October 19, 1939, had an important reservation which exempted Turkey from action involving her in war with the U.S.S.R. France and England began at once to back up their guarantees to these eastern European states by extending them large credits for the purchase of war materials and by negotiating new commercial agreements with them.[36]

The tortuous negotiations between Britain, France, and Russia were unsuccessful. The lack of attention paid to Russia during the Munich crisis had not strengthened Franco-Russian ties or increased Russian confidence in democratic protestations against fascism. Now the guarantees to Poland and Romania, countries with which Russia had a score to settle, did not help matters. This was above all true when Poland made it clear that she was not anxious for assistance which involved the use of Russian troops on Polish soil. The U.S.S.R. apparently also wanted support for contemplated mutual assistance pacts with the Baltic states. Great Britain and France hesitated to approve these since they feared, quite rightly, that they would mean the end of the independence of these small nations. But it was the successful conclusion of Russo-German negotiations which were being carried on at the same

---

[36] Dean, Vera Micheles, "Europe's Diplomatic Tug of War," *Foreign Policy Reports*, XV (July 15, 1939), p. 107.

time (August, 1939) that sent the English and French delegations scurrying home from Moscow.

On April 28, 1939, Hitler got around to answering Poland's repeated refusal to accept Germany's proposals. He publicly demanded the same things which Ribbentrop had secretly proposed to the Polish ambassador on October 25, 1938: (1) return of Danzig to the Reich, (2) Polish trade rights to be guaranteed, (3) German extraterritorial motor road and railway across the Corridor, and (4) a twenty-five year non-aggression pact between the two states. He berated Great Britain's new guarantee to Poland as an attempt to encircle the Reich with enemies and denounced the German-Polish Pact of 1934, as well as the German-British Naval Agreement of 1935.

Germany's ties with Italy were strengthened when the Axis agreement of 1936 was converted into a formal alliance on May 22, 1939. Each party pledged unrestricted military support in case of "one of them becoming involved in warlike complications with another power." In a secret clause of the agreement, Italy apparently stipulated that she needed three years to recover from the Ethiopian and Spanish Wars. Should war break out before then, she would not automatically be bound to give aid to Germany.[37]

Within Germany, notably in army circles, there was always a group who favored a pro-Russian policy. To meet the new diplomatic situation in Europe, these advisers urged Hitler to reverse his bitter anti-communist attitude. It was apparently with great hesitancy and real reluctance that Hitler gave in.

The negotiations were made easier when Molotov replaced Litvinov as Russian Commissar of Foreign Affairs on May 3. Rumors spread, but the world was not prepared for the shock it received when a far-reaching German-Russian trade accord was signed on August 19, to be followed by a German-Russian non-aggression pact on August 23. The two signatories undertook to refrain from any act of aggression against each other for a period of ten years, to consult on matters of common interest, and to adjust any conflict that might arise between them. There were additional secret understandings along general lines as to how things were to shape up in Eastern Europe.

---

[37] Hitler at this time apparently acceded to the Duce's wish that the Italo-German frontier be purified by the repatriation of Germans in South Tyrol. Actually the formal agreement was not signed until October 21, 1939. It has never been carried out completely and many of the German Tyrolese still remain in their old homes. See Eugene M. Kulischer, *The Displacement of Population in Europe* (Montreal: International Labour Office, 1943), pp. 17-19; "The Exchange of Minorities and Transfers of Population in Europe Since 1919," *Bulletin of International News*, XXI (August 19, 1944), 658-661.

German attack on Poland. Britain continued to back Poland and on August 25 signed the definitive mutual assistance pact with that country. Hitler, protected by his non-aggression pact with Russia, pushed on to settle the dispute with Poland. Disorders, alleged and real, broke out in Danzig and Poland and were given much publicity in the German press.

Hitler served notice that his patience was at an end. Unless Poland agreed to negotiate on the basis of his demands, events would have to take their course. The British and French ambassadors attempted to mediate. As a last concession, Germany demanded that a Polish representative with full powers be sent to Berlin to negotiate by the evening of August 30. Knowing what had happened when Chancellor Schuschnigg of Austria went to Berchtesgaden in February, 1938, and when President Hacha of Czechoslovakia went to Berlin in March, 1939, the Polish statesmen were determined not to enter such a conference.

Hitler had now increased his demands. As before, Danzig was to be returned to Germany. Now, however, a plebiscite was to be held in the Corridor in which persons domiciled in that area on January 1, 1918, or born there before that date could vote. Whichever country was defeated in the plebiscite should be entitled to extra-territorial highway and railway communications, the Germans with Danzig and East Prussia, the Poles with Gdynia, which was in any case to remain a Polish city.

The different official document collections, when placed side-by-side, give a pretty clear picture of the last minute efforts to stave off the war. Ever since October, Hitler had been trying by negotiation to obtain Danzig and some sort of solution of the Corridor problem. Now as then the Poles were determined not to meet his demands. England and France did not feel, after their experience with the Munich agreement, that they could urge Poland to give in. They favored thrashing the whole thing out at a conference which would probably not have met for several weeks. Yet there is no indication that either Germany or Poland would have modified its position.

Hitler was determined to end once and for all this most detested of all the territorial settlements made by the Treaty of Versailles. The Poles felt equally strongly that to give in on Danzig and the Corridor would mean the end of their independence. The German and Polish armies were mobilized. Fall rains might ruin for the Germans the still untested *Blitzkrieg* of air and tank power. On September 1, 1939, the German armies marched.

In his speech before the Reichstag that same day, Hitler reiterated his demands and added: "I am determined to fight either until the present Polish Government is disposed to effect this change or until another Polish Government is prepared to do so." Would the Polish Government yield? Again Mussolini attempted to arrange a last-minute conference. An immediate armistice was to leave the armies where they then stood. A conference to be called within two or three days would decide the issues of the conflict. Hitler agreed to consider the proposition. England and France expressed favorable views but demanded, as an essential condition for the conference, that Germany evacuate any Polish territories that had been occupied. Mussolini knew that this condition would not be acceptable and gave up the effort at conciliation.

At Warsaw, the government did not for one minute weaken in its determination to fight it out. Messages were sent to Britain and France urging them to give their promised support. On September 3, England led off by declaring war against Germany, to be followed some hours later by France. Italy declared at once that she would take no military action, a position she was entitled to take according to the secret reservation of the Italian-German alliance. Hitler publicly approved of this position, since Germany felt capable of dealing with Poland alone and Italian neutrality might aid in localizing the conflict. After the fall of Mussolini, however, Hitler denounced the group of Italians who had made it impossible for Mussolini to enter the war in 1939.

The Second World War
From the Invasion of Poland to the Fall of France

The Russian role. As the German army surged ahead, Russian mobilization quickened and on the morning of September 17 the Red army crossed the Polish frontier. The official Russian position was that the Polish State and Government had ceased to exist and that the Russian armies were coming to aid their brother Ukrainians and White Russians. This of course was pure fiction, as the Polish Government was still on Polish soil, directing a fighting Polish army.

The Russian forces soon met the advancing Germans, and it was clear that a definite boundary line would have to be drawn. Ribbentrop flew to Moscow and there on September 28 the final German-Russian partition of Poland was arranged.[38] Germany surrendered most of Lithuania to Russia, but the eastern boundary of Poland was pushed

---

[38] For an analysis of the Russo-German agreements of August and September, see David J. Dallin, *Soviet Russia's Foreign Policy 1939-1942* (New Haven: Yale University Press, 1942). pp. 55-63.

somewhat farther east than had been foreseen in the August 23 agreement. Even so, Russia obtained more territory than the famous Curzon demarcation line of 1920 had proposed. In all, Russia received 75,500 square miles, with a populaton of about 7,000,000 Ruthenians, 3,000,000 White Russians, 1,000,000 Poles, and 1,000,000 Jews. On October 22, staged elections were held and by overwhelming majorities the people approved incorporation into the White Russian and Ukrainian Republics of the U.S.S.R.

Russia also undertook to establish her long-planned spheres of influence along the Baltic. Russian forces were moved up to the frontiers of Estonia, Latvia, and Lithuania, and their respective governments were asked to negotiate a mutual assistance pact. Estonia signed on the dotted line September 28, Latvia on October 5, and Lithuania on October 10.

In each case Russia obtained the right to establish air and naval bases and to maintain certain garrisons. Russia promised not to interfere with the governments of the respective states or to attempt any propaganda. Expansion of trade relations was foreseen. The Lithuanians were consoled by the return of Vilna to their administration. All in all, if these agreements had been kept, the Baltic states would have maintained an adequate degree of independence.

The Finns were determined that they would grant Russia no bases, nor would they sign a mutual assistance pact. The Russians wanted two things above all: first, a naval base on the Hankö Peninsula which would enable them to dominate the Gulf of Finland; second, expansion of Russia's frontier in the Karelian Isthmus. The Finns refused the former absolutely, but they expressed their willingness to withdraw their frontier in the vicinity of Leningrad for about thirteen miles. This by no means met the Russian desire for the territory up to and beyond the strong Mannerheim line of fortifications.

The Scandinavian states and also the United States sent messages to Moscow expressing their hope that Russia would not molest Finnish independence. A series of unsuccessful negotiations followed. On November 26, 1939, Russia charged Finland with a serious frontier violation. On November 29 Russia withdrew her minister from Helsinki and began to bomb the city.

It was nothing new to begin hostilities without declaring war, but Russia now presented the world with a strange situation. The Soviet authorities immediately recognized a new Finnish People's Government under the leadership of Otto Kuusinen. This quisling regime requested military assistance from Russia, and on December 2 a mutual assistance pact, similar to that concluded by Russia with the three smaller Baltic states, was signed.

In the eyes of the Soviet authorities they were not at war with Finland. For this reason they permitted no foreign diplomats to take over the protection of Finnish interests at Moscow. This was also the reason why Russia refused to participate in the session of the League of Nations which was called on an appeal from Finland. The League recommended that all members should give what aid they could to Finland and gave force to their condemnation of Russia by expelling her from membership. Other nations resigned, but Russia was the only country ever to be expelled from the League.

World opinion was definitely against Russia. President Roosevelt took the lead in the United States in castigating Soviet authorities, words which sound strange when read in conjunction with the words of praise showered upon Stalin during the second Finnish-Russian War. A "moral embargo" was placed on the shipment of airplanes to Russia, to be followed within the next few weeks by a long list of other forbidden articles.

While withstanding the onslaught of the Russian forces, the Finns never stopped trying to re-establish relations with the Russian Government. The "Blitz" victory expected in Moscow did not materialize, and it was necessary to take far more extensive military measures than had been planned. Germany and Sweden were largely responsible for restoring contact between the legitimate Finnish Government and the Soviets at the end of January, 1940.

An additional complication appeared when Great Britain and France offered to send troops to aid the Finns. They proposed to land in Norway and cross through Sweden to Finland. Both of these countries were opposed to this procedure and that was the primary reason why Finland did not apply to the Allies for help. Yet the chances of armed aid to the Finns increased steadily during the end of February and the first days of March. This fact, along with Stalin's desire to straighten out his position in the Balkans, influenced him to make peace on March 12, 1940.

He obtained even better territorial terms from the Finns than he had demanded in October. Finland was forced to surrender the entire Karelian Isthmus with its important city of Viipuri, various islands in the Gulf of Finland, and a strip of land along the western shore of Lake Ladoga, so that henceforth this body of water was entirely surrounded by Russia. The Hankö Peninsula was leased to Russia as a naval base for thirty years at an annual rental of 8,000,000 Finnish marks. Finland undertook to build certain connecting railways to Sweden that the Russians desired and accepted various other stipulations. The one thing she escaped was the signature of a mutual assistance pact.

Germany's eastern policy. Having come to an agreement with Russia, Germany incorporated directly into the Reich those territories which Poland had taken from Germany in 1919, but with considerable additions. The rest of what had been Poland was labeled the Government General of Poland. It was of course under German domination.

No doubt realizing what was in store for the Baltic states, Hitler, on October 15 and 30, 1939, signed protocols with Estonia and Latvia arranging for a voluntary "return" of the Baltic Germans to the Reich. Similar agreements were later negotiated with Lithuania and with Russia in regard to Germans resident in the part of Poland annexed by Russia. Most of these repatriated Baltic Germans were settled in the territory which Germany had annexed from Poland, and from which the Poles were removed in one fashion or another.[39]

On April 9, 1940 the invasion of Denmark and Norway was launched. This was followed on May 10 by the invasion of Luxemburg, Belgium, and the Netherlands. The campaign culminated within two months in the fall of France. Italy had entered the war on June 10, just in time to be considered in the armistice negotiations with France which were concluded on June 22. The unexpectedly rapid success of German arms had deep repercussions in Eastern and Central Europe.

From the Fall of France to the Invasion of Russia

Russian policy. In spite of repeated assurances to Romania during the previous six months that her territorial integrity would be respected, Russia presented an ultimatum on June 26, 1940, demanding Romanian evacuation of Bessarabia and northern Bukovina within four days. The latter territory had never been in Russia's possession, but a large percentage of its population was Ruthenian and it was strategically important because of its position between the recently acquired Polish territories and Bessarabia. The Romanians could do nothing but give in. The defeat in the west had made the French guarantee valueless, and no help was to be expected from Britain. Henceforth Romania sought refuge with the Axis.

Stalin now decided it was high time to exact his full demands on the

---

[39] Kulischer, *Displacement of Population,* Ch. I; "The Exchange of Minorities and Transfers of Population in Europe Since 1919," *Bulletin of International News,* XXI (August 19, 1944), pp. 661-663; Helmreich, E. C., "The Return of the Baltic Germans," *American Political Science Review,* XXXVI (August, 1942), pp. 711-716.

Baltic states. On June 15, 1940, Lithuania was presented with an ultimatum in which she was charged on rather slim grounds with violation of the mutual assistance pact of October, 1939. The right to station
a larger number of troops within the country and the formation of a
pro-Russian government was demanded. Similar demands were made
on Latvia and Estonia on June 16, and by the evening of the next day
Russian troops had occupied all three states.

Russia made no such far-reaching demands on Finland, but Finnish-
Russian relations were far from cordial. There were numerous differences over the peace treaty. Russia sponsored a Society for Peace and
Friendship between Finland and Russia, but Finnish police broke up
its organized demonstrations. Finland had to accept Russian demands
that she enter into no defensive agreements with Sweden and Norway,
that Russian troops could be transported on Finnish railways to the
Hankö Peninsula, and that the Åland Islands be demilitarized. Finland, however, was able to stall off Russia's attempts to gain control of
the nickel mines in the Petsamo region. Germany loomed more and
more as Finland's sole "protector" against complete annihilation by
Russia.

The Axis and Danubian problems. After the Russian annexation of
Bessarabia and part of the Bukovina, Hungary actively pushed her
claims on Romania. The last thing Hitler and Mussolini wanted was
war in the Balkans, because it would cut off very vital supplies. They
also felt it was high time to call a halt to Russian expansion. To stabilize the whole region, Ribbentrop and Ciano met at Vienna and
worked out a settlement.

Under the terms of this Vienna Award of August 30, Romania was
to cede approximately the northern half of Transylvania to Hungary,
about 16,000 square miles with a population of two and one half millions. More than a million of these were Romanian and provision was
made for them to ask for Romanian citizenship. Germany and Italy
undertook to guarantee the new boundaries of Romania uncondition-
ally, although rectification in favor of Bulgaria was expected. "By this
guarantee," the Romanian foreign minister explained in a broadcast,
"we tie ourselves indissolubly to the Axis powers. Henceforth our politics will not know any other policy than the policy of the Axis, in which
we place all our hopes." [40] German troops soon occupied strategic
points within Romania to give substance to this guarantee.

[40] "Rumania and the War," *Bulletin of International News*, XXI (January 8, 1944), 7; see
also "The Dismemberment of Rumania," *Bulletin of International News*, XVII (September 7,
1940), 1145-1148; Mosely, Philip E., "Transylvania Partitioned," *Foreign Affairs*, XIX
(October 1940), 236-244.

The Soviet authorities had at different times supported Bulgaria's claims to the southern Dobrudja. But it was actually because of German and Italian pressure that Romania on August 9 turned back to Bulgaria the territories obtained from her in 1913. Ethnographically, southern Dobrudja is largely Bulgarian and provision was made for some exchange of the remaining population.

The Pact of Berlin. On September 27, 1940, Germany, Italy, and Japan concluded the "Pact of Berlin", in which each assumed the obligation to help the others in the event of "being attacked by a power at present not involved in the European War or in the Chinese-Japanese conflict." This treaty was obviously aimed at the United States, and from that moment on, one of the objectives of American diplomacy was to get Japan to denounce it.

In order to quiet Russian fears, Article V specifically stated that the treaty did "not in any way affect the political status which exists at present as between each of the three contracting parties and Soviet Russia." Molotov's visit to Berlin, November 12-15, 1940, was meant to show the world that Russian-German collaboration had not been impaired. Yet it seems clear from what information we have that, although practically all European problems were discussed, no mutual agreement was reached on any of them. Everywhere in Eastern Europe, Russia and Germany were colliding.

Hardly had Molotov left than King Boris of Bulgaria arrived in Berlin for a conference. No far-reaching commitments were made at the time, but collaboration paved the way for the infiltration of German technicians and "tourists" into Bulgaria. It was only in March, 1941, that Bulgaria joined the Pact of Berlin and German troops were openly permitted to enter Bulgaria.

In November, 1940, Hitler had already succeeded in gaining the adherence of Hungary, Romania, and Slovakia to the Pact of Berlin. Only Yugoslavia hesitated. Germany made an outright offer to Belgrade in March of 1941. The Axis powers would not request the right to march or transport troops over Yugoslav territory, but they did demand coöperation in the transport of supplies. In return Yugoslavia was to receive the province of Salonica and thus get an outlet on the Aegean. The government of Regent Paul signed the Pact of Berlin on March 22.

This act aroused a storm of opposition, especially in Serbian circles. A *coup d'état* followed, resulting in a new government under young King Peter. Great Britain, the United States, and Russia all welcomed this change. Churchill was endeavoring to create a Yugoslav-Greek-Turkish bloc. Roosevelt offered lend-lease aid and Russia ceremoniously signed a non-aggression pact with the new government. Friendly relations were mutually pledged should either be attacked by a third power and Russia also promised to deliver certain military equipment.

Hitler's Balkan campaign. On April 6, 1941, Hitler struck at Yugoslavia and Greece, and five days later Hungary joined in the attack. Within eleven days the Yugoslav campaign was officially ended, although Germany by no means controlled all of the mountainous terrain to which many patriots retreated.

Yugoslavia was then partitioned.[41] Bulgaria took over Macedonia as far north as Skoplje. The Italian puppet Kingdom of Albania was enlarged by adding some districts around Lake Scutari and the plain of Kossovo. Italy herself seized the valuable harbor of Cattaro, many islands along the coast, most of Dalmatia, and the part of Slovenia lying mostly south of the Save River. Germany annexed the rest of Slovenia. Hungary took the triangle of territory between the Drave and Tiza Rivers. The rich Banat and various other territories were occupied by Germany. An "independent" Kingdom of Croatia was established under the leadership of Pavelić, a protegé of Italy whose name is associated with the assassination of King Alexander and Barthou at Marseilles in 1934. Croatia eventually chose an Italian prince as king, but he was never crowned. Rump Montenegrin and Serbian states, both smaller than in 1912, were placed under Italian and German occupation, respectively.

By the end of April the Greek War was over, except for the conquest of Crete and various other islands in the Aegean. British aid had been too little and too late. Greece was occupied mostly by Italian forces, although Germans held key positions. Western Thrace was occupied by the Bulgarians, who formally annexed it in October, 1941.

Russia did not relish being crowded out of the Balkans. On April 11, at the height of the Axis Balkan campaign, Russia signed a non-aggression pact with Japan, a pact which in many ways gave Japan the same green light that Hitler had obtained by his pact with Russia of August, 1939. Stalin attempted to negotiate with the Turkish Government, but here again German military successes paved the way for diplomatic gains. On June 18, a treaty of friendship—which fol-

---

[41] "The Division of Spoils in Yugoslavia," *Bulletin of International News*, XVIII (December 27, 1941), 2008-2010.

lowed several trade agreements—was signed by Turkey and Germany. From Hitler's standpoint, this amounted to insurance of Turkish neutrality if war broke out with Russia.

The Invasion of Russia

Expansion of hostilities. While maintaining a façade of friendship, both Russia and Germany concentrated troops along their frontiers. On June 22, 1941, the Germans attacked. Hitler was back at his old stand and summoned the nations of the world to a crusade against communism. Italy, Romania, and Slovakia declared war the same day. Russia claimed that German forces stationed in Finland had attacked her and retaliated by bombing Finnish cities. This led to a Finnish declaration of war on June 25. Hungary followed suit the next day, and Albania the day after.[42]

On July 12, 1941, just twenty days after the German attack, an Anglo-Russian alliance was concluded. It was a short document in which each party pledged assistance to the other in the prosecution of the war and promised not to make peace without consulting the other. The United States also immediately adopted a friendly attitude and made provisions for extending material aid to the new champion "in the fight against aggressors." Russian funds in the United States, which had been frozen only ten days before, were freed by President Roosevelt on June 23. The German armies surged ahead. The Baltic states, eastern Poland, Bukovina, and Bessarabia were overrun and German armies moved deep into Russian territory.

On July 30, 1941, Russia concluded a treaty with the Polish government-in-exile, the very government which Moscow had declared non-existent on September 17, 1939. The Soviet-German treaties of 1939, involving territorial changes in Poland, were considered to have lost their validity. A Polish army was to be organized on Russian soil and the two signatories pledged each other "aid and support of all kinds in the present war against Hitlerite Germany." This was confirmed and strengthened by a Russian-Polish Declaration on December 4, 1941.[43]

Policy of the United States. President Roosevelt meanwhile began to intervene more actively than ever in the war. Roosevelt and Churchill, after a dramatic conference at sea, issued the Atlantic Charter on August 14. It was supposedly a blueprint for the freedom of the

---

[42] Dallin, *Soviet Russia's Foreign Policy,* pp. 378-379, 385-388.
[43] For text of the agreements, see Vera Micheles Dean, "European Agreements for Post-War Reconstruction," *Foreign Policy Reports,* XVIII (March 15, 1942), pp. 9-10.

world. This was followed the next day by a joint letter to Stalin suggesting a conference on mutual aid, which met in due course at Moscow on September 29. On November 12, Finland rejected the American request for cessation of hostilities with Russia. Great Britain, in order to show her complete solidarity with Russia, declared war on Finland, Hungary, and Romania on December 6, 1941. The next day the Japanese attacked Pearl Harbor, and the United States progressed from passive to active participation in the war. In accordance with their alliance agreement with Japan, Germany and Italy declared war on the United States on December 11. Hungary, Romania, and Bulgaria took the same step two days later.

A joint United Nations declaration was signed by twenty-six states on January 1, 1942. This document reaffirmed the principles of the Atlantic Charter, although Russia made significant reservations.[44] In the round robin of declarations it should be noted that Russia remained at peace with Japan, likewise Bulgaria with Russia, and the United States with Finland.

Plans for future federations. On January 15, 1942, the Greek and Yugoslav governments-in-exile announced their agreement on plans for a Balkan Union, which it was hoped the other Balkan states would eventually join. A nucleus for a similar Central European Union was set forth on January 23, 1942, in an agreement outlining a future Confederation of Poland and Czechoslovakia. Soviet leaders frowned upon these plans, for they opposed all combinations among the states along their borders that did not originate in Moscow.

Turning of the Tide

Axis defeats. Axis armies in 1942 swept all the way to the Volga and to the borders of Egypt; but the surrender of the German armies at Stalingrad in January, 1943, and the North African campaigns of that winter and spring set the tide of battle flowing in the opposite direction. A succession of military defeats forced Mussolini from office. The King of Italy and Marshal Badoglio signed an armistice on September 8, 1943. Many of the Italian troops which were garrisoning the Balkans also accepted the armistice. At times they skirmished with the Germans who moved in to take over. The disorganization resulting from Italy's surrender aided the mounting activity of the under-

---

[44] Dallin, *Russia and Postwar Europe,* pp. 135-143. Churchill in subsequent speeches has also revealed limitations in the Charter; for example, that it does not apply to India or the British Empire, nor to the defeated states, nor does it forbid a system of imperial preference tariff rates.

ground forces operating in the Balkans which are discussed elsewhere in this volume.

Great power conferences. The year 1943 was marked by important conferences between leaders of the most powerful of the United Nations. Two of them were most significant for Central-Eastern Europe: the Moscow conference of the foreign secretaries of Russia (Molotov), Britain (Eden), and the United States (Hull), on October 19-30; and the Teheran conference of Stalin, Churchill, and Roosevelt on November 28-December 1.

At the first of these it was decided to set up a European Advisory Commission to study various questions and make joint recommendations to the various governments. The only specific declaration of policy made publicly was the determination of the three governments to restore Austrian independence. The Austrians were reminded that "in the final settlement, account will be taken of efforts that Austria may make toward its own liberation." [45]

The second conference made no public announcement of policy in Eastern Europe, but it seems probable that some decisions were reached along general lines about future boundaries. On their return from Teheran, Churchill and Roosevelt interviewed Turkish statesmen, whom they found still unwilling to enter the war.

Problems of Central-Eastern Europe

Russian-Polish relations. The most perplexing and difficult boundary problem was that of Poland. The agreement to organize a Polish army on Russian soil had not worked well and most of the Polish forces were eventually evacuated to the Middle East. Many of the Polish officers known to have been in Russian prison camps could not be located. When the Polish government-in-exile became too insistent in its inquiries about these men, Stalin broke off diplomatic relations on April 26, 1943.

Moscow immediately threw its support to a newly organized "Union of Polish Patriots." Great Britain and the United States attempted discreetly to restore relations between the Polish government-in-exile and the Moscow authorities. Czech leaders were also alarmed by the rift, and, since they had determined to hitch their wagon to the Red Star of Russia, they broke off the negotiations which they had been conducting with the Poles. Soon the Czech-Polish Confederation Pact of January, 1942, was a dead letter. On December 12, 1943, "an agree-

---

[45] Dean, Vera Micheles, "From Casablanca to Teheran—with Texts of Documents," *Foreign Policy Reports,* XIX (February 15, 1944).

ment of friendship, mutual assistance, and post-war coöperation" was signed between the U.S.S.R. and Czechoslovakia. This treaty, along with the Soviet pledge of the previous February to restore the pre-Munich frontiers of Czechoslovakia, definitely placed Czechoslovakia within the Russian orbit. The Poles were invited to adhere to this agreement, but refused to do so.

Russia consistently maintained that her frontiers of June, 1941, which included parts of Finland, all of Estonia, Latvia, and Lithuania, pre-war Poland east of the German-Russian demarcation line of 1939, Bessarabia, and part of Bukovina, were not to be questioned. It was, therefore, a concession on her part when it was announced on January 11, 1944, that Russia would accept a new Polish frontier corresponding to the Curzon line of 1920. This constituted a small sacrifice of territory.

The Polish government-in-exile, located in London, was not disposed to accept this settlement, especially since there was a question as to who should control the new Polish state. On July 23, 1944, a Russian-supported "Polish Committee of National Liberation" was formed to take over the government of Poland. The Union of Polish Patriots was merged with this new government, which took its seat at Lublin. Great Britain and the United States, which still recognized the Polish government-in-exile, renewed their efforts to bring about a Polish-Russian reconciliation. It was not, however, so much a matter of boundaries as of control which made agreement difficult. In spite of repeated conversations and changes of personnel in the London Polish government, no accord could be reached between it and the Russian-sponsored group. In the summer of 1945, after five years of war and the final defeat of Germany, the Polish question was still far from settled.

Finland. After the Russians had been driven out of former Finnish territory, the second Finnish-Russian conflict remained more or less static until 1944, when the Russians again began to advance. Several attempts were made by the United States to get Finland to withdraw from the war. Serious peace negotiations failed in the spring of 1944. Dissatisfied with continued Finnish-German coöperation, the United States broke off diplomatic relations with Finland on June 30. Finally, on September 4, the Finns laid down their arms.

Under the formal armistice agreement, Finland had to withdraw to the 1940 frontiers and in addition had to surrender Petsamo and the valuable nickel mines in the north. Instead of a naval base at Hankö, the Russians this time acquired a fifty-year lease on the Porkhala Peninsula, only eight miles from Helsinki. Finland was forced to pay in goods an indemnity of $300,000,000 within six years. Relatively this was a heavier demand for reparations than was made on any country after the First World War. The Germans were given until September 15 to withdraw what troops they had left in Finland, and the Finns assumed the obligation of removing those who remained after that date. This led to armed clashes between the two former allies.

Romania. The pronounced deterioration of Germany's military position during the summer of 1944—marked by the great Russian offensives, the Allied capture of Rome, and the invasion of Normandy on June 6—led to German political reverses in the Balkans. On August 2, Turkey severed diplomatic relations with Berlin. On August 23, King Michael of Romania announced the removal of Marshal Ion Antonescu as premier and the acceptance of armistice terms offered by the Soviet Union, Great Britain, and the United States.

The formal armistice signed later gave Russia her 1940 frontiers and a $300,000,000 payment to be made in goods within six months. Other provisions enabled Russia to obtain a stranglehold on the Romanian economy, at least for the duration of the war. In return, Romania was promised the restoration of the major part of Transylvania. Romania now pressed an attack against her former allies—Germany and Hungary.

Bulgaria. Bulgarian statesmen, seeing the handwriting on the wall, did their best to extricate themselves from the war. Officials were sent to Cairo to negotiate with United States and British officials. These negotiations were knocked into a cocked hat when Russia suddenly declared war on Bulgaria on September 5, 1944. The Bulgarians immediately requested an armistice, but it was not accorded until four days later after Bulgaria had declared war against Germany. The Russians occupied most of Bulgaria in their efforts to cut off the Germans in the south of the Balkan peninsula.

The formal armistice between Bulgaria and the Soviet Union, the United Kingdom, and the United States was subsequently signed at Moscow on October 28, 1944. Bulgaria agreed to evacuate all former Greek and Yugoslav territory (but not the Dobrudja, which had been acquired from Romania) and to lend her aid in every way against the Germans. Unlike the Finnish and Romanian armistices, no definite reparation payments were set, although provision was made for payment of damages to be determined later. War criminals were to be tried—an undertaking which the new Bulgarian Government carried out with gusto. Although an Allied Control Commission was established at Sofia, Bulgarian affairs were dominated by the Russians.

Within a few months, representatives of official United States agencies were expelled from Bulgaria, no American reporters were permitted in the country, and representatives of the State Department were virtually restricted to the confines of Sofia.

Greece. Even before the collapse of Bulgaria, the Germans had begun their withdrawal from Greece, although they left garrisons on Crete and other Aegean islands. During August a Greek Government of National Unity under Premier Papandreou had been laboriously patched together from various Greek political factions. Great Britain acted as sponsor and supported the government when it returned to Greece on October 18, 1944.

Attempts to disarm the various Partisan bands and to bring them under the authority of the established government led to civil war. The E.L.A.S., the armed forces of the communist-dominated E.A.M. organization, threatened to seize power. On December 5, armed conflict broke out between these Greek insurgents and the British forces of occupation. In spite of severe criticism from large sections of world opinion, Prime Minister Churchill persisted in his policy of breaking the armed power of the E.L.A.S. It was clearly established that Greece was to be in the British sphere of influence, at least until the Greeks could express their will at a free election to be held as soon as conditions warranted. On February 13, 1945, an agreement was reached between the Greek Government and the opposing factions. Partisan bands were to surrender their arms and a general political amnesty was offered—except for collaborators with the Axis.

Hungary. The rapid advance of the Russian armies led Admiral Horthy to issue a public appeal for an armistice on October 15, 1944. Thereupon Ferenc Szalasi, head of the fascist Cross Arrow organization, ousted Horthy and established a new government bent on further military coöperation with Germany. Not many Hungarians supported the new regime. By December, the Russian armies were besieging Budapest and a Provisional National Assembly was "elected" in the areas under Russian control. This assembly met at Debreczen and established a Provisional National Government with General Bela Miklos as premier. It was this government which signed an armistice agreement with Russia, the United Kingdom, and the United States at Moscow on January 20, 1945.

The Hungarians renounced all territory they had taken since 1937, agreed to coöperate against the Germans, and accepted an obligation to pay $300,000,000 in reparations within a period of six years. The armistice of course did not affect the supporters of the Szalasi regime and some Hungarian troops continued to fight side-by-side with the Germans. Budapest was defended from house to house and it was not until February 13 that the Russians could announce the total occupation of the city. The Red army was then free to push its drive toward Vienna.

Although an Allied Control Commission was supposed to supervise Hungarian affairs under the armistice terms, Stalin turned over northern Transylvania to Romania on March 12, 1945. This was done to bolster the Romanian Government of Premier Peter Groza, which had just been placed in office by Soviet manipulation.

Yugoslavia. On September 28, 1944, Moscow announced that an agreement had been reached with Marshal Tito for the Russian army to enter Yugoslavia. Belgrade was occupied by October 20. In the struggle for the liberation of Yugoslavia, Marshal Tito thus definitely won out over General Draga Mikhailovitch, leader of a rival guerrilla faction.

The Yugoslav government-in-exile had to come to terms with Tito. On November 1, 1944, Tito and Dr. Subasitch, head of King Peter's government in London, reached an agreement. A democratic federated Yugoslavia was to be established. Until it was possible to determine by plebiscite whether or not King Peter should return, the royal power was to be exercised by a regency council named by the king. Peter threatened to balk at this arrangement, particularly when some of his appointments to the regency council were vetoed by Marshal Tito. Timely advice from both London and Washington, however, caused the king to yield in February, 1945. The Tito-Subasitch government was definitely under the leadership of the former, but the strength of his popular support is hard to gauge.

Czechoslovakia. The advance of the Russian armies freed first sub-Carpathian Ruthenia and then sections of Slovakia from German control. In March, 1945, the Czech government-in-exile under Beneš left London and established its headquarters at Košice after a lengthy stop in Moscow. Prague and most of Bohemia and Moravia were not liberated until the final German surrender in May.

International conferences. From August 21 to September 28, 1944, delegations from the Soviet Union, Great Britain, and the United States met at Dumbarton Oaks, near Washington, D. C., to draw up a tentative charter for a future World Organization. In discussions lasting from September 29 to October 7, China's adherence to the proposals was elicited. Russia did not participate in this second session because of her desire to remain aloof from any possible involvement in the Far

Eastern War.   Various matters remained unsettled at this conference, notably the question of how voting powers should be exercised.

These points were part of the agenda at the conference of Stalin, Churchill, and Roosevelt, held at Yalta in the Crimea (February 4-12, 1945).   The official communique indicated that military plans for the final defeat and occupation of Germany were reviewed.   Progress was made on various points in connection with the Dumbarton Oaks proposals and it was agreed that a conference should be called at San Francisco on April 25, 1945 to continue work on this plan.

At Russia's insistence only those nations which had declared war on the Axis by March 1, 1945, were to be invited to this conference and entitled to become charter members of the new World Organization. A rash of war declarations soon followed in consequence.   Only two need be mentioned here.   On February 23, Turkey announced her declaration of war to be effective March 1.   Finland declared on March 1 that she had considered herself at war with Germany ever since she had begun, in accordance with the armistice terms, to drive German troops from Finnish soil on September 15, 1944.   Every country of Central-Eastern Europe, with the exception of Austria and Albania, which had no recognized governments, was then at war with Germany.

At Yalta, lip service was again paid to the Atlantic Charter.   Poland's eastern frontier was to be essentially the Curzon line, and she was promised very substantial additions from East Prussia and German territory extending to the Oder River.   The three conferees agreed that the base of the Lublin Polish government should be broadened and a representative democratic government established.   This was to be the prelude to the holding of "free and unfettered elections as soon as possible on the basis of universal suffrage and the secret ballot . . . all democratic and anti-Nazi parties . . . [having] the right to take part and to put forward candidates."   It is not surprising, considering the different conceptions of what democracy means in Moscow, London, and Washington, that the Russian Foreign Minister and the British and American ambassadors at Moscow, who were to superintend the reorganization of the Lublin government, made slow progress.   Meanwhile the Polish government-in-exile denounced the Yalta Agreement and refused to disappear from the scene.   The Polish problem, original cause of the Second World War, was still far from settled when Germany surrendered, May 8, 1945.

Of the Central-Eastern European countries, only Russia, Czechoslovakia, Yugoslavia, Greece, and Turkey were represented at the San

Francisco Conference when it met on April 25, 1945. Finland, Hungary, Romania, and Bulgaria were barred as former enemies of the United Nations. Latvia, Lithuania, and Estonia had been swallowed by Russia. Albania had no government, and the provisional coalition Austrian regime, set up by Russia in April without consulting the western Allies, was not recognized by Britain and the United States.

Russian Foreign Commissar Molotov put up a hard fight at San Francisco for the admission of the Moscow-sponsored Polish provisional government, but the United States and Britain were adamant in their refusal of this demand. They took the position that the Warsaw regime could not be considered representative until it had been broadened in accordance with the Yalta Agreement. In general, at the time of the San Francisco Conference, it appeared that practically all of Central-Eastern Europe (except Greece and possibly Turkey) was definitely within the orbit of Russian influence.

Bibliography

Basch, Antonin, *The Danube Basin and the German Economic Sphere* (New York: Columbia University Press, 1943). Well buttressed with production and trade figures.

Dallin, David J., *Soviet Russia's Foreign Policy 1939-1942* (New Haven: Yale University Press, 1942); *Russia and Postwar Europe* (1943); *The Real Soviet Russia* (1944). Very valuable.

Fischer, Louis, *The Soviets in World Affairs. A History of Relations Between the Soviet Union and the Rest of the World,* 2 vols. (London: Jonathan Cape, 1930). Contains much information on many out-of-the-way subjects.

Gathorne-Hardy, G. M., *A Short History of International Affairs 1920 to 1938* (London: Oxford University Press, 1938). Probably the best one-volume survey of the period.

Graham, Malbone W., *New Governments of Central Europe* (New York: Henry Holt, 1924); *New Governments of Eastern Europe* (1927). Very useful accounts of the revolutionary movements which preceded the establishment of the different new governments.

Keith, Arthur Berriedale, *The Causes of the War* (London: Thomas Nelson and Sons, 1940). A readable and opinionated survey by a distinguished English professor.

Lee, Dwight E., *Ten Years. The World on the Way to War 1930-1940* (Boston: Houghton Mifflin, 1942). The best account of this important decade.

McInnis, Edgar, *The War* (New York: Oxford University Press, 1940-   ). Scholarly annual volumes surveying military and diplomatic events of the war from September to September.

Morrow, Ian F. D., *The Peace Settlement in the German-Polish Borderlands. A Study of Conditions Today in the Pre-War Prussian Provinces of East and West Prussia* (London: Oxford University Press, 1936). Although concentrated on the years 1920-1934, this study also includes excellent historical summaries of earlier periods.

Roucek, Joseph S., ed., *A Challenge to Peacemakers* (Philadelphia: American Academy of Political and Social Science, 1944). Published as volume CCXXXII of *The Annals,* this group of studies deals with the problem of nationalism in each of the countries of Central-Eastern Europe. Attention is called particularly to the very useful bibliography on pp. 177-181.

Royal Institute of International Affairs, *South-Eastern Europe. A Political and Economic Survey* (London: Oxford University Press, 1939). Has a good brief summary of foreign relations 1918-1939 and special chapters on the internal politics, economics, trade, and finance of each country.

Schacher, Gerhard, *Central Europe and the Western World* (London: George Allen & Unwin, 1936). Good on economic problems.

Schuman, Frederick L., *Europe on the Eve. The Crisis of Diplomacy* (New York: Knopf, 1939); *Night Over Europe. The Diplomacy of Nemesis 1939-1940* (New York: Knopf, 1941). Includes many interesting details and sidelights in his account of diplomatic events; apparently written without the need of meeting a word limit.

Temperley, H. W. V., *A History of the Peace Conference of Paris,* 6 vols. (London: Henry Frowde and Hodder & Stoughton, 1921-1924). The standard history of the peace conference.

Toynbee, A. J., *Survey of International Affairs, 1920-* (London: Oxford University Press, 1925-). Annual volumes sponsored by the Royal Institute of International Affairs summarizing world affairs and giving texts of important documents.

Wheeler-Bennett, John W., *The Forgotten Peace, Brest-Litovsk, March 1918* (New York: William Morrow & Co., 1939). A very readable, solid study.

See bibliographies of other chapters, particularly Chapter I. Attention is also called to the many excellent *Foreign Policy Reports,* and to the articles in *The Bulletin of International News* published fortnightly by The Royal Institute of International Affairs.

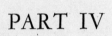

PART IV

CHAPTER XV

AUSTRIA (1918-1938)

A Tragic History

IN WORLD WAR I, Austria cracked up before Germany. Paralyzed by hunger and economic disorganization, and above all by the unwillingness of the oppressed nationalities of the empire to be ruled by the Habsburgs, the Austro-Hungarian monarchy disintegrated under the double impact of military disaster and internal revolt. The Austrian republic emerged from the war with 14.2 per cent of its former territory and about 14 per cent of its former population. It became a land-locked state, extending 230 miles along the Danube. With nearly nine-tenths of its territory gone and all of its relations with the rest of the Danube Valley disrupted, easy-going Austria slipped into a state of coma, unable to live and forbidden to die—since the Allies forbade an Austro-German *Anschluss*. Decay set in. Vienna with nearly 2,000,-000 inhabitants became an oversized head; the rest of Austria, with less than 5,000,000 people where the old empire had over 50,000,000, was the dwarfed and sickening body. Until the coming of Hitler, many Austrians believed that the forbidden *Anschluss* with Germany would be a lesser evil than their independence.

The history of Austria between the two wars is the history of bitter tragedy. The *Gemütlichkeit* of Vienna, which deluded and benumbed so many of the chroniclers of the scene, and the ever-recurring hope inspired by this or that change in government, or by one or another of many financial expedients, served only to highlight the tragic elements in the drama. It is classic drama, too, for the denouement is the result not only of the machinations of the villain of the piece but of the blunders of its heroes as well. To watch the cumulative effect of well-intentioned but ineffective statesmanship at home combined with blindness and hostility abroad is to watch the gradual unfolding of scenes whose only end could be March, 1938.

The general recognition of the fact that Austria's tragedy was Europe's tragedy, that Austria's failure would be Europe's failure, gave emphasis to the stark drama that was played for twenty years in the once-proud domain of the mighty Habsburgs. Of all the states that the settlements of 1919 brought into a new or reorganized existence, none maintained such a tenuous hold on life through the long armistice as did dismembered Austria. When the slender thread of life snapped, it was the signal for the end of a period. It required no great statesmanship to see—though it must be confessed that even this modicum of statesmanship was not in evidence in some of the great governments of the world—that the moment the Germans were installed at the Brenner, Mussolini had only two alternatives. He could fight as Hitler's ally or he could fight against him. With neutral Austria between them, the Abysinnian campaign, even the Spanish war, could with some rationalization be disregarded by the European chancelleries as matters of no vital concern to them. But only blindness or dullness can account for their failure to make the extinction of Austria, rather than the invasion of Poland, the *casus belli*. Mussolini's refusal to come to Austria's aid, as he had done at the time of the Dollfuss murder, was warning enough that he and the German dictator had come to terms.

The Organization of Austria

The boundaries of the Austria that lasted for twenty years after 1918 were not solely the work of the diplomats at Paris. The Treaty of St. Germain was not signed until October 16, 1919, but long before that the physical and political character of Austria had been determined.

"It was no treaty that set up separate governments at Prague, at Budapest, and at Vienna, for those separate governments had existed since before the German Armistice. And no Peace Conference could have joined together the fragments of an empire which its peoples had put asunder." [1]

Although the process of disintegration had been operative in the old Austro-Hungarian Empire since early in the year, it was not until October 27, 1918, that Emperor Charles frankly admitted his inability to hold it together any longer. On that date he asked President Wilson for an armistice and promised the recognition of the independence of Poland and Czechoslovakia. This action was independent of any action that Germany might take and was, therefore, a termination of the Dual Alliance of 1879. Professor Lammasch, a liberal and a long-time

[1] Miller, David Hunter, "The Adriatic Negotiations at Paris," *Atlantic Monthly*, Vol. 128 (August, 1921), p. 270.

advocate of federalism as a solution of the Empire's racial and geographic problems, was asked to form a ministry whose sole function was to be the liquidation of the Empire. During the short life of the Lammasch government, October 26 to November 11, the German deputies of the lower chamber of the *Reichsrat* had been meeting separately in the assembly hall of the Lower Austrian Provincial Legislature in the *Herrengasse*. When the abdication of Emperor Charles was announced on the morning of November 11, Austria was therefore already a functioning state. On November 12, amid tremendous enthusiasm and by a unanimous vote, the Provisional National Assembly abolished the Monarchy and declared German-Austria to be a democratic Republic.[2]

Among the first problems of the new government was the matter of boundaries. Chancellor Renner was compelled to say to the Provisional National Assembly, two days after the Republic was declared: "We need to decide what is the territorial extent in order to be able to administer. We cannot collect taxes until we establish where they are collectable."[3] But Austria, a defeated power and completely demilitarized by the Armistice, was in no position to determine her boundaries for herself. It was one thing to profess sovereignty over all the German-speaking peoples of the old Empire, but it was quite another to compete successfully with the new governments of Poland, Czechoslovakia, and Yugoslavia. These states were considered members of the winning side in the war and their claims to territory, whether or not such claims violated the precious principle of "self-determination," carried weight where weight was important. They employed ethnographic arguments when the ethnography was in their favor, but they could turn readily to economic, historical, or ideological arguments when the ethnography was on the other side.[4]

The first formal expression of opinion by the Austrian Provisional Assembly on the matter of boundaries was the law of November 22. With some naïveté, the Assembly by this Act claimed jurisdiction over all territories in the old Empire which had a German majority, resting this claim upon President Wilson's insistence that racial homogeneity should be the basis for the new international frontiers. Such an Austria would have contained more than 9,000,000 people, with large economic resources and valuable trade outlets.

[2] Strong, David F., *Austria, October 1918-March 1919* (New York: Columbia University Press, 1939), pp. 91-116.

[3] *Ibid.*, p. 124.

[4] Beneš, Eduard, *My War Memoirs*, Translated by Paul Selver (Boston: Houghton Mifflin Co., 1928), pp. 480 ff.

But it was foolish to assume that the other Succession States, with their favorable diplomatic position, would accept Austria's own delimitation of frontiers. They proceeded to occupy the border territories which they claimed; Austria, perforce, had to acquiesce. Within a week of the time that German-Austria laid claim to the German areas of the Empire, she found herself actually in possession only of the old Alpine Provinces with a population of some 6,000,000. Some minor adjustments based upon plebiscites and negotiation were subsequently made, but the Austria which was readmitted to the public law of Europe by the Treaty of St. Germain on October 16, 1919, was virtually the residue that had been left after the claims of its neighbors had been granted.

Not only the territory, but also the government had been established long before the Allies announced their terms to Austria. The Provisional Assembly recognized its lack of constituent authority to determine the permanent government for the new state, but it felt free to discuss the basic problems involved and to frame what it chose to call a provisional constitution. The three major parties in the Provisional Assembly (the Social Democratic Party, the Christian Socialist Party, and the German National Party) were in reasonable agreement on fundamentals although, as was to be expected, the Christian Socialist Party found it hard to break completely with its monarchical, Catholic-Christian past. The German National Party had no program for constitutional reform and was in fact less an integrated party than a collection of German nationalist groups. The provisional constitution that evolved through October and November, 1918, was, therefore, almost completely an expression of the political philosophy of the largest element in the assembly, the Social Democratic Party.

The framework of the new government was agreed upon in assembly sessions on October 21 and October 30. On the former date it was decided to select three presidents, one from each of the major parties. The three candidates were nominated without opposition at this sitting and were elected at the session of October 30. On the latter date, the organs of government were described and their functions were outlined. A Council of State composed of twenty deputies was to be responsible for the administration of all laws passed by the Assembly; a Chancellor was to be the parliamentary representative of the Council before the Assembly; and a Notary was to validate the enactments of the Assembly.

A resolution on this same date recognized that supreme legislative authority in the new state rested with the Provisional National Assembly, and that a constituent national assembly would be elected in the future by general and equal suffrage. With this resolution the revolution was complete, because the authority of the Habsburgs was nowhere recognized; monarchical Austria broke with its past and at once attempted to create a constitutional republic with a responsible ministry. The formal declaration which made German-Austria a democratic republic was delayed until the session on November 12, at which time it was adopted by unanimous vote amid the tremendous enthusiasm of the deputies and the crowded galleries.

The problem of the election of a new assembly with constituent authority was complicated by the uncertainty of Austria's territorial limits. The Provisional Assembly was compelled to lay out districts and to allocate seats in preparation for the election. To restrict its election plans to the areas which were not claimed by neighboring states would be to admit the validity of their claims. To extend the election to the whole Germanic area claimed by the resolution of November 22 would be to endanger international relations just at the time that Austria's very existence was dependent upon support from abroad. A practical and realistic compromise was adopted on December 18, 1918. Election procedures were provided for the whole area claimed, but the Council of State was given authority to select the proper number of deputies for those areas, if any, where it was impossible to hold elections.

On Sunday, February 16, 1919, the Austrian people went to the polls to make a free choice of representatives whose business it would be to guide the little state through the next two years, to make peace with the Allies, and to solve the many and various problems that were pressing on every side. The results of the election were disappointing to the Social Democrats. Their preponderance in the capital had led them to hope that they would have a clear majority in the new body. They could claim only 69 of the 159 seats, while the Christian Socialist Party gained 63 and the German Nationalists 25. The minor parties in the campaign elected two representatives. The geographic distribution of party strength, which was to have such tragic results during the next twenty years, is evidenced by the fact that the Social Democratic Party elected two-thirds of the Vienna delegation but only one-third of the non-Viennese members, whereas the Christian Socialist Party had less than one-quarter of the Vienna votes but practically one-half of the delegates outside the capital. Real statesmanship was going to be necessary if a bloody contest between the national capital and the provinces was to be avoided.[5]

---

[5] For a detailed treatment of the political events through the winter of 1918-1919, the reader is referred to Strong, *op. cit.,* Part II, Chapters I, II, and VII.

Political and Economic Problems

Austria's history for the twenty years between the two World Wars was conditioned largely by plain facts of geography and population. The post-settlement Austria was not only a small state in both area and population, it was also an economic and political anachronism. Vienna was still the great city it had been before the war, a city of more than two million people, but its *hinterland* now included little more than four million people as compared to the fifty million it had served economically, politically, and culturally in the days of the Habsburgs. Its food and raw materials had come from the four corners of the old empire; its products and its influence had had an equally wide market. The new government had to try to evolve an economy that would support the dismembered state and at the same time maintain its capital city in the standard of living to which it was accustomed.

This task was complicated and made all but impossible by the narrow nationalism of Austria and its neighbors. The close economic integration within the old Austro-Hungarian Empire had not only permitted but encouraged the development of specialized production in its various parts. It was sound to specialize when fuel, food, and industrial products could move freely. But the breakup of the empire left each of the component areas sadly deficient in essential commodities, and the impossibility of re-establishing a free movement of goods resulted in very severe hardships.

Of all the new states created in whole or in part out of the imperial domain, Austria found itself in the most desperate straits. The disproportion of urban and rural populations, the mountainous and unfertile character of such agricultural areas as remained, the complete inadequacy of native fuel supplies, the total disruption of normal trade routes of which Vienna had been the center, the hostility of the neighboring states due to Austria's old leadership and present claims to territories still in dispute, the disillusionment and despair resulting from the defeat, and the tragic lack of social and economic cohesion among the Austrian people themselves—all these were significant factors in explaining Austria's peculiar position within the old Habsburg territories.

The disproportion of urban and rural populations has already been mentioned. But the natural difficulties resulting from the size of Vienna in relation to the rest of Austria when hostilities ceased were aggravated by an actual increase in the Viennese population during 1919. Not only did the number of German-Austrians who returned to Vienna after the war exceed the number of non-Germans who left for their own national states, but the number of refugees from Czechoslovakia, Poland, Hungary, and Romania was so great as to increase seriously the per capita shortages of food and fuel.[6]

The food situation was probably as bad in Austria as in any part of post-war Europe. Kurt Schuschnigg describes it as "just a little too much for people to die on, and not enough to live on."[7] Austria had always been a large importer of food even before the loss of much of her best agricultural territory. It was obvious that her very existence now would be dependent upon outside supplies. The single item of milk will do as well as any for purposes of illustration. Before the war the city of Vienna consumed approximately 900,000 liters daily; this was reduced by 1916 to 145,000 liters. During January, 1919, the deliveries had shrunk to 75,000 and the following month to 30,000 liters daily. It was officially decreed that the consumption of milk must be limited to children under two years of age.[8]

The shortage of coal for industrial and domestic use, while not so obviously serious as the shortage of food, was probably even more disruptive of Austria's economy. Native coal before the war had come almost exclusively from the territories that Austria lost to its neighbors. Repeated efforts were made by successive Austrian governments to negotiate arrangements with Poland, Czechoslovakia, and Yugoslavia for increased shipments of coal, both anthracite and lignite. Their lack of success was due both to Austria's lack of barter goods and to its neighbors' desire to retain their fuel to build up their own industries.[9]

But all the other causes of Austria's inability to solve its problems rest finally on the tragic and suicidal lack of cohesion—economic, social, religious, and ideological—of the Austrian people themselves. Their inability to submerge their differences in the larger national interest was, in the end, *the* cause of Austria's demise; and no attempt to make Nazism, Fascism, or Communism the *bête noir* of the piece will satisfy the record. An adequate analysis of the seven millions or less who constituted the Austrian population is, of course, quite out of the question in this brief discussion, but some attempt must be made to understand the tensions and the discords, the stresses and the strains, that for

[6] Pasvolsky, Leo, *Economic Nationalism of the Danubian States* (New York: The Macmillan Company, 1928), p. 96. Vienna *Reichspost*, Dec. 25, 1918, p. 3; Jan. 29, 1919, p. 7. Vienna *Neue Freie Presse*, Jan. 29, 1919, p. 8.

[7] Schuschnigg, Kurt, *My Austria* (New York: Alfred A. Knopf, 1938), p. 58.

[8] Strong, *op. cit.*, p. 183.

[9] For a complete analysis of Austria's pre-war coal situation, see Emil Homann-Herimberg, *Die Kohlenversorgung in Österreich wahrend des Krieges* (Wien: Holder-Pichler-Tempsky, 1925). For the futile efforts to solve the post-war problem, see Strong, *op. cit.*, pp. 185-192.

twenty years made futile every effort to discover and develop the national interest.

The economic stratification of Austrian society was both feudalistic and capitalistic. Feudalism had contributed the great estates of the nobility with their peasant workers; capitalism had contributed modern industrialization, with its owner-manager class at the top and the proletariat at the bottom. Two per cent of the independent landowners owned thirty per cent of the tillable soil in 1934, and two per cent of the non-agricultural independent operators employed fifty-seven per cent of the workers and salaried employees.[10] It requires no Marxist to discover latent trouble here. As in other European countries, much feudal accumulation of wealth had been invested in modern industry, so that the same man was apt to be both a great hereditary landlord and an industrial capitalist.

The rigidity of Austrian social classification was probably no more marked than that of other European states, but in conjunction with the other factors under discussion it contributed its share to the lack of homogeneity in the whole population. The feudal and royal character of class distinction had carried over from the Empire in spite of the fact that there was little place for it in the spirit and letter of the democratic constitution of the new state. The rapid development of equalitarian doctrines, both native and imported, gave to the traditional social classes an anachronistic character that was exploited by the parties of the Left.

In the field of religion, the divergence of loyalties was polar in its intensity. The Catholic Church was not only the dominant religious authority; it was practically without competition among the great majority of the Austrian people who professed Christianity. Where, then, is to be found the basis for religious strife? The answer lies in the fact that a large percentage of the population was Jewish and that another large percentage had deserted the Church for the dialectic of Karl Marx. The generalization can be made that the workers of Vienna and of the industrial area running as far south as Wiener-Neustadt were consciously and militantly anti-clerical in their attitude toward religion. To these should be added the coal miners from the Styrian fields, making an industrial proletariat that comprised more than a third of the total population. The Church retained its historic influence in the rural areas, both with the peasant and landowning classes. As else-

---

[10] For an excellent analysis of the social and economic stratification of the Austrian people, see Emanuel Januschka, *The Social Stratification of the Austrian Population*. Translated by Robert Lorenz under the joint auspices of the Works Progress Administration and the Department of Social Science, (New York: Columbia University Press, 1939).

where in post-war Europe, colors came to signify groups, and the clerical "blacks" were as bitterly hated in the workers' councils in Vienna as
were the socialist-communist "reds" in the ranks of Prince Starhemberg's *Heimwehr*.

But religion only added fuel to the political and ideological flames
that raged in little Austria from the moment of its severance from the
Habsburg Empire to its incorporation into Hitler's *Reich*. Again the
alignment is largely along geographical lines. The urban and industrial areas had accepted one or another of the then-current interpretations of the philosophy of Karl Marx. Communism, of the extreme
Russian variety, never had a large following, but the rank and file of
the city workers were at least doctrinaire Socialists. Their political
organization was the Social Democratic Party and their mouthpiece
was the Vienna *Arbeiter Zeitung*.[11] Their strength lay in their numbers, in their geographical concentration, in the ability and intelligence
of their leaders, and in the fact that they had a program and the courage of their convictions. But their strength was also their weakness—
the fact that they were concentrated in Vienna made both them and the
capital city the focal point of attack; if they could be defeated in Vienna,
they were defeated in all Austria.

The rural provinces supplied support for the conservative elements
to whom Marxism in any dress was anathema. But the anti-Marxist
forces were themselves hopelessly splintered into a chaos of conflicting
ideas. The Christian Socialist Party represented the largest body
among these forces. Its leaders were either Churchmen or Catholic
laymen who frankly accepted the leadership of the Church. Its political mouthpiece was the Vienna *Reichspost* and its program was a united
Austria under Christian-Catholic direction.[12] Its mass support came
from the peasantry. But this clerical party by no means spoke for all
the anti-Marxist elements in the population. Fascism imported from
Italy, Nazism imported from Germany after 1933, and a native brand
of authoritarianism all competed for the support of conservative, anti-
socialist sentiment.

Two other divisive forces reinforced and complicated the fractures
in the Austrian population. These were anti-Semitism and the idea of
Anschluss. Anti-Semitism was nothing new in the realm of the Habsburgs. The panic of 1873 had stirred up great anti-Jewish feeling
which had been exploited for political purposes by Karl Lueger in his

---

[11] The program of the Social Democrats was outlined in a series of eight articles in the
Arbeiter Zeitung under the general title of *"Der Weg zum Socialismus,"* in January, 1919: Jan. 5,
p. 1; Jan. 9, pp. 1-2; Jan. 10, p. 2; Jan. 14, p. 2; Jan. 16, pp. 1-2; Jan. 19, pp. 1-2; Jan. 22, p. 1.
[12] The platform of the Christian Socialists was set forth in the *Reichspost*, Dec. 25, 1918, p. 1.

fight for control of the Christian Socialist Party. But Karl Lueger's death in 1910 and the natural lessening of class tensions during the first years of the war had caused a subsidence of racial prejudice until the debacle of 1918.

During the bitter struggle for power that followed the creation of the republican state in 1918, anti-Semitism again appeared as a whipping boy for politicians and politico-economic factions that needed political capital. After 1933, the brutal racism of Hitler found a ready market in Austria. The concentration of the Jews in the cities and their heavy influence in the Social Democratic Party made them an easy target for the whole galaxy of clerical, conservative, Nazi, Fascist, agrarian, and anti-socialist groups.

The idea of *Anschluss* was equally divisive. Unquestionably the vast majority of Austrians favored it immediately after the war, and its prohibition by the Treaty of St. Germain only made it seem the more desirable. If it had been permitted by the Allies in 1919, it might well have changed the whole course of European and world history. But as the debate over it became more embittered, in Austria, in Germany, and before the League of Nations and the World Court, issues were raised that could not easily be resolved. In Austria, opposition developed among the clerical factions because of the heavy Protestant population of Germany; fear and dislike of Prussia and "Prussianism" frightened many others; many Viennese, particularly the leaders of the Social Democrats, were afraid of losing their importance and identity in the larger German state. Finally, the rise of Hitler meant an acceptance of Nazism the moment that Austria attached herself to Germany. Instead of the overwhelming majority which had favored *Anschluss* at the beginning of the period, by 1938 its supporters were limited to the active Nazis who saw in it the only means of winning control of Austria.[13]

Surrounded by hostile states, cut off from trade outlets, compelled to bear the odium of the Habsburg tradition, and overwhelmed by economic problems at home, Austria was denied even an honest effort to work out her salvation by the lack of social cohesion among her people and her consequent inability to discover her national self-interest. Austria could not follow a definite road because her people could not agree on a destination.

---

[13] For a complete discussion of the *Anschluss* question to 1936, see M. M. Ball, *Post-War German-Austrian Relations. The Anschluss Movement, 1918-1936* (Stanford University Press, 1937).

Austrian Culture

Austria's particularist feeling, in combination with other factors, was strong enough to resist absorption into the *Reich* until 1938. It is true that Austrian literature has been closely bound up with that of the German people as a whole, yet it preserved characteristics of its own.

Hugo von Hofmannsthal (1874-1929) was the last great Austrian lyric poet. The leader of expressionist writers was Franz Werfel (1890-   ) now living in Hollywood; his *Jakobosky and the Colonel* was a sensational Broadway play in 1944 and several of his novels have been best sellers (*The Song of Bernadette*). Stefan Zweig, a biographer and literary critic, is known for his *Marie Antoinette,* while the late Arnold Zweig (who committed suicide in Brazil) was world-famous for his novel *The Case of Sergeant Grischa*. Perhaps the most illustrious name in post-war Austrian literature was that of Arthur Schnitzler (1862-1931), who, with Jacob Wassermann, dealt especially with current life in Vienna and its social problems. Among their rivals, Hermann Bahr, Raoul Auernheimer, Felix Salten, Paul Zifferer, and Ernst Lotha should be mentioned. In opposition to the Schnitzler group were those who followed Rudolf Hans Bartsch. Their novels focussed mostly on the provinces, and they shared Bartsch's power of giving speech to nature and his sympathy with life in the country and small cities.

In the field of drama, the naturalism of the Schnitzler school and the new romantic style of Hofmannsthal had to share leadership with the primitive strength of the Tyrolese Karl Schönherr. Society comedy continued to be cultivated by Bahr, Salten, Auernheimer, Kurt Frieberger, and the Shaw apostle Siegfried Trebitsch. Mell and Georg Terramare attempted to revive the mediaeval morality play, suggested by Hofmannsthal's arrangement of *Jedermann* in 1912.

The pre-war reputation of Vienna for musical creativeness continued under the Republic. Arnold Schönberg was the leading post-war Austrian composer. He introduced a new system of melodic construction which divides the scale into 12 tones, none of which is more important than the others. The composer called his music "expressionistic." Like expressionistic painting and drama, it is difficult to understand. Ernest Krenek, born in Vienna of Czech parents, achieved international fame with his jazz opera *Jonny spielt auf* (*Johnny Strikes Up*) and is today on the staff of Vassar College. The great annual festival at Salzburg gathered music lovers from all parts of the world.

Although Vienna was a terribly poor city after World War I, it was a great musical center. Students came there to study from all over the world. The great name of Sigmund Freud (1856-1940) is outstanding in the field of psychoanalysis.

Austrian Political History

As we have seen, the election of February 16, 1919, returned a slight plurality of Social Democrats to the constituent assembly. Two of their number, Karl Seitz and Karl Renner, became President of the Assembly and Chancellor of the Republic, respectively. The problem of framing a new constitution was suspended in order to make the Austrian instrument fit in with the constitution of the German *Reich*, which was then being drafted. But the terms of the Treaty of St. Germain, announced in September, specifically prohibited any union of the two German states without approval of the Council of the League of Nations, so the Austrian constituent assembly had no choice but to proceed with its task. On October 1, 1920, the constitution of the Federal Republic was announced.

It was the Christian Socialists who had insisted upon the federal form of the new state. Their natural fear of industrialized and socialistic Vienna was shared by the provinces, who were not inclined to accept domination by the capital. The *Bundesrat,* or upper house, was expected to preserve the federal idea with its representatives from the nine *Länder,* or provinces, elected by the provincial diets. The Chancellor and cabinet were to be responsible to the lower house (*National-rat*), elected by universal suffrage of all citizens over twenty. Until 1929 the President was elected by the two houses meeting as a Federal Assembly, but in that year a constitutional amendment provided for popular presidential elections.

The Social Democrats lost their plurality in the first elections held under the new constitution, and the Christian Socialists organized the government with the support of the German nationalist groups. Dr. Michael Hainisch became the first President and the chancellorship alternated during the early period of the Republic between the Christian Socialists and the Pan-Germans.

The man who above all others set the course for Austrian policy both at home and abroad came into power as Chancellor in May, 1922. Ignaz Seipel, an erudite Catholic priest, was a complete embodiment of the Austrian clerico-political tradition. Sincere, scholarly, courageous, he was at once both intensely patriotic and intensely loyal to his Church. By no liberality of definition can he be called a great statesman, because he failed in the one great task that confronted Austrian statesmanship throughout the long armistice: the task of uniting the Austrian people. Whether the fault was his or whether it lay with the Social Democrats need not be argued here. It is the sort of argument for which history can give no answer; the sort on which only *ex parte* chroniclers can afford to be dogmatic.[14] But there can be no doubt that it was Monsignor Seipel who drew the plans from which Dollfuss and Schuschnigg attempted to build an Austrian state—and failed.

The immediate and inescapable responsibility of Seipel's government was to rescue the Austrian fiscal system. After a tour of European capitals, the new Chancellor addressed an effective appeal to the League of Nations in September, 1922. At that time the morass of inflation had carried the Austrian crown to an exchange rate of 77,000 to one with the American dollar and it was apparent even to Austria's late enemies that the very existence of the little Danubian state was dependent upon outside assistance. After much deliberation, the First Geneva Protocol provided that seven European states would advance $130,000,-000 for twenty years and that Austria would accept a League commissioner to supervise the reorganization of her finances. The schilling replaced the old crown, and by 1926 the League supervision was withdrawn because of the satisfactory progress that had been made.

But this fiscal rehabilitation had been accomplished at no small domestic cost. The rapid deflation infuriated the Social Democrats and they did everything in their power to obstruct the program. A series of crippling strikes and an unsuccessful attempt on his life induced the ailing Chancellor to resign in 1924. His successor and disciple, Rudolf Ramek, was unable to find a solution for the social and economic problems that produced more than a quarter of a million unemployed and brought into the limelight with new bitterness the issues of anti-Semitism and *Anschluss*. In 1926 Seipel again accepted the onerous task of forming a government. It was in this second period of power that his policies and tactics began the process of alienating the Pan-Germans without attracting the Social Democrats, so that he and his Christian Socialist successors, Dollfuss and Schuschnigg, were inevitably driven to the necessity of authoritarianism if they were to retain power. With both the Social Democrats and Pan-Germans in oppo-

---

[14] Out of the extensive literature on both sides of the question the reader is referred for the clerical side to Kurt Schuschnigg, *My Austria*. The best anti-clerical treatment of the argument by an eye-witness is G. E. R. Gedye, *Betrayal in the Balkans* (New York: Harper & Brothers, 1939).

AUSTRIA

sition, the clerical governments were compelled to rely increasingly on the well-organized but unpredictable *Heimwehr* and on the unorganized and poorly led agrarians.

The existence within Austria of the two rival organizations, the *Heimwehr* and the *Schutzbund,* is perhaps the most striking single evidence of the inadequacy of the official government of the state. Military in character and political in purpose, they constituted two opposing armies, each of them twice as large as the military force permitted to Austria by the Treaty of St. Germain.

The *Heimwehr* was agrarian in personnel and conservative in its approach to domestic policies. Its strength came almost exclusively from the non-industrialized areas and its economic and political ideology were confused at best. It was strongly touched by Pan-Germanism in its earlier years, although it became the bitter enemy of Nazism after the rise of Hitler. While it was always militantly anti-socialistic, factions within it were also bitterly anti-clerical. What unity of principle it contained sprang from the ardent nationalism of its leaders, nationalism that did not shy away from an alliance with Mussolini as a hedge against Hitler and which seriously considered the restoration of the Habsburgs as the surest guarantee of Austrian independence. Its leaders were many, but certainly the most colorful and most characteristic of its emotional and unpredictable nature was Prince Ernst Rudiger von Starhemberg.[15]

The *Schutzbund* was the semi-military arm of the Social Democrats. Vienna was naturally its center and its inspiration but its members came from other industrial areas and from the Styrian mining districts as well. It was better disciplined than the *Heimwehr* and its program was the program of the Social Democrats. As a frankly class-conscious organization, its purpose was to protect the socialist accomplishments in the city of Vienna and to advance the socialist program throughout the Republic. Armed clashes between these two private armies were frequent and the consequent casualties added bitterness and intensity to domestic politics.[16]

In 1932 there came to the head of the Austrian state the first of the two Chancellors destined for martyrdom at the hands of Nazi brutality, Dr. Engelbert Dollfuss. Born of a peasant family in Lower Austria,

---

[15] Starhemberg's book is as revealing by its omissions as by its contents. E. R. von Starhemberg, *Between Hitler and Mussolini* (New York: Harper & Brothers, 1942).

[16] The acquittal of three members of the *Heimwehr* on the charge of killing two Socialists in 1927 was the same sort of *cause celebre* as the Sacco-Venzetti trial in Boston or the Billings-Mooney affair in California. It was one of the most significant causes of the unwillingness of the Social Democrats to coöperate with the governments of Seipel, Dolfuss, and Schuschnigg.

Dollfuss had worked his way through a law course at the University of
Vienna, had emerged from the war with an officer's rank, and had risen
rapidly in national politics as a member of the Christian Socialist Party.
Tiny in stature, engaging in personal contacts, and courageous both
spiritually and physically, he vigorously attacked the problems confronting him.   The Lausanne Protocol provided another international loan
to stabilize finances; reform of the civil services reduced government
expenses and removed the worst features of the old Habsburg bureaucracy; successful efforts were made to attract foreign tourists; public
works were undertaken both to make Austria more attractive to visitors
and to provide work for the unemployed; and trade agreements attempted to find an outlet for Austrian products in exchange for the raw
materials and foodstuffs so badly needed.

But Dollfuss, like Seipel before him and Schuschnigg to come later,
could find no formula for the unification of the Austrian people.   The
Social Democrats and the Pan-Germans were both in opposition and his
majority of one in the lower house, when he formed his government,
soon proved inadequate.   When the speaker, Dr. Renner, and the two
deputy speakers resigned in 1933, thereby preventing a meeting of the
Nationalrat, Dollfuss resorted to authoritarianism.   President Miklas
invested him with emergency powers and he proceeded to govern by
decree.

During the thirteen months from June, 1933, to July, 1934, domestic
politics in Austria degenerated into undisguised violence.   The *Schutzbund* had been dissolved by official decree in April, and in May the Communist Party had been abolished.   In June, after Nazi bombs were
thrown at a special police force, Dollfuss ordered all Nazi "brown
houses" closed. After Hitler's special agent in Austria, Theodor
Habicht, had been expelled, the German Nazis continued their campaign by incendiary radio programs from Munich and by tons of propaganda leaflets dropped from planes.   A young Austrian Nazi grazed
the arm of Dollfuss in an unsuccessful attempt at assassination.

Meanwhile the government's fight with the Social Democrats became more embittered.   The dissolution of the *Schutzbund* had been
followed by the creation of the "Fatherland Front."   This was the Chancellor's offer to the young men of Austria who felt the need of a military
organization and who were responsive to a purely patriotic appeal.   It
was to be non-partisan and was to take the offensive against all subversive and anti-national movements.   But its allegedly non-partisan
character was unconvincing to the workers in view of the fact that the
Schutzbund had been dissolved, but the *Heimwehr* was allowed to re-

main active under the leadership of von Starhemberg. On February 11, 1934, when Dollfuss decreed the dissolution of all political parties, the workers' leaders decided that the time had come to hit back. They countered with a general strike, to which the government replied with martial law. In a short but bloody battle the government forces, with the aid of the *Heimwehr,* crushed the socialist opposition. On February 15, the workers in the Karl Marx Hof, the largest of the famous municipal dwelling houses built by the socialist government of Vienna, surrendered and socialism went underground.

Dollfuss took this opportunity to legitimize the authoritarian state he had already created. On May 1, 1934, a new constitution was proclaimed. It made no attempt to disguise its undemocratic character, for its preamble began: "In the name of God Almighty, from whom all law emanates, the Austrian people receives this Constitution for its Christian, German, Federal State." The influence of Italian Fascism was apparent in its "corporative" character and in the elaborate system of councils designed to nullify any attempt at popular control.

It was apparent that strong government was necessary if the Nazis were to be kept within the law. Throughout the spring and early summer of 1934, they became an increasing menace both to national and individual security. Destruction of railways, terminals, power houses and other essential installations was climaxed on the afternoon of July 25 by a carefully planned *Putsch.* One group of Nazis seized the government radio station and a second group entered the chancellery and assassinated Dollfuss. But the Nazi victory was short-lived. The police and the *Heimwehr* laid siege to the chancellery and the conspirators were forced to negotiate for their surrender. The terms, arranged by the German Minister, provided that they should be given safe-conduct to the German border. When it was learned that Dollfuss had died, the Austrian government considered the situation sufficiently altered to cancel the safe-conduct. Otto Planetta, the man who had fired the shot that killed the Chancellor, and several others were tried and hanged, thereby becoming sainted heroes of the German *Reich.*

At the time of the Dollfuss murder, the Vice-Chancellor, Prince Starhemberg, was on one of his frequent visits to an Italian pleasure resort. He flew immediately to Vienna, expecting to be placed in charge of the government. President Miklas, however, chose Kurt von Schuschnigg, the Minister of Education. The new Chancellor found it easy and natural to continue the Dollfuss program. A devout Catholic, an ardent patriot, and a competent constitutional lawyer, he saw in the Nazi menace a threat to his religion as well as to his state. He

struggled valiantly to make the Fatherland Front an all-Austrian program, but he failed. The remnants of the Social Democrats were suspicious of his clerical associations, and the Nazis were openly defiant.

In a final effort to come to terms with Hitler, terms that would enable
an independent Austria to exist, he went to Berchtesgaden in February,
1938. That visit was the beginning of the end. The terms that the
German dictator laid down required the inclusion of Nazis in Schuschnigg's cabinet and in the Fatherland Front. Dr. Arthur Seyss-Inquart
became Minister of the Interior, and almost immediately left for a conference with Hitler in Berlin!

Events moved rapidly. On March 9, Schuschnigg suddenly announced a plebiscite of the Austrian people on the question of independence. The election was to be held the following Sunday, March
13, too soon for the Nazis to bring their strong-arm election methods
into action. Hitler's reply was immediate—unless the plebiscite was
cancelled, his troops would march. What was Dr. Kurt von Schuschnigg to do? To ignore the ultimatum was to throw a handful of poorly
organized troops against Hitler's mighty war machine. Mussolini had
made it clear that Austria could expect no such support as he had given
her in 1934, when he had sent troops to the Brenner Pass at the news of
the Dollfuss murder. Schuschnigg's decision was to make a brief,
emotion-filled speech in which he took leave of the Austrian people.[17]
Seyss-Inquart assumed power and invited Hitler to send in the German
army to preserve order. Thus, on March 12, 1938, the ex-Austrian who
had made himself master of all Germany added some seven million
people to his Third Reich. Austria had become the first in what was
to be a long list of conquered states, a victim of her internal confusion, of
the ineptitude of her statesmen, of the stupidity of her friends, and of
the brutality of her enemies.

After five and one-half years of first-hand experience of the "blessings" of the Nazi regime, all but a small minority of unscrupulous
careerists and SS scoundrels had but one overwhelming desire: to get
rid of the Germans and see the end of the war. Fortunately for the
majority, the great Allied Powers took thought for Austria and decreed
her rebirth at Moscow in November of 1943.

When the Red Army liberated Austria, early in 1945, Moscow announced the formation of an Austrian provisional government headed

---

[17] The reader is again referred to Kurt Schuschnigg, *My Austria*, for a full account of these
last days, including Schuschnigg's two radio addresses, March 9 and March 12. See also the
exciting Eugene Lennhoff, *The Last Five Hours of Austria* (New York: Frederick A. Stokes
Company, 1938).

by Dr. Karl Renner—the same man who was Chancellor of the first Austrian government in 1918 and whose resignation as speaker of the *Nationalrat* had paved the way for the Dollfuss dictatorship. His Cabinet was a coalition of Social Democrats, Christian Socialists, and Communists. Since Russia had not consulted the United States or Great Britain about the formation of this government, the western Allies were reluctant to recognize it. But in general the prospects for Austria are brighter than at any time since the little Republic was first proclaimed.

Bibliography

Allizé, Henry, *Ma Mission à Vienne, Mars 1919-Aôut 1920* (Paris: Librairie Plon, 1933). This contains some excellent material on the economic, fiscal, political, and population problems during the first months of the Republic.

Almond, Nina, and Lutz, Ralph Haswell, *The Treaty of St. Germain. A Documentary History of Its Territorial and Political Clauses* (Stanford University Press, 1935). This work contains in translation all the essential documents and is a prerequisite to any serious work on the Balkans during the post-war period.

Ball, M. Margaret, *Post-War German-Austrian Relations. The Anschluss Movement, 1918-1936* (Stanford University Press, 1937). While the movement for *Anschluss* is the central theme of the book, it does not exclude the other phases of the German-Austrian relationship.

Bullock, Malcolm, *Austria, 1918-1938. A Study in Failure* (London: The Macmillan Company, 1939). This is an account, in readable, narrative form, of the essential story. Contains no bibliography and no footnotes.

Fuchs, Martin, *Showdown in Vienna. The Death of Austria.* Translated by Charles Hope Lumley (New York: G. P. Putnam's Sons, 1939). This is an objective account of the last days of the Republic.

Gedye, G. E. R., *Betrayal in Central Europe* (New York: Harper & Brothers, 1939). An English foreign correspondent gives a detailed, if somewhat subjective, account of the fall of Austria.

Lennhoff, Eugene, *The Last Five Hours of Austria* (New York: Frederick A. Stokes, 1938). This is an exciting story. The book contains enough background to explain the events of the last day.

Pasvolsky, Leo, *Economic Nationalism of the Danubian States* (New York: The Macmillan Company, 1928). This is a Brookings Institute work and is indispensable.

Schuschnigg, Kurt, *My Austria* (New York: Alfred A. Knopf, 1938). The tragic story of the author's well-intentioned but futile efforts to preserve an independent Austria.

Strong, David F., *Austria, October 1918-March 1919* (New York: Columbia University Press, 1939). As indicated by the title, this is a detailed study of Austria during the first winter after the war.

Chapter XVI

HUNGARY (1918-1945)

History

BETWEEN 1918 and 1938, Hungary was a potato-shaped land just south of Czechoslovakia and about as big as the state of Ohio. The peace-makers of 1919 carved off a peel more than twice as big as what they left. "At first sight Hungary looks like a land of gorgeous musical-comedy costumes and uniforms, from General Ratz down to Prince Festetics' hereditary doorman. But behind all the braid and medals, swords and plumes, are a country, a character, and a cause that are anything but comic. A fierce, fighting people, they are sometimes called the Prussians of the South." [1]

To understand the present position and problems of Hungary, it is appropriate to review its history as distinct from that of Austria or Austria-Hungary.

More than a thousand years ago, some 25,000 warrior Magyars rode into the great mountain basin of the Carpathians. A mysterious, non-Slav people, they came from Central Asia, a mixture of a Finnish-Ugrian and Asiatic-Turkish stock. The fertile Danubian plain they found inside the natural mountain fortress was empty of all but a few human remnants of a hundred wars. Their first reconnoitering party reached the territory of modern Hungary in 892. Árpád, "a Magyar chief of extraordinary military ability and political sagacity," [2] carried out his plan to cross the Carpathians and occupy the Danube valley. By the year 900 the conquest was completed and the Magyar warrior tribes controlled the strategic points of the basin. This control was a decisive factor in the shaping of Central-Eastern Europe because it drove a wedge between the two main groups of Slavs (Yugoslavs and northern Slavs) and also because it ensured the relative isolation of the Slovaks until quite recent times. For Árpád united his forces with the

---

[1] "Hungary, The Kingless Kingdom, Wooed by Germany, Clamors for Lost Lands," *Life*, September 12, 1938, pp. 51-61; contains excellent pictures also.
[2] Pribichevich, Stoyan, *World Without End* (New York: Reynal & Hitchcock, 1939), p. 34.

German King Arnulph against Svatopluk's Great Moravia and defeated this outstanding figure of Czechoslovakia's history. The Magyars thereupon seized Slovakia and kept it until 1918.

This success incited the Hungarians to start raiding the Balkans, Italy, Austria, Switzerland, southern Germany, and France. All Europe trembled before the dreaded plague. The Germans called them Hungarians because they were "hungry" (*hungrig*). But the methodical Germans finally defeated them at Augsburg (955). Thereafter the Hungarians settled down. Recognizing the political advantages of Christianity, they adopted the new religion.[3] St. Stephen (997-1037), the most prominent figure in early Hungarian history, received the gift of the Holy Apostolic Crown in the year 1000 from Pope Sylvester II. The Crown of St. Stephen has ever since remained the symbol of the Hungarian state. Stephen from the first looked to Rome rather than to Byzantium. He consolidated the new Kingdom and abolished the ancient Magyar communism. Lands hitherto held by tribes were distributed among individual owners and tribal chieftains were replaced by officials appointed by the king.

The "minorities" policies of the early Hungarians is worth noting. The Hungarians, as the conquering race, were the ruling class. They owned all the land, enjoyed all the political rights, and paid no taxes. All Hungarians were equal and directly subject to the king. The conquered aliens (the Slovaks, the Wallachians-Romanians of Transylvania, and the Ruthenians) had no political rights, did all the work, and paid all the taxes.

But the Magyars behaved differently toward invited foreigners. They settled Szeklers, their own people, in Transylvania (who later became a part of the Hungarian minority in post-war Romania), with the privilege of autonomy and even land communism. In the early part of the thirteenth century, German settlers from the Rhine, erroneously called Saxons, were imported as "King's Guests" to build farms and cities and were granted extensive self-government (their descendants became a German minority of 80,000 in post-war Romania). They built seven cities, and so the region where they still live is called the *Siebenburgen* (Seven Towns).

In general, the Hungarians followed the policy laid down by St. Stephen in a memorable letter to his son and heir, advising him that the new settlers, whom it was his policy to welcome, should be "held in

---

[3] It is interesting to note that Slovakia became Christian sooner than the central Magyar plain. See R. W. Seton-Watson, *A History of the Czechs and Slovaks* (London: Hutchinson & Co., 1943), p. 251.

honor, for they bring fresh knowledge and arms; they are an ornament and support of the throne, for a country where only one language and one custom prevails is weak and fragile." The Hungarians honored this advice until the nineteenth century, when the directly opposite policy of unreasoning assimilation was adopted. As a result, all of the neighboring nationalities helped to dismember Hungary in 1918.[4]

Hungary's early social system was based on three main classes: the land-owning Hungarians, the privileged Germans, and the land-working Slav and Wallachian serfs. As time went on, the country gradually adopted feudalism and a few people began to own most of the land. Here was the beginning of the well-known class of Hungarian magnates. The original class division along racial lines disappeared, and the mass of the Hungarian peoples became subject to a few feudal lords. By the thirteenth century, the royal power had become quite weak. The landlords oppressed the peasantry and fought each other as well as the king.

The possession of Transylvania became one of the most difficult problems of post-war Europe (see Chapter 8). The Romanians claim that Transylvania was an integral part of ancient Dacia until it was subjugated by the Magyars in 1003. But the Hungarians claim that Transylvania was settled by the Magyars, by their cousins the Szeklers, and by Saxons transplanted by Magyar kings to the slopes of the Carpathians. They insist that Romanian elements only infiltrated later.[5] Hence the Magyars contend that Transylvania has always been an integral part of Hungary.

Croatia and Slavonia were conquered under the rule of St. Ladislaw and Koloman. In 1102 the ruling Croat nobility recognized Hungarian kings as their own, in exchange for perpetual confirmation of their feudal rights. Thereafter Croatia maintained a kind of autonomy under the Hungarians until 1918.

Hungarian propogandists have always made much of the Golden Bull, which was promulgated in 1222. They like to compare it to the Magna Carta of 1215 and celebrate it as the origin of Hungarian constitutional liberties and parliamentarianism. It granted the rights of due process of trial, exemption from taxation, armed resistance to the king for breach of compact, and the like. But these liberties were granted only to the landed gentry; the document was actually a guarantee of the power of the nobles over the people. In fact, until 1918,

---

[4] Cited by R. W. Seton-Watson, *op. cit.*, p. 252.
[5] For the Hungarian case, see Eugene Horváth, *Transylvania and the History of the Roumanians* (Budapest, 1935), pp. 5-9.

the Hungarian Constitution made a legal distinction between the landed nobles (the nation) and the plebeians without citizens' rights (the peasants).[6]

It is true that several kings tried to reassert the royal authority and Béla IV began to reacquire the royal estates given to the nobility. The times, however, were not favorable for curbing the great lords. The Tartars were advancing. The discontented nobles rallied half heartedly to the king's aid, but when a decisive battle had to be fought against the Tartars in 1241, disaster followed. The last king of the Árpád dynasty died in 1301. The Anjous of Naples ascended the throne but they too achieved no lasting success in curbing the nobles.

Under Louis the Great (1342-1382), Hungary reached the zenith of her world position and territorial expansion. But the menace of the approaching Turks was steadily increasing, although Hungary enjoyed brilliant international prestige under kings of foreign blood in the fourteenth and fifteenth centuries. Matthias Corvinus (1458-90), the last powerful king of independent Hungary, was of domestic descent. He founded a fine library of precious manuscripts (*Corvina*), managed the nobles with a firm hand, and won fame in numerous peasant legends.

In 1526 a large Ottoman army invaded Hungary. Louis II Jagello, at the head of poorly equipped Hungarian troops, lost the Battle of Mohács (1526). In 1541, the Turks occupied Buda and large districts of Hungary. The country was then divided into three parts: (1) the west was under the rule of the Habsburg King of Hungary (Ferdinand I, elected in 1527); (2) the east became the independent Hungarian principality of Transylvania; and (3) the rich central plain of Hungary was annexed by the Turkish Empire. After the defeat of Vienna (1683), the Turks withdrew into the Balkans and the Habsburgs occupied all of Hungary.

Habsburg rule of Hungary led to forceful Catholicization and Germanization. Soon nearly all the Protestants, who had accepted this religious conversion after the Battle of Mohács, were exterminated— except in Transylvania, where Calvinism was dominant for 200 years as a symbol of opposition to the Habsburgs. By the middle of the eighteenth century, however, Catholicism had won all of Hungary.

The Hungarians did not like Austrian rule. There were many rebellions, all originating in Transylvania. The most successful one was that of Francis Rákóczy, who was elected prince by the Hungarian Diet in 1704. After his defeat, the Habsburgs were recognized as kings of

---

[6] Pribichevich, *op. cit.,* p. 57.

Hungary in return for a general amnesty and guarantee of constitutional rights. But the Magyar nobles resented the attempts of Vienna to improve the lot of the peasantry as an encroachment on Magyar national rights.

Unlike other European countries, Hungary used Latin as its official "national" language until 1844, when Magyar was made the official language by law. It was, therefore, only in the nineteenth century that nationalism stressed the Magyar character of the multi-racial kingdom.[7] Up to then there had been no serious national conflicts, although there were Slovaks in the northwest, Ruthenians in the north, Romanians in the East, Croats in the southwest, and Serbs in the Banat and the Backa, together with Catholic peasants from southern Germany (Swabians).

After the French Revolution, Magyar nationalism became self-conscious through the noble bodyguard at the Emperor's Court in Vienna. The reform of the Magyar language followed and gave impetus to Magyar poetry and *belles-lettres* represented by the works of Kölcsey, Vörösmarty, Berzsenyi, Petöfi, Kemény, Jókai, and others. Simultaneously, political nationalism developed in aspirations for independence from Austria.[8] Hungarian leaders, especially Louis Kossuth, evaluated their nationalism in terms of liberalism.

In 1848 the Hungarians revolted against Austria. The nationalistic hopes of Kossuth came to nothing, however, as the Austrian Emperor Francis Joseph II quelled the rebellion with the aid of a Russian Army —a matter the Hungarians have never forgotten. For twenty years Austria governed Hungary despotically until Francis Deák signed the famous *Ausgleich* (Compromise) in 1867 (see Chapter II). The Compromise gave Magyar nationalism new impetus. It also opened a new era for all the non-Magyar nationalities, who were handed over to the unrestricted political control of the now dominant Magyars.

The status of non-Magyars was theoretically regulated by the Law of Equal Rights of the Nationalities (1868). This was the work of Deák and Eötvös, who regarded assimilation as the ideal solution of racial problems, but wanted each race to develop its own language and culture without hindrance. In reality, this Law was a dead letter from the

---

[7] For more details, see Hans Kohn, *The Idea of Nationalism* (New York: The Macmillan Co., 1944), pp. 527-534; Rustem Vambéry, "Nationalism in Hungary," *The Annals of The American Academy of Political and Social Science*, CCXXXII (March, 1944), pp. 77-85.

[8] It ought to be noted that Alexander Petöfi, the inspired poet of the Magyar Revolution, and Louis Kossuth were both of the Slovak origin. The first was the son of purely Slavic parents and only Magyarized his original name of Petrovic when he was a student; Kossuth came from lesser "gentry" stock of Košuty, near St. Martin, the very heart of Slovakia. Cf. R. W. Seton-Watson, *op. cit.*, p. 259.

outset. When power fell into the hands of extremists, notably Koloman Tisza (who ruled Hungary from 1875 to 1890 as the all-powerful
leader of the Liberal Party, the mouthpiece of the gentry), drastic
nationalistic policies were promoted by the peculiar franchise and electoral practices which gave predominance to the ruling clique. It was
assumed that Hungary was a Magyar national state, although the proportion of the population who spoke Magyar barely topped 50 per cent
in the census of 1910. "This assumption . . . was based on the theory
that the Magyar ruling classes were sustaining the 'nation,' which on
the other hand included the ruling caste and everybody who professed
their theory. Anyone disagreeing with this theory or disapproving the
policy of the ruling caste was considered a traitor." [9]

Hungary was seething before World War I. All of Hungary's
minorities objected to the *Ausgleich,* which handed their fortunes over
to the Magyar aristocrats. The latter, in turn, would not forgive the
Slavs and the Romanians for fighting on the side of the Habsburgs
during the revolution of 1848. Nationalistic lines of antagonism were
made sharper by social and economic divisions. The ruling landowners exploited the common people, the minorities as well as the
mass of Hungarians. Hundreds of thousands of emigrants left for
America. In 1914, three-fourths of the male population in Hungary
could not vote.

As one-half of the Austro-Hungarian Monarchy, Hungary was defeated in World War I. The Treaty of Trianon deprived her of 75
per cent of her territory and 60 per cent of her population. Slovakia,
in the north, was taken by Czechoslovakia; Transylvania in the east by
Romania; Croatia and other areas in the south by Yugoslavia; and
Burgenland in the west by Austria.[10] In spite of Hungarian propaganda claims, the Slovaks, Romanians, and Yugoslavs were not just
grabbed by their respective countries. The inability of Hungary to
solve her problem of racial heterogeneity induced them to seek union
with their respective co-patriots across Hungary's borders.

Geopolitical Aspects

Shifts of Hungarian territory have been spectacular in both World
Wars. Before World War I, Hungary had a population of more than
20,000,000 and an area of 125,609 square miles. The Allied victors cut

---

[9] Vambéry, R., *op. cit.,* p. 79.

[10] While all these regions were chiefly inhabited by non-Hungarian populations, considerable
Hungarian minorities were included: 1,480,000 in Romania, 500,000 in Yugoslavia, and some
700,000 in Czechoslovakia.

Hungary down, as noted above, and took away valuable mineral resources and timberland. In 1938-39, the partition of Czechoslovakia restored to Hungary parts of western Czechoslovakia, wild, mountainous Ruthenia, and the fertile farm lands of southern Slovakia. In 1939, Hungary formally joined the Axis. By the end of 1940, nearly half of Transylvania, with its fields of natural gas and its wealth of gold, silver, lead, copper, and zinc, was returned to Hungary by Romania under Nazi pressure. Hungarian forces invaded Yugoslavia and added their strength to the German invasion of the Soviet Union in 1941. In all, Hungary regained territory larger than West Virginia, with a population of roughly four and a half million people—including more than a million Romanians.

As the Balkan back door to Germany, Hungary found herself occupied by the Russians in 1944. The Carpathian Mountains that rim Hungary's recently acquired Ruthenian district and stretch deep into Romania did not stop the Red Army. West of this mountain barrier, the plains of Hungary spread out into open, flat terrain, broken only by the north-south course of the Danube and the Tisza. The Danube, cutting through the heart of the country, is a natural corridor leading from the Balkans into Austria, and thence into the center of formerly Nazi-held Europe. Railways converge at Budapest from all directions, making Hungary a center of communications between the Balkan nations and middle Europe.

The defeat of Hungary in World War I and the agony that followed brought no change in the policies of Hungary's rulers toward their minorities. According to the census of 1930, the population of Hungary was 8,688,117. Of the total, 92.1 per cent were Magyar, 5.5 per cent were German, the rest were Slovaks, Romanians, Croats, Serbs, and others. The Treaty of Trianon guaranteed minority rights to racial or national groups, but Budapest nevertheless persisted in the practice of de-nationalizing minorities. The theory of "a single and indivisible Magyar nation," embodied in a law passed in 1868, has never been abandoned. The national minorities had no political representation and no autonomous political existence. Even the Germans had to be content with only 10 per cent of their children attending purely German schools. Religiously, Hungary was divided into 64.9 per cent Roman Catholics, 27 per cent Protestants, 5.1 per cent Jews, and 2.3 per cent Greek Catholics. In general, Hungary's national minorities were not treated as fractions of the nation who differed from the Magyars and had the right to maintain their ethnological individuality; they were regarded as groups of citizens speaking an alien language who were to be Magyarized.

Economic Factors

Some 60 per cent of all Hungary is cultivated land. Another 20 per cent is meadow and pasture. This amazingly high percentage of useful land makes Hungary a food reservoir—just what the Nazi government needed. Its resources also include hides for leather, timber, and valuable minerals. The leading crops are wheat, corn, rye, sugar beets, potatoes, and fruits. Poultry, livestock, and the rich fishing preserves along the Danube and Lake Balaton contributed to Hungary's value as a larder for the Axis countries on a blockaded continent. Coal and bauxite, the ore from which aluminum derives, have been Hungary's greatest mineral assets. The production and processing of petroleum in fairly large quantities is a recent development. Hungarian oil output was multiplied nearly twenty times between 1937 and 1938, and is believed to have been pushed much higher since.

Social Conditions

Hungary was, in 1945, still a land of big estates, governed in semifeudal style by their seigneurs, although many thousands of peasants have been settled on small holdings since 1918.[11] Thirty-six Magyar magnates owned a million acres of land; the 1,200,000 peasants who were set on their own farms owned a total of 950,000 acres. Moreover, the large landowners paid only 10 pengoes in taxes per acre; the peasant paid 16 pengoes.[12]

Hungary's non-royal Prince George-Tassilon-Joseph Festétics of Tolna, Lord of Keszthély, Saint George, Csurgó, and so forth, cousin of the British Duke of Hamilton, was one of Hungary's biggest landowners. He owned nine great farms on both sides of Lake Balaton in western Hungary; worked 500 farm laborers, 600 woodsmen. He paid them in goods, not in money. The only larger landholder was Prince Paul Estherházy, who owned some 100,000 acres.[13] A Land Reform Act taxed them one-sixth of their land, divided 430,000 acres among some 400,000 peasants and war veterans (averaging an acre apiece).

Socialism was sternly repressed among the peasants but some reforms

---

[11] One of Hungary's arguments was that the land reforms of Czechoslovakia and Romania were directed against Hungarians. The fact is that Magyar peasants in both countries received allocations of land. It is true that most of the great estates in Transylvania, taken from Hungary, were owned by Magyars or Germans. These were duly expropriated, with very inadequate compensation. But Romanian landowners were just as unlucky as Magyars or Germans.

[12] Newman, Bernard, *The New Europe* (New York: The Macmillan Co., 1943), p. 443.

[13] For documentary pictures, see *Life* (September 12, 1938), pp. 52-53.

have been carried out under an iron paternalism. Peasants are allowed to vote, but only in public. (Townspeople get the secret ballot.)[14]

Cultural Development and Education

Because of its separate racial origin, the Magyar language is entirely different from all others in Central-Eastern Europe. The first impression of a foreigner listening to it is one of complete unintelligibility. The oldest written records in Magyar go back as far as the twelfth and thirteenth centuries. At Buda, sister city to Pest—together the present city of Budapest—books were printed as early as 1473. János Cséri of Apáca, born in Transylvania, a pupil of Descartes, wrote his books of philosophy in Magyar. The first Hungarian minstrel, Bálint Balassa, created Hungarian lyrical poetry in the sixteenth century. Nicolaus Zrinyi, the great epic war-poet of the seventeenth century, wrote the first national war song. In the reign of Maria Theresa, several Hungarian guardsmen returned from Vienna full of new impressions and inaugurated a great revival in national Hungarian literature.

In the nineteenth century, Ferenc Kázinczy initiated a movement for the reformation of the Magyar language. When the national Hungarian struggle for liberty broke out in 1848-1849, a powerful array of talent arose in the service of liberty and poetry. Sándor Petöfi (1823-1849), who died on the battlefield at the age of 26, was the greatest of them. Some of his works have been translated into English (*Selected Lyrics,* and *The Apostle,* both New York, 1912). N. P. Endre Ady (1877-1919), the adored and popular champion of modern lyric poetry, took the role of Baudelaire and Verlaine in Hungarian literature with his strong temperament and irrepressible individuality. Imre Madách (1823-1908) wrote *The Tragedy of Man,* a classic program piece of the Hungarian theater and a philosophic treasure of the Hungarians, as *Faust* is of the Germans. Ferenc Molnár is known the world over for his clever modern plays.

Maurice Jókai (1825-1904) was the creator of Hungarian novels. His richly colored language, his narrative talent, and his friendly joviality are also available in translation (*Black Diamonds,* New York, 1896; *A Hungarian Nabob,* New York, 1899). Kálmán Mikszáth (1849-1922) was a master of the lyric prose of realism and melancholy, a classic sculptor of Hungarian figures of a bygone day (*St. Peter's Umbrella,* London, 1906). Ferenc Herzeg's plays are often on the

---

[14] Beynon, E. D., "Migrations of Hungarian Peasants," *The Geographical Review,* XXVII (April, 1937), pp. 214-228, is a good survey of the social system of peasant Hungary.

program of Hungary's theaters; he is a shrewd, keen-eyed sketcher of the middle class. Jenö Heltai, poet and novelist, is a master of quiet, profound irony (*Csardas,* London, 1932).

The homeland of Liszt can also boast of Ernst von Dohnányi, whose pianoforte, chamber, and orchestral music is often performed in America. Zoltán Kodály has incorporated the rich Magyar folk music into his many beautiful compositions. Bela Bartók was the greatest of Hungarian folksong enthusiasts. Franz Lehár is world-famous with his *Merry Widow, The Count of Luxemburg,* and *Gipsy Love.*

Hungary's over-production of intelligentsia was an outstanding post-war problem. A solution was sought in the *numerus clausus,* restricting Jewish enrollment in the universities and higher schools to 5 per cent in the early twenties. The Jews, incidentally, dominated the cultural and commercial life of Hungary until anti-Semitic restrictions were put into effect.

Political System

When reading Hungarian accounts of the political system of Hungary, one must constantly guard against what we know in this country as "double talk." Hungarian spokesmen describe their system as a "democracy"—and yet by all modern standards it is semi-feudal. Hungary has a parliament, but it is run by great landowners confirmed in their power by a law requiring public ballots in the rural districts (the first completely secret poll in Hungarian history was held in 1939). Hungary calls itself a Kingdom, although there is no king and no dynasty, and when Charles, the last Emperor of Austria-Hungary, tried to return to his Kingdom he was twice prevented from doing so by his "Regent," Admiral Horthy. The latter, who ruled the country in the absence of a hypothetical king, insisted on wearing his admiral's uniform although Hungary has not even a seacoast.

Until the appearance of the various National Socialist groups after 1933, Hungarian politics could be interpreted in terms of the relationship between the magnates (great landed proprietors) and the more numerous gentry (or small landowning and official class).[15] Between 1867, the year of the *Ausgleich,* and the end of World War I, almost the only point at issue between these two groups was the question of Hungary's relations with Austria. The Liberal Party (and especially the extreme Right, composed of the magnates and the higher Catholic

---

[15] A good survey is Royal Institute of International Affairs, *South-Eastern Europe* (New York: Oxford University Press, 1939), pp. 57-66.

clergy) held to the Austrian connection as a safeguard of Hungarian independence, whereas the Party of Independence was more nationalistic and wanted to get rid of the Habsburgs. Neither party was interested in social reforms.

When the Austro-Hungarian Empire was dissolved in 1918, Hungary first tried to save herself by forming a Socialist Republic under Count Michael Karolyi, who was unable to bring order out of chaos. Then the Communists, headed by the notorious Béla Kun and his "Lenin boys," terrorized Hungary. The "White" Counter-Revolution was just as brutal. A Romanian army seized this occasion to march on Budapest to secure Romanian gains and laid the foundation for additional antagonism between Magyars and Romanians. Finally the internecine strife and bloody reprisals were brought under control by a conservative group under Admiral Horthy. Since Béla Kun was a Jew, this was made the pretext for growing anti-Semitism, culminating in Fascist measures, although many of the anti-Semites are of Jewish origin. (Imrédy, the Hungarian Prime Minister who passed the first restrictive measures, had to resign because his opponent discovered that he was part-Jewish). The country was weak for a decade due to the successive "Red" and "White" terrors. At the end of 1919, the old reactionary political system was reinstated, except for the substitution of a Regent, Admiral Horthy, in place of the King.

Horthy's Regime

Nicholas Horthy de Nágybanya was born in 1868. He was commander of an Austrian cruiser squadron in World War I, fought the British in the Otranto Straits, and became Vice-Admiral in command of the Austrian fleet in 1918. He organized a White Army against the Hungarian Soviet Republic in 1919, defeated the Communists, and assumed the title of "Administrator of the Realm" in 1920. He twice balked attempts by ex-Emperor Charles of Austria to reclaim the throne (the second time by armed force). Horthy controlled Hungarian laws through the House of Lords, to which he named 43 members outright and many more indirectly. His followers of the National Union Party completely dominated the Lower House.

In 1919, during the Red and White Terrors of the civil wars, he came riding into Hungary on a white horse (a performance which he repeated when Hungary re-acquired Transylvania). His powers were undefined. He issued decrees and appointed judges and other officials. The Hungarian crown is a civil person in the eyes of the law, so that while it exists the kingdom exists, regardless of whether or not there is a king in Budapest. In 1920 Horthy was elected regent for life. In 1933 his powers were increased by conferring upon him the rights enjoyed by the king with regard to the dissolution, cloture, and adjournment of parliament.

Under Horthy there was only one real political platform in Hungary —the return of its "Lost Provinces," a platform also accepted by all the Hungarian Nazis. All Hungarian political groups were committed to the restoration of "indivisible" Hungary, even though this would involve the unwilling return of non-Magyar minorities.

This was in accord with the Hungarian nationalistic ideology: the Sacred Crown of St. Stephen is still the source of all law, and all lands ever ruled by the Crown of St. Stephen must be restored to the Kingdom. Economic distress plus nationalistic pride emotionalized the eternal cry of the Hungarians for this "revisionism," expressed in the slogan: "Nem, nem, soha!" (No, No, Never). The children of Hungary were taught to recite: "I believe in one God; I believe in one Fatherland; I believe in one divine hour coming; I believe in the resurrection of Hungary. Amen." This propaganda gained some sympathy in England, which receded when Hungary started to lean toward the Axis. Even the humblest peasant supported the program.

After 1920, for the next twelve years, Hungary was governed by three magnate Prime Ministers: Count Teleki (July 1920-April 1921); Count Bethlen (April 1921-August 1931); and Count Guyla Károlyi (August 1931-September 1932). They found their support in a Party of National Unity of the whole propertied class.

During the five years after 1932, the gentry and middle-class elements began to predominate. General Gömbös (1932-36) represented the gentry and strong anti-Legitimists. He showed marked sympathy with the rising power of Nazi Germany. On his death, he was succeeded by his former colleague, Darányi, who was confronted by many Hungarian National Socialist movements. Each of them appealed to the landless section of the population with promises of revolutionary agrarian and electoral reforms and offered the panacea of anti-Semitism to the official and professional classes (which were suffering from low incomes and a plethora of university-trained candidates for the very limited number of posts available). These local fascists found support among the poorest peasantry and workers, the anti-Semitic middle classes, the unemployed intellectuals, and the Army. Against them were ranged the big landowners, the churches, the constitutionalists, the orthodox Social Democrats, and the Jews.

The incorporation of Austria into the Reich in March, 1938, brought in the government of Dr. Imrédy (1938-1939). Another aristocrat, Count Teleki, took his place in 1939. He declared his intention of carrying out Dr. Imrédy's policy, including the anti-Semitic and agrarian measures. But the German influence in Hungary's internal affairs was increasing and the government was forced to make concessions to the German minority.

Hungary Under Hitler's Auspices

In 1939, the "revisionist" policy of Hungary began to get results. Hungary lined up with Germany with a greedy eye on old possessions. The first dividend was paid in March, 1939, when Hungary grabbed Carpatho-Ruthenia as Germany swallowed Czechoslovakia. Then, in satisfying succession, came nearly two-thirds of Transylvania from Romania, and the Yugoslav Banat, granted to Hungary by Germany as a reward for letting German troops march through to invade Yugoslavia in 1941.

But there were disadvantages to being a satellite. His country's treachery in aiding the invasion of her Yugoslav neighbor drove Count Paul Teleki to suicide. In 1942, after successful campaigns in Russia, Hungary's troops met disaster supporting the German flank on the Don River before Stalingrad. Ten Hungarian divisions were lost in the winter slaughter and thereafter the Hungarian Army counted for little in Russia.

Nazism, strange to say in view of Horthy's alliance with Hitler, was anathema to Horthy and his reactionary followers. For them the rise of Nazism meant the ascendancy of the gutter element. But at the same time the Fuehrer represented the dynamic force in Europe that could change frontiers. Horthy and his friends swallowed their pride and joined the Nazis. But they paid a stiff price. Horthy put his country's railways and munitions factories at Germany's disposal and promised to aid the Germans in defending the Carpathians against the Russians, if the need arose. In 1944, that need did arise when Hitler moved his soldiers into Hungarian Transylvania to try to hold the passes against the victorious Red Army. But the Horthy regime was unwilling to be reminded of its 1940 bargain, since Horthy's followers were then urging him to adopt the Darlan-Victor Emmanuel-Badoglio strategy.[16]

In 1944 the question came up how to make peace with the Allies— and still to keep the territories acquired with Hitler's help. But Hitler decided not to wait for Horthy's change of mind. At 3 A.M., March 19, 1944, German parachutists fluttered down in the dark on Budapest and other Hungarian airfields. On the fiftieth anniversary of the death of Hungary's greatest nationalist and patriot, Louis Kossuth, German ground troops crossed Hungary's borders and smashed resisting garrisons. Horthy's country was conquered by her erstwhile ally.

The Germans first attempted to form a government under former Premier Béla Imrédy, then settled on Field Marshal Doeme Sztojay, Hungarian Minister in Berlin, as Premier with a Cabinet of ten reliable collaborators. They took the place of Premier Nicholas Kallay's government. But the real authority, military and civil, rested with SS leader Dr. Edmund Veesenmayer, Field Marshal Baron Maximilian von Weichs (German commander-in-chief in the Balkans), and Hungarian industrialists.

In 36 hours Hungary had lost every vestige of independence. Her fate was the inevitable outcome of tortuous, opportunist diplomacy, the same fate that confronted Bulgaria and Romania.

In October, 1944, Horthy reached a conclusion, helped in his decision by the thud of Russian feet marching toward Budapest. On October 15, the Budapest radio announced that the Regent had accepted Allied armistice terms. Three hours later, Horthy was overthrown and a new Hungarian alliance was proclaimed with Germany. A rabid Nazi, Ferenc Szalasi, was named Regent. The new puppet government found itself beset on all sides. A reign of terror swept the Hungarian capital as the German press reported Admiral Horthy, his family, and close associates to be "enjoying the right of asylum" somewhere in the Reich. By early November, Russian troops had reached panic-stricken Budapest in a four-pronged offensive. The city was completely encircled by December 27, and fell in February, 1945, after a three-month struggle.

Meanwhile, on January 20, 1945, a new Hungarian Government, set up under Russian auspices in Debreczen, signed an armistice with Moscow. The terms included cession of all territorial gains since 1937 (sections of Czechoslovakia, Romania and Yugoslavia); reparations ($300,-

---

[16] For Tibor Eckhardt's aspects of this strategy, see Joseph S. Roucek, "The 'Free' Movements of Horthy's Eckhardt and Austria's Otto," *Public Opinion Quarterly*, VII (Fall, 1943), pp. 466-476.

000,000 in commodities payable in six years—two-thirds to Russia, the rest to aggression victims); the establishment of an Allied Control Commission in Budapest; and a Hungarian declaration of war against Germany with a pledge of at least eight divisions.

Bibliography

Almond, Nina, and Lutz, R. H., *The Treaty of Trianon* (Palo Alto, Cal.: Stanford University Press, 1935). A careful review of the history and provisions of the Treaty.

Apponyi, Albert, and others, *Justice for Hungary* (London: Longmans, 1928). Hungarian propaganda on behalf of "revisionism."

Eckhardt, Ferenc, *A Short History of the Hungarian People* (London: Grant Richards, 1931). Factual and brief.

Jászi, Oscar, *Revolution and Counter-Revolution in Hungary* (London: King, 1924). An important account of the three Hungarian revolutions of 1918-1919, by one of Karolyi's Ministers.

Kosary, D. G., *A History of Hungary* (New York: Benjamin Franklin Bibliophile Soc., 1941). Up to 1940 by a Hungarian professor.

Macartney, C. A., *Hungary and Her Successors* (New York: Oxford University Press, 1937). One of the most dependable studies.

Pribichevich, Stoyan, *World Without End* (New York: Reynal & Hitchcock, 1939). Probably the most valuable survey from the standpoint of social history.

Vambéry, Rustem, *The Hungarian Problem* (New York: The Nation, 1942). A Hungarian liberal attacks the ruling clique of Hungary.

Wiskemann, Elizabeth, *Prologue to War* (New York: Oxford University Press, 1940). A dependable account of the Reich's penetration of the Danubian countries.

Wolfe, Henry C., *The German Octopus* (Garden City, N. Y.: Doubleday, Doran, 1938). Chapter 17 is an excellent journalistic account of Hungary's general problems.

Chapter XVII

CZECHOSLOVAKIA (1918-1945)

Geopolitical Position

THE "new" Czechoslovakia which appeared on the map of Europe after 1918 consists partly of the so-called "historical lands" of Bohemia, Moravia, and Silesia (constituent parts of the one-time Kingdom of Bohemia), and partly of Slovakia and Carpathian Russia (Ruthenia), both of which formerly belonged to Hungary. The historical lands were slightly increased at the expense of Germany by the addition of the district of Hlučín, and at the expense of Austria by the addition of the districts of Valtice and Vitoráz. On the other hand, by a decision of the Conference of Ambassadors of July 28, 1920, the eastern part of Silesia and a part of the Slovak districts of Spiš and Orava were assigned to Poland. Carpathian Ruthenia was incorporated in the Republic as an autonomous territory.

A description of Czechoslovakia is impossible without a series of contradictions. For example, Czechoslovakia was ranked among the minor states, and rightly so to a certain extent, for it was no bigger than Belgium or Holland from north to south. But from west to east it was as long as the whole of Germany from the frontiers of Bohemia to the Gulf of Danzig, or as England from the Orkneys to Plymouth, or as France from Calais to the Pyrenees, or as Italy from the Alps to the Gulf of Taranto.

The line from west to east is very significant. It marks as great a distance in terms of civilization as would a line drawn from Manchester or Lille to the Caucasus. In the western part of the Republic, one finds the typical features of the whole northwest of Europe—extensive and highly specialized industry, intensive and rationalized agriculture, a life completely urbanized and even mechanized. But in passing from west to east, Czechoslovakia becomes steadily more rustic, picturesque, and primitive. In the extreme eastern part, one could walk for days through ancient forests, armed with a gun against bears, without meeting a single soul beyond an occasional herdsman or seeing more than an occasional hamlet of wooden cottages, akin to the remotest villages of Russia. The distance between Prague and Carpathian Russia represents a greater disparity in civilization than could be found in any other country of Europe.

The Czechoslovak Republic is situated on the great watershed between the Black, Baltic, and North Seas, approximately in the geographical center of Europe. In shape it resembles a long wedge with the thick end in the west and the thin end in the east. Its location in the center of Europe placed it at the very heart of history's mêlée. Many collisions of races, of cultures, of ideas have involved this area. The northern frontier of the Roman Empire passed through it; migrating tribes of Gauls, Germans, and Slavs poured over its frontier heights. It was here that Turkish and Tartar incursions from the Orient were halted. Here in the sixteenth century stood the eastern bulwark of Roman culture, and here in the twentieth century, just as it happened a thousand years ago, the Eastern and Western Churches came into contact. Here also arose the Reformation, and the war broke out on this soil between southern Catholicism and northern Protestantism which practically exterminated the nation and swept its culture away.

Surrounded by far more powerful and belligerent states, the frontiers of Czechoslovakia shook before the battering-rams of conquerors. Sometimes these frontiers were thrust forward to the shores of the Baltic or again down to the Mediterranean, in order that the nation might secure breathing space after the pressure to which it had been subjected. Two historical events illuminate the honor and the tragedy of this central situation: first, the Hussite Wars, in which a nation of peasants armed with flails succeeded in defending their country against the world; second, a few decades later, the ideas of King George of Poděbrady, who drew up a scheme not unlike the League of Nations in the fifteenth century.

Here, too, in a way were situated the crossroads of nature. No geological age left this small land untouched. The border of the southern region of wine, maize, and tobacco extends to the very threshold of the forests of the north. Most prominent of all, however, the face of the earth bears witness to the toil of men for a thousand years. Every inch of soil is intensively tilled and utilized. A concentrated chessboard of fields sweeps unbroken over hill and dale to the frontiers.

Czechoslovakia has often been hailed as a new nation. Yet in 1929 it was able to celebrate the thousandth anniversary of the old Czech state—a state older than that of William the Conqueror. Hus and

Comenius bear witness to the high level of Czech culture at the threshold of the modern era, but it was only one hundred years ago that this same nation again began to re-create a literature of its own. At the time when Voltaire and Lessing were writing, the Czechs did not even possess spelling-books for their children in their own language. The schools were German and the towns were Germanized. Only the villages preserved the national tongue—and they were villages of serfs. Eighty years ago Prague did not possess a Czech theater. Sixty years ago the ancient Czech University at Prague was recalled to life.

The population of Czechoslovakia is composed largely of workers and peasants, that is, of people bound to the land and to sources of production. In essence, it is a nation of "stay-at-homes" rather than adventurers. Yet its sons fought for the liberty of their country in both World Wars on the battlefields of Serbia, in Lombardy, in the Argonne, in the Urals, in Siberia, in the Near East, in Africa, in England.

During the last few centuries, the Czechs and Slovaks have had to struggle, consciously and desperately, for their national existence and for their language against the Austrian Germans and the Magyars under Habsburg rule. It was an exhausting, embittered, daily fight against de-nationalization and humiliation. During both World Wars, their burdens were increased by brutal regimes of terror, by mass executions, and by prisons filled with Czechs and Slovaks from the leaders of the nation down to women and children.

On October 28, 1919, this nation of rebels won its freedom but took no revenge. Two or three days after the revolution, the Czechoslovak Government offered seats in the Convention Parliament to the German minority which, however, refused all coöperation.

These general lines of Czechoslovakia's historical, geographical, and political development should be kept in mind by all who desire a real understanding of Czechoslovakia's problems after 1918.

Formation of the New State

Czechoslovakia came into existence as an independent state on October 28, 1918, as a consequence of the revolt of Czechs and Slovaks both abroad and at home against the Austro-Hungarian Empire—a revolt which accelerated the collapse of the Habsburg Monarchy. From the standpoint of its founders, the Republic was the fruit of the revolutionary will of the Czechoslovak people to gain independence and unity. This motive was propounded by Professor Thomas G. Masaryk at the beginning of the First World War, when he organized revolutionary activities against the Austro-Hungarian Monarchy. He became the leader of this revolution not only because he embodied the will of the people but primarily because he gave the Czechoslovak cause a constructive ideology related to the war efforts of the Allies. For Masaryk the First World War was a world revolution in which the ideals of humanitarianism and democracy struggled against autocratic principles, a fight against oppression and obsolete privileges of all kinds. Such a contest inevitably evoked a responsive echo from Czech history, rooted as it is in the evolution of democratic ideas and humanitarian aims culminating in the self-determination of small nations. Hence the Czechoslovak legionnaires in Siberia, France, and Italy fought not only for the freedom of their nation, but also for world-wide recognition of the precepts of freedom, justice, and equality. Masaryk taught that the French, English, American, and Italian democracies had to win and that Czechoslovakia's future depended on democracy in action.

The development of Czechoslovakia between 1918 and 1938 was based on the continuity of the moral principles and democratic policies fostered under the leadership of President Masaryk and Minister of Foreign Affairs Dr. Eduard Beneš, who became President in 1935. These two men were united not only by the affinity of their ideological convictions but also by the bonds of sincere personal friendship. They held office for a longer period than any other European statesmen after World War I, a fact which gave the Republic unusual stability during its formative years. It is true that Czechoslovakia's dependence on the democracies at the time of Munich brought the country to the brink of destruction. But despite this temporary set-back, Beneš continued to coöperate with Great Britain, the United States, and the Soviet Union and refused to collaborate with the forces of aggressive Nazism, thereby paving the way for Czechoslovakia's resurrection from the grave of Munich in World War II.[1]

Thanks to a series of fortunate circumstances and particularly to the

---

[1] In his speech, "What Are We Fighting for?" delivered at the Chicago Stadium, May 23, 1943 (reprinted in: Czechoslovak Sources and Documents, No. 4, August, 1943, *President Beneš on War and Peace,* New York: The Czechoslovak Information Service, 1943, pp. 71-80), President Beneš expressed this as follows: "It was our fate in Czechoslovakia to be a citadel of democracy placed next to a powerful country whose leaders believed in the totalitarian order. . . . European democracy failed to realize its peril in time. . . . We in Czechoslovakia paid a very high price for the extra year of so-called peace which the Munich decree gave to Europe. We do not say that the price was too high. We accepted the democratic way of life . . . (But) democracy has a genuine hatred of war. . . . We had to face the Anglo-Saxon hatred of war at the time of the Munich crisis . . . Through their own blundering and evil intentions the Axis Powers have brought into being the grand alliance known as the United Nations which is bound to be triumphant to the end . . . It will be triumphant because the spirit of humanity and the trend of historical events are on its side. . . . We believe that the war collaboration with the Soviet Union will bring the United Nations into post-war collaboration in peace and democracy . . ."

well-conducted revolutionary movement that resulted in its establishment, the Czechoslovak state was represented at the Peace Conference which met in Paris in January, 1919. Its authority was based on recognition by the Allied Powers, which had already virtually agreed on the frontiers of the future state. Negotiations regarding Czechoslovak territorial demands were conducted smoothly, on the whole. The "historical" boundaries of the Czech lands were accepted and Slovakia was incorporated in the new state. Carpathian Ruthenia was added, at the request of its population, in the form of an autonomous territory.

Constitutional Democracy

Masaryk's democratic ideology met with an enthusiastic response among the masses and was expressed in the temporary Constitution of November, 1918, which established a democratic Republic and abolished privileges of nobility, birth, and class.

The Constitution in its final form, voted by the National Assembly on February 29, 1920, was to have the distinction of being the only charter of its kind in Central Europe to survive for two subsequent decades. In the surrounding countries, constitutions were radically modified or abolished. The fundamental law of Czechoslovakia was framed under the influence of Masaryk's ideology of "humanitarian nationalism." Copied in part from the United States Constitution, it was redolent of Jeffersonian ideals of democracy and government by the consent of the governed. But it was also modernized by a strong dash of nationalism and socialism.[2]

The Constitution created a centralized rather than a federative state. Only the territory of Carpathian Ruthenia was guaranteed extensive autonomy. The latter's population was composed largely of Ukrainians, for the most part illiterate in 1919, as a consequence of Magyar oppression. Prague therefore never established a Ukrainian Diet (until after Munich), fearing that it would be dominated by the well-organized Hungarians and Jews, although a modest autonomy was granted by the appointment of local governors from the very beginning. The first governor was an American of Ukrainian extraction, but in 1923 a native Ukrainian succeeded to the office.

The legislative power in Czechoslovakia was granted to two houses of parliament elected by popular vote: deputies for a term of six years, senators for eight. The President of the Republic was elected by both houses of Parliament, sitting in joint session, for a term of seven years. The Constitution permitted only two presidential terms, but an excep-

---

[2] The text can be found in *International Conciliation,* October, 1922, No. 179.

tion was made to permit President Masaryk to be re-elected as long as he would accept office. He served for seventeen years.

The Cabinet, appointed by the President, was made responsible to the Chamber of Deputies, while the Senate was to exercise the functions of amendment and moderation. A permanent committee—two-thirds of the members taken from the House of Deputies and one-third from the Senate—was to take the place of the National Assembly during its vacations. The presidential powers were subordinated to those of the Assembly.

In addition to a special section devoted to the so-called "fundamental rights and liberties of citizens," an outstanding chapter of the Constitution was devoted to safeguards for racial and religious minorities. In general, it incorporated the provisions of international treaties for the protection of minorities.[3]

Politics

As far as the Czechs were concerned (and, to a large extent, the Slovaks also), Czechoslovakia was a real progressive democracy—the only one east of Switzerland. Its political system was as firmly established as any in Europe up to Munich.

Voting was based on proportional representation, as in France. Parties presented their lists all over the country. The votes they gained in each constituency were added together and seats in Parliament were allotted according to the total number of votes in the country. Since the parties nominated their own candidates and arranged their names according to a specific order on "bound lists," the ruling cliques of the parties had enormous power.

This was one of the evils of Czech political life.[4] The voters could choose only among the "bound lists" of the different parties, and could not vote as they liked, in the American fashion, for individual candidates or groups of candidates other than those represented by the lists. Party membership cards played far too important a part in securing civil service and private jobs. All big political parties possessed a complicated apparatus of organization which touched the interests of the

---

[3] A very useful short summary of the accomplishments of Czechoslovakia's democracy is Brackett Lewis, *Democracy in Czechoslovakia* (New York: American Friends of Czechoslovakia, 1941). For more about the problem of Czechoslovakia's minorities, see Joseph S. Roucek, *The Working of the Minority System under the League of Nations* (Prague: Orbis, 1928); Joseph S. Roucek, "Czechoslovakia and Her Minorities," chapter IX, pp. 171-192, in *Czechoslovakia: Twenty Years of Independence,* edited by R. J. Kerner (Berkeley, California: University of California Press, 1940).

[4] Roucek, Joseph S., "The Working of Czechoslovak Constitutional Democracy," *World Affairs Interpreter,* VIII (July, 1937), pp. 157-167.

electorate at all points. They owned daily papers and possessed strong economic organizations (building, production, and consumer coöperative societies).

Proportional representation—theoretically the most advanced and progressive democratic system possible—had another disadvantage. It greatly increased the number of parties by giving representation to small minorities. In all, there were over twenty significant parties. Slovaks, Germans, Hungarians, and Poles each had their own parties and their own deputies in Parliament, and could vote for them even when they lived in predominantly Czech districts.

The system, therefore, gave protection to national minorities. But it meant also that no one party was ever strong.enough to form a government by itself. The Government of Czechoslovakia was government by coalition. The Prime Minister usually belonged to the strongest party at the time. The other Ministries were assigned to the parties according to their electoral strength. This meant that the ideological program of each party was modified in practice and that the government acted according to compromises worked out among the parties represented in it. Since all Cabinet decisions had to be unanimous, every measure had to be more or less satisfactory to Socialists, Catholics, town workers, and farmers as well as to Czechs, Slovaks, and Germans. (The Communists, the Poles, and the Hungarians were consistently in opposition—joined at times by other groups—the Germans, the Slovak Autonomists, and other minor elements.) The result was that no party was ever satisfied. But the country, as a whole, carried out its political processes with a minimum of upheaval and without sudden changes. Continuity in the Presidency also helped to maintain stability.

There were eleven Cabinets from 1918 to 1938, but only seven Prime Ministers. One of them was a Social Democrat (Tusar), one a Czech Socialist (Beneš), and the last four were Agrarians (Švehla, Udržal, Malypetr, and Hodža).

The complications of operating a multi-party coalition, and of reaching acceptable compromises on a multitude of policies, laws, and appointments, led to the formation of a council of party leaders. Called the "Five" or the "Seven" (according to the number of parties in the coalition at the time), it had no constitutional standing but its decisions were invariably accepted and given legal form by Parliament or Cabinet as necessary. Although this shadow cabinet was criticized as an undemocratic institution, it actually represented the decisions of the parties participating in the government and made the coalition system workable.

The composition of the four Parliaments from 1919 to 1935 was as follows:[5]

	April 1920	November 1925	October 1929	May 1935
CZECHOSLOVAK PARTIES:				
Agrarian(a)	40	46	46	45
Social Democratic(b)	74	29	39	38
Progressive Socialist	3			
Czech Socialist(c)	24	28	32	28
National Democratic(d)	19	13	15	17
National Union			3	
Trades and Crafts	6	31	12	17
Czechoslovak Catholic(e)	21	23	25	22
Slovak Catholic(f)	12		19	22
Fascist				6
	199	183	191	195
OTHER PARTIES:				
Communist(g)		41	30	30
Sudeten German(h)				44
German Socialist Democratic	31	17	21	11
" Agrarian	13	24	16	5
" Christian Socialist	9	13	14	6
" Nationalist	12	10	7	
" National Socialist	5	7	8	
" Democratic	2			
" Trades			3	
Hungarian National(i)	1		4	
" Christian Socialist(i)	5	4	5	9
Hungarian-German Social Democrats	4			
Independent			1	1
	82	117	109	105

(a) Founded 1899; its leader, Antonin Švehla, was Prime Minister 1922-1926 and 1926-1929; he died in 1933.

(b) The chief worker's party, founded 1878; early members were persecuted by Austria; workingmen obtained the right to vote only in 1896.

(c) Founded in 1896 with a Socialist program, but one which rejected Marxism. Membership consisted largely of the upper working classes, office employees and some professional people. It had a strong women's section. Dr. Beneš belonged to this group.

(d) Founded in 1918, it represented largely the interests of industry, financial circles, property owners; its leader Dr. Kramář was Prime Minister during the Constitutional Assembly. This party combined with the National Union before the 1935 elections.

(e) Founded in 1922, the leader was Msgr. Šrámek, who became Prime Minister of the Czechoslovak government-in-exile in London in World War II. The Catholic clerical parties were the only ones unable to unite Czech and Slovak wings in one party.

(f) Founded in 1918, it was always the strongest party in Slovakia; it included 2 Deputies of the Ruthenian party, 1 of the united Polish parties, and 1 of the Slovak Protestant Party.

(g) Split off from the Social Democratic Party in 1921, but lost votes heavily.

(h) The party of German Nationalists with a Nazi form of organization and propaganda. Founded and led by Konrad Henlein; it secured 56% of the German-speaking votes in 1935.

(i) Represented together about 60% of the Hungarian vote, the remainder being scattered among the Agrarian, Social Democratic, and Communist Parties.

[5] Based on Brackett Lewis, *Democracy in Czechoslovakia*, pp. 14-15.

Several tendencies in the alignment of parties in the various coalitions during the first two decades are worth noting. The Social Democratic (Workers') Party was overwhelmingly the strongest in the first election, and its leader Tusar was the first Premier. It lost heavily when its Marxist wing seceded in 1921 to form the Communist Party, but recovered later and constituted the third largest group in the last Parliament. The Communist Party won the second largest representation in its first parliamentary elections (1925), but later fell to fourth place. The Agrarian Party grew gradually, even after the death of its founder and Premier, Švehla, and was the largest group in Parliament, after 1925. It also attracted members from the city populations because of its power and its non-socialist tendencies.

The various nationalities in the population of the Republic were fairly represented in the House of Deputies, as can be seen in the following table:

(The last two columns give the proportion of the last House belonging to each nationality and their proportion of the total population.)[6]

	1920	1925	1929	1935	Proportion of Deputies Per Cent	Population Per Cent
Czechoslovaks.........	199	207	208	206	68.66	66.9
Germans...............	73	75	73	72	24.00	22.3
Hungarians............	9	10	8	10	3.33	4.8
Ruthenians............		6	6	8	2.67	3.8
Polish................		2	3	2	0.67	0.6
Jews.................			2	2	0.67	1.3
	281	300	300	300	100.	99.7

[6] *Ibid.*, p. 17.

Note, however, that not all of the deputies of minor nationalities sat in Parliament for their separate national parties. Some of them represented the larger general parties: Social Democratic or Communist. The table indicates that Germans and Poles had a slightly larger representation in the Lower House than their proportion of the total population would warrant.

The same plan of proportional representation applied to provincial, district, and town administrations. In the Provincial Board of Bohemia, there were 83 Czechs and 37 Germans; in that of Moravia and Silesia, 44 Czechs, 14 Germans, and 1 Pole; in Slovakia, 49 Slovaks and 5 Hungarians; in Ruthenia, 16 Ruthenes and 2 Hungarians. In 46 districts and 3,363 towns, Germans were in the majority in the governing councils and the Czechs and Slovaks had only a minor voice in public affairs. As a matter of fact, complaints by Czech minorities in

German-speaking communities about their treatment in the use of school or relief funds were as loud as those of the German minority groups elsewhere.

In spite of Czechoslovakia's basic differences in national, religious, social, and economic elements, her parliamentary system functioned successfully and gave the Republic one of the most stable governmental forms in Europe under the mellowed leadership of Masaryk. But "The Grand Old Man" of Czechoslovakia was well advanced in years in the second decade of his country's independence and decided to retire.

Beneš Takes Up Masaryk's Task

The Presidential standard was slowly hauled down from the tower of Lány Castle at one o'clock on December 14, 1935, as the signal that Masaryk had resigned the Presidential office he had held for seventeen years. Recommending Dr. Beneš as his successor, the President said in his resignation: "Four times I have been elected President of the Republic. This fact may give me the right to ask you . . . always to remember that states can be maintained only by respecting those ideals which brought them into being." Justice, he emphasized, must "be equal for all citizens regardless of race and religion."

The title "President Liberator" was conferred upon him by the Cabinet and there was a solemn feeling throughout the nation that a memorable chapter in Czechoslovakia's history had closed. Parliament granted him the use of Lány Castle for his lifetime and a continuation of the emoluments he received as President. The 85-year-old Masaryk was happy that the destinies of his country had been placed in the hands of Beneš, in whom he had had supreme faith since the outbreak of the First World War had brought them together.

Of all the creators of Czechoslovakia, Beneš in western eyes was the greatest after Masaryk himself. This little man, slender, alert, with cool eyes, a teetotaler and non-smoker, served the robust young democracy from its birth in 1918 right down to 1938—twenty years without a break. He was Foreign Minister for seventeen years and President for three.

Beneš was an international figure of world-wide reputation, holding such positions as General Rapporteur of the Geneva Disarmament Conference and President of the League of Nations. In 1931 he was the only statesman in Geneva who protested the Japanese aggression against China on behalf of the idea of collective security. He also created the Little Entente, an anti-Hungarian alliance with Yugoslavia and Romania, and the alliance with Russia was concluded under his Presidency. He was responsible for Czechoslovakia's steady orientation to France and England as a sincere and devoted friend of the Western democracies. In short, he was the best-known European after Briand, a pillar of the League, and the foremost spokesman of the small nations in international gatherings.

To understand Dr. Eduard Beneš, it is necessary to review his career. The son of simple Czech peasants, he was the youngest of ten children. His older brother, Vojta Beneš (who helped to organize the Czechoslovak National Council of America in World War I as he did during World War II), helped him to get an education. In 1905, at the age of 21, Beneš left Prague to study in Paris, London, Berlin, and finally in Dijon, where he received his doctorate in 1908. His student days help to explain his pro-French sympathies.[7] He then taught economics in the Czechoslovak National Academy in Prague, and at the age of 28 he was appointed lecturer in sociology in the Charles University of Prague.

In 1914 he met Masaryk, and Beneš, also a savant although only 30 years old, became Masaryk's closest collaborator. When the latter went abroad to organize revolution, Beneš at first remained behind to keep open the line of communications between Prague and Masaryk through Switzerland. Through spies in strategic places and friends banded together in a secret society, "Maffia," he kept Masaryk informed of Austria's moves. He split postcards into halves and inserted cipher messages between them, having them joined together by a bookbinder. He also received the latest news from the Austrian Ministry of the Interior, as the Minister's valet was a sympathizer who pilfered state secrets. With his help, the details of the mysterious proceedings of the Vienna Ministerial Council appeared a few days later in the enemy press, much to the consternation of the Austrian leaders. A broken leg saved Beneš from service in the Austrian army. When he began to be suspected by the Austrian police, he escaped to Switzerland with the help of a forged passport.

His new task was to make the Allies conscious of Czechoslovakia, and Beneš did a highly successful job on the lecture platform, in newspapers, salons, Masonic lodges, foreign offices, and university circles. Whereas Masaryk was the beloved philosopher and spiritual architect of his people's house of liberty, it was Beneš the indefatigable, Beneš the hard-headed and thick-skinned, Beneš the mercurial, who sat on

---

[7] For Beneš' career and ideology, see Joseph S. Roucek, "Eduard Beneš," *Social Science*, X (April, 1935), p. 2000, and "Fiftieth Anniversary Birthday of Dr. Eduard Beneš," *World Affairs. Interpreter*, V (July, 1934), pp. 154-158, and "Eduard Beneš as a Sociologist," *Sociology and Social Research*, XXIII (September-October 1938), pp. 18-24.

Balfour's doorstep, who tirelessly haunted Clemenceau, who pestered Lord Robert Cecil, who beleaguered Lord Derby until he had obtained formal assurance from each of them that they would recognize an independent Czechoslovak army. He and Masaryk won their big victory when the establishment of an independent Czechoslovakia became a cardinal point in the peace terms laid down by English and French leaders and by President Wilson. By the time Beneš was 35 years old, he was on intimate terms with the leading statesmen of Europe and used this acquaintance to very good advantage at the Paris Peace Conference and in post-war international conferences.

Beneš had a few vociferous opponents at home (after 1918), people resentful of his position as the Republic's "peripatetic Foreign Minister" and as the most influential personality next to Masaryk. His unremitting labors on behalf of the League of Nations and international understanding, so necessary for the preservation of a small country, turned out tragically when France, the country which Beneš trusted most, helped to sell Czechoslovakia "down the river" at Munich. The most tragic figure of the whole grim drama, Beneš bore himself with dignity and unflinching fortitude to the end.

Beneš could not know that the departure of Masaryk from the Czechoslovak Presidency was also a concluding phase of the era of democratic idealism in Europe. With Masaryk's death on September 14, 1937, there passed the last great leader who had hoped that an era of collective security, international coöperation, and enlightened nationalism could transform the slaughterhouse tendencies of Europe into the sweet reasonableness of internationalism.

Czechoslovak Resources

The Republic has a variety of scenery and natural resources. The mountain-rimmed Bohemian plateau counterbalances the mountainous and heavily forested eastern sections, with river valleys leading down to the Hungarian plain. The country's natural resources are represented first and foremost by deposits of pit-coal and lignite which give some districts—particularly those around Moravská-Ostrava and Most—a typical mining aspect. In fact, with the exception of platinum, Czechoslovakia has practically every useful mineral, including iron ore (produced chiefly in Slovakia), copper, silver, lead, and gold. An important source of radium ores as well as of finished radium is world-famous Jáchymov (Joachimsthal). Salt is found in Carpathian Ruthenia and in Slovakia, and the output almost suffices to meet the needs of home consumption. China clay of excellent quality found in northwestern

Bohemia gave rise to a famous porcelain industry, centered around Karlový Vary (Carlsbad), a fashionable health resort for Europe's ruling houses and aristocracy since 1795. Naphtha, obtained in Moravia and Slovakia, is used mainly for the production of heavy lubricant oils.

Czechoslovakia benefits by having more or less of an equilibrium between agriculture and industry. Industrial output is somewhat more important than agricultural output in the western part of the Republic, but agriculture predominates in Slovakia and particularly in Carpathian Ruthenia.

Czechoslovakia contains almost 100 per cent of the porcelain industry of the former Austro-Hungarian Empire, 92 per cent of its sugar industry, 92 per cent of its glass industry, 87 per cent of its barley output, 75 per cent of its cotton industry, and 46 per cent of its alcohol production. As to the mineral resources of the former Monarchy, three-fourths of the coal output, two-thirds of the graphite beds, almost all of the silver mines, and the chief gold mines are in Czechoslovak territory.

The capacity of Czechoslovak industries was greatly in excess of home consumption until 1938, so that the country depended principally on its industries for its favorable balance of trade. Czechoslovak exports exceeded imports by $35,000,000 in 1937. From Prague came machinery and refined sugar. Brno (Brunn), the capital of Moravia, exported textiles and the excellent light arms produced in the Czechoslovak Arms Manufacturing Company plant. Bustling Moravská-Ostrava, in Silesia, was the Czech Pittsburg. Bratislava, the capital of Slovakia, was the site of the Nobel dynamite works. Plzeň (Pilsen) workers brewed the world-famous Pilsen beer and produced heavy machinery, locomotives, and railroad equipment in the main Skoda foundry. At Zlín (near Brno) was located the mammoth shoe factory of the Báťa family, whose competition so greatly disturbed America's high tariff advocates in 1938. Glass-making had been a famous Bohemian industry since the sixteenth century and thousands of workers in north Bohemia were engaged in it. The manufacture of glass bijouterie was important also, especially glass beads exported to Africa, America, and elsewhere. The textile trade was highly developed and the musical instruments and laces turned out in the Ore Mountains are known all over the world.

All in all, some 75 per cent of the whole industrial plant of the former Austro-Hungarian Monarchy was located in Czechoslovakia. This was not, however, entirely advantageous to the Republic, since it created extremely complex problems of customs barriers between the points of production and those of former consumption, of competition with new industries on former Austro-Hungarian territory which used to consume Czech-made goods, and of finding new markets to replace the old. Hence Czechoslovakia was most anxious for international agreements which would make frontiers less of an obstacle to trade and personal travel. The Czechoslovaks imported Swedish alloying metals, American cotton and copper, and East Indian rubber, and exported Czech glassware and shoes to India, South America, and the United States. The railway system taken over from Austria-Hungary was an economic handicap, as it was built when the centers of communications were Vienna and Budapest. Czechoslovakia therefore has no railroads or roads running the length of the country. But these difficulties were somewhat offset by the internationalization of the Danube, and the country was given special Elbe River privileges with a free port at Hamburg.

Social Policies

When the Czechoslovak people, hitherto subjected to Habsburg rule, organized an army of over 100,000 volunteers and offered their services to the Allies in World War I, they did so not only to re-establish their own national freedom through the victory of the Allies but also to create a democratic country where farmers, workers and the middle class could assert themselves. Most Czechoslovaks looked forward to a progressively more democratic social system. One of the first laws enacted by the Prague Parliament when the country was established in 1918 was the Land Reform Law. This law abolished the old feudal land system and land was redistributed among those who were eager to cultivate it, so that over half a million new farmers were created. The limit of independent ownership was 150 hectares of arable land. The original owners were reimbursed on the basis of the average value of 1913 to 1915. The land thus acquired by the state was sold to 235,000 landless cottagers, craftsmen, and soldiers; 415,000 people who had less than 25 acres were allowed to round out their holdings. These owners then formed the backbone of the Agrarian Party, which developed an agricultural policy of self-sufficiency with rigorously restricted imports and controlled exports.

The Land Reform also had other repercussions on the internal and foreign policies of the country. Since practically all of the Czech nobility was wiped out or exiled in 1620-1621 and the new aristocracy was German or Hungarian in language and sympathies, the representatives of these minorities charged that the whole plan was designed to dispossess them and made frequent complaints to the League of Nations. Another complaint was that German applicants were intentionally overlooked in making allotments. This might have been true, but the point was that the Germans were concentrated in mountainous districts along the German frontier, where arable land was limited and where there were few large estates to be divided.

Another important reform created a system of social insurance which covered all wage earners and salaried persons, both men and women. The ramifications of social welfare, under the supervision of provincial headquarters and supported by the Ministry of Social Welfare, touched every town of the Republic with mothers' clinics, the feeding and clothing of undernourished children, and a multitude of other activities. All employees, moreover, had medical care at the expense of their insurance funds. Czechoslovakia's system of social insurance was so highly regarded that it served as a model for the systems introduced in France, Greece, and elsewhere. The father of the Czechoslovak system, Prof. Dr. Emil Schoenbaum, developed social insurance in many Latin American countries after 1939.

The government did not tend to develop a top-heavy business structure. Nine-tenths of the 718,000 industrial establishments employed from one to five persons each; only some 2 per cent of the total employed more than twenty persons each. Possibly two-thirds of the income-producing wealth of the country belonged to companies employing less than twenty persons. The Báťa shoe factories were the only undertaking based on complete employer individualism of the Henry Ford variety.

Practically all workers belonged to unions, and "work committees" of employees were recognized by law. There were labor courts, and the work week was limited to forty-eight hours. The worker and the employer contributed in equal amounts to a health-insurance fund and there were various provisions for accident and old-age insurance. Boys under 16 and girls under 18 years of age could not be employed at heavy labor; no one under 16 and no woman could be employed in mining or other dangerous occupations. One week's holiday with pay each year was assured to all persons in any employment.

The struggle against unemployment included valiant efforts to regain or discover new foreign markets, organized assistance to foreign trade, the financing of a large number of public works, and tax concessions for private building and repair activities. The larger cities organized labor corps of unemployed young men 18 to 24 years of age, who worked on parks, sport fields, and other non-competitive undertakings. Remuneration was in the form of goods and a small allowance, and the boys continued to live at home. Many industries were linked up with an extensive network of agricultural coöperative societies, made up of one-third of all landowners. Another great network of consumers' coöperatives served 886,000 people in the cities and towns. They were grouped in five central associations, one of which was German for the German-speaking part of the population.

Education

The low state of literacy was a sad inheritance from the Austro-Hungarian Monarchy. In the Slovak province of Czechoslovakia, for instance, as many as 57 per cent could not read and write. It was the conscious policy of the Hungarian feudal lords to keep the people in ignorance on the premise that as long as they were ignorant they would remain powerless. During the twenty years of Czechoslovakia's independence, practically every other Slovak community received a new school.

During the post-war years, considerable international attention was drawn to the Sokol Congresses, scheduled every six years. The Czechoslovak Sokol, oldest gymnastic organization in the world, was founded in 1862 by the philosophers Dr. Miroslav Tyrš and Dr. Jindřich Fugner. The name Sokol (meaning falcon) was adopted because it is the traditional name and symbol for Czech folksong heroes. During the years of Habsburg dominance, Sokol groups helped to keep Czech nationalism alive. When the First World War broke out, their members filtered into Allied armies and formed Sokol legions to fight against their old masters. During the two decades of Czechoslovakia, the 460,000 male members were welded together by means of adult education, gymnastic training, and democratic spirit, constituting a storehouse of well-trained manpower for their country's army of 180,000 men. All in all, the Sokol numbered some 800,000 men, women, and children—one out of every 20 in the population—organized in 3,265 local branches. Their periodic public performances in flashing uniforms—shirts of Garibaldi red, gray Czech jackets, and little round red capes with falcon feathers slung from their left shoulders—never failed to arouse national enthusiasm.

The Sokols were just one branch of the numerous educational activities of the country. In line with Masaryk's unceasing emphasis on the preservation of democracy through universal education, the Republic established middle-school and university education in Slovakia, where it was practically non-existent before 1918. Special schools were established for minorities; 96.2 per cent of all German children, 94 per cent of all Hungarian children, and 92.5 per cent of all Polish children attended purely German, Hungarian, and Polish schools. They were taught in their own languages by teachers of their own nationality. The University in Prague and the German Polytechnic Institute in Brno were supported by the state—as were all minority schools. Two new universities were established: Masaryk University of Brno and Comenius University of Bratislava. Scholarships were provided for poor but gifted students.

Adult education received tremendous impetus with the setting up of educational committees in every community to conduct libraries, lectures, and courses for adults, under the Masaryk Institute of Adult Education. One of the results of such efforts was that illiteracy in Czechoslovakia (7.5 per cent in 1921 and 3.25 per cent in 1930) was lower than in any other country of Central and Eastern Europe.

Cultural Trends

Since the independence of Czechoslovakia was built on the cultural basis of national consciousness, the cultural development of post-war Czechoslovakia was indissolubly linked with the period of the national re-awakening concerned with the creation of a literary language and the popularization of Czech historic ideas. As we have seen, the Czechs had developed a truly magnificent nationalistic culture before 1914 (Josef Dobrovský, Josef Jungmann, František Palacký, Pavel Josef Šafařík, Jan Kollár, Karel Havlíček).

Modern Czech literature was founded in the eighteen-thirties by the author of the poem *Máj*, Karel Hynek Mácha, a master of musical verse and the creator of magnificent images. He was the first Czech writer to express the torment of the modern soul under the influence of intellectual nihilism.

Modern Czech poetry had its beginnings at the end of the eighteenth century and incorporated Slavonic literary tendencies. It was invigorated by romanticism and the cult of folk poetry, and great enthusiasm was shown in the collection of popular ballads and legends. The *Echoes* of František Ld. Čelakovský were based on Russian national songs, and Karel Jaromír Erben wrote *The Bouquet*. The historical novels of Sir Walter Scott influenced Czech prose fiction. Characters taken from the Czech countryside were portrayed by Božena Němcová, who boldly opened up new paths in her popular novel *Grandmother*. Many dramas by Josef K. Tyl, who gave great impetus to the development of the Czech theatre, are very popular because of their Czech spirit and universal appeal.

Regarding literature as a means of fortifying the people in their struggle toward better conditions, these early writers placed their faith in national tradition. The next generation set itself the task of modernizing Czech life and literature. After cosmopolitan beginnings, their work shows a strong tendency toward a new kind of nationalism that was not satisfied with sentimental words and the thoughtless cult of tradition. The literary leader of this generation was Jan Neruda, a poet with a simple diction but deep feeling, who was the mystically inspired singer of the national destiny. He wrote tales of old Prague which are full of local color. His friend Vitězslav Hálek described village life, while Karolína Světlá wrote novels on the Czech national revival in Prague and on the countryside. Fantasy combined with realism is the distinguishing feature of the short stories of Jakub Arbes, the majority of which deal with Prague. The generation of the '6os thus established the Czech novel and improved the drama, which began to develop rapidly after the Czech theatre in Prague became an independent institution.

Considerable progress was effected in the 70's by the literary group connected with the periodical *Lumír*. The new endeavors were stimulated by the study of foreign literatures, particularly French and Russian. In the 90's, attention began to be paid to the literature of the countries of Northern Europe. In 1883 the University of Prague was divided into a German and a Czech section; the same year saw the opening of the new National Theatre in Prague. After long years of painful effort, the Czech Academy was established with an independent section for art.

Translator of an enormous number of modern poetical masterpieces as well as an original poet, dramatist, and prose-writer, Jaroslav Vrchlický was at home in all the literatures of the world. A spirit of the Renaissance and a lover of sunny, joyful existence, he produced splendid Parnassian verse which later became the subject of sharp literary polemics. A similar feeling for poetical beauty and mysticism was evidenced by Julius Zeyer who wrote poems—mainly epics—prose, and dramas. The favorite writer, however, was Svatopluk Čech, who composed epics, academic in form but giving expression to the national troubles of his people. His colorful, sonorous, and rather rhetorical verse was widely read and had a powerful effect on Czech life. A contemporary of Vrchlický was J. V. Sládek, a lyric poet who was valued also for his translation of Shakespeare. The simple, religious soul of the Slovak peasant and the influence of the process of Magyarization were fully described by the Slovak poet Hviezdoslav.

A trend from romanticism to realism was discernible in fiction and the drama alike before World War I. Alois Jirásek, who lived to see the liberation of his native land, wrote powerful historical novels and dramas on the past life of the Czech nation, particularly on the Hussite period, the years after the defeat of the Battle of White Mountain, and the national rebirth. Together with Svatopluk Čech, he contributed most to the inspiration of the nation in its struggle for independence. His friend, Zikmund Winter, portrayed in detail the period prior to the Battle of White Mountain. Life of the Slovak gentlefolk was described by Hviezdoslav's friend, Světozar Vojanský, who was strongly influenced by the Russian realists. The life of the lower-middle classes of Prague was portrayed with humor by Ignatc Herrmann. One of the best modern Czech novelists was K. M. Čapek-Chod, who combined a clear psychological insight into everyday life with brutal realism.

Among the poets, the mood of the age was expressed most fully in the verse of J. S. Machar, sometimes bitterly ironic and at other times sharply aggressive. He passed from an uncompromising criticism of Czech political life before World War I to a description of the development of world history. One of the most original and influential figures among Czech poets was Petr Bezruč, who described the desperate condition of the Czech inhabitants of Silesia, languishing under the oppression of foreign capitalists and imperialists. Apparently born out of his time, Otakar Březina dealt in his poems with the problems of life and death and the cosmic mysteries. The poetry of Antonín Sova was infused with dreams of a new world civilization arising on the ruins of the old order.

The First World War formed a dividing line in Czech literary development. The soul-stirring experiences of the war years naturally left their mark on the literary work of the period despite the watchful Austrian censorship. In 1917, prior to the opening of the Vienna Parliament, the Czech writers sent a bold manifesto to the deputies inaugurating a definite revolutionary policy. They were headed by Jirásek, and the poet and dramatist Jaroslav Krapil. Viktor Dyk was a spokesman for the oppressed Czechs in his poems and novels. Literary work was also produced in the foreign legions, especially in Russia, and the impressions and experiences of the legionnaires thereafter formed the basis of a special literature (Rudolf Medek, Josef Kopta, František Langar).[8]

Czechoslovak literature started on a new period in 1918 with a truly rich background. Many authors of the pre-war school were still popular with the masses, but a large group of young authors were eager either to tell about their war experiences in their novels or to integrate Czech literature with the latest world trends. The outstanding representative of the "old school," Jirásek (1851-1930), whose novels treated outstanding epochs of the nation's past with epic strength of narrative, lost his popularity—only to regain it again with the resurgence of Czech nationalism after the Munich tragedy in 1938.

The Czech writer who was best known internationally was Karel Čapek (1890-1938), who died of influenza at the age of 48. His tendency was to oppose the traditions of excessive Central European nationalism with the idea of cosmopolitanism, and he tried to achieve his goal by using fantastic, Utopian themes. His play *R.U.R.*, a protest against the growing mechanization of spiritual life, was produced in New York in 1922 and made him famous throughout the English-speaking world.[9] In fact, the word "robot" was added to the English vocabulary by this play. His gently satirical *Letters from England* is ranked among the best books on the English character. Čapek also published his conversations with President Masaryk.

Jaroslav Hašek's *The Good Soldier Sweik* is internationally known for its sarcastic personification, in the figure of Private Svejk, of the senselessness of war and the coarseness of the military machine. The maturest figure in Czech post-war prose is Vladislav Vančůra, who restored the epic, in its most fundamental form, to the modern Czech short story and novel.

The most outstanding Czech essayist, F. X. Šalda, concentrated on literary criticism but also wrote novels, drama, and poetry; he was second only to Thomas G. Masaryk in his influence on the Czechoslovak intelligentsia. Another well-known essayist was Otakar Fischer. Outstanding among Czechoslovak poets in the twenty year period of independence were Jiří Wolker, Vítězslav Nezval, Jaroslav Seifer, Josef Hora, František Halas, and Laco Novoměský. Lyric poetry is probably the most brilliant achievement of modern Czechoslovak literature.

The destruction of Czechoslovakia which began with the Munich agreement and culminated in the German occupation of March 15,

---

[8] For more details, see Egon Hostovský, "The Czech Novel Between the World Wars," *The Slavonic and East European Review*, XXI (1943), pp. 78-96.

[9] Roucek, Joseph S., "Requiescat Karel Čapek," *Books Abroad*, XIII (Spring, 1939), pp. 171-172.

1939, temporarily ended all creative art in the young nation. Karel Čapek survived Munich by only a few weeks; his brother was thrown into a concentration camp by the Nazis. Vladislav Vančůra was executed and Ivan Olbracht died. Karel Poláček was dragged to some spot in Poland. Egon Hostovský lived in exile in America. Others had to be silent.

Possibly the best-known creative activity of the Czechoslovak people has been music. One cannot listen to any American radio station for long without hearing a tune by some Czechoslovak composer—Bedřich Smetana, Antonín Dvořák, Rudolf Friml, Bohuslav Martinů, and others.[10] Bedřich Smetana (1824-1884) has been the outstanding Czech composer, but his fame has only been recognized during the last few years in America with periodic presentations of the *Bartered Bride,* a melodic opera centered around the peasant customs of Bohemia, and of a cycle of symphonies under the title of *My Country.* Antonín Dvořák (1841-1904) has become one of the best known composers of our age, mainly because of his *New World Symphony.* Zdeněk Fibich (1850-1900) is known in the United States for his *Poem* (entitled, for some reason, *Moonlight Madonna*). Leo Janáček (1854-1928), was a composer of stormy temperament who applied himself to popular themes. The leading composers of the post-war period have been Josef Bohumil Foerster, with his intimate lyrics of a noble and delicately cultivated mind, Vitězlav Novák, Josef Suk, and Otakar Ostrčil. The world-famous violin school of Otakar Ševčik produced several internationally known artists—Jan Kubelík, Jaroslav Kocina, František Ondříček, Ševčik himself, all taught in America in the post-war years. The distinguished composer Martinů is now living in America.

The Czechoslovak engraver best known in America is T. S. Šimon, who has made many charming color etchings of American scenes. Max Švabinský's portraits and etchings have also been very popular in the United States. Joza Úprka won fame at home and abroad as a painter of the Slovak peasant and his national costumes. Dušan Jurkovič has adapted the popular architecture of Slovak wooden churches to provide ideas for modern buildings. The name of Alfons Mucha is also known to American art lovers. His series of monumental pictures, "The Slavonic Epochs," glorifying outstanding events in Slavic history, were exhibited in America's leading cities under the auspices of the late Charles R. Crane, a close friend of President Wilson and former

---

[10] Hostovský, *op. cit.,* p. 96.

United States Minister to China. An elemental talent, great power, and stylistic discipline featured the work of the sculptor Jan Štursa.

The Munich Period

Former President Masaryk lived long enough to see his country threatened from without. He lived to consent to restrictions on the democracy that to him was a religion. He lived to see the German minority as dissatisfied in Czechoslovakia as the Czechs had been in Austria. The movement for German autonomy certainly could not have been avoided even if the concessions made after Hitler came to power had been offered earlier. Masaryk was one of the few statesmen who had reckoned on a German comeback and saw his worst fears realized. He lived to see the world made unsafe for democracy, but he died believing in the worth of human beings.

Czechoslovakia's geographical position and its German minority proved a source of grave weakness. Lying directly across the transversal Eurasian Axis—the Hamburg-Prague-Budapest-Constantinople-Basra road—a continuation and extension of the German Kaiser's dream of *Drang nach Osten,* Czechoslovakia was a thorn in the flesh of the German geopoliticians and their spokesman, Adolf Hitler. It happened to be "the greatest natural fortress of Europe" (as Bismarck had shrewdly remarked), and Hitler intended to be its master in order to reach the food-growing plains of Hungary and the Ukraine, the Romanian oil fields—and points east.

The surprise of the 1935 elections was the appearance of Konrad Henlein's "Sudeten" Party with the backing of more than half of the German-speaking voters. However, Henlein was at first opposed by the German Social Democratic, Christian Socialist, and Agrarian groups.

The roots of Henlein's movement can be traced originally to the defeat of Germany and Austria-Hungary in 1918, when the Czech servants became the masters and the former German masters did not like the change. The discontent of the Germans was in evidence from the beginning. On October 29, 1918, the German deputies from Bohemia held a special meeting in Vienna and declared "German-Bohemia" to be a part of "the state of German Austria." A Nationalist deputy, Dr. von Lodgmann, was elected as *Landeshauptmann,* and it was decided to convoke a Diet at Reichenberg (the main German center in northeast Bohemia). The very next day another German province was proclaimed under the name of "Sudetenland"—afterwards to be used in a more comprehensive and less accurate form—with its center at Troppau; and in the first days of November two smaller mushroom governments sprang up. But the first enthusiasm for union with Germany cooled off as the Austrians noted the chaos and financial insecurity in the Reich.

The Czechs naturally resented the German reactions. When the new state was formed, President Masaryk had to deal not only with German discontent but also to some extent with Czech chauvinism. In the process, Masaryk crushed the Kramar Party, which represented extreme Czech nationalism. In any case, the German minority was treated more generously than that in any other Central European country. The Germans used the German language in Czechoslovakia's Parliament (just as the Hungarians spoke Magyar). Their periodicals, particularly *Bohemia*, spent twenty years attacking the Republic and especially its foreign policy without interference from censorship.

Economic causes played an important role in Czech-German fiction. The Czechoslovak Germans subscribed heavily to the Austrian war loans, which were honored "only" to 75 per cent by the new Czech state. Moreover, the German-speaking bankers and industrialists did not believe that Czechoslovakia would survive and speculated heavily on the German mark. They were wiped out in 1923 and had to be rehabilitated by the Prague banks, which increased Czech influence and German resentment. Since Hitler offered them the possibility of regaining their dominant status, Nazism began to appeal to many "Sudeten" Germans.[11]

The economic crisis after 1929 gave powerful impetus to this underlying mentality. The effects of the world depression were severe all over Czechoslovakia, but were especially catastrophic in the heavily industrialized districts of north Bohemia, inhabited primarily by Germans, which before the war had been the workshop of the Habsburg Monarchy and since the war had been forced by the contraction of the domestic market to seek outlets abroad. The "Sudeten" districts quickly became industrial graveyards, partly as a result of Germany's own system of self-sufficiency (*Autarky*). Furthermore, a larger proportion of Germans than Czechs were engaged in industrial occupations in Czechoslovakia, hence the Germans were more affected by the depression.

[11] For more details, see Joseph S. Roucek, "The Case for Czechoslovakia," *World Affairs Interpreter,* IX (October, 1938), pp. 235-243; and "Czechoslovakia—the Watchdog of Europe's Peace," *Social Science,* XIII (October 1, 1938), pp. 277-283; Josef Chmelar, *National Minorities in Central Europe* (Prague: Orbis, 1937), and *The German Problem in Czechoslovakia* (Prague: Orbis, 1936); S. Grant Duff, *German and Czech* (London: New Fabian Research, 1937); Elizabeth Wiskemann, *Czechs and Germans* (New York: Oxford University Press, 1938), and *Prologue to War* (New York: Oxford University Press, 1940).

The Germans claimed that they were discriminated against in administrative positions and in private industry. They also complained that government funds were spent more lavishly in Czech areas than in German districts. But the attitude of the Germans themselves in the early years of the Republic was at least partly responsible for that. While the German Nazis blamed everything on a malicious outer world and the Jews, the "Sudeten" Germans blamed the Czechs for all their troubles. Hitler aroused new hopes in the hearts of Germans, particularly those who thought they would again be "top-dogs" in his "reorganized Europe." Many Germans no doubt believed that the Czechs were deliberately taking advantage of their distress to turn the screws on them, to capture or ruin their industries, and generally to further the Czech national cause at the expense of a defenseless minority. There may have been discriminations here and there—but the roots of the trouble were far beyond the control of the Czechs.

The elections of May, 1935, gave 44 seats out of a total of 72 German mandates to Henlein, the "Fuehrer" of the Czechoslovak Germans. Henlein continued to profess his allegiance to the Czech state up to the last moment. German Centrists (Catholics) and Agrarians joined with Henlein in the general excitement that followed the annexation of Austria in March, 1938. Before Munich, therefore, fifty-five representatives of Henlein were opposed by eleven German Social Democrats and five German Communists in the Czechoslovak parliament. The municipal elections of May, 1938, also under the shadow of the *Anschluss,* and particularly under the terror caused by Hitler's threat to invade Czechoslovakia during the night of May 20-21, 1938, gave more than 75 per cent representation to Henleiners, whose pre-Munich demands proclaimed the allegiance of the party to the totalitarian philosophy of Nazism. They demanded recognition of the German minority in Czechoslovakia as a legal entity and asked for autonomy. In the sphere of foreign affairs, the Sudeten Germans demanded that Czechoslovakia give up her alliance with Russia.

The diplomatic aspects of Munich are dealt with in other chapters of this book. Suffice it to say that, as we now know, Hitler had decided to settle the problem of Czechoslovakia in his own way. While professing loyalty to Czechoslovakia, Henlein was taking orders from Hitler and his demands grew bolder in their defiance of the Czech authorities and shriller in their demands upon President Beneš and Premier Hodža. The latter, in turn, urged on by Chamberlain's and Daladier's "appeasers," were compelled to make an increasing number of concessions.

The tactics of Hitler's representatives were painfully simple: the more concessions Prague made to Henlein, the greater the disorders by the "Sudeten" Germans; the more disorders, the louder Henlein's cries of persecution and torture; the louder the cries, the greater the ire of Hitler, determined to re-establish "law and order" in Czechoslovakia. German newspapers and radio broadcasts shrieked a crescendo of recitals of the tortures of Germans in Czechoslovakia, to the accompaniment of sneers and epithets directed at Beneš. After every new concession granted by Prague at the insistence of London and Paris, the Ministers from France and Britain counselled further surrenders to Henlein's demands. The real purpose of Lord Runciman's "private" mission, as we learn from Sir Neville Henderson's *Failure of a Mission,* was to convince the Czechs that they ought to yield. While Lord Runciman was deliberating in August, 1938, chiefly at the Chateau of the Prince of Hohenlohe, clashes between Germans and Czechs grew in intensity.

While Hitler's puppets provoked riots and demonstrations throughout the Sudeten area, smoke was thrown in the world's eyes by the spacious presentation of the problem as one involving "self-determination." Was it worth while, argued Hitler's mouthpieces, to go to war simply to prevent the application of this Wilsonian principle? Although this was not the issue at all, many "peace-lovers" throughout the world wanted to believe Hitler.

After Hitler's hysterical outburst at Nuremberg, Chamberlain[12] flew to see Hitler at Berchtesgaden on September 15. This was the first step which eventually led to the Canossa of the Democracies at Munich on September 30. Since the sixth century, the Bohemian mountains had served as a barrier against the eastward push of Teutonic tribes, but never had its protective power been of such world-wide concern as in 1938. Chamberlain and Daladier handed their protective fence over to Hitler.

The "Second" Republic of Czechoslovakia

During October, 1938, the Czechoslovak government was compelled to surrender the Sudeten region to the Reich, pursuant to the dictates of Munich. Contrary to the popular conception, Czechoslovakia had not acquired this territory from Germany. It was a land where Czechs and Germans had lived together for eight centuries, an area that had never in history been a part of the German Empire nor an

---

[12] Chamberlain, Neville, *The Struggle for Peace* (New York: G. P. Putnam's Sons, 1939), p. 275.

autonomous province in former Austria-Hungary. It is also worth noting that Munich brought Hitler substantially more than he had asked for in the Godesberg Memorandum-ultimatum that Britain and France had found so repugnant and over which they were prepared to make war.

The international commission, "composed of Germany, the United Kingdom, France, Italy, and Czechoslovakia," was really a cardboard organization created to satisfy public opinion momentarily in France and Britain. The German delegates simply dictated their demands. Furthermore, during October, 1938, Poland sent an ultimatum to Prague and its troops took over the districts of Těšín and Bohumín in Silesia. During November, certain large portions of Slovakia and Carpathian Russia were allotted to Hungary. Altogether under the terms of Munich and Vienna, Czechoslovakia lost roughly one-third of its previous area and one-third of its population. Its area was reduced from 54,236 square miles to 38,180 square miles and its population from 14,729,000 to 9,807,000.[13] It should be noted, from the standpoint of "racial justice" and "self-determination," that 738,502 of the 2,822,899 souls ceded to Germany were Czechoslovaks. Hungary acquired 992,492 inhabitants, of whom 288,803 were Czechs and Slovaks, 25,261 were Ruthenians, 13,608 Germans, and 51,578 Poles. Poland took 230,282 people, of whom only 73,303 were Poles; 134,311 being Czechs and Slovaks, and 17,351 Germans.

Since the presence of Dr. Beneš in Prague was considered a source of irritation to Hitler, the President resigned his post under German pressure on October 5 and departed by plane for London on October 22. A new cabinet under General Syrový, a one-eyed hero of the World War Czech Legions, was formed the day before. A Germanophile Agrarian-inspired movement started the sudden anti-Beneš sentiment in Prague and university students in Prague destroyed a bust of ex-President Masaryk. On November 30, Dr. Emil Hácha, an unimaginative and uninspiring President of the Supreme Court, was elected the new President of the country as a "dark horse," since he had not been connected with any political group. Syrový was succeeded by Rudolf Beran, a very shrewd self-made Agrarian leader. He was granted dictatorial powers on December 14 by Parliament, controlled by the Party of National Unity which had absorbed the dissolved Agrarian Party, the Czechoslovak Socialist Party, the Czechoslovak Small Traders'

---

[13] Based on Joseph S. Roucek, "The 'Second' Republic of Czechoslovakia," *The Journal of Geography,* XLVIII (March, 1939), pp. 89-98; and "Europe After Munich," *Social Science,* XIV (January, 1939), pp. 17-22; Martha Gellhorn, *A Stricken Field* (New York: Duell, Sloan & Pearce, 1940), is a moving story of Prague during the Munich crisis of 1938.

Party, the Clericals, and the National League. Growing Nazi influence was indicated in the government order abolishing the Communist Party.

Slovak Autonomists

A little more than a week after Munich, Hlinka's Slovaks demanded autonomy.

The religious issue was partly responsible for difficulties which arose between the Czechs and the Slovaks. Shortly after the foundation of the Republic, there was a large exodus of Czechs from the Roman Catholic Church, since Catholicism was associated with the Austrian regime. But anti-clericalism soon subsided and complete religious toleration was practiced in Czechoslovakia. At first the Slovak Clerical Party, under Hlinka, coöperated in the same way as the Czech Clericals under Monsignor Šrámek (later the Prime Minister of the government-in-exile in London). But after a while Hlinka moved into the opposition, partly for political and partly for personal reasons. A Roman Catholic priest, he was a brave and devoted Slovak in pre-war Hungary. But in Czechoslovakia he preferred "Slovak" to "Czechoslovak" patriotism. When he died, in August, 1938, his place as leader of the Slovak Autonomist Party was taken by Tiso, also a priest, who was to become Hitler's quisling.

It must be noted, however, that Hlinka's party never had a majority of the Slovak votes. Probably most Slovaks were not even aware that he was working for the destruction of the Republic. Dr. Hodža, the Agrarian Prime Minister, Dr. Dérer, and other leading Slovaks never supported Hlinka's demands. Hlinka based his stand on the Pittsburgh manifesto signed by Masaryk and American Slovaks in America at the end of World War I.[14] The autonomists claimed that premises of autonomy made in this document had been broken; the "centralists" maintained that none of the signatories had any mandate to sign such a document and that the final clause made the whole arrangement contingent upon its endorsement by constitutionally elected representatives of both Czechs and Slovaks at home after the war.

At any rate, Czechoslovakia was reconstituted in 1938 as a federal union of the Czechs, the Slovaks, and the Carpatho-Russians, with central departments of national defense, foreign affairs, and finance. In addition to the legislative bodies for the provinces of Bohemia-Moravia, Slovakia, and Carpathian Ukrainia, there was to be a joint legislative

---

[14] For the best pro-Czech analysis of the Pittsburgh Agreement by a Slovak political leader, see Ivan Dérer, *The Unity of the Czechs and Slovaks. Has the Pittsburgh Declaration Been Carried Out?* (Prague: Orbis. 1938).

parliament (but this was never formed). The Slovak Diet of 63 members, limited dictatorially to followers of the Slovak People's Party, was elected on December 18, 1938, under Premier Tiso. A similar fascist pattern appeared in Carpathian Ukrainia, where only the People's Party was allowed to exist.

Protectorate

Although the Prague Government went a long way to meet most of the German demands, Berlin's pressure became steadily more insistent. The 400,000 Germans left in the new Czecho-Slovakia were entrusted with "a special mission," and the Vienna radio station incessantly broadcast anti-Czech propaganda inciting the Slovaks to secede, although Slovakia's free status in the federal union met all the important demands of the Slovak autonomists.[15] The Germans tried to create the impression that Czechoslovakia was collapsing from within and that they were needed to protect the victims of Czech "brutalities" and of "plundering Hussite mobs." They found followers in Durčanský, Mach, Murgas, and a few other hitherto little known Slovak politicians, who began agitating for a sovereign Slovakia. On March 12, 1939, Prague decided to intervene in Bratislava against the Slovak extremists by deposing Dr. Tiso, the Catholic Premier, and appointing Karel Sidor, the heir to the patriotic tradition of Father Hlinka, as his successor.

Berlin was obviously displeased with the bloodless liquidation of what it had hoped would be a revolt. On March 13 the discharged Slovak Premier was summoned to Berlin and confronted with an ultimatum asking him to proclaim the independence of Slovakia. Berlin also ordered Dr. Hácha to convoke the Slovak Provincial Parliament so that it could make decisions concerning the future status of Slovakia. The Slovak Parliament refused on March 14 to vote on separation from the Czechs.[16] Three times, in fact, the Parliament voted against secession. Then the German Commissar Karmašín told Tiso that German batteries placed across the Danube would shell the city. After this threat, the Slovak Parliament proclaimed the independence of Slovakia.

The creation of a separate Slovak state split the Ruthenians from the Czechs, and the provincial government at Chust had to proclaim its

[15] Josef Hanč, "Czechs and Slovaks Since Munich," *Foreign Affairs,* XVIII (October, 1939), pp. 102-115, is a valuable summary of this period.

[16] For the most complete story of the separation of Slovakia from Czecho-Slovakia, see V. S. Hurban, "Slovakia, Springboard to the East," *The New York Times,* February 11, 1940.

independence also. "Never has a people declared itself 'free' so reluctantly as did the half million Ruthenes of this tiny province." [17] Premier Vološín thanked the Czechs "for their twenty years of support which helped us to strengthen our national consciousness and culture progress." After 24 hours of independence, Hungarian troops invaded Carpathian Ruthenia, and on March 16 Premier Teleki announced its incorporation into Hungary.

Meanwhile Dr. Hácha followed Tiso to Berlin on March 14. Hácha, "an old and weak man," was granted an interview with Hitler at one in the morning. A German doctor, ordered in attendance, had to revive him twice. At 4 a.m. he was terrorized into signing on the dotted line, placing "the destiny of the Czech people and lands trustfully in the hands of the Fuehrer . . . in the interests of pacification." But long before Hácha arrived at Hitler's chancellery, German troops were already sweeping across Bohemia and Moravia. In fact, German S.S. troops had occupied two Czech cities even before Hácha's arrival in Berlin. By manipulation of the train service, Hitler's train reached Prague before Hácha's next morning, and on March 15 the constitution of Bohemia and Moravia into a German protectorate was announced to the Czechs.

Hitler then undertook to "protect" Slovakia also and signed a treaty at Vienna on March 18, 1939, with Dr. Josef Tiso, legalizing Germany's military occupation of the country. Special political status was reserved for the small German minority of about 100,000 and the posts of a German Under-Secretary of State was created in the government.

The fiction of the independence of Bohemia-Moravia and Slovakia was kept up for a while. The Czech President had his own cabinet, appointed with the protector's "approval." The protector's office, a vast and complex apparatus with 16 divisions, was in reality the exclusive source of legislative and administrative power. All the Germans in the province were under the jurisdiction of Reich laws, and the extension of German laws for the defense of the Reich to the entire territory of the protectorate confirmed Nazi supremacy. A planned policy of denationalization was practiced by moving Czech workers to the Reich and sending their children to German schools. The property of Czechs who had fled abroad and of Jews was given to Germans. A Reich office had to approve all property transfers and all state properties were sequestered. Germans from the Baltic states were resettled around Prague, breaking up compact Czech communities.

Slovakia's fictitious independence was expressed in a new Slovak

---

[17] Hanč, *op. cit.*, p. 105.

constitution of July, 1939. It described the country as a Christian National Republic and permitted the existence of only one party, Hlinka's former separatists. Every citizen was compelled to belong to one of the five "corporations" (agriculture, industry, finance, the professions). The Senate was composed of representatives of the corporations, delegates from Hlinka's People's Party, the members of the Cabinet, and delegates sent by Parliament. The President was elected by Parliament for seven years, with powers resembling those of rulers in the authoritarian states.

Czechoslovakia Fights Back

Under German rule, the Czechs were denationalized, murdered, executed, transplanted from their homes—in short, taught in every way that they were "inferior" to the "master race" which was determined to cripple them permanently as a nation and to exploit them on their way to the grave.[18] But the Czechs resisted bravely by all means available to them and profited from their experiences as fighters against their oppressors during previous centuries.

The Czech technique of resistance ran all the way from the mildest and yet one of the most effective methods, that of grumbling, with gestures and expressions of dissent (such as the refusal of Czech girls to dance with German soldiers), to organized and active violence[19] (such as the killing of Heydrich). This mass opposition was strengthened by six factors: (1) a well-developed ideology of Czechoslovak nationalism, integrated with memories of independence and democratic ideals; (2) the leadership provided by intellectuals living abroad; (3) moral and material support by the descendants of Czechoslovaks who had settled abroad, especially in America; (4) conditions in America and Britain favoring the promotion of the Czechoslovak cause; (5) the memory of living ·generations of the successful ways and means whereby Czechoslovakia had gained its independence in 1918; (6) the favorable development of the war through the military victories of the Soviet Union, the United States, and Great Britain.

Reinhard Heydrich—Heydrich the Hangman—Deputy Reich Protector of Bohemia-Moravia, was attacked and fatally injured by two assailants at 2:04 P.M. on May 26, 1942, on the outskirts of Prague.[20]

[18] Czechoslovak Ministry of Foreign Affairs, *Czechoslovakia Fights Back* (Washington, D. C.: American Council on Public Affairs, 1943), is a careful record of these policies.

[19] Roucek, Joseph S., "Methods of Meeting Domination: The Czechoslovaks," *American Sociological Review,* VI (October, 1941), pp. 670-673.

[20] For details, see Harold Kirkpatrick, "Death of the Hangman," *Life,* XVI (May 22, 1944), pp. 49-55.

For the death of this perverted sadist, second in power only to Gestapo Chief Heinrich Himmler and perhaps even more hated than he, the enraged Nazis unleashed savage reprisals. They literally wiped out the village of Lidice, thus perpetuating its name for eternity.

Beneš Carries On Abroad

While the Nazis drenched Czechoslovakia in blood and terror, the experiences of the liberation movement abroad in 1914-1918 enabled Dr. Beneš to carry on in the same tradition after 1939. But the diplomatic problems were quite different this time from those in 1914-1918. In 1939 the Czechoslovak Republic had existed, although dismembered and occupied by the Germans as a result of the Munich agreement. It was necessary, therefore, to secure recognition of the non-validity of that agreement. The second difficulty was due to the fact that Czechoslovakia's governmental machinery had remained in Czechoslovakia, making it essential to secure recognition of an executive and a government which could represent the Czechoslovak people in their fight against Germany. Beneš undertook that task.

The Beneš government attained this status gradually. On March 27, 1939, President Roosevelt, in writing to Dr. Beneš to acknowledge receipt of a telegram concerning the occupation of Prague by the Germans, addressed him simply as "My dear Dr. Beneš," not as "President Beneš." This established his status of the moment, so far as the White House was concerned, as a private individual. The first recognition of any kind given to Beneš as an official character came on November 9, 1939, after the outbreak of the war, when the French government of Daladier recognized a committee composed of Dr. Beneš and seven other personalities as "qualified to represent the Czechoslovak people." On December 20, 1939, Viscount Halifax, British Foreign Secretary, added his country's recognition of this committee.

On July 21, 1940, shortly after the defeat of France, the British government recognized the Czech committee as the "Provisional Government" of Czechoslovakia. Canada followed suit on October 12.

A year later, on July 18, 1941, Britain went all the way and extended "full recognition to the Czechoslovak Republic." On the same day Russia signed an agreement with the Czechs, in which the group was referred to as the "Government of the Republic of Czechoslovakia." The United States recognized the Czech group as a "Provisional Government" only in a note from American Ambassador in London John G. Winant to Czechoslovak Minister of Foreign Affairs Jan Masaryk on July 30, 1941, and was still referring to it as such in the lend-lease agreement concluded with the Czechs on July 11, 1942. Not until October 28, 1942, did American Ambassador Biddle inform Jan Masaryk that the United States was finally according his group "complete and definite legal and diplomatic recognition." The three big powers were finally all agreed on the status of the Czechoslovakia headed by President Beneš.

Thanks to the ways by which London was able to keep in touch with the occupied territory, the Czechoslovak Government was familiar with the wishes of the Czechoslovak people and directed its policy accordingly. Czech broadcasts reached large sections of the people in the protectorate and underground papers printed news about the activity and proclamations of the Czechoslovak Government. Internal resistance continued, especially after 1943. Mass desertions started in the Slovak Army forced by the Germans to fight against the Russians. In August, 1944, it was necessary to put Slovakia under martial law to quell a rising revolt.

In line with swiftly moving events, František Němec, Minister of Reconstruction, left London for Moscow in the middle of August as head of a Czechoslovak Government delegation for the administration of liberated Czechoslovak territories. On September 13, 1944, the Slovak National Council, which had been formed more than a year before, came out into the open and carried on the government of freed Slovak territory. Two days later contact was made between Red Army patrols and Slovak partisan forces operating in the Carpathian Mountains, and Soviet forces, aided by units of the Czechoslovak brigade in Russia, crossed into Slovakia.

In October, 1944, Minister Němec moved his headquarters as the representative of the Czechoslovak Government in London to Užhorod, the liberated capital of Carpathian Ruthenia. President Beneš and his Cabinet followed him to the liberated sections of Czechoslovakia in April, 1945—by way of Moscow. The experiences of Beneš during Munich taught him that the future of Czechoslovakia would depend more on the collaboration of his country with the East than with the West. The Soviet-Czechoslovak Treaty signed on December 12, 1943, a continuation of a pact of mutual assistance with the Soviet of May 16, 1935, was a practical expression of this belief.

Bibliography

Beneš, Eduard, *My War Memoirs* (Boston: Houghton Mifflin, 1928). A readable account of Beneš' techniques and of his political philosophy.

————, *Democracy Today and Tomorrow* (New York: The Macmillan

Co., 1939). A review of Beneš' experiment in democratic statesmanship and his hopes for the future of democracy.

Čapek, Karel, *President Masaryk Tells His Story* (New York: Brentano's, 1935). Probably the best introduction to Masaryk's personality and philosophy.

Duff, S. G., *Europe and the Czechs* (New York: Penguin Books, 1938). A readable survey of the events leading up to Munich.

George, G. J., *Europe and the Czechs* (New York: Penguin Books, 1938). The story of the betrayal, by a Czech.

Hanč, Josef, *Tornado Across Eastern Europe* (New York: Greystone, 1942). By an able Czechoslovak diplomat.

Kerner, R. J., Editor, *Czechoslovakia, A Record of Two Decades* (Berkeley, Cal.: University of California Press, 1940). Probably the best introduction to all aspects of Czechoslovakia in English.

Krofta, Kamil, *A Short History of Czechoslovakia* (New York: Macmillan, 1934). By an outstanding Czech historian.

Masaryk, T. G., *The Making of a State* (New York: Stokes, 1927). Indispensable for an understanding of Masaryk's philosophy.

Nosek, Vladimir, *The Spirit of Bohemia* (New York: Brentano, 1927). A general review of Czech history, literature, and art.

Seton-Watson, R. W., *A History of the Czechs and Slovaks* (London: Hutchinson & Co., 1943). Indispensable.

Spinka, Matthew, *John Hus and the Czech Reform* (Chicago: University of Chicago Press, 1941; *John Amos Comenius* (Chicago: University of Chicago Press, 1943). The best introductions in English to these two great Czech historic figures.

Thomson, S. H., *Czechoslovakia in European History* (Princeton, N. J.: Princeton University Press, 1943. A valuable history of Czechoslovakia in relation to the part its land and people played in the whole European scene.

Wiskemann, Elizabeth, *Czechs and Germans* (New York: Oxford University Press, 1938). Fair to both sides.

CHAPTER XVIII

POLAND (1918-1945)

Restoration of Poland's Independence

ON NOVEMBER 11, 1918, commonly accepted as the date of the restoration of Poland's independence, the liberated areas, comprising former Congress Poland, Western Galicia, and the adjacent Cieszyn (Teschen) region of former Austrian Silesia, were ruled by four separate Polish authorities. Each of them was an outgrowth of local conditions. Warsaw and the rest of the former German zone of Congress Poland was governed by a Regency Council, appointed by the Germans, through a Cabinet composed of National Democrats. This Council had also unsuccessfully claimed authority over the former Austrian zone of Congress Poland. There, however, another type of government was established after the downfall of the Habsburg Monarchy—the so-called "People's Government"—a democratic Polish Cabinet composed of Socialists, Peasant Party representatives, and independent Democrats under the chairmanship of the Socialist leader, Ignacy Daszynski. This government, which ruled from Lublin, issued an inaugural Manifesto which was later accepted by Polish democrats as the basic statement of their aims. Western Galicia and Cieszyn Silesia (the Teschen region) were ruled by temporary governments composed of representatives of various Polish parties.

In order to enable Poland to take over the parts of the country which were still under foreign rule or were being fought for, it was essential to consolidate these regimes. This was made possible by Pilsudski's return from German internment. He was immediately appointed to command the troops which owed allegiance to the Regency Council. A few days later, the Council transferred all its powers to Pilsudski and resigned. Pilsudski himself assumed the title of "Chief of State," and appointed a Cabinet headed by the Socialist Moraczewski. But he had to deal also with the Polish National Committee in Paris under the Chairmanship of the National Democratic leader Roman Dmowski,

who had organized it after leaving Russia. The latter was recognized
by the Western Allies and controlled the Polish Army in France. The
famous pianist, I. J. Paderewski, acted as a negotiator between the
Dmowski Committee and Pilsudski's regime. The two bodies com-
promised by appointing Paderewski Premier, and his government was
recognized by the Western Powers.

Territorial Settlements in the West

When the first government of the Polish Republic was formed, the
western provinces of Poznan and Pomerania were still under German
rule. After a few weeks of hard fighting, the Germans were driven
from Poznan. When the final boundaries between Poland and Germany were drawn (Treaty of Versailles, 1919), Poznan and Pomerania
were given to Poland, except for a few counties and the city of Danzig,
which became a "free city" under League of Nations protection.

There were, however, other areas in dispute between Poland and
Germany, such as Upper Silesia. Detached from Poland in the fifteenth century, it had nevertheless remained basically Polish, ethnically
and liguistically, although many Germans had settled in its industrial
cities and many Poles had become Germanized. After World War
I, Upper Silesia was high on the list of Polish claims against Germany.
The Peace Conference originally decided to grant these claims. However, repeated German protests that Upper Silesia was indispensable to
the German economy,[1] as well as certain British apprehensions caused
by Poland's special relations with France, led to the decision to arrange
a plebiscite in the contested area instead.

The preparations for the plebiscite lasted two years and were openly
sabotaged by German civil servants in Upper Silesia. Two uprisings
of the Polish population finally forced the authorities to conduct the
plebiscite in March, 1921. The results proved inconclusive, and it was
decided to partition the area. The first plan for partition, however,
was unfair to the Polish population. This led to a third uprising,
which resulted in a new partition plan accepted by both Poland and
Germany. The final arrangement gave Poland important collieries,
steelworks, and factories, but it left many predominantly Polish industrial and rural communities under German rule.

Plebiscites were also held in two contested East Prussian areas in
which the Polish language predominated. They took place at a moment when Poland was gravely endangered by Russian invasion, for

---

[1] This was not true, for even before 1914 a considerable part of the output of Upper
Silesian industry was consumed by the Polish rather than the German market.

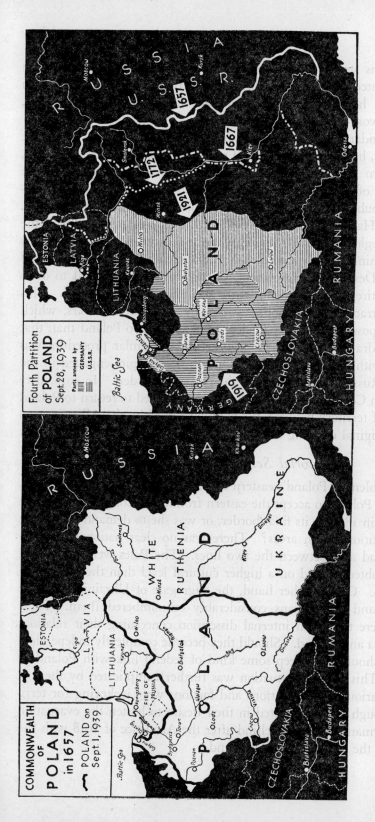

The boundaries of Poland at various periods in the past. The boundaries of the new Poland have been defined, on the East by a Polish-Soviet treaty, as comprising the Curzon Line, with minor modifications; on the West by the Potsdam Declaration, "pending the final settlement," as embracing "the former German territories west of Swinemünde, and thence along the Oder River to the confluence of the western Neisse River and along the western Neisse to the Czechoslovak frontier, including that portion of East Prussia not placed under the administration of the U.S.S.R. . . . and including the former Free City of Danzig." (*Maps used by permission of the Polish Government Information Center.*)

the Russians stood before Warsaw. Moreover, German propaganda misrepresented Poland to the predominantly Protestant East Prussian voters as a hotbed of Catholic religious intolerance. Consequently, Germany won these areas.

The boundary between Poland and Czechoslovakia, fixed by nature and history, had only two disputed spots: the Cieszyn (Teschen) area, and the two formerly Hungarian counties of Spiš and Orava. The population of these areas is predominantly Polish, but the Czechoslovak Republic claimed them for historical and economic reasons. When the Habsburg Monarchy collapsed, the Poles and Czechs of the Teschen region made a temporary arrangement which divided the region administratively into Polish and Czech zones pending a final decision. Despite this agreement, Czechoslovak troops tried to overrun the entire area in January, 1919, and brief fighting ensued. This led to protracted negotiations, assisted by the Allied Powers, which finally proposed a boundary far less advantageous to Poland than that originally drawn by the local negotiators. A similar procedure was followed with regard to Spiš and Orava. Its energies engaged in the war with Russia, Poland accepted the proposed borders. In 1938, after the Munich Conference, Czechoslovakia was forced to return to Poland the strip of territory between the boundary fixed by the Allies in 1920 and the original dividing line.

Territorial Settlements in the East

The problem of Poland's eastern boundaries presented many difficulties. Was Poland to accept the eastern frontier of Congress Poland, as organized in 1815, as its final border, or was she to demand the return of pre-partition Polish areas? There was no clear national majority in the broad area between the two lines. The Poles were numerous, and undoubtedly stood on a higher cultural level than the rest of the population. On the other hand, the aggregate of Ukrainians, White Russians, and Lithuanians considerably outnumbered them. These peoples were torn with internal dissension concerning their relations with Russia and Poland. Should they become completely independent states, or should they keep some kind of federal link with Poland or Russia? This involved situation was further complicated by the fact that the various administrations and factions were jockeying for territory, although all were united in their desire to hasten the evacuation of the German troops left behind after the Armistice of 1918 with the consent of the Allied High Command.

In 1919, the question became urgent. German troops had withdrawn, and Soviet troops, at that time abhorred and fought by the Western Powers, were advancing. The Allied Supreme Council attempted
to solve the situation by fixing a temporary boundary. This line,
known as the "Curzon Line" (after the British statesman who later
proposed it as a permanent border), corresponded roughly to the eastern border of Congress Poland as established in 1815. The territory
west of the Curzon Line was considered unquestionably Polish, but the
territory east of it was considered in dispute between Poland and Russia and subject to settlement by the Western Allies. The Curzon Line,
however, was not accepted by either of the parties concerned.[2]

In the meantime, a war was being fought in Eastern Galicia. That
area, only fragments of which had ever belonged to Russia, had been
delivered by Austria after the downfall of the Habsburg Monarchy to
the local Ukrainian Committee which called itself the "Western
Ukrainian Government." The Polish population, notably in the city
of Lwow, revolted. Polish troops, hastily organized in uncontested
Polish areas, came to their assistance. After several months of hard
fighting, they drove the Ukrainian troops out of the country and established a Polish administration, which was subsequently recognized by
the Western Allies.

The Allied decision regarding the Curzon Line and the elimination of the so-called "Western Ukrainian Government" did not, however, bring peace to Poland's eastern frontiers. Repeated armed clashes
between Polish and Soviet troops alternated with negotiations, in the
course of which several tentative boundaries were proposed. Finally,
in the spring of 1920, fearful that the then anticipated victory of the
"white" (counter-revolutionary) Russians over the Soviet Government
would lead to the re-establishment of an imperialist Russia and ex-
orbitant new claims against Poland, Pilsudski decided to forestall the
danger by establishing a separate Ukraine and White Russia[3] as buffer
states.

In order to set up a Ukrainian Republic, Polish troops advanced into
that country and occupied Kiev. This interference in foreign affairs,

---

[2] The Soviet Government even declared, in its note of July 17, 1920, that it regarded the
Curzon Line as unjust to Poland. See: Stanislaw Grabski, *The Polish-Soviet Frontier* (New
York: Polish Information Center, 1944), pp. 22-23.

[3] The name "White Russians" (with a capital "W") designates a Slavic people centered around
the Soviet city of Minsk. The Poles and the Lithuanians are the White Russians' western
neighbors, the Russians their eastern neighbors. The designation "white Russians" (with a
small "w") is usually applied to the Russians who rose in arms against the Soviet Government
after its establishment in 1917.

disapproved by the majority of the Polish people, almost cost Poland her recently recovered independence. Kiev, the capital of the Ukraine, the richest Soviet Republic, is the cherished national symbol of ancient Russia. Its occupation by the Poles, coupled with the threatened loss of the Ukraine, temporarily lessened the intensity of the Russian civil war and gave Soviet troops an opportunity to launch a counter-offensive. This operation carried the Red Army to the suburbs of Warsaw, and a Polish Communist Government under Russian auspices was established behind the Russian lines. However, before the Western Allies had time to intervene (it was then that the "Curzon Line" was proposed as the permanent Russian-Polish border) the Poles counter-attacked. Just as the Russians had used all of their strength to drive the Poles from Kiev, so now the Poles marshalled all of theirs to drive the Russians from Warsaw.

After several more months of fighting, peace was finally concluded between Russia (including the Ukraine, which had decided to remain with Russia) and Poland. The Treaty of Riga, drawn up at that time (1921), established a boundary which remained in effect until 1939. This boundary, a typical compromise, lies about halfway between a line originally proposed by Dmowski (at one time in the course of the negotiations Russia herself had proposed a line similar to that suggested by Dmowski) and the Curzon Line.

After the establishment of an independent Lithuanian Republic in 1918 and 1919, the only point of dispute between it and Poland was the city of Vilna and its surrounding area. Lithuania claimed it for historic reasons, since Vilna had been Lithuania's capital for centuries. Poland claimed it because the overwhelming majority of its inhabitants are Poles. In 1919 and 1920 Vilna changed hands frequently. Finally, after a Polish coup d'état (organized by General Zeligowski) and subsequent negotiations, an autonomous administration was established in Vilna and its environs under the name of Central Lithuania. The original plan was to establish a federation of Western Lithuania, the area generally known as the Republic of Lithuania, and Central Lithuania. But after protracted negotiations, conducted through the League of Nations, the Central Lithuanian legislature voted to rejoin Poland.

On March 15, 1923, the legality of Poland's eastern borders, as described above, was recognized by the Conference of Ambassadors, the successor body to the Supreme Allied Council. Thus Poland's geographical shape became fixed and its place on the map established for the following sixteen years.

Geopolitical Situation

Post-war Poland (meaning Land of Fields) was about as big as Spain. Its 150,965 square miles were flat and mostly at sea level. Situated centrally in Europe (diagonals joining the four extreme corners of Europe intersect near Warsaw), Poland is at the same time the most easterly country in Europe linked up with western civilization. Because of this special position, Poland in the course of history has had to assume the role of an intermediary between Eastern and Western Europe in the domains of culture, civilization, and political life.

This geopolitical situation dictated Poland's post-war international policy. Lacking geographic barriers, Poland could be squeezed by the pincers formed on one side by Germany and on the other by Soviet Russia. Its frontiers, with the exception of the famous Pripet Marshes in the east, were open. This absence of a natural frontier was the dominant fact in Poland's relations with its two great neighbors. Both of them used Polish territory, which they had seized and attempted to de-nationalize a hundred years before, as their battleground.

Poland ranked sixth in Europe in the size of its population, which grew from 27,000,000 to 35,000,000 after Poland was recreated as a republic. Poland's natural increase of population was the highest among the major countries of Europe, amounting to 1.3 per cent per annum. In the period from 1918 to 1939, illiteracy was reduced from 35 per cent to 18 per cent.

The Economics of Poland

Agriculture. Although the predominant position of agriculture in Poland's economic life gradually declined between 1918 and 1939, Poland was nevertheless primarily an agricultural country, with 69 per cent of the population living on farms. Poland's most important agricultural product is rye, but it is also a large producer of potatoes, wheat, oats, sugar beets, barley, and a variety of other crops. In output, Poland occupies a place between the capitalist countries of the West, with a high level of agricultural production, and the more backward countries of Central and Eastern Europe. There are sharp regional differences in its agricultural productivity. Western Poland approaches Western European levels, while eastern Poland is closer to Balkan standards. Livestock breeding was also of considerable importance in the Polish economy and showed a steady increase in the period under discussion.

Polish agriculture was characterized by a vast number of uneconomic dwarf farms, existing side-by-side with large estates. There were few medium-sized farms in Poland. According to the census of 1921, large estates exceeding 100 hectares (approximately 250 acres) accounted for no more than 0.6 per cent of the total number of landholdings, but occupied 43 per cent of the total land area. It must be noted, however, that much of the land area of the large estates consisted of forests and lakes, that many of the large estates were publicly owned (public estates included much barren land, notably in the mountainous south), and that about 25 per cent of the land belonging to large estates was parcelled among the peasants between 1921 and 1939. Allowing for the above, we can estimate that about 20 per cent of the total land under cultivation belonged to privately owned estates exceeding 100 hectares, unquestionably a very high percentage. About 10 per cent of the total area under cultivation belonged to medium estates of 20 to 100 hectares (50 to 250 acres), and 5 per cent was publicly owned. This left 65 per cent of the total area of arable land belonging to small farms of less than 20 hectares (50 acres), and less than one-half of this area belonged to dwarf farms not exceeding 5 hectares (12 acres). These petty holdings, however, accounted for 64 per cent of the total number of landholdings. Despite a marked improvement between 1918 and 1939, the social structure of Polish agriculture was therefore still extremely top-heavy at the outbreak of the Second World War.

The weakness of this structure, coupled with the relatively low productivity of Polish agriculture, caused a permanent depression in the Polish countryside. The low living standard of the peasantry was in turn highly detrimental to the efforts of Polish industry to enlarge its domestic market. Moreover, the great number of petty holdings, which provided no opportunity for the efficient utilization of the time and energies of the owners and their families, resulted in latent unemployment throughout Polish rural districts, a situation further aggravated by the existence of several million landless farm laborers. This vast supply of manpower, available to the large landowners and medium farms, inevitably depressed agricultural wages. Between 1920 and 1939, however, some progress was made in the parcelling of large estates. That fact, coupled with the gradual absorption of "superfluous" rural manpower by expanding industry, promised some improvement in the Polish villages.[4]

[4] Kagan, George, "Agrarian Regime of Pre-War Poland," *Journal of Central European Affairs,* III (October, 1943), pp. 241-269. For the ownership structure of Polish agriculture, see Wladyslaw Malinowski, "Note on the Agrarian Regime of Pre-War Poland," *Ibid.,* IV (April, 1944), pp. 71-75.

Industry. When Poland was re-established in 1918, it inherited a rather chaotic industrial system. In formerly Russian territory, a large textile industry and a moderately developed metal industry existed in and around the cities of Lodz and Bialystok. The great coal mines in former Prussian Upper Silesia produced more coal than Poland needed, and they were not the only coal mines in Poland. A system of modern steel plants was centered around these mines. Poznan province—also a former Prussian possession—had a considerable sugar refining and packing industry. Oil extraction and refining were an important part of the economic life of southern Poland, which was also the home of a growing chemical industry as well as the center of an important lumbering and saw-mill industry.

Much of Poland's industrial equipment had been destroyed during the World War of 1914-1918, and had to be replaced. But Polish industry was rebuilt haphazardly, looking backward instead of to the future. The most glaring example of this was provided by the Lodz textile industry, which was reconstructed along pre-1914 lines. It was equipped to produce cheap textiles in huge quantities for the Russian and Asiatic markets, although these were virtually non-existent after the restoration of Poland's independence. As a result, the Polish textile industry never worked at full capacity and a large proportion of its workers were chronically unemployed. Meanwhile, especially during years of prosperity, many better textiles were imported from abroad, for the Polish urban population was dissatisfied with the poor quality of domestic textiles.

The currency inflation in the early years of the republic was a boon to Polish industry. It either completely cancelled or greatly reduced industry's pre-1914 indebtedness and also that incurred for reconstruction purposes. However, the severe depressions of 1924-1925 and 1930-1935 greatly handicapped further industrial development. Most of the new factories established between 1924 and 1939 were connected, directly or indirectly, with defense preparations and enjoyed the support of the government. Those which did not belong in this category were often owned by foreign capital.

Two of the most noteworthy aspects of the ownership structure of Polish industry were so-called "étatism" (or "statism") and the participation of foreign capital. Even apart from such enterprises as the National Tobacco, Spirits, and Salt Monopolies, regarded as sources of revenue, and defense plants directly owned by the State, the State's participation in Polish industry was considerable. It was usually exercised through the government-owned banks which advanced credits to various private enterprises. When the indebtedness became too great to be repaid, it was converted into capital participation by the Government bank. Enterprises in which the Government had an influence, whether directly or through the instrumentality of State-owned banks, usually retained their former legal structure and continued to function as stock companies, with the Government represented on the Board. The purpose of this State participation in business was not to obtain additional revenues, but to strengthen the Government's control over markets in addition to the power it exercised through its tariff and quota policies. Government-owned industrial enterprises often participated in cartel agreements.[5]

No picture of Polish economic life would be complete without mention of Polish handicraft industries, with their 200,000 shops and 375,000 artisans, working to supply many of Poland's domestic needs.

Commerce and Foreign Trade. The village and small-town general store was the mainstay of Polish domestic commerce. The rather low living standard did not encourage the establishment of specialized stores, which were limited mostly to the cities and larger towns. Co-operatives also existed and offered serious competition to privately-owned stores in some places.

Polish foreign trade underwent substantial changes between 1921 and 1939. At first it was limited almost exclusively to exports of Polish raw materials and unprocessed agricultural products, and imports of luxury goods, machinery and cotton for the textile industry, and certain other essential raw materials. After a few years, coal became one of the most important items of Polish export. Many other items which were at first exported unprocessed were later exported in finished form. Thus, boards and furniture replaced logs, and canned pork replaced live pigs as export commodities. In imports, additional machinery and more raw materials soon took the place of luxury goods, which became severely restricted.

The Polish balance of trade fluctuated. However, even in years when trade was active, the balance of payments was almost invariably passive, due to the payments made from reserves of gold and foreign exchange to service foreign debts and investments. Foreign exchange controls were established in 1936, mainly to obtain control over these movements of funds.

Communications. Poland has a fairly adequate network of railroads, most of which are important from a domestic point of view only, al-

---

[5] On foreign-capital participation in Polish industry and banking, see note on page 416.

though a few are vital parts of the European rail system. The Polish railways, Government-owned and operated, functioned quite smoothly and rated high among European carriers. But road transport was underdeveloped, mainly because the high prices of cars, trucks, and gasoline prohibited competition with the railroads.

Polish foreign trade was conducted principally (up to 78 per cent) by sea transport, mostly by means of foreign ships, since Poland's merchant marine was small.

The Danzig Question

The port of Danzig (Gdansk), situated at the mouth of the Vistula, is Poland's natural and traditional port. It was about to become part of Polish territory in 1919, as it had been between 1466 and 1793, but certain Governments objected to this at the Versailles Conference, mainly because the population of Danzig was predominantly German. The problem of Danzig was finally solved by its designation as a "Free City." It was completely independent politically in internal affairs, but in foreign affairs and economic matters it was a part of the Polish system and was included within Polish tariff barriers. Its means of communication with Poland, including railways and mails, were placed under Polish control, while the port was to be administered by a joint Council. Despite the advantageous position thus attained by Danzig, most of the city's German population strenuously objected to being severed from the Reich. The establishment of the economic links between Danzig and Poland, as provided in the Treaty of Versailles, took years of negotiation and had to surmount stubborn opposition. Even after Poland had concluded an agreement with the Danzig Senate (its governing body), German nationalists persisted in sabotaging common interests.

The unsatisfactory situation in Danzig was widely recognized in Poland. It was finally decided to build another port, on Polish territory, to enable Poland to dispense with Danzig's unwilling services if that became necessary. The new port, built near the village of Gdynia, was soon to overshadow Danzig and become the most important trade port on the Baltic. This Polish decision had an important effect on Danzig, whose people, fearful that Polish trade might by-pass their city and flow through Gdynia, visibly changed their attitude toward Poland.

In the meantime, Polish exports, most of which went to Germany and Austria before 1925, changed their direction and began to flow to Great Britain (foodstuffs and timber) and the Scandinavian countries (coal). Since sea transport is cheapest for goods shipped from Poland to Great Britain and the Scandinavian countries, Poland's maritime trade increased so greatly that both Gdynia and Danzig, which now took first and second place, respectively, among Baltic trade ports, were fully employed in handling it.

After a Nazi administration took over in Danzig, relations between Poland and its old port deteriorated considerably. Subsequently, Nazi-provoked incidents in Danzig and German demands for the return of Danzig to the Reich played an important role as Nazi pretexts for World War II.

Social and Political Structure

Since agriculture is the basis of the Polish economy, the countryside is the basic factor in Poland's national life. Socially, the Polish rural population is divided into peasants and landowners. Since most peasants own their farms, the essential difference between the two groups does not lie in the ownership status, but rather in the size of the holding (100 hectares is considered the dividing line by most Polish sociologists and statisticians), and in the fact that most of the owners of large estates are descendants of the old Polish gentry.

The landowners—the gentry—were omnipotent economically, socially, and politically in pre-partition Poland. They had great influence even during the partition period, either because the constitutional set-up of the empires which had divided Poland permitted them to retain their dominant position, or because their leadership had long been passively accepted by the rest of the nation and was challenged rarely and ineffectively. Economically, however, the landowners' position was seriously weakened when the foreign rulers of Poland instituted land ownership by peasants.

In independent Poland, their economic position deteriorated further. Many estates were cut down by the agrarian reform laws, or by voluntary sales made by the owners in anticipation of the subdivision of their land. Even greater economic losses resulted from the insistence of most large landowners on continuing grain production, which had become much less profitable since competing Canadian and Argentine grain had deprived Polish grain of its traditional markets in Western Europe. Uneconomic grain production led to serious difficulties, including heavy debts. Relatively few of the big landowners took advantage of the opportunity to change to more profitable livestock breeding and dairy production, an opportunity that the peasants understood and utilized much more rapidly.

Despite the deterioration of their economic position, the influence of the landowning classes was still extensive in the social sphere, partly because the urban middle class patterned its way of living upon that of the landowners. In the field of politics, the influence of the landowners infiltrated primarily through their association with high government officials, some of whom were men of their own class. Even those who belonged to other groups tried to please them because of their traditional social prestige. The Conservative Party, maintained by the landowners in association with some industrialists, was of little consequence politically and never attempted to face the electorate in free elections after 1918, for it had no popular backing. Whatever representation the Conservative Party had in Parliament or other public bodies was achieved by combining with other parties or by appointment.

Many landowners supported the National Democratic Party, an essentially middle-class party, and were often able (particularly during the early years of Poland's independence) to gain more influence through it than through the Conservative Party. On the whole, throughout the period of independence, the landowners preferred to exercise their power through organizations not essentially their own. This technique reached its peak a few years after the establishment of Pilsudski's semi-dictatorship (1926), when the landowners were extremely potent behind the scenes.

The peasants, the most numerous class in Poland and the core of the nation, were relative newcomers to Polish politics. There were isolated and localized instances of peasant political activity in earlier times, but it was only at the turn of the present century that the peasants as a whole became a conscious social group.

By the end of the nineteenth century, however, the peasants had begun to develop social consciousness in Galicia (Austrian Poland). This consciousness expressed itself in the creation of coöperatives, in insistence upon the rights of the villages to self-government, and, above all, in political activity. Independent peasant candidates were frequently elected to the Austrian Parliament and the Galician Diet. Gradually the Peasant Movement emerged, which was to become one of the most powerful elements in Polish political life. It originated in Galicia. Prussian and Russian Poland soon followed suit, although their Peasant Movements did not have the strength and cohesion of the Galician movement.

Because it had developed in the three separate parts of Poland, with their diverse traditions, the Peasant Party did not at once achieve organizational unity in independent Poland. The various regions had peasant parties of their own, and some of these expanded beyond their regional limits and competed with local groups. This tendency to competition was strengthened by the fact that individual peasant leaders usually exerted a strong personal appeal and often looked for mass support outside their normal geographic areas. Another competitive factor entered the picture when economic differentiations began to develop among the peasants. Various political groups began to identify themselves with particular strata of the peasant population rather than with specific geographic regions. As a result, bitter strife often arose among the various peasant groups, but their representatives in Parliament always remained united on basic issues and thus wielded considerable power.

After the establishment of Pilsudski's semi-dictatorship in 1926, political pressure on all groups which opposed the regime increased. This pressure led to a growing realization that the best opportunity for the re-establishment of democracy lay in the coördinated activity of all democratic and peasant groups. The regional peasant parties therefore merged into a unified Peasant Party (1931). Since no free national election has been held since its formation, and since local and village elections were inconclusive because the personal element was so important in them, the Peasant Party has never been able fully to demonstrate its strength. However, a trend was apparent even in the local elections, in which the Peasant Party swept dozens of counties.

The Peasant Party was not the only political party active among the peasants. The Socialist Party also found many supporters among landless peasants and petty landholders. Socialist influence among the peasantry was especially strong in industrial regions, where peasants often worked in factories during the winter. The National Democratic Party also sought support among the peasants, but succeeded only in a few small and clearly defined geographic areas.

Organizational activity among the Polish peasants was not limited to politics, especially in the last years before the Second World War, when the coöperative movement made astonishing progress throughout the Polish countryside, contributing greatly to the improvement of economic standards. A widespread educational movement, with many "Folk Universities," also took root. In both the coöperative and educational fields, the Polish peasants looked abroad, especially to Denmark, to supplement their own creative spirit and experience. All these improvements combined to fuse the peasants, particularly in the years preceding World War II, into a group completely independent of all others socially and ideologically. This development was especially apparent in the Peasant Youth Movement.

While the population of the Polish countryside is divided into only two distinct social groups, the situation in the cities is very different. There we find not only the two classes which emerge with the capitalist system of production—capitalists and workers—but also a number of intermediate groups of shopkeepers, artisans, professional men, civil servants, and white collar workers. These latter may be combined into two larger groups: the petty bourgeoisie, roughly corresponding to the lower-middle classes of the English-speaking nations, and the "intelligentsia." Although the Polish countryside is basically more important than the towns, the latter have been far more active in the political and cultural fields.

The capitalists in Poland—factory owners, bankers, corporation executives—though not numerous, were very class-conscious. They included a number of foreigners, mostly Polonized Germans. Among the native Poles, a high percentage were of Jewish descent. Their influence was limited almost exclusively to the economic field. In the cultural and social field they tried to emulate the landowners, with whom they insistently sought to associate either by drawing them into their business enterprises or by purchasing landed estates of their own.

The Polish capitalist group was well organized by industries and regions, with a general organization commonly called "the Leviathan" as a central agency. It corresponded approximately to the National Association of Manufacturers in the United States. The most important of "the Leviathan's" activities were representation of its membership before governmental agencies, protection of the members' interests, and research for their benefit.

The government's penetration into Poland's economic life and the dependence of business on government policies necessitated close and continuous contact between business and government agencies, a function which the "Leviathan" performed with considerable effectiveness. Probably because of their success on this apparently non-political basis, the Polish capitalists made few attempts to influence political life directly. They limited themselves to support of the Conservative Party, and, less frequently, of the National Democratic Party. Many industrialists supported the Pilsudski clique when it became the ruling group in Poland.

The workers were undoubtedly the most active political group in Poland. Some of them were descendants of city artisans, transformed into wage-earners by the emergence of factories. Others stemmed from the poorer gentry. Most of them, however, were landless peasants who had come to the cities to work for wages, which, low as they were, represented an improvement over the misery they had endured at home. The three elements quickly combined and a solid working class came into being.

We have seen how the Polish Socialist Party developed in Congress Poland and Galicia while they still belonged to Russia and Austria, respectively. In independent Poland, these regions remained the center of the Socialist movement, although it also made large inroads in the formerly Prussian part of Poland, notably Silesia, and in the seaboard city of Gdynia. In the early democratic years of the Republic, the Socialist Party had considerable influence in Parliament and in local government; it also had many representatives in the Social Security Offices, which were at that time administered by directors elected by workers and employers. However, when it became clear that the Socialist Party would uncompromisingly oppose the dictatorial tendencies of the Pilsudski regime, established in 1926, the regime decided to destroy Socialist influence by transferring the functions of local governments and Social Security Offices to appointed central government officials. This resulted in loss of patronage and considerable damage to the Socialist organization. Further deterioration was brought about by the economic depression of 1929-1932 and by political pressure on the part of the authorities, exercised mostly in smaller cities.

The Polish Socialist Party was at its lowest ebb in the years immediately after 1930. The Socialist organization did, however, retain considerable influence among the workers. A few years later, when the masses became disillusioned with the Pilsudski regime, and when the upward economic trend made a drive for higher wages possible, the Socialist Party, together with the trade unions, took a leading part in that drive and combined it with political action aimed at the overthrow of the dictatorship and the re-establishment of democracy. In a matter of months, the Socialist Party again became the focal point of the democratic opposition, which attracted citizens of high standing even from outside the ranks of labor. The municipal elections of 1938 and 1939 —the first elections in many years that were not marred by an inequitable electoral system or fraud—showed that the Socialists were by far the strongest political force in the Polish cities, in most of which they won either majorities or pluralities of votes and council seats.

The Socialists were not the only political party active among the workers.[6] Most of the other parties sought the workers' votes, but only three could be regarded as small-scale and local rivals of the Socialists: the Communist Party, the National Labor Party, and the Christian Democratic Party.

The Communists, generally weak throughout the country, never won more than two or three per cent of the total electorate.[7] But since most of their votes were concentrated in a few communities, they were able to elect representatives to Parliament and local governments. Sometimes the authorities disqualified their ticket for technical reasons, a method widely used by the administration whenever it wanted to check the electoral success of any political party. The Communist Party of Poland was not only faction-ridden—many of its supporters became disillusioned after the struggle between Stalinists and Trotskyites—but also spy-ridden. This eventually led to the dissolution of the party by the Comintern in 1937.

The influence of the National Labor Party, a non-socialist reform party, was limited mostly to formerly Prussian Poland. It developed a strong nationalistic feeling coupled with a bitter antagonism to German-dominated labor organizations, with which the Polish Socialists coöperated. In restored and united Poland, its power was steadily declining.

The Christian Democratic Party was basically a Catholic middle-class party, somewhat akin to the German Center Party and the Austrian Christian Socialist Party. Enjoying the support of the Catholic clergy, it was for a time very influential among religiously inclined workers. Most of this influence disappeared later when the antagonism between the Catholic Church and the Socialist Party became less sharp. In recent years, the Christian Democratic Party was able to retain its influence among workers only in Upper Silesia, where it

---

[6] Gross, Feliks, "The Polish Proletariat and Socialism," *Journal of Central European Affairs,* IV (October, 1944), pp. 241-261.

[7] The Communist Party, as such, was outlawed in Poland, but Communist candidates were able to run for office as individuals.

had taken deep root because of the great popularity of its one-time leader, Korfanty.[8] Shortly before the outbreak of war in 1939, the National Labor Party and the Christian Democratic Party merged into the Christian Labor Party, a democratic movement which looked for inspiration to the Papal encyclicals on social problems.

Polish labor was very political-minded and it was, therefore, in the political parties that its desires and aspirations were best expressed. The trade union movement was also of great importance and its membership greatly exceeded that of the political parties. The trade unions concentrated on collective bargaining and grievance adjustment machinery. Some of the unions were organized on a craft basis, others on an industrial basis. However, the existence of several competing trade union federations, with attendant jurisdictional disputes, undermined their influence and efficiency to some extent.

The Polish Trades Union Congress was by far the strongest of all the trade union federations. It was, in theory, non-partisan, but most of its leaders were Socialists and it coöperated closely with the Socialist Party. The other federations were also connected with political parties. Some of them were simply vote-catching agencies for their respective parties rather than bona-fide labor organizations. The stiff rivalry between the various federations resulted in high membership figures. Reliable data indicate that about half of all the industrial workers in Poland were unionized in 1938. The greatest influence in union activities was wielded by the Polish Trades Union Congress which also had the largest membership.

Poland, like other Central and Eastern European countries, had a special social group called the "intelligentsia." It consisted of persons of greatly varied economic status and occupations, but with the common factor of at least a certain minimum of formal schooling (secondary schooling was usually deemed sufficient to place a person within this group), and a non-manual occupation. Thus, it included professional people, civil servants, teachers of all grades, and white collar workers. As a social group, the intelligentsia had several origins. At first it was made up of educated burghers and impoverished noblemen who came to the cities in search of non-manual jobs. Later, many peasants' sons who had secured an education and professional jobs found their way into its ranks, with Jewish professionals following

---

[8] Wojciech Korfanty represented Silesian workers in the German Parliament before 1914. After 1918 he became the chief leader in the struggle of the Silesian Poles for the reunion of Silesia with Poland. His personal popularity, derived from his contribution to that national success, enhanced the fortunes of his party.

them closely. However, the various constituent elements of the intelligentsia soon consolidated, forming a distinct social group.[9] Its members often patterned themselves on the gentry in their way of living.

The influence of the intelligentsia in Polish life derived not so much from their own political organization, the Democratic Party, which was in and out of politics and never achieved much importance, but rather from their leadership of most of the other political parties. This group also staffed the administrative offices of the state and shaped the minds of youth in the schools.

The intelligentsia reflected almost all political currents in Poland. Some of the group played an important part in building up the ideology and strength of the Pilsudski regime. It was only in the last pre-war years that a general leftward trend became apparent among them.

The lower-middle class was another distinct social group in the Polish towns. It was composed mostly of persons active in the professions which had originated before the industrial revolution, such as shop-keeping and artisanship. These were joined later by a considerable number of lower-grade civil servants whose positions did not require a degree of education which would place them among the intelligentsia. Because their economic security was constantly menaced by the process of industrialization and commercial consolidation, members of this group took an essentially reactionary position in Poland's political life and were the backbone of every reactionary movement, including the National Democratic Party.

This party, which was the chief political outlet for Polish circles that advocated coöperation with Tsarist Russia before 1914, soon became the foremost reactionary force in independent Poland. While at first it paid lip service to a moderate form of political democracy, it split soon after Fascism appeared on the international political scene. The majority of its members looked to Fascism as a model to be followed in Poland. Some of these Fascist forces, notably the younger elements, broke away from the National Democratic Party and formed the National Revolutionary Camp (commonly known as the *Nara*).[10] The rest remained within the Party to combat the more conservative old-timers. This factional struggle, which divided the National Democratic Party, was still in progress when the war broke out in 1939. National Revolutionaries as well as Fascist-minded National Demo-

---

[9] Gross, Feliks, *op. cit.*

[10] There were also other Fascist groups, such as the Polish Phalanx.

crats soon adopted Fascist organizational forms and tactics. They roamed Polish cities in uniforms, attacked the political meetings of their opponents, beat them up in the streets, and generally introduced terroristic methods. Both these groups were very active and had a following among university students, which, together with their hoodlum tactics, placed them more in the public eye than their real strength and membership warranted.

Whatever their disagreements of political theory, all National Democrats were united against cultural progress and the rights of labor. In Parliament, their representatives consistently opposed progressive legislation and advocated a variety of anti-labor measures. In economic life, they often supplied strike-breakers. This attitude was determined both by the connection between the National Democratic Party and the "Leviathan" in the early years of the republic, and by the antagonism of the lower-middle classes to organized labor, prevalent throughout continental Europe between the two World Wars. Whenever the National Democrats made one of their unsuccessful bids for labor support, this antagonism was naturally played down.

The National Democratic Party was also strongly anti-Semitic. The National Revolutionaries openly organized anti-Jewish demonstrations and advocated the expulsion of Jews from Poland. The anti-Semitic element overshadowed all others in the Nationalist propaganda and was practically the only one employed during periods when the general trend of public opinion was to the Left.

The National Democratic Party was the main political expression of the Polish lower-middle class. Its only rivals were the Christian Democrats. The latter refused to have any ideological or political connection with Fascism, especially in the last years before the war. Moreover, because of their continued efforts to gain influence among the workers, they could not afford to take the anti-labor attitude characteristic of the National Democrats. Their anti-Semitism was hardly more moderate than that of the National Democrats, but it did not take such brutal forms.

The widespread anti-Semitism of the Polish lower-middle class was almost certainly the result of acute economic competition between Gentile and Jewish shopkeepers and artisans, just as the anti-Semitism of Gentile professionals was a reaction to the competition of their Jewish colleagues. Only an expansion of Poland's economic life could have brought about a broadening of opportunity sufficient to reduce the intensity of competition in these fields.

The Minorities

The inhabitants of Poland were not all of Polish extraction. In eastern Poland there were numerous Ukrainians and White Russians who frequently constituted local majorities. The Jews were scattered throughout Poland, though mostly concentrated in towns and cities. Western Poland was honeycombed with German settlements. There were also small groups of other minorities—Lithuanians, Czechs, Russians—but these were not important enough numerically to exercise any influence. In round figures, as of January 1, 1939, Poland had 35,500,-000 inhabitants, which included approximately 5,000,000 Ukrainians, 1,900,000 White Russians,[11] 800,000 Germans, and 3,400,000 Jews (about 400,000 of the latter listed themselves in the census as being of the Hebrew religion, but of Polish nationality).

The Ukrainians lived in southeastern Poland, where areas with a Ukrainian majority were intermingled with others predominantly Polish. The cities, particularly Lwow, were almost exclusively Polish in character. Most of the Ukrainians were peasants and few of them achieved the status of intelligentsia or factory workers. The Polish Ukrainians were divided in religion. Those who lived in Galicia (under Austrian domination before 1918) were Catholics (of the Greek rite), whereas those who lived in formerly Russian areas were Russian-Orthodox. The Galician Ukrainians were the most active politically, for the same reasons that made the Polish Peasant Party of Galicia the leading element in the Polish Peasant Movement.

In 1918 and 1919, a Polish-Ukrainian war was waged over the future of eastern Galicia. It was won by Poland and left considerable bitterness on both sides. Most Ukrainians refused to accept the outcome of the war and its recognition by the League of Nations, and retained their aspirations for independence. Many Poles, for their part, became suspicious of the Ukrainians and sought to restrict their educational and economic opportunities, a situation which the Ukrainians tried to counteract by developing their own coöperative movement.

There were several Ukrainian political parties. They varied in their approach to economic and social questions, but were united in advocating an independent Ukraine to include all the areas inhabited by Ukrainians. Only the Ukrainian Communists, who called themselves

---

[11] About 800,000, included in the total of 1,900,000 White Russians, designated their nationality as "local people" in the census.

the "Communist Party of Western Ukraine," urged the union of all these areas with the Ukrainian Soviet Republic. Intransigeant Ukrainian youths frequently terrorized the Poles, burning their homes and crops and bringing down severe reprisals by the Pilsudski government.

The White Russians[12] lived in northeastern Poland, east of the Vilna area, which was inhabited by Poles. Practically all White Russians were peasants. Their national feeling was much less intense than that of the Ukrainians. Many of them voted for Polish parties in elections.

The Polish Jews were distributed all over Poland, but their ratio to the total population was highest in the large cities, and generally higher in eastern Poland. There were comparatively few Jews in western Poland. Only a small proportion of Jews lived in rural districts, either as farmers or as shopkeepers. The Jewish urban population included shopkeepers, handicraftsmen, workers, professionals, and capitalists. They were particularly well represented in retail trade and the handicrafts, and it was in these fields that they offered the greatest competition to Gentiles.

It was mainly because of their concentration in Poland that the Jews clung together, continuing to use their own language—Yiddish—and developing a culture and educational system of their own. About 10 per cent of the Polish Jews, however, regarded themselves as part of the Polish nation and used the Polish language in everyday life. These assimilated Jews took an active part in Polish political and cultural life, but the anti-Semitism of Polish Rightists soon limited their participation to progressive Polish parties.

The non-assimilated Jews had political groups of their own. The Jewish Socialists ("Bundists"), Zionists, Labor Zionists, and the Religious Federation (Orthodox Jews) were the most important among them. For some time their strength was fairly evenly balanced, with the Zionists somewhat in the lead. But the municipal elections of 1938-1939 showed that the Jewish Socialists were gaining the confidence of the majority of Polish Jews.

An active and creative cultural life developed among the non-assimilated Polish Jews. Novels, poetry, periodicals, and scientific works in large numbers were published in Yiddish, and the Jewish stage attracted large audiences. There were also many schools with instruction in Yiddish. The cultural centers of non-assimilated Polish Jewry were in Warsaw and Vilna. In the latter city, the Jewish Scien-

---

[12] See footnote #3.

tific Institute (YIVO—at present in New York) carried on extremely productive research work.

There was greater social diversity among the Germans in Poland than among the almost exclusively rural Ukrainians and White Russians, or the almost exclusively urban Jews. Some of the Germans were farmers, usually owning medium-sized farms, others were industrialists or skilled factory workers.

After the establishment of Polish independence, a considerable proportion of the Germans in Poland professed loyalty to the republic but worked against it secretly with the support of the authorities in the German Reich. This type of activity was enhanced after the Nazis took over Germany. Despite initial protestations of friendship, the Nazis were always preparing to attack Poland.

The social diversity of the German minority in Poland was reflected in the variety of their political parties. Practically all the German parties were represented among the Germans in Poland, but only the Socialists and the Catholic Center coöperated with their Polish counterparts.

When the Nazis came to power in Germany, they seized control of several important German organizations in Poland which had been subsidized by the German Government and were thus dependent upon it. This gave the Nazis an effective springboard from which to gain unchallenged superiority among the Germans in Poland. They either took over the other German parties directly or simply disbanded them and absorbed their members into the Nazi organization, which adopted the respectable name of "Young German Party." Nazi propaganda among the Germans in Poland was not limited to persons who had been active in German organizations, but also sought to appeal to Poles of German origin, no matter how many generations back. Emphasizing the racial myth and the master-race legend, the Nazis were able to arouse pro-German feeling even among persons who had always regarded themselves and been regarded as Poles. The Nazi fifth column in Poland was based on this element.

Political Trends

While Poland was fighting the Battle of the Frontiers, Moraczewski's government, appointed by Pilsudski, proclaimed a liberal electoral law on November 28, 1918. It provided suffrage for both sexes on the basis of proportional representation. The Sejm (Diet), elected on January 26, 1919, met without the representatives of Poznan, who went to Warsaw only after the conclusion of the Versailles Treaty, but with the former deputies to the Austrian Reichsrat from Eastern Galicia. It was almost equally divided between the multiplicity of Right and Left parties, most of which had existed before the re-establishment of independent Poland (the Polish Socialist Party, the Peasant Party, the National Democratic Party, and the less important National Labor and Christian Democratic Parties).[13] Soon after its first meeting on February 10, 1919, at which the National Democrat Trampczynski was elected speaker, the Diet introduced a temporary "Little Constitution," confirmed the office of the "Chief of State," and voted its confidence in Pilsudski, with the provision that he exercise executive power through a Cabinet which he was to appoint in consultation with the Diet. Both the Chief of State and the Government were made responsible to the Diet, which assumed supreme legislative authority and control over the executive powers.

The governments which followed that of Paderewski (which was in office when the Diet first met) were either coalition Cabinets weighted to the Right, or Cabinets of experts and officials who lacked a solid body of supporters in the Diet and had to depend upon different Parliamentary groups for the enactment of each policy they proposed. The sole exception was the Cabinet of National Defense, headed by the peasant leader W. Witos as Premier and the Socialist leader Daszynski as Vice Premier. This Cabinet, in which all parties were represented, was appointed at a moment of grave national danger in 1920, when Russian armies were within ten miles of Warsaw. It survived peace with Russia by only a few weeks and was succeeded by another Cabinet composed of moderate professors and officials.

These early Cabinets did not continue the social reforms begun by the Socialist-led administrations of Daszynski and Moraczewski. The unexpected show of voting strength by the National Democrats precluded expansion of the progressive legislation introduced by decree before the first meeting of the Diet. However, the strong demand for agrarian reform forced the passage of a bill, in 1920, which limited the size of landed estates to 100 hectares (approximately 250 acres) in western and central Poland, and to 400 hectares (approximately 1000 acres) in the parts of Poland which had a lower level of agricultural productivity. The enforcement of this law was extremely slow and cautious.

The Diet's work centered primarily upon the future constitution. After a bill proposing a federal government structure was rejected, the principle of a unified democratic and parliamentary republic was

---

[13] Several lesser parties, such as the Conservative, Democratic, and Center parties, were also represented in the Diet by a few deputies each.

adopted. Considerable discussion was finally followed by the promulgation of a genuinely democratic constitution on March 17, 1921.

The constitution resembled that of the French Republic, except for the role and the powers of the Senate.[14] Executive authority was carefully limited. The Senate was given the right to revise the acts of the Sejm, but a majority of the Sejm could overrule the Senate. Both houses were elected for five-year terms by universal adult suffrage on the basis of proportional representation. Executive power was vested in a President, elected for a seven-year term by the National Assembly (both houses in joint session). The President was to appoint a Cabinet responsible to the Parliament. The Bill of Rights provisions were among the most complete in modern European constitutions. But, like the French constitutional laws of 1875 upon which it was modelled, the Polish Constitution failed to include adequate provisions for resolving a deadlock between the executive and the legislature. This fact, further aggravated by the failure to specify a deadline for the passage of budget legislation, finally proved fatal to the constitution.

Polish Political Life, 1922-1939

The first Polish Parliament, elected in 1922, did not have any clear political majority. The National Democrats, together with the Conservatives and Christian Democrats, were by far the strongest group in both Houses, but the Left and Center could outvote them if and when they were able to enlist the support of the 80-odd deputies representing the national minorities.

The first important political act of the new Parliament was to elect Poland's constitutional President. Pilsudski, irritated by a protracted struggle with the Sejm over the right of nominating Cabinets during the time when he was fighting the war with Russia, made it known that he would not be a candidate for the Presidency. He believed that the constitution did not give the President adequate powers. The post fell to the candidate of the Left, Gabriel Narutowicz, a well-known liberal engineer. He was elected by the votes of the Polish Left, the Peasant Party, and the representatives of the minorities. The incensed National Democrats then began to insist that no majority in the Polish Parliament should be considered valid unless it consisted of purely Polish votes. This violent campaign caused high tension. A few days after his inauguration, President Narutowicz was murdered by a member of the National Democratic Party. He was succeeded by Stanis-

---

[14] In old Poland, the name Diet was used to designate jointly the House of Deputies and the Senate. In modern Poland, only the House of Deputies is known as the Diet.

law Wojciechowski, one of the leaders of the Polish coöperative movement and a former member of the Socialist Party.

There were several Cabinets during Wojciechowski's term. Some consisted of experts and civil servants who carried out the tasks of their office without following any political program and obtained acceptance of their bills by majorities which shifted with the nature of the legislation proposed. Other Cabinets were "Parliamentary" and consisted of political leaders. These were the result of short-lived parliamentary combinations, mostly between parties of the Right and the Peasant Party. Pilsudski was appointed Marshal and Inspector General of the Polish Army, but resigned when his proposal that the Inspector General should be the actual Supreme Commander of the Armed Forces was rejected by the Cabinet (May, 1923).

In May, 1926, Wincenty Witos returned to form a third Cabinet, in which an anti-Pilsudski general was appointed Minister of War. Pilsudski organized a revolt of the troops that had remained faithful to him. He was supported by his close friend General Rydz-Smigly and also by the Socialist Party and trade unions.[15] The latter joined with him because the government was generally suspected of encouraging a coup by nascent Fascist groups. The support of the Railwaymen's Union proved especially useful, since it delayed the trains carrying reinforcements for the government and brought in reinforcements for Pilsudski. After three days of street fighting in Warsaw, both the President and the Cabinet resigned. M. Rataj,[16] the Speaker of the Diet, became acting President and appointed a new Cabinet conforming to Pilsudski's wishes.

When Pilsudski seized power in 1926, his avowed aims were to strengthen the executive powers, to eradicate official corruption, and to reorganize the high command of the Polish armed forces. But what he really wanted, in addition to the above, was a decisive voice in all major political decisions, especially those concerning foreign policy. If he could achieve this aim, the technical title and nature of his position were unimportant to him. A man of modest tastes and an old-time conspirator, Pilsudski hated publicity and ostentation. His favorite method of public expression was by press interviews, although he generally preferred to state his views in private and have his plans carried out by others.

Pilsudski's original plans undoubtedly called for the execution of his

---

[15] Pilsudski was also supported by the Communist Party at that time.

[16] Executed by the Germans in 1940, together with his friend, the Socialist leader M. Niedzialkowski.

political designs within the framework of the existing constitutional set-up. He declined to run for the Presidency. Instead, a learned and respected but politically unknown professor of chemistry, Ignacy Moscicki, hand-picked by Pilsudski, was elected President. A few weeks later, a constitutional amendment was passed providing a mechanism for breaking deadlocks between the legislature and the executive by giving the President the right to dissolve Parliament.

Pilsudski's idea was to obtain Presidential appointment of Ministers who belonged to no political parties or had only loose connections with them and who would command the respect of Parliament. He hoped thereby to secure passage of legislation he deemed necessary, at the same time keeping party politics out of executive departments. Minor legislation in which he was not interested was to be left to Parliament. Men personally connected with Pilsudski and planted by him in responsible positions in almost all political parties were counted upon to keep their respective parties in line.

Kazimierz Bartel,[17] a professor of engineering and formerly a democratic deputy, was appointed Prime Minister. Popular among the deputies of the Left and Center, he seemed to be the most appropriate person to carry out Pilsudski's original tactical plan. He later resigned and was reappointed several times. Each time his return to office was interpreted as a resumption by Pilsudski of his original tactics of coöperating with Parliament on his own conditions. For himself, Pilsudski selected the office of Minister of War and Inspector General of the Armed Forces. He was also Prime Minister on two occasions.

Pilsudski's plans, however, did not work out in practice. The parties of the Left, which had helped Pilsudski with his coup, soon discovered that he meant to rule Poland dictatorially, preserving only the appearance of constitutional government. They were also indignant over Pilsudski's open alliance with the Conservative Party and offered strong opposition. Pilsudski realized that he would need his own political group in Parliament if he was to go on with his program. Accordingly, he delayed parliamentary elections for almost two years while he set up a political organization he could rely on for unconditional support.

This brings us to the core of the problem. Up to 1926 and 1927, Pilsudski enjoyed the support of Leftists. Their first loyalty, however, was to their own parties and they abandoned Pilsudski when it became clear that a struggle between him and the parties of the Left was unavoidable. But Pilsudski also had other supporters, much less numer-

---

[17] Executed by the Germans in 1941.

ous but loyal to him alone. This group consisted of his former soldiers, members of the Polish Legions of the First World War. Many of them became professional soldiers after the war and soon developed the arrogance characteristic of that class; others, mostly intellectuals, returned to civilian life. All of them were convinced that they alone, led by Pilsudski, were responsible for the re-establishment of an independent Poland to the exclusion of everyone else. They resented all political activities by persons outside their clique and considered themselves the only group fit to govern Poland. They resented even more any opposition to Pilsudski, especially from such former sympathizers as Socialists and other Left-wing groups. The arrogance of the Pilsudski faction was rationalized and justified by students of Pareto's theory of the elite, since these people came to regard themselves as the national elite.

Every elite must of course have a source from which it periodically renews itself. That source in Poland was provided by the intelligentsia, the social element most sympathetic to the Pilsudski veterans. The Polish intelligentsia, while furnishing much of the leadership of all political groups, lacked a powerful political instrument of their own; this vacuum was filled by Pilsudski's group. The fact that a large number of the intelligentsia were employed by the government or by organizations dependent upon it probably accelerated the process of enlisting their support. This situation continued until Pilsudski's death and, to some extent, even afterwards.

Most of the intelligentsia thus placed themselves in strong opposition to the peasants and workers who fought for democracy and against dictatorship. They also developed the conviction that all power in Poland should belong to them. Some sociologists compare the arrogance of the Polish gentry of pre-partition times with that of the Polish intelligentsia in the Pilsudski period, finding similar characteristics and attitudes in the two groups. Others liken the basic ideological approach of the Polish intelligentsia to that of the American "Technocrats."

As noted above, Pilsudski postponed parliamentary elections until 1928 in order to permit this support to consolidate and to win additional backing from various other quarters. When the polls were tabulated, the Pilsudski supporters (under the name of "Non-Partisan Pro-Government Bloc")[18] emerged as the strongest single group in both Houses, but with only one-quarter of the total number of seats. Unable

---

[18] Usually referred to as *B.B.W.R.*, the initials of the Polish name of the group. Also known as the *Sanacja*.

to improve their position in spite of a number of electoral frauds, they were defeated in the organization of the Diet when the Socialist leader Daszynski was elected Speaker by the combined vote of the Left. Pilsudski had Bartel reappointed Premier, but the democratic parties were determined to prevent the establishment of dictatorship, even in disguise. An issue was soon created when the Board of Audits discovered that huge sums of money had been spent by the Treasury without parliamentary authorization, and that part of this money was used to cover the electoral expenses of the Pilsudski faction. The Minister of Finance was impeached and tried by the Tribunal of State.

At that point, it became clear that Pilsudski could not be a dictator and still preserve the appearances of parliamentary rule. He once tried to intimidate the Diet by crowding the lobby with officers, but Speaker Daszynski refused to open the session until the officers left the building. Pilsudski attempted to strengthen his hand by obtaining the appointment of a new Cabinet, selecting the Ministers from a particularly aggressive group known as the "Colonels" because most of them had held that rank in the army. The issues sharpened. The parties of the Left and Center united in the battle to save democracy in Poland. Mass demonstrations were held throughout Poland, but in the very midst of the campaign the Diet was dissolved (1930), and the deputies were thus deprived of parliamentary immunity. About twenty of them, including the most active leaders of the democratic opposition, were arrested and taken to the fortress dungeon of Brest, where they were mistreated and threatened with death.[19]

New elections were called, but the administration had seized control of the election machinery. In many constituencies opposition tickets were thrown off the ballot, leaving only the *Sanacja* (Pilsudski) ticket. The electoral campaign of the opposition was further severely handicapped by a ban on most meetings called by the democratic parties, by repeated seizures of opposition papers and their printing plants, by intimidating voters at the polls, and, finally, by fraud in the tabulation of votes. Despite these tactics, the Pilsudski group was credited in the official announcement with only 40 per cent of the votes cast. However, as a result of the elimination of opposition tickets wherever these were most likely to win, the *Sanacja* captured just over one-half of the parliamentary seats.

The opposition parties had lost the struggle for power. If they were ever to win office again, they had to start from the beginning. That

---

[19] Ten of these deputies were tried for allegedly plotting sedition and sentenced to various terms in jail.

was not easy. By that time the administration, substituting appointed commissioners for formerly elected mayors and social security directors, had secured a monopoly of all sources of patronage (it already controlled the jobs in direct government service and the railroads). Moreover, the depression of 1929 had caught up with Poland (a year late) and the people's attention was taken up with fighting it rather than with political issues, which were shelved for the time being.

For almost the first time since its restoration, Poland had an administration which commanded a majority in Parliament, a homogeneous Cabinet and a civil service completely loyal to it. The people expected that this government would be able to do something to alleviate their suffering. But the government made the situation even worse, if possible, by stubbornly continuing its one-sided deflationary policy, which ruined the peasants and increased unemployment until every third potential wage-earner was out of work. At the same time, persons connected with members of the government and those in important economic positions enjoyed ostentatious luxury. Resultant popular disillusion gave new strength to the opposition parties, which, however, were unable to prevent the adoption by Parliament of laws restricting civil liberties and limiting the existing progressive social legislation.

The climax of the Pilsudski clique's legislative activities was the adoption of a new constitution in 1935. While not overtly Fascist, this constitution was strongly authoritarian. Technically, legislative power was still vested in Parliament, but the President was given extensive rights to legislate by decree as well as the right to appoint a part of the Senators. Furthermore, the new electoral laws made it practically impossible for opposition parties to obtain the election of their candidates.

The old Polish constitution required a two-thirds majority for the adoption of constitutional amendments and changes. Lacking such a majority, the Pilsudski faction engineered a parliamentary incident, causing the opposition deputies to leave the House. Thereupon, the Pilsudski forces quickly passed the new constitution, crowding all three readings into one meeting. This procedure aroused much indignation in Poland, but, since the President signed the bill and since there is no judicial review of legislation in Poland, the new constitution became law in spite of serious misgivings advanced by the opposition.

Pilsudski had long been ill and died (May 12, 1935) a few weeks after the passage of the new constitution. Some of his followers hoped that his death would end the anomalous situation where an individual, technically only one of the Ministers, exercised virtual dictatorship. They urged that the new constitution be permitted to function, with the President duly exercising his powers under it. Others opposed the change, supporting the bid of Marshal Rydz-Smigly, Pilsudski's successor as Inspector-General, for the place that Pilsudski had occupied in Polish life since 1926. The followers of Marshal Rydz-Smigly won, and President Moscicki continued his merely nominal functions.

In the meantime, the economic situation had improved. Conditions permitted increases in salaries. A re-established trade union movement gained strength and a wave of strikes swept the country. The aims of the strikes were more than economic. At that time, and especially after Pilsudski's death, demands for the re-establishment of democracy were voiced with increasing insistence by the peasants and workers and by the Peasant and Socialist Parties which represented them. Since the new electoral law made it impossible for them to gain representation in Parliament, mass action was the only course open to them. Moreover, the increasing sympathy shown by Marshal Rydz-Smigly toward Fascism and Fascist elements, including the National Revolutionary Group, caused many former Pilsudski supporters to come over to the opposition. They either joined one of the existing parties, or the newly reorganized Democratic Party.

The increased activity of the opposition forced the Fascist followers of Marshal Rydz-Smigly repeatedly to postpone their projected coup, in preparation for which they had created a "National Unity Party." [20] It was slated eventually to become the official party of a Fascist regime. The adherents of this party, however, were limited to reactionary Pilsudski supporters and to certain other Rightists who had joined it because it seemed more likely to establish Fascism in Poland than the National Democratic Party (which, incidentally, had by that time dropped the "Democratic" from its name).

The autumn of 1938 saw much feverish discussion of ways and means among the followers of Rydz-Smigly. It was a time of national and municipal elections. Because the electoral law made it practically impossible for the opposition parties to obtain representation in Parliament, they boycotted the national elections as they had in 1935. In both elections, no more than half of the eligible voters went to the polls. The national elections of 1938 naturally ended in a complete "victory" for the *Ozon*. A few weeks later, however, municipal elections were held, in which the opposition parties participated. This time the opposition, especially the Peasant and Socialist Parties, swept the country, showing clearly that the power of the *Sanacja* was only the result of special privilege, pressure, and fraud.

[20] Known in Poland as *Ozon* or *O.Z.N.*, from the initials of the party's name in Polish.

The democratic victory in the municipal elections of 1938 and 1939 (held in communities which had not elected their administrations in 1938) checked whatever plans Marshal Rydz-Smigly and his followers had developed for changing Poland's authoritarian constitution into an outright Fascist or near-Fascist regime. The threat of war, which became apparent early in 1939, was another obstacle. But despite the opposition's repeated demands for a democratic revision of the constitution, or at least of the electoral law, nothing was done about them. The outbreak of war found only followers of the *Ozon* in office, under the presidency of Ignacy Moscicki, who had been elected in 1926 and re-elected in 1933.

Polish Cultural Life, 1918-1943[21]

The restoration of Poland's independence in 1918 wrought far-reaching changes in Polish cultural life.

Lyric poetry was the outstanding form of literature during the first ten years of Poland's independence. It was represented by a group of poets called the "Scamanderists" (a name derived from the literary monthly *Scamander*). They achieved considerable success in modernizing the language of Polish poetry, mainly by revitalizing it with elements of the modern urban language and by introducing variety into the rhythm and structure of their verse. They pioneered in the use of blank verse, novel rhymes, bold metaphors, and similar poetic forms. The "Scamanderists" proclaimed themselves to be "the poets of today," which to some extent linked them with the Italian futurists and the Russian revolutionary poets. Such leading Polish poets as Julian Tuwim, Antoni Slonimski, Jan Lechon, and Kazimierz Wierzynski were members of the "Scamanderist" group. Other prominent Polish poets, like Kazimiera Illakowicz, Maria Pawlikowska, and Wladyslaw Broniewski, were also connected with the group, although much more loosely.

Novelists continued the realist pattern established before the period of independence, but they used a new realistic technique. Zofia Nalkowska attempted a new form, which she called "written reality," but later returned to an emphasis on plot. Maria Dabrowska used in *Nights and Days* the old form of chronicle-novel. Jozef Wittlin is not only an outstanding poet, well known for his translation of Homer's Odyssey, but also the author of the lyrico-epic novel *Salt of the Earth*, which has been translated into many foreign languages. This novel

---

[21] Contributed by Professor Manfred Kridl, Smith College.

presents an excellent picture of the early days of the First World War. The historical novel is best represented by Zofia Kossak Szczucka, whose book *Blessed Are the Meek* has been translated into English. Julius Kaden-Bandrowski is the author of many novels which stand between realism and anti-realism, such as *The Black Wings* and *Mateusz Bigda.* Ignacy Witkiewicz, abandoned the realistic pattern both in his novels and more especially in his plays.

Karol Hubert Rostworowski, author of *Judas,* was considered the foremost Polish playwright. *The Quail,* a play by the novelist Zeromski, and two plays by Nalkowska were sensationally successful. Contemporary comedy is represented by Wlodzimierz Perzynski and Antoni Cwojdzinski. The latter brought scientific problems to the stage, writing plays about the theory of relativity and Freud's theory of dreams.

The humanities and the sciences also made considerable progress. The following Polish leaders in these fields are well known abroad: Tadeusz Zielinski, professor of classical philology; the historian Marceli Handelsman; and the logicians Lukasiewicz and Kotarbinski, pupils of Kazimierz Twardowski, a recognized authority in the field of philosophy. Others worthy of mention are Sierpinski, Steinhaus, Banach, and Tarski, the chief representatives of the "Polish School of Mathematics"; Mme. Sklodowska-Curie; the chemist Kazimierz Fajans; the anthropologist and sociologist Bronislaw Malinowski; the sociologists Znaniecki and Czarnowski; the astronomer Banachiewicz; the bacteriologist Weigel; and the Sanskrit scholar A. Gawronski.

K. Irzykowski and T. Boy-Zelenski were the most prominent literary critics. In painting, a definite swing away from impressionism developed when painters began to emphasize the element of structure. The modern school of painting embracing various trends achieved considerable success in Poland.

Extensive activity both in private housing and in the erection of public buildings gave impetus to the development of modern architecture. Many old buildings, however, were carefully restored in their traditional appearance and architectural forms.

Much emphasis was also placed in independent Poland upon folk art, which was encouraged both in building and in artistic textiles.

Contemporary Polish music is best represented by Karol Szymanowski, who was very popular abroad, especially in Germany, and was considered by foreigners to be the foremost Polish composer since Chopin. He wrote symphonies, concertos, an opera, and a ballet. Many younger performers also gained wide fame: the pianists Jozef Hoffman and Artur Rubinstein, the harpsichordist Wanda Landowska, the violinist Bronislaw Huberman, and the conductor Artur Rodzinski. The impact of Poland's military defeat in 1939 was disastrous to Polish culture, especially since the Germans deliberately set out to destroy it. But Polish cultural life did not disappear. It continued both in the Polish underground and in exile, chiefly in Great Britain and the United States, where a number of poets and novelists found refuge. Several hundred Polish books were published in exile, including both novels and poetry. There were also Polish scientific societies in exile, which carried on the tradition of Polish science. The development of Polish culture under these conditions gives forceful proof of its vitality. It could not be crushed even by the trials and misfortunes it had to endure after 1939.

International Relations and the Coming Blitzkrieg

Poland was originally France's closest ally in Eastern Europe because of Poland's constant search for security, but there were times when their relations were strained and marred by mutual recriminations. The changes in Polish-French relations illustrated the changing methods by which Poland struggled to achieve security, as well as changes in the French attitude toward Central-Eastern European problems.

As far back as 1924, Germany adopted a double-faced line in foreign policy. With France and the other Western democracies, she was pliant and full of apparent good will, assuring them of her peaceful intentions and acceptance of the prevailing balance of power.[22] Toward Poland, however, Germany pursued an aggressive policy which had two aims: to convince the Western democracies that Poland should not be accepted as a full-fledged and permanent participant in European international life; and to prove that Germany had been grievously wronged by the territorial decisions concerning her frontiers with Poland, notably in Pomerania (the so-called Polish Corridor) and Upper Silesia.[23] Repeated incidents and frictions were engineered along the German-Polish border. The Polish minority in Germany was subjected to ruthless persecution and Germanization. Partly as a result of this propaganda, England and France gradually lost interest in maintaining the existing balance of power in Central-Eastern Europe,

---

[22] Boas, George, "Stresemann, Object Lesson in Post-War Leadership," *Public Opinion Quarterly*, VIII (Summer, 1944), pp. 232-43.

[23] Roucek, Joseph S., *Misapprehensions About Central-Eastern Europe in Anglo-Saxon Historiography* (reprinted from the *Quarterly Bulletin of the Polish Institute of Arts and Sciences in America*, January, 1944), analyzes the various causes which made the Anglo-Saxon world look down on Eastern Europe, partly under the influence of German propaganda.

a fact that was soon realized in Warsaw. But Poland's foreign policy was not changed even by Pilsudski (after his seizure of power in 1926), although his feelings toward France were notoriously cool.

The turning point came in 1933, when Hitler seized power in Germany. Pilsudski secretly proposed a preventive war against Germany. But France rejected Pilsudski's proposal, leading him to the conclusion that she was not interested in Eastern Europe and that Poland must henceforth seek her own safeguards independently. The spokesman of the new policy was Colonel Joseph Beck, who had shortly before been appointed Minister of Foreign Affairs.

Beck opened negotiations with Germany for a non-aggression pact which was concluded in 1934, almost two years after the signing of a similar pact with the Soviet Union. The subsequent French proposal for an Eastern Pact of Security in which Russia would participate was interpreted by Pilsudski as additional proof that France wished to reduce her commitments in Eastern Europe and dilute them by accepting Russia as a partner in underwriting Eastern European security. Poland rejected the French proposal and placed ever-increasing reliance on friendly relations with Germany. Later, during the Munich crisis of 1938, the failure of France to come to the rescue of Czechoslovakia was again interpreted in some Polish circles as proof of the soundness of Polish policy toward Germany. At the same time, Beck abandoned Warsaw's former reliance on the League of Nations and collective security and switched to the bilateral-pact school of foreign relations, of which Berlin was a leading advocate.

Polish public opinion was divided on the question of Beck's German policy, which was strongly attacked from many quarters. The democratic opposition strenuously opposed the shift away from the League; other groups, such as the traditionally Francophile conservative National Democrats, urged the maintenance of the Polish alliance with France. The democratic opposition was not able to force Poland's return to the collective security policy, but it nevertheless prevented further commitments with Germany. Berlin was unable to draw Poland into the Anti-Comintern Pact. However, Poland maintained friendly relations with the various states in the Fascist orbit, including Hungary and Italy. Polish diplomacy was helpful to Italy in the Abyssinian crisis, for Poland was the first nation, outside of the Italian satellites, to recognize the Italian conquest of Abyssinia.

Relations between Russia and Poland were never cordial. After the Treaty of Riga, several other treaties were concluded by Warsaw and Moscow, including one which made the Kellogg Anti-War Pact effective between them immediately, without waiting until the pact obtained the necessary number of ratifications. A Russo-Polish non-aggression pact, signed in 1932, was extended for ten more years in 1935.

As Polish-German relations improved, Polish Soviet relations deteriorated. No country could simultaneously enjoy the friendship of both. Russian-Polish relations were especially strained during the Munich crisis, when Poland's position made Soviet military intervention on Czechoslovakia's behalf impossible. Later they improved somewhat until the German-Soviet non-aggression pact was signed.

Friendly relations with Czechoslovakia were prevented by Polish resentment of Czechoslovakia's attack on the Polish section of the Cieszyn (Teschen) region in Silesia in 1919, when Poland was engaged in war against the Ukraine and Russia. The Poles also resented the subsequent pressure upon them to accept the annexation of that region by Czechoslovakia. When this resentment began to disappear, partly because of Czechoslovakia's considerate treatment of the Polish minority, Poland and Czechoslovakia were already aligned in opposing political blocs as a result of Beck's new foreign policy. Beck forced Czechoslovakia to return the Teschen area to Poland during the Munich crisis; but Polish public opinion was shocked and critical, and the method of recovery was condemned. Several months later, after the complete occupation of Czechoslovakia by the Germans, thousands of Czech refugees streamed into Poland and met with a cordial reception.

Poland had no diplomatic relations with Lithuania until 1938, as the Lithuanians refused to recognize the acquisition of the Vilna district by Poland. Lithuanian diplomats considered their country in a state of war with Poland and repeatedly petitioned the League of Nations to compel Poland to restore the contested area to their country. Only in 1938, when the German threat became imminent, was Polish pressure able to force Lithuania to re-establish diplomatic relations.

Poland's relations with other countries had no decisive impact on her foreign policy. However, particularly in Colonel Beck's time, certain of these relations had repercussions beyond their original importance. Thus, Poland's support of Hungary contributed considerably to the bitterness between Czechoslovakia and Poland. There was little cordiality in Poland's relations with Great Britain before 1939. The Poles frequently suspected British diplomacy of pro-German leanings. The events of 1939 completely changed this attitude.

From 1934 to 1939 Hitler repeatedly urged Poland to join Germany in an attack on Soviet Russia, promising her large territorial gains in

Eastern Europe. Although Poland accepted French and British pledges of military aid in March, 1939, she rejected Moscow's proposals two months later for a mutual assistance pact or participation in collective negotiations with England and France. War became inevitable when Poland, by rejecting German claims upon Polish territory and upon Danzig, showed herself ready to become the first nation to oppose Hitler's expansionist tendencies with armed force rather than compromise on the territorial issue.

Then came the Russian-German non-aggression pact. At dawn on September 1, 1939, German land and air armies attacked Poland without any declaration of war, crossing the frontier at 14 points from East Prussia, West Prussia, Silesia, Moravia, and Slovakia. Germany bombed all Polish airfields and 61 towns within the first few hours. The war lasted 35 days, from September 1 to October 5, 1939. The siege of Warsaw lasted 19 days in spite of heavy air and artillery bombardment. Warsaw surrendered on September 27. This was the penalty Poland paid for being the first country to abandon the policy of endless concessions and the first to have the courage to say *No* to Hitler.

On September 17, 1939, Soviet troops also crossed the Polish border. Polish resistance was extremely weak, partly because most of the troops were engaged against the Germans, and partly because of the rumor that the Russians were coming to help Poland. The Russians advanced westward into Poland until they met the Germans, and both armies proceeded to mop up the remnants of the resisting Polish troops. The Soviet authorities explained Russia's intervention by the need to protect the life and property of the Ukrainian and White Russian inhabitants of Eastern Poland. Later on, it was explained that the Soviet Government knew that the Germans would subsequently attack Russia and was therefore anxious to obtain an additional security zone. In view of this fact, it becomes immaterial to what extent the Russian action contributed to the defeat of the Polish troops, a large part of whom were taken prisoner by the Germans and the Russians. Even before organized Polish resistance had ceased, Germany and the Soviet Union partitioned Poland once again, each taking about one half of Poland's territory.

The German-occupied zone was inhabited by a compact population of 19 million Poles. There were also two million Jews in the German zone, and Germany created a Jewish reservation around Lublin as a vast concentration camp not only for Polish but also for German Jews. The Russian-held area was soon incorporated into the Soviet Ukrainian and White Russian Republics, on the basis of plebiscite-type elections to local National Assemblies.

Poland Fights Abroad and at Home

The Polish Government fled to Romania. President Moscicki resigned, nominating M. Raczkiewicz in Paris as his successor. Wladislaw Raczkiewicz formed a new Polish Government, at Angers in France, from among exiled Polish politicians. General Wladyslaw Sikorski was appointed Premier; Count Zaleski, ex-Foreign Minister of Poland's anti-German period, was made Foreign Minister. Marshal Edward Rydz-Smigly, interned in Romania, was dismissed from his post as Commander-in-Chief and Inspector-General. The Polish Army was reorganized by enlisting Poles who lived in France and other foreign countries.

Upon his appointment as Premier, General Sikorski (who had parted company with Pilsudski when the latter began to show dictatorial tendencies) immediately got in touch with representatives of the four main opposition parties (the Polish Socialist Party, the Peasant Party, the Christian Democratic Labor Party, and the National Party) and formed a cabinet. All the parties pledged themselves to support Sikorski's cabinet, and this pledge—upheld by the underground organizations of these parties within Poland and defined in a joint statement of democratic principles—became the basis of the Polish government-in-exile. However, General Sikorski's cabinet contained not only representatives of the four former opposition parties, but also non-party men, as well as some former Pilsudski followers.

Sikorski's cabinet assigned itself the task of rebuilding and reorganizing the Polish Army. Thousands of Poles enlisted, arriving from Poland, from internment camps all over Europe, and from the Polish colony in France. Polish troops participated in both the Norwegian and French campaigns of 1940. But the defeat of the French armies caused heavy casualties and many of the Polish soldiers were either taken prisoner or interned in Switzerland.

The capitulation of France forced the Polish Government to move to Great Britain. Its main task was again to rebuild the Polish armed forces, starting with the remnants that were evacuated from France to England. They were reinforced by new recruits, trickling in from Poland through a modern version of an "underground railway," by volunteers from Polish communities all over the world, and, above all, by Polish prisoners of war and deportees returned by Russia after the re-establishment of diplomatic relations between Poland and the Soviet Union in 1941. Some units fought in the Libyan campaign and the Polish Air Force played an honorable part in the Battle of Britain in 1940. The Polish Navy and merchant marine also rendered important services to the Allies.

When Hitler attacked Russia in 1941, General Sikorski immediately proposed the restoration of diplomatic relations with Moscow. The resulting treaty cancelled the Soviet-German non-aggression pact and all other agreements between Germany and Russia, including the one that partitioned Poland and established the Ribbentrop-Molotov line. Russia also promised to release Polish prisoners of war and deportees and to permit the organization of Polish military units in Russia. But despite the additional diplomatic instruments concluded between the two countries, relations failed to develop satisfactorily. Russia still regarded eastern Poland as part of the Ukrainian and White Russian Soviet Republics, although she made it plain that she considered the so-called Curzon line, rather than the Ribbentrop-Molotov line, as the Soviet-Polish border.[24] Poland's government insisted on the frontier established by the Treaty of Riga, but preferred to postpone discussion of territorial issues until after the war. Russian diplomacy demanded immediate acceptance of the Curzon line.

The territorial question was not the only dispute between Poland and Russia. The Russian pledge to release Polish prisoners, deportees, and internees was not completely fulfilled. Furthermore, while Russia had agreed to the establishment of a Polish welfare organization on its territory to take care of the liberated Poles, Soviet authorities repeatedly interfered with Polish welfare activities and eventually greatly limited their scope. Finally, by unilateral declaration, the remaining Polish refugees and deportees were deprived of their Polish citizenship by the Soviet Government. Friction also arose in connection with the organization of Polish military units in Russia. The Polish Command, having charged that the Russians had supplied these units with inadequate matériel and rations, decided to evacuate them to Iran. The Russians, on the other hand, objected to the fact that the Polish units already organized were not sent into battle.

The major reason for Russia's diplomatic break with Poland was the so-called Katyn affair. At Katyn, a Russian village under German occupation, Nazi authorities reported the discovery, in 1943, of the corpses of about 10,000 Polish officers, who had been taken prisoner by the Russians in 1939. Despite repeated inquiries, these officers had not been accounted for when Polish prisoners of war were liberated by Russia in 1941. The Germans alleged that the officers had been massacred by the Russians in 1940, the year in which the relatives of the officers lost contact with them, and in which letters sent to them began to

---

[24] The Curzon line, in some sectors, is slightly to the east of the Molotov-Ribbentrop line. In the version proposed by the Soviet Government, the Curzon line is extended into Galicia, the eastern part of which is also claimed by the U.S.S.R.

be returned. The Polish Government, anxious to learn the truth, appealed to the International Red Cross for an inquiry. The Soviet Government, offended by this act, immediately severed diplomatic relations with Poland, accusing it of furthering Nazi propaganda. The Soviet authorities stated that the officers had been left behind at the time of the Soviet retreat before the Great German offensive of 1941, and that they had subsequently been murdered by the Germans.

The rupture in Polish-Russian relations was regarded as a major rift among the United Nations, especially after the emergence of the Soviet-sponsored Union of Polish Patriots in Moscow, obviously groomed by the Soviet Government for use, at the proper moment, as a substitute for the Polish Government. General Sikorski actively endeavored to heal the breach, but died in the midst of his efforts in an airplane crash over Gibraltar on July 4, 1943. After a short cabinet crisis, Mr. Stanislaw Mikolajczyk, hitherto Deputy Prime Minister, was appointed to succeed General Sikorski as Prime Minister, and General Sosnkowski was appointed Commander-in-Chief of the Polish Armed Forces.

Mikolajczyk, in turn, was plagued by the same problem. He visited Stalin, but in spite of the efforts of Prime Minister Churchill and Foreign Secretary Anthony Eden to work out a solution, he refused to sign an agreement fixing Poland's future frontier along the so-called Curzon line, west of Vilna and Lwow. On November 25, 1944, he proposed to negotiate further with the Soviet Union, but his colleagues advocated a policy of waiting. Weary of the endless trials of his office, Mikolajczyk resigned, although he was "probably the only man in the London Polish colony who would be acceptable to Moscow as head of a government combining the government-in-exile and the provisional government functioning inside the country with headquarters in Lublin." [25]

When the Underground Governed Poland

The German-occupied part of Poland was divided into two areas. One of these was incorporated directly into the German Reich; the other was named the "Government General" and placed under an administration of a quasi-colonial type. Subsequently this area was also proclaimed to be a part of the "Greater" German Reich.

The incorporated area (western Poland) was regarded by the Nazis as a purely German region, from which all Poles must be expelled. Several weeks after the annexation, in the winter of 1939-1940, mass deportations of Poles began. Nearly 9,000,000 of the approximately

---

[25] Daniel, Clifton, "Polish Premier Quits as Cabinet Refuses to Yield on Soviet Border," *The New York Times*, November 24, 1944.

10,000,000 inhabitants of the area were Poles. About 20 per cent of these were gradually deported to the Government General. Many were also taken to Germany for forced labor.[26] The Jews were either driven out of the area or confined to ghettoes. The Germans—both those recently arrived from the Reich and local inhabitants—were given a preferred status over the rest of the population. The extermination policy against the Poles included expropriation of Polish-owned real estate and industrial establishments. Most of the confiscated property was distributed among German settlers—including some who had been evacuated from the Baltic countries. All forms of Polish cultural and social activity were suppressed; the schools were Germanized; all Polish books were confiscated from public and private libraries and most of them were destroyed. A similar policy was developed in the Government General (central and southern Poland). In both sections, police terror reigned supreme. The many concentration camps throughout the country were always filled to capacity, both with people arrested on specific charges, and those rounded up without reason or explanation.[27]

The harshness of the Nazi treatment confirmed the theory that the Germans were trying to reduce the defeated nations numerically in order to secure a biological advantage over them regardless of the outcome of the war. The treatment of the Jews was particularly cruel; in 1942, the Germans decided to exterminate the Polish Jews completely and to turn Poland into a vast execution place for Jews from all European countries.[28]

After Soviet-occupied eastern Poland was annexed to Russia, Soviet legislation was gradually introduced there, bringing about radical political and social changes. Because the land and factory owning elements in eastern Poland were mainly Polish, the harsh consequences of the changes in social structure were principally felt by the Poles. Polish cultural activity as such was not directly suppressed under Soviet rule, but it was placed under strict control. Polish schools were permitted to continue, but preferential encouragement was given to the Ukrainian and White Russian educational systems, which took over a considerable part of the Polish educational facilities. For instance, the Ukrainian language was established as the medium of instruction in most departments of Lwow University.

---

[26] Wachenheim, Hedwig, "Transfer of Populations in Eastern Europe," *Foreign Affairs*, XX (1942), pp. 705-718.

[27] *Oswiecim, Camp of Death* (New York: Polish Labor Group, 1944). For additional information on German rule in Poland, see Chapter XXVIII of this book.

[28] *The Mass Extermination of Jews in German-Occupied Poland* (published for the Polish Ministry of Foreign Affairs by Roy Publishers, New York, 1943).

Mass deportations were the harshest factor of Soviet rule in eastern Poland. At first, they mainly affected members of the educated classes and persons who had been active in political life. Most of the former administrative personnel was jailed. Later the deportations spread to persons of no especial prominence, who were included without any stated or apparent reason. When the deportations assumed proportions too great to be continued in silence, the Soviet press officially explained that recent social changes in the Soviet-occupied areas had rendered a large part of their population non-essential.

The number of deportees is variously estimated at between one and two million. Most of them were taken to northern Russia, Siberia, or Central Asia, and put to work at lumbering or farming in these distant regions. A large proportion of the deportees was sent to compulsory labor camps. The methods of the Soviet authorities, who rounded up thousands of people without warning and separated families, caused much additional bitterness. Although Ukrainians were also numerous among the deportees, it is obvious that the principal aim of the deportations was to weaken the Polish population. The great majority of those deported were Poles, both Gentile and Jewish. Moreover, the high percentage of professionals, white collar workers, and refugees from German-occupied areas among the deportees also confirms the political character of the action. Many of the deportees were unable to survive the journey, which sometimes lasted for weeks, or to adjust themselves to the unaccustomed conditions into which they had been forced. We have already seen what became of the survivors after the re-establishment of Polish-Russian relations.

A tiny part of Soviet-occupied Polish territory, including the city of Vilna, was ceded to Lithuania by the Soviet Government. The Lithuanians immediately began to "Lithuanize" this area, but had not proceeded far before all of Lithuania, including Vilna, came under Soviet rule in 1940.

The first Polish underground cells were formed almost before the cessation of organized resistance in 1939. Their original purpose was to spread information received from abroad over secret radio sets, but their functions were soon expanded. Within a short time, the cells were consolidated into larger organizations, most of which were political and military in character. The underground political organizations were continuations of pre-war political parties and groups, although, for reasons of safety, some of them used other names. Delegates of the underground organizations of the four major Polish political parties represented in the Polish Government worked together as an advisory political body, which maintained regular contact with the government through its delegate to the home front. This delegate resided in Poland and had the rank of Deputy Prime Minister. He also headed the underground administrative apparatus which carried out the government's orders in Poland. However, after 1943, important Left-wing underground groups went into opposition and became independent from the official underground administrative apparatus. These organizations later became the nucleus of the Lublin provisional government.

The Poles from the beginning adopted an uncompromising attitude toward the occupying power. In no sphere of political life was there any collaboration with the Germans. Numerous attempts by German officials to stabilize relations with the Poles, to achieve some measure of political collaboration between the Polish nation and the occupation authorities, or to develop some form of Polish political administration which would coöperate with the Germans, were consistently and resolutely rejected. There was not one Pole in the administration of the general government; not one Pole agreed to serve as a provincial governor, or head of a county administration, or even to accept an appointment as a town mayor. In no sector of political life did the Poles submit to the invaders.

On the other hand, the organization of the Polish underground administration was remarkably thorough. Its basic principle was nonrecognition of the German occupation and the continuity of the legal existence of the Polish state. Accordingly, all the essential authorities, departments, and institutions of a modern democratic state were preserved in Poland, although they had to function underground. The foreign occupation also made it necessary for the legal government of Poland to maintain its headquarters abroad, for effective protection of Polish interests could be achieved only under conditions of security which made daily collaboration with the other United Nations possible. The Polish Government therefore represented not only the Polish refugees, but the entire Polish nation. Strict adherence to this principle made the Polish underground movement probably the strongest of its kind in occupied Europe.

While the underground political parties continued their ideological activities,[29] developing new platforms[30] and publishing clandestine periodicals, the underground administration had certain definite tasks to

---

[29] While all old parties were represented in the underground, considerable changes took place in their relative strength. A pronounced shift to the democratic Left was evident by 1942, thanks to the additional support of elements which had been indifferent politically before the war, as well as some former Pilsudski backers. The Underground Labor Movement was by far the strongest of all the underground political parties in Poland.

[30] *Program for People's Poland* (New York: Polish Labor Group, 1943); Winifred N. Hadsel, "Post-War Program of Europe's Underground," *Foreign Policy Reports*, Nov. 15, 1943.

carry out in the field of disseminating information, directing sabotage activities, and conducting guerrilla and psychological warfare. It performed these tasks with the assistance of special cells of the underground political movements and a regular underground army, which was steadily growing in strength, preparing for the uprising against the Germans and for its part in the fight waged on Polish soil by the German and Soviet armies. Special underground courts of law were also established to try the few Poles who coöperated with the Germans; as well as Germans guilty of especial cruelty or dishonesty. The sentences of the underground courts were faithfully carried out and respected by all Poles.[31] The Warsaw uprising in August, 1944, constitutes the culminating point of the underground struggle. Besieged Warsaw fell again, after a German counter-offensive had prevented Soviet aid from reaching the city.

Yalta and Its Sequel

In November, 1944, as noted previously, Prime Minister Mikolajczyk had to resign because of wide differences of opinion within his Cabinet about the solution of the Polish-Soviet rift. President Raczkiewicz appointed a new Cabinet, headed by Tomasz Arciszewski, a former Socialist leader, who had recently arrived in London after serving in one of the most important posts in the Polish underground movement. The Peasant Party, of which Mikolajczyk was Chairman, refused to participate in Prime Minister Arciszewski's Coalition Cabinet (composed of representatives of the National Party and the Christian-Democratic Labor Party, and of three Socialists), which continued, technically, to be recognized by almost all foreign governments that recognized its predecessor. The new Cabinet's intransigeant attitude toward the Soviet Union, however, estranged much of the sympathy formerly given to the governments of General Sikorski and Prime Minister Mikolajczyk. The Soviet Government reacted by authorizing the Polish Committee of National Liberation (first at Lublin and later at Warsaw) to become the Polish provisional government. It assumed authority in the areas liberated during the Soviet winter offensive of 1945.

An acute awareness of the threat to United Nations' coöperation resulting from Poland's two governments—the exile government in London, recognized by Great Britain, the United States and almost all

---

[31] Malinowski, Wladyslaw R., "The Pattern of Underground Resistance," *The Annals of the American Academy of Political and Social Science*, CCXXXII (March, 1944), pp. 126-134; Malinowski, "Underground Resistance in Poland," *International Post-War Problems*, I (March, 1944), pp. 263-276; Malinowski, "The Polish Underground Labor Movement," *Ibid.*, I (June, 1944), pp. 427-438; Jan Karski, *Story of a Secret State* (Boston: Houghton Mifflin Co., 1944).

other nations, and the provisional government administering liberated
Poland and recognized by the Soviet Union—led to a discussion of the
Polish problem by President Roosevelt, Prime Minister Churchill, and
Marshal Stalin at the Yalta Conference in February, 1945. Without
consulting the London government, the "Big Three" decided to recognize the Curzon line (with minor corrections in Poland's favor)
as the Polish-Soviet border. Poland was to be granted territorial compensation at Germany's expense.

As to the Polish government, the Yalta Conference decided that:
"The provisional government . . . in Poland should be reorganized
on a broader democratic basis with the inclusion of democratic leaders
from Poland itself and from abroad. This new government should
then be called the Polish provisional government of national unity."
A commission consisting of Soviet, British, and American representatives was "authorized . . . to consult . . . with members of the present
provisional government and with other members from Poland and
from abroad with a view to the reorganization of the present government along the above lines. The Polish provisional government of
national unity shall be pledged to the holding of free and unfettered
elections as soon as possible on the basis of universal suffrage and secret
ballot. In these elections all democratic and anti-Nazi parties shall
have the right to take part and to put forward candidates."

The Soviet interpretation of this formula differed from the understanding of the American and British Governments. As a result, the
Molotov-Harriman-Clark Kerr Commission made no progress. The
Soviet delegation at the United Nations Conference at San Francisco
(April-June, 1945) urged admission to the conference of representatives
of the Warsaw regime. The United States and Britain refused. The
situation was further complicated by the casual Russian announcement
of the arrest of 16 Poles, reported to be leaders of the underground
movement, on charges of diversionary activity.

To ease the growing tension, President Truman dispatched Harry
Hopkins to Moscow to confer with Marshal Stalin and his colleagues
on Polish and other problems. One of the fruits of the Hopkins mission was the resumption of negotiations for the reorganization of the
Polish provisional government in accordance with the Yalta Agreement.
Eight Poles who were not members of the Warsaw government were
invited, including Mikolajczyk and Wincenty Witos (who had been
Prime Minister of Poland before the Pilsudski coup). The Peasant
and Socialist parties were represented, but members of the Arciszewski
cabinet in London were pointedly ignored.

The negotiations resulted in the formation of a new provisional

Polish government, announced on June 22, 1945, a few days after 12 of the arrested Poles had been convicted and given relatively light prison sentences and 3 had been acquitted. The new cabinet included Mikolajczyk as Deputy Premier. This was the first real indication that a workable solution to the problem of Polish-Russian relations might be found. Other indications followed soon after. On August 17, 1945, the Soviet Union and the new Polish Government signed a frontier treaty which outlined the final shape of the Polish-Soviet border. Another treaty was concluded which provided for the restoration of Polish nationality to Polish refugees and deportees in Russia, and for their repatriation. Even before this, acting on the initiative supplied by the Soviet Union, the Potsdam Conference of the "Big Three" had given Poland considerable territory in Eastern Germany, up to the Oder and Neisse Rivers, and had thus re-established Polish rule in old Slav lands.

Bibliography

Books on Poland (Supplement to *The Polish Review,* New York: Polish Government Information Center, 745 Fifth Avenue, New York 22, 1944) is the best classified bibliography of recent publications on Poland.

Allyn, Emily, *Polish-German Relations in Pomerania and East Prussia* (reprinted from the *Bulletin of the Polish Institute of Arts and Sciences in America,* 1944).

Black Book of Poland (New York: G. P. Putnam's Sons, 1942). Documentary—and especially for those who "just cannot believe it."

Buell, R. L., *Poland: Key to Europe* (New York: A. A. Knopf, 1939). One of the best introductions.

Cambridge History of Poland from Augustus II to Pilsudski (1697-1935) (Cambridge: Cambridge University Press, 1941). Indispensable for any serious student of Polish history.

Dyboski, Roman, *Modern Polish Literature* (London: George Allen and Unwin, 1924); *Poland* (London: Benn, 1933). Professor of English Literature at the University of Cracow, maintains the high level of scholarship for which Cracow is famous.

Evans, John, *The Nazi New Order in Poland* (London: V. Gollancz, 1941).

The German Fifth Column in Poland (London: Published for the Polish Ministry of Information by Hutchinson and Co., 1941).

Gotlib, Henryk, *Polish Painting* (London: Minerva Publishing Co., 1942).

Graham, M. W., *New Governments of Eastern Europe* (New York: Henry Holt, 1927). Prints in the Appendix 36 documents on Polish history, 1914-1917.

Halecki, Oskar, *A History of Poland* (New York: Roy Publishers, 1943). A standard text by an outstanding Polish historian.

Humphrey, Grace, *Poland Today* (Warsaw: M. Arct Publishing Co., 1935). A delightful little book written by a keen observer. Very informative.

Kot, Stanislaw, *Five Centuries of Polish Learning* (Oxford: Basil Blackwell, 1941). Three lectures delivered at Oxford University.

Kridl, Manfred; Malinowski, Wladyslaw R.; and Wittlin, Josef, editors, *For Your Freedom and Ours* (New York: Frederick Ungar Publishing Co., 1943). Selections on "Polish Progressive Spirit Through the Centuries."

Lednicki, Waclaw, *Life and Culture of Poland* (New York: Roy Publishers, 1944). A study of the national, political, and religious life of Poland during the last four centuries as reflected in the works of her writers.

Lord, Robert H., *The Second Partition of Poland* (Cambridge, Mass.: Harvard University Press, 1915). A standard work on the subject.

Machray, Robert, *The Poland of Pilsudski* (New York: E. P. Dutton, 1936). On the period between 1914-1936; on the laudatory side.

Mendelsohn, Solomon, *The Polish Jews Behind the Nazi Ghetto Walls* (New York: Yiddish Scientific Institute, 1942); *The Battle of the Warsaw Ghetto* (New York: Yiddish Scientific Institute, 1944); "The Jewish Underground Labor Movement in Poland," *International War Problems,* I (June, 1944), pp. 439-445.

Morton, J. B., *John Sobieski, King of Poland, and the Defeat of Islam* (London: Eyre and Spottiswoode, 1932).

Patterson, E. J., *Poland* (London: Arrowsmith, 1934). Clear, factual, popular treatment.

Phillips, Charles, *Paderewski* (New York: The Macmillan Co., 1934). A good biography.

The Polish White Book. Official Documents Concerning Polish-German and Polish-Soviet Relations, 1933-1939 (London: Republic of Poland, Ministry for Foreign Affairs, 1940); *German Occupation of Poland* (New York: Greystone Press and Roy Publishers, 1942).

Rose, W. J., *Poland* (London: Penguin Books, 1939). Interesting, informative, and readable.

Segal, Simon, *New Poland and the Jews* (New York: Lee Furman, 1938).

Slocombe, George, *A History of Poland* (London: Thomas Nelson and Sons, 1941).

Smogorzewski, Casimir, *Poland's Access to the Sea* (London: George Allen and Unwin, 1934). A clear presentation of one of Poland's serious problems.

Thomas, W. J. and Znaniecki, Florian, *The Polish Peasant in Europe and America,* 2 vols. (New York: A. A. Knopf, 1927). A standard work.

Wanklyn, H. G., *The Eastern Marchlands of Europe* (New York: The Macmillan Co., 1942).

Wheeler-Bennett, J. W., *The Forgotten Peace* (New York: W. W. Morrow & Co., 1938).

Note by the Editor

Extensive sections of Dr. Ehrenpreis' manuscript have been eliminated or condensed by the Editor for lack of space and in order to avoid duplication with material contained in other chapters. Sections devoted to foreign-capital participation in Poland's economic life and to the Polish currency system have been eliminated altogether, while the following sections have been condensed: domestic politics, 1919-1926; Poland's relations with Great Britain; German rule in occupied Poland; the struggle of Warsaw, 1939, 1943, 1944. For this information, see bibliography.

Chapter XIX

SOVIET RUSSIA (1918-1945)

A Nation with a Great Future

SOVIET Russia possesses all the requisites for development into one of the greatest powers in world history. With a population now estimated at close to 200 millions,[1] a huge and growing system of industrial production, vast acreage devoted to agriculture, and enormous deposits of minerals and petroleum (still largely undeveloped), the U.S.S.R. is already overcoming the devastation caused by the war and is well on the way to becoming one of the strongest and most cultured nations on earth. The elimination of Germany and Japan as threats to her national security will facilitate her internal development in the arts of peace and permit her a much freer hand in external affairs.

The Soviet Union's territory comprises one-sixth of the land area of the globe and lies in a favorable geocentric position dominating the world's largest contiguous land mass. Comparatively free from attack from north and south, yet able to move unimpeded to the outer limits of her European-Asiatic base, the U.S.S.R. will have attained, as a result of the war and her fortunate geographical position, the utmost political and economic security of which a modern national state is capable. The tolerant policy of the Kremlin toward Russia's scores of nationalities has apparently removed the problem of racial conflict from the arena of Soviet politics.[2] As one of the leading members of the United Nations, whose sacrifices for victory were far greater than those of any other nation, the U.S.S.R. will exercise great influence on the peace settlements and on the nature and functioning of the post-war organization to preserve the peace.

In 1944, the U.S.S.R. ranked among the top three or four nations in industrial capacity. Russia has improved her people's health, built

---

[1] Including territorial acquisitions resulting from the war. See A. Grajdanzev, "Labor in the Post-War Reconstruction of the Soviet Union," *The U. S. S. R. in Reconstruction* (New York: American-Russian Institute, 1944), pp. 126-127.

[2] Kohn, Hans, *Nationalism in the Soviet Union* (New York: Columbia University Press, 1933).

From Russia Through the Ages *by Stuart Ramsay Tompkins, copyright, 1940, by Prentice-Hall, Inc.*

libraries, raised her literacy to about 80 per cent—and trained a huge and most formidable army. No nation in history has ever done so much so fast.

Like the United States, the U.S.S.R. is a vast melting pot—but in a different way. The 16 Soviet Republics of the Union of Soviet Socialist Republics are just the beginning. There are 189 races and peoples in the Soviet Union. They speak 150 languages, practice 40 religions, inhabit 74 assorted regions, territories, autonomous republics, and Soviet Republics. Depending on their location, they wear reindeer fur, Moslem veils, ordinary coats and trousers.

Roughly three-quarters of them are Slavs: Great Russians, Ukrainians (or Little Russians), White Russians. These peoples constituted three of the original four republics which joined to form the Soviet Union in 1922. The fourth was the Transcaucasian Republic, which later split into the Georgian, Armenian, and Azerbaijan republics. From the lofty, windy plateau of Central Asia, in the shadow of the high Pamirs, came Turkmen, Tajiks, and Uzbeks to establish three more border republics in 1925. Slope-eyed Kazakhs and Kirghiz were found ready to form Soviet Republics in 1936. The five youngest republics grew out of the war. When Hitler attacked Poland, the Red Army moved westward, converting the three independent Baltic countries of Estonia, Latvia, and Lithuania into Soviet states. There was a solemn plebiscite. Next, Russia took Bessarabia back from Romania (she had lost it in World War I) and renamed it the Moldavian Republic. Finally the Russian part of the Karelian Isthmus, plus a slice of Finland conquered in 1940, was set up as the Karelo-Finnish Republic, and the pattern of border buffer republics was complete. (Between Russia proper and China lies the Mongolian People's Republic, neither completely in nor quite out of the Soviet Union, but a buffer state just the same).

Looking at a map of the Eastern Hemisphere, we see the U.S.S.R.'s expanse of land stretching from mid-Europe to the Pacific. The largest republic of the Union is the gigantic Russian Soviet Federated Socialist Republic, with well over 6,000,000 square miles. The R.S.F.S.R. (or Russia proper, as the big unit is popularly known) occupies nearly four-fifths of the Soviet Union's entire area. It includes Moscow, Leningrad, Stalingrad, and other key Russian cities.

One outstanding fact about Russia is its modernity. For instance, the Russians are great aviators. Russian electric plants are among the most up-to-date in the world, and Soviet architecture is very advanced.

This love of modernity is especially important when we think of the tremendous resources of Russia. Known Soviet coal reserves reach the astronomical figure of 1,650,000,000,000 tons (21 per cent of the world's supply). Prospected oil fields total 61,000,000,000 barrels (55 per cent of the world's supply); iron ore beds amount to 10,600,000,000 tons (20 per cent of the world's supply); forest reserves total 2,500,000,000 acres (33 per cent of the world's supply). Russia has the largest black-soil area in the world—247,000,000 acres. These facts have been established only within the past 20 years, and the land is not yet completely surveyed.

Within 20 years, mostly within the space of two Five Year Plans, the Soviet regime quadrupled the industrial capacity of the nation. But the story of these accomplishments is also a story of bloody political upheavals.

World War I and the Russian Revolution

The outbreak of World War I soon revealed Russia's unreadiness to meet the situation, both as to military preparedness and national morale. The test of battle exposed to the public gaze the pitiful inadequacy of governmental arrangements to provide transportation, supplies, and weapons to the armies in the field. Quarrels between the bureaucracy and the army increased the confusion which the weak Tsar Nicolai and his scheming consort proved totally unable to handle. Disastrous defeats of Russian armies by the Germans coupled with startling public revelations of the control exercised over the royal family by the crafty Rasputin brought widespread forces of discontent to a head. The disintegrating movement was spurred by professional revolutionaries of leftist parties, both at home and in exile.

In the crisis, the Duma displayed unexpected initiative. A Progressive Bloc was organized, consisting of middle groups in the Chamber, which vigorously criticized the inefficient conduct of the war. This in turn caused still further popular disaffection, especially among the middle classes. Outbreaks of strikes and food riots in Petrograd and other cities in February, 1917, demonstrated the complete helplessness of the government. Liberal parties in the Duma set up a Provisional Government under Prince Lvov and forced the Tsar to abdicate. The parties which supported the Provisional Government aimed at continuation of the war and establishment of a liberal democracy.

Meanwhile, radicals of the Social Democratic and Peasant parties created councils of soldiers, sailors, and workers. These groups, with plans based on experience in the abortive revolution of 1905, took advantage of the rights of free speech and free press (established since February) to agitate for a Communist revolution. Under the leadership of Lenin and Trotsky, the revolutionists promised an immediate end to the war, division of the land among the peasantry, and bread.[3]

Shifts to the Left by the Provisional Government brought Kerensky into power and additional Socialist representation in the cabinet, but these changes could not stem the rising tide of revolution. Bolshevik leaders, delayed in their plans for calling a constituent assembly, staged huge demonstrations and propagandized the army and the navy. Defeated in the coup of July 1, 1917, the Soviets profited by growing economic and military disorganization, the Kornilov rebellion, and the gradual shift of peasant and labor support to the Socialist cause. By October, disaffection in the military forces had reached a point where the Bolsheviks could take over the government with hardly a struggle.

Communist Ideology

Russian Communist doctrine is based upon the "scientific" socialism of Karl Marx, modified somewhat by the rulers of the Soviet State, Lenin and Stalin. Marxian ideology is founded upon a subversion of Hegelian dialectic and, for purposes of elementary study, may be considered under the heads of (1) dialectical materialism; (2) economic interpretation of history; (3) war of the classes; (4) concentration of wealth; (5) dictatorship of the proletariat; and (6) the withering away of the state. These doctrines may be summarized as follows:

1. Dialectical materialism. Influenced by Hegel's theory of the conflict of opposites in ideas and Darwin's doctrine of survival of the fittest, Marx posited a material world where goods are scarce and life is a struggle for power to acquire and control life's necessities and luxuries.

2. Economic interpretation of history. In contravention of democratic doctrine, Communists place principal emphasis upon material things. Human beings, they contend, value economic goods first and moral and spiritual things second. They insist that the fundamental human relationship is one of economic determinism, in which the struggle for economic goods gives rise to moral and spiritual institutions and values which are created and maintained by ruling classes in order to rationalize, justify, or defend their control over the economic system of a given community. On this premise, all historical institutions and developments can be explained in terms of the struggle of human individuals, groups, and classes for the lion's share of available economic goods.

3. Conflict of classes. As society progresses to higher cultural levels,

---

[3] Harper, S. N., *The Government of the Soviet Union* (New York: Van Nostrand, 1937), pp. 28-29; and G. Vernadsky, *The Russian Revolution* (New York: Holt, 1932), p. 63.

human groups are merged into comparatively fixed classes with at least a modicum of common interests. These interests involve a struggle, usually between haves and have-nots, for control of the State and the economic goods at its disposal. Thus, at any given time, the State is merely the political organ of a given national community controlled by and representing the interests of the classes then dominant in the community.[4]

Generally speaking, society progresses from a stage of control by the few to the stage of control by the many. The economic system which prevails reflects the methods employed by the ruling class to exploit the masses for their benefit. Capitalism and liberal democracy represent the stage of control by the middle classes (bourgeoisie). Behind the façade of democratic liberties, according to Marxians, the employing class exercises basic control over the economic system which constitutes the means by which essential economic values are created. Through their control of the economic system, capitalists are able to exploit the working classes by paying them less for their labor than the values it creates (surplus value theory); and to dominate the government, thus permitting enactment and enforcement of legislation which protects the property values and wealth-creating machinery under their control.[5]

4. *Concentration of wealth.* Capitalism, however, sows the seeds of its own destruction. Exploitation of the workers results in the concentration of wealth in the hands of the few. This in turn leads to overproduction and underconsumption of goods, resulting in periodic crises or depressions which tend to grow more and more serious as capitalism reaches the stage of maturity. Attempts by employers of a given nation to find markets abroad for their surplus capital and consumption goods lead to imperialism and war with other nations. The resulting conflagration paves the way for the disintegration of the capitalist system and consequent revolution.[6]

5. *The dictatorship of the proletariat.* This tendency is enhanced by the intensified struggle of the propertied few, intent upon holding their gains, with the increasing numbers of dispossessed workers who, as the Communist Manifesto puts it, "have nothing to lose but their chains." The movement proceeds until the proletarian masses rise up against their oppressors, seize control of the government and the economic sys-

---

[4] Lenin, V. I., *State and Revolution* (New York: International Publishers, 1932), Ch. I; and J. Stalin, *Marxism and the National Question* (New York: International Publishers, 1932), pp. 17-20.

[5] Lenin, *op. cit.,* pp. 12 ff.

[6] Stalin, *op. cit.,* p. 137 ff.

tem, and establish a dictatorship of the proletarian workers. The proletarian dictatorship is posited as a stage of tutelage which continues until all traces of capitalistic ideology have disappeared; the bases of class conflicts have been eliminated through "liquidation" of all classes except the one great class of workers; and the masses have learned to practice the Communist golden rule: "From each according to his ability; to each according to his needs."

6. *The withering away of the State.* When this ideal stage shall have been reached, the State, in the sense of an agency of force to coerce the masses on behalf of a ruling class, will wither away—because it will no longer be necessary. According to present views, the U.S.S.R. is still in the preparatory phase—not only because Russia has not yet reached a sufficiently advanced stage of internal development to allow relaxation of Socialist discipline, but also because dangers from abroad have not so far permitted the Soviets the security necessary to achieve the goal of Communism. In reality, the trend has been reactionary, toward a strong national state exercising close control and strict discipline over the economic and social system.

Revolutionary Communism and Lenin

The saint of Russia's Communism is Vladimir Ilyitch Lenin, leader of the Russian Revolution. Born on April 22, 1870, the son of a college teacher, he became a lawyer and joined the Labor movement. He adopted the alias of Lenin (his real name was Ulyanoff). As a strict Marxist he led the radical, uncompromising (Bolshevik) wing of the Russian Socialist Party which broke away from the moderate faction in 1903. Living in exile at Paris, Vienna, and Zurich from 1907 to 1917, he advocated a revolutionary course at Socialist congresses.

After the Russian Revolution in March, 1917, the German General Staff saw its chance to get rid of the Russian enemy and transported Lenin across Germany in a sealed car. Lenin arrived at Petrograd in April, 1917, and took command of the Bolshevik Party. Together with Trotsky, he organized a first uprising in July, which proved abortive, and a second on November 7, 1917, which overthrew the moderate Kerensky Government. Lenin became President of the Council of the People's Commissars, as the Government was now called, and proletarian dictatorship was henceforth exercised by the Workers' and Soldiers' Soviets (Councils), although there were only 1,400,000 industrial workers in Russia at that time—about 1.2% of the population.

Civil war followed and Lenin hastened to conclude peace at all costs with Germany and Austria (the so-called Brest-Litovsk Treaty) so as to have a free hand in the struggle.[7] The civil war lasted till 1921 and ended with the victory of the Bolsheviks, who had meanwhile adopted the name of Communists. All privately owned land was confiscated and redistributed among the peasants. In 1922, Lenin was shot at by a woman member of the Anti-Bolshevik Social-Revolutionary Party and wounded. The wound was not fatal, but his health was poor thereafter. Lenin fell ill from overwork in 1923 and died on January 21, 1924. His body was embalmed and has been permanently exhibited in the Lenin mausoleum in Moscow. Petrograd was renamed Leningrad in his honor.

The Soviet Government had to modify its radical policies even before Lenin's death. Disorganization and falling off of production in the factories and the reluctance of the peasants to turn over their products without payment produced an economic collapse. This crisis, coupled with intervention by the Allies in Siberia and on the Murmansk coast, the war with Poland, and the civil war against Admiral Kolchak, Wrangel, and Denikin, compelled the new regime to shift its position.

Period of the NEP

Lenin announced that a temporary retreat to capitalistic practices was necessary and proclaimed a New Economic Policy (NEP). In March, 1921, the grain levy was replaced by a tax on grain which made it possible for the farmers to sell their surplus grain in free markets. In order to facilitate such sales, the price system was restored and stabilized on the basis of a new monetary unit called the "chervonets" (equal to 10 rubles). Private traders were allowed to operate in the markets, but the Government continued to expand its control over large-scale industry.

As a result of this policy, production and trade began to expand and prices to drop. By 1927, production had reached its pre-war volume, but the old machinery was beginning to wear out. It had become evident to Bolshevist leaders that the new regime, if it was to survive, must have the economic strength to provide for the welfare of the people and the military power to hold off its enemies.

Concentration upon "socialism in one country" was expedited by the death of Lenin and the ensuing victory of Stalin over Trotsky. Optimistic beliefs of Communist leaders that they could engineer a world revolution were shown to be fallacious by the course of events. Stalin's

---

[7] Dennis, A. L. P., *The Foreign Policies of Soviet Russia* (New York: Dutton, 1924), Ch. II.

policy of concentrating on socialism within the U.S.S.R. constituted another momentous shift of direction for the Soviet regime.[8]

It had become obvious, however, that the mere seizing of power by the Communists and the taking over of the factories could not of itself install the Socialist system. The people, clearly, were not yet mentally ready for it. They must be trained in Socialist ideology, as well as in coöperative productive endeavor. The readiness of the merchants and upper-class peasants to enrich themselves under the NEP indicated the tremendous task before the Communists. Particularly irritating to them was the problem of individual ownership of agriculture, which was still the predominant feature of the productive system that blocked the way toward socialism.[9]

The Five Year Plans

Soviet leaders therefore decided upon a policy of complete socialization: ideological, industrial, agricultural, and social. In general, their plan involved: (1) complete socialization of industry and agriculture through elimination of private ownership of factories and land; (2) "liquidation" of class enemies by means of imprisonment, exile, or death; (3) elimination of all capitalist ideology by monopolistic State control over the press, the schools, and other modes of expression, and by the overthrow of established religion; and (4) use of all channels of communication to inculcate Marxian ideology.

All of these steps were taken more or less simultaneously, but principal emphasis was placed upon the Five Year Plans for industrial reconstruction. The first Five Year Plan was started in 1928. It established advanced goals for rapid industrialization of the country under a master plan worked out by the Bolshevists. Foreign engineering experts were employed, but all capital equipment had to be provided by increased production and rigid control over the consumption of goods. Particular emphasis was placed upon heavy industry.

The socialization of industry was accomplished without great difficulty, but the program for the socialization of agriculture assumed monumental proportions. Rich peasants were exiled to Siberia and their lands expropriated. Poorer peasants were dragooned into giving up their private holdings and combining in "collectives" which were

---

[8] Florinsky, M. T., *World Revolution and the U. S. S. R.* (New York: Macmillan, 1933), pp. 1-28, 100, 110-111.

[9] Lawton, L., *An Economic History of Soviet Russia*, Vol. II (London: Macmillan, 1933), pp. 310-311, 401-404.

worked as coöperative enterprises with mechanized implements. Peasant resistance to the dictatorial tactics of Bolshevik representatives led to the slaughter of herds, reduction of crops, and rebellion in some of the villages. By 1932, more than 60 per cent of all peasant holdings were collectivized.

In the field of industry, new factories, power plants, and natural resources were developed at a rapid rate. The hostility of her neighbors and fear of war impelled Soviet leaders to drive ahead at a feverish pace. The second Five Year Plan continued the expansion of heavy industry, but an effort was also made to devote more time and money to cultural, welfare, and educational activities. By 1937, it was estimated that over 80 per cent of the total production of Russian industry was turned out by newly created plants. Expenditures for social welfare, education, housing, and social security increased enormously. The wages of workers and incomes of farmers also rose substantially.

Though the gains were truly remarkable, Red leaders recognized that the per capita output of the Soviet Union was still far behind that of the principal Western nations. Therefore the goal of the third Five Year Plan was to equal if not to surpass production in those countries. Emphasis was placed on machine-building—especially in the armament field—and on output of iron and steel. The latest scientific and technical discoveries and methods of industrial organization were used. Efforts were made to develop higher skills among the workers and to secure greater labor productivity.

By 1940, agriculture had been completely collectivized. New land was opened up for cultivation in central Siberia and the food supply was substantially increased. New steel and armament plants were established in the Urals, mines were developed, power stations were built in regions free from danger of attack. The outbreak of the war did not prevent the continuation of new construction. Production did not decline even when most able-bodied men were drafted into the armed forces. Hours of labor were increased and the seven-day work week was restored, but the stimulus of labor discipline to which the government had had to resort before the war was no longer needed when the country was invaded. Russia's ability to provide for the needs of her armed forces and civilian population surprised the world.[10]

---

[10] Mandel, W., "Wartime Changes in Soviet Industry," *The U. S. S. R. in Reconstruction, op. cit.,* pp. 89-90; Mary Van Kleek, "Planning and Reconstruction," *loc. cit.,* pp. 36 ff.; and J. N. Hazard, "The Impact of War on Soviet Political and Economic Institutions," in H. Zink and T. Cole, *Government in Wartime Europe* (New York: Reynal and Hitchcock, 1942), pp. 132-133.

The Communist Party

The Communist Party of the Soviet Union constitutes an elite organization with a severely restricted membership—chosen with particular regard for loyalty, discipline, and devotion to duty. The party, as its rules frankly state, constitutes the leadership of the proletarian dictatorship in Russia, acting under discipline to effectuate its program through all organs of government in the building of a socialist society.[11]

Membership in the party was so arranged that industrial workers, Red Army men, and collective farmers were given first consideration. The four categories set up by the party congress of 1934 placed industrial workers of five years' working experience in class one; those with less than five years' experience, agricultural workers, Red Army men with working experience, and engineers and technicians in class two; collective farmers, artisans, and elementary school teachers in class three; and all other employees in class four. Persons in class one had to be sponsored by three party members of five years' standing, those in the other classes by five members of ten years' standing. In 1939, this rather complicated and overcautious provision was replaced by a requirement that all applicants (except former members of other political parties) must be recommended by three party members of three years' standing who had known the applicant for at least one year. Persons so recommended are accepted by the party cell and approved by the party committee of the city or county.

Party members are duty-bound to obey all rules of the party and orders of party superiors, know socialist ideology and work diligently to spread it among the masses, and set an example to others both in their personal life and at work. Special training for the Communist elite is provided in party educational institutions established at all levels. The 1939 amendment to the rules gives members the right to criticize other members at party meetings, to vote and hold office in the party, to obtain information, and to defend themselves if accused of misconduct.

Because of the small size of the party, worthy persons have been encouraged to belong to an organization of "Sympathizers" who actively coöperate with the party in carrying out its program. Soviet leaders have tried to obtain as many new members as possible from the ranks of the *Comsomol,* a youth organization composed of boys and girls

[11] Rappard, W. E., et al, *Source Book of European Governments* (New York: Van Nostrand, 1937), Pt. V, pp. 34-35.

from 14 to 23 years of age. This group is heavily indoctrinated in Communist ideology and has the duty of leavening the mass of youth with it as well as furnishing a nucleus from which party members are drawn.

Comsomols in turn get their members from the *Pioneers,* composed of children from 10 to 16 years of age, over whom they exercise supervision. Below the *Pioneers* are the *Octobrists* between the ages of 8 and 10. The aim is to insure training of the younger generation in the tenets of the new regime so that habit, inclination, belief, and zeal will combine to inspire the youth of Russia to work for the success of socialism. Soviet progress in this endeavor led fascist dictatorships to copy the Communist youth program slavishly.

Party organization begins with local party cells of three members or more in village, factory, or workshop. Members of cells constitute Communist shock troops with the special duty of supervising productive enterprises and promoting party aims in their localities. Delegates from the cells are elected to party bodies on higher regional levels, each with its party conference, bureau, and secretary, until the national level is reached. The All-Union party Congress, which meets (in theory) every three years, tops the party hierarchy.

Authority over everyday affairs is delegated on paper to a Central Committee, which in turn appoints three powerful agencies: (1) the Secretariat, headed by Stalin, who has occupied the office of Secretary-General since 1922; (2) the Organization Bureau; and (3) the Political Bureau. Through these committees, whose members are designated by Stalin, the Central Committee exercises general supervision over all activities both of the party and of the Government. Under the revised party rules of 1939, a Committee of Party Control was created as a subsidiary of the Central Committee. This agency acts in coöperation with the Soviet Control Committee, an arm of the Government, which was raised to the status of a full-fledged Commissariat in 1940. Through these two committees, party and Government were indissolubly linked together.

By means of his position as Secretary-General of the Communist Party and his control as party leader over the party members who predominate in all government agencies on a national level, and by the close integration of the party machinery with that of authoritative government agencies, Stalin was able to exercise dictatorial authority in the U.S.S.R. until 1940, despite the fact that he occupied no official governmental position. When the war broke out, however, he evidently felt that this control was not sufficiently direct, because he took over the premiership and control of the military forces and retained them throughout the course of the war.

Under party rules, members are sworn to adhere to party policy. Discussions and criticism is permitted, if constructive, prior to the adoption of a policy, but, once decided upon, no deviation from the party line is permitted. Suggestions as to detailed methods of the application of policies are encouraged, particularly among workers in the fields and factories, but not proposals which obviously would result in deflection from the party's general aims. Adoption of a one-party system did not prevent factional conflicts. These led to frequent purges of party membership, starting with expulsion of the Mensheviks, then of Trotsky and his followers in 1924, and finally a number of minor purges between 1924 and 1933.

Stalin

Joseph Vissarionovitch Stalin was born in 1879 in a village near Tiflis, in the Caucasus, the son of a Georgian cobbler. He was educated at a church college at Tiflis with a view to becoming a priest, but preferred to join the socialist revolutionary movement in the Caucasian oilfields. A member of the Bolshevist Party from the beginning (1903), he adopted the alias of Stalin ("man of steel"), his actual Georgian name being Djugashvili, and was repeatedly imprisoned and exiled to Siberia. After the Russian Revolution in March, 1917, Stalin went to Petrograd, where he became a member of the Political Bureau of the Communist Party and Commissar of Nationalities in the Soviet Government. In 1919 he became General Secretary of the Central Party Committee.

After Lenin's death in January, 1924, a struggle for the succession began between Stalin and Trotsky. Stalin formed the "Troyka" with Zinovieff and Kamenieff against Trotsky. After having ousted Trotsky, he then collaborated with the right-wingers under Rukoff and Kalinin to eliminate the influence of the Zinovieff group. By 1927 Stalin had achieved full control of the party. The ideological background of the long intra-party struggle had been the divergence of opinion between the Trotskyite faction, which advocated an immediate drive for world revolution, and the Stalinite faction favoring "socialism in one country," meaning the development of Russia's internal resources along socialist lines. The adherents of a "national" Communist policy under Stalin prevailed and the Five Year Plans were carried out under Stalin's guidance on the basis of orthodox socialism.

Stalin's desire to strengthen his position and to close ranks in the face of the menace of war resulted in a wholesale purge of party members of all ranks between 1934 and 1938. It was precipitated by the murder of S. M. Kirov, a friend of Stalin and a member of the Political Bureau. Hundreds of high-ranking members of the party, the Government, and the military forces were investigated; forced or persuaded to confess disloyal, seditious, or traitorous acts; tried; and sentenced to be imprisoned or executed.

Most of the old-guard Bolsheviks were eliminated in this way. New leaders were mostly of the younger generation trained under the Soviet system. The effect of the purge upon the rank and file of the party and the people was so great that the party congress, meeting in 1939, changed the rules to redefine the rights of party members, abolish mass purges, shorten terms of party office, and increase the power of local party organizations over local economic affairs. Annual conferences of local party organizations on a national level were also encouraged.[12]

The Third International

The Third International, organized in 1919 and composed of Communist parties in all countries, was actually an instrument of the All-Union Communist Party of the U.S.S.R. to spread its propaganda in favor of world revolution abroad. Its headquarters were in Moscow. Hence Bolshevik leaders were in a position to exercise a predominating influence, although the Soviet Government persistently denied that it was in any way connected with the Comintern. Dissolution of the Third International by its Congress on May 22, 1943, however, indicated the close connection between the existence and activities of this body and the Soviet regime, since the obvious purpose was to free the U.S.S.R. from the taint of the Red terror and to make possible a closer rapprochement with England and the United States.

The Constitution

The vast bulk of the U.S.S.R., with its large number of different nationalities and national territorial units, has necessitated recognition of regional and cultural differences from the beginning. Therefore it is not surprising that these should bulk so large in the framework of the constitution. In the reaction against Tsarist absolutism, the Communist ruling oligarchy sought to secure support by recognizing in theory the right of each nationality to exercise autonomy in its own affairs, while at the same time it crushed ruthlessly the attempts of opposition elements to establish independent governments. This recognition was

---

[12] Duranty, W., *The Kremlin and the People* (New York: Reynal and Hitchcock, 1941), Chs. II-VI.

carried over into the constitution of 1924 and is repeated in the constitution of 1936.

In form, the U.S.S.R. is a federal state like the United States and Switzerland, with all powers not specifically delegated to the federal government belonging to the constituent republics. However, there are a number of significant differences which operate to make the Russian system unlike other federal systems.

As a consequence of the revolution, Russia has emerged as a socialist, proletarian state in which all productive instruments of any consequence are owned either by the state or by coöperatives. Private ownership and its income from interest, rent, and profits, has been almost entirely eliminated (except for small plots of land, homes, household chattels, and personal effects). Since competition between individual enterprises no longer regulates production, planning by the national government has had to be substituted. This necessitates a government with ample power to deal not only with political but with economic matters. Hence so-called federalism, which in Western parlance implies wide political autonomy and still broader exemption from national interference with economic affairs, becomes, in Russia, the regimentation of all political, economic, and ideological phases of life, except in a few cultural spheres where the dictatorship feels it is safe to permit greater freedom of action.

In the constitution of 1936, the U.S.S.R. is given power over international relations; war and peace; admission of new republics; observance of the federal constitution by member republics; changes of boundaries of Union Republics; creation of new autonomous republics and regions; military affairs; foreign trade; internal security; national planning; national taxation and finance; banks; industry, agriculture, and trade of national significance; transportation and communications; money and credit; insurance and national accounting; criminal and civil law; citizenship and amnesty acts. In addition, the national government may determine fundamental principles for the use of the land and natural resources and may regulate the public health policies of Union Republics. This imposing array of federal powers makes it quite clear that local autonomy in Russia consists in the method of administering the laws rather than in a division of powers between national and local governments.

Some concession to decentralization is seen in the constitutional provisions that (1) the sovereignty of Union Republics is restricted only by the powers expressly given to the national government by the constitution; (2) each Union Republic has the right to secede from the Union;

and (3) the territory of the Union Republics may not be changed without their consent.   The right of secession, however, has become a dead letter.[13]

More important still, amendment of the constitution is accomplished by a two-thirds vote of the Supreme Council of the U.S.S.R. (Art. 146). Thus, the national government alone determines the allocation of power between itself and Union Republics.

Recent amendments to the constitution permit Union Republics to exchange diplomatic representatives and make agreements with foreign states and to raise and maintain armies of their own.   These changes seem intended to relax the tight controls of the central government and perhaps to induce other countries of eastern Europe to join the U.S.S.R.[14]

The Supreme Soviet of the U.S.S.R.

Soviet governmental organs have no counterpart in western Europe or America.   They rest rather upon the firm foundation of Russian precedent.   The legislative function in Russia under the Tsars remained in a state of arrested development, by western standards, and Soviet experiments have not so far changed the picture appreciably. Nor does Soviet political theory accept the idea of a separation of powers, as in the United States, preferring to vest all powers in one central body which is divided into legislative and executive branches.   The constitution of 1924 established an All-Union Congress of Soviets composed of representatives from provincial and city Soviets, which in turn were made up of delegates from lower bodies.   Industrial workers were given preference by allotting them one representative for every 25,000 workers, whereas peasants received one for every 125,000 of the rural population.

Theoretically, this huge body of more than 2000 members held ultimate governmental power, but because of its size and infrequent meetings, primary legislative authority resided in the Central Executive Committee, chosen by the All-Union Congress.   This Committee consisted of the Council of the Union, a body of several hundred members selected on the basis of population; and the Council of Nationalities, a smaller chamber with 5 representatives from each union and autonomous republic, and one from each autonomous region.

---

[13] Rappard, et al, *op. cit.*, V, 110-111; and Florinsky, *op. cit.*, p. 843.

[14] "Autonomy," *Information Bulletin, U. S. S. R. Embassy*, XIV:19 (February 15, 1944), pp. 6-7; Irving Brant, "The New Russian Enigma," *New Republic*, CX:9 (February 28, 1944), pp. 272-274; and "Autonomy and the Soviet Union," *Business Week*, No. 755 (February 19, 1944), pp. 113-116.

The Central Executive Committee, as the highest legislative, executive, and administrative authority of the U.S.S.R., had power to appoint and control the Presidium and the Council of People's Commissars, and to pass upon all legislative proposals and decrees issuing from these and similar bodies in the Union Republics. The Presidium, an executive committee of 27 members, exercised all of the powers of the Central Executive Committee between its sessions, which were supposed to be held at least three times between the sessions of the All-Union Congress. It supervised observance of the constitution and execution of the laws, had power to approve or veto decrees of the Council of People's Commissars or of individual Commissars, and could suspend any laws of Union Congresses, subject to approval by the Central Executive Committee. It also decided all conflicts between the Council of People's Commissars and the Central Executive Committees of Union Republics.

The Council of People's Commissars of the U.S.S.R., under the constitution of 1924, consisted of the heads of the various administrative departments. It was designated as the executive and administrative organ of the Central Executive Committee, with power to issue decrees binding upon the entire territory of the U.S.S.R. It could also examine decrees of individual Commissars of the U.S.S.R. and of Central Executive Committees of Union Republics. It was made responsible for its acts to the Central Executive Committee and Presidium of the U.S.S.R., but did not go out of office as a body on a vote of lack of confidence.

By the Constitution of 1936, the All-Union Congress was eliminated. The Supreme Council, elected for four years, possesses all legislative power. The Council of the Union (the lower house) is now chosen by the voters on the basis of one deputy for every 300,000 of the population. The Council of Nationalities (the upper chamber) is elected by the voters of each regional unit on the basis of 25 deputies for each union republic, 11 for each autonomous republic, 5 for each autonomous region, and 1 for each national district. Deputies are immune from arrest except by vote of the Supreme Council, or of the Presidium if the Council is not in session.

The chambers are co-equal in legislative powers. Their sessions are co-terminous and are called twice a year by the Presidium. Each house elects a chairman and two vice-chairmen as its officers. Differences over legislation between the two houses are settled by a conciliation committee made up of an equal number from each body. If no agreement is possible, the constitution provides for dissolution of the chambers by the Presidium of the Supreme Council, which then fixes dates for new elections. In practice, no dissolution has occurred to date.

The Presidium of the Supreme Council, now consisting of 37 members, including the chairman, 11 vice-chairmen, and 24 ordinary members, is given much broader authority by the 1936 constitution. Although it no longer has power to legislate, the Presidium interprets national laws; dissolves the Supreme Council and holds new elections in case of differences between the two chambers; conducts referenda on its own initiative or on request of a single Union Republic; awards decorations and honors; exercises the power of pardon; appoints and removes the highest officers of the military forces; declares war in case of attack or to fulfill treaty commitments if the Supreme Council is not in session; declares general or partial mobilization; ratifies treaties; appoints and recalls diplomatic representatives; and receives foreign diplomats. In addition, the Presidium acts in place of the Supreme Council when the latter is not in session, vetoes decisions and acts of the Councils of People's Commissars of the U.S.S.R. and the Union Republics, and appoints and dismisses individual commissars on recommendation of their chairmen.

The Council of People's Commissars is left substantially unchanged by the new constitution as to methods of selection and organization, except that the chairman of the Commission of Soviet Control and the heads of the Committees on Art and Education are added to it. Commissars are obligated to give oral or written replies to questions addressed to them by deputies of the Supreme Council.

Commissariats are either All-Union or Union-Republic. The former enforce and administer directly national laws throughout the entire territory of the U.S.S.R. in such matters as foreign affairs, transport, communications, foreign trade, industry, armaments, shipbuilding, and so forth. Union-Republic Commissariats act through their counterparts in the various Union Republics on matters delegated to them, including food, light industry, agriculture, forests, farms, health, justice, and so forth.

Government in Subordinate Territorial Units

In general, the same type of organization prevails in the Union Republics and other local units as in the national government. The degree of standardization of governmental forms indicates the chief difference between the constitutions of American states, for example, and the republics of the Soviet Union. In the United States, state constitutions are originated and adopted locally. Hence great variations in form and function prevail among the states. In the U.S.S.R., on the other hand, there is one uniform constitution for all the republics, thus indicating its central origin and a resulting lack of local spontaneity and opportunity for innovations in political affairs. Concentration of power at the center is also shown by the hierarchical character of governmental administration. Beginning at the top, the higher Soviets exercise supervision over the lower until primary territorial units are reached. In the United States, on the other hand, state governments are largely independent of national control in the exercise of their powers.

Popular Participation in Politics

The constitution of 1936 removes all religious, economic, and political disqualifications formerly applicable to non-Bolsheviks and grants universal suffrage at the age of 18. The only exceptions are criminals and the insane. Deputies to Soviets on all levels are subject to direct election by the voters. Citizens in the armed services are eligible both to vote and to run for office. Balloting is secret. Both men and women are eligible as candidates for office if sponsored by a Communist Party organization, trade union, coöperative, cultural society, or youth organization.

However, it is illegal for any party, other than the Communist, to sponsor candidates—this would be considered a treasonable act. Outright opposition to government policies is also forbidden, although criticism of the personal conduct of candidates or of details of administration is permitted. Each incumbent running for re-election is required to give an account of his work, and political problems are called to the attention of voters during campaigns. Elections are held at places of work, or in districts for non-workers, under the supervision of electoral commissions established on each regional level. Under these conditions, elections in the U.S.S.R. could hardly be said to be free in the Western-democratic sense of the term.

Rights and Duties of Citizens

The bill of rights of the 1936 constitution goes much farther than the American Constitution, at least on paper, in granting rights and privileges to the people. Not only are all personal and judicial rights substantially conceded, but the citizen is guaranteed the right to work, to rest, to social security, free education, and equal rights for women. Private property rights are eliminated under the system of socialist production, except for small domiciliary and personal holdings. Soviet leaders have made a substantial effort to achieve the goals of economic comfort set forth in the constitution. Although retarded by the war, they have made some progress in that direction. But so far as the rights of free speech, free press, free association, and inviolability of the person are concerned, the obvious facts belie the written word. The great problem of Russian socialism is to make economic welfare compatible with political freedom. The record of the great purge, the operations of the Ogpu, control of the press, liquidation of anti-Communist organizations, and the use of "labor discipline" all indicate that in these respects the bill of rights expresses ideals for the future rather than accomplished facts.

The duties of citizens include respect for the constitution and the laws of the land, observance of labor discipline and social obligations, safeguarding of state property, universal military service, avoidance of treasonable or seditious acts, and defense of the fatherland.[15]

The Judiciary

Courts created by the constitution of 1936 include the Supreme Court of the U.S.S.R., the Supreme Courts of Union Republics, territorial and provincial courts, courts of autonomous republics and provinces, district courts, special courts created by act of the Supreme Council of the U.S.S.R., and People's Courts. Each of these is elected by the Councils of the respective territorial areas for periods of five years, except the People's Courts, which are chosen by the voters directly for terms of three years. Judges are theoretically independent, but can be recalled by the bodies which elected them, or subjected to criminal prosecution by the State Prosecutor of the U.S.S.R. with the permission of the Presidium of the U.S.S.R. The Supreme Court of the U.S.S.R. reviews decisions of lower courts. It also exercises original jurisdiction over conflicts between republics and cases of sedition and treason against the Soviet Union. Similar functions are performed by the higher regional courts.

The principal trial courts are the People's Courts, presided over in each case by a judge and two public assessors selected from lists prepared by local Soviets and serving for short periods. Trials are public and accused persons have the right of defense.

Laws administered by the courts have now been thoroughly recodified and socialized. They are frequently revised. The tendency is to increase the severity of punishment for political offenses, although the rehabilitation theory of correction has been applied in criminal

---

[15] "Constitution of 1936," Chs. X, XI, in Rappard, *op. cit.*, pp. 125-129.

cases. Economic disputes are usually settled by special arbitration boards.

The enforcement of the laws and supervision of the courts is in the hands of the Prosecutor of the U.S.S.R., appointed by the Supreme Council for a period of seven years. Prosecutors on all other levels are appointed by the U.S.S.R. Prosecutor for seven-year terms, except district and urban prosecutors, who are appointed by prosecutors of the Union Republics with approval of the U.S.S.R. Prosecutor. Thus law enforcement is much more highly centralized in the U.S.S.R. than in the United States or Switzerland.

The Ogpu

The judicial protection provided by the regular system of courts does not apply to political offenders accused of counter-revolutionary activities or subversive offenses against the regime. These may be apprehended by the State secret police, subjected to summary secret trial, and executed; or made to sign confessions before a public trial, as in the case of the famous treason trials, and then executed.[16] Originally called the Ogpu, the secret police were later designated as the NKVD.

Cultural Achievements[17]

The need for internal propaganda has developed a vigorous Soviet art. Posters have launched a school of easel painters and muralists, and public monuments have established sculpture, an art which is new to Russia. In literature, novelists and poets like Aleksei Tolstoi, M. A. Sholokhov, and Ilya Ehrenburg have a tremendous following. In music, the U.S.S.R. leads the world in having the largest number of

[16] Lyons, E., Stalin, Czar of All the Russias (Philadelphia: Lippincott, 1940), Chs. XXII-XXIV.

[17] "Special Issue on Russia," Life, XIV, No. 13 (March 29, 1943), is the best-illustrated survey of Russia's history and growth under the Soviets. See also L. S. Kaun and E. S. Simmons, et al., Slavic Studies (Ithaca, N. Y.: Cornell University, 1943); Paul Miliukov, Outlines of Russian Culture (Philadelphia: University of Pennsylvania Press, 1942); John Cournos, et al., A Treasury of Russian Life and Humor (New York: Coward-McCann, 1943); E. J. Simmons, An Outline of Modern Russian Literature (Ithaca, N. Y.: Cornell University Press, 1943); Deana Levin, Children in Soviet Russia (Forest Hills, N. Y.: Transatlantic Arts, 1943); V. I. Seroff & N. Galli-Shohat, Dmitri Shostakovich (New York: A. A. Knopf, 1943); B. G. Guerney, et al., A Treasury of Russian Literature (New York: The Vanguard Press, 1943); Avrahm Yarmolinsky, A Treasury of Great Russian Short Stories (New York: The Macmillan Co., 1944); Helene Iswolsky, Soul of Russia (New York: Sheed & Ward, 1943); Science in Soviet Russia (Lancaster, Pa.: Jacques Cattell Press, 1944); Alexander Kaun, Soviet Poets and Poetry (Berkeley, Cal.: University of California Press, 1943); H. W. L. Dana, Drama in Wartime Russia (New York: National Council of American-Soviet Friendship, 1944); Soviet Art in Wartime (Washington, D. C.: Embassy of the U.S.S.R., 1944); F. D. Cornford & E. P. Salaman, Eds., Poems from the Russians (Forest Hills, N. Y.: Transatlantic Press, 1944); V. N. Ipatieff, Modern Science in Russia (reprint, Journal of Chemical Education, 1943, vol. XX).

great modern composers, including Shostakovich, Miaskovsky, Proko-fieff, and Gliere. Artists are the highest-paid group in Russia, and Aleksei Tolstoi is reputedly the richest man in the Soviet Union. To their honors, which include the Order of Lenin and such titles as "People's Artist," have recently been added annual Stalin prizes in cash.

Education

The fathers of the revolution attempted to make as complete a break with the past in the field of intellectual and artistic work as in the political and economic spheres. Since the revolutionary aim was the creation of a new society differing completely in direction, scope, and structure from the liberal, capitalistic societies of the Western world, the Bolshevists saw clearly the need of breaking with the basic tenets of these societies and the means of transmitting these tenets to the younger generation. This could only be accomplished by seizing control of all channels through which ideas were communicated and changing completely the ideological bearing of the concepts transmitted through educational agencies.

Most important of these channels of communication of ideas were the schools. Since existing categories of knowledge were cast in the mold of nineteenth-century attitudes and conceptions, and since the school systems which transmitted them were staffed by teaching personnel steeped in the attitudes, doctrines, and teaching methods of the past, it was obvious to Soviet leaders that the entire structure and staffs of the schools must be fundamentally altered. Consequently the old school systems were abolished and most of the teachers and professors were killed, exiled, or sent to prison. This created an embarrassing hiatus in educational facilities for a time, but the revolutionary enthusiasts were not disturbed by that.

The idea of group education was applied on a large scale, combined with the notion of bringing the toiling masses into the schools, and students into the practical everyday work of production. The organization of schools was changed to accomplish this end and teachers were subordinated to the will of the classes they were supposed to teach. Principal emphasis at this time was placed upon the dissemination of Marxian doctrines. These practices, however, led to several unfortunate results: (1) lack of teachers and of teacher-control over the classes, combined with too little regard for the tools of learning, resulted in graduates poorly prepared for the practical tasks of everyday life upon which so much depended in the way of production of badly needed goods; and (2) overemphasis on theory produced little effect upon students unprepared to deal in abstractions and led to neglect of more urgently needed practical studies.

In consequence, a thorough revision of the educational system took place in which many of the features of the old system were restored. The teacher was given greater authority, knowledge of practical subjects was stressed, and less time was given to indoctrination. Even so, special care was taken in all schools to orient students toward the prevailing Marxist or Stalinist doctrines, and great efforts were made to school the masses (especially the industrial workers) and to expand the educational system as widely as possible.

By 1941, the Soviet government was spending 12 times as much on education as the tsar's government had spent in 1914. Instead of the 91 universities and colleges existing in Russia in 1914, mostly in St. Petersburg and Moscow, there are now 750 such institutions scattered over the entire Soviet Union. Instruction at all levels is carried on in 75 languages. Attempts are made to reach all workers through courses sponsored by labor unions and workers' clubs. Schools are also provided for migratory workers, nomadic peoples, and children living in isolated sections of the Arctic region or in the great forests.

The pressing need for engineers and technicians has led to the creation of many technical schools and colleges operated by the Commissariats which supervise the types of technical production for which the students are trained. The immense educational effort of the U.S.S.R. is rapidly creating a well-educated and intellectually alert Russian citizenry, thoroughly imbued with the nationalistic and patriotic conceptions of the regime.

Literary Trends

The early emphasis on "proletarian" literature which extolled the revolution, depicted the evils of capitalistic society, featured the selfish and corrupt capitalistic exploiters in Russia who refused to coöperate in revolutionary reforms, and proclaimed the new era of the toiling masses, has now been jettisoned. Soviet writers today glorify the tremendous sacrifices of the people in the great patriotic war, their amazing accomplishments in production, their sufferings under the yoke of the invader, their love of country and of family. Many of the older Russian writers, such as Tolstoi, Turgenyev, and Chekhov, have been restored to favor. Foreign works are printed in large numbers, although writers and contents are carefully selected. Today nearly 700,-000,000 books and pamphlets are printed in the Soviet Union. The

State Press prints nearly half of them. Public libraries have also expanded rapidly.

Since the revolution, the entire press has been completely controlled by the party line, i.e., the newspapers cannot express sentiments which conflict in any way with the accepted policies of the regime. Some newspapers are State-controlled, others are party-controlled, and still others are sponsored by unions, clubs, organizations of factory workers, or collectives. The function of the press is mainly informative, educational, and ideological. Hence its tone tends to be didactic and its material dry and tiresome. Too much space is given to long reports of officials, citations of facts regarding productive achievements, and statements of official policy.

There is much uniformity among newspapers, which indicates the dictated character of the material. The only criticism permitted is that which pertains to inefficiency, corruption, dishonesty, and kindred failings in the various phases of economic production. Little original writing of literary merit is published. Much of the reporting is in the form of letters which workers from all over the Soviet Union are encouraged to write, telling of their local problems, living conditions, and sentiments.

The war has stimulated the press to print war stories, cartoons, verses and jokes about the war, and accounts of the deeds of both military and civilian war heroes. In spite of the government-dictated character of the press, the people buy newspapers eagerly and their circulation has expanded greatly. Today more than 8000 newspapers serve nearly 40,000,000 readers.

The Arts

In the theater, the system has stressed the work of collective groups rather than individual actors. Group discipline and precision are remarkable. Dramatic themes have rotated around the Revolution in its various aspects and the creative activities of the new Soviet system. Motion pictures have followed the same trend. The quality of dramatic performances has greatly improved and attendance at the theater and cinema has notably increased. By 1941, there were 850 theaters in Russia, well distributed throughout the Union. A considerable proportion of these were especially for rural areas and audiences of children. Theatrical efforts are actively encouraged by the government, the *Comsomols,* and the trade unions.

In recent years, a craze for amateur art has swept the country, particularly, for native folk dancing. Schools, clubhouses, and factories all encourage it. The same is true of choral singing—nearly every form of association has its chorus.

Radio

The radio stations of the U.S.S.R. are of course owned and operated by the government. The principal stations are in Moscow and Khabarovsk. News, weather forecasts, entertainment features, music, and statements of government leaders are broadcast from these and smaller stations. Local stations help to organize and motivate community activities. Advertising features which mar American programs are omitted, but government-sponsored propaganda takes its place. Thus, in every phase of communications, the government controls and directs the thinking of the people.

The U.S.S.R. in World War II

Soviet Russia was much misunderstood and resented not only by the United States but also by other "civilized" nations in the post-war years. The Soviet Union, as the standard-bearer of revolutionary communism and the mainstay of the Third (Communist) International, whose objective was the struggle for world revolution, was feared by all the so-called "capitalist" powers. It was, in fact, this fear of communism which enabled Hitler to ride into power in Germany and to pretend that Germany was saving the world from communism.

Hitler's accession to power made Germany a grave potential danger to Soviet Russia, whose leaders started searching for collective security. But the appeasement policies of the democracies, culminating in the Munich Agreement of September, 1938, closed the doors to any Russian participation in joint action against Hitler. Moreover, it indicated to Soviet authorities that the Chamberlains and Daladiers hoped to save their democracies from Nazism by encouraging it to spend its force against Russia. Munich also demonstrated the weakness of the democracies in the crisis. The absence of Soviet Russia from Munich was largely ignored by the press and the public of the democracies—a fact never forgotten by Soviet leaders, who also recalled that Russian representatives had not been invited to the Versailles Peace Conference after the First World War.

With the German danger growing in the summer of 1939, the British and French tried to save themselves by attempting to reopen negotiations with the Soviets. Thereupon Stalin made his deal with Hitler— a deal which led to the initial steps of the Second World War and which resulted in the partition of Poland by Germany and Russia. In short, the Soviet-German agreement was the determining factor in unleashing the war of 1939.

The gloating by Russia's enemies over disunity in the U.S.S.R. because of the bloody purges of 1936-1937 proved unfounded. Moreover, the belief of some writers that the adoption of the constitution of 1936 and Soviet support of the League of Nations and the sanctity of treaties demonstrated a change of heart on the part of the Soviet Union was only an illusion. The U.S.S.R. had remained a totalitarian dictatorship playing a very realistic game of power politics.

Hitler's war against Great Britain and France proved, however, to be only the prelude to the seizure of the Ukraine and the Caucasus, long desired by German statesmen hungry for land and raw materials. The U.S.S.R. was to be pushed eastward and the Ukraine was to furnish space and resources for German expansion. Stalin's awareness of these plans was obvious from Russia's acquisition of the Baltic states, eastern Poland, and Bessarabia, which were seized as an aftermath of the non-aggression pact with Germany. In June, 1941, Hitler's hordes attacked Russia (though the invasion was somewhat delayed by Yugoslavia's unexpected resistance to Hitler's demands for capitulation).

Hitler's decision proved to be the greatest mistake of his career. Russia was able to bear the whole weight of Hitler's mighty war machine. In spite of frequent Russian appeals, no second front was established until June, 1944. But already in January, 1944, the Red Army had crossed the pre-1939 Polish border for the first time in the midst of a great winter counter-offensive. On August 18, 1944, the first Russian troops crossed the German border. Russia also extended its conquests and influence in Central-Eastern Europe by knocking Romania out of the war in the same month; and by forcing the Finns to sign an armistice on September 4, and the Bulgarians on September 9. In the fall of 1944, the Russians started attacking Budapest. In April, 1945 the Russians took Berlin.

The Red Army's victories increased Russian demands on the Allies—demands which irritated many Americans, particularly the former isolationists who had been pointing to ever-growing figures of lend-lease aid to Russia and to Moscow's neutrality toward Japan. Russia's friends, on the other hand, were not slow to emphasize that Russia had borne the main brunt of Hitler's attack and that she was the first nation able to stop Hitler's *Blitzkrieg* tactics (with Allied help, of course).

The war with Nazi Germany compelled the Soviet Union to devote its productive energies to the life and death struggle with Fascism. From a normal expenditure for defense of about one-tenth of the

State's budget, armament costs gradually increased to about one-third in 1940. Climbing to over 50 per cent by 1943, total war costs were expected to reach 70 per cent of the budget in 1944. Large areas of European Russia and the Ukraine were overrun and devastated by both German and Russian armies. Factories, power stations, mines, dams, and village industries were destroyed. Livestock was killed or carried away, food supplies seized, crops destroyed, schools, museums, libraries, and institutions of higher learning burned or used for military purposes. Hundreds of thousands of men and women were carried away to Germany for labor service. Millions of men were killed or wounded in battle and millions more diverted from productive peacetime pursuits to the armed services. Brutality, starvation, and disease wrecked the lives of millions, raising grave problems of health.[18] As the German tide was stopped at Stalingrad and ebbed slowly back from Russian soil, Soviet leaders began to plan and work to reconstruct the devastated areas while the war was still going on.

Problems of Reconstruction

The automatic controls of demand, supply, and price which are supposed to maintain the private enterprise system on an even keel do not function in a socialist economy where land and capital are collectivized and production for profit is abolished. Hence national planning, or the budgeting of natural resources, labor, and capital, is inevitable.

National planning in the U.S.S.R. is in charge of the State Planning Commission, successor to the Supreme Economic Council, and now a department of the Council of People's Commissars of the U.S.S.R. Similar planning agencies exist on each level of government. The general principles of the plan to be adopted are outlined by high party and government leaders and transmitted to the State Planning Commission. The latter, using the vast information at its disposal, prepares a unified plan which is submitted to government leaders for approval, then passed on to subordinate planning agencies, collective farms, and factories for criticisms and suggestions. It is finally revised by the higher agencies and put into effect.

Soviet planning during the periods of the three Five Year Plans aimed at complete socialization of industry and agriculture, transformation of the U.S.S.R. into a highly industrialized state, and substantial improvement in the living standards of the people. Critics point to serious errors by the planners, such as the overbuilding of industrial plants and

---

[18] Kazakévich, V. D., "Financing War and Reconstruction," *The U. S. S. R. in Reconstruction, op. cit.,* p. 148.

underbuilding of transportation facilities (especially railroads) to carry their products, lack of coördination among various phases of the plans, and uneven achievement of goals. These mistakes evidently arose from inaccurate estimates of the productive capacity of labor, inefficiency of technicians and managers, the retarding influence of an unwieldy bureaucracy, and such intangibles as the resentment of workers and peasants at low incomes, heavy taxes, high costs of living, and the dictatorial methods of the regime.[19]

To a large degree, the ability of Soviet Russia to survive in the postwar world and succeed in its socialist experiment depends upon the success of socialist planning. The task of reconstruction covers all phases of life. Even after all repairs have been made, the U.S.S.R. still has far to go before it can equal or surpass the productive capacities and living standards of the most advanced western nations. Nevertheless, great strides have been made in the desired direction. The record shows that, within the brief span of 20 years, the Soviets have succeeded in converting Russia from an agricultural to a highly industrialized state, advancing in capital construction at a rate much faster than the United States and other capitalistic countries. The tempo has been somewhat slackened in some sectors during the war, but it has increased in others.

By 1944, power, industrial, and arms production had increased several times over pre-war figures, while costs declined, but the U.S.S.R. barely held its own in agricultural output.[20]

Planners during the war, working through the "vertical" controls of the various Commissariats, "geographical" or community controls, and special agencies, are devoting primary attention to the reconstruction of devastated areas. Their plans cover the restoration of wrecked mines, coal fields, schools, railways, farms, and homes, and the replacement of livestock. Scientific methods and artistic designs are being applied to housing construction and town planning.

After the war, the aim is a Fifteen Year Plan which will undertake to achieve the ultimate goal of Communism for Russia. This grandiose objective is to be reached, Soviet leaders declare, without borrowing from abroad. In other words, all war costs are to be liquidated, devastation repaired, and a sufficiently high goal of production attained to permit plenty for all, so that relaxation of controls by the government

---

[19] Yugow, A., *Russia's Economic Front for War and Peace* (New York: Harpers, 1942), Ch. I; and M. T. Florinsky, *op. cit.*, pp. 865-880.

[20] Benediktov, I., "Soviet Agriculture in Three Years of War," *Information Bulletin, Embassy of U. S. S. R.*, IV:73 (June 27, 1944), pp. 5-6; and "Soviet Industry Stands Test of War," *loc. cit.*, IV:80 (July 15, 1944), p. 6.

may permit the "withering away of the state." This goal, they insist, will be secured even if the strict rationing and labor controls now imposed upon the people must be continued.

In the light of past experience, the project outlined above seems utopian. The greatest weakness of the socialist regime in Russia has been in the field of industrial organization and production. Throughout the period of the Five Year Plans, the industrial system suffered from over-centralization of control. Individual industries were grouped into trusts, trusts into syndicates, and syndicates into combines. All of these functioned under industrial Commissariats of the U.S.S.R. and the Union Republics, topped by a political dictatorship which was harsh in its methods and not too patient about results. Too much centralization led to a top-heavy superstructure with divided responsibility and an army of bureaucrats who practiced nepotism and graft, floundered in red tape, and ate up any surpluses produced by the workers. Reaction against this inefficient "functional" organization led to purges of the guilty ones, and a shift to greater emphasis on the responsibility of individual plants and managers. Greater supervisory power was accorded to local party and government agencies also, but without noticeable results.

Lack of training of workers, technicians, engineers, and managers was a potent cause of failure throughout. This led to faulty organization of work, poor quality of products, frequent shut-downs, lack of coördination, and high costs. The result was decreased total production. The government's need to save capital led to reduced wages and higher prices. Socialist inducements for labor efficiency proved inadequate. Faced with lower "take home" wages and higher costs of living, workers began to leave their jobs or engage in a "slow down."

Realizing that medals, honors, and coercion were insufficient, the government then turned to capitalistic practices. Piece-work wages were offered to stimulate labor efforts. When this did not produce adequate results, "Stakhanovism" (a speed-up system) was introduced. These methods led to some increase in labor efficiency but tended to split the workers into classes with increasingly large wage differentials. Under the "speed up," young workers burned themselves out while the basic difficulties remained unsolved.

Still trying to increase labor productivity in the face of impending war, severe labor discipline was restored in 1939-1941. Foremen were given dictatorial powers, hours were increased, wages were cut, and it was made a crime for workers to leave their jobs without good cause. These controls have not been relaxed during the war. Nevertheless, the German invasion worked an amazing transformation in the zeal and energy of the laboring masses of Russia. Although most of the younger men were drafted into the armed services and their places were taken by women, old men, and boys, and in spite of the hardships of moving to new locations to the east out of reach of the enemy, labor productivity increased substantially during the war years in practically all phases of effort.

When the will to work was present, men found they could do wonders even with the inadequate tools and processes available in the early years of the war. These are now being rapidly replaced by up-to-date machinery and methods. The people have been equally effective in the work of reconstruction. The question now is whether their high morale can be carried over into peacetime.

Agricultural Problems

The situation in agriculture has been comparable to that in industry. The resentment of peasants at forcible collectivization during the 30's led to a tremendous drop in agricultural output. After collectivization was fully achieved, by 1938, heavy taxes (in kind) on collectives, forcible collections, low prices paid for farm goods, and so forth, coupled with top-heavy staffing of collectives, caused peasant incomes to drop to very low levels. This in turn led to dissatisfaction and the lowering of labor efficiency. Peasant demands for the right to work land of their own finally forced the government to legalize this practice in the 1936 constitution. Subsequently, peasants have increased production on their private holdings (up to 2.5 acres) with the tacit acceptance of this capitalistic practice by the regime. State farms have not been successful, on the whole. Collective farms have been fairly successful, but peasants are irritated by high government exactions and by the great differences in returns between rich and poor collectives—a situation which has resulted in class distinctions among the peasants.

The scorched earth policy of the Russians in their retreat before the advancing Germans in 1941, followed by the destruction wrought by the Germans during their occupation of Soviet territory and eventual retreat, left the areas involved almost totally in ruins. Practically all livestock was moved away or slaughtered, most buildings were destroyed, crops were burned, tractors and other equipment rendered useless.

As the Germans were driven back, the Soviet Government issued a directive on August 1, 1943, for the rehabilitation of the liberated regions. The plan called for the transfer of 600,000 head of cattle from the east to be distributed to the collective farms. To put the livestock industry back on its feet, 1,000,000 more were to be added eventually. The housing project called for the construction of 300,000 homes and agricultural buildings, the establishment of lumber mills, and the repair of machine and tractor stations together with replacement of the tractors themselves. According to reports from Russia, this plan has been more than fulfilled.

The rapid pace of restoration was due largely to the fact that the factories of the Urals and Central Siberia were untouched by the invasion. Production from these factories was most helpful. So were contributions of seed, machinery, and livestock from collective farms in the east, state grants, voluntary subscriptions, and the use of industrial equipment and skilled workers from the east. All of these, added to the prodigious efforts of the inhabitants of the liberated areas, made possible the amazing transformation. Though supplies of grain were below normal in earlier war years, current reports indicate bumper harvests on the way.[21]

Trade Unions

The great question for Soviet Russia after the war will be whether the Russian people are willing to continue the tremendous sacrifices they have been called upon to make during the past 20 years. Under the dictatorship, they have been deprived of the means of protecting their interests against exploitation by the Communist ruling class. The old type of trade unions were "liquidated" at an early stage. Workers were forced to join Communist unions by discriminations in favor of members of these organizations. Lack of worker interest in such associations has caused the regime to extend itself to try to encourage them. At present, labor unions in Russia make collective wage agreements with factory managers, supervise observance by factories of labor legislation, possess and administer their own resorts and rest homes where members may spend their vacations, control the operation of all social security legislation, maintain cultural and educational facilities for members, and afford them legal advice. The list of functions is truly imposing, but the fact remains that the unions cannot act independently to further the interests of labor as a group.

---

[21] Valin, L., and Goodstein, S., "Problems of Agricultural Rehabilitation in the Liberated Regions of the Soviet Union," *The U. S. S. R. in Reconstruction, op. cit.*, pp. 98ff.

Large Families

To the extensive list of benefits accorded to workers and their families, including vacations with pay, health protection and social security, the U.S.S.R. has recently added increased state aid to mothers of large families. State allowances have been enlarged to provide for a grant of 400 rubles for the birth of a third child, up to a grant of 5,000 rubles and a monthly allowance of 300 rubles for the birth of an eleventh child. These benefits are accompanied by maternity medals and increased maternity leaves for expectant mothers. Increased taxes are to be imposed on unmarried men and women and on families with not more than two children. Finally, marriage and divorce laws have been tightened. All connubial relationships must be legalized and divorce is made more difficult by the subjection of applicants to a public hearing and a court decision.

Church and State in Soviet Russia

The facts indicate that, instead of progressing toward Communism, the Soviet regime has been reverting in many important respects to the practices of capitalist regimes. This is true of religion as well as of policies concerning industry, agriculture, and the family. Stalin's restoration of the Greek Catholic Church to its former status as an established Church in September, 1943, marks a complete reversal of the original Communist plan to eradicate religion. After 1917, the Soviet regime made war on the Church, confiscating its buildings, restricting its activities, and subjecting its clergy to persecution. In addition to disestablishing the Church, Red leaders actively fostered the teaching of atheism. Church elections were prohibited after 1925 in order to prevent the selection of a new Patriarch.

The policy of persecution was continued until the danger of war forced the Kremlin to seek the support of organized religion in the battle against Fascism. In 1939, Christianity was declared by party leaders to be compatible with Marxism. Manifestations of loyal support by Acting Patriarch Sergius led the government to permit convocation of a Church Council in 1943, which formally elected Sergius as Patriarch. The Patriarchate was then connected with the Council of People's Commissars, becoming in effect a branch of the Russian Government. Under these conditions, freedom of religion in Russia will be handicapped by a state-managed Church.[22]

[22] Timasheff, N. S., "The Church in the Soviet Union, 1917-1941," *Russian Review*, 1:1 (November, 1941), pp. 20-30; M. Karpovitch, "Church and State in Russian History," *loc. cit.,*

Communist ideology is being employed to preach utopian ideals to the people and now religion is restored to its historic role of "administering the opiates" necessary to produce docility on the part of the masses. Thus, the indictment of Marx against the use of religion by governments may be applied against the heirs of the Marxian tradition enthroned in the Kremlin. The war psychosis, increased emphasis on patriotism, and loyalty to the fatherland work to the same end. In this way the cycle of revolution followed by reaction is being completed.[23]

Post-War Soviet Foreign Policy

Under Stalin's skillful direction, the Soviet ship of state is being maneuvered in new directions which are destined to have a profound influence upon the future of the world. As a consequence of Russian successes in the Second World War, new territory has been acquired in Finland, the Baltic States, Poland, and Romania. Moreover, Soviet power and influence is spreading over all of eastern Europe and the Balkans, with the exception of Greece, and even into Germany itself. As the Yalta agreements have demonstrated, the Anglo-American Allies have had to yield to Russian demands in this area. Along with easy peace terms extended to the conquered satellites of Nazi Germany (Romania, Bulgaria, Hungary, and Finland), the Kremlin has smoothed the way for rapprochement by all of the states of Central-Eastern Europe with the U.S.S.R., which may lead in some cases to their entry into the Soviet Union.

Soviet expansionist aims have been reformulated and are now presented convincingly to show that the Soviet Union has eradicated the two basic evils of imperialism: oppression of minorities and enslavement of the working classes of dependent territories. Russian propaganda now contends that the wide cultural toleration of minorities in the U.S.S.R. has created a novel form of nationalism whereby the widest nationalistic differences can be practiced under a common political sovereignty, thus permitting an indefinite expansion of Soviet territorial jurisdiction without interference with native, regional, or racial *mores*. Moreover, Soviet apologists maintain that the Soviet Socialist system of production assures equality of treatment of all workers, regardless of nationality, and the absence of "capitalistic" exploitation. To conform with this new expansionist ideology, the Kremlin has

---

III:2 (Spring, 1944), pp. 18-20; and S. B. Fay, "What Does Stalin Want?" *Current History*, V:27 (November, 1943), pp. 205-207.

[23] Lyons, E., "Soviet Foreign Policies," *American Mercury* (March, 1943), pp. 367-373.

initiated certain political innovations which work in the same direction. While frowning upon any post-war confederations in Eastern Europe which might be aimed at Russia, the Kremlin has negotiated treaties of peace and friendly coöperation with Czechoslovakia and Yugoslavia and has invited other nations in the area to join with her in similar agreements. The constitution of the U.S.S.R. has been changed to permit member republics to form and maintain their own standing armies and to carry on diplomatic relations with foreign states. Pan-Slav conferences held in Moscow have been revived, and re-establishment of the Greek Catholic Church helps to promote a friendly spirit in the Balkans.

These steps clearly indicate the Kremlin's intention to maintain a "security sphere" in Central-Eastern Europe, encouraging some states voluntarily to enter the U.S.S.R. and promoting in others governments friendly to the Soviet Union. In order to guarantee their friendliness, Soviet authorities have been promoting the organization of working class groups in all of these states which they hope will ultimately gain control of their respective governments. This project is being speedily carried out in all of the territories under Russian occupation.

The spread of Soviet influence will not stop short at Germany's eastern boundaries. Soviet leaders, including Stalin, have long desired to win Germany for communism. If this aim could be achieved, Soviet fear of a war of revenge would be removed and Germany could be used as a base for the spread of Socialist doctrines over all of Europe and the world. Soviet propaganda is endeavoring to place war guilt upon Nazi leaders and to absolve the German workers, many of whom they hope to propagandize and use as a nucleus for the new anti-Hitlerite order in Germany.

The "hard" peace at which Russia aims envisages severe punishment of all Germans found guilty of atrocities, and complete reparation for destruction wrought in Soviet territories by German arms. But the Russians do not contemplate destruction of the German nation, elimination of its heavy industries, or the turning of German workers into serfs. They figure that socialist propaganda is always most readily accepted by industrial workers, and besides, Russia needs the output of German industry.

Thus, if Stalin's plans are realized, the nations of the Central-Eastern area, including Catholic Austria (which Russia hopes to bring into the Soviet orbit), will be forced to accept Red domination in place of that of Nazi Germany. Soviet suzerainty, however, will be, according to all indications, much more tolerant, more constructive, and less oppressive than the German yoke. The Central-Eastern European peoples will be freer, within limits, to conduct their own affairs, live their own lives, and enjoy the fruits of their own labor.

The basic background of this expansionist policy was Russia's eternal search for security. Remembering the Allied anti-Russian policy after the First World War, the appeasement policy of the Chamberlain era, and Munich, the Soviet Union is building a post-war Europe in which she will be safe against any aggression. Meanwhile, she is trying to ascertain whether the United Nations, represented primarily by the United States and Great Britain, will be able to create a post-war world in which the Soviet Union will wish to become a partner.

In general, the Russians are showing a disposition to coöperate with the United States and Great Britain in the formation and maintenance of a world organization to maintain peace. Contrary to the predictions of hostile critics, the Soviet delegation did not try to break up the United Nations Conference at San Francisco. On the contrary, despite considerable tension on various issues, the Russian Government made some rather notable concessions to assure the success of the Conference. The Soviet Union faces a long and staggering task of reconstruction. There is every indication that it sincerely desires peaceful and friendly relations with the other great powers.

Russia and the United States

The revival of the historic friendship between the United States and Russia symbolized by the Teheran and Yalta meetings (December, 1943, and February, 1945) of President Roosevelt and Premier Stalin has led many Americans to hope that an enduring peace may arise on the basis of this accord. Although the political systems of the two countries have always been at opposite poles, a fact which has produced periods of dangerous ideological conflict, an appraisal of history nevertheless reveals that the foreign policies of the two nations have run along parallel lines. Passing reference may be made to the similarities between the Russian and American peoples and to the respective continental position of the two nations.

But, more fundamentally, their interests have been very much the same and the threats to those interests have arisen from the same quarters. During the greater part of the nineteenth century, Russian aims coincided with those of an emergent America in opposition to Great Britain and in the desire to uphold the freedom of the seas. Common objectives of trade and commerce have also served to bring about a "parallelism" in policy. Finally, the two powers have twice found themselves arrayed against a common enemy—Germany—in war. Little more than this can be inferred from the story of Russian-American relations; yet it is the history of a friendship based upon the realistic appraisal of each nation's interests. Similar harmony may be expected in the future if equally realistic judgments are made, although responsibilites henceforth will be international rather than solely national in character.

Bibliography

Central Committee of the Communist Party of the Soviet Union, *History of the Communist Party of the Soviet Union* (New York: International Publishers, 1939). Latest official history of the party.

Chamberlain, W. H., *Soviet Russia* (Boston: Little, Brown, 1931). A sympathetic discussion by the former Moscow correspondent of the *Christian Science Monitor; Russia's Iron Age* (Boston: Little, Brown, 1934). A critical account by the same author; continued in *The Russian Enigma* (New York: Charles Scribner's, 1943).

Cournos, John, *et al., A Treasury of Russian Life and Humor* (New York: Coward-McCann, 1943). An anthology of nineteenth-century Russian literature, interpreting the Russian character and qualities.

Dana, H. W. L., *Drama in Wartime Russia* (New York: National Council on American-Soviet Friendship, 1944).

Dobb, M. H., *Soviet Economy and the War* (New York: International Publishers, 1943).

Duranty, Walter, *U.S.S.R.; The Story of Soviet Russia* (Philadelphia: J. B. Lippincott, 1944). The panorama of Soviet Russia and future prospects, presented by a correspondent who spent many years in Russia.

Eulau, H. H. F., "The New Soviet Nationalism," *Annals,* CCXXXII (March, 1944), pp. 25-32. A very significant analysis of Russia's contemporary objectives and the rise of the new nationalism.

Florinsky, M. T., "Russia—the U.S.S.R.," in J. T. Shotwell, *et al., Governments of Continental Europe* (New York: The Macmillan Co., 1940). A satisfactory longer treatment of the Soviet government and its problems.

Goodall, George, Ed., *Soviet Russia in Maps* (Chicago: Denoyer-Geppert Co., 1943).

Guerney, B. G., Ed., *A Treasury of Russian Literature* (New York: The Vanguard Press, 1943). Selections in practically every field of the rich literature of Russia from its beginnings to the present.

Harper, S. N., *The Government of the Soviet Union* (New York: D. Van Nostrand, 1937). One of the best short introductions to the subject.

Hazard, J. N., "The Impact of War on Soviet Political and Economics Institutions," in H. Zink and T. Cole, *et al., Government in Wartime Europe* (New York: Reynal & Hitchcock, 1941). Valuable for its survey of events between 1939 and 1941 in Russia.

Hindus, M. G., *Mother Russia* (Garden City: Doubleday, Doran, 1943). Hindus writes revealingly about Russian bravery and what has made the people so heroic.

Hrdlicka, Ales, *The Peoples of the Soviet Union* (Washington, D. C.: Smithsonian Institute, 1942). The best short introduction to this field.

Hyde, N. V., and Fillmore Hyde, *Russia Then and Always* (New York: Coward-McCann, 1944). A history of Russia, stressing the continuity of what the authors, a Russian scholar and her American husband, feel are the basic elements of Russian life, a coöperative society and continental solidarity.

Ives, Vernon, *Russia* (New York: Holiday House, 1943). A simplified history and geography of Soviet Russia.

Kerner, R. J., *The Urge to the Sea* (Berkeley, Cal.: University of California Press, 1942). The role of rivers, portages, ostrogs, monasteries, and furs in the expansion of Russia and in the building of a vast Eurasian empire is emphasized.

Kerr, Walter, *The Russian Army* (New York: A. A. Knopf, 1944). A picture of the great Russian Army by the former Moscow correspondent for the *N. Y. Herald-Tribune,* who was in Russia during the Battle of Moscow and the Battle of Stalingrad.

Lengyel, Emil, *Siberia* (Garden City, N. Y.: Doubleday, Doran, 1943).

Lenin, V. I., *The State and Revolution* (New York: International Publishers, 1932). Presents the ideology of Leninism.

Lyons, E., *Stalin, Czar of All the Russias* (Philadelphia: J. B. Lippincott, 1940). Examines critically Stalin's policies during the great purge.

Pares, Sir Bernard, *Russia and the Peace* (New York: The Macmillan Co., 1944). A summary and answers to questions on Russia most often asked of this English author.

Rappard, W. E., et al., *Source Book on European Governments* (New York: D. Van Nostrand Co., 1937). This collection of source materials on Russia cannot be overlooked.

Segal, Louis, *Russia* (Forest Hills, N. Y.: Transatlantic Arts, 1944). A panoramic view of Russia's history from her founding in 862 A.D. to the present day, including a calendar of events covering 1,000 years.

Steiger, A. J., "The Soviet Middle East," *Survey Graphic,* XXXIII (February, 1944), pp. 72-78. Contains much valuable information on Soviet construction in Central Siberia.

Strong, Anne L., *The New Soviet Constitution* (New York: Henry Holt, 1937). A good translation of the constitution of 1936 and a useful but uncritical account of earlier constitutional developments.

Timasheff, N. T., *Religion in Soviet Russia* (New York: Sheed & Ward, 1943). A well-documented account of the survival and growth of religion in Russia in spite of the Communist assault on it.

Trotsky, Elon, *The Revolution Betrayed* (New York: Doubleday, Doran, 1937). A bitter indictment of Stalin's rule.

The U.S.S.R. in Reconstruction (New York: American-Russian Institute, 1944). The many articles on recent Soviet developments bring the reader up-to-date.

Vernardsky, G. V., *A History of Russia* (New Haven, Conn.: Yale University Press, rev. ed., 1944). Covers Russian history from 1917 to 1943.

Yarmolinsky, Avrahm, ed., *A Treasury of Great Russian Short Stories* (New York: The Macmillan Co., 1944). An anthology of the outstanding short stories of the great Russian writers of the nineteenth and pre-Soviet twentieth centuries; a biographical note on each author and a critical introductory essay by the editor are also included.

Yugow, A., *Russia's Economic Front for War and Peace* (New York: Harper's, 1942). An excellent recent analysis of Soviet economic problems.

CHAPTER XX

FINLAND BETWEEN WORLD WAR I AND
WORLD WAR II

Developments from 1918 to 1922

As ALREADY noted in Chapter VI, Finland achieved independence for the first time in history in 1918 when she was able to break away from Russian domination as a result of the Russian Revolution of 1917. Although Finnish independence was assured for the moment, it was not at all certain that it could be maintained indefinitely without fighting. Finnish history had long been filled with conflicts with Russia, and in 1918 the chances were that new conflicts would arise.

Early in the nineteen-twenties, there was some reason to hope that the new League of Nations and its peace machinery might supply the means by which such conflicts could be avoided. Later, however, that hope died. In 1921, when Finland appealed both to the Council of the League of Nations and to the Permanent Court of International Justice for support in her efforts to protect the Finnish people in Eastern Karelia, she learned that both institutions were impotent when it came to dealing with Soviet Russia. In the Russo-Finnish War of 1939, the League's condemnation of Russia was an empty gesture, and Finland knew that she would have to fight for her independence if she wished to maintain it.

In 1918, that independence was achieved only after bitter and bloody fighting against Red Finnish and Russian forces. The "Red Revolt," as this struggle was called, was finally put down by the temporary government.[1] Not until the fighting was over was it possible to set up a new constitution and to elect the first president, Professor K. J. Stålberg (1919-1925).[2]

The new government[3] had long and distinguished antecedents.

[1] Hannula, J. O., op. cit., especially Chapter V.
[2] For a list of Finnish presidents, see Finland Yearbook, op. cit., pp. 60-63, 67, 73, 82.
[3] Ibid., pp. 66-71.

The Constitution of 1919 embodied the main principles of an earlier governmental act adopted in 1906, which in turn found a precedent in the Act of 1808.[4] The latter was adopted by the Diet of Bårgo, in which Russia ratified the old Swedish system of government then in force in Finland. The Act of 1919 was further amplified in 1928 and in 1935.

The new government, like its predecessors, was democratic and virile, for it continued to function without interruption through the two recent wars between Finland and Russia. In form it was a combination of the European and American systems. The president was chosen by an electoral college and was the chief executive to whom the cabinet was responsible. The Diet, on the other hand, was unicameral, possessed of full legislative responsibility, and had most of the powers of other European parliaments. Its acts were generally reviewed by a Grand Council of forty-five members. The judiciary was independent.

The broadest principles of suffrage were observed and political parties had free opportunity to express themselves. Local government was centralized under provinces and the Department of the Interior.

As the new government was being formed, basic principles were laid down by which future policies were to be guided. One of the early decisions concerned territorial expansion. As far back as the first rumblings of the independence movement, agitation had begun for a union of the Fenno-Baltic lands. The agitation became articulate at the time of the war for independence in 1918, especially in the area inhabited by the Karelian Citizens League, which had its headquarters at Viborg. Such a union envisioned the creation of a Greater Finland[5] by combining Finland, Eastern Karelia, Ingria, Kola, Estonia, and the Åland Islands into a single state.

The thought behind this agitation was that the scattered Finnish people would thus be combined into a single logical unit. Many benefits would flow from such a union. Russia would be excluded from the Baltic and yet not suffer any infringement of her legitimate interests. The naval burden upon all of the small Baltic states would be lightened. A balance of power would be reached in the north, and the danger of Bolshevism would be removed from Europe.

The majority of the Finnish leaders realized fully that, fascinating as these thoughts might be, they were hardly realistic. The Åland Islands alone remained with Finland. Estonia had been set up as an

---

[4] *Ibid.,* Chapter VI.

[5] *The Greater Finland* (Publication No. 1, The Karelian Citizens League, Helsingfors, 1919).

independent state. The rest of the territory in question was retained by Russia, although she did promise Finland that she would respect the autonomy of the Eastern Karelian population, a promise she subsequently broke in Ingria and Porajärvi in 1921.[6] It became apparent that Finland could not embark upon a program of aggrandizement even if she wished to do so. So the agitation for a Greater Finland ceased and the government, which had never given the movement any encouragement, still stood for the retention of existing frontiers. The firm roots of this policy could be seen a generation later in 1941-1943, when Finnish troops were not permitted to cross the Svir River nor to attack besieged Leningrad.

Three serious border problems challenged both regents, Pehr Svinhufvud[7] and Gustav Mannerheim, later President Stålberg. These were the Åland Island question, the issue of Eastern Karelia, and relations with Estonia.[8]

The Åland Island Question[9]

These islands are an archipelago lying off the western shore of Finland. Their strategic importance was attested by the Treaty of Paris, ending the Crimean War, which forbade Russia to fortify the Åland Islands. The population is Swedish, although they are only a small part of the total Swedish population of Finland. It was this Swedish population which asked for a plebiscite during the turbulent days of 1918, by which they hoped to signify their wish to be reunited with Sweden. There were indications that the Swedish Government might approve such a plebiscite. Finland, however, demonstrated that, although the Åland population was incontestibly Swedish, its wishes were not shared by the rest of the Swedish population of Finland, and that any plebiscite which might be held, in order to be just, should cover all the Swedish people in Finland.

After considerable discussion and negotiation, in which all the interested major powers except Russia participated, an international conference was called in October, 1921, to deal with the matter. Finland promised to respect certain guarantees of autonomy for the Åland peoples, in return for which she was given full possession of the Islands,

---

[6] Kalijarvi, Thorsten V., "The Question of East Carelia," *American Journal of International Law*, 18:1 (1924), pp. 93 ff.

[7] For the most illuminating account, see Errki Räikkönen, *Svinhufvud, the Builder of Finland. An Adventure in Statecraft* (London: Alan Wilmer, 1938).

[8] *The Greater Finland, op. cit.*

[9] Kalijarvi, *Contemporary Europe, op. cit.*, p. 482.

although she was not allowed to fortify them. A few years later the neutralization provision was lifted; but the rest of the terms were observed until the outbreak of war in 1939.

Eastern Karelia

The second problem had to do with the Finnish people who lived in the Russian provinces of Eastern Karelia, particularly in Ingria and Porajärvi, on the eastern and southeastern borders of Finland.[10]

There were very few Russians in this area. The people were Finnish in language, culture, and sentiment. They desired union with Finland and Finland wished to incorporate them into her territory. In 1918, due to the interference of British General Maynard and Rear Admiral Kemp, Finland and the peoples of the Eastern Karelian provinces were unable to effect a union. When the British intervention was lifted, Russia became less lenient about permitting border areas to break away and decided to retain possession of Eastern Karelia. As already stated, Russia promised to respect the autonomy of the people in the territory, but failed to do so. Finland appealed to the League and to the Permanent Court of International Justice on behalf of the Karelian population, but was told in an advisory opinion of the Court that there was nothing the Court or the Council could do unless Russia permitted them to take jurisdiction. Russia refused to do this.

The Estonian Question

Less serious as an issue, but more challenging from the standpoint of policy, were Finnish relations with Estonia.[11]

The question here was whether or not the two countries should merge into a single state. The people were of the same racial stock, and the agitation for a union of Finland and Estonia was expressed in deeds as well as in words. Thus, two regiments of Finnish volunteers aided Kostantin Päts to bring order to Estonia in the late winter of 1919. The question was disposed of by the Peace of Tartu, February 2, 1920, between Estonia and Russia, in which Estonia was recognized by Russia as an independent state. Indeed, the matter of union had been definitely settled almost a year before in the Estonian Constitutional Assembly of April, 1919, which decided that Estonia should follow her own national interests.

---

[10] See reference in footnote 6.
[11] *Greater Finland, op. cit.*, pp. 27-28.

Foreign Policies[12]

These three border issues involved certain basic principles which went into the making of Finnish foreign policy. They showed that Finland believed in aiding her neighboring states, that she saw value in closer bonds with the rest of Scandinavia, and that she needed aid from other countries.

Finnish foreign policies were shaping up in other ways as well. When France and Poland promoted a Baltic Entente, similar to the Little Entente, Finland was interested in it because it fitted the spirit and purpose of her own objectives. Finnish friendship for Germany was motivated first by appreciation for the part which German troops had played in freeing Finland from Russia; and second by the hope of finding an ally against the powerful eastern neighbor.

Of all the countries in the world, Finland considered the United States to be her best friend. Not only had thousands of Finns come to the United States during the last century to escape Russian persecutions and become citizens of this country, but more recently the Hoover Relief Mission and American loans had proved to be real blessings. Many Finns who had lived in the United States had returned to the land of their birth and had brought with them an American influence, spreading it into all walks of life. Trade and travel opportunities beckoned, with the result that the closest relations between the United States and Finland were sought and developed.

Finnish Russophobia needs no further elaboration, but there were certain added aspects of Finnish foreign policy which depended upon this feeling and attitude to some degree. For example, Finland was in danger of becoming involved [13] in any war in which Russia might be engaged in Eastern Europe.

A warm friendship with the United States could not suffice to keep Finland out of such a conflict. Therefore, she sought support in a closer union with her neighboring states; in the advocacy of collective security, particularly under the League and the Permanent Court of International Justice; and in the cultivation of international good will. Moreover, Finland looked to the West rather than to the East for her contacts.

---

[12] Jackson, J. Hampden, *Finland* (London: George Allen and Unwin), 1938.

[13] Dean, Vera M., *European Powers Struggle Over Finland* (New York: Foreign Policy Association Bulletin, 1940), 19:21.

Developments from 1922 to 1939

The period from 1918 to 1922 was devoted to laying the foundations for a life of national independence. The period from 1922 to 1939 was filled with events which led to political and economic stability.

When the Red forces were suppressed in Finland in 1918 and 1919, the Communists rapidly lost all power. In 1923 they had sunk so low as a political party that they were deprived of legal status. This decline was followed by efforts to revive the party which again aroused old fears of Russia and disturbed both President Lauri K. Relander (1925-1931) and the Diet.[14]

The spark which touched off momentous events was an announcement in 1929 that the Communist Youth Movement was to be revived. The immediate and spontaneous reaction was a blast of protests from the pulpits, from the province of Lapua, and particularly from the farmers. The Diet wished to enact repressive measures, but the Social Democrats would not agree, thus preventing positive action. Premier Kallio resigned and Pehr Svinhufvud took the helm. The Diet was dissolved and elections were held. The Finnish people refused to support either the Communists or those who wanted to take repressive measures against them.

Not satisfied with this attitude, two of the anti-Communist leaders, Vihtori Kosola and Kurt Wallenius, organized a revolt with a view to seizing control of the government. The Lapua Movement, which they founded, was a great help to the Germans later. The revolt was short-lived and Finland survived the disturbance. There was to be no repetition of the bloody days of 1918 and 1919. Communism was a dead issue and the Finnish people did not fear its resurgence within their own ranks in the year 1930.

How much of this disturbance could be attributed to underlying economic distress is difficult to say, but Finland was then experiencing (1928-1934) the same economic depression[15] as the rest of the world. It ushered out President Relander and brought in President Pehr Svinhufvud (1931-1937).

Finland's method of meeting the crisis was to establish a committee of experts, who recommended a series of restrictive measures in 1930. These measures included the abandonment of the gold standard, a reduction in the standard of living, and certain restrictions on imports

---

[14] *Finland Yearbook, 1939-1940*, p. 9.
[15] *Ibid.*, pp. 167-171.

and exports. The prescription worked, and the crisis came to an end in 1934. The Finnish economy was soundly based.

But settlement of economic problems and the establishment of internal political stability were not enough. The Finns also wanted protection against dangers from abroad. The Lapua Movement, the deterioration of the system of collective security, and the rising might of Russia caused Finland to adopt a new Conscription Act [16] on June 30, 1932, under which every able-bodied Finn was obliged to serve at least 350 days in the armed forces upon reaching the age of 21. The defense forces were defined by this act as consisting of the Civic Guard, the Frontier Guard, and the Coast Guard.

Broad as was the scope of the act, it is significant that at no time between 1935 and 1939 did expenditures for defense exceed those for education by any substantial amount. The act was designed solely for defense, as could be seen when Finland steered a course of careful neutrality between England and Germany after their agreement of 1935. She might readily have cast her lot with either.

Economic Growth, 1919 to 1939 [17]

During the generation between the achievement of independence and the first Russian War, Finland made substantial economic progress by developing her chief resources: timber, water power, and minerals.

In agriculture, while the farm population did not increase appreciably, growth took place in tilled areas, cereal crops, hay, and potatoes. Cattle and dairy products expanded in quantity and quality. This was true particularly of butter and cheese. Pigs, grain, and cattle feed could also be added to the list.

Transportation expanded. Both railways and shipping profited. Life and fire insurance swelled and many new industrial opportunities developed. The timber industry and the manufacture of plywood were enlarged. Sawmills increased, and half of their output was exported. Marked growth also took place in pulp producing, cellulose making, paper manufacture, metal work, cement production, glass fabrication, brick making, cotton textiles, woollen cloth, and in nickel and iron output. [18]

Both exports and imports grew. Imports consisted chiefly of ma-

[16] *Ibid.*, pp. 72-76.
[17] Lindgren, Verner, *Twenty Years of Economic Reconstruction in Finland* (Reprint from *Unitas,* Helsinki, Oy. Pohjoismaiden Yhdyspankki, 1939).
[18] See the very useful map, *Finnish Trade Review,* 1 and 2 (January-March, 1939), p. 5. The whole issue is useful.

chinery, foodstuffs, luxuries, and some raw materials. Exports were timber, butter, cheese, eggs, and foodstuffs.

Financial conditions also improved. Finnish capital replaced much of the foreign capital invested in Finnish enterprises. Debts were reduced, the exchange was bolstered, and venture capital was attracted to Finland. All in all, the twenty years of economic reconstruction after 1917 were of great benefit to the country, making it possible for Finland to survive the two disastrous wars of 1939 and 1941.

The Recent Wars with Russia[19]

The following facts should be noted as an explanation of Finland's relations with Germany and Russia before and during World War II. In January, 1918, a Red revolutionary government was formed in southern Finland, and a civil war ensued. The White Finns under General (later Field Marshal) Baron Carl Gustav Mannerheim, a Swedish-Finn, who had served in the Russian Imperial Army, defeated the Red Finns when the German expeditionary force under General von der Golz landed in Finland. Thereupon, the Finns elected the German Prince Friedrich Karl of Hesse as King of Finland, but Germany's defeat in November, 1918, prevented him from taking possession of Finland's throne.

As a democratic republic Finland prospered—and had a very good reputation in America as the only country which paid her debts to the United States. In 1930, Parliament outlawed the Finnish Communist Party.

In October, 1939, with a view to strengthening her strategic position, the Soviet Government presented Finland with demands aiming at the establishment of Russian naval bases on Finnish islands in the Gulf of Finland and on the Finnish mainland at Hankö, the cession of the Arctic port of Petsamo and other frontier adjustments, and additional demands similar to those which the other Baltic states had been forced to accept. Finland refused part of these demands, feeling that there was little difference between defeat in war or the loss of independence and national identity by yielding to Russian demands.

Russia invaded Finland and the Finns held the aggressors (as most of the world and the League of Nations branded the Russians) at bay from November 30, 1939, to March 12, 1940. But the fight was hopelessly uneven and in the Treaty of Moscow new frontiers were fixed for Finland which deprived her of 10 to 12 per cent of her territory, includ-

---

[19] Chamberlin, William Henry, "The Tragic Case of Finland," *The American Mercury*, August, 1944, pp. 7-15.

ing Viipuri, (Viborg), Kuusamo, Salla, and the Rybachi Peninsula. This area contained the Karelian Isthmus and the area freely granted to Finland by Russia in the Peace of Dorpat in 1920. In addition, Finland had to lease the strategic port of Hankö to Russia. Agriculture, fishing, forestry resources, mines, manufacturing establishments, power plants, and valuable harbors were included in the ceded areas.[20]

Finland thereafter faced a terrific problem of reconstruction. She experienced increasing pressures and demands from Russia, which now began to interfere in Finnish local affairs and to make demands on Finland for additional concessions.[21] President Ryti, who had succeeded President Kallio in 1940, found no respite from these Russian demands. He discovered that Russia's peace pressures were almost as devastating as her war claims; and it began to look as though the days of Finnish independence were numbered.

On June 22, 1941, after Germany attacked Russia, the latter began to bomb Finnish territory. On June 25, Russian forces openly attacked Finland.[22] It should not be forgotten that Hitler had already proclaimed to the world, in his speech announcing the beginning of hostilities with Russia, that Finland and Romania were his allies. Moreover, German troops had been allowed to use Finnish transportation facilities to take up positions all along the Russian front.[23]

On June 26, Finland declared that a state of war existed with Russia and Finnish troops fought their way forward until they occupied the Karelian Isthmus and stood at the banks of the Svir River. The Hankö Peninsula was recaptured, and during 1941 and 1942 it looked as though Finland might recover all of her lost lands.

All through the conflict Finland insisted that she was fighting Russia only. However, under Russian pressure, England declared war upon Finland. As the tide of war changed and Russian victories followed in rapid sequence, the Finnish situation grew more and more serious. In 1943 and 1944, as the Russian forces rolled the Germans back, the United States sought to bring about peace between Finland and Russia. In the summer of 1944, Finland's fate seemed sealed when the Russians opened an offensive against her. Ribbentrop thereupon visited President Ryti and in July, 1944, secured from him a written assurance that the Finns would not withdraw from the war if the Germans sup-

---

[20] *The Finland Yearbook, 1940-1941, op. cit.*

[21] *Finland Reveals Her Secret Documents,* Official Blue-White Book of Finland (New York: Wilfred Funk, 1941). The foreword summarizes the situation.

[22] *Ibid.*

[23] Russia had wrung a similar concession from Finland after the Peace of Moscow, by which her troops were permitted to use Finnish railways for military purposes.

plied them with troops and munitions. However, the Russian armies pushed the Germans to the Baltic and shut off the flow of weapons, so that Germany could not help Finland.

In August, Field Marshall Baron Mannerheim was designated President of Finland, replacing Ryti.[24] On September 19, 1944, the terms of the armistice between Finland and the United Nations were agreed upon. They restored the 1939 eastern border, but transferred to Russia the port of Petsamo and the nearby nickel mines, and required Finland to lease the Porkkala Peninsula to Russia for 50 years. Finland was also required to pay an indemnity of $300,000,000 (in goods) to Russia in six years, turn out the German troops, permit Russia to fortify the Åland Islands, turn over much of her shipping to Russia, and place herself under United Nations (Russian) control. These were hard terms, but the Finns made an earnest effort to fulfill them by interning the German troops who remained in Finland after September 15, 1944.

Germany, however, refused to remove her soldiers and attacked the Island of Suusaari, whereupon Finnish troops were sent into action to rid the country of the German forces. In March, 1945, Finland declared war upon Germany. Events forced a definite change in Finnish foreign policy. Before the elections of March, 1945, it was announced that henceforth Finland's policy must be one of friendship with Soviet Russia by whose consent Finland still remained a free state. The national elections at that time reflected this basic change in Finland's attitude.

Art, Science, Literature[25]

Finland has a rich peasant culture, which is expressed in handicrafts of wood, gaily colored textiles and tapestries, folk poems, songs, proverbs, riddles, tales, and melodies.

The national monument of Finnish literature is the famed *Kalevala,* collected and edited by Elias Lönnrot. During the last century and a half, corresponding rather closely to the rise of Finnish nationalism, a substantial number of authors have appeared and left their contributions. Among the more recent are such men as Aleksis Kivi, whose long novel, *Seven Brothers,* has left a deep impression on Finnish thought. Some others are Arvid Järnefelt, a disciple of Tolstoi; Jo-

---

[24] *Newsweek,* 24:7 (August 14, 1944), pp. 50-52, for the correct facts. See also *Time,* 44:7 (August 14, 1944), p. 36, for the correct interpretation.

[25] For a summary, see Kalijarvi in *Contemporary Europe,* pp. 488 ff. For detailed treatments, see Konrad Hahm, *Die Kunst in Finland* (Berlin: Deutsche Kunstverlag, 1933); Hans Grellman, *Finnische Literatur* (Breslau: Ferdinand Hirst, 1932); and *Finland Yearbook, 1939-1940, op. cit.*

hannes Linankoski, the author of the ballad *Helkavirsia;* Mika Waltari, a prolific writer; K. A. Tavastjerna, a lyric poet; Hjalmar Procopé and Bertel Gripenberg, poets; and Runar Schildt, the pessimist.

The Finnish press is active and numbers approximately 800 newspapers and periodicals. Like the press in most European countries certain Finnish newspapers are identified with specific political parties. Thus, *Vaasa* is an organ of the Coalition Party, *Kaleva* of the Progressive Party, *Ilkka* of the Agrarian Party, *Kansan Lehti* of the Social Democratic Party, and *Vasabladet* of the Swedish Party.

Pictorial art has produced the paintings of Albert Edelfeldt, Akseli Gallen-Kallela, Eero Järnefelt, Magnus Enckell, Juho Riisanen, and T. K. Sallinen; the sculpture of Väinö Aaltonen; and the wood carving of Hannes Autere.

Finnish music has achieved a great reputation and needs little comment except to mention that it has been built by the Finnish people and by such composers as Jean Sibelius, Armas Järnefelt, Aare Merikanto, and Selim Palmgren. It includes chamber music, opera, tone poems, scenic sketches, symphonies, and vocal and instrumental compositions.

There has also been a considerable advance in Finnish architecture. The excellent work of E. Saarinen and A. Lindgren, as typified in the railroad station in Helsinki and the National Museum Building, are world-famous. So are the works of L. Sonck and others. The arts and crafts should definitely be included in the list of major Finnish achievements.

Health, Welfare, and Social Service[26]

Social welfare in Finland includes not only the care of the destitute, crippled children, and the mentally deficient; but it also covers care for waifs, strays, chronic inebriates, the blind, and needy seamen. These categories and others are covered in the present poor law, passed in 1922 and known as the Poor Persons Assistance Act. This law went back for precedent to an act of 1879 and the precedent for the care of needy children was an act of 1852. Maternity aid was provided for in 1937.

Medical care and health regulations fall under the supervision of a Medical Board. These deal with protection against infectious diseases, venereal diseases, and tuberculosis. Care for school children begins with the teaching of cleanliness. Voluntary health leagues and societies are encouraged.

In addition to these measures, a wide range of compulsory and subsidized social insurance is in vogue. The compulsory types include

---

[26] Laati, Iisakki, *Social Legislation and Activity in Finland* (Helsinki, Oy. Suomen Kirja, 1939).

such items as workmen's compensation insurance, unemployment compensation, insurance against industrial diseases, old age insurance, insurance against motor vehicle accidents, and insurance of fishing gear. The voluntary kinds include the familiar annuity types with customary fire and life. Enlightened and effective laws govern insurance transactions.

The Coöperative Movement[27]

One of the principal means by which the Finnish people, individually and collectively, made rapid economic progress in the generation following the First World War was through the aid of coöperatives. As in the other Scandinavian countries, the Finnish system of coöperatives was extensive and effective. Finnish coöperatives really began with the Pellervo-Seura, founded by Hannes Gebhard in 1899. They now include stores with a central wholesale society (SOK or Consumer Wholesale Society), of dairies dealing in cattle, butter, cheese, and milk; slaughter houses; poultry growers' societies; credit societies of the German Raiffeisen type; export coöperatives; and forest owners coöperatives.

Finland is a comparatively poor country and possesses limited capital. Through coöperative effort, therefore, large classes of people have been able to profit in a way which would otherwise have been closed to them unless they had brought in extensive foreign capital.

Women[28]

No account of recent Finnish history can make a pretense at completeness without a reference to the status of women. Finnish women for many years have enjoyed far greater freedom and rights than the women of any other country. In 1906 they acquired the right to vote and since that time have been extensively represented in the Diet.

It is interesting that even with this greater freedom they prefer to serve in local communities, where they hold many positions of responsibility and trust. As far back as 1871 they attended Finnish universities. They possess extensive organizations and for years have led in European activities for their sex. They have been particularly strong in the feminist movement, especially at the end of the last and the beginning of the present century. Political parties have their women's unions. The greatest single woman's organization, embracing many

---

[27] For a helpful discussion of this subject, see Henry H. Bakken, *Coöperation to the Finnish* (Madison, Wisconsin: Mimir, 1939).

[28] *Status of Women in Finland in 1935* (Helsinki: Liike ja virkanaisten liitto r. y. Julkaisu-Publikation 1, 1936).

sub-groups, is the Martha League. Perhaps the organization best known to the world at large, due to its activities during the two recent Russian wars, is the *Lotta-Svärd*.

Education[29]

The Finnish people possess an unusually high degree of literacy. This was due to the influence of the Church in a very substantial measure. The beginnings of popular education can be traced back to the Reformation. In 1718 Gezelius the Younger reported extensive literacy as the result of an Act of 1686, which required that a person must be able to read in order to be admitted to Holy Communion. In the nineteenth century, public education was stimulated, and in 1866 Cygnaeus drew up the basis for an elementary school system.

When compulsory elementary school education was inaugurated in 1937, it stimulated a rapid increase in both pupils and teachers. There had been a steady growth in both groups since 1918. As a result, a teachers' college for elementary schools, serving both men and women, was founded in Jyväskylä in 1934. At the time this school was established there were 1950 teachers and 59,778 pupils in the elementary schools of Finland. There are also a number of people's colleges, workmen's institutes, and correspondence schools under government supervision.

Secondary school education was begun by the Catholic Church before the Reformation, and has since developed into three distinct types: (1) for boys, (2) for girls, and (3) co-educational. Teacher training is carried on in a special school. Most of these secondary schools have two programs: (1) the lycée course which leads to the University, and (2) a middle school course, which leads to trade schools.

Vocational training is offered in forestry, commercial affairs, trade, wood-turning, the operation of sawmills, navigation, and several similar subjects.

At the apex of the educational system are the universities, the State University at Helsinki and the two private ones at Turku. There are also a technical college, commercial colleges, and a sociological college.

Outside the school system proper there are a large number of learned and scientific societies. Examples include Suomen Tiedeseura, Academia Scientiarum Fennica, Historical Society of Finland, Swedish Literary Society, Finnish Society of Chemists, and the Society for Jurisprudence.

---

[29] *Finland Yearbook, 1939-1940, op. cit.,* pp. 89 ff.

Finnish Nationalism[30]

Over the centuries, the Finnish people have developed a strong individuality and nationalism. Since independence was achieved in 1918, this nationalism first took the form of making the Finnish language paramount over Swedish. Later it expressed itself in a powerful and stubborn defense of Finland against invasion. How completely language lines faded into the background at that time may be seen in the leadership of Mannerheim and Svinhufvud, for they were both members of the Swedish group. Recent Finnish nationalism is grounded in culture, language, and a fear of foreign powers.

Conclusions

Finland today has a high standard of literacy and culture, and social welfare measures are advanced. Her government is basically democratic, as may readily be seen in the uninterrupted functioning of the Diet throughout the wars with Russia and in the Lapua crisis. In these matters, whatever the racial stock may be, Finland shares with Norway, Denmark, and Sweden a common Scandinavian heritage of thought, culture, politics, and social activity.

Finland is desperately depressed economically and physically as a result of five years of war. Her reconstruction problems are unusually severe. Furthermore, in international affairs she leads a precarious existence which can only find permanent improvement in a closer union with the other Scandinavian states or in a new system of collective security of unprecedented effectiveness or in both of these combined. All of which means that Finland is a small country located in an unenviable strategic position in a world of power politics.

Bibliography

Aalto, *Architecture and Furniture* (New York: Museum of Modern Art, 1938). A short and reliable treatment of a specialized subject.

Bugbee, Willis N., *The Spirit of Finland* (Syracuse, N. Y.: Bugbee, 1940). A eulogy.

Constitution de la Finlande (Helsinki: V. K., 1924). A useful document for the understanding of Finnish government.

Die Entwicklung Finnlands als selbständiges Reich (Helsinki: Oy. Suomen Kirja, 1939). A short account of the Finnish struggle for independence.

Finland Reveals Her Secret Documents on Soviet Policy, March 1940-June 1941. Official Blue-White Book of Finland (New York: Wilfred Funk, 1941). Documents covering relations between Finland and Russia between the two wars of 1939 and 1940.

---

[30] See section in Chap. VI for references.

Guide to Finland, ed. by I. Leiviskä & Levämäki (Helsinki: Oy. Suomen Kirja, 1938). Useful maps and text.

Hippaka, T. A., *Indomitable Finland, Educational Background* (Washington, D. C.: Daylion, 1940). If taken together with *Finland Yearbook, 1939-1940,* this is reliable and illuminating.

Rothery, Agnes, *Finland, the New Nation* (New York: Viking, 1936). One of a popular series. Well done and reliable.

Schumacher, Jack, *Die Finnen, das grosse Sportvolk, Wege zu den Erfolgen der finnischen Sportgrössen* (Berlin: Wilhelm Limpert Verlag, 1936). A treatment of Finnish athletics and sport.

Sommer, William, *Geschichte Finnlands* (Munich and Berlin: R. Oldenburg, 1938). Rather more extensive than most accounts of Finnish history. Reliable and helpful, especially for interpretations.

CHAPTER XXI

THE BALTIC STATES (LITHUANIA, LATVIA, ESTONIA) FROM WORLD WAR I TO WORLD WAR II

German Withdrawal

Wﬁ the collapse of Tsarist Russia and the defeat of Germany in the First World War, the three Baltic states (Lithuania, Latvia, and Estonia) set out on their high road of independence. Not regarded at the outset in the light of Wilsonian principles of self-determination but rather as part of a "cordon sanitaire" directed against Russia, a rampart in the socio-political struggle between West and East, the new nations were slowly recognized by the western powers. (The United States formally recognized the new Baltic order only in July, 1922.)

When Germany denounced the Treaty of Brest Litovsk, her agreement with the Allies stipulated that the Germans would remain in the Baltic area until directed by the Allies to withdraw. German forces had occupied Lithuania in 1917 and Latvia and Estonia during 1917 and February, 1918. Following the armistice of November 11, 1918, Germany began a gradual withdrawal of troops in the Baltic. As they departed, the Bolsheviks returned in an attempt to restore Russian rule. White Russians, aided by the Baltic Germans, organized counter-revolutions; German troops under von der Goltz returned and sought to recover power; and finally Russo-German freebooters of the Bermond-Avaloff-Verkolich forces raided the region.

Peace and order were established only after bloody conflicts. With the sword and sacrifice, the Baltic lands were cleared of enemy forces both from within and without. Germany gave some help against the Russians in the beginning; but it was English naval support and French military might which finally strengthened the hand of existing authorities sufficiently to restore order. The German evacuation was ended late in 1919 under the supervision of an inter-allied mission. Lithuania made a formal peace with Russia in the Peace of Moscow, 1920; Estonia in the Peace of Tartu, 1920; and Latvia in the Peace of Riga, 1920.[1]

Lithuania (1920-1939)[2]

After centuries of foreign rule, the Lithuanian Declaration of Independence placed responsibility upon the Taryba for setting up an independent government and the governmental machinery to operate it. The Allied and Associated Powers never evinced any inclination to reestablish the old Lithuanian state. It was the pressure of Lithuanians abroad, especially in the United States, which made independence possible. A constitution (October, 1918) established a new government consisting of a national assembly, a president, a prime minister, and a cabinet. The strength of this new government was tested when its organization of sharpshooters (*Shauliai*) cleared the land of alien enemies.

The Government was first quartered in Vilna, but, after a *coup* by the Polish General Zeligowski, it was moved to Kaunas. There in 1920 the Seimas, or constitutional assembly, ratified the Declaration of Independence and modified the Provisional Constitution. By August, 1922, the changes were complete, and the new Constitution was finally adopted. The Seimas became the supreme power. The Government was divided into the executive branch, including the President and the Cabinet, and the legislative, including the Seimas and the judiciary. The form was originally democratic.

In December, 1926, the Nationalist Party ended the democratic regime and established a dictatorship which overthrew the Constitution and set up Smetona as President and Voldermaras as Prime Minister. With the aid of his "Iron Wolf" supporters, Voldemaras drove all opposition out of office and initiated a new Constitution on May 15, 1928. Although Voldemaras in turn was driven out in 1929, the Nationalist Party remained in power with Smetona at its head. The new Premier was Juozas Tubelis. In 1936, the Seimas was reduced in size and power. A new Constitution, promulgated on May 12, 1938, left the dictatorship unimpaired.[3]

The new Lithuania had great difficulty in establishing normal conditions after 1920 because of differences which arose with Poland over the

---

[1] "The Baltic States," *The Contemporary Review*, CCCXXXIV (July, 1929), pp. 182-189.

[2] Zadeikis, P., *Introducing Lithuania* (New York: Lithuanian Government, 1933), pp. 5-22; also J. J. Hertmanowicz, *op. cit.*

[3] Joseph S. Roucek, *Contemporary Europe* (New York: D. Van Nostrand, 1941), pp. 438-444; Robert Machray, "The Baltic Pact, Vilna and Memel," *The Nineteenth Century*, DCXCIX (May, 1935), pp. 583-596.

city and border area of Vilna (Vilnius).[4]   This region, where the Lithuanians and the White Russians merge, lies on the eastern edge of
Lithuania. The city of Vilna was the ancient capital and spiritual
home of the Lithuanians, but during the centuries of Lithuanian union
with Poland the population had become chiefly Polish.

When the German and Russian armies withdrew from the eastern
section of Lithuania in 1919, the boundary line with Russia was not
established. Poland and Russia entered into a treaty at Riga in 1920,
which transferred to Poland the part of Lithuania that included Vilna.
But the Lithuanian Government had been in possession of the city of
Vilna ever since the Russians had driven out the Poles in the summer
of 1920. Conflict now broke out between the Poles and Lithuanians
over this area, with the result that the League of Nations proposed a
division of the territory between them by the so-called "Curzon Line."
This would have given the City of Vilna to Lithuania. Poland apparently acquiesced. As late as October 7, 1920, Poland signed the non-
aggression pact of Suvalki with Lithuania, which confirmed a similar
line.

On October 9, 1920, evidently under orders from Marshal Pilsudski,
although he claimed to be operating as an independent leader, the Polish General Zeligowski invaded the territory and City of Vilna and
seized it, presumably for himself but actually for Poland. Then followed a most complicated and unsuccessful series of negotiations involving the League of Nations, the Council, the Assembly, and all the
other paraphernalia of peace. Zeligowski held firm, and Poland refused to disclaim or to oust him. Thus Poland acquired Vilna and
held it until the Second World War and the Fourth Polish Partition.

Lithuania still considered herself to be at war with Poland, and this
unsolved problem remained an obstacle to a peaceful Lithuanian foreign policy for years. It disrupted Lithuanian internal relations and
delayed reconstruction. The Polish aggression gave Poland a strip of
territory running to the borders of Latvia, thus cutting Lithuania off
from her eastern neighbor, Russia. Lithuania, during her independent
existence, never recognized the Polish seizure by any statement or action. In 1938, normal diplomatic relations between the two countries
were re-established, but only because Lithuania had reason to believe
that Poland would open hostilities unless she gave in.[5]

---

[4] *The Vilna Question, Consultations* (London: Hazell, Watson, and Viney, 1929); also J. J.
Hertmanowicz, *op. cit.*, Pt. I, pp. 11-20.
[5] Eliot, George Fielding, "Baltic Bickerings," *Current History*, XXXXVIII:5 (May, 1938),
pp. 36-38.

Memel [6] was another cause of controversy. Memelland or Klaipeda (as the Lithuanians call it) is a strip of territory running northward from the Niemen River to the Port of Memel. In ancient times it had been inhabited by the same tribes as those living in Lithuania proper. Since 1410, it had been held by Germans with the exception of brief periods of warfare. When World War I came to an end and the new Lithuania was established, Memel was about the only outlet to the Baltic Sea available to Lithuania. In a vague set of agreements, the Allied and Associated Powers gave Lithuania reason to believe that she would be given the territory of Memel. As the discussion seemed interminably protracted, Lithuania took a page out of Poland's book and forced the issue by sending her own Budrys into Memelland on January 10, 1923, to seize it for Lithuania as Zeligowski had seized Vilna for Poland. The move was eminently successful.

In 1924, the Allied and Associated Powers recognized Lithuania's sovereignty over the area and provided articles of autonomy for the people of Memel. The situation was impossible for both Lithuania and the Memellanders. Lithuania interpreted the promise of sovereignty as giving her a free hand to rule the land. The people of Memelland, though a mixture of Germans and Lithuanians, were predominantly in favor of German rule and wanted a rigid adherence to the provisions of autonomy. Germany, as she gathered strength, took the side of the local population. There could be little hope for an amicable solution as long as all sides remained firm in their respective positions. Finally, in 1939, Hitler took possession of Memel, eliminating Lithuania's only seaport, over a quarter of her industry, three-quarters of her export trade, and almost three-quarters of her import trade.

The economic development [7] of Lithuania was greatly handicapped between the two world wars. She presumably set her house in order between 1918 and 1920, during which time she was ridding herself of Bolshevism. From 1920 to 1938 she was technically at war with Poland with a large part of her productive manpower under arms. In 1939, she was stripped of her only seaport and with it a substantial part of her economic life.

In spite of these difficulties, economic progress was made. Agriculture,[8] which gave work to approximately three-quarters of the people,

[6] Kalijarvi, Thorsten V., *The Memel Statute* (London: Robert Hale, Ltd., 1937).

[7] *Contemporary Europe, op. cit.;* Vogel, *op. cit.,* for this and other material as well. See E. J. Harrison, *Lithuania, 1928* (London: Hazell, Watson, and Viney, 1928).

[8] For a summary treatment of the economic problems of all these states in 1927, see Eugene Van Cleef, "Some Economic Problems in the Baltic Republics," *Geographical Review,* XVII:3 (July 1927), pp. 434-447.

expanded to even geater limits. Production increased in potatoes, rye, oats, barley, wheat, peas, flax, hemp, horses, cattle, sheep, hogs, and poultry. In 1922 a Land Reform Law was enacted which divided the large landed estates into small parcels. This law was modified to some extent in 1927. Meanwhile, as elsewhere in Europe, the coöperative movement flourished. In 1920, there were only 253 coöperatives in all of Lithuania. By 1929, the number had increased to 2200. Consumer, credit, dairy farming, agricultural, and producers' coöperative associations were particularly active.

World War I had wiped out the humble industrial activities of Lithuania, but revival and new growth began immediately after the war. By 1929, eight thousand industrial plants employed 33,000 workers. They were chiefly of the food-producing types, including livestock raising and slaughtering. Sawmills abounded. There were also clothing shops, metallurgical factories, and establishments for the production of matches, tobacco, liquor, soaps, leather, textiles, cement, and fertilizers. The peat industry grew and the electrification of the Niemen River was undertaken.[9]

Commerce and trade more than doubled in the decade from 1920 to 1930. Exports and imports were carried on chiefly with Germany and Great Britain; but also with Czechoslovakia, Latvia, Holland, Russia, and the United States.

Loans increased fifteen-fold and deposits nine-fold between 1923 and 1932. State finances were stabilized and increased. In short, Lithuania in one generation had not only gained her independence, but had become sound, solvent, and well established; a credit to herself and her people, entitled to live a free and independent life.[10]

Independence gave the Lithuanians the opportunity for which they had longed—and longed all the more fiercely because it had been so persistently denied them. Education,[11] which had been choked off under imperialist Russia, was spurred on by freedom. By 1930, some 2,656 elementary schools had been established. In addition there were 90 high schools and 47 senior high schools (comparable to American senior high schools and junior colleges combined), 11 teachers' colleges, 3 secretarial schools, 3 agricultural schools, and several other types. A

---

[9] For the excellent Lithuanian condition in the midst of world-wide depression, see *Monthly Labour Review*, XXXIV:4 (April, 1932), p. 808; for Latvia and Estonia, see pages 11, 53, 1179, and 1181 of *ibid*.

[10] On this whole section, see *Introducing Lithuania, op. cit.;* also *Ten Years of Lithuanian Economy, Report of the Chamber of Commerce, Industry, and Culture* (Kaunas: Vilniaus, 1938).

[11] Chapter VII; also Alvin C. Eichholz, *The Baltic States, Estonia, Latvia, and Lithuania, A Short Review of Resources, Industry, Finance and Trade* (Washington, Trade Information Bulletin, 1928), 569; K. Masilianus, "Education in Lithuania," *School Life*, XXIV:6 (March, 1939), pp. 171-175.

new state university was set up at Kaunas to take the place of the Vilna school of ancient lineage and fame.

Literature flourished, as has been indicated in Chapter VII. One hundred and twelve newspapers were published, including the *Lietuvos Aidas, Lietuvos Zinios, Rytas, Musu Rytojus,* and *Trimitas.*

Cultural organizations included an opera house, ballet, and art societies. A school of music, a theater, a museum, and libraries were among the excellent products of post-war Lithuanian activities.

Sports and athletics gained a large following and athletic organizations sprang up everywhere. Wrestlers, gymnasts, football players, and other specialized sports enthusiasts formed their own associations. Trap and rifle shooters, hunters, and fishers also banded together.

One of the finest tributes to the value of the freedom for mankind was the tremendous achievement of Lithuania during her brief revival as an independent state. The Lithuanian people both at home and abroad combined to build an enlightened modern state which, despite troubled foreign relations, was able to create a government, to improve economic conditions, to develop educational and cultural institutions, and to expand foreign trade. It was an excellent record, for the task of reconstructing ruined cities and communications was prodigious.[12]

The pressure of Communism from one side and National Socialism from the other was a constant menace. Promises had been given by both Russia and Germany to respect Lithuanian independence and territorial integrity. In spite of these promises, Lithuania was to experience another tragedy in her long history of misfortune

Latvia

Latvia, after gaining her independence, adopted a coat of arms, resumed the use of her ancient flag, and undertook agrarian reforms in 1920. Her new government, set up in 1922, consisted of a single-chamber legislature, a president, and an independent judiciary. Perhaps the greatest weakness of this government was a system of proportional representation which permitted any seven citizens to form a party and any hundred citizens to nominate a candidate for a district. The result was a Seima, or Legislature, with about twenty different parties and with constant confusion of policies and governmental objectives.[13]

---

[12] Some of the spirit can be caught from the excellent and authoritative statement of P. Zadeikis in "An Aspect of the Lithuanian Record of Independence," The *Annals,* CCXXXII (March, 1944), pp. 49-51. For a diametrically opposite view and one which is deeply prejudiced, bordering on an apologia for the Soviets, see Gregory Meiksins, *The Baltic Riddle* (New York: Fischer, 1943).

[13] Pollock, James K., "The Constitution of Latvia," *American Political Science Review,* XVII:3 (August, 1923), pp. 446-448.

This weakness caused the development of nationalist party movements and set a social democratic movement against them. As far
back as 1918 the Civil Guards or *Aizsargi*[14] had been organized into a
powerful military society, upon which the nationalist groups gradually
came to depend for support. The Nationalists by 1927 had also developed a society known as *Pehr Konkrusts*. The Social Democrats answered these moves by organizing a *Workers Sporting Club,* an armed
and uniformed organization. It was the aim and purpose of the Social
Democrats to choke off any possible usurpation of the government by
the Nationalists. The strife between the two groups increased in intensity and tempo until drastic action was required if violence was to be
avoided.

The decision was taken on May 15, 1934, when Premier Ulmanis, the
leader of the Peasant Union, dissolved the Seima, forbade party activities, prohibited strikes and lockouts, and proclaimed martial law. The
support of the *Aizsargi* made this possible and also enabled Ulmanis to
have himself elected President in 1936, when President Kresis finished
his term of office. This Government continued itself in power by
emergency decrees until 1938. In that year it made the temporary
arrangement permanent by the "Law of Defense of the State."

The new government placed all executive and legislative power in
the hands of the President and the Cabinet. A State Council was organized in addition to the Seima, and this Council embodied the boards
of the National Chambers, which were organized on the old guild lines
of agriculture, industry, commerce, artisans, labor, professions, and the
arts. The State Council was actually composed of the Economic Council and the State Cultural Council. The Economic Council met for the
first time in January, 1938, while the State Cultural Council, consisting
of the Chamber of Art and Literature and the Chamber of Professions,
was established on May 5, 1938. Special emphasis was given to education, coöperative enterprises, and economic planning.

While domestic political conditions were disturbed, progress was
made in foreign relations[15] which justified all Latvian claims to independence. Latvia entered into treaties with scores of states and settled
her frontiers with Lithuania and her other neighbors during the early
1920's. Like all other small states, she became a loyal and enthusiastic
supporter of the whole system of collective security, including the

---

[14] See *Contemporary Europe, supra cit.,* p. 441; "Two More Little Hitlers," *New Republic,*
LXXIX:1016 (May 30, 1934), pp. 60-62.
[15] Bilmanis, Alfred, "Free Latvia in Free Europe," The *Annals,* CCXXXII (March, 1944),
pp. 43-48; also Alfred Bihlmans, *Latvia in the Making, 1918-1928* (Riga: Riga Times, 1928).

League of Nations, the Permanent Court of International Justice, and the International Labor Office. This included arbitration and all forms of pacific settlement of international disputes. She entered into the Baltic Union, but found that she had much more in common with Estonia than with the other states. In 1921, Latvia and Estonia entered into a treaty of alliance and in November, 1923, they augmented it with a military convention. In 1934, they enlarged this agreement to cover representation of the two countries by a single delegate at international conferences and conventions. On November 3, 1934, the so-called "Treaty of Good Understanding and Coöperation" capped the whole structure of close mutual relations with Estonia.

Latvia's general development during her independence[16] was marked by a policy of leniency toward minorities, which were permitted to set up special schools under a law passed in 1919. In 1929, the Celmins ministry even went so far as to grant a subsidy for the erection of a German war memorial, which caused a cabinet crisis. After 1934, however, the Nationalist Government tended to be less lenient with minorities than its predecessors.

Like her neighbors, Latvia liquidated the large pre-war landed estates early in her period of independence. These lands were then divided among small holders, being sold or leased to them on reasonable terms. No compensation was paid for the land taken and the original owners were allowed to retain only between 125 and 250 acres of their former property. Also like her neighbors, Latvia took over the forests and declared them to be state property.

In agriculture, schools were set up, machinery was introduced to replace manpower, stock was bred and blooded, seeds were developed, cereal growing was expanded, dairy products were carefully inspected, and government participation was encouraged in every branch. The government took a benevolent attitude towards all agricultural development, and rapid strides were made toward placing the country on a self-sufficient basis so far as food supply was concerned.[17]

Lumber, pulp, plywood, and match industries were encouraged. A large government dam for water power was constructed at Kegums. Trade relations improved. The Latvian merchant marine consisted of about 200,000 tons of shipping in 1939.

Religious instruction was carried on in the schools, each denomination being entitled to special instruction if there were ten or more chil-

---

[16] Offutt, Milton, "Latvia's Ten Years of Independence," *Current History*, XXIX:4 (January, 1929), pp. 700-701.

[17] For the effect of the depression on Latvia, see "Wages and Cost of Living in Latvia, 1930 to 1937," *Monthly Labour Review*, XLV:1 (July, 1937), pp. 204-207.

dren of its faith in the school.   Latvian illiteracy fell from 25.7 per cent
in 1920 to 7.91 per cent in 1935, showing that the educational program
had been remarkably successful.[18]   Compulsory education in the elementary schools and an excellent system of secondary schools and vocational schools were largely responsible for these favorable figures.
Progress was made in the arts and cultural subjects under the stimulus
of independence, which expanded national individuality.   A number
of Catholics in the Latgallian province were covered by a concordat
between the Vatican and Latvia dated May, 1922.

Estonia[19]

The development of Estonia followed much the same pattern as that
of Lithuania and Latvia.   A period of reorganization began immediately after gaining independence.   A government was established and
given legal form in the constitution of June 15, 1920.[20]   It provided for
a president, a state assembly, and an independent judiciary.   The constitution was particularly noteworthy for its long list of "Fundamental
Rights of Estonian Citizens."   Another section, "On the People," also
contained further rights, as did other sections of the same instrument.
In fact, the whole constitution was built around the people.

Contrary to the treaty of peace with Estonia, the Soviet Government
harbored Communist leaders and their newspaper, which featured constant propaganda for the return of their party to Estonia.   In 1924, they
organized an open revolt in the capital of Tallinn; but the government
was able to suppress the rebels and to maintain order.   In spite of this
agitation and in spite of other difficulties, Estonia achieved economic
prosperity and was remarkably free from unemployment at the time
the rest of the world was going through the great depression.   The
Estonian budget remained balanced at all times.[21]

New to independent existence and freedom of government, the Estonians had their first taste of a governmental upheaval in 1931.   A
group of ex-servicemen, known as the "Liberators," sought a stronger
executive and wished to bring about a change in the method of voting,
since the preferential list system did not satisfy their objectives.   As in

---

[18] Kronlins, Janis, "The Latvian Schools and Their Attainments," *School Life*, XXIV:9 (June,
1939), pp. 266-269.

[19] Pullerits, Albert, *Estonia, op. cit.*, for the best general treatment.

[20] See the *Constitution of the Estonian Republic*, published by the *Baltic Review* (London:
no date).

[21] Kaiv, Johannes, "Esthonian Nationalism," The *Annals*, 232 (March, 1944), pp. 39-42. See,
for example, the wage rates for 1927 and 1938 in *Monthly Labour Review*, XXXIX:3 (September, 1934), pp. 733-734; Joseph S. Roucek, "Constitutional Changes in Estonia," *American Political Science Review*, XXX:3 (June, 1936), pp. 556-558.

the case of the *Pehr Konkrusts* in Latvia, they ran into direct conflict with the Social Democrats, who wanted no executive. The issue was debated at considerable length without being presented to the people, during which time the Agrarians sought to compromise the conflict. Finally, in 1933, the issue was placed before the people, who elected by an overwhelming majority to follow the lead of the Liberators by strengthening the executive. A new constitution was adopted and Konstantin Päts assumed the presidency.

In January, 1934, the victory of the Liberators was made complete by another overwhelming victory in the municipal elections. Shortly thereafter, however, they were turned out of office when President Päts, following in the footsteps of Smetona and Ulmanis, seized complete power and made General Laidoner Commander-in-Chief of the Army. The reason for this act was the fear that the Liberators were turning to German National Socialism, and President Päts stated that he was taking "democracy into safe keeping." [22] The rule he set up was benevolent. Labor continued to possess the right to strike and the people suffered few restrictions. The most significant change was the cessation of all political activities except on the part of the government.[23] In 1938, a new Constitution legalized the new form of government. It was looked upon in some quarters as a return to democracy, and in others as merely legalizing the dictatorship.

Much of what has been said about Latvia applies equally to Estonian foreign relations.[24] This little country supported collective security, meticulously observed its international compacts, settled its disputes amicably, and combined these policies with a studied neutrality in conflicts which in any way affected her. Like Latvia, Estonia granted favorable treatment to Russian trade, although here as in Latvia the Russians made little use of the privilege. On the whole, Estonia acquired an excellent reputation as an independent state.

Estonia's record for generous treatment of minorities within her boundaries is unexcelled. In 1925, a Law of Cultural Autonomy permitted any minority of more than 3,000 people to set up its own council for the control of educational, cultural, and charitable matters. Jews and Germans took advantage of this privilege.

---

[22] Thompson, Ralph, "Estonia Rejects Dictatorship," *Current History*, XLIV:1 (April, 1936), pp. 97-98.

[23] Kaiv, *op. cit.* See also *Contemporary Europe, op. cit.,* pp. 440-441. The ignorant or Machiavellian criticism of Estonia's dictatorship as Fascist is contradicted by the calm statement that it was an "authoritative government" directed against Fascism. See *The Literary Digest,* CXX:11 (September 14, 1935), p. 17.

[24] Kaiv, *op. cit.*

Land reforms were similar to those in Latvia and Lithuania. Education, too, followed the same beneficial course as in Latvia. Agricultural reforms and governmental paternalism with regard to agricultural development were the same as in Latvia. Estonia also made substantial industrial progress, setting up a sound economic life for her people.

Estonia has one especially valuable resource—oil shale, which is refined and produces gasoline and lubricating oil. She also has important paper and pulp mills, cement industries, and phosphate deposits for fertilizer. Naturally these are small compared with larger resources or enterprises in neighboring lands. They were, however, sufficiently significant to give Estonia a valid base for economic development. Music, literature, and arts all flourished.[25]

Baltic Confederation

All three of the small Baltic countries realized at the outset of their independence how relatively weak they were in a world of power politics. The Allied and Associated Powers also realized it, as did Poland. In August, 1920, at a time when the treaties of peace were being signed with Russia and a period of stability was beginning, five states—Finland, Estonia, Latvia, Lithuania, and Poland—met at Riga to see if it would be possible to establish a confederation. This conference was followed by several others until about 1925.[26]

The conference in 1920 not only examined military and naval possibilities, but attention was also given to a common currency, united trade policies and programs, unified systems of exchange, and measures aimed to bring the states closer together.

Unfortunately, little came of these moves. There were several good reasons for this. The languages of these peoples were not alike, although much of their history dovetailed. Their social and political problems were much alike, especially because of their centuries of experience with Russia, but they were at different stages of development and culture. Moreover, Finland, as noted in Chapter VI, decided that her main historic, geographical, and cultural interests were tied with those of the Scandinavian states. Lithuania and Poland were at loggerheads over the problem of Vilna. Lithuania was predominantly agri-

---

[25] Pullerits, op. cit.; some travel literature is also available. Especially useful are *Visit Esthonia* and *Tallinn;* E. R. Saiv, "Esthonia After Twenty Years," *The Fortnightly,* CXLIII (March, 1938) pp. 343-349; Peter Alexander Speek, "Education in Esthonia," XXIV:7 (April, 1939), pp. 206-209.

[26] Bowman, Isaiah, op. cit., pp. 442-443; Piip, Antonius, "The Baltic States as a Regional Unity," The *Annals,* CLXVIII (July, 1923), pp. 171-177.

cultural and could do little to change its status. Estonia and Latvia did more to cultivate industry. Lithuania also had a special problem in Memel, first with the Allied and Associated Powers and later with Germany. In short, a common background to force these states into a confederation of defense was lacking. While the pattern for a confederation could be found, as could that of an entente in the experience of the nations to the south, it was not acceptable to the Baltic peoples.

In retrospect, it is doubtful that a confederation would have had the least effect on events from 1939 on. The attacks of Russia and Germany on Poland and Finland would undoubtedly have been duplicated by similar attacks on the three Baltic republics if they had attempted any resistance.

Submergence in Russia and Germany

Having traced the history of Lithuania, Latvia, and Estonia from the earliest times through their independence, it is apparent that their histories merge at times and then separate. Even during the generation of independence between the two world wars, they followed much the same course. All three began with liberal constitutions. All three passed through a decade of republicanism during which their constitutions were found lacking in one respect or another. All three experienced the assumption of supreme power by a president who remained in office and changed the constitution. In each case, the president was encouraged to do this by a group of nationalists organized into a party in opposition to the Social Democrats. These assumptions of power have sometimes been described as the establishment of dictatorships on the Fascist model. This sort of generalization is hard to substantiate without a preliminary definition of the meaning of Fascism. But, Fascist or not, all three countries developed economically and raised the standards of living of their people. All three reduced illiteracy, fostered the arts and sciences, and experienced the thrill of national existence.[27]

As they had prospered together, so they also suffered together in renewed tragedy. In March, 1938, Poland forced Lithuania to yield on the question of Vilna and to re-establish normal diplomatic relations. On March 22, 1939, Lithuania was forced to yield Memel to Germany for a compensation of $120,000,000 in machinery and equipment and the free use of the port. Non-aggression pacts were signed between

[27] Kaiv, *op. cit.*; Zadekis, *op. cit.*; Bilmanis, *op. cit.*; Bowman, *op. cit.*; Vogel, *op. cit.*; and Meiksins, *op. cit.*

Germany and Lithuania, Latvia, and Estonia. Incidentally, all three countries had similar non-aggression treaties with Russia.[28]

Then, as the Second World War approached and the Allies and Germany jockeyed for Russian support, the Germans outmaneuvered the British and French. On August 23, 1939, the Russo-German Treaty was signed, which gave Hitler security to move against Poland in September, 1939. This was the chance that Russia had long awaited. In addition to sharing in the partition of Poland, she invited the three Baltic states to send delegations to Moscow and there instructed them that there were "pressing problems" to discuss. The discussions were simple demands for garrison rights and transportation facilities and the cession of strategically important territory. In return, Russia "permitted" these countries to continue their independence and to retain their own armies while Russia supplied those armies with materials at favorable rates. Lithuania was given Vilna, which Russia had just obtained in the Polish partition.

The shadow of things to come was cast by the German exodus from the Baltic. In October, 1939, Germany signed agreements with Estonia and Latvia providing for the movement of all Germans from those two Baltic states. The transfer of property and the relocation of populations were covered, most of the migrants being settled in East Prussia.[29] Such a movement of people could only presage one of two things. Either the Germans were moving out to give the Russians a completely free field, or the people were being moved because conflict was anticipated. The chances were that the first was the reason in this case.

The Russian garrisons moved in without much disturbance. Then in May, 1940, Russia complained to Lithuania that Russian soldiers had been waylaid and beaten. In June, Russia demanded that Lithuania reconstitute her government so that it would be more friendly to Russia, also that Russia be granted additional privileges. Russia likewise accused Lithuania of entering into a military alliance with the other Baltic states directed solely at Russia. Lithuania was helpless. She was taken over by a new form of Machiavellian imperialism.

The same thing occurred in Latvia and Estonia. Smetona fled to Königsberg, but Ulmanis and Päts remained in their own countries,

---

[28] Machray, Robert, "Baltic Trends," *The Fortnightly*, CXLV:1 (June, 1939), pp. 73-81.

[29] "La Transfert des populations," *L'Esprit international*, XIV (April 1940), pp. 163-186; "The Baltic States Without Germans," *The Nineteenth Century*, DCCLVIII (April 1940), pp. 434-439; Rolf Gardiner, "German Eastward Policy and the Baltic States," *Contemporary Review,* CXLV (March 1934), pp. 324-331.

where only members of the Working People's Bloc were permitted to vote in the elections of July, 1939.

Undoubtedly this rim of states was essential to Russia for strategic and military purposes when she went in and took them. The charges Russia made against them were typical power politics pretexts for aggression. Mass arrests followed the Russian assumption of control and thousands were deported from all three countries. The "set-up" elections were interpreted by Russia as requests to join the Soviet Union and in August, 1940, the three countries were "accepted" by the Soviet Supreme Council as the fourteenth, fifteenth, and sixteenth Soviet republics. Sovietization began at once. The advances of the past generation were wiped out and the nationalization of banks, property, and agriculture began.[30]

The new governments set up under the Russian aegis were headed by Premier Gedvilas in Lithuania, Professor Kirchensteins in Latvia, and Dr. Vares in Estonia. The Communist Party, which had been illegal in all three countries for twenty years, came out into the open and seized power. Communists were released from jail and glorified.[31]

Collaboration with the new Soviet master differed in the three countries. Coöperation was slowest to develop in Lithuania. It was easier to secure in Latvia and Estonia. Social Democrats and the more radical intelligentsia were converted into Communists as the states became Soviet Socialist republics. They adopted the Soviet form of political organization. The ministries were not particularly changed as to form, but were drastically altered in purpose and methods.

Industry and agriculture were completely reorganized. Much property and many economic enterprises were nationalized. The system of free enterprise and the right of the individual to carry on his own economic activities were abolished. Owners of land were prevented from disposing of their property freely. State-owned tractor and agricultural machinery stations were established. Small farms were amalgamated into collective farms (kolkhozy) and State farms (sovkhozy). In short, the whole economic set-up of the Baltic states was subjected to sweeping changes.

But the Russians were not permitted to bring their sovietization to a conclusion at this time. Barely nine months had elapsed after they took

---

[30] The Russians took over control of all means of communication and, by imposing the strictest censorship, prevented any news of activities from reaching the outside world. For a similar statement to the above, see Bilmanis, *op. cit.*, p. 47.

[31] Meiksins, *op. cit.*, pp. 118-119. His Chapter IX should be offset by the more mature and balanced treatment in Bilmanis, *op. cit.*

over control in the Baltic when the German conquest swept into the area and reached Riga and Tallinn in July, 1941. The Russians had killed thousands and deported thousands to Siberia to forced labor camps. The new German rule over the three countries, which were organized into the German province of Ostland,[32] was also harsh, resulting in the killing of more of the people and the deportation of additional thousands to Germany to work in German factories. Both Russians and Germans enlisted citizens of the Baltic states in their armed forces.

Ostland was the area covered by the three Baltic states and White Russia. The territory was governed by a German Commissioner responsible to the German Minister for Occupied Territory. H. Lohse was appointed to that post on July 17, 1941, and during the rest of that year he issued the orders on which German rule rested until it was replaced by the returning Russians. Each of the states constituted one of four administrative districts with its own individual commissioner.

Late in July, the Commissioner for the Ostland called upon the people to place their resources at his disposal for the restoration of order and employment. This was followed by the announcement that the Commissioner had taken over all executive power without any intention of interfering with the military authorities. In this same order he announced that he was taking over all property "of the U.S.S.R., of the states forming part of it, and of bodies corporate, associations, and unions, including all claims, shares, rights and interests of all kinds . . ." [33] Shortly thereafter this order was followed by the announcement that private ownership, taken away by the Russians, would be restored. In order to do this, the property actually belonging to the Soviet Union would be confiscated. All property had to be registered with an administrator. A system was established for the handling of confiscated property. New German companies were given special privileges and were responsible only to the Commissioner.

Sovietized urban property was confiscated. Business undertakings had to have the approval of the Commissioner before they became binding if they pertained to real estate, farming, insurance, or a number of other undertakings. Organizations were set up to enforce these measures. An Economic Chamber for Ostland was created. Other organizations were established to take over the Soviet associations, particularly those which dealt with producing and marketing.

---

[32] An excellent treatment of this whole subject will be found in the *International Labour Review*, XLIX:2 (February, 1944), pp. 171-190.

[33] "The Baltic Republics and White Russia Under German Occupation, 1941-1942," *International Labour Review*, XLIX:2 (February, 1944), p. 173.

Handicrafts, retail trade, and small private enterprises were encouraged. Their promotion was attempted through handicraftsmen's unions, which regulated the price of the articles as well as the methods of their production. In many ways this represented a return to the old guild economy. A license was required for such undertakings as well as for any small industry, which was described as one that employed twenty people or less. Wherever these enterprises had been nationalized by the Russians, they were to be handed over to their original owners in return for the payment of the current cost.

As far as possible, the Germans cancelled the changes made in the agriculture of the Baltic republics by Russia between 1940 and 1941. Wherever the Soviet state had held possession of farms, the Germans took over. An order of September 13, 1941, attempted regulation of both the small farms and the large collective farms. Holdings detached from large private farms by the Russians were returned to the original holding, and the occupiers were regarded as tenant farmers. Administrators were appointed for the abandoned lands. Instead of changing the state farms and the tractor stations they were simply transferred to German possession. The whole agricultural organization and its administration was placed under the Ostland Land Management Association, which managed, operated, and improved the state farms. Wages for agricultural workers were regulated, and so was marketing.

Needless to say the whole population was subjected to rationing. Labor was recruited for work in Ostland and laborers were required to register. Employment cards were issued. In the latter part of 1942, labor was made compulsory in agriculture for inhabitants between the ages of 18 and 45. This order applied to the Ostland area proper. Price and wage controls were set up and organizations were established to deal with the wage tax, fines imposed on the worker by the employer, hours of work, and rights of association and assembly.

The old Estonian, Latvian, and Lithuanian insurance societies,[34] which were about to be replaced by the Soviet insurance system, came to an end with German rule. Old-age pensions and disability insurance were doubled. War workers were favorably treated. And, as everywhere under Nazi rule, no payments could be made to "Jews and Bolsheviks."

In the summer of 1944, the Russians began the drives which eventu-

---

[34] "Compulsory Accident Insurance in Lithuania," *Monthly Labour Review*, XLIII:5 (November, 1936), pp. 1146-1148; "Sickness and Accident Insurance for Workers in Esthonia," *Ibid.*, XXXII:6 (June, 1931), pp. 77-81; "Old Age, Invalidity, and Survivors Insurance for Professional Workers in Estonia," *Ibid.*, XLI:1 (July, 1935), pp. 41-42.

ally carried them to the Baltic Sea, and the Baltic states once again came under Soviet control. Fighting went on in this area until the spring of 1945. As sections of all three countries were restored to Russian dominance, the process of communization, interrupted in 1941, was completed. Censorship blotted out all except scraps of occasional news, and what did leak out revealed that the Baltic peoples were once more undergoing political changes, peaceful wherever possible, but under compulsion when peaceful methods would not suffice.

The Future

Thus, in a span of less than thirty years, Lithuania, Latvia, and Estonia have been successively the subjects of Russia; free and independent democracies; dictatorships; the conquered territory of Russia; the conquered territory of Germany; and again the reconquered territory of Russia. They have experienced revolution, warfare, upheavals in their basic economies and social structures, violent changes in political systems, mass deportations and killings, forced labor, and other hardships. The terrific toll in life, resources, raw materials, equipment, and institutions cannot even be approximately estimated.

Nationalization and the confiscation of private property, the sapping of the strength of independent political institutions, the loss of cultural and intellectual advances, and the limitations on freedom have changed these states completely. It seems futile to assess the problem in terms of who may or may not be to blame. German and Russian assertions about the benevolence of their respective rules can hardly be sustained by an objective study of the facts.

After all, Lithuania, Latvia, and Estonia sought only independence and freedom.[35] They did not wish Russian or German rule. But it is hardly likely that considerations of power politics and Russian ambitions will permit them any restoration of freedom except as defined by Marx and the Bolshevik philosophy.

Although the United States has refused, up to the time of writing, to acknowledge the Russian acquisition, and has allowed the diplomatic representatives of the Baltic states to remain in Washington, Stalin is evidently determined to assure the most strategically advantageous boundaries for Russia. Great Britain answered Russia's request for the recognition of the Soviet acquisitions by explaining that it was impossible for Britain to recognize territorial changes until after the war. By the summer of 1945, it was apparent that there was very little chance

---

[35] *Life*, XXXIII:24 (June 12, 1939), pp. 21 and 22, for a statement made in the coolness of objectivity.

of modifying Moscow's decision to keep the Baltic states as part of the Soviet Union.

Bibliography

Akzin, Benjamin, "Choices Before the Baltic States," *Foreign Affairs,* XV:3 (April, 1937), pp. 495-508. A useful summary as of 1937.

Bates, Mary Estella, *Bulletin of Bibliography,* Vol. 17 (Boston: F. W. Faxon, 1943). Pages 6 and 7 give a workable bibliography in English on Lithuania. This may be used in conjunction with "Modern Books on Lithuania," *The Literary Journal,* LVII:17 (October 1, 1932), pp. 816-818.

Benedictsen, Age Meyer, *Lithuania* (Copenhagen, 1924). Comment in Chapter VII.

Bihlmans, Alfred, *Latvia in the Making, 1918-1928* (Riga: Riga Times Edition, 1928). Excellent handbook of useful information.

Hale, Richard W., *Letters of Warwick Greene* (Boston: Houghton Mifflin, 1931). Some background on the formation of the independent Baltic republics.

Henman, Gabriel, *Aspects Juridiques de l'Independance Esthonienne* (Paris: A. Pedone, 1938). A splendid treatment of the achievement of independence, the Baltic confederation, and similar matters.

Hoetzsch, Otto, "The Baltic States," *Foreign Affairs,* X:1 (October, 1931), pp. 120-133. A realistic evaluation of the Baltic states in their power politics relationships.

Ten Years of Lithuanian Economy, Report of the Chamber of Commerce, Industry, and Crafts (Kaunas: Vilniaus, 1938). A clear-cut demonstration of the progress made during a generation of independence.

The Baltic States, A Survey of the Political and Economic Structure and the Foreign Relations of Esthonia, Latvia and Lithuania (London: Oxford University [Royal Institute of International Affairs], 1938). Authoritative, scholarly, but does not cover the more recent phases.

Vitola, H., *La Mer Baltique et les états baltics* (Paris: Domat-Montchrestién, 1935). Background for both Chapters VII and XXI.

THE BALKANS (1918-1945)

THE Balkan states after World War I consisted of Romania, Yugoslavia, Bulgaria, Albania, and Greece. The new political boundaries undoubtedly left fewer people separated from their fellow-countrymen by national frontiers than before. But there were still permanent minority groups throughout the Balkans whose continuous agitation did much to disturb the political atmosphere of the region. This was especially true when the Great Powers utilized the dissatisfaction of these minorities as a weapon in the constant game of power politics.

Balkan history is not easily understood by the Westerner, for it is personal to a degree that the Anglo-Saxon mind can never grasp. Balkan politics is first and foremost a contest among personalities. The royal courts, backed by their armies, ruled their respective countries in much the same way as former Turkish pashas. That is why the court camarillas and the army played such a preponderant role in the internal political struggles of all these countries between the two World Wars.

As a result, power in the Balkans has tended to remain concentrated in the hands of dominant minorities, while the majorities became increasingly self-conscious and aggressive in their political demands. These majority groups consisted of peasants, a growing middle class, industrial and agricultural workers, and national minorities. But they failed to become effectively mobilized, since personalities are more important in Balkan politics than mass movements expressed in terms of parties. Political parties were often mere loose associations grouped around personal leaders. Generally, they lacked coherent programs and spent their greatest efforts in arousing the rampant nationalism of the masses to a high pitch.

This is in part explained by the lack of organization and of a clearly defined ideology which is usually associated with an agricultural society. Geographical isolation, with its inevitable corollary of suspicion, also played a part. No explanation could be complete, however, without taking into consideration the fact that even the most enlightened of the Balkan states are only now emerging from the traditions of feudalism. It is true that the Balkan constitutions provided for parliamentary democracy, but this was mostly window-dressing. The borrowed forms of democracy had no real background in the political evolution of the Balkans.

The personal character of Balkan politics is intensified by the fact that officialdom fights bitterly to retain its position against the hazards of political change. There is an excess of people qualified for administrative work. The Balkan governments were founded by educated nationals who were, in the early years of self-rule, completely absorbed by governmental bureaus. Within a few post-war years, the bureaucracy was overgrown, the peasant was resentful, and there was a consequent tribalization of political groups into warring bureaucratic wings anxious to retain or obtain the only middle-class anchorage—the office of *fonctionnaire*.

Underneath the whole system of the Balkans is the peasant—paying heavy taxes, groaning under weighty burdens, but carrying on. He has suffered and been imposed upon for so many centuries that he has even forgotten his occasional bloody revolutions of the past and has kept going in the post-war years without audible protest—although the Romanian National Peasant Party made a vain bid for enduring political power. The important fact remains that—although the proportion of the agricultural groups ranges from 60 to 90 per cent in the Balkans—the political make-up of the Balkan states failed to mirror the social structure. Only in Romania did the National Peasant Party have a chance to rule briefly in the thirties. Otherwise the states were actually run by the town and city intelligentsia, merchants, small industrialists, and bankers.

The political contests among these privileged groups were very bitter and frequently assumed the aspects of minor wars, especially during elections. The spoils system presented its worst features in the Balkans. This system utilized parliament as a sort of appendage to impress outsiders and the populace with its theoretical democratic practices. In actual application, the system nearly always featured a monopoly of political power by one party, headed by the ruler.

However, a definite distinction between the dictatorial system in the Balkans and those in Russia, Germany, and Italy should be noted. In the latter countries, totalitarian regimes were openly supported by a political ideology which gave full endorsement to the Communist, Nazi, Fascist doctrines, respectively. In the Balkans, the ideology theoretically supported democratic principles as expressed in constitutional cliches and proclamations.

The basic social divisions agitating post-war Balkan politics were, consequently, hard to discern. The forces of agrarianism and of the towns were most glaringly in opposition in Romania and Bulgaria. In Albania, a small group of intelligentsia and the new bourgeoisie were trying to get the upper hand over the landowners. In Greece, the monarchistic-republican issue was complicated by the dividing line runing between the forces of the more aggressive refugees and the inhabitants of the old Greece. In Yugoslavia, the forces of decentralization and tribalism were opposed to the domination of Belgrade, headed by· the Serbs.

World War II gave birth to liberal movements throughout the Balkans which seriously disturbed the peace of mind of kings and politicians who hoped to re-establish the old regimes in their respective countries after the war. It appeared by 1945 that the peoples of the Balkans (with the possible exception of Romania) were staunchly republican and vehemently opposed to royalty. They were aiming for governments that would try to raise the standard of living of workers and peasants rather than of the royal cliques. Many Balkan spokesmen believed that it was imperative to establish new governments, totally different from those that ruled their respective countries before the invasion by Hitler's armies and "tourists."

All of the conflicting forces described above operated within the framework of Europe's power politics. Behind the moves of Balkan foreign ministers there always was the heavy hand of a Great Power interested in shifting slightly, for its own benefit, the precarious balance upon which the fragile structure of Balkan peace was built.

Post-war Balkan history can be divided into four definite periods. The first, lasting from the "great parade" to the rise of Hitler's Reich, was characterized by the efforts of Italy to replace French and British influence in the Balkans—a region then seething with enmities among its states. The second period witnessed the struggle between centripetal schemes for Danubian coöperation with Franco-British encouragement. The third was formally inaugurated by the Munich Pact of October 1, 1938, which confirmed the ascendancy of Germany's renewed *Drang nach Osten,* the retreat of the Western democracies in the Balkans, and the forceful extension of German supremacy foreshadowed in the second period. The fourth period brought Russian domination in place of German.

Hitler's conquest of the Balkans was bound to be only temporary. Although the authoritarian regimes of the Balkans were but precursors of Hitler's rule, Nazi overlordship only increased the instability of the area. Both Nazis and Fascists deepened existing antagonisms by playing one faction against another, by favoring one nation at the expense of its neighbors. The results of this policy were widespread sabotage, guerrilla warfare, and mass executions. Russia's dramatic return to the Balkans in 1944 indicated the broadening of Soviet influence in southeastern Europe. This new variation of Pan-Slavism was inaugurated by Moscow's support of the guerrilla forces of Marshal Tito.

The original Pan-Slav idea—the possibility of uniting all Slavs under the leadership of the greatest Slav nation, Russia—obtained a foothold in the Balkans during the later days of the Ottoman Empire. Russia employed it first as a weapon against Turkey and then against Austria-Hungary and Germany. Balkan Slavs have traditionally looked to Russia as the mother state. During the last century, Pan-Slavism helped—when it suited the Tsars—to obtain the liberation of the Slavs from Turkish rule. Even today, many Serb peasants believe that imperial Russia collapsed after her entrance in the last war to save Serbia and to free the Croats, Slovenes, and Bosnians from Viennese domination.

Sentiment has always been overbalanced by logic in the analysis of Pan-Slavism. This is made clear when we remember that Pan-Slavism did not prevent two wars between the Serbs and Bulgarians since 1912, Czech seizure of Tešín from the Poles after World War I, and the Polish recapture of Tešín after Munich, the anti-Russian policies of the Bulgars, the antagonism of the Yugoslav royal family to Communist Russia, and the traditional hostility between Poles and Russians. But by 1945 Russia had returned to the Balkans as the determining factor. While Greece remained under British influence, Russia's word was final everywhere else in the Balkans.

CHAPTER XXII

ROMANIA (1918-1945)

Geopolitical Situation

AFTER World War I, Romania was a Latin island almost surrounded by Slavic and Magyar seas. Here East and West intermingled; Byzantine and Gothic, minaret and cross, stood side by side. Romania sheltered alike the Transylvanian shepherd with his ten-foot horn and the Bucharest boyar with his aristocratic palace.

But Romania's new possessions gave her trouble because of the inevitable minority problems. Out of Romania's 19 million people, about 4.5 million were national minorities: 1.4 million Hungarians (in Transylvania); 800,000 Germans (mostly in Transylvania); 400,000 Bulgars (in the Dobrudja), 300,000 Russians (in Bessarabia); 200,000 Turks and Tartars (in the Dobrudja); and 900,000 Jews scattered all over the country. These minorities were a constant source of friction and bad feeling. The Romanians endeavored to absorb the foreigners by attempting to wipe out all traces of their origins. The minorities charged that they were oppressed. The neighboring states (particularly Hungary) were incensed and hoped to regain their losses. And Russia, while she agreed not to go to war over Bessarabia, did not recognize Romania's claim to the territory.

There were also religious divisions. The national Church of Romania is the Orthodox Church, but freedom of worship was recognized by the constitution. In 1938 there were about 13,200,000 members of the Orthodox Church; 1,426,800 Greek Orthodox; 1,200,000 Roman Catholics; 720,000 Reformists; 400,000 Lutherans; 75,000 Unitarians; 1,500,000 Jews; 260,000 Moslems; and 140,000 others.

Economic Factors

The economic wealth of Romania rests chiefly on agriculture—and oil. She had to pay for this wealth when Hitler started driving for world conquest, for Romania could satisfy the most pressing hungers

of Nazi Germany—wheat for the stomachs of its people and oil to run
its machines. Romania, with one-sixth of the population of Germany,
produced almost as much wheat, both on the fertile plateau of Transylvania and on the black soil of Old Romania.

The country produced far more oil and natural gas than all the rest
of non-Soviet Europe combined, though three-quarters of it was wasted
by poor management. The oil bubbled out of the ground east and west
of Ploesti on the southern side of the Transylvanian Alps, right in front
of the Predeal Pass. And Romania also had coal, iron, lead, zinc,
copper, mercury, bauxite, aluminum, antimony, gold, silver, salt, and
graphite. It has only lately begun the long process of learning how
to exploit these assets.

Romania was and still is overwhelmingly a backward agricultural
country trying hard to learn about machinery. Almost 80 per cent of
the population were peasants. The majority of them lived on small
holdings producing no more than the bare minimum necessary for
existence. Before the agrarian reform (1919-1921), 42 per cent of the
cultivable land belonged to large estates (about 250 acres or more)
and 58 per cent to small farms. After the reform, the former percentage dropped to 11.2, and the latter increased to 88.8. But the peasants
had to borrow money at interest rates ranging from 30 to 50 per cent
to buy seed and tools. The agricultural per capita debt became the
highest in the world.

In addition to other assets, Romania also had vast forests. The country underwent rather extensive industrialization—but suffered from
lack of credit and the extremely low purchasing power of the people.
Moreover, the transportation system was insufficient to take care of the
needs of the sprawling kingdom.

Social Conditions

It is impossible to understand Romania (or the rest of the Balkans)
without remembering that Turkey ruled the whole region up to a century ago. Many bad habits hang on. Until after World War I, ver-
min infested even the big hotels. Tips (*baksheesh*) were necessary to
get a locomotive engineer to drive his train, a station master to let it
go through. Statesmen were also known as pickpockets. A fairly
respectable profession (particularly in fashion during Hitler's time)
was that of assassin. But in the twenty years after the war, Romania
cleaned herself up considerably.

The most important move was to hand out nearly 90 per cent of
Romania's farm land to the peasants. Much of this was taken from

Hungarian and Tsarist aristocrats and from the Catholic Church, whose properties Romania had received in the peace treaties. The superior civilization of the Hungarian peoples west of the mountains was a de-Balkanizing influence for Romania after 1918. Finally, Romanian oil attracted capital from Britain, France, and Italy, as well as America, and Romanian oil and wheat bought great quantities of machinery from Germany.

But by the end of the second decade of Romania's independence, all this civilizing took an unfortunate turn. After the war, the government filled the higher schools with peasant boys on free scholarships. The great majority of them grew up to be violent reactionaries and joined a fascist, anti-Semitic organization called the Iron Guard.

Cultural Development

In the twenty years after the war, Romania made considerable strides in cultural advancement, based on a rich cultural background.

The origin of the Romanian language dates back as far as the fourth century and was in general use among the population in the ninth century. The first printing office was founded by Lutheran Saxons in Transylvania. The first Romanian book was a catechism printed in 1544 in Sibiu in Cyrillic letters, followed by another one in Cluj. The first complete translation of the New Testament appeared in Alba-Julia in 1648.

By the end of the seventeenth century, Romanian had become the authorized language of the Church. After 1727, Romanian was also recognized as the language of the law-courts. In Moldavia and Wallachia, the theater played an important role in promoting the use of the language as a means of rallying the new generation against the tyranny of a Greek court.

The development of Romanian intellectual life can be traced in the history of its literature. The chroniclers Miron Costin, Ion Neculce, and Dimitrie Cantemir, who recorded the history of the Princes and Principalities, were followed at the end of the eighteenth and the beginning of the nineteenth centuries by a phalanx of philologists and historians who strove to bring out the Latin origins of the Romanian language and people. Then came the classic authors, who sought to enrich the written language with neo-Latin elements or with the beautiful products of folklore. However, it was only after it had passed through Titu Maiorescu's sieve of severe criticism that Romanian literature gave forth its triple blossom of genius—the poetry of Mihai Eminescu, the prose of Ion Creanga, and the drama of I. Caragiale.

Painting went through a similar evolutionary process. Under the influence of the West, painting was freed from ecclesiastical art (Theodor Aman, Tatarascu, and Andreescu) in the nineteenth century. It drew inspiration from the Barbizon school and brought out the picturesqueness of the Romanian landscape (N. Grigorescu); and it fathomed the depth of the Romanian soul and the Romanian love of colors (Luchian). Peasant art and customs have always enchanted all students of Romania's life. Enesco's Romanian symphonies are world-famous and have been heard more and more in America in recent years.

Political Forces

After 1918, still another turbulent stream entered the maelstrom of strife: the rivalry between "new province" Romanians and "old kingdom" Romanians. Before the First World War, Romania was an L-shaped land of 50,715 square miles. The peace treaties rounded it out into a circle of 122,282 square miles, making it the largest of Europe's small countries.

The Romanians in the western province (Transylvania), even though they had been kept in an inferior position by Hungarians, Germans, and Jews, considered themselves "European" and felt superior to the "Balkan" Romanians from the old kingdom with their "Byzantine culture." However, practically all political power was retained by "old kingdom" men and the capital is the "old kingdom" city of Bucharest. The "new" Romanians felt a bitter enmity against the "old" Romanians, which gave rise to regional friction such as once existed between the northern and southern parts of the United States.

The minority question cursed Romania not only nationalistically but also socially. Foreigners dominated most of its cities and controlled many of its financial, mercantile, and industrial enterprises. Most of these foreigners were intellectually superior to the Romanians and lorded it over them. They were cultured, wealthy, and dominant— whereas the Romanians were ignorant, poor, and dominated. In most of the country, the Romanians were peasants or shepherds, wearing hand-woven clothes, with their long, flowing shirts outside their trousers. They had no white collars or shiny shoes. They lived in villages or on the outskirts of towns and were not allowed to penetrate into urban centers. Very few attended the universities—and even fewer held high positions.

In 1918, political power passed into the hands of the Romanians, but foreigners still retained economic and financial dominance. Business, banks, and factories were controlled to a large extent by non-Romanians. In every single new-province city, the Romanians were in a minority. The best houses were inhabited by people of other nationalities. Most of the local press was printed in foreign languages. The Romanians were still considered inferior in large parts of their own country.

All this helped to arouse intense Romanian hatred of foreigners and especially of Jews. The Jews owned, controlled, and wrote a large part of the newspapers. They managed many of the theaters. They conducted much of the country's business and once owned most of the banks. They were the innkeepers and moneylenders in a number of the villages. They used to fill the universities and occupied leading places in all the professions. Being diligent and capable, they got ahead, so they appeared to be rich in the midst of wretchedly poor Romanians. Most young Romanians could not rise in the over-filled professions and imagined it was the foreigners, especially the Jews, who blocked their path. The reaction developed into a terrific nationalistic and anti-Semitic torrent.

The early post-war period saw a slow change in the strained relations between the peasant and urban classes. The franchise introduced the town politician into the village, and increased trading activities brought the peasant into frequent contact with urban communities. A growing group of the young intelligentsia became sincerely interested in rural life and stressed the national importance of the Romanian village.

The agrarian reform of 1919-21 and the agitation of the National Peasant Party started to change the mentality of the peasant. This party took the place vacated by the Liberals on the Left of Romanian politics, becoming the chief democratic element in the nation. Dr. Juliu Maniu became its leader. The National Peasant organization developed its agrarian ideology in juxtaposition to the mercantilism of the Liberals. It advocated parliamentary democracy; coöperative organization of peasant economy in production, marketing, and credit; subordination of industry to the interests of agriculture; and coöperative education of the peasant. Firmly entrenched in the villages, the party was the chief opponent of fascism and other forms of authoritarianism in Romania.

These, therefore, were the forces in Romania's political whirlpool. The wretched, illiterate masses opposed a rich and favored elite; peasants opposed city-dwellers; the long-frustrated natives opposed foreigners who had dominated them; and adroit, experienced "Balkan" Romanians lorded it over the softer and more pretentious "European" Romanians.

Trends in Political Fortunes

When World War I ended, the Liberals, headed by the Bratianu family, rode on the wave of popular acclaim and royal approval. Ion I. C. Bratianu (1864-1927) and Vintila I. C. Bratianu (1867-1930), the sons of the "Grand Old Man," controlled the Liberal Party, which replaced the Conservatives in power. They represented entrenched urban wealth and the "educated" minority, and they protected financial, industrial, and commercial interests. The party opposed foreign domination of Romanian financial and commercial enterprise, as well as oil concessions to foreign companies. It advocated the so-called "royal parliamentarianism" typical of the Balkan states—monarchic authority within the framework of a parliamentary system, with the king as a governor, not as a mere conciliator. In and out of the government, the Bratianus gave the orders and "made" the elections. Ion Bratianu pushed through the constitution of 1923, which was theoretically very democratic, and forced the abdication of Crown Prince Carol, who threatened to dispense with him once he came to power.

But gradually the Liberals lost their grip. The strain of growing economic and financial difficulties forced Ion Bratianu to resign in 1926. A year later King Ferdinand died—and four months later Bratianu was also carried to his grave. His brother Vintila headed the reconstructed government under the Regency. But the strength of the Liberal Party had passed with King Ferdinand and Ion Bratianu. In November, 1928, Maniu's National Peasant Party came into power.

Temporarily this shifted the center of political gravity from the Right to the Left, from mercantilism to the peasantry. Romania had the first peasant government in her history. Within a few weeks, press censorship and the state of siege were abolished; anti-Semitic riots were stopped; and the political, administrative, and financial systems began to be reorganized. Tendencies of centralization gave way to revived local autonomy, and the minorities were treated more liberally. The elections of December, 1928, were free and fair.

But Maniu lasted only two years. His intention of building a new democratic political and economic structure collided head-on with the heritage left by the Liberals. The bureaucracy boycotted the new cabinet. The public was sharply critical of the higher tax rate. The world-wide agricultural crisis forced Maniu to temporize—and to repatriate Carol, who had been living in exile with his Magda Lupescu. Maniu engineered the repatriation as a preventive measure against the restoration of the Liberals under Vintila Bratianu, Carol's foe.

King Carol

In June, 1930, Carol returned to Bucharest by airplane to displace his little son, King Michael. With the help of Nicholas, his brother and one of the regents, and with the support of the army and Maniu's adherents, Carol had the parliament confer the title of Prince of Alba-Julia on his son and proclaimed himself King Carol II.

When Maniu insisted that Carol keep his promise to make up with his wife, Helen, and to terminate the Lupescu affair, Carol got tired of his moralizing Premier and thereafter started replacing Premiers in quick succession. Carol deliberately promoted political instability in order to create the impression that the "old" political parties, led by "old stagers," were incapable of government. For example, there were eight cabinet crises between 1930 and 1933. The eighth cabinet was presided over by I. G. Duca, who was assassinated by three student members of the Iron Guard.

At first, Carol was received with joy by his longsuffering people. They looked upon him as a leader who would establish justice, punish grafters, and enable all Romanians to prosper. Naturally, Carol could not make such dreams come true, even if he had been a perfect ruler, which he was not. Carol's reign was marked by personal domination. He allowed no one to share mastery with him. For a while he preserved the forms of parliamentarianism, but he used them as an instrument to increase his personal authority. As soon as he found himself unable to dictate the popular suffrage, he abolished the constitution.

Carol's personal domination seemed all the more obnoxious to many because it appeared to be exercised through a small group of court favorites, of which Madame Lupescu was a leading member. She came to be a symbol of autocratic royal power; an emblem of frustration of the popular will.

Popular dissatisfaction was expressed through four main channels. First was the National Peasant Party, led by the honest, fearless ex-Premier Juliu Maniu, a "new province" Romanian devoted to democracy. Next came the fanatical, terroristic fascist party called "All for the Fatherland." It was led by a fiery, revolutionary, ruthless youth called Captain Corneliu Zelea Codreanu, and was made up of desperate boys and girls determined at all costs to make Romania over. This dynamic popular force in Romania enjoyed the allegiance of most students, many young officers, and many young priests. It was terribly in earnest and stopped at nothing. Third came a branch of the Liberal

Party, led by George Bratianu, a member of Romania's most famous political dynasty. The fourth group was the violently anti-Semitic National Christian Party led by a poet, Octavian Goga, and a professor, Constantine Cuza.

After the end of 1933, Carol governed Romania through his able personal representative, George Tatarescu, and the Liberal Party, of which Tatarescu was the secretary. The cabinet, the parliament, and the party faithfully carried out the king's wishes and all went well— for them—until their term of office expired in the winter of 1937, after which new elections were held. For the first time in all Romanian history, the people voted out a government on December 20, 1937. The king's personal regime received less than 38 per cent of the votes. The masses, defying coercion and intimidation, broke all precedents, violated all traditions, and defeated a government at the polls.

In order to gain time to work out a new plan, Carol temporarily placed power in the hands of the rabid anti-Semitic agitator, Octavian Goga. When everything was ready, he restored the old Liberal cabinet with a few alterations and under the nominal leadership of the Patriarch Miron Cristea. Since the people had once voted this cabinet out, the king could keep it in power only by disfranchising the people. He did this by abolishing the old constitution, placing the country under military control, and asking the nation to accept a new constitution by open voting.

The fake plebiscite held on this constitution ran true to fascist form. All parties were banned and parliament was abolished. The king was a dictator in form as in fact, and the regime which had evoked unprecedented popular opposition was continued.

King Carol meant business as a dictator. He got tired of the agitation of the Iron Guard. Thousands of Iron Guard followers were arrested. Codreanu was suddenly hauled before a court martial and was sentenced to ten years' penal servitude on May 19, 1938. All other parties felt the heavy royal hand.

In this three-sided contest for power between the king, Nazism (supported by Hitler), and the adherents of parliamentary democracy, Carol had the upper hand for a while. The world was surprised but little shocked to learn, on November 30, 1938, of the sudden demise of Codreanu and 13 of his closest associates in the Iron Guard, all convicted murderers. On the way to a judicial investigation, the trucks carrying the prisoners, according to the official report, were ambushed by Iron Guard sympathizers in a densely wooded section of the road.

The guards, instructed to shoot, used machine guns to mow down the convicts because they were "trying to escape." The police thereafter continued their merciless drive against the terrorist Iron Guard.

Meanwhile the king, acting through a newly organized National Renascence Front, proceeded to a wholesale reorganization of many key departments of the nation's life. The first corporative parliament under the new constitution was chosen on June 1, 1939, and assembled on June 7. The powers of parliament were limited to the examination of bills submitted to it by the cabinet, which was directly responsible to the king. But strong democratic and underground fascist and communist movements continued to agitate for Carol's overthrow. The Iron Guard struck at Carol again on September 21, 1939, amid the confusion caused by the collapse of Polish resistance to the joint German-Soviet attack and the flight of thousands of Polish refugees across the Romanian border. Six Iron Guard members assassinated Premier Armand Calinescu in Bucharest as a prelude to a country-wide uprising, instigated from Berlin. The government exacted terrible reprisals.

As soon as France fell in June, 1940, King Carol, who had changed his mind in the preceding months about as fast as he changed uniforms, decided the time had come to cast his lot with Germany. He scrapped his "Party of National Rebirth" in favor of a new "Party of the Nation," which the Iron Guard was invited to join. Carol even announced that "officials responsible for killing Iron Guardists in recent years will be punished." The king hoped that conciliation of the pro-German Guard would win him Hitler's favor.

Then there was the trouble with Russia over Bessarabia. In 1940, Stalin was pushing his frontier to the west against the day of inevitable war with Germany. Carol decided to become a warm public admirer of Hitler, in the hope that the Fuehrer might scare Stalin away.

The Propaganda Ministry lost its head completely. Its incoherent attempts to reassure the people reached a climax in the following story, circulated throughout the country:

"Rumanian citizens will remember that in the last war the Russians, then our Allies, guzzled all the liquor they could get their hands on. Rumanians will remember that Russian drunkenness brought them several defeats. Informed quarters in Bucharest revealed today that the General Staff has moved big stocks of cheap brandy and vodka into the frontier regions. It is certain that Russian troops, if they come in, will repeat their performance of the last war and will be totally unable to function because of drunkenness.[1]

The panicky government had to give up Bessarabia to Russia in July, 1940. Northern Bukovina was engulfed at the same time, although the

---

[1] Parker, Robert, *Headquarters Budapest* (New York: Farrar & Rinehart, 1944), p. 225.

territory had formerly belonged to Austria-Hungary. As the German octopus tightened its tentacles on the country, in August, 1940, Bucharest had to yield southern Dobrudja to Bulgaria. On August 31, 1940, the Rome-Berlin Axis forced Romania to cede a portion of Transylvania to Hungary.

The measures adopted by Carol in attempting to stave off German politico-economic domination paralleled in many ways those resorted to by Hungary and other states in southeastern Europe exposed to expansive Nazi pressure. While avoiding an open break with the Reich, Carol angled for support from Britain, France, the Soviet Union, and even Italy. At the same time he sought to check German propaganda within his kingdom by adopting much of the Hitlerian social and economic program and establishing a totalitarian state under his own, rather than German, control. But all this was futile. Carol again fled into exile on September 6, 1940, after surrendering his power to General Ion Antonescu. He took with him a fortune in gold and jewels in a bullet-riddled train made up of cars borrowed from the Orient Express.[2]

Antonescu

Under Antonescu, Romania became a pro-fascist military dictatorship overnight, with only insignificant authority vested in King Michael, the son and nominal successor of Carol II. Antonescu established the Iron Guard as the only recognized party of the state and took the title of "Conducator." The constitution of 1938 was abolished on September 6, 1940, and six days later Romania was proclaimed a "National Legionary State."

But Antonescu's regime was unable to preserve order. At the end of 1940, armed legionnaires of the green-shirted fascist, anti-Semitic Iron Guard broke into the gloomy Jihlava fortress prison. They dragged out 64 Carolists and lined them up in front of a long trench from whose top they had just ripped a concrete slab. In the frosty dawn they opened fire and watched the bodies crumple to earth. Theirs was a mission of revenge. From the trench they had removed the bodies of Iron Guard founder Corneliu Zelea Codreanu and 13 other Guardists, executed on the same spot just three days less than two years before. Then blood lust rushed through the whole disaster-sickened country. One-time Premier Professor Nicolas Iorga, tutor of King Carol and

---

[2] The period of the Nazi penetration is well-described in Countess Waldeck, *Athene Palace* (New York: Robert M. McBride, 1942); see also Pavel Pavel, *Why Rumania Failed* (London: Alliance Press, 1944); Robert Parker, *Headquarters Budapest* (New York: Farrar & Rinehart, 1944), an unreliable but exciting account.

eminent historian, "the teacher of the nation," was found dead on the outskirts of the oil fields near his country home at Valeni-de-Munte. Though both Romanian and German troops promptly occupied key buildings in Bucharest, murder followed murder as the days sped by. The riots quickly turned from political to racial hysteria and thousands of Jews perished. Civil war came next, and army and Iron Guard battalions battled in the streets in open warfare. This gave Germany another pretext to send additional troops into the stricken country.

On November 23, 1940, Antonescu's government signed the Axis Tripartite Pact, following by three days its far-from-beloved neighbor, Hungary. This signature was not, however, a world-shaking event; it merely confirmed a growing trend.

Antonescu had a difficult time convincing the Romanians of the usefulness of his policies. Sabotage mounted steadily. An uprising was reported in January, 1943, and another one in February, following the announcement that there had been 400,000 casualties among Romanian troops fighting in Russia. Heinrich Himmler had to dispatch his right-hand man, Dr. Ernst Kaltenbrunner, to take over the direction of Romanian police forces because of mounting unrest within the country. All this was happening in spite of the fact that, when the Axis forces overran the Soviet Union's Ukraine, Romania not only recovered part of the 1940 cessions but also won an extra prize in a slice of the U.S.S.R. east of the Dniester River.

At the turn of 1944, the dependence of the German military machine on Romanian oil production placed an additional stamp of importance on reports of internal dissension among the Romanian people and even among members of the government itself. Antonescu found it necessary to have himself appointed supreme judge, so that all "justice" in Romania could be invested in himself alone. Persons accused of economic sabotage were either executed or sent with their families to Transdniestra (the area generally including Bessarabia and the rest of the territory beyond the Dniester River almost to the Axis-held Russian city of Odessa). But these violent measures could not suppress growing dissatisfaction among the people, who could not forget that their country had lost not only its richest province (Transylvania), but also 400,000 of its sons on the field of battle—for Hitler. Marshal Antonescu, the "architect of a new Romania," seldom appeared in public any more. The sporadic but highly effective raids on the Ploesti oil fields by Allied aircraft resulted in terrific damage.

In the early half of 1944, Romania became a battleground of the Soviet armies.

Romania Changes Horses in Midstream

On August 23, 1944, London broadcast the electrifying news that Romania had accepted Allied armistice terms and ended her war with the Soviet Union, Britain, and the United States. Long desirous to get out of the war, the group behind King Michael had waited for this opportunity, presented to them by the weakened position of Germany and the new Russian drive. However, the story behind this important step reads much like a fiction thriller. It was a Romanian super-melodrama that could hardly be matched in its bizarre qualities.

Michael, the 22-year-old king, had previously attempted no less than seven times to get rid of Marshal Antonescu. The eighth—and successful—attempt was originally scheduled for August 26th. While preparations were in progress, word leaked out that Antonescu was leaving for the front. So the king sent for the dictator on August 23. Michael received the dictator in his study and had him arrested and imprisoned in the small vault where Carol used to keep his stamps. Allied headquarters in Cairo was asked to bomb Bucharest on August 26—the day when the royal coup was expected—and to give instructions to spare the royal palace.

Michael's new cabinet, besides Premier Sanatescu, included Juliu Maniu, George Bratianu (leader of the Liberal Party), Lucretiu Patrascanu (Communist), and Constantin Petrescu (Socialist).

Like Italy, Romania hoped at first to terminate its alliance with Germany peaceably. But on August 24, Nazi bombers swooped down on Bucharest. On August 25, 1944, Romania declared war on Germany and was accepted by the Allies as a co-belligerent on the same footing as Italy. In September, lawyer Lucretiu Patrascanu signed an armistice in the Kremlin which officially took Romania out of her war against the Allies and into an approved war against Germany and Hungary. She had a promise of the return of northern Transylvania if she did her part in recapturing that rich, disputed region from the Hungarians. Among other things, Romania undertook to place 12 divisions under Russian command; to fight until Germany was defeated; to pay $300 million in kind in six years as reparations to Russia; to honor damage claims submitted by the other Allies; to restore Bessarabia and northern Bukovina to Russia; to abolish all fascist organizations; to free all anti-fascists; to intern all Axis nationals; to restore in good order all property seized from Allied nationals; to permit a Russian-managed Allied Control Commission to supervise the government and press until a peace was signed.

By the end of 1944, Moscow's influence in Bucharest had obviously increased. The Russians behaved better than the former ally—Germany; this was the key to their popularity. King Michael, who certainly was not sympathetic to Moscow, continued in office, and the first Romanian Cabinets had a decided Right-wing tinge. After the regime of General Konstantin Sanatescu, General Radescu's cabinet took office on December 5, 1944. But Russian pressure grew steadily. Radescu's government disappeared on February 28, 1945, after Russia charged that it had not been purging pro-Germans and war criminals as provided in the armistice terms. The Communists had been growing more and more aggressive ever since Romania surrendered and they cracked Radescu's coalition with demands for a new "National Democratic Front." In Bucharest, armed Reds attacked the royal palace, the Ministry of Interior, and the Premier's office. Martial law had to be declared throughout Romania. The revolt was organized by Anna Parker, formerly a Left-wing trade-union organizer in the United States, where her husband, a Romanian by birth but a Soviet citizen, worked in the personnel department of the Amtorg—Russia's official trading corporation in the United States.

King Michael, hoping for Anglo-American support against growing Soviet pressure, asked the immensely wealthy old Anglophile, Prince Stirbey, a leader of the big Peasant Party and the negotiator of Romania's armistice, to form a cabinet. He failed. Then the choice came around to where the Reds wanted it: the six-party National Democratic front, formed by Communists and their associates. Dr. Petre Groza, well-to-do but radical leader of an organization grandly called the "Ploughmen's Party of the Front," was the Leftist selection for Premier. This procedure was contrary to the Crimea agreement whereby the United States, Great Britain, and Russia had agreed that all three would participate in policy-making within liberated or former enemy countries. But Stalin's satisfaction with the new government was expressed by his making a present to Romania of northern Transylvania (in March, 1945), an area which had been seized by Hungary with Hitler's permission. The Russian influence was paramount in Romania in the spring and summer of 1945.

Bibliography

Beza, Marcu, *Byzantine Art in Roumania* (New York: Charles Scribner's, 1940). 29 color and 67 monochrome reproductions from originals.

Clark, C. Up., *United Roumania* (New York: Dodd, Mead & Co., 1932). Valuable for a survey of various aspects of Romania's life, including its literature.

Ghyka, M. C., *A Documentary Chronology of Roumanian History* (New York: William Salloch, 1942).

Graefenberg, R. G., *Athene Palace* ("By Countess Waldeck") (New York: McBride, 1942). Lively picture of Bucharest in the dramatic days before Carol stepped out and Hitler stepped in.

Iorga, Nicolae, *A History of Roumania* (New York: Dodd, Mead, 1926). The standard account in English of Romanian characteristics and national history. Not particularly well-organized, and rather weak on the recent period.

Madgearu, Virgil, *Rumania's New Economic Policy* (London: King, 1930). A National-Peasant leader explains the attitude of his party toward agriculture, tariffs, capital, and so forth.

Marie, Dowager Queen of Rumania, *The Country That I Love* (New York: Brentano, 1925). Chatty sketches of people and places, including shrewd appraisal of the former Romanian rulers, King Charles and "Carmen Sylva."

Mitrany, David, *The Land and the Peasant in Rumania* (New Haven: Yale University Press, 1930). The agrarian problem in its historical and social setting.

Patmore, Derek, *Invitation to Roumania* (New York: The Macmillan Co., 1939). A pleasant picture of the country, the people, and their problems, by an Englishman impressed with the historical function of the feudal aristocracy.

Pavel, Pavel, *Why Rumania Failed* (London: Alliance Press, 1944). A National-Peasant Party representative surveys Carol's rule.

Roucek, Joseph S., *Contemporary Roumania and Her Problems*. (Stanford, Cal.: Stanford University Press, 1932); *The Politics of the Balkans* (New York: McGraw-Hill Book Co., 1939), Chapter III, pp. 26-54.

Roumania Ten Years After (Boston: Beacon Press, 1928). Social and political conditions as seen through the eyes of the American Committee on the Rights of Religious Minorities.

CHAPTER XXIII

YUGOSLAVIA (1918-1945)

Economic and Social Factors

APART from Romania's oil resources, Yugoslavia has the richest mineral supplies of all the Balkan countries. They were exploited largely by French and British capital—and later by the Germans. But manufacturing remained of minor importance, although there has been some development since World War I. Basically, agriculture was the main support of Yugoslavia's population, although livestock raising, forestry, and mining contributed substantially to the national income. Roughly 80 per cent of the population were peasants. Only 32 per cent of land holdings were above 12.3 acres—the minimum for existence. More than a million peasants, or nearly 10 per cent, were landless and had to earn their living as migratory seasonal workers. The nearly 80 per cent of the population engaged in agriculture received only 50 per cent of the national income, while the 11 per cent in industry received 32 per cent, and the 3 per cent in commerce and banking received 11 per cent. In general, the peasant standard of living was very low.

Nationalistic and Racial Factors

The kingdom was formed in 1918 through the union of pre-war Serbia, Montenegro, and the former Austro-Hungarian provinces of Croatia, Slovenia, Bosnia, Herzegovina, and Dalmatia. Out of the total population of 14 million (according to the 1941 census), nearly 12 million were composed of three closely related Slavic nationalities: Serbs (about 6.5 million), Croats (approximately 4 million), and Slovenes (over 1 million). But there were also large minorities. In Bosnia lived some 800,000 Moslems (of Slavic origin), who considered themselves partly Serbs, partly Croats, and partly "Yugoslavs." Along the northern frontier were half a million Germans and close to half a million Hungarians. The rest of the population was made up of Albanians and Turks. The Macedonians were officially counted as Serbs.

There were many elements of controversy besides the all-important Serb-Croat problem. There was religious strife between Greek Orthodox Serbs, Roman Catholic Croats and Slovenes, and Moslems; increasing activities and demands of the pro-Nazi German-speaking minority; agitation by small Yugoslav Nazi groups on the one hand and by the illegal Communist movement on the other; harsh economic exploitation of the peasants. For years a deep gulf divided the government, controlled by a Serb military oligarchy of pro-Nazi and anti-Soviet tendencies, and the masses of the people, who were in the main staunchly democratic, friendly toward the Soviet Union, and eager to coöperate with the Anglo-French "anti-aggression" front.

The Perpetual Serb-Croat Conflict

But the worst of all Yugoslav problems from the very beginning of the new state in 1918 to the present time has been the issue between centralism, represented by the Serbs (first by Nicholas Pashitch's Radical Party) who wanted a "Greater Serbia," and the proponents of some form of regionalism and federalism, headed by the Croat Peasant Party of Dr. Matchek and the late Stephen Raditch.[1]

Despite their geographical proximity and their racial and language affinity, the Yugoslavs before 1918 did not constitute parts of the same state and did not participate in the same cultural, economic, political, and religious development. The unfavorable geopolitical situation of the Balkans was conducive to such centrifugal tendencies. High, hardly penetrable mountains and useless river systems, geomorphological and climatic variety favored cultural differentiation rather than integration. The new state was unable to impose spiritual unity on its various tribal members, because these Slavs had lived to the end of the First World War in five different states—Austria, Hungary, Serbia, Montenegro, and Turkey. The strange processes of history had divided the branches of the western, eastern, and northern political and cultural spheres. When the new state was created, the old tribal instincts were already too deeply rooted not to influence the political attitudes of the leaders.

The Croats joined the new kingdom with some enthusiasm. They hoped to create a new political-economic state, but they wanted it to be more than a simple extension of victorious Serbia toward the west. The enactment of the Vidovdan Constitution without the consent of

---

[1] Pribichevich, Stoyan, "The Nazi Drive to the East," *Foreign Policy Reports*, XIV (October 15, 1938), p. 174.

the Croats ignited the growing antagonism between Zagreb and Belgrade, and the latter began to utilize the advantages of its dominant position as the capital. Experiences with the new centralistic and overstaffed bureaucratic administration revived the already deeply-rooted tribal enmity.

Although both Serbs and Croats have the same literary language, both consider themselves special cultural groups. The Croats and Slovenes use the Roman alphabet, while the Serbs write in Cyrillic. The territorial-historical elements are also important. The thousand-year tradition of a more-or-less independent Croat Kingdom, united with even fresher memories of the wide autonomy which was enjoyed by the Croats in former Hungary, taught the Croats to talk constantly about "justice" and to complain incessantly, often naïvely and often in hardly articulate terms. The Croats have been jealous of their separate entity, suspicious of the dominant Serbs, and have no intention of allowing themselves, after the hard fight against Magyarization, to be "Balkanized." A form of political autonomy had been for generations the most cherished weapon in the Croat's nationalistic struggle against the ever-encroaching Magyar.

These differences in political mentality are enhanced by religious differences. The Serbs are Greek Orthodox; the Croats and the Slovenes are Catholics. The latter have always sought their inspiration from Rome, which organized its followers in a rigid system of religious obedience, holding in obeisance also the politics and intellectual life of these provinces. Many Croat and Slovene politicians, like Dr. Koroshets, also wore priestly robes. In contrast, the Orthodox Church of the Serbs was run rather loosely and concerned itself much less with politics and secular affairs, though it was nationalistic in its outlook. The upper classes of Serbia, mostly educated abroad, saw to it that religion did not play a large part in their affairs, and they were quite indifferent to the religion of the masses as long as it supported nationalistic aims. Religion, for the Serb, is identified with his nationalism; but so is the Catholicism of the Croat, who despises his Serb cousin in Belgrade as a "non-believer" and an "infidel."

The gulf is widened also by cultural differences. Belonging to the "western" cultural zone, the Croat and the Slovene are convinced that they have an "older" and "higher" civilization than the Serb, who in their eyes is little more than a "barbarian," a ridiculous and under-civilized upstart. The percentage of illiteracy, which is much smaller in Croatia than in Serbia, provides another argument for the Croat, who was educated under the influence of Vienna.

The Serb, on the other hand, cares little for arguments about "culture." His sufferings and sacrifices during the past centuries have imbued him with an obsession for his nationalistic cause. He remembers the famous retreat of the Serbian armies during the First World War, which left bloody footprints in the snow of the Balkan mountains. His historical experience has taught him to be swift to draw the sword and to be slow to put it down. And, after all, were not the Croat regiments, in the service of the Austro-Hungarian Empire, shooting at him while he was dying for the liberation of his country? "Cultural" arguments are therefore less convincing to the Serb than active deeds.

Serb-Croat antagonism was further nourished by differences in economic standards. The highly industrialized sections of Croatia and Slovenia, which had received financial support from Vienna and Budapest for their development, felt bitter because their economic interests and taxes were sacrificed to support the almost purely agricultural systems of Serbia, Bosnia, Herzegovina, Montenegro, and Macedonia— another symptom of backwardness at which to point the finger of scorn. They resented the fact that the "Sava Banovina" is only a second-rate periphery of Belgrade, although the numerical proportion of the Croats to the Serbs is roughly 4:5. They wanted to have a larger representation of the Croat element in the administration of the state, in the army, in the foreign service, and in political appointments in general. Public corruption and the censorship more than irritated the Croat, whose resentment, after the death of Raditch, found its symbol in the person of Dr. Matchek.

Parliamentary Decay

Although the kingdom was faced with a dangerous international situation from the beginning of its existence, the political life of the nation, the framework of which was defined by the constitution of 1921, dominated Yugoslavia's efforts at parliamentary democracy. Petty politics and politicians dominated the Constituent Assembly. The parties represented in it were essentially a continuation of old parties, resting on regional orientation instead of on a program which could cope with national questions. Consequently governmental coalitions never lasted very long and never comprised representatives from all districts of the kingdom.

The parliamentary life of the first decade of Yugoslavia's existence was nothing but a succession of crises, with changes of cabinets averaging nearly three a year. During the ten years of the parliamentary regime Yugoslavia, in fact, changed 20 ministries, 24 governments, and 130 ministers. Cabinets usually lasted only a couple of months; only two succeeded in remaining in office as long as eleven months. There were governments which held office only for one month, and some for only two weeks. Twenty ministers each changed from three to five quite different ministries, and there were some who headed six different ministerial departments.

The fundamental task of the parliament, constructive legislation, was almost wholly neglected for political disturbances which increased from year to year. Although different parliaments were returned three times by new elections—1923, 1925, 1927—they never succeeded in giving the country uniform legislation. The different laws which had been operative before the union in the various provinces were still in force when the dictatorship tried to cut the Gordian knot. Nepotism and inefficiency ruled supreme. Membership in a party or a government was considered more valuable as an opportunity for personal revenue and advantages than as a call to serve the interests of the new nation. The limited horizon of the pre-war politicians restricted their approach to the entirely new problems of the kingdom. Cabinets were governed by illogical inconsistencies, and went from one extreme to another. Raditch, for instance, went from jail into a position as a cabinet minister, only to break his oath and attack the government again in a few months.

In general, struggling personalities overshadowed all other political considerations and programs lacked any social *raison d'être.* The differences between the Serbs and Croats, the fundamental issue of Yugoslav politics, really defied solution, due in part to the intransigeancy of the Serbs and in part to the short-sighted policy of Raditch. Additional bitterness was created by the extension of the bureaucratic system of Belgrade to the rest of the new kingdom. The excessive centralization was not adapted to the regional requirements of administrative autonomy. Intrigue became endemic, and personal jealousies led to a great deal of treachery. Newspapers printed reckless, slanderous, and vitriolic statements about men in public life. Most of the dailies were provincial in character and reflected local interests only. The elections were under great official pressure and corruption, and gerrymandering was a common electoral practice.

The conflicts between a policy of Yugoslav centralism and the practical allegiance of the old parties to regional tendencies produced a crisis of state on June 20, 1928. A supporter of the government killed and wounded several members of the Croat Peasant Party. Raditch died of his wounds. His followers withdrew from Belgrade and set up their own parliament at Zagreb, where they passed resolutions refusing to recognize the "rump" parliament at Belgrade. When the tenth anniversary of the founding of the state was celebrated on December 1, the Croats refused to participate. Quite obviously, the only way out of this political *impasse* was the one offered by the King—a dictatorship.[2]

Alexander's Dictatorship

In January, 1929, King Alexander proclaimed a dictatorship and appointed a non-party military man as Premier. The dictatorship was intended to give the government an opportunity for political reorganization. The country was divided into new administrative districts, and its name was officially changed to Yugoslavia (it had been known as the "Kingdom of the Serbs, Croats, and Slovenes"). Numerous other reforms were inaugurated in the hope of creating a government which, while centralized in Belgrade, would no longer be based on old racial and regional subdivisions. The Serbs, who at first favored these administrative reforms, later argued that they interfered with democratic institutions. On September 3, 1931, the government promulgated a constitution which provided some elements of parliamentary rule—under a one-party system. But there was growing opposition to the existing system, characterized by extreme centralization and ruthless promotion of Serb interests.

On October 9, 1933, King Alexander was assassinated in Marseille by a Macedonian terrorist. Croat and Italian complicity was suspected. He was succeeded by his 11-year-old son Peter. A regency of three men, headed by Peter's uncle, Prince Paul, was named to rule during the King's minority. Prince Paul was the real ruler of Yugoslavia from 1934 to 1941.

The Stoyadinovich Government

Paul appointed Dr. Milan Stoyadinovich as Premier with instructions to "conciliate" the Croats. Minor concessions were offered, but the Premier balked at the demand of Dr. Vladimir Matchek for the dissolution of Parliament and the free election of a Constituent Assembly to draft a new constitution based upon democracy and federalism. Stoyadinovich retained the authoritarian 1931 constitution, but relaxed somewhat the repressive character of the dictatorship. At the same

---

[2] Adamic, Louis, *My Native Land* (New York: Harper & Bros., 1943), thinks that the Serbian conception of a centralized state was imposed upon Yugoslavia by Belgrade's 200 families, the *charskya*.

time he embarked upon a new foreign policy that brought Yugoslavia into closer relations with Italy and Germany and aroused further distrust of the government among pro-democratic Serbs and Croats alike.

In September, 1937, Matchek's Croatian Peasant Party united with the Serb liberal parties on a definite program of opposition to the government. A year later, the question whether to side with Germany and Italy, or with France and Czechoslovakia, had become a major issue between the government and public opinion. The government's ban on all meetings relating to foreign politics only intensified public resentment. This was apparent in the 1938 elections, which increased the Croat-Serbian opposition vote and reduced the government majority. The newly elected Croat deputies again refused to take their seats in Parliament.

This electoral set-back to Premier Stoyadinovich, coupled with the growing danger of a European war, led to the resignation of the cabinet. Dragisha Cvetkovich, a cabinet officer under Stoyadinovich and a member of the latter's Radical Union (government) Party, was charged with the task of reaching an early accord with the Croats. The proposed concessions to the Croats led to a schism in the government party in June and July of 1939. On the other hand, Dr. Matchek threatened Croat secession from Yugoslavia and acceptance of a German protectorate unless his demands were granted. The compromise settlement of August 24, 1939, after years of bitter controversy, followed. An autonomous Croatia, comprising 26½ per cent of Yugoslavia's territory and 28½ per cent of her population, was set up. This was regarded as the initial step toward a federal state of Yugoslavia. Dr. Matchek joined the cabinet of "national union" as Vice-Premier. But even this far-reaching settlement did not fulfill all Croat aspirations. Powerful Serb elements remained firmly opposed to Croat autonomy.

Meanwhile the international situation was getting more dangerous for Yugoslavia every day. Yugoslavia was already being conquered economically by Germany.

Cultural Life

The emphasis on politics in Yugoslavia's life should not blind us to Yugoslav contributions in the world of art, music, and literature. The thirteenth and fourteenth centuries were the Golden Age of Yugoslav art. About a thousand churches and fortresses and about ten thousand frescoes and ikons from that period have been preserved. Dalmatia, which was open to Western influences, has many magnificent examples of architectural and sculptural work from that time. The Turkish invasion cut short the normal development of Yugoslav culture. During the last two centuries, Yugoslav art has become more and more similar in style and ideals to the art of Western and Central Europe. One of the greatest figures among contemporary European sculptors is Ivan Mestrovich.

The whole of Yugoslavia is exceedingly rich in folk music and traditional songs. Many beautiful Croat folk melodies were used by Haydn as motifs for his many symphonies. One of the earliest of the polyphonic masters, Jacopus Gallus (1550-1591), was a Slovene. The Ljubljana Philharmonic Society was founded in 1702 and is the oldest in Central Europe. Musical life was greatly encouraged and given a national character during the nineteenth century by the work of some inspired collectors of national folk melodies. A collector whose works are still in the repertoire of all Yugoslav choral societies and who attained a world-wide reputation was Stefan Mokranjac (1855-1934). The leading figure among the modern composers of symphonic music is Josip Slavenski, whose works—Balkanophonia, Religiophonia—have been successfully performed in western Europe.

Yugoslav national ballads were first revealed to the world in the work of the father of Yugoslav literature, Vuk Stefan Karadjich, with the assistance of Kopitar, the great Slav philologist, and were translated by Jacob Grimm and Goethe. They have been the object of sincere admiration by music lovers ever since. The national epics have been one of the most important elements in maintaining the national consciousness of the people.

During the nineteenth century, the main currents of European thought and literature gradually reached the Yugoslav lands, where the writers started to use the national language and to study the national folk literature. The greatest Yugoslav poet of the century was Peter Petrovic Njegos, Prince-Bishop of Montenegro (1813-1851). His *Mountain Wreath,* a dramatic epic, has been translated into all the principal European languages. Ivan Mazuranich's *Death of Smail Aga Cengic* is one of the most remarkable creations of Yugoslav literature. The great representative of the Yugoslav movement in the second half of the nineteenth century was the famous Bishop Josip Juraj Strosmajer (1815-1905). The most noteworthy short story writer of the time, however, was Laza Lazarevich (1851-1890), whose stories have been many times translated into English. The greatest novelist of our time was Bora Stankovich (1876-1927), whose novel *Tainted Blood* has been translated into many European languages. Mestrovich helped to create a nationalist art movement (Racki the painter, Rosandich and Panich the sculptors, and Pletchnik the architect).

The Collapse

The story of how Yugoslavia resisted Nazi maneuvers and eventually
started a national revolution against the government which wanted to
use "appeasement" tactics is one of the heroic tales of World War II.[3]

Negotiations for Yugoslavia's adherence to the Rome-Berlin-Tokyo
alliance were nearly concluded under Prince Paul's pressure. But at
one o'clock on March 27, 1941, while all Belgrade slept, tanks, trucks,
and artillery units moved swiftly to strategic points throughout the
capital. The regent and the Cvetkovich government were overthrown
and taken into custody. Seventeen-year-old King Peter II assumed full
powers, with General Dushan Simovitch, popular lady's man and vet-
eran of the heroic Serbian Army of the First World War as premier.
Matchek agreed to become vice-premier.

At 5:15 A.M., Sunday, April 6, 1941, the full fury of the German
Blitzkrieg struck at Yugoslavia.[4] In a few days, the Yugoslav Army,
cut up by the Nazi hordes, was divided by Simovitch into guerrilla
parties—the kind of fighting carried on by Serbian *comitadjis* for centuries against Turkish and Habsburg rulers.

The twelve days of *Blitzkrieg* led to the division of the country.
Serbia and the Banat was under German military rule. On August 29,
a puppet government under General Milan Neditch was set up. On
May 3, 1941, Italy annexed the greater part of Slovenia as the province
of Ljubljana. On July 12, 1941, a "Constituent Assembly" at Cetinje
proclaimed an independent Montenegro under Italian protection. On
April 10, 1941, the independence of Croatia was declared, and eight
days later the first government of Dr. Ante Pavelitch as *Poglavnik*
(Leader) and Prime Minister was announced. The Duke of Spoleto,
a nephew of the King of Italy, was proclaimed King of Croatia on May
18 as King Tomislav I. By the treaty of May 18, Italy also took possession of the Dalmatian coast and most of the Adriatic Islands. The
Hungarians seized the northern section of Yugoslavia, known as the
Voivodina, and the Bulgarians occupied South Serbia (Macedonia).
King Peter's government went into exile.

---

[3] For more details, see Joseph S. Roucek, "Hitler Over the Balkans," *World Affairs Interpreter*,
XII (July, 1941), pp. 136-152; Nicholas Mirkowich, "Yugoslavia's Choice," *Foreign Affairs*, XX
(October, 1941), pp. 131-151; Robert St. John, *From the Land of the Silent People* (Garden
City, N. Y.: Doubleday, Doran, 1942); Leigh White, *The Long Balkan Night* (New York:
Charles Scribner's Sons, 1944).

[4] For details, see Paul W. Thomson, *Modern Battle* (New York: Penguin Books, 1942),
Chapter 7, "War for the Passes," pp. 122-165.

Dissensions and Guerrilla Warfare

When Hitler invaded Yugoslavia in April, 1941, he was greatly aided by internal dissensions. Certain elements which had long been opposed to the domination of the Serbs gave him considerable assistance. On the eve of the invasion, in fact, the country was so divided on the issue of yielding to Hitler's demands that it took a major internal upheaval to bring about resistance. Hitler would undoubtedly have subdued Yugoslavia even if the country had been united, but there can be no question that his task was rendered much easier by widespread internal strife.

After the surrender, the country was split into no fewer than 10 different sections. The Germans fanned racial hatreds between the Serbs and Croats, virtually producing a condition of civil war. No fewer than 300,000 murders, perhaps even more, have taken place within the boundaries of Yugoslavia since the spring of 1941.

During the early period following the surrender, all resistance to the Axis appeared to be centered in a group known as the "Chetniks," led by Dragha Mikhailovich, then a colonel in the Yugoslav army. The Chetniks took whatever arms they could gather and fled to the mountains, where they organized guerrilla opposition to the invaders. To the outside world, the Chetniks typified the highest form of heroism, and Mikhailovich became the symbol of resistance to tyranny. The Chetniks received the blessing of the United States and England. Mikhailovich was promoted to the rank of general and named Minister of War in the cabinet of the government-in-exile in London.

As long as the Chetniks were the only organized group effectively fighting the Axis, few problems arose and it was logical for the Allies to support them. But reports soon began to seep out of Yugoslavia to the effect that another guerrilla group, known as the "Partisans," were also combatting the Axis. Led by a mysterious figure nicknamed "Tito" (whose real name was Josip Broz), the Partisans became more and more prominent. Not only did they meet the conquerors in battle, but, like the Chetniks, they engaged in acts of sabotage, destroying railroads and bridges and generally harassing the Germans and Italians. It is estimated that Germany had to keep as many as 20 divisions in Yugoslavia to keep the country from boiling over.

For a time, it is reported, the forces of General Mikhailovich and those of Tito agreed to work together, but their period of coöperation was short-lived. Ancient feuds flared up and the two groups frequently fought each other instead of the common enemy. The Partisans accused the Chetniks of promoting the pre-war cause of a Greater Serbia and of reorganizing the country at the expense of other racial groups. The Chetniks were also charged with aiding the enemy. That was the reason given for the execution of a number of Mikhailovich's followers.

The Chetniks, for their part, accused the Partisans of trying to weaken the country by fomenting dissension and starting civil war. They asserted that the Partisans were nothing but Red bandits, trying to reshape the country on communist lines. The Chetniks claimed to have the undivided support of England and the United States, in view of the fact that those countries supported the Yugoslav government-in-exile in which their leader Mikhailovich was Minister of War. On the other hand, the Partisans claimed the backing of the Soviet Union. The issue thus became international in scope and threatened to divide the major Allies.

At the beginning of 1944, Yugoslavia was in the throes of a triangular ideological conflict—Tito, Matchek, and Mikhailovich—in which the Serbs and Croats were fighting out old grudges. The Serbs, moreover, were divided within their own ranks by Rightist trends that caused their Left wing to side with the Croats in the Partisan forces. King Peter's government was completely helpless to end the fratricidal strife. A little earlier, the British had become disgusted with Mikhailovich, who insisted on his cautious "wait-to-strike" strategy, and assigned liaison officers to Tito's forces in the summer of 1943. The British were also anxious to show Moscow that friends of the Soviet Union were automatically their friends. Then, with the support of Washington, British diplomacy started to coördinate the two Yugoslav factions by forcing the elimination of the Serbian nationalist officers who surrounded young King Peter. The Soviet Government, although it officially recognized King Peter's regime in Cairo, as did all the other United Nations, had been supporting the Partisans from the beginning.

On June 1, 1944, Dr. Ivan Subasich, a Croat, was appointed Premier by King Peter. He met with Marshal Tito on Yugoslav soil and reached an agreement with him, with the result that Mikhailovich was dismissed from his army post in August. The exiled government recognized Tito as head of his provisional administration inside Yugoslavia. Tito agreed that the Yugoslavs should get a chance to vote for whatever kind of government they wanted at the end of the war. Meanwhile, Peter could continue to call himself king.

Hopes for a Federated Yugoslavia

During 1944, Tito's shadow government flitted from town to town to avoid the Germans. But while it ran, it also ran a large part of Yugoslavia—and the Allies were doing business with it. It was headed by a Communist, but it was definitely not a Communist government.

It had been brought into existence in 1943, at Jajce, with a four-point program: (1) the creation of a federated Yugoslavia, composed of the six states of Croatia, Slovenia, Serbia, Bosnia and Herzegovina, Montenegro, and Macedonia; (2) establishment of "truly democratic" rights and liberties; (3) inviolability of private property; (4) no revolutionary economic or social changes.

This was a program that could rally most Yugoslavs, and the agreement with the exiled government in London was recognized as paving the way for peaceful settlement of Yugoslavia's internal difficulties. The Subasich government was composed of only six men: two Serbs, two Croats, and two Slovenes. Two of the Ministers came from Tito's forces. Subasich himself took the portfolios of Prime Minister and Minister of War (the latter post had been held for two years by Mikhailovich). The blacksmith's boy of Klanjec became Marshal and Provisional President of Yugoslavia.

Tito's new government, called the "National Committee of Liberation" was scarcely more Communistic than its program. Only five out of seventeen cabinet officers were Communists. Among the non-Communists were Foreign Minister Josip Smodlaka, a friend of Czechoslovakia's great Thomas G. Masaryk and former Yugoslav Minister to the Vatican; and the Rev. Vladho Zecevich, Minister of the Interior, an Orthodox priest who commanded a detachment of Chetniks until 1941, when he switched from Mikhailovich to Tito.

There was a minor revolt in the king's government at the turn of 1945—by the king himself. Peter made a bold and rather reckless move by abruptly dismissing Premier Subasich, who had meanwhile reached an agreement with Marshal Tito about a new government under a regency. He took this action without having consulted Prime Minister Churchill, who previously had blessed the Tito-Subasich accord.

King Peter's gesture resembled King Canute's in commanding the waves to recede. Since Marshal Tito and the coalition already held effective power in Yugoslavia and had the approval of England and Russia, the young monarch was tackling overwhelming odds. Premier

Subasich made it plain that he would ignore his dismissal and go ahead with plans for the new government. He was warmly supported by the British, who welcomed the departure of another troublesome exiled regime. Peter soon changed his tune. Since Tito had indicated he would make no more concessions to the king, the latter consented to transfer his power to a regency and approved a new cabinet formed by Subasich.

The key points in the Yugoslav crisis were: (1) the British Government's determination to prove that the original British-Russian agreement on joint influence in Yugoslavia was still in effect; and (2) President Roosevelt's statement of January 6, 1945, that "no temporary or provisional authorities in the liberated countries (should) block the eventual exercise of the people's right freely to choose the government and institutions under which, as free men, they are to live." This principle was confirmed at Yalta (February, 1945) and there appears to be a fairly good prospect, at the time of writing, that it will work out in practice. If so, federalism may well prove the right prescription to cure Yugoslavia's chronic racial indigestion.

Bibliography

Adamic, Louis, *My Native Land* (New York: Harper & Bros., 1943); *The Native's Return* (New York: Harper & Bros., 1934). Probably the most readable introductions to the history of Yugoslavia, in spite of their occasional mistakes.

Baerlein, Henry, *The Birth of Yugoslavia* (London: Parsons, 1922), 2 vols. Voluminous description of Serbia before the war, the struggle for unification, and post-war difficulties.

Beard, Charles A., and Radin, George, *The Balkan Pivot: Jugoslavia*. (New York: MacMillan, 1929). An excellent survey of the Yugoslav government and administration as it existed until King Alexander's *coup d'état*.

Buchan, John, Ed., *Yugoslavia* (London: Hodder, 1923). A volume in the Nations of Today series, giving an historical survey and an outline of resources and conditions.

Graham, Stephen, *Alexander of Yugoslavia* (New Haven: Yale University Press, 1939). A very readable introduction to the history of the House of Karageorgevitch.

Haumant, Emile, *La formation de la Yougoslavie* (Paris: Bossard, 1930). A general history of the Southern Slav peoples from the fifteenth century to the end of the war; well-informed and detailed.

Laffan, R. G. D., *Yugoslavia Since 1918* (London: Yugoslav Society, 1929). A good survey.

Loncar, Dragotin, *The Slovenes* (Cleveland: American Jugoslav Printing and Publishing Co., 1939). On the neglected topic of social history.

Morison, W. A., trans., *The Revolt of the Serbs Against the Turks* (1804-

1813) (New York: The Macmillan Co., 1942). The first translation of these Serbian epics.

Schmitt, B. E., "July 1914, Thirty Years After," *Journal of Modern History,* XVI (September, 1944), pp. 169-204.

St. John, Robert, *From the Land of the Silent People* (Garden City, N. Y.: Doubleday, Doran, 1942). Indispensable on the period of Nazi invasion.

Vojnovic, Lujo, *Dalmatia and the Jugoslav Movement* (New York: Charles Scribner's Sons, 1919). The story of Dalmatia's struggle against Venice and the Habsburgs, and its part in the Serbo-Croat movement. Written by a Ragusan patriot and scholar.

Voshnjak, Bogumil, *A Bulwark Against Germany* (New York: Revell, 1919). The fight of the Slovenes for national existence, by one of their wartime spokesmen.

West, Rebecca, *Black Lamb and Grey Falcon* (New York: Viking Press, 1941), 2 vols. A lengthy discourse on nearly all aspects of Yugoslavia's history.

CHAPTER XXIV

BULGARIA (1918-1945)

Geopolitical Factors

BEFORE the First World War, Bulgaria was the largest country in the Balkans. Territorial losses following the peace treaties in 1919 cost the defeated country strips of territory awarded to Yugoslavia, Greece, and Turkey, leaving a diminished Bulgaria of only 39,825 square miles. Thousands of refugees from the ceded regions created problems in the remainder of the country, which was further hampered by the loss of its only access to the Mediterranean with that block of Aegean coastal region which was transferred to Greece.

With the exception of Albania, Bulgaria thus became the smallest of the Balkan nations, but it occupies a location in southeastern Europe where two great natural routes cross—routes that have been used for invasion and trade since the days of the Roman Emperor Trajan. One is the overland road running southwest from central Asia by way of Russia and Romania into Greece. The other is the time-worn path running northwest from Asia Minor to Central Europe. Jumping the Dardanelles, this route follows the battle-marked valleys of southeastern Europe from Turkey to the Danube and Germany.

Three F's—farming, forestry, and fishing—provide Bulgaria's chief means of support, although industry has been encouraged by the government in recent years, and there are valuable mineral deposits. Coal is the most important mineral product. Manufacturing is still in its infancy. When the world had peace to enjoy luxuries, Bulgaria was famed as a perfumer to milady. For years it supplied three-fourths of the world's attar of roses. But essentially Bulgaria is a nation of farmers; about four-fifths of its population make their living from the soil. Farms are for the most part extremely small, and farm implements are generally primitive. White oxen or black water buffaloes pulling plows are seen more frequently than tractors.

On the whole, Bulgaria has no minority problems.[1] Most of the more than six million people are Bulgars, although Turks formed a minority estimated at eleven per cent of the population. Another four or five per cent consisted of Romanians, Greeks, Armenians, Serbians, and a few Jews. Religiously, Bulgaria's population is predominantly Greek-Orthodox.

In the boundary settlement after World War I, in which Bulgaria was allied with the Central Powers, this nation lost to Greece the southern patch of land that gave it access to the Aegean Sea. But Bulgaria has never ceased to lay claim to this area, plus certain others (especially Macedonia) in Yugoslavia on the west.

Cultural Background

The liberation of Bulgaria in 1878 created a favorable atmosphere for literary production. Ivan Vazov's literary accomplishments are known far beyond the frontiers of Bulgaria. P. K. Yavorov was one of the most brilliant Bulgarian lyric poets. Cyril Christov, a lyric poet, is a master of sentimental and frivolous verse. Today the doors have been thrown wide open to the influence of the literatures of Western Europe. The advance-guard of Bulgarian poetry is represented by such names as Nicolai Liliev, Todor Traianov, Dimtcho Debelianov, and Ludmil Stoyanow. Two young Bulgarian women, Dora Gabe and Elisabeth Beltchewa-Bagriana, have produced works characterized by artistic simplicity. Among the most talented modern writers of fiction are A. Strashimirov, Elin-Lein, Jordan Yovcov, Dobre Nemirov, Georgi Raitchev, Nicolai Raniov and C. Constantinov, A. Karailyjtchev, and V. Polianov.

The Bulgarian National Opera became the center of Bulgaria's musical life. The National Musical Academy in Sofia was also an important factor. Dobri Christov has written fine solo and choral songs in the spirit of folksongs and the symphonies of Petko Stainov and Pancho Vladigherov are performed in many European musical centers.

Bulgarian plastic art is a comparatively recent creation. There were icon paintings of a very high order a hundred years ago and Zachari Zograv (1810-1861) was the best painter of his day. But practically all Bulgarian art has been produced since the liberation. The greatest of the older artists is Ivan Mrkvichka, a Czech, who came to Bulgaria shortly after the liberation as an instructor in painting. Another worth

[1] The Greco-Bulgarian Convention of 1919 was a specific attempt to encourage the emigration of Greeks from Bulgaria and of Bulgarians from Greece. See S. P. Ladas, *The Exchange of Minorities* (New York: The Macmillan Co., 1932).

noting is the late Anton Mittov, for a long time director of the Art School in Sofia, whose paintings of folk life are among the best in Bulgaria. Boris Denev and Nichola Tanev specialize in old Bulgarian towns. The late Nichola Petrov, Ivan Michov, and Constantin Sharkelov are excellent landscape painters. Peter Morosov's pictures of Bulgarian scenes, places, and types are known to foreigners visiting the country. The very gifted Boris Gheorhiev is both an excellent portraitist and a mystic symbolist. Jeco Spiridanov, Ivan Lzarov, and Andrei Nicolov are the foremost Bulgarian sculptors.

Agrarian Dictatorship

Ever since World War I, from which Bulgaria emerged as the Cinderella of the Balkans—reduced in territory, population, and economic potentialities—the country has been waiting for a good fairy. Its situation has never been stable—internally or externally. Surrounded by suspicious neighbors, Bulgaria has had to face a series of frontier incidents and frequent threats in post-war years.

Disturbed social conditions were reflected in the social structure of the Kingdom. As in all other Balkan countries, there was a wide gap between the standard of living of the village peasant and that of the city dweller. The large cities (there are only a few of them) have many of the conveniences found in Western Europe, but the peasant ekes out only the barest necessities of life from his toil. Before World War II, he could not even sell or exchange these for other needed products. To a considerable extent, each peasant household is a self-contained but very primitive economic and social unit. Additional troubles came with the invasion of the country by hundreds of thousands of refugees from Macedonia, Thrace, and the Dobrudja.

But despite wars and social and economic unrest, the population of Bulgaria has been growing steadily. Since Bulgaria became independent, it has more than doubled its population; the density may be compared to that of the state of Ohio—although it does not possess the industrial resources of the latter.

There was also the eternal problem of a growing "intellectual proletariat" composed of young men who, having received a secondary or university education, did not wish to work upon the land of their fathers, yet could not find "white collar" jobs. The few who had positions, were very limited in their purchasing power because of extremely low salaries.

In the early period after World War I, nationalism, militarism, and conservatism went completely out of fashion. When Tsar Ferdinand

and his politicians were discredited in 1918, the peasantry was ready to take over. The short-lived cabinets of Malinov and Todorov gave way to the government of Stambuliski (October, 1919-June, 1923), and the peasants were in the saddle.

Alexander Stambuliski was the son of a peasant who borrowed a small sum from his schoolteacher (later his wife) and went to study agriculture in Germany. By the time he was 23, he became editor of the chief organ of the Agrarian Party, a descendant of the Agrarian League founded in 1898 as an early protest against the rule of the bourgeosie. Elected to the *Sobranye* in 1908, he soon became known as a brilliant orator. His primitive and forceful eloquence had an irresistible appeal to his peasant audiences. His dogged opposition to the Tsar earned him a death sentence in 1915, although it was subsequently commuted to life imprisonment.

After the flight of Ferdinand, this rugged peasant of Herculean proportions, with small, alert eyes and a top sergeant's mustache, became prime minister in time to sign the Treaty of Neuilly of 1919. Until 1923 he ruled Bulgaria with a rod of iron, favoring the peasant over the townspeople. He had the war cabinet ministers condemned to death, jailed or exiled all other political chiefs, and carried on a systematic persecution of the nation's "learned." A Peasant Guard ("Orange Guards") was established to protect the "Green Dictatorship" against uprisings.

Stambuliski must be credited with the introduction of the labor service system, his efforts to carry out loyally the terms of the peace treaties, and the improvement of Bulgaria's relations with Yugoslavia. But his conviction that a union of all South Slavs under peasant leadership would bring universal peace and harmony met fierce opposition on the part of the Macedonians. They joined army leaders and bourgeois politicians in a *coup d'état* of June 9, 1923, in which Stambuliski was shot.

The Bourgeois Domination

The revolt was put through by a merger of the various bourgeois parties united against their common foes, the agrarian reformers and Left-wing revolutionists. People branded as "radicals" and "communists" were brought to trial and many were executed. Both Agrarians and Marxists retaliated with riots. A period of civil war followed, which abated only gradually. The thin layer of the bourgeois class again reasserted its power and has kept it ever since—though its ranks have always been divided into numerous personal followings. The town, therefore, again ruled the village in Bulgaria after 1923. Officially, all elections were "free." But the government used various devices to make sure that it won safe majorities.

Until recent years, a very unhealthy influence in Bulgarian politics was exerted by the illegal secret Macedonian organization (*IMRO*) and by the military. The long series of murders and executions perpetrated by the *IMRO* is something hardly comprehensible to a Western observer who does not favor fascist methods. There was open warfare in the streets of Sofia and many were killed who dared to question the wishes of the *IMRO*. Although the Bulgarian Government always disclaimed any connection with the *IMRO,* there is reason to believe that King Boris was in close touch with this organization for years.

The whole Macedonian question was complicated by the fact that the population of Bulgaria included some six or seven hundred thousand Macedonians (or citizens of Macedonian origin). The inability or reluctance of the Sofia government to take strong measures against the terrorists can be partly explained by public sympathy for the Macedonians, who claimed that they were fighting for the liberation of Macedonia from Yugoslavia.

King Boris III (1918-1943)

When Boris III ascended the throne on October 3, 1918, at the age of 24, the First World War was still raging outside the kingdom and inside it there was strife verging almost on anarchy. But Boris at first had the confidence of his people, among whom he had been reared and whose army he had served. With courage and tact, he succeeded in establishing order. Unlike Ferdinand, who ruled unconstitutionally but never formally abandoned parliamentary government, Boris twice permitted dictatorship to rule the country without protest during the first 16 years of his reign. From 1919 to 1923, though Parliament was retained, the royal authority was reduced almost to the vanishing point under the Agrarian Premier Stambuliski, as noted above. After Stambuliski was murdered, reactionaries headed by Professor Tsankov instigated a White Terror. For the next ten years near-fascist and fascist groups, many of whom hated the king, maneuvered for power. In 1934 these movements culminated in a *coup d'état* which forced Boris to dissolve Parliament and establish a dictatorship. In the following year, Colonel Gheorgiev, who had engineered the *coup d'état,* was accused of setting himself up as sole dictator.

Throughout all these years there were disorders and border disputes, and sometimes there was a grave threat of civil war. In 1921 a bomb exploded near the king as he was watching a parade in Sofia. In 1925 revolutionaries ambushed his automobile, killing his chauffeur and another occupant. The king himself, though a bullet grazed his mustache, took the wheel and drove into the nearest town for military aid. The next day General Gheorgiev was killed. A bomb exploded at his funeral in the Cathedral in Sofia, killing 123 persons and wounding 323. During 1924 alone there were 200 assassinations in Bulgaria. The Macedonians contributed their full share to Bulgaria's reputation for political terrorism.

Yet Boris scorned danger and rarely remained in his palace. Often he drove through the countryside and stopped to chat with peasants. Boris inherited an aptitude for botany, natural history, and mechanics from his father. His chief hobby was driving locomotives. In 1930, after gaining the Pope's consent to his wedding, on condition that all the children of the marriage be brought up in the Roman faith (a pledge he eventually broke), Boris, a Greek Orthodox, married the third daughter of King Victor Emanuel III of Italy. An heir to the throne, Crown Prince Simeon, was born on June 16, 1937.

After the Gheorgiev dictatorship, Boris tried to re-establish parliamentarianism gradually. Premiers followed one another and Boris carefully played each faction against all other factions. Parliament was never again a governing body, but elections were held, and the assembly proved to be an important mouthpiece for public opinion.

In May, 1938, parliament met for the first time in three years. To prevent a resurgence of the old political parties, whose inefficiency and corruption were at least partly responsible for the 1934 coup, candidates at the parliamentary elections were not permitted to represent parties. However, a considerable number of opponents of the government were elected. This parliament had no authority. It was purely an advisory body unable to enact laws or to overthrow the government. But it persistently harassed the government with demands for the restoration of its legislative powers and made effective use of the growing revisionist sentiment among the people. In October, 1938, the Macedonians killed General Payev, the chief of the General Staff, and attempted a *coup d'état,* but it failed and thousands were arrested.

The tragedy of King Boris was that, like his father before him, he picked the wrong horse. When Boris made a trip to Berlin in the fall of 1940, he set in motion a pattern of events similar to that which followed the unfortunate decision of Ferdinand I, when he pushed Bulgaria into an alliance with the Central Powers in World War I.

That decision eventually forced Ferdinand, formerly Prince of Saxe-Coburg-Gotha, to abdicate his throne and brought Bulgaria to the brink of ruin. Boris' decision, whether caused by personal inclinations or an external compulsion too strong to resist, cost him the loss of his people's confidence and provoked seething discontent within his country.

The die was cast on March 1, 1941, when Bulgaria signed with the Axis in a ceremony at Vienna. The familiar Nazi infiltration tactics had already begun and Boris became, as he had been twice before in his reign, a puppet king. On the other occasions he had been an amiable puppet, but this time he was beset from the outset with worries, trying to keep peace within his country and stalling for time against growing German insistence that he send Bulgarian troops to fight the Russians.

One of the probable reasons for Boris' decision to join the Axis was his father's influence. Ferdinand, who had been living since his abdication on his ancestral estate in Coburg, was always a vehement Germanophile. Boris was not. It was said of Bulgaria that "the king is pro-Ally, the Army pro-German, and the people pro-Russian."

Neither the king nor the people had any desire to enter World War II. But Bulgaria was bound to become a pawn in the game of power politics because of her location in the heart of the Balkans. The Germans had long coveted control of this strategic area. Moreover, the greater part of Bulgaria's exports were going to Germany and most of her finished goods came from Germany. Hitler's Reich thus dominated the Bulgarian economy, overcoming French and British competition by typical Nazi methods.

The Nazis shrewdly fostered the Bulgarian Revisionist Movement, concentrating first on the Dobrudja (in 1940), and then, when Italy began the war in Greece, helping the Bulgarians to secure a corridor through Thrace to the Aegean. Finally, Germany supported Bulgaria's claim to western Macedonia. After that, the Germans gave the Bulgarians a bad shock by presenting a bill for services rendered. This was a peremptory demand for free passage of German troops through Bulgaria. For the last time Boris temporized, but it was too late. By the spring of 1941 he gave in, and German troops marched through his country, using it as a base for the swift campaign against Greece and Yugoslavia.

Later Boris had to join the other Axis satellites in declaring war on the United States and Great Britain on December 13, 1941. But although he introduced all the usual nazi measures against democrats and Jews, he refused to declare war on Russia. Bulgaria had always had a real historic, linguistic, and racial sympathy for Russia, which not even the advent of Communism could upset. Russia's entry into Poland was hailed in Bulgaria as the beginning of Slavic self-determination, and Bulgaria sent thanks to Moscow after she got southern Dobrudja from Romania. But if Bulgaria's heart dictated Moscow, her head dictated Rome-Berlin—which was a bad mistake. As the German lines sagged in Russia and the Mediterranean, Berlin demanded greater help from Sofia.

Bulgarian public opinion did not accept these arrangements without protest. Deputies got up in parliament and denounced the Nazi pressure. The people were so strongly opposed to any Nazi occupation that Premier Filov had to make a speaking tour around the country to explain the situation and attempt to allay unrest. There was much sabotage, and many Bulgarians, despite their traditional hatred of the Yugoslavs, joined the forces of the Yugoslav Partisans.

Boris died on August 28, 1943, and his six-year-old son succeeded him as Tsar Simeon II. Boris' 25-year reign had begun and ended in war and chaos—and the king died under highly suspicious circumstances. It was reported that Boris had returned in broken health from a stormy visit with Adolf Hitler. Sofia and Berlin denied there had been such a visit, but no one could forget other men who had left the Fuehrer's presence the worse for wear. At Berchtesgaden in 1938, just before the annexation of Austria, stubborn Chancellor Kurt Schuschnigg had been shattered by hysterics and threats. At Berlin in 1939, on the eve of Czechoslovakia's dissolution, phlegmatic President Emil Hácha had collapsed after 45 minutes of the Fuehrer's ranting.

During the twenty-five years of his reign, Boris had had eleven prime ministers: one Conservative, one Left-wing Agrarian, one Fascist, three Democrats, one Republican, one general, one aged and intriguing courtier, one able professional diplomat, and one professor of archeology. Two of these men died natural deaths, one was brutally murdered, and one died at a public meeting in the very act of denouncing the king's dictatorial policy. The rest were still living in 1943. One was a German agent, one was in prison for anti-German activities, one was the leader of the *Sobranye* opposition, two were sunk in the oblivion their insignificance deserved, one was Bulgarian Minister to Switzerland, and the remaining one was the prime minister. With the exception of the last two, still in the king's service in 1943, all of them had been in prison more than once. Only two of the eleven, as leaders of the National Assembly majority after more or less free elections, represented the people's choice.[2]

---

[2] Padev, Michael, *Escape from the Balkans* (Indianapolis: Bobbs-Merrill Co., 1943), pp. 90-91. See also the section, pp. 235 ff., dealing with George Dimitrov, later head of the Third International.

Another Bulgarian Defeat

When Boris died, more German troops marched into Bulgaria. A regency council chosen by Berlin, although the *Sobranye* later confirmed the selection, replaced the late king. Prince Cyril, Boris' brother, was one of the four regents. Another was Professor Filov, a Nazi mouthpiece since 1940 and one of the ablest men in the Balkans. Filov and the council ruled by terrorist methods, but kept an apprehensive eye on Soviet Russia. The main thing that made the Bulgarians hesitate to give up when their ultimate defeat became assured in 1944 was the uncertainty of retaining the loot they had gained from Axis partnership—Thrace and Macedonia.

After Romania capitulated in 1944, Bulgaria hastened to get on the peace bandwagon. However, Sofia got thoroughly tangled up in her efforts to get out of the war. The government sent emissaries to Cairo to confer with representatives of England and the United States. This looked to Moscow like an attempt to flirt with the Allies and at the same time to coöperate with Germany on the quiet. So Moscow suddenly declared war against Bulgaria on September 5, 1944. The astounded government in Sofia asked for an armistice six hours later. The Russians gave them the silent treatment on this question, then demanded that Bulgaria declare war on Germany. After four hours of indecision, the Red Army crossed the Danube, swiftly taking the key Bulgarian ports of Varna and Burgas. The Muraviev government fell and a new one formed by Col. Kimon Gheorghiev promptly declared war on a Germany too busy elsewhere to retaliate.

The new Fatherland Front Government had no intention of establishing a Communist regime, although Communists were included in it. Anton Yugov, Communist Minister of the Interior soon proclaimed several outstanding reforms promulgated by the government: equal rights for women; separation of church and state and freedom of religion; religious tolerance and civil marriage; the immediate restoration of the original democratic constitution; and free elections for a new parliament.

On October 28, 1944, Bulgaria signed an armistice with Russia, the United States, and Great Britain—leaving Hitler with only one ally in the European war at that time (Hungary). The former Axis satellite was forced to give up the portions of Greece and Yugoslavia that she had acquired in April, 1941, and, as the first step in making reparations, to make food immediately available for the relief of the population of Greek and Yugoslav territories that had suffered as a result of Bulgarian aggression. (Southern Dobrudja, which the Germans forced Romania to give to Bulgaria in 1940, was not mentioned in the armistice terms). Two Bulgarian armies, commanded by Generals Stanchev and Stojchev, started fighting the Germans side by side with the Red Army and the Yugoslav People's Army of Liberation.

Internally, Bulgaria came into the Russian sphere of influence. Although the Communists represented hardly more than two per cent of the people of Bulgaria, their party was the most active and important in the new government. More than 100 persons were condemned as war criminals. The parade to the execution wall included three former regents (Prince Cyril, brother of the late Tsar Boris III and uncle of the boy King Simeon II; ex-Premier Professor Bogdan Filov, who preferred making history to teaching it; and Lieutenant General Nikola Mikhov, who had held the mistaken belief that the German Army was invincible), two ex-Premiers, twenty-two Ministers, nine Royal Counselors, 66 ex-deputies. To jail for life, with his property confiscated and a fine of 3,000,000 leva, went Bulgaria's last war Premier, Konstantin Muraviev, Agrarian and liberal, who landed Bulgaria in a three-day war with Russia while trying to remain neutral.

The new regime lost no time in proclaiming its Russophile sentiments and welcoming Soviet troops to Sofia. An interesting sidelight was the fact that the Metropolitan of Bulgaria, Mgr. Stephen, gave the Russians an impassioned address of greeting. Still more important, there was a complete repudiation of the "Greater Bulgaria" ideology, which had poisoned relations between Bulgars and Serbs for generations. Since the Macedonian districts were lost, Sofia publicly committed itself to the creation of an autonomous Macedonia. While the plan might have gained the approval of Marshal Tito, the proposed solution was irritating to Greece, whose part of Macedonia has become overwhelmingly Greek as the result of the exchange of populations with Turkey and the mass evictions of the Jewish Sephardim community. This argument remains to be settled. It is evident that Russian influence will be paramount in Bulgaria for a long time to come, and that the Soviet Union's ideas about Balkan readjustments will be accepted.

Bibliography

Black, C. E., *The Establishment of Constitutional Government in Bulgaria* (Princeton, N. J.: Princeton University Press, 1944). A valuable scholarly introduction.

Buchan, John, Ed., *Bulgaria and Roumania* (London: Hodder, 1924). A volume in the Nations of Today series. The treatment is largely historical, with a rather brief review of economic life and conditions.

Logio, G. C., *Bulgaria, Problems and Politics* (London: Heinemann, 1919). A general review of Bulgarian politics before and during World War I, by an author violently opposed to Ferdinand and the militarists and warmly sympathetic to Stambuliski and his group.

Manning, C. A., "The Literary Scene in Bulgaria," *Books Abroad,* XIV (Summer, 1940), pp. 237-239.

Markham, R. H., *Meet Bulgaria* (Sofia: The Author, 1931). One of the best readable studies.

Mosely, P. E., "The Post-War Historiography of Modern Bulgaria," *Journal of Modern History,* IX (September, 1937).

Pasvolsky, Leo, *Bulgaria's Economic Position* (Washington, D. C.: Brookings Institution, 1930). With special references to the reparations problem and the action of the League.

Petroff, B. G., *Son of the Danube* (New York: The Viking Press, 1940).

Roucek, Joseph S., *The Politics of the Balkans* (New York: McGraw-Hill Book Co., 1939). See Chapter VII, "Bulgaria," pp. 118-137, and Chapter VIII, "Macedonians," pp. 138-151.

Todorov, Kosta, *Balkan Firebrand* (Chicago: Ziff-Davis, 1943). Memoirs of a Bulgarian politician and revolutionist.

CHAPTER XXV

ALBANIA (1918-1945)

Geopolitical and Economic Factors

AT THE end of the First World War, Albania was in a difficult position. The Italians declined to leave. But President Wilson's refusal at the Peace Conference to countenance either the partition of Albania or the establishment of an Italian mandate saved the harassed country. In January, 1920, an assembly at Lushnja protested against partition and elected a regency council. The Italians were driven out in August of that year. After the Italian eviction, Albania had 20 years of comparative peace and independence before Italy invaded the country again in 1939.

This little fragment of the old Ottoman Empire is slightly larger than Vermont and has a million inhabitants. It occupies a 200-mile strip of land which separates Yugoslavia's Dalmatian coast from Greece. This seemingly favorable location has been a liability to the people of the area since Roman times. Stronger powers always kept the region in subjection until the Balkan War of 1912 ended more than four centuries of Turkish domination.

Albania is a land corridor into the Balkan Peninsula—but with mountain barriers blocking the way. It dominates the narrow water gate between the Adriatic and the Ionian Sea, and is only about 47 miles across the Strait of Otranto from the "heel" of Italy's "boot." Brindisi, troop embarkation port in southeastern Italy, is 79 miles from Albania's port of Valona, and about 105 miles from Albania's capital, Tirana. The distance is less than that from New York City to Albany. Ever since 1914, Italian forces have literally camped on Albania's doorstep. From June, 1917, when Albania's independence under Italian protection was declared, until the end of 1944, the history of Albania was primarily an account of Italy's waxing or waning influence in the pint-sized Balkan country.

Under Turkish rule, Albania was kept in a primitive state. Rug-

weaving was virtually its only industry.   Since teaching in the Albanian
language was forbidden, education remained stagnant.   Under Zog's
domination in the nineteen-twenties and 'thirties, the country was
slowly coaxed from its slow-tempo agricultural existence toward the
machine age.   But progress was hampered by the barricade of mountain chains, some more than a mile high, which cut Albania off from
her neighbors.   Only two rivers are even partially navigable, and these
dwindle away to bone-dry stream beds in summer.   Horseback travel,
important enough to support big horse fairs, was the only means of
penetrating the country's barbaric highland fastnesses until the First
World War made roads for troop movements a matter of life or death.
In 1933, Albania had over a thousand miles of motor roads, with more
than 2000 bridges across mountain torrents.   While several air routes
were in regular use, chiefly between the capital and the ports, the country's first railroad was not built until after the 1939 occupation by the
Italians.

The region along the Adriatic has been handicapped by the problem
of malaria.   Most Albanians are farmers and stock-raisers.   With
primitive methods of agriculture, they cultivate less than 1,300 square
miles of the country's total area of 10,620 square miles.

Albania has considerable mineral wealth.   Although largely undeveloped, it was an important source of supplies for the Axis countries.
In 1938, Albania ranked sixth among Europe's producers of oil.   Mines
in the mountains of the north were producing copper at the rate of
40,000 tons a year in 1940.

Under Zog, Albania adopted many Western customs in recent years.
Polygamy was forbidden by law, along with the Moslem veil which
once hid all women's faces.   Much of the modernization can be traced
to Albanians who lived for a while in the United States.   Those who
returned to their native land with their savings built modern homes,
equipped with electricity, steam heat, telephones, and up-to-date plumb-
ing.   Their sons played football until the war brought an end to games,
and their daughters attended American movies and expected Albanian
shops to stock lingerie like that worn by American movie stars.

King Zog

The "Snowy Land" of the twentieth century reversed the usual historic procedure by changing its government from a republic to a monarchy.   The turn-about occurred in 1928, when the President for the
preceding three years became King Zog I.

Ahmet Bey Zog was born on October 8, 1895, of a family whose founder came from northern Albania to Mati (in central Albania) toward the end of the fifteenth century. Ahmet Zogolli (who later dropped the "olli," which signifies "son of") was educated at a military school at Monastir and at Galatza Serai. He was only sixteen when the First Balkan War broke out, but a very important Albanian in the eyes of the Turks, for upon the death of his father he became chief of the Mati tribes. The tribesmen refused to fight against the Serbs except under their chieftain. So Zog was taken out of school and put at the head of his tribes, which he led against the Serbian invaders who had burned his family's dwellings. When the Prince of Wied arrived, Zog was known as his supporter.

When the First World War broke out, Zog unfurled the ancient eagle banner of Skanderbeg and swept down upon the Albanian plain, driving the Serbs before him. He agreed to coöperate with the Austrian armies and distinguished himself on the battlefield in a series of astonishing feats of daring. Once he captured a whole company of the enemy single-handed. He was lavishly decorated and was rated one of the most notable of Albanian heroes.

Young Zog marched on Albasan in 1916, where the Albanian patriots summoned a provisional National Assembly and elected a Commission of Initiative under his presidency. The Austrians, however, interfered with his plans to restore the Prince of Wied's government. At first he commanded the Albanian forces coöperating with the Austro-Hungarian armies. But when it was discovered that he had vague intentions of conspiring with the Bulgarians to re-establish Albanian administrative independence, he was invited by the Austrians to Vienna for a council of war and then treacherously interned.

At the end of hostilities he returned to Albania, which was in a chaotic condition. Although only in his early twenties, Zog was instrumental in driving an Italian army of occupation out of Valona, halting another Yugoslav invasion, crushing numerous tribal insurrections, and securing the recognition of Albania's independence by the Great Powers. All this was accomplished with inadequate supplies of arms and ammunition and hardly any financial resources. Moreover, he had to cope with the constant threat of foreign and internal intrigues.

Zog's abilities pushed him ahead with dazzling speed. From March 27, 1921, to November 20, 1921, he was Minister of the Interior. In December, 1921, he again held that office. In December, 1922, he became Prime Minister. Thereafter, with the exception of a brief interlude in 1924 when Fan Noli's revolt drove him out of power temporarily, he ruled the country, climbing the official ladder as Commander-in-Chief, Premier, Dictator, first President of the Albanian Republic, and finally King. He became President on January 31, 1925, and was proclaimed Zog I, King of the Albanians, on September 1, 1928.

Zog's campaign to modernize Albania can be favorably compared to President Kemal's in Turkey. He promulgated a civil code based on French law, abolished polygamy, and inaugurated state control over marriage, divorce, and education. A new penal code, modeled on the Italian example, replaced the Ottoman code. The promotion of national consciousness was pushed by the compulsory use of a common language for schoolbooks, newspapers, and literary works. Previously they had been printed in local dialects. Another national aim was achieved by legal recognition of the native Christian Albanian Church, which uses the Albanian language and ritual. The Law of Agrarian Reform of 1930 laid the foundation for a nationalistic class of small peasant proprietors. The country was stabilized by the pacification of outlying districts. In foreign policy, Zog favored Italy and received regular support from her, but he was by no means a puppet in the hands of Mussolini.

King Zog ruled as an autocrat, but he used his power with a sense of moderation. He was firm with his enemies, but conciliatory when he felt that conditions permitted it. His ardent patriotism eventually won the support of nearly all Albanian patriots except the extreme reactionaries. Personally he was quiet and retiring, but completely fearless. As the only European ruler who established a kingdom in the post-war period, he displayed a high degree of political acumen and consistency. Zog belonged to a faded world which accepted democracy by hearsay only, but in that faded world he did the work consigned to him with zest and urbanity.

Before Zog reached the peak of his gradual rise to power, Albanian politics was chiefly concerned with the disposal of foreign invaders during and after the First World War. Soon afterward the struggle of personalities assumed violent form. Basically it represented a conflict between conservative elements and progressives who wanted to imitate the liberal methods of western Europe and America, where some of them were trained. But as Zog asserted his leadership, the issue crystallized around his own personality. Gradually his most dangerous opponents were eliminated. Most of them went into exile or were liquidated by violent means. From another point of view, Zog's government represented the domination of the new bourgeois and professional classes and the intellectuals over the landowning beys, who were gradually losing ground. The agrarian laws, if enforced, would be the death-knell of their influence and political power.

It is impossible to form a totally unfavorable opinion of Zog's rule. It united "the form of democracy with the reality of a not unpopular despotism." [1] Zog's supporters found it easy to get out of prison, elections were a farce, and members of the king's own tribe, the Mati, were allowed to remain armed. But Zog's acceptance of a British gendarmerie, his suppression of brigandage and vendettas, his encouragement of education, and his appointment of a "new gang" of young men of liberal ideas as ministers under Mehdi Frasheri in 1935, with an Anglophile foreign minister, were hopeful signs.

Zog's marriage to the Hungarian-born daughter of an American mother was popular. But Zog's title of "King of the Albanians," analogous to the Greek "King of the Hellenes," alarmed Yugoslavia as implying claims to the Albanian minorities in that country.

The Italian Occupation

Albania had an eternal financial problem. Having failed to obtain financial assistance from the League of Nations, Zog turned to Italy, which granted Albania a series of loans beginning in 1925. Zog had to pay for this help by signing a treaty in 1926 which gave Mussolini the right to intervene, "on Albania's request," in the country's foreign and domestic affairs. Another treaty was signed a year later. But the Italians claimed that King Zog "did little to show appreciation for Italy's moral and material aid to his government and his people." [2]

In April, 1939, two weeks after Hitler occupied Czechoslovakia, Italy's legions invaded Albania. Zog had to flee with his wife and his newly-born heir to the throne. On April 12, the Albanian Assembly offered the crown to Italy's King Victor Emanuel III. The new constitution of Albania, proclaimed on June 3, 1939, vested all executive and legislative functions in the Italian King, assisted by the Supreme Fascist Corporative Council. Rome of course assumed control of Albania's foreign relations.

In 1940-1941 Albania became a principal battleground of the Greek-Italian war. By March, 1941, Greek forces had occupied a large part of the country. But on April 23, 1941, the German Army forced the Greeks in Albania to capitulate.

---

[1] Robinson, Vandeleur, *Albania's Road to Freedom* (New York: W. W. Norton, 1942). For more details, see The Royal Institute of International Affairs, *South-Eastern Europe* (New York: Oxford University Press, 1939), pp. 87-89.

[2] Italian Library of Information, *The Kingdom of Albania* (New York, August, 1939), p. 14.

During 1943, native resistance to Axis rule grew rapidly. In March, the weary and disgusted Italians gave up the pretense of administering Albanian civil affairs in a "peaceful" manner. Guerrilla and patriot bands played the dominant role in bringing about this failure of Italian administration. Raids on Italian military convoys and garrisons became very frequent after 1942. The shaky position of the puppet Albanian premiers was demonstrated at the time of the statement by Secretary of State Hull on December 10, 1943, and reiterated by Russia's Molotov, pledging the return of freedom to Albania and praising the resistance of the patriots. The traitor-premier Kruja protested vehemently against "the interference of the Allies in the intercourse between Albania and Italy." His concern over the effect of the Allied statement was well-founded, for his cabinet collapsed a few weeks later.

Political instability characterized Albania thereafter. Two quisling governments were set up within a week after Kruja's resignation. The Italians finally found it necessary, having exhausted the available supply of prominent traitors, to appoint Maliq Bashati as premier. He had been Minister of the Interior in the first cabinet that came to power after the invasion.

Additional evidence to prove the lack of collaboration between the Albanians and the Fascists was forthcoming during the summer of 1943. At that time the Italian authorities sought to raise an Albanian legion to fight in Russia, but not a single man volunteered. At the same time the Italians demanded contributions of wool to make uniforms for the coming Russian winter, but Albanians burned the warehouse in Durazzo where the wool was stored. All Albanian drivers were forbidden by guerrilla leaders to transport Axis soldiers under penalty of death. Then Italy surrendered and anarchy descended upon Albania.

In June, 1944, the Germans opened a full-scale drive against the various patriotic and guerrilla movements, calling in a division and a half of Nazi troops. They were supported by Albanian quislings. The guerrillas vanished into the hills and the German offensive against the Albanian Partisan Army of National Liberation in southern Albania spent itself without achieving its chief aim—liquidation of the Partisan movement. While fighting was in progress, a national congress was elected. It met and nominated an anti-Fascist committee to administer all territory liberated from the Germans. Hoxha was named president and Myslim Pza vice-president.

Up to August, 1944, Allied intervention had managed to stave off a serious civil war between rival guerrilla groups by promoting the idea of independence, which the King of Italy had already conceded. In that month, Bedri Spahui, head of the mission of the National Army of Liberation to the Allies, reported that there had been an open break within the patriot forces. The nationalist faction under Abas Kupi, which wanted King Zog back, accused the opposition group of joining the Balli Kombetar, or collaborating elements, in working openly with the Germans.

This was the situation when Allied forces landed in Albania in the fall of 1944. At that time, in a 40-room mansion outside London, Albania's King Zog and his half-American Queen Geraldine held a modest court but kept sensitive ears cocked toward the Balkans. Zog was eager to go home.

On December 2, 1944, Colonel General Enver Hoxha, who headed both the Partisan Army and the government as Premier, entered the liberated capital of Tirana. The arrival of the government in the capital on the thirty-second anniversary of Albanian independence, was the signal for three days of national rejoicing. Hoxha pledged a democratic regime and promised to fight to preserve the nation's southern boundaries. This was a reaction to a statement by Greek Premier Papandreou to the effect that Greece would seek a portion of southern Albania in post-war settlements. In January, 1945, King Zog, who had been living in Great Britain since 1940, declared that he would approve the creation of a new government for Albania "if and when the proposal were made."

Bibliography

Baerlein, Henry, *A Difficult Frontier* (London: Leonard Parsons, 1922). The general relations between the Serbs and Albanians as a setting for a discussion of the Serbo-Albanian frontier established by the Ambassadors' Conference in November, 1921.

Bareilles, Betrand, Durham, M. E., and others, *Albania and the Albanians* (Paris: Chapelot, 1920). A general survey of the land and the people, by sympathetic writers.

Cassavetes, N. J., *Epirus and Albania, 1919* (New York: Oxford University Press, 1919). The Northern Epirus question as it was stated at Paris by Greece.

Chekrezi, C. A., *Albania Past and Present* (New York: The Macmillan Co., 1919). The expansion of a thesis prepared by an Albanian student at Harvard, with emphasis on events during and just after World War I.

Federal Writers' Project of the Works Progress Administration of Massachusetts, *The Albanian Struggle in the Old World and New* (Boston: The Writer, Inc., 1939). One of the best short surveys.

Ismail, Kemal Bey, *Memoirs* (London: Constable, 1920). A picture of old-school diplomacy by an Albanian statesman, cousin of the Grand Vizier, Ferid Pasha Vlora, and himself at one time in Turkish service. He played an important part in preparing Albanian independence and was Premier in the first cabinet in 1912.

"Recognition of Albania Spotlights Balkan Troubles," *Geographic School Bulletin*, XXIV (December 17, 1945).

Robinson, Vandeleur, *Albania's Road to Freedom* (New York: W. W. Norton, 1942).

Roucek, Joseph S., "Albania As a Nation," pp. 107-109, in *The Annals of The American Academy of Political and Social Science*, CCXXXII (March, 1944), "A Challenge to Peacemakers."

Stickney, E. P., *Southern Albania or Northern Epirus in European International Affairs, 1912-1923* (Stanford: Stanford University Press, 1926). A scholarly introduction.

Swire, Joseph, *Albania. The Rise of a Kingdom* (London: Williams and Norgate, 1929). The most extensive history of modern Albania, but in form hardly more than a chronological handbook.

CHAPTER XXVI

GREECE (1920-1945)

Geopolitical Factors

MODERN Greece occupies a very important strategic position in Europe. With an area of 50,146 square miles—approximately the size of the State of New York—and a population of 7,800,000—a little more than that of New York City—the country is located in the southernmost part of Europe with the Ionian and the Adriatic seas to the west, the Aegean Sea to the east, and the Mediterranean Sea to the south. Greece is bounded on the north by Albania, Yugoslavia, and Bulgaria; on the east by Turkey. Because of her geographical situation, Greece straddles the Mediterranean route and is necessarily of special interest to a great sea power, such as Great Britain, with which she maintains an identity of interest in both commerce and politics. These two countries have been traditionally friends ever since the Greeks won their independence at the beginning of the nineteenth century.

The Greek constitution designates the Orthodox Church as the religion of the State, but guarantees complete freedom of worship to all faiths. The population is remarkably homogeneous. In 1937, there were 126,000 Moslems, 72,790 Jews, 35,180 Roman Catholics, 18,600 Albanians, and 9,000 Protestants. The rest of the more than seven million people were Greek Orthodox. Of the latter, 33,635 were Armenians who came as refugees from Turkey at the end of World War I, 19,700 were Kutsovlachs, and 16,775 were Bulgarians.[1] This absence of large racial minorities, unique in Central-Eastern Europe, was achieved by a compulsory exchange of populations in 1923 between Greece and her two neighbors, Bulgaria and Turkey, when over a million Greeks emigrated to Greece from Asia Minor and about 50,000 came from Bulgaria. In addition, some 60,000 Greek-Russians sought refuge in Greece after the Bolshevist revolution. All of these people were Greeks by race and belonged to the Greek Orthodox Church,

---

[1] *Annuaire Statistique de la Grèce* (Athens, 1937), p. 71.

whose administration is vested in a Holy Synod consisting of the Metropolitan of Athens and 12 other metropolitans or archbishops.

For a variety of reasons, means of communication in Greece have always been limited. There are only 2,692 kilometers of railroads. Of the total, 1,474 km. of standard gauge railroads are state-owned, 842 km. comprise the Peloponnesus line, and 253 km. the Thessaly line. A short electrical line, principally for passengers, connects Athens and Piraeus. Coastwise shipping, required by law to be of Greek registry, carries a great deal of passenger and freight traffic. Air travel is handled by one Greek line and a number of foreign lines. The network of 17,742 km. of roads includes 9,965 km. of national highways, 3,954 km. of county roads, 1,838 km. of municipal roads, and 1,985 km. of tourist roads.[2]

Economic Factors

Greece is mostly rugged and mountainous, with few plains and fewer rivers. The climate is mild the year round. The density of population is 54.73 per square mile—the lowest in this part of the world except for Turkey, where the density is only 22.03 persons per square mile. In spite of a marked movement from the country to the cities, 67 per cent of the Greek population in 1938 was rural, 33 per cent was urban. Only about 45 per cent of the population was gainfully occupied. Of those employed, 54 per cent were engaged in agricultural or related pursuits, 25 per cent were wage earners, and the remaining 21 per cent were professional people, civil servants, and domestics.

The arable land does not exceed 20 per cent of the total area. Small landholdings have prevailed since 1917, when large properties were expropriated and distributed to the peasants. This was the first stage in the program of agrarian reform, which was speeded up by the settlement of the exchanged populations from Turkey and Bulgaria in 1923. Further subdivision of landholdings were prohibited by a law passed in 1939. The coöperative movement was legally authorized in 1914. It was predominantly rural—some 65 per cent of the agricultural population were members of coöperatives or were served by them. In 1938, 300,000 members were associated in 9,611 coöperatives, of which 6,270 were rural and 3,341 urban. There were 4,476 credit associations; 1,684 workers' productive and labor associations; 946 housing and construction groups; 625 consumers coöperatives; 514 processing and productive groups; and 493 marketing associations.

Industrial development is hampered by an inadequate supply of coal

[2] *Ibid.*, p. 251 ff.

and raw materials. Well-developed manufacturing industries, in order of importance, are the textile, mechanical, chemical, building material, and tobacco industries. The first general system of social insurance for commercial and industrial workers was established by law in 1934. It provided financial protection against sickness, accidents, maternity, disability, old age, and tuberculosis, as well as life insurance. This insurance was made compulsory for all employees in urban areas designated as insurance centers; persons employed in agriculture, forestry, and stock raising were excluded. Workmen's compensation was introduced in 1914; it covered wage-earning and salaried employees when injured in the course of their employment. Seamen were protected by special insurance against disability, old age, accidents, death from tuberculosis and heart diseases, sickness, and unemployment. No government plan for the payment of family allowances existed except for a collective agreement covering bank employees, signed in 1937, which included salary scales based on length of service, family allowances, and increments.

A large part of the Greek Government's income derives from heavy consumption taxes, such as import duties, fees, monopolies, excise and turnover taxes. The yield from direct taxation is relatively small and collections are difficult. All taxes collected in 1939 represented 24 per cent of the entire national income, calculated by the Supreme National Council at 55 billion drachmas or $400,000,000. The fiscal year runs from April 1st to March 31st. The budget for 1938-39 amounted to 12.7 billion drachmas or $80,000,000, of which 30 per cent went to the Ministry of Finance, 17 per cent was appropriated for war, 12 per cent for communications, 7.8 per cent for education, 7 per cent for hygiene, 6.5 per cent for the Ministry of the Interior, and 5 per cent for the navy. The service on the national debt in foreign exchange, though greatly reduced, absorbed about 30 per cent of the budget in that fiscal year.

Social Conditions

In Greece, the family is patterned on a patriarchal tradition. The father, as its head, exercises a high degree of moral authority. Until recent years, women were concerned almost exclusively with domestic duties. Those who were employed were engaged mostly in domestic service. Since World War I, however, a large number of women have been absorbed into industrial and commercial enterprises, others have taken up various professions, and many more have engaged in government service. The new economic power thus acquired has enabled women to assert a social freedom approaching that of their menfolk. Divorce, however, is relatively rare.

Living conditions, in contrast with those of neighboring states, are fairly high because of coastal industries and the merchant marine (which is the ninth largest in the world), the cultivation of intensive crops of tobacco and currants, and the relatively high efficiency of workers. Housing is that of a civilized but poor country. Marble, wood, stucco, and brick houses range in elegance and form from the villas of the wealthy to the simple one-room abode of the impoverished peasant. Electric lighting has been widely introduced and gas ranges are common, but electric appliances, running water, bathrooms, and other modern facilities are still considered as luxuries, especially in small towns.

Demands for food, clothing, and shelter are comparatively simple. Consequently there is little need for public charity in normal times. Indeed, charity is not looked upon favorably and few are willing to undergo the stigma of being public charges, no matter what their economic difficulties. There are always relatives, near and distant, to lend a hand. The staple diet features olives and olive oil. Lamb is the commonest meat, and fish is consumed in great quantities; these are accompanied by bread, macaroni, rice, lentils, and leafy vegetables. Ordinarily breakfast is short and simple, lunch a more elaborate affair, and supper the important meal of the day. The latter is usually eaten quite late in the evening, since time is taken out after lunch for a mid-day rest.

As to personal traits, the Greek is a born democrat—a characteristic surviving from ancient times. Titles of nobility are unknown and castes non-existent. Instead, ancestry, wealth, and learning form the trinity of class consciousness and privilege. The Greek does not participate in any significant fraternal or tribal organizations. His personal character is dominated by five outstanding qualities: (a) a love for liberty which he places above personal considerations; (b) a keen sense of honor and a personal dignity that make him an intelligent social being; (c) a degree of honesty that does not prevent him from being as shrewd as any other trader in business transactions; (d) an outspoken friendliness that inspires trust and confidence and endears him to strangers; and (e) a single-minded idealism that transforms him into a bold fighter and a dependable worker. Gambling, though of little consequence, is legalized, and the Lottery of the National Navy finds wide appeal among rich and poor alike.

Popular entertainment used to consist chiefly of puppet-shows, public dancing, sitting at a cafe sipping Greek coffee or "ouzo" (the Greek gin distilled from grapes), and talking politics. Puppet-plays have been largely displaced by the movies. Public sports are mostly identified with track meets, mass calisthenics, and indoor exercises. The peculiarly national game is soccer-football and loyalties are strong in intercity or international matches, but there is little commercial exploitation of this or any other sport.

The most important national holidays and festivals are connected with the Church. They are topped by the celebration of Holy Easter and the Assumption of the Virgin Mary. There are numerous shrines to the latter throughout Greece; pilgrims from all parts of the country flock to them in thousands during the festivals, of which that of the island of Tinos is the most renowned.[3] In case of illness or accident, people from all walks of life often vow that, if they recover, they will journey each year to a particular shrine. This custom is a relic of ancient times. Once made, the pledge is faithfully fulfilled year after year. In addition, a number of religious festivals attain local prominence because churches are named in honor of important saints and also because of the fact that the Greeks generally celebrate the name day of their saint rather than the date of their birth.

Cultural Development

With the single exception of the grammar, modern Greek approximates the language as spoken and written by the ancients. It made its way into the army and the civil service of the Byzantine Empire in the seventh century and developed into the spoken or *demotiki* language of modern Greece during the reign of Emperor Michael III in the ninth century, when the cycle of the Acritic epics was inaugurated. These ballads, having been expressed in a dynamic, expanding language, were passed from generation to generation by word of mouth. They are found today incorporated in all the principal neo-Hellenic dialects throughout the contemporary Hellenic world. Not less remarkable than the uniformity of language and character is the similarity of custom, of lore, and of superstition; in short, of everything which is most ancient and most national in Greece today. But the language remains the chief connecting link with the past. According to Kostis Palamas, unquestionably the poet laureate of contemporary Greece (1859-1943), the *demotiki* "is the language of life and the language of truth."

---

[3] It was on August 15, 1940, while Tinos was crowded with worshippers, that the light cruiser *Elli* was torpedoed and sunk without warning by an Italian submarine, causing a large number of casualties.

Elementary education covers six years; it is free and obligatory. Secondary or preparatory education is divided into classical studies, pursued in the so-called "Gymnasium" (the Greek equivalent of the French *Lycée*), and commercial studies; it varies from four to six years. All education is directed and supervised by the Ministry of Education and Religions. Athens is the educational center of the country. Among its higher institutions of learning are the National University, the Polytechnic Institute, the Superior School of Commercial Science, the Superior School of Political Sciences, the School of Eveloidon for army cadets, and the School of Dokimon for midshipmen. All of these are State-supported. After World War I, a second university was founded in Salonica. In addition, there are three so-called American Colleges; the Athens College for boys, the Helleniko College for girls, and the Anatolia College in Macedonia. The American Farm School, so-called "House" School after its founder Charles House, also in Macedonia, trains young people in farming. Finally there are in Athens the British Archaeological School, the French Archaeological School, and the American School of Classical Studies. The latter possesses a magnificent library, the *Gennadion,* built largely with funds supplied by the Carnegie Foundation. However, illiteracy is still high, especially among women and people living in the rural areas.

Arts and Letters

In the world of arts and letters, contemporary Greece occupies a most enviable position. Her large literature is distinguished for portraying the fortunes of the nation, for reflecting language disputes and social upheavals, and for bearing the impress of Western schools of thought.

A limited number of references will show the general trend. Rigas (1757-98) was a man of action, passionately devoted to the liberation of his people, while Bilaras (1771-1823), a poet and a prose-writer, was instrumental in introducing the spoken or "demotiki" language into the literature of the day. His work was ably carried on by Professor Psihari (1854-1929) of the University of Paris, who was in turn damned and praised as the father of modern Greek. Of the Phanariotes, the two brothers, A. and P. Soutsos (1803-63 and 1806-68, respectively), excelled in satire, comedies, philosophy, and patriotic novels. The so-called "Old School" of Athens was influenced by the struggles of the young nation. It is represented by George and Achilles Parashos (1822-86 and 1838-95, respectively), Paparigopoulos (1843-73) and Bikelas (1835-1908). On the other hand, the "New School" of Athens, founded by Kostis Palamas (1859-1943), the poet laureate of Greece, with a tremendous output of poetry, shows vigor and originality and competes with the best elsewhere. It is graced by many poets and writers, such as Malakasis, Sikelianos, Skippis, and others. Xenopoulos (1862-   ) is a prolific playwriter, while Nirvanas (1866-   ) is the classic example of artistic newspaper writing depicting everyday life.

In music, Byzantine chorals and popular songs found expression in the compositions of Lavrangas, Calomiris, Mitropoulos (the latter an internationally known orchestra conductor), and other composers. Theotocopoulos (El Greco) is well-known as a painter, while Dimitriadis has done creditable work in sculpture. One of the latter's works, the Discus-thrower, was donated by a Greek-American to the City of New York and set up in Central Park.

History After World War I

The First World War came to an end for all but one of the Allies with the signing of the Armistice in 1918. For Greece, it continued for four more years in the plains of Asia Minor, where Greek troups were sent under an Allied mandate to liberate the Greek people who had inhabited the Vilayet of Aidin for centuries and to stamp out the Turkish insurrection. This insurrection was led by the Turkish Nationalist Kemal Pasha, who was aided and abetted by France and Italy with military equipment and other help. Such perfidy on the part of two allies to a gallant nation shocked the world; it resulted in the massacre of over one million Greeks and in the catastrophe of Smyrna under the guns of the Allied navies anchored there. The Greeks, who had drive the Turks to the outskirts of Ankara, were forced to retreat and finally to evacuate Asia Minor, leaving their people to the mercy of the advancing enemy.

Two significant events which followed this catastrophe shaped the destinies of Greece during the short period between the two World Wars. First, the influx of Greek refugees from Asia Minor, Bulgaria, and the Black Sea region taxed the resources of the nation to the limit. Continuous wars since 1912 had depressed trade and agriculture, had increased the national debt, and had dislocated the entire national economy. The task of reconstructing the war-torn country and settling more than a million and a half refugees would have baffled even a financially healthy nation with ample natural resources. But Greece showed an astonishing power of recovery. With the assistance of the League of Nations and her friends in America, she went ahead to solve the problem. Within a comparatively short period, her new citizens became wage-earners and successful farmers, thus aiding the rehabilitation of the country.

The second event concerned the abolition of the Constitutional Monarchy and the establishment of a Republic that lasted from 1924 until 1935, when the revolutionary cycle in Greece was completed with the restoration of the Monarchy which bore the constitutional imprint of 1864.[4] The new Republic was born of military disaster rather than instigated by widespread popular opposition to the Monarchy as an institution. It lived eleven turbulent years marked by parliamentarianism, army *coups d'état* and popular discontent resulting from the worldwide economic crisis of the thirties. It hardly had a chance to blossom and bear fruit.

Barring the army *coups d'état*, which were universally repudiated by a people imbued with true democratic traditions, the party strife that developed during these years was no more than a duplication of what was going on all over Europe in an effort to meet and solve manifold post-war problems. A parallel can easily be found in the party strife of France, which was waged by an inordinately large number of parties ranging all the way from extreme Right to extreme Left, in contrast to the two major party system across the Channel in Britain and across the Atlantic in the United States.

The Royalist-Republican dispute, aggravated by personal animosities and aggrandizement, became the fundamental issue in Greek politics. It hinged on the personality of M. Venizelos, who became Prime Minister in 1928 as the representative of Republicanism and remained in control until 1933. The bad economic situation of Greece and the discontent produced by defects and abuses in administration finally brought his regime to an end.

In 1933 the Royalists returned to power. A Republican revolt in March, 1935, was suppressed by General Kondylis, who became Prime Minister by a *coup d'état* in October of the same year. A stage-managed plebiscite showed 97 per cent in favor of the restoration of the Monarchy. King George returned from London and politely dismissed General Kondylis.

The last general elections in Greece were held on January 26, 1936, after the return of the king. They gave no majority to any single party. As a result, a coalition party government was formed, first under Professor Demerjis and later, after his death, under General Metaxas,

---

[4] Kaltchas, Nicholas, *Introduction to the Constitutional History of Modern Greece* (New York: Columbia University Press, 1940), pp. 149 ff.

the leader of a small parliamentary group. Metaxas forthwith presented a comprehensive program, adjourned Parliament, and promised to govern under an Enabling Act. On August 4, 1936, however, accusing the Communists of threatening to call a general strike, the Premier declared a state of emergency, dissolved the Chamber, and continued to govern by royal decree. Thus the Metaxas dictatorship was born. It was in the midst of reconstructing the life of the nation, financially, internally, and militarily, when the Fascist blow involved Greece in World War II.

Greece and World War II

At the outbreak of World War II, Greece's relations with her neighbors were quite friendly on the whole. The ill-feeling resulting from the Turkish war of 1922 and the expulsion of the Asia Minor Greeks had been replaced by cordial relations. Although Bulgaria wanted direct access to the Aegean Sea, Sofia made a declaration of neutrality soon after the beginning of the war. The Greek-Albanian frontier in the Epirus was not a burning issue, and Greek-Yugoslav relations were extremely friendly. There was, however, a distinct and well-founded Greek mistrust of Italy. Moreover, Germany was more than faintly interested in Greece, and Goering, Goebbels, and Schacht had visited the country together with numerous trade agents and "tourists."

In the Nazi *Drang nach Osten,* the Balkans formed a first-rate sphere of influence for Hitler. But Mussolini thought differently; he held that Dalmatia, Croatia, and Greece should fall to Italy's share of the spoils. How these two modern "conquistadors" ultimately settled their differences is not known, but Mussolini believed that his chance lay in getting there first. And he did—though he often later wished he hadn't.

He made a good beginning in Albania, his faithful ally, by landing his legions on Good Friday, April 7, 1939, to prepare the way for the final attack against Greece. Thereupon Britain and France offered Greece a territorial guarantee against aggression—a gesture at no time demanded by the Greek Government. This was followed by a note signed on September 12, 1939, by the Duce himself, in which he solemnly declared that "no military action whatsoever" was contemplated against Greece.

But a year later, at 3:00 A.M. on October 28, 1940—"another day that will live in infamy"—an Italian ultimatum was handed to Prime Minister Metaxas demanding a decision by 6 A.M. Actually, the Italian hordes in Albania had crossed the Greek frontier at 5:30, discounting in advance the emphatic refusal of the Greek premier to heed the ultimatum. Mussolini was in a great hurry. He felt confident that his armies, strongly reinforced and far superior to the Greeks in both equipment and numbers, would rapidly overrun Greece. He was "misled." His legions were held and in four weeks defeated and chased back to the edge of the Adriatic—as gallant a campaign by a resolute people fighting for their homeland as World War II produced.

After five months of frustration and defeat, Mussolini was finally rescued by his Axis partner in crime—and with him, a number of proud and bemedalled generals: Soddu, Visconti-Prasca, Cavallero, and even Badoglio himself. All met the "contemptible little" Greek army—and regretted it. On April 6, 1941, the German hordes attacked from Bulgaria—a country adept at stabbing friends and neighbors in the back— and through Yugoslavia—a house divided among the Serbs, the Croats, and the fifth columnists. In spite of the belated but eager help of the British, the Nazis succeeded in occupying the entire Greek mainland within a month. A three-pronged rule of occupation was introduced: the Nazis stayed in the large cities and ports, such as Athens, Piraeus, Salonica, and Patras; the Italians took over the outlying districts; and the Bulgarians sneaked up, for their share in the spoils, into western Thrace and Greek Macedonia (except for Salonica).

Though the mainland was quickly overrun by the Nazis, the king and his Tsouderos government, with the remnants of the army, transferred to the island of Crete, where they continued the unequal fight for four more weeks. By doing so, the Greeks gave the British time to prepare against the Axis menace in Egypt and delayed by that much the Nazi attack against the Soviets. The king and his government were finally forced to abandon Crete and go into exile in London and then in Cairo. They waged war from there until October, 1944, when the government under Premier George Papandreou, a former Venizelos adherent, returned to Athens, following the defeat and expulsion of the Nazis.

The Cost of the Axis Occupation

The modern rule of tyranny over Greece lasted from April, 1941, to the fall of 1944. It exacted a terrible toll in lives and wealth. Over half a million of the Greek population died of starvation; almost 75,000 people were shot by German, Italian, and Bulgarian firing squads; and 350,000 were arrested or sent to the dreadful concentration camps that dotted the country from one end to the other. No less than 150,000 innocent men, women, and children were forced to abandon their homes in Thrace and Macedonia in favor of Bulgarian settlers, and a great number of them were carried to Bulgaria for slave labor and eventual extermination. Approximately 1600 cities, towns, and villages, including numerous monasteries and churches of irreplaceable antiquity, were razed to the ground either for sheltering guerrilla patriots, for assisting Allied airmen to escape, or for other reasons. As a result, more than a million and half people—one-fifth of the population of Greece—were rendered homeless and destitute. Another million are suffering from tuberculosis, malaria, and other diseases. Of the Greek merchant marine, consisting at the start of the war of 450 freighters (2,600,000 tons), 69 passenger ships (150,000 tons), 716 sailing ships (over 30 tons each), and 1,100 other small boats of all kinds, Greece lost through enemy action 364 freighters (2,100,000 tons), 65 passenger ships (110,000 tons), 19 salvage tugs, and most of her sailing vessels, a total of well over two million tons. For a nation of limited resources, these losses were appalling. They pointed up the inevitability of a long and arduous road to relief, reconstruction, and rehabilitation, a road impossible to travel without substantial Allied assistance.

Despite all this, the morale of the Greek people remained high during the occupation. Guerrilla bands were harassing the Italians and Bulgarians as early as the autumn of 1941. One important guerrilla group was the ELAS (National Popular Liberation Front), controlled by the EAM (National Liberation Movement), a left wing organization which had formerly opposed Metaxas. Other large bodies were the EDES (National Democratic Greek Army), which favored monarchical principles, and the EKKA (National Movement of Social Progress). After the Italian collapse, EAM secured the lion's share of abandoned Italian arms. Fighting, skillfully fomented by the Germans, took place between the forces of EAM and EDES during 1943-1944.

The guerrilla civil war was only one of the political differences in Greece. The whole problem of the form of the Greek Government came to a head. King George II was unpopular with the underground movement in Greece and was asked not to return until a plebiscite had been held to determine the future of the Monarchy. Unrest and distrust of British motives with regard to King George mounted rapidly in liberal Greek circles everywhere.

Liberated Greece

In September, 1944, the ELAS and the EDES finally established fighting unity, both recognizing the authority of the government-in-exile. Thus a coalition government came into being, representing all anti-Nazi political movements in Greece.

In 1941, British forces had joined the heroic Greek armies in a vain effort to stem the German tide. In October, 1944, they were back again. Working hand in hand with those Greek underground forces that did not know the word surrender, they chased the Germans before them. By the beginning of November, the whole of Greece was liberated. After three and a half years in exile, the Greek Government returned to Athens.

But Premier Papandreou found himself confronted by political as well as humanitarian problems. The EDES were anti-Bulgarian and anti-Russian. As Rightists, they wanted Greece to profit from the war by annexing as much neighboring territory as possible; they also wanted the nation to continue in Britain's sphere of influence and to get British support for an expansionist program. The EAM, as leftists, had wider popular support. Although dominated by the Greek Communist Party, their ideas pointed toward a democratic rather than a Soviet system of government. They were friendly toward Russia and concerned more with internal reforms than with territorial expansion.

Greece's forty-two days of civil war from December 3, 1944, to January, 1945, were among the saddest and most tragic events of World War II. Upon her liberation, Greece was in a situation analogous to that when she attained her independence in 1829, after an eight-year war against the Ottoman Empire. Everything was in ruins. Everything had to be rebuilt: homes, towns, communications, finances, economy, institutions. How did the tragedy of civil war come about on top of this catastrophe?

The civil strife in Greece developed between the National Liberation Front (EAM), and its military arm, the ELAS, on the one hand, and the government-in-exile which returned to Athens on October 14, 1944, with the support of British military forces, on the other. The roots of the conflict can be found in the British policy toward Greece.

The British had kept a tight grip on the Tsouderos government in Cairo for the three years it remained the nominal Greek Government. Churchill's desire to keep this government in being until the liberation and to maintain King George II on the Greek throne was frankly stated in successive public addresses. He succeeded at Casablanca in obtaining an agreement from President Roosevelt that, as between Britain and the United States, Britain was to have complete charge of Allied military operations and corollary diplomatic policy in the Middle East and the Balkans.

Meanwhile, in Greece, the National Liberation Front became the most powerful resistance movement and left no doubt regarding its views on the question of the king: he was not to return to Greece until a plebiscite should decide whether he was to be restored to the throne. They also made it plain that the Tsouderos government, in their eyes, was a shadow government drawing its authority solely from the king, a successor to the Metaxas dictatorship, a regime in no way representative of the fighting people of Greece. When this became clear to the British Foreign Office, its policy veered away from support of the EAM and shifted to EDES, whose leadership acknowledged the authority of the king.

On the return to Athens, the Greek government of British choice, headed by George Papandreou, found control of the country in the hands of the EAM. But the ELAS troops were barred from Athens, and the Greek Mountain Brigade fighting in Italy and alleged to consist of pro-royalist elements was quickly brought to Athens by the British. All resistance forces were directed by the British General Scobie to surrender their arms and disband by December 10. The EAM asked that the Mountain Brigade be also disbanded; the government retorted that these forces were part of the regular Greek army. The resulting civil war and British armed intervention served the general purpose of proving that the policy of separate spheres of influence of the Great Powers was a fatal mistake.

The bloody conflict forced Churchill's dramatic Christmas Day plane trip to Athens. On his return to London on December 29, 1944, Churchill summoned King George and urged him to agree to a Regency. The next day George appointed Archbishop Damaskinos as Regent. By his declaration the king virtually renounced his throne, unless the people of Greece, in a free election, should call him back to rule.

Damaskinos' first act was to accept the resignation of the Papandreou Cabinet. A new government was formed under General Nicholas Plastiras. On February 12, a Peace Protocol was signed between the EAM and the government which secured Greek unity. But it is clear that the Monarchy-Republic issue, which plagued Greece before, during, and after World War I, was still the basic question of Greek politics in 1945.

Claims and Aspirations of Greece

In view of what happened in 1940-41, Greece is demanding that certain of her claims, just and long past due, be recognized by her allies

and redeemed—preferably before the Peace Conference. Amply safeguarded by the Atlantic Charter and the Declaration of the United
Nations, these claims cover mainly the unredeemed Greeks of the
Dodecanese Islands, those living in northern Epirus, certain territorial
adjustments in the frontiers of Greece and Bulgaria, and the islanders
of Cyprus.[5]

The Greek claim on the Dodecanese Islands, where Hippocrates was
born, is underlined by the principle of nationality. According to an official report,[6] their aggregate population of 140,000 was "over 80%
Greek Orthodox . . . bitterly opposed to the . . . Italian occupation."
The remainder comprised Turks, Jews, and a limited number of families of Italian officials. The Turks, who occupied the islands before
1912, have not raised any objection to the Greek claim of incorporating
the islands into the Greek nation, to which they belonged from time
immemorial. As for the Italians, it took a Second World War to drive
them out of their illegitimate possession, while anti-fascist Italian leaders, such as Count Sforza and the Mazzini Society in the United States,
openly admit that the islands must be returned to Greece at the earliest
possible moment, at long last carrying out the resolution of the United
States Senate of May 17, 1920, to the effect that the Dodecanese, "where
a strong Greek population predominates, should be awarded to
Greece."

The claim on northern Epirus is also endorsed by the Senate resolution, because it is likewise based on ethnological grounds. It dates
back to ancient times, when the territory was a center of Hellenic culture and continued as such down to the time of the Ottoman rule and
thereafter. Its population of 225,000 is predominantly Greek, and the
three principal cities of Koritsa, Argyroskastron, and Aghioi Saranta
are as Greek as Athens itself. After the war of independence of 1821,
many attempts to liberate Epirus were frustrated, mainly because of
Italian pressure to keep the way open into the Balkan peninsula
through this backdoor of Albania. This plan was put into operation
by Mussolini through the occupation of Albania in 1939, followed by
the attack on Greece in 1940. Thus, on additional grounds of national
defense, the Greeks are resolved to press their demand for a just and
honorable solution of the Albanian question.

The same reasoning applies to the claim for a territorial readjustment

---

[5] Diamantopoulos, Cimon P., "Greece's National Aim: The Historical and Ethnological Background," *The Annals* of The American Academy of Political and Social Science, CCXXXII
(March, 1944), pp. 110-115.

[6] "Report of the American Territorial Experts to the Paris Peace Conference," January 21,
1919.

of the Greek-Bulgarian frontier in the so-called Petrich Department. The object is to prevent future attacks on Greece by Bulgaria, a country that in 30 years has embarked three times upon wars of aggression and has pursued policies of rape and murder in order to satisfy her so-called "legitimate" aims, all dominated by a desire to enslave alien peoples and to confiscate their properties. As a matter of national defense, Greece has a strong claim against a neighbor who cannot be trusted. The solution of the Bulgarian problem must parallel that imposed on Germany.

The question of the return of the island of Cyprus to Greece is inexorably bound up with post-war settlements. Cyprus was ceded to Britain by Turkey in the Treaty of Berlin of 1878, and has remained in British hands ever since. Prime Minister Churchill did not intend to preside over the dissolution of the British Empire, but Cyprus is predominantly Greek and should be united with the Greek nation. The difficulty may be overcome by granting the British a naval base by an arrangement similar to those in the Caribbean and in Newfoundland between Britain and the United States.

Full satisfaction of these claims is dictated by the principles for which the United Nations have fought. The birthplace of true democracy, Greece has been fighting tyranny for all mankind for over 3,000 years. She is now at the crossroads of history. Only complete restoration of both her lands and her people will take her back on the road of prosperity and will enable her to occupy the position she deserves in the councils of the new world emerging from the "tears and sweat" of the war.

Bibliography

Abbott, G. F., *Greece and the Allies, 1914-1922* (London: Methuen, 1922).
————, Ed., *Greece in Evolution* (London: Unwin, 1909). Studies prepared under the auspices of the French League for the defense of the rights of Hellenism.
Alastos, Doros, *Venizelos: Patriot, Statesman, Revolutionary* (London: Lund, Humphries, 1942).
Baird, H. M., *Modern Greece* (New York: Harper's, 1856). A narrative of a residence and travels with observations on Greek antiquities, literature, language, politics, and religion.
Benjamin, S. G. W., *The Turk and the Greek* (New York: Hurd & Houghton, 1867). Creeds, races, society, and scenery in Turkey, Greece, and the isles of Greece.
Casson, Stanley, *Greece Against the Axis* (Washington, D. C.: American Council of Public Affairs, 1943).

Cline, M. A., *American Attitude Toward the Greek War of Independence* (Published by the author, Georgia, 1930).

Cunliffe-Owen, Betty, *Silhouettes of Republican Greece* (London: Hutchinson, 1928). Chats on post-war Greek life and conditions, with special reference to the refugee problem.

Dewing, H. B., and Capps, Edward, *Greece and the Great Powers* (Washington, D. C.: American Friends of Greece, 1924). A brief survey of developments in Greece during and after World War I.

Finlay, George, *A History of Greece* (Oxford: Oxford University Press, 1877), 7 vols. From its conquest by the Romans to the present time.

Gibbons, H. A., *Venizelos* (Boston: Houghton Mifflin, 1920).

Levandis, J. A., *The Greek Foreign Debt and the Great Powers, 1821-1898* (New York: Columbia University Press, 1944). Scholarly.

Mavrogordato, John, *Modern Greece* (New York: The Macmillan Co., 1931). A good introduction.

Mears, E. G., *Greece Today* (Stanford: Stanford University Press, 1929). An excellent survey setting forth the post-war problems, with emphasis on economic questions.

Miller, Walter, *Greece and the Greeks* (New York: The Macmillan Co., 1941). A survey of Greek civilization.

Miller, William, *Greece* (New York: Scribner's, 1928). One of the best historical accounts in English; also his *The Ottoman Empire and Its Successors, 1801-1936* (Cambridge: Cambridge University Press, 1936).

Mitrany, David, *The Effect of the War in Southeastern Europe* (New Haven: Yale University Press, 1936). A standard study of this field.

Newman, Bertrand, *The New Europe* (New York: The Macmillan Co., 1943). A very readable survey of modern problems.

Papassoterious, P. J., *Greece Back to Democracy* (New York: 1928).

Walker, A. H., *A Primer of Greek Constitutional History* (Oxford: Blackwell, 1902).

CHAPTER XXVII

TURKEY (1918-1945)

Geopolitical Factors

THE present area of Turkey, within the frontiers fixed by the Treaty of Lausanne of 1923, is 296,346 square miles (of which 13,012 square miles are in Europe). This is approximately equal to the combined areas of New York, Pennsylvania, Ohio, Illinois, Indiana, and Michigan. The *sanjak* of Alexandretta was ceded to Turkey by France on June 23, 1939 (area 1,930 square miles). The frontiers run from the Black Sea along the rivers Tundza and Maritsa to the Aegean Sea, comprising Turkey-in-Europe or Eastern Thrace. This region is bounded by Greece on the south and west, by Bulgaria on the north. Eastward from the Black Sea, the Turkish frontiers meet those of the Caucasian Soviet Republics of Armenia, Azerbaijian, and Georgia, then run south of Mount Ararat to Persia, Iraq, and Syria. The Mediterranean forms the western boundary of Anatolia (a Greek name meaning "land of the sunrise") and Asia Minor. The landscape of Turkey-in-Asia consists mostly of mountains, valleys, and plateaus. There are few lakes and marshes. Turkey's chief cities are the new capital of Ankara with 166,500 population; Constantinople or Istanbul with 883,600; Smyrna or Izmir with 220,530; and Adana with 90,000.[1] The total population of Turkey was given by the census of October 20, 1940, as 17,870,000.

Turkey's strategic position derives from the possession of Istanbul and the Straits on the land route between Asia and Europe, commanding the passage between the Mediterranean to the south and the Black Sea to the north. The city and the Straits have cost humanity more in blood and suffering than any other single place. Since 1815, they have been an outstanding objective of diplomatic intrigue. Rivalries, hatreds, and suspicions radiating from the Straits caused a number of wars in the nineteenth century. Possession of Constantinople was the

---

[1] *Annuaire Statistique de Turquie* (Ankara, 1936/37).

main Russian goal in the First World War; the same eternal city and the narrow Straits upon which it stands are an important stake in the peace settlements to follow the Second World War.

After the conquest of Constantinople in 1453, the Turks excluded all foreign ships from the "virgin waters" of the Black Sea by closing the Bosporus until the arrival of the Russians in 1774 forced the opening of the Straits and broke Turkish power to command such a monopoly of shipping. The same privilege of free passage was conferred on the other powers as a matter of course, although the Turkish right to prohibit warships from passing through the Straits was retained. This right was recognized by treaty in 1840, and was reaffirmed in the Convention of the Straits of 1841 to the end that: "So long as the Porte is at peace, His Highness (the Sultan) will admit no Foreign Ships of War into the Straits."

The Treaty of Lausanne (1923) provided for the demilitarization of both the European and Asiatic shores of the Bosporus and the Dardanelles and insured freedom of passage under an International Straits Commission, presided over by Turkey and acting under the auspices of the League of Nations. Later, the Convention of Montreux of 1936 abolished the commission, transferred its functions to Turkey, and empowered her to refortify the Dardanelles and to close the Straits to warships of all nations during a war in which she was not a belligerent.[2]

Turkey-in-Europe is well-served with railways and the main line carries the Orient Express to Istanbul. Turkey-in-Asia has four main rail lines. One runs to Ismid, Eshi-Shehir, and Ankara; another from Eshi-Shehir to Afion-Karahisar and Smyrna; a third from Smyrna to Konia and Adana; and the fourth from Smyrna to Panderma on the sea of Marmora, and thence south to Aidin and Egirdir. The total rail trackage in 1937 was 6,849 kilometers, or 4,619 miles, of which only 509 kilometers were privately owned, as against 2,352 kilometers privately owned in 1924. The tendency has been for the state to buy in all private lines and to extend rail transportation as fast as rails can be laid. Coastwise shipping is confined to 125 Turkish ships, aggregating 190,800 tons. It is forbidden to vessels of foreign registry. There are two main air lines, the Aero Espresso and Air France. Turkey possesses 25,274 miles of national highways and county and municipal roads.

---

[2] Shotwell, J. T., and Deák, Francis, *Turkey at the Straits* (New York: Macmillan, 1940), *passim*. See also: Birge, J. K., "Turkey Between Two World Wars," *Foreign Policy Reports*, XX, No. 16 (1944); Tobin, C. M., *Turkey, Key to the East* (New York: Putnam, 1944); Frechling, L. E., "Allied Strategy in the Near East," *Foreign Policy Reports*, XVII, No. 22 (1942).

Economic Factors

A few decades ago, Turkey was sparsely populated, backward in its industrial and agricultural development, anemic in its finances, and untouched by the enlightenment of the West, with the notable exception of the Christian populations inhabiting Turkey's large cities and dotting the western shores of Asia Minor. In the interior, agriculture was the natural occupation of a primitive, land-loving peasantry, who enjoyed a good climate, sheltered coastlands, fertile river valleys, and a rich productive soil. After the revolution, Turkish leaders realized that improvements in agriculture were urgently needed. To that end, they introduced agricultural implements and machinery, built mills and factories, and established banks and credit coöperatives supervised and often owned by the state.

Only about 20 per cent of the total area of Turkey is under cultivation, engaging approximately 81 per cent of the population. The most important product is tobacco, followed by cereals, figs, olive oil, and livestock. The country is rich in coal, with an annual output reaching three million tons; it enjoys a world monopoly in meerschaum and has large sources of copper, manganese, and emery; it contributes a quarter of the world's chrome output; and it produces such other minerals as gold, zinc, tin, and salt. Fisheries constitute an important factor in its national wealth.

In 1929 an appropriation of $120,000,000.—a rather large sum for Turkey—was authorized to provide funds for new railways, ports, breakwaters, irrigation, and reclamation. This was followed in 1934 by an industrial five-year plan which sought to set up such basic production industries as steel, copper, and chemicals, to turn out such consumption goods as textiles, and to exploit the mineral wealth of the country. It was supplemented by a four-year industrial plan in 1938 which aimed to enlarge the steel industry, to industrialize eastern Turkey, to modernize certain Black Sea harbors, and to build up the merchant marine.[3]

The financial situation of Turkey is complicated by her heritage from the past. Although Turkey paid no reparations for World War I, she is still saddled with a very large foreign debt. The bulk of the revenue is derived from direct taxation, most of it internal. Tariffs are low. Indirect taxes are also heavy and the prosperity of the country suffers from the inability of new enterprises to survive taxation in their early stages. National defense is by far the largest item

---

[3] Lengyel, Emil, *Turkey* (New York: Random House, 1941), pp. 424 ff.

of expense, averaging between one-third and one-half of both ordinary and extraordinary budgets. It amounted to 44 per cent in 1931-32, but went up to 57 per cent in 1937. Since then it has overshadowed all other state expenditures, of which 26 per cent goes to the public debt, 8 per cent to public instruction, and 4 per cent to public health and welfare.

Taxation was originally borne chiefly by the rural population, and this fact in itself was a serious cause of friction between farmers and city people. In order to win over the peasant, who did not regard the reforms of the Kemalist regime with enthusiasm, the government abolished tithes, which lay heavily on the agricultural classes, and reduced military service to 18 months. The resulting deficit was met by a heavier taxation of the urban population. In 1942, it took the form of a tax on wealth which provoked widespread repercussions inside the country and abroad.

This so-called "Varlik Vergisi Law" assessed the wealth and extraordinary profits of all persons possessing wealth and earning profits, citizens and aliens alike, who resided in Turkey and were between 18 and 55 years of age. It did not apply to women, invalids, and farmers. Those unable or unwilling to pay were compelled to work in any part of the country in public service, which simply meant forced labor and concentration camps. By this capital levy the Turks sought to provide needed funds for their national defense, to halt inflation, and, most significant of all, to reduce the influence and prestige of Turkey's so-called "minorities"—Greeks, Armenians, Jews, Italians, et al. The law was administered by special commissions required to enforce the assessments within 15 days from the date of notification, otherwise to send delinquents to camps of public service established for the purpose. In the closing days of 1943, such camps "housed" about 30,000 inmates.

Strong protests by the Greek Government and friendly "advice" given to President Inonu by President Roosevelt and Prime Minister Churchill at the Cairo Conference in December, 1943, resulted in halting further execution of the law and the release of the people held in concentration camps. The law did not prevent inflation, but it did bring in from collections in Istanbul alone, where the effect on minorities was catastrophic, the sum of 344,000,000 Turkish pounds as compared to estimates for the entire country given out by Premier Saracoglou himself of not more than 250,000,000 Turkish pounds.[4]

---

[4] *Turkish Official Gazette*, No. 5255 of November 12, 1942, and C. L. Sulzberger, *The New York Times*, September 9, 10, 11, 12, and 13, 1943.

Social Conditions

The people of Turkey have lived for centuries under two handicaps. One was the doctrine of *kismet*, which meant a fatalism inculcated by Islam and characteristic of most countries in the East. The other was the oppression of the environment, both physical and human. The latter was represented by government officials and money-lenders. Villagers and townspeople were compelled to borrow from usurers at ruinous rates; they were robbed by dishonest tax collectors; they were periodically required to contribute their horses to the army and their meager savings to the Sultan's treasury.

The outstanding achievement of the Nationalists has been the introduction of a number of reforms carried out with great zeal and singleness of purpose. The Turkey of today bears little resemblance to the Turkey of yesteryear. The old dynasty of the Osmanlis was expelled; the Caliphate was abolished; all educational and scientific institutions were attached to the Ministry of Public Instruction; ecclesiastical seminaries and their vast properties were confiscated for state purposes; religious corporations were eliminated; missionary activities were suppressed; foreigners were guaranteed equal rights; the so-called capitulatory or extra-territorial system (see Chapter XIII) was scrapped; the fez and the turban for men were removed and women were unveiled; all ancient fashions of salutation and salaam were discarded; Persian and Arabic words and phrases were banished from Turkish literature; harem and eunuch practices were destroyed; the Moslem Friday was barred in favor of the Christian Sunday; old festivals vanished; and everything reminiscent of the *ancien régime* was regarded with disfavor. Even the old titles of Pasha, Bey, and Effendi were abolished in 1934 and everybody was required to adopt a family name.

Next came the overhauling of judicial administration, which in the past had been so deficient and so ridden with fraud and corruption as to justify fully the extra-territorial rights of foreigners. The old system of law, before the National Assembly revised the constitution, was based on the Sunni Moslem law that was religious in both origin and sanction. It did not apply to infidels (non-Moslems).

This was changed in 1924 and a new judicial system was organized on a secular basis. It was followed in 1926 by a new Civil Code based upon the Swiss Code, a Penal Code along Italian lines, a Commercial Code, and a Debtors Law. Among other things, these changes brought about the abolition of polygamy, granted equal rights to

women, and liberalized marriage and divorce. It is symptomatic of
the change in Turkish jurisprudence that divorces, which were unknown among Moslems before 1920, numbered 2,127 in 1930 and 21,-
693 in 1936.

The most troublesome question that modern Turkey inherited from
the defunct Empire was the problem of minorities. This was partly
solved in 1923 by an exchange of populations between Turkey and
Greece, although it caused a serious dislocation of the Turkish national economy. Whatever minorities still remain are concentrated
in Istanbul. They are estimated at 180,000 Greeks, 80,000 Armenians,
4,000 Bulgarians, and 71,000 Jews, of whom 9,000 are scattered throughout Turkey. Statistics as to the total number of Kurds, Circassians,
Armenians, Arabs, and other nationalities living in the interior of
Turkey are not available.

In this connection, it should be noted that modern Turkey has abandoned the old Ottoman idea of ruling many races and nationalities as
distinct and separate groups or minorities. Instead, it has adopted an
uncompromising nationalism which seeks to assimilate all subject
races and, if this is impossible, to exterminate or expel them. This
policy provoked a serious revolt by the Kurds in the eastern part of
Anatolia in 1924-25. It was crushed with much loss of life and
wealth. The Kurds, who had a highly developed sense of nationality
and fiercely resented Kemal's reforms, were almost exterminated.

Cultural Developments

Nomadic life, and then world conquest, left little time for the Turk
to engage in arts and letters. It was from his neighbor—the Persian—
that he learned to appreciate the lyrical word. In early poems, he
glorified the Prophet and sang the bliss of love. Subsequently, he
kept the flames of the conquering spirit ablaze by chanting about the
victories of the past. The growth of letters in any other form was
banned; literature and Islam were mutually inclusive. This explains
why letters and revolt grew together. The leader of the new literati,
Ziya Gokalp, became the Voltaire of the Turkish revolution. The
Turks began learning languages, their bookstores were flooded with
translations, and new cultural horizons inspired the young people.

The bulk of the population, however, still remains illiterate. In
1935, illiteracy was given at 76.7 per cent for men and 91.8 per cent
for women. It is not surprising that the law of 1929, which introduced the compulsory use of Latin characters in place of the old

Arabic, was not such a gigantic educational problem as it would have been in any more educated country. Education is fostered by an ever-growing number of public schools, which are patterned after the British elementary schools. Higher education is provided by a Law School in Ankara, Istanbul University, and 15 other vocational schools for mechanical training, agriculture, forestry, and other specialized subjects. Outstanding foreign institutions of higher learning include the American College for Women and Robert College, both in Istanbul, founded and maintained by the Near East College Association of New York. Their graduates are admitted to post-graduate studies in the United States without further examination.

Dictatorship

In October, 1923, Turkey became a Republic, with Mustapha Kemal Pasha as its first President. Although national sovereignty theoretically resides in the National Assembly, Kemal showed decided tendencies toward a personal dictatorship. As a result, an opposition was fathered by Reouf Bey and Kara-Bekir Pasha to keep the young republic on a more democratic basis. It was called the Republican Progressive Party (1924). When the Kurds revolted at the harsh measures of the government in carrying out Kemal's reforms, the latter seized the opportunity to strike at the opposition by enacting the so-called "law of maintenance of order." The revolutionary tribunals of independence were revived; a reign of terror overtook the opposition; freedom of speech, press, and assembly was evaded. In general, Kemal wielded unbounded power.

Such activity was possible under the constitution of 1921, revised in 1924 and amended in 1934. Its provisions vest ultimate executive and legislative power in the Grand National Assembly of 429 deputies, who are elected for four years by universal suffrage. The executive power is directly exercised through the President, elected for four years by the assembly, and through a council of ministers chosen by the President. In practice, therefore, the President has absolute powers under the constitution. Moreover, he is the titular head of the only legal party, the People's party.

This merger of Party and State was further strengthened in 1936, when much of the party organization was dissolved, all of its provincial chairmen were replaced by the provincial governors, and the office of the national secretary general of the party was taken over by the Minister of Interior. The constitution was amended on February 5,

1937, to include all of the six basic principles of the Party by proclaiming that "Turkey is a Republic which is nationalist, populist, statist, secular, and revolutionary."

In other words, Party and State in Turkey are both synonymous and co-terminal. The result is an omnipotent but paternal government. The affairs of the nation are administered for the general welfare by representatives duly elected by the people; the latter, however, are given no alternatives either of program or of candidates. The enemies of the party are enemies of the state and by the same token enemies of the people.

There is some justification for this development. Self-government in the Empire as a whole would have meant the peaceful coöperation of many embittered and oppressed peoples with the masters who had long tyrannized over them. This could never be more than a summer night's dream. It is not surprising that the experiment of constitutional government in Turkey today still has far to go before a true democratic form of administration can be evolved. It is of necessity that "Turkey is still being ruled by an autocratic oligarchy under the outward veil of constitutional government." [5]

Republican Leadership

The overwhelming defeat of Turkey in World War I was followed in the short interval of three years by a revival that was almost miraculous. After their victory over the Ottoman Empire, a foregone conclusion from the outset of the war, the Allies incorporated in the Treaty of Sèvres of August 10, 1920, all their plans for the extinction of the old House of Osmanli from Europe and Asia Minor alike. It was a humiliating treaty; its harsh terms surpassed any the Osmanlis had imposed on subject peoples in previous years. When it was ratified by the Sultan, both he and the treaty were denounced by Kemal and his Nationalists, who succeeded in arousing the people to revolt by adopting a National Pact, setting up a National Assembly, and establishing a rival government in Ankara.

The extraordinary renaissance that followed was due to a combination of forces and events. The most dynamic factors that contributed to the success of the revolution, however, were the genius, the energy, and the intense nationalism of one man—Mustafa Kemal Pasha, who started as a revolutionary at the turn of the century. His personality dominated and won the support of his countrymen both in peace and in war. He was unquestionably "the first among Turks."

---

[5] Toynbee, A. J., and Kirkwood, K. P., *Turkey* (New York: Scribner's, 1927), p. 186.

For whereas the Treaty of Sèvres wrote the death-warrant of the sprawling colossus of the Ottoman Empire, which was "sick unto death," the subsequent Treaty of Lausanne wrote a new chapter of freedom for Turkey "having performed in action its will to live." Primarily through the efforts of one man, there emerged a nation as vigorous and progressive as its parent, the defunct Empire, was feeble and reactionary; a country as compact and homogeneous as its progenitor was unwieldy and composite.

The Republic was proclaimed on October 29, 1923, and a new constitution, affirming toleration and freedom of conscience, was promulgated the following year. The architect of the amazing revival—Kemal—was elected president of both the Assembly and the Republic. In 1934, this leader of men adopted the family name of Ataturk or "Father of Turks" and changed the Arabic name Kemal to Kamal. He died in 1938 at the age of 58.

Kamal was succeeded by his lifelong friend and collaborator, Ismet Inonu, the present president—a soldier, a statesman and a "National Chief." A professional soldier like Kamal, he was a brilliant Chief of Staff of the Nationalist forces, which he joined in March, 1920, and further distinguished himself immediately after the war at the ensuing peace talks. The armistice conference revealed him as a clever diplomat, while the peace negotiations at Lausanne, where he stubbornly held out against the Allies, enhanced his reputation as a shrewd negotiator. As Foreign Secretary for a year and subsequently as the first Prime Minister of the new Republic, he held office with one short interruption from 1923 until his resignation in 1937. The following year he was elected unanimously to succeed his "Ghazi" in the presidency and was re-elected in 1943. He is now ably assisted by his Prime Minister, Shukru Saracoglou, an ex-corporation lawyer.

World War II

Under the Mutual Assistance Pacts of 1939 between Turkey and Britain and Turkey and France, the Allies agreed to assist Turkey in case of aggression by a European Power. Turkey, for her part, undertook to join them in case of an act of aggression by a European Power leading to war in the Mediterranean or in the event that these two powers became engaged in hostilities on account of their guarantee given to Greece and Romania in April, 1939.

Why Turkey did not join World War II, in spite of the acts of aggression committed by both Italy and Germany leading to war in the Mediterranean, is a moot question for historians. There are facts available, however, which may give a clue to Turkey's role in this most terrible war of all time.

Turkey had been a traditional stronghold of German diplomacy in the Near East, for her geopolitical situation invites the casting of lines to southeastern Europe and deep into the heart of Asia and Africa. After 1909, the Kaiser's diplomats very quickly marched with the "Young Turks." With the beginning of Kemal's rule, however, the German Foreign Office entered a difficult period. The creator of the new Turkish Republic was a cool realist. Unlike some other authoritarian leaders, he was not deluded by successes, but remained moderate and constructive. More than that, he understood Balkan problems. After casting off the Ottoman ties, he strove mightily, especially with Venizelos and Papanastassiou, both liberal leaders of Greece, for a Balkan union. This took the form of a non-aggression pact, signed in 1934 by Turkey, Greece, Romania, and Yugoslavia.

On Hitler's assumption of power, an attempt was made to expand German propaganda in Turkey, concentrating at first on profit-channels. When the British-Franco-Turkish pacts were concluded, Hitler's patience was not exhausted, nor did he indulge in his customary raving about reprisals. Instead, he sought to win over Ankara by economic and diplomatic methods, by resorting to Dr. Schacht's tradition, and by dispatching as his personal representative his stirrup-holder von Papen. The latter, known as the "sly fox," was received without fear by the Turks.

Von Papen's "gifts" of foreign territories were rejected politely but firmly, as the Turks were not seeking expansion. However, the standard Nazi cliché of the menacing and imminent danger of Bolshevism was sufficiently successful to create a rift between Ankara and Moscow. The Adana and Cairo Conferences helped to clear the air and obtain some gains for the Allies, which can be summarized as limited exports to the Reich (especially chrome) and a strict neutrality toward all belligerents.[6]

Turkish policy was influenced by two events in 1944. In March, the British cut off their supply of tanks, small arms, aircraft, and other equipment to Turkey, presumably on the ground that they were out of patience with Ankara's dilatory tactics in making up its mind whether to come into the war on the side of the United Nations, or to sit it out as a neutral after the Swedish pattern. Too many Turkish interests had long been doing too good a business to welcome entrance into the

---

[6] Jackh, Ernest, *The Rising Crescent* (New York: Farrar and Rinehart, 1944), *passim*.

war. Opposed to them were other Turks who fervently supported the
United Nations on the bandwagon principle that it would be fatal for
Turkey to be on the outside during the period of reconstruction.

The second event that tipped the scales in Turkish calculations was
the successful invasion of Normandy and the opening of a second front
in Europe by the Allies. By that time the Turks were both angry and
anxious. They were angry because they suspected that hidden deals
were being made behind their backs. They were anxious to enter the
war in return for certain political guarantees regarding Turkey's participation in the peace conference, the safeguarding of her post-war
frontiers, and her dominant Black Sea naval position. The Allies
could not give iron-clad guarantees of the sort Turkey desired and
could not see the need for them in view of the Atlantic Charter.

The breaking off of diplomatic relations by Turkey with tottering
Germany on August 2, 1944, was symptomatic of the course of international events at that time. In January, 1945, Turkey virtuously
"added a new link" to its "policy of assistance to the Allied cause" and
made another delayed bid for recognition at the peace table. Ankara,
in response to "requests" from the Allies, announced the severance of
diplomatic and economic relations with Japan.

Turkey's entry into the war at the eleventh hour (February 23, 1945)
was a direct reflection of the Yalta Conference. The action had no
military importance. Ankara made the decision because the "Big
Three" threatened to exclude it and other neutrals from the world
security conference at San Francisco. Hence Turkey's declaration of
war had more symbolic than actual significance, and was plainly intended to obtain a voice for Turkey in the peace settlements.

But Stalin did not permit the delayed "coöperation" to become a
definite integration of Turkey's foreign policy with that of Russia. In
March, 1945, while Soviet troops were edging forward in Central-
Eastern Europe, Russia denounced her 1925 non-aggression treaty with
Turkey. Relations with Turkey, said Moscow, "needed considerable
improvement." The "improvement" Stalin has in mind is undoubtedly designed to bring Turkey closer to the Soviet orbit. Russia especially wants freer use of the Dardanelles as a warm-water outlet to the
sea.

The Straits are important to Britain also, as a factor in the security
of the British Empire. The future of the Dardanelles, and of Russo-
Turkish relations in general, are vital to the prospects of stability and
enduring peace.

Bibliography

Abbott, G. F., *Turkey, Greece and the Great Powers* (London: R. Scott, 1916). A study in friendship and hate.

Armstrong, Harold, *Turkey in Travail* (London: Lane, 1925). A most valuable record of experiences and observations in Turkey between 1916 and 1923, by an English officer captured at Kut.

Djemal, Pasha, Ahmad, *Memories of a Turkish Statesman, 1913-1919* (New York: Doran, 1922). An important volume of memoirs about Turkey in the war period, written by one of the controlling Triumvirate.

Earle, E. M., *Turkey, the Great Powers and the Bagdad Railway* (New York: Macmillan, 1923). A study in imperialism.

Emin, Ahmed, *Turkey in World War* (New Haven: Yale University Press, 1930). Traces the breakdown of the old regime and the rise of the Young Turks; then surveys economic aspects of the war, takes up racial problems and questions of reform, education, and health; ends with a succinct analysis of the nationalist movement.

Eversley, G. J. S., and Chirol, Sir Valentine, *The Turkish Empire* (London: T. Fisher Unwin, 1923). A new edition of the general narrative.

Furniss, E. S., *A New State Faces a Difficult World* (New Haven: Yale University Press, 1940). The position of Turkey today.

Gordon, L. G., *American Relations with Turkey, 1830-1930* (Philadelphia: University of Pennsylvania Press, 1932). An economic interpretation.

Halidah Abid, Khanum, *Turkey Faces West* (New Haven: Yale University Press, 1930). Stresses the vicissitudes of the Turkish people and their cultural progress.

Howard, Harry, *The Partition of Turkey, 1913-1923* (Norman, Okla.: University of Oklahoma Press, 1913). A careful study.

Jackh, Ernest, *The Rising Crescent* (New York: Farrar & Rinehart, 1944). The new political life of Turkey and the men who helped to bring about her reformation.

Lengyel, Emil, *Turkey* (New York, Random House, 1941). A very readable introduction.

Levonian, Lufti, *The Moslem Mind* (Boston: Pilgrim Press, 1929). An unusual and highly interesting discussion of Turkish mentality and the background of recent changes.

Mears, E. G., *Modern Turkey* (New York: Macmillan, 1924). A coöperative work, one of the most useful books in English.

Mikusch, Dagobert von, *Mustapha Kemal* (New York: Doubleday, 1931). One of the best biographies of Mustapha Kemal.

Miller, William, *The Ottoman Empire and Its Successors, 1801-1927* (Cambridge: Cambridge University Press, 1927). One of the standard English books on the subject.

Monroe, W. S., *Turkey and the Turks* (London: Bell, 1908). An account of the lands, the peoples, and the institutions of the Ottoman Empire.

Ostrorog, Leon, Hrabia, *The Angora Reform* (London: University of London Press, 1928). Reviews the rise of Turkish nationalism.

Price, Clair, *The Rebirth of Turkey* (New York: Seltzer, 1923). One of the best of the earlier books.

Tobin, Chester M., *Turkey* (New York: Putnam's Sons, 1944). A sympathetic portrayal.

Toynbee, A. J., and Kirkwood, Kenneth, *Turkey* (New York: Scribner's, 1927). Traces chiefly the nationalist revival.

Ward, Barbara, *Turkey* (New York: Oxford University Press, 1942). Shows mainly Turkey's reactions to the developments of World War II.

Webster, D. E., *Turkey of Ataturk* (Philadelphia: American Academy of Political and Social Science, 1939). One of the most useful volumes in English.

PART V

PART V

CHAPTER XXVIII

CENTRAL-EASTERN EUROPE UNDER GERMAN OCCUPATION

German Aims and Plans

FOR generations, the Germans have envisaged a German Middle-European state of sufficient size and power to make the Teutons the masters of Europe. At first this idea was expressed in terms of Pan-Germanism, which sought to include all German minorities within a reasonable distance of the central German core in one solid bloc. The ideology of this concept was demonstrated in World War I, when German plans for a *Mittel-Europa*, stretching from the North Sea to Asia Minor and including most of Central-Eastern Europe, were brought to light. The purpose was obviously to enable the Reich to break out of the ring with which her enemies had encircled her and gain access to the surplus raw materials and foodstuffs of the Balkans and Asia Minor and finally to the markets of the world by way of the Mediterranean and the open seas beyond.

Though this project was defeated, Reich leaders never abandoned it. The immediate objective of German expansionist planning was always domination of the small countries of Central-Eastern Europe lying at Germany's doorstep. By 1918, German power theorists had led the people a long way toward acceptance of the idea of the unscrupulous use of force to secure German ends. But it remained for the Nazis to carry Hegel's concept of the God-state and the anti-Christian teachings of Nietzsche, Von Treitschke, and Spengler to their logical conclusion.

To the budding power theories of Germany's empire builders, founded on the abstractions of German romanticists and nationalists, were added the Darwinian doctrine of survival of the fittest and the Marxian materialistic interpretation of history which reduces Hegelian dialectic to a matter of the economic conflict of classes. Haushofer gathered up these disconnected but parallel doctrines, already thoroughly grounded in German thinking, and fused them into his system of geopolitics. Under Haushofer's influence, German master-planners gave up the outworn argument of Pan-Germanism and replaced it by an older notion, now revitalized by the geopoliticists and referred to as "space-politics" or national *lebensraum*.

Fundamental to this way of thinking was the power-postulate that the nation-state, inhabited by a putatively superior race with productive capacity and superlative culture, has a natural right to subject neighboring states to its purposes if this is necessary, in its own view, to realize its utmost capacity as a people. German leaders were obsessed with the fear of resumption of the blockade by the sea powers in event of another war. They realized that Germany, on her existing territory, would never be able to assume a place on a level with other world powers unless she could have unhampered access to the means to establish military supremacy over her rivals.

To a power-state, such as Germany came to be, *Lebensraum* meant not only access to the material instruments of war-making, but a completely unified political and economic space in which the larger aims of the master race could be pursued without obstruction.[1] The idea, as such, was obviously not new, but the methods employed were unprecedented in modern times. The cold, inhuman calculation and unexampled barbarity of the policies employed required a major rationalization to justify them.

This was supplied by the Nazi race-doctrine. According to this principle, the individual becomes a mere cell in the blood-stream of a racial community and his worth can be measured only as a living, contributing part of the national blood-brotherhood. Different races vary tremendously in intelligence and capacity for civilized life and should be graded in function according to their capacities. The "Aryan race" has been the ruling race throughout history, and of all the Aryan race the Teutons are the least contaminated with inferior blood. The Teutons, therefore, are the highest and most deserving of all the races of mankind. The stock must be kept pure by preventing mixtures with racial inferiors. Races occupying lands needed by the master race for *Lebensraum* must be subdued by force, if necessary, and made to serve the needs of the conquerors.

No moral scruples should deter the masters from employing any means necessary to gain their objectives, since these take precedence over the rights of racial inferiors whose contributions to human progress have been valueless. Yet races differ in worth, from those who may be classed as associates to the lowest scum of mankind, the Jews,

---

[1] Rauschning, H., "Hitler Could Not Stop," *Foreign Affairs*, XVIII:1 (October, 1939), pp. 7-8.

upon whom was heaped the blame for most of mankind's ills.[2] The attack upon the Jews was used to justify initial acts of Nazi violence against persons and property, thus giving release to the vengeance and envy complexes of the propertyless masses, supplying the Nazis with immediate wealth without resort to unpopular heavy taxation, and furnishing them with an opening wedge for further encroachments upon the institutions of subject peoples.

The practical aspects of the German plan involved a number of difficulties. These included: (1) the methods to be employed to secure the desired territories; (2) the political organization of subject nations in their relation to the Reich; (3) the economic organization for most efficient use of the goods and services of conquered peoples; and (4) treatment of captured populations in terms of assimilation, de-culturization, elimination, or utilization for labor or military purposes.

In general, German foreign policies prior to World War II aimed primarily to break up military alliances against the Reich and to immobilize enemy states in order to permit the unhindered conquest of Germany's intended victims. Through intimidation, threats, propaganda, and force, Hitler seized territories almost at will. Nations brought under Germany's sway were classified and treated according to their utility in the Nazi master-plan.

The basic idea of this plan was to create in Europe a mutually compensating economic system in which the manufactured products of a highly industrialized German Reich, plus its Polish and Czechoslovak adjuncts, would balance the agricultural products of the remaining portions of Greater Germany, compelled to specialize in agrarian pursuits. Success in this grand design, however, depended upon obliteration of existing national states, diversion of the loyalties of their peoples to the Reich, and the coöperation of all of the diverse national groups with German plans. Not only the national but the economic interests of the non-German peoples in the area were at variance with the Nazi scheme. Permanent degradation of all of these peoples to the role of agricultural serfs, who would live in poverty in order to support their German masters in affluence, offered them few economic inducements.

There was also the problem of securing food surpluses in territories which were not self-sufficient in terms of food. Only in some of the Balkan States was there a surplus of food production, and their con-

---

[2] Schuman, F. L., "The Political Theory of German Fascism," W. E. Rappard, *Source Book on European Governments* (New York: Van Nostrand, 1937), pp. 161-162.

tributions were not sufficient to meet the needs of the Third Reich, expanded far beyond normal by the needs of war and bound to increase in the future in proportion to the demands of the 200 million Germans envisaged by Reich leaders as constituting the optimum population of the Greater Germany to come.[3]

The existence of this problem no doubt contributed to the Nazi desire to reduce the size of populations in various sections. To this should be added the perennial conflict of Germans versus Slavs, rendered critical in the German mind by the more rapid increase of Slavic populations vis-à-vis the Germans. As a result of their clever tactics and the mistakes of their opponents, the Germans suddenly found huge masses of Slavs in the fallen countries of Central-Eastern Europe at their mercy. Nazi leaders saw in this fact an unprecedented opportunity to rectify the unequal racial balance and rid themselves of extra mouths to feed at a single stroke.

Nevertheless, the growing need for manpower for war purposes placed a check upon their urge to wholesale murder. Hence Berlin's policies throughout the period of occupation were somewhat inconsistent. In their attempts to reconcile opposing purposes, Reich planners differentiated between various national groups and sub-groups but sometimes shifted abruptly, often in unaccountable ways. Austrians, Hungarians, Czechs, Romanians, and Bulgarians were allowed to live, though subjected to rigid political control and economic exploitation. Czechs, Poles, Slovaks, and Slovenes were given large doses of German *Kultur*. But Jews, unreconciled Poles and Czechs, Serbians, Greeks, and Russians, unwilling to submit to slavery or incapable of being Germanized, were ruthlessly eliminated.

Germany Moves In

Austria. Possession of Austria was necessary to Hitler in order to block any possibility of aid to Czechoslovakia from the West, and to enable him to make use of Austrian manpower and wealth in his campaign to dominate Europe. Since the Treaties of Versailles and St. Germain had orphaned Austria, that country had remained isolated from the rest of Central-Eastern Europe—partly because of the reluctance of her leaders to make common cause with Germany's foes, and partly because of the unwillingness of Austria's neighbors to include her in their systems of alliances. A considerable proportion of Austrian opinion in Austria, including the Catholic Church and its political agencies, and many influential members of the ruling classes, favored

---

[3] *Europe Under Hitler* (London: Oxford University Press, 1941), pp. 10-11.

anschluss with Germany. The appeasement policies of the Allies strengthened this stand. Despite socialist opposition, the National Socialist movement was therefore allowed to develop unhindered in Austria. Just before the annexation, 25 per cent of the Austrian people were counted as Nazi supporters.[4] That made it easy for Hitler to move in on Austria. Italian opposition was overcome by Hitler's encouragement of Italian expansionist aims in Africa and his promises to Mussolini to redress Italy's territorial grievances in Europe.

As noted in Chapter XV, Hitler sent an ultimatum to Austria in March, 1938, demanding that the proposed plebiscite to determine the attitude of the people toward union with Germany be canceled. As a result, Premier Schuschnigg resigned and was replaced by Seyss-Inquart, Austrian Nazi leader. The latter then called upon Hitler for military support to maintain order. Nazi troops thereupon marched into Austria without opposition.[5]

Czechoslovakia. The seizure of Austria exposed Czechoslovakia's southern flank to the Nazi advance and gave great impetus to the growth of National Socialism among the Sudeten Germans. Henlein, their leader, had previously confined himself to demands for autonomy for his group. But after Germany's absorption of Austria, he began to demand that Czechoslovakia give up her alliances and her attitude of obstruction to Germany's march to the East, and coöperate wholeheartedly instead with Nazi leaders and their work of spreading National Socialist doctrines in the Sudeten area. Pro-*anschluss* supporters had increased from about two-thirds to nearly 85 per cent of the Sudeten Germans in May, 1938.[6]

Prolonged negotiations between the Czechoslovak government and the Sudeten Party followed. The obvious eagerness of French and British appeasers to yield to Germany's demands regarding Czechoslovakia weakened the latter's stand. In August, Lord Runciman arrived in Prague. Aided by Sir Neville Henderson, the British Ambassador to Germany, he took charge of the negotiations. The British policy was obviously aimed at getting Prague to yield peacefully to Nazi demands, so that France could evade her commitments to her ally. In September, ignoring substantial Czech concessions, Hitler threatened to intervene if the Sudeten affair was not settled immediately.

[4] Czernin, Ferdinand, "Austria's Position in Reconstructed Europe," *Annals*, CCXXXII (March, 1944), p. 74.

[5] Hanč, J., *Tornado Across Eastern Europe* (New York: Greystone, 1942), pp. 173 ff.

[6] *Ibid.*, pp. 181-182.

Panicky *démarches* between the French and British foreign offices resulted in France's betrayal of her treaty obligations and Chamberlain's weak-kneed yielding to Hitler's demand for the entire Sudetenland. The shameful agreement of Munich followed, when France and England signed away Czechoslovakia's independence. Left to face mighty Germany alone, the Czechs were forced to give up the Sudetenland and additional territory to Poland and Hungary. The subsequent invasion of all of Czechoslovakia in 1939 was the inevitable result.[7]

Poland. When the Nazi legions took up positions on the eastern Czechoslovak frontier, Poland's doom was sealed. Threatened from the north, west, and southwest by the *Wehrmacht,* there was little that Poland could do, either by diplomacy or war, to hold back the oncoming flood. To be sure, French and British leaders, frightened at last by the duplicity and avid lust for power of the German war machine, had guaranteed Poland against a German attack. But Hitler was now entrenched behind the Siegfried Line and was confident of his ability to hold off the Western Allies until Poland's armies were defeated.

Russia was immobilized by the non-aggression pact of 1939 and later placated by the division of Polish territory. The question of Danzig and the Polish Corridor offered a convenient excuse.[8] Despite Russia's refusal to coöperate, the British refused to re-enact another Munich and on August 31, 1939, German armies invaded Poland. Within a month, Polish armed resistance was crushed. By the German-Soviet agreement, Poland was split approximately in half, Germany taking the western part to a line defined by the Narva, Vistula, Bug, and San Rivers.

Romania. The year that elapsed between August, 1939, and August, 1940, permitted Germany partially to digest her Polish prey. Occupation of Slovakia by German troops put Hitler on Romania's borders, thus opening the way into the Balkans. At the Fuehrer's demand, a conference was held in Vienna on August 30, 1940, presumably to prevent a war between Romania and Hungary over disputed territory. Actually, Romania was confronted with the alternative of being treated like Poland or of yielding Transylvania to Hungary and accepting German occupation and complete control of her economic resources, which were already being exploited by the

---

[7] *Ibid.,* pp. 184-201.
[8] See Floyd A. Cave, "The U.S.S.R. and Asia," in *Modern World Politics* (New York: Crowell, 1942), pp. 466, 468.

Nazis under an agreement signed in March, 1939. Unable to resist, King Carol left the country and Antonescu, the Nazi quisling, took over the reins of power.[9]

Hungary. Committed to a revisionist policy because of her losses in World War I, Hungary received further inducements from Hitler to throw in her lot with the Axis Powers. Rewarded by cessions of territory from Czechoslovakia and Romania, the Hungarian government readily signed the Tripartite Pact in November, 1940, opened her territory to German troops, and reorganized her government to conform to the Nazi model.

Bulgaria. Hitler's designs on the Mediterranean and the Near East required the subjection of Bulgaria, Yugoslavia, and Greece to German control. Mussolini's dismal failure in the campaign against Greece necessitated Berlin's intervention to prevent Greece from being used as a base of British operations in the Balkans and to permit its use by the *Wehrmacht* as a point of departure for attacks against the British in the Eastern Mediterranean area.

So the squeeze play was worked again with Bulgaria as the victim. The usual swarm of Nazi agents invaded the kingdom, working up pro-German sentiment and dividing public opinion. A slice of Greek territory in Thrace was held out to King Boris as bait. The din of pro-German agitation drowned out the voices of the pro-Russian peasants. The government began to pass pro-Axis legislation. Finally, on March 1, 1941, hoping to gain territory and economic advantages, Bulgaria signed the Tripartite Pact and granted free passage to German troops through her territory.[10]

Yugoslavia. The most convenient route to Greece and the Port of Salonica, desired by Hitler as a base for operations in the Near East, was via the Vardar River Valley in Yugoslavia. Besides, German plans called for the absorption of Slovenia into the inner ring of Greater Germany and the use of Serbia as a dumping ground for surplus populations removed from other areas. Since Yugoslavia was now virtually surrounded by Axis forces, the only problem was to bring about her downfall as quickly and cheaply as possible. Nazi *agents provocateurs* began to stir up animosities between Serbs and Croats and between Greek Orthodox and Roman Catholics. When the Nazis judged that the Yugoslav government had reached the

[9] Strausz-Hupé, R., "Rumanian Nationalism," *Annals,* CCXXXII (March, 1944), pp. 88, 90; and Bosch, A., *The Danube Basin and the German Economic Sphere* (New York: Columbia University Press, 1943), pp. 213-215.

[10] Hanč, J., *op. cit.,* pp. 242-243, and Anastasoff, Christ, "Bulgaria's National Struggles," *Annals,* CCXXXII (March, 1944), p. 105.

proper pitch of anxiety, Hitler suddenly demanded, in March, 1941, that Yugoslavia should join the Tripartite Alliance. In return, she would receive guarantees of continued independence.

Under the proposed agreement, Yugoslavia would be compelled to desist from all anti-Axis activities, place all of her exports under German control, and disband her military forces. Overcome with fear as a result of Germany's invasion of Bulgaria and persuaded by his reactionary friends, Prince Paul, disregarding the advice of his associates, signed the agreement.

The popular uprising that followed placed young King Peter on the throne and led to armed resistance against the Nazi invaders. Lack of preparedness and defection of the Croats weakened Yugoslavia's fighting power. On April 13, 1941, Belgrade was taken by the Nazis and organized resistance came to an end.[11]

Greece. Germany attacked Greece at the same time she made war on Yugoslavia. Opposition of the small Greek Army (aided by about 10,000 British troops) was soon overcome. Seizure of Greece (and later the island of Crete) gave Germany her long coveted vantage point for an attack against Allied positions in Africa and the Near East.

Turkey. On April 18, 1941, Germany concluded a non-aggression pact with Turkey whereby the latter agreed to refrain from all acts of hostility against the Reich. With Turkey immobilized by the friendship accord and Britain on the defensive, Hitler felt free to attack Russia.

The U.S.S.R. Hitler's eagerness to seize the riches of the Ukraine and his wish to eliminate the Red Army from his flank as he moved farther into the Near East, as well as Germany's urgent need for the plentiful supplies of petroleum in the Caucasus, led the Fuehrer into his ill-fated war against the Soviets. On June 22, 1941, Hitler's forces attacked the Soviet Union. Much of Western Russia and the Ukraine were overrun and occupied for a time by the German Army.

Political Reorganization of the Occupied Territories

Territories considered industrially developed or necessary to German industry because of valuable raw materials within their borders, and which were capable of being Germanized, were incorporated directly into Germany. The Nazi aim, where this step was taken, was to split up and disintegrate the national territory of the peoples to be absorbed, so as to render united action on their part impossible.

---

[11] Hanč, J., *loc. cit.,* pp. 244-246.

By a German law and an Austrian constitutional amendment of dubious legality, Austria was incorporated into the inner core of Greater Germany under the name of *Ostmark*. German laws were made applicable to the new acquisition and the Austrian economy was speedily linked with the Nazi Four-Year Plan. Seyss-Inquart was designated as Reich's Regent and his cabinet became the government of the new province. Herr Buerckel was made Reich's Commissioner to supervise Austrian affairs and coördinate Austrian activities with those of the German homeland. In April, 1939, the *Ostmark* was subdivided into seven administrative areas corresponding roughly to the historic Austrian provinces, each of them headed by a Regent with sharply limited powers.

In the case of Czechoslovakia, the country was ripped to shreds. First, the Sudeten borderlands were seized by Berlin, under the Munich Agreement. Then the Czechs were forced to cede 3,064 square miles of territory in Ruthenia to Hungary, and Teschen was claimed and obtained by Poland. As a result, 19,000 square miles of territory, inhabited by nearly 5,000,000 people, were lost to the Czechs.

Incited by the Nazis, Slovak autonomists demanded freedom for Slovakia. Fearing complete disintegration, the Czech parliament consented to a constitutional change which established a separate government for Slovakia under a federal form of state to be called the "Czecho-Slovak Republic." In November, 1938, Prime Minister Joseph Tiso stated his desire for Slovakia to become a totalitarian state. Political parties were dissolved and only one party list was presented in the elections held in December. Tiso's government received a 95 per cent majority. The Slovak government supported by Germany, then began to demand complete independence, along with the separation of Czech and Slovak military forces. The federal government refused to comply and sent armed forces into Slovakia to maintain order, at the same time dismissing Tiso's government. Berlin intervened, stating through the press that the action of the federal government was contrary to the interests of the German minority in Slovakia and threatening to withdraw German protection unless Slovakia proclaimed her independence. The intimidated Slovak parliament weakly submitted and on March 14, 1939 proclaimed Slovakia's independence.

Next, President Hácha and Foreign Minister Chvalkovský of Czechoslovakia were summoned to Berlin and compelled, on March 15, to sign a declaration accepting annexation by the Reich.[12] Nazi

---

[12] For material in this section, see Czechoslovak Ministry of Foreign Affairs, *Four Fighting Years* (London: Hutchinson, 1943), Ch. I.

troops marched into Prague. On March 16, Hitler's decree establishing the Protectorate of Bohemia-Moravia was promulgated.

Ostensibly creating an autonomous state by setting up a Czech cabinet, the decree fully insured German control by providing that the President must enjoy the confidence of the Fuehrer in the discharge of his office. This aim was even more fully secured by setting up a Hitler-appointed Reich Protector in Bohemia-Moravia, whose primary duty was to insure that Hitler's orders were obeyed. To that end, the Protector was given a veto on all Czech legislation "which might injure the Reich," power to confirm or reject appointments to the Czech cabinet, and authority to issue decrees with the force of law. In addition, the Protectorate was excluded from participation in managing its own foreign relations; its military defense was entirely in German hands and Reich military garrisons were maintained in the territory; and all communications, postal facilities, telephones, and customs were German-administered. Economic affairs were under a German Minister of Economics and Labor in the Czech "government," and German advisors were designated for each Czech Minister.[13]

Local government was also completely reorganized. In June, 1939, a decree was issued dividing Bohemia-Moravia into 19 administrative districts, each headed by a German sheriff responsible to the Protector. Provincial legislative bodies were abolished, and local councils were forced to accept German advisors. German mayors replaced Czechs in many cities. No act of any Czech official could go into effect without German approval. In May, 1942, administration of the affairs of local governments was substantially turned over to the Nazis when Czech officials were largely replaced by Germans. The civil service was purged of anti-Nazis and all government employees were required to be proficient in the German language. Two failures to pass examinations in German resulted in dismissal. German officers were placed in charge of Czech police forces.[14]

The so-called "Independent Government" of Slovakia differed only slightly from the Czech Protectorate in its relations to the Reich. The government was somewhat less restricted by German control and, because it was more coöperative in its attitude, suffered somewhat less from German persecution. On March 15, 1939, Prime Minister Tiso invited Germany to place Slovakia under its protection. Nazi troops entered the country, established garrisons, took up positions along its

---

[13] *Ibid.*, pp. 33-34, 36, 38, and Czechoslovak Ministry of Foreign Affairs, *Two Years of German Oppression in Czechoslovakia* (London: Unwin, 1941), pp. 30-32.

[14] *Four Fighting Years, loc. cit.*, pp. 36-38.

frontiers, and constructed fortifications. Slovak military and foreign affairs were subjected to German supervision by the treaty of March 23, 1939. Hitler then allowed Hungary to seize 400 square miles of additional Slovakian territory along the Hungarian frontier.

In practice, the German Ambassador and Military Mission dictated the affairs of Slovakia. Political, economic, and monetary matters were disposed of largely at the pleasure of the Germans. After the Salzburg meeting, in July, 1940, Slovakia was reorganized on National Socialist principles. Parliament was emasculated and legislative powers were transferred to the cabinet; *Gauleiters* were appointed for administrative districts; the Hlinka Guard was transformed into an Elite Guard; compulsory labor camps were instituted; religion was brought under state control; and anti-Jewish measures were adopted. German advisors were installed in all Slovak offices. Thus the Slovak state became a helpless tool of the Nazis.[15]

In the case of Poland, as a consequence of the German-Soviet victory, Germany received 72,866 square miles of Polish territory containing 22,250,000 people. The Nazi plan was to split up this territory into two sections, the western part to be incorporated into the Reich and the eastern part made into a "protectorate." The western part destined for absorption consisted of 35,714 square miles of territory and 10,740,000 people. This area was organized for purposes of administration mainly into two provinces: the *Reichsgau Wartheland,* made up of Poznan and a part of central Poland, and the *Reichsgau Danzig-Westpreussen,* comprising the Free City of Danzig and its hinterland territory. In addition, a section of north central Poland was incorporated into East Prussia as the *Gau Ostpreussen.* Polish Upper Silesia was added to the *Gau Oberschlesien.*

The Government General covered an area of 36,862 square miles and contained a population of 11,485,000 people. Its capital was Cracow and it was headed by a Governor General appointed by Hitler. Four administrative areas were created: Cracow, Lublin, Radom, and Warsaw. A Commander was placed at the head of each district with full powers over ordinary governmental affairs as well as the Elite Guard and the police. Each district was divided into town and rural areas with a delegate in charge of each. Local communal associations were provided with officials appointed by the delegate.[16] The Cracow regime was separated from the Reich by a customs frontier

---

[15] *Ibid.,* pp. 141-147.
[16] Polish Ministry of Information, *Polish White Book* (New York: Greystone, 1941), pp. 82-85; and *The Black Book of Poland* (New York: Putnam, 1942), pp. 9-12.

and evidently was originally intended as a dumping ground for Jews and other recalcitrant groups. Later, when the annexationist policy in Western Poland failed, the distinction between the two sections tended to break down.

Germany's war against Russia enabled her to take over the three Baltic States of Estonia, Latvia, and Lithuania. Previously swallowed up in the huge maw of the U.S.S.R., these little states were helpless against Germany. Unwillingly, they were lumped together in another Reich province called the *Ostland* under a Reich Commissioner located at Riga.

The greater part of Slovenia in northern Yugoslavia was also annexed and formed into a district under a German *Gauleiter*.[17] Croatia and Serbia were split apart and quislings were liberally employed to do Germany's dirty work. In Croatia, Germany allowed Italy's influence to prevail superficially. Organized at first as the "Independent State of Croatia" that country was made a part of the Italian imperial domain in 1940, nominally under the Duke of Spoletto as King.[18] In reality, the traitor Pavelitch, leader of the notorious Nazi-supported Ustachis, became the real ruler of the state. Supplied with German money and arms, Ustachis followed the German Army, attacking and murdering thousands of innocent Serbs. The Nazis hoped in this way to create a permanent breach between the two peoples.[19]

In Greece, a quisling government was established after the departure of King George's government into exile. Political affairs were dictated largely by the German Army of Occupation. Eastern Macedonia and Thrace were given to Bulgaria, while three of the western Greek provinces were handed over to the Italians.[20]

As has been previously noted, Hungary and Romania set up puppet governments under close German supervision. In the case of occupied Russian territory, it remained under German military control until the Nazis were finally driven out.

In general, German governmental practices in the occupied territories were characterized by brutality, dishonesty, nepotism, and flagrant corruption. German administrators not only expressed the in-

---

[17] Loewenstein, K., "Government and Politics in Germany," in J. T. Shotwell, et al, *Governments of Continental Europe* (New York: MacMillan, 1940), pp. 459-460.

[18] Hanč, *op. cit.*, pp. 275-276; and Clissold, J., *The Slovenes Want to Live* (New York: Yugoslav Information Center, 1942), p. 30.

[19] Hanč, J., *op. cit.*, pp. 259-260; and Adamic, L., *My Native Land* (New York: Harper, 1943), pp. 34-36.

[20] Xydis, S. G., *The Economy and Finances of Greece Under Axis Occupation* (Pittsburgh: Hermes Printing Co., 1943), pp. 10-11.

tention of their Nazi masters to use subject peoples and their property with cynical disregard of their rights and interests, but they also took advantage of their positions to fatten their private fortunes through blackmail, torture, robbery, exploitation of black markets, and every conceivable form of corrupt practice. So-called "German efficiency" ended up in the most gigantic form of political and economic racketeering in history.[21]

Law and Justice in the Occupied Regions

The German conception of law and justice for so-called "inferior races" was well exemplified in Bohemia-Moravia and the Polish Government General. Obviously, in German eyes, the Anglo-Saxon conceptions of the rule of law and equality before the law had no place within the confines of Greater Germany. In the Czech Protectorate, three kinds of law applied to the inhabitants: (1) German law to the degree that this was extended to the territory; (2) Protectorate law, consisting of decrees of the Protector; and (3) the old Czech law, insofar as it covered matters not superseded by the other two categories. The German intent was to displace Czech law by German as soon as possible. This threefold legal system created confusion among the citizens, a fact which played into the hands of the Gestapo.

Two kinds of citizens were created. Sudeten Germans were made Reich citizens subject to German law and courts alone; Czechs and Jews were designated as Protectorate nationals subject to all three forms of law and to both German and Czech courts. Czech courts were definitely subordinated to German tribunals. All cases affecting German interests were under the jurisdiction of Reich tribunals if they involved administrative, political, or criminal matters. Decisions of any Czech court could be nullified by the Reich Protector and the case turned over to a German judge. In this way, a suit by a Czech against a German could be invalidated. On the other hand, any suits by Germans against Czechs were instituted in German courts. Much Czech property was transferred into German hands by this unequal procedure. German criminal law was extended to the Protectorate and the Czechs were prevented from using the courts for redress of grievances.

Independent Czech judges were in many instances sent to prison for sustaining the rights of Czech citizens. German corporations were given the protection of Reich courts and civil laws. Even if a Czech could get his case into court (in the great majority of cases he was

---

[21] "Europe: How Germany Rules It," *Fortune*, XXIV:2 (December, 1941), p. 134.

prevented from doing so by the Gestapo or German political authorities), he had very little chance of obtaining justice.[22]

In the Government General of Poland, much harsher legal measures were applied to the Poles and Jews. Two legal jurisdictions and two categories of citizenship, the German and the Polish, were created. German citizens were exempted from jurisdiction of Polish law and courts and given positions of privilege over the Poles. Under German criminal law as extended to the Poles, sentences were made more severe, and the list of crimes was widened to include offenses against the security and authority of the Reich; against the lives, health, honor, or property of German citizens; against ordinances of the Governor-General; and misdemeanors committed in buildings or places occupied by German authorities. Death sentences or long prison terms were meted out to persons listening to foreign radio programs, singing the Polish national anthem, uttering insults against Hitler, or predicting German defeat.

Special courts were established in each of the four districts to try grave offenses under German criminal law. Defense attorneys could be appointed but were not required. German attorneys could practice before courts of the Government General. In large cities, another series of German courts were created to handle ordinary business. Polish citizens of the Protectorate could take their civil cases into Polish courts, but the decisions of these tribunals were subject to revision by German courts, to annulment by the head of the Division of Justice of the Government General, or they could be sent to German courts for retrial. The Polish Supreme Court and Labor Conciliation Courts were abolished.[23] Thus, in law as well as in fact, Germans in the occupied territories were given the status of a ruling class and the legal machinery provided by Nazi ingenuity made the crushing of all rights of the subject peoples an easy matter.

Methods of Economic Plunder

Nazi techniques of economic exploitation exhausted every device for squeezing the last ounce of wealth and unit of energy from the victims. Certain patterns may be seen over the entire occupied area, with variations to meet different conditions in different countries.

The record indicates that the squeeze was applied to every phase of the economic systems, including expropriation and use of public and private lands, financial resources, capital goods and equipment, the

---

[22] Two Years of German Oppression in Czechoslovakia, op. cit., pp. 37-40.
[23] Polish White Book, op. cit., pp. 90-95; and The Black Book of Poland, op. cit., pp. 90 ff.

revenue system, raw materials and foodstuffs, and labor resources. German plans included both immediate and long term objectives. The former involved the use of all available resources for the purpose of winning the war. The latter included the planning and allocation of economic activities over the whole of Greater Germany, with a view to securing a maximum of production for the ultimate enrichment of the German ruling class. Conflicts between short and long term aims arose in many instances, resulting in confusion and misguided effort. As the war progressed and Nazi fortunes declined, war demands assumed greater importance, with long term objectives receding into the background.

Initial steps in the system of organized plunder instituted by the Nazis included skimming the cream of liquid wealth, to meet the high cost of warfare, by a German "pay-as-you-go" plan. Economic experts travelled with German forces as they advanced into fallen territories to indicate the properties to be taken. Deriving their original experience in this field from the Saar and Rhineland occupations, Nazi planners introduced a series of special economic units especially trained in this field under the "War Economy and Armament Board of the High Command of the Armed Forces," which was headed by a high-ranking military commander. After the invasion of Poland, this organization assumed major proportions. Trained in economics, business, and engineering, its members were required to get as much for the German war machine as possible within a limited period of time. Trainloads of raw materials taken from stock piles, machinery, money, and public and private valuables of various kinds were shipped to Germany.

Wealth not shipped away was conserved by the economic troops who soon came to be attached to every fighting unit. Other units in the guise of representatives of the Reichsbank took over all financial transactions between Nazi troops and resident populations. Special occupation marks and occupation notes without monetary backing and negotiable only within the country where circulated were foisted upon local business men and the people generally. An arbitrary rate of exchange was fixed, overvaluing German money compared to local money so that, even if the occupation currency was redeemed, subject peoples would stand to lose heavily. Property sales by the inhabitants were forbidden in order to give the Germans time to buy up as much local property as possible.[24]

[24] Hediger, E. S., "Nazi Exploitation of Occupied Europe," *Foreign Policy Reports*, XVIII (June 1, 1944), pp. 66-69.

Nazi land policies involved the wholesale confiscation of property in occupied territories for the use of German settlers. In Czechoslovakia, the seizure of land started in the Sudeten area in 1938. Properties of Czechs and Jews who had fled for fear of persecution for political or racial reasons were declared forfeit and German families were settled on them. Heavily mortgaged properties were bought up with paper marks and resold to Germans. Czech occupants of land were expelled and both land and capital assets were appropriated in exchange for occupation currency. By 1939, it was estimated that 370,-000 acres had been restored to big German landowners—thus nullifying the effects of the Land Reform Act of 1919.

When the Germans invaded Bohemia-Moravia, they appointed Nazi officials to controlling positions over forests and state lands. The technique of "Aryanization" was then employed as an entering wedge to get control of private landholdings. In spite of opposition by Czech authorities, most of the properties held by Jews had been taken over by Nazi authorities by 1942. A program of Germanization was instituted. Czech strips separating sections held predominantly by Germans were eliminated—the Czech occupants being compelled to move out in favor of German colonists brought into the area from other sections or from the Baltic regions. Czech owners were compensated for their land, but at sacrifice prices.

In order to expedite the land program, a German Settlement Society was organized and located at Prague. Strips of land were purchased in such a way as to split Czech settlements apart with German wedges. War demands, coupled with the extreme opposition of Czech peasants and the failure of German settlers to get satisfactory results from their farming, slowed down the settlement program in 1941-1942. Disobedience of Czech peasants to German demands for production and delivery of foodstuffs resulted in heavy penalties for the Czechs.[25]

In Western Poland, the German design was to root out or destroy the Poles until people of German nationality predominated in the region. Over-population of rural areas was an impediment to the Nazi plan to derive a surplus of foodstuffs for urbanized Germany, hence a general reduction of rural population in all of the occupied areas to 85-90 per square mile (compared to existing populations of 150-200 per square mile) was set up as a goal.[26]

Nazi methods employed here followed the Czech example. All

---

[25] *Four Fighting Years, op. cit.,* pp. 39-42.
[26] "The Survey," *New Europe,* III:2 (February, 1943), p. 24.

state forests and lands were confiscated. Then Jewish properties were "Aryanized," and this was followed by seizure of Polish-owned private lands. The original plan called for the expulsion of at least 5,000,000 Poles to the Government General and settlement of German colonists in their places. Actually around 1,500,000 Poles were uprooted and banished from their homes, taking nothing with them except a few personal possessions. Many died of brutal treatment on the way to Central Poland. Those that survived were relegated to the status of serfs.

About 500,000 German settlers were moved in to take the places of dispossessed Poles. They were brought from the Baltic States, from Soviet-occupied Poland, from the Government General, from Soviet-occupied portions of Romania, and some from Western Germany. By 1942, the ambitious German colonization scheme for Poland had died a natural death. Its demise was due to several causes: (1) Germany's intense preoccupation with the Russian war; (2) Polish resistance to Nazi measures; and (3) reluctance of German farmers to accept land in outlying territories.[27]

In Slovenia, lands, crops, and livestock were taken forcibly and the dispossessed peasants were moved into Serbia. A special bureau was established to locate selected German families on the vacated lands. These families came from northern Italy, from Soviet-occupied Romania, from Italian-occupied Slovenia, and from the Reich itself. Farm families were grouped into villages and lands were operated as common village estates. Even the German colonists were dissatisfied.[28]

In all occupied countries, farmers (whether native peasants or Germans) were required to raise crops suitable for the German warmachine and contributing to national self-sufficiency. Industrial crops such as soy beans, flax, and sunflowers for vegetable oils were grown in Southeastern Europe. Sugar beets and cotton crops were specified for the Balkans and Czechoslovakia. Live-stock production was discouraged in order to conserve cereals. Peasants were ordered to turn over specified quotas to the Germans on pain of heavy penalties.[29]

---

[27] The Black Book of Poland, op. cit., pp. 202-214.

[28] Furlan, Boris, Fighting Yugoslavia (New York: Yugoslavia Information Center, 1943), pp. 19-20.

[29] Hediger, E. S., "Nazi Economic Imperialism," Foreign Policy Reports, XVIII (August 15, 1942), p. 146; and Munk, F., op. cit., pp. 36-40.

Manipulation of Finances

One of the first steps after occupation of a country was the seizure by Nazi agents of national and bank-owned gold reserves and foreign exchange. This practice was followed in all of the countries invaded or annexed. In Austria, it has been estimated that nearly $70,000,000 in gold and foreign exchange was appropriated by the Germans. In Czechoslovakia, German economic experts took immediate control of the gold reserves, foreign exchange, and bank securities, and began cashing them in. Czechoslovak authorities estimate that at least $400,-000,000 was extorted from these sources. Upon demand of Nazi authorities, the Bank of England turned over about $25,000,000 worth of Czechoslovak gold to the German government.[30]

All Czech money, first in the Sudeten area, and later in Bohemia-Moravia, was seized and used to finance the German acquisition of Czech capital assets, banks, industries, land, and so forth. German decrees prevented Czechs from selling their property and froze all the pre-invasion contractual obligations of Czechs, thus preventing disposal of jeopardized property and making it easy for the Germans to buy it with stolen Czech money or bogus marks. Upon the capitulation of a country to the *Reichswehr,* its army equipment became the property of the Reich. In the case of Austria and Czechoslovakia, the yield on this property, which was sold to other countries in Southeastern Europe, was estimated at $200,000,000. The total for all of the occupied countries was very substantial. Approximately $4,000,-000,000 worth of gold, foreign exchange, bank securities, and military equipment was taken by the Nazis.[31]

The Nazi plunderbund always got control of all banks and banking activities in the occupied areas at once. Certain large German banks began to buy up native banks in the occupied territories as rapidly as they could absorb them. The *Deutsche Bank* took over local banks in the principal cities of Austria, Serbia, the Czechoslovak Protectorate, Slovakia, Bulgaria, Romania, Croatia, Greece, Poland, and Hungary. The *Dresdner Bank* obtained branches in all of these states and in Latvia. The *Commerz Bank* owned banks in Greece, Poland, the Baltic States, Romania, Croatia, and Serbia. The *German Labor Bank* also had extensive holdings throughout the occupied territories.[32]

The banks thus obtained were acquired in various ways. Their

---

[30] *Europe Under Hitler, op. cit.,* pp. 32-33; and *Four Fighting Years, op. cit.,* pp. 52-54.

[31] *Europe Under Hitler, loc. cit.*

[32] *The Penetration of German Capital Into Europe* (London: Interallied Information Committee, 1942), pp. 6-7.

stock was purchased with confiscated money or phoney currency. Jewish banks were "Aryanized," their owners driven away and deprived of their property without compensation. Berlin banks began to demand payment on securities held by them of the banks destined for spoilation. Since their assets had been confiscated, the local banks were unable to make good on their obligations and were taken by foreclosure. Branch banks were forcibly seized and their assets confiscated, in many cases, and the parent banks were then compelled to consent to absorption or close their doors.

German banks already located in a particular area expanded their issues of capital stock and took over the business of closed native banks. Through threats and intimidation, many banks were pressured into increasing their voting shares, which were then bought up with fiat money on the markets in sufficient amounts to enable German bankers to obtain a controlling interest.

According to Munk, only one bank escaped acquisition by the Germans in Czechoslovakia. All other large banks were taken over by German banking institutions, after which they were required to exchange whatever liquid assets or credit they had for Reich treasury bills. In a comparatively short time, the great bulk of Czech bank assets consisted of these bills. In this way, Czech wealth was siphoned into the vaults of the Reich.[33]

In western Poland, all Polish banks were taken over by the Germans. Branch banks of German concerns were established in their places. All Polish coöperative credit banks were liquidated and replaced by "peoples' banks" created for the purpose of absorbing the savings of peasants and workers.

In the Government General, some Polish banks were allowed to continue in operation subject to severe restrictions. Hampered by German interference, the Polish banks gradually lost ground. In the Ukraine, an Issue Bank was established in March, 1942, which began to circulate occupation notes to finance the purchase of agricultural machinery by German settlers. A system of "popular savings banks" was also created.

In the annexed territories of Yugoslavia, all existing banks were forcibly taken over and supplanted by Viennese banks already operating in the area. Here also "savings banks" were set up and the coöperative credit system was manipulated to German advantage. In Croatia, the entire banking system was absorbed by a combination of large German Banks. Similar policies were followed in Serbia. In

---

[33] Munk, F., *op. cit.*, pp. 126-127.

the Baltic States, three large concerns: the *Dresdner, Commerz,* and *Gemeinschaftsbank Ostland,* took over all banking operations.

In the German satellite states of Hungary, Bulgaria, and Romania, local banks were compelled to allow German companies to buy up French shares and other available securities until German concerns held a controlling interest in many cases. The German octopus thus spread its tentacles over all phases of the productive life of the satellite countries. Similar techniques were employed in Greece.[34]

Establishment of German control over the banking systems of the occupied countries was accompanied by measures to prevent people from using up their savings too rapidly. Withdrawals from bank accounts were strictly limited to amounts sufficient for a minimum of daily needs. Insurance companies were taken over by the Nazis and their tremendous savings were used to advantage by the Reich's money masters.

The stream of stolen wealth flowing toward the Reich was accelerated by exchange manipulation. Rates of exchange were arbitrarily set by German authorities at values which discriminated against the currencies of the occupied countries by from 5 to 63 per cent.

This accomplished a double purpose for the Germans: it enabled them to buy up all manner of valuable assets in the occupied areas at bargain prices; it forced the victims to pay more money for goods from the Reich than they were worth. Since their only possibility of trade was with the Reich, the victims had no choice but to submit to what amounted to outright robbery. To make the situation worse, local banks still under control of native owners were forced to accept nearly worthless *Reichsmarks* in exchange for valid assets. Citizens of occupied countries also had to accept German fiat money. Realizing its worthlessness, they tried to get rid of it as quickly as possible. Prices rose rapidly until inflation became general.[35]

As if these crushing measures were not enough, the Nazi junta assessed costs of occupation against all the nations occupied by Germany in Central-Eastern Europe. These costs were set far above the actual expenditures of occupying forces. The intention here was obviously to exact a perennial form of tribute from the enslaved peoples. Hediger estimates the total revenue from occupation costs of all occupied countries at $4,500,000,000 per year, of which exactions

---

[34] *The Penetration of German Capital Into Europe, loc. cit.,* pp. 8 ff.
[35] *Europe Under Hitler, op. cit.,* pp. 35-38.

from the countries of Central-Eastern Europe formed a substantial proportion.[36]

In addition, special taxes and levies were imposed upon the unfortunate victims. In Czechoslovakia, the Reich government seized the proceeds from indirect taxes and sent them to Germany. This larceny was continued year after year. Authoritative estimates place total German gains from this source at $240,000,000. A war contribution of approximately $70,000,000 was imposed upon the Czechs. A special tax on alcoholic beverages, expected to yield about $20,000,000 per year, was decreed in the Protectorate. With extension of the German Customs Union to Czechoslovakia after October, 1940, German indirect taxes were applied to that country, amounting to a 10 per cent levy on the national income. Similar practices were followed in Poland. No doubt to emphasize Polish inferiority, a 15 per cent income tax was levied upon all Polish workers.[37]

The Nazi Industrial Blitzkrieg in Central-Eastern Europe

Plans of the plunderbund to concentrate most industrial production in Germany proper were modified by the demands of war. In order to escape the ravages of Allied bombing, war industries were moved into the Czech Protectorate and Slovakia until a considerable proportion of Nazi production was centered there by 1942. Croatia was also used as a base for expansion of production in the chemical industry.

After 1938, Reich experts began to take over all industrial and mining facilities in the occupied territories. Huge industrial combines were organized to control and operate such plants in the interests of the Reich. Outstanding among these was the Hermann Goering Works. Originally subsidized by the German government to develop iron mines in Germany, it was used by Goering, the head of the Four Year Plan, as a means of concentrating control of all types of industrial plants in the Reich considered essential for war. When Austria was annexed, the Goering concern was on the scene from the start. Absorbing Jewish holdings as fast as they were "Aryanized", the Goering Works obtained possession of every type of large-scale business.

From there, the Goering Works spread its tentacles into practically every German-occupied country. It specialized in mines and metallurgy, machinery and armament production, and inland waterway

---

[36] Hediger, E. S., *op. cit.,* p. 139.
[37] *Europe Under Hitler, op. cit.,* pp. 27-30; and *Four Fighting Years, op. cit.,* pp. 57-58.

navigation. Other great German cartels operating in the occupied areas on a grand scale were the I. G. Farbenindustrie and the Kontinentale Oel A. G.[38] A number of smaller associations were formed with Nazi leaders on their boards of directors, and even corporations owned and operated directly by the Nazi Party, to develop the vast spoils now available to Germany. The average capital of German joint stock companies was doubled between 1933 and 1940 to handle the new business.[39] By means of such business organizations, the Nazi plunderbund was able to get control over all raw materials, coal, iron, nickel, magnesite, chrome, oil wells, and other vital products in the occupied regions.

Practically all large productive plants were taken over by German trusts and all others were organized under German control. The process of acquiring ownership was comparatively simple. Preliminary seizure of the banks had given ownership, in many cases amounting to a controlling interest, in the securities of many local concerns. In other cases, local businesses were required to increase their stock issues and these were then bought with occupation marks. In Western Poland, practically all business property, both large and small, was confiscated without compensation. In the Government General all Jewish firms were liquidated, as were large businesses generally. A few were permitted to function under German supervision. Many businesses producing for civilian use were closed and the machinery shipped to Germany.

In Bohemia-Moravia, all Czech business was placed under German domination. A German was appointed Minister of Industry, Trade, and Business, and all industrial activities were brought under his control. Organizations of Czech businessmen were dissolved and reestablished along similar structural lines, but with Germans in key positions. Chambers of Industry, Trade, and Handicrafts, organized on Reich models, topped these agencies. Governing boards of the Chambers were appointed by the Minister of Industry, Trade, and Business. Nazi representatives were placed on all committees of the associations, membership of businessmen in the associations was made compulsory, and association funds were appropriated for German use.

In the satellite states of Bulgaria, Hungary, and Romania, large German cartels extended their control over local business. Through

---

[38] Munk, F., *op. cit.*, pp. 40-43, 143-144; and *Penetration of German Capital Into Europe, op. cit.*, p. 5.

[39] *Penetration of German Capital Into Europe, loc. cit.*

Reich-owned or -controlled banks, financial flotations enabled Nazi combines to buy up properties and engineer amalgamations, or to purchase majority voting rights in industrial, chemical, and mining companies, until the industrial systems of these countries were dominated by German monopolies.[40]

Manipulation of Prices, Foodstuffs, Raw Materials, and Manufactured Goods

Prices and supplies of goods were regulated by the conquerors to suit their political ends. In order to conserve foodstuffs and other needed goods, to insure that the master race would get sufficient supplies, and to eliminate undesirable elements, the peoples of Central-Eastern Europe were placed under strict rationing so low in some cases as to be equivalent to a death sentence by starvation.

Provisions for rationing varied with the country involved. For example, ration allowances in Czechoslovakia were much lower than those of the Germans, but they were fairly adequate compared to those of the Poles or Greeks. In Poland the allowance was 680 calories a day compared to the standard allowance of 2,400 calories. Jews were permitted only 400 calories a day. As a result of these starvation diets, the mortality rate was appalling. The weekly death rate in Warsaw increased from 251 in 1936 to 1,184 in June, 1941. Typhus and tuberculosis spread alarmingly, particularly among the Jews. The infant mortality rate among the Poles increased by over 42 per cent between 1937 and 1939.

In Greece, as in the other invaded areas, reserves of foodstuffs were carried away by the Germans. But in this case, nothing was left for the Greek population and there were hundreds of thousands of deaths from starvation. More than half of the population was reduced to a daily diet of 250 calories a day. Very few infants were able to survive. Conditions in Yugoslavia also were very bad because of Nazi plundering.[41]

Prices were varied to suit the end in view. Black markets were encouraged and many Nazis in the armed forces and government services actually contributed to them from their surplus stores stolen from local populations in order to reap the huge profits involved. Since rations were cut so low, many people with hidden funds used

[40] For additional material on this section, see R. Tirana, *The Spoils of Europe* (New York: Norton, 1941), Ch. 19.

[41] *Rationing Under Axis Rule* (New York: United Nations Information Office, 1942), pp. 3, 5-6, 8-9, 12-16; and Lynn, H. Z., "Biological Extermination of Polish Youth," *Polish Review*, III:38 (October 18, 1943), pp. 4-5.

them to buy supplies from the black markets, but those without funds had no such recourse.

Social and political prices were also employed, involving higher prices for persons of means on the legitimate markets, although, where goods were strictly limited in quantity, prices became less important than food coupons. Political prices were fixed in such a manner as to discriminate in favor of German citizens and against non-Germans. Finally, racial prices were set to increase the burdens of races of lower status and to make invidious comparisons between them and races on higher levels.[42]

Reserves of foodstuffs in all of the occupied territories were seized and transported to the Reich. Peasants were given annual quotas to fill and compelled to turn them over to the Germans under threat of dire penalties if they failed or inducements of more favorable treatment if they complied. Strict rationing of civilian needs permitted Reich agents to siphon stock piles, reserves, and annual production quotas of raw materials and manufactured goods to Germany. All productive facilities were converted to war purposes except for a limited number of factories and workshops. Businesses which refused to comply were closed and their facilities were shipped to other places.

Slave Workers for the Reich

Possession of all of the material resources of the victimized nations was of little use without labor to work them. This became one of the greatest of Nazi problems, not only because of the growing shortage of workers due to the enormous wastage of manpower in war, but also because of the unwilling attitude of the working people who became subject to their political control. Never noted for magnanimity in their methods, pressure for output of war goods as well as ideological promptings caused the Nazi overlords to use the most brutal methods of compulsion to force workers to bow to their will.

Preliminary steps usually involved the breaking up of independent labor unions and the organization of a Labor Front on the Nazi model in each occupied area. These tactics were not very successful. In the Czech Protectorate, Nazi attempts to win over labor leaders as quislings for the Labor Front were defeated by the refusal of these men to betray their comrades, even under the most severe persecution. Instead, the unified union became a center of resistance to the Nazi

---

[42] Munk, F., *op. cit.*, pp. 110-111.

invaders. Nazi brutality was softened somewhat in this case with bribes and concessions because of the German need to move industries into Czechoslovakia to escape Allied bombings. Nevertheless, hours of labor were increased to 60 hours a week plus overtime, Czech workers were compelled to carry work cards and could not leave their jobs except with the consent of the employment office.

Czechs and Slovaks had a somewhat easier time than Poles, Russians, and Jews. Destined for ultimate extinction, Jews were not counted as part of the permanent working force. Poles and Russians were treated with the barbarity which the Nazis considered fitting for such degraded races. Czech workers, permitted to volunteer for labor in the Reich at first, were eventually subjected to compulsory labor in both the Protectorate and the Reich, including men between 16 and 65 and women between 17 and 45 (except mothers of families). Slovak workers were theoretically free from German compulsion, but actually the quisling government coöperated with the Nazis in sending about 100,000 workers to the Reich.[43]

In dealing with the Poles, both in the annexed area and the Government General, the Nazis did not allow scruples of any kind to deter them in their hunt for laborers. Compulsory legislation of 1939-1940 subjected all Poles from 14 to 60 to labor conscription. Because workers were reluctant to go to Germany voluntarily, they were transported by force.

The favorite method of the Gestapo was to stage raids on Polish restaurants and meeting places where the younger and more vigorous persons of both sexes were rounded up and shipped to Germany. House to house searches were staged, both in the towns and in the country. When these devices failed, quotas were fixed for each town and village and severe penalties were assessed against them if they failed to meet requirements. Estimates of the number of Poles shipped to Germany ranged as high as 1,500,000 in April, 1943. Hundreds of thousands more had been added by 1944.

The treatment of Polish workers in the Reich was brutal in the extreme. Czechs and Slovaks were comparatively well off. The Poles were made to wear distinguishing badges and Germans were forbidden to associate with them. If sick, the Poles were shipped home at once. They were assigned to work in groups and lived in barracks isolated from other workers. Labor cards, which served also for identification, were required. Poles could not use public conveyances without special police permission or attend church services in company with

---

[43] For further material on this section, see *Four Fighting Years, op. cit.*, pp. 94-96, 150.

Germans. Clothing allowances were restricted to bare essentials. Poles were forbidden to belong to labor organizations or to serve as worker representatives or shop foremen. Paid strictly by piecework, they were prevented from sharing in overtime pay, travel pay, or bonuses. Family and children's allowances, granted to German workers, were denied the Poles as were also income tax exemptions. Remittances to Poland were handled by their employers. Holidays were suspended in the case of Polish workers, and child labor legislation did not apply to Polish children. These measures confirm the German plan to exterminate the Poles.[44]

Similar tactics were employed against Russian workers. V. M. Molotov, in the Spring of 1943, presented documentary proof to the heads of the Allied governments that hundreds of thousands of Russian citizens in the German-occupied areas had been kidnapped and transported to the Reich, where they were treated even more brutally than the Poles.[45] In addition to compulsory labor recruits, millions of prisoners of war from Russia, Poland, Czechoslovakia, and other countries of Central-Eastern Europe were compelled to work on war projects for their German masters. The Soviet government, in particular, complained repeatedly about the illegal and inhuman Nazi treatment of Red Army prisoners of war.[46]

Women, heretofore exempted from warlike measures, were treated with savage disregard of civilized standards by the Nazis. Polish and Russian women were compelled to be servants in the homes of Germans and laborers on the farms of the Reich under appallingly harsh conditions. Those who resisted in any way were sent to concentration camps (where few survived), tortured, shot, or burned to death. In Czechoslovakia, after the murder of Heydrick, the whole village of Lidice, including women and children, was destroyed. In Yugoslavia and Greece, German troops attacked and burned entire villages, mercilessly slaying women and children. Particularly revolting was the Nazi practice of organized rape, to which Russian and Polish women were subjected. Not only were these practices carried out in the territories, but young women, taken ostensibly for labor service, were sent to German military camps for use as prostitutes. Slovene women were also victimized in this way.[47]

---

[44] *The Black Book of Poland, op. cit.,* p. 95 ff., and *Polish Fortnightly Review,* No. 65 (April 1, 1943), pp. 1-8.

[45] *Information Bulletin, U.S.S.R. Embassy,* No. 52 (May 15, 1943), pp. 1-4.

[46] See the files of the *Information Bulletin, U.S.S.R. Embassy* for 1943.

[47] *Axis Treatment of Women* (New York: United Nations Information Office, 1943), pp. 3, 8-10, 12-14, 19-26.

Germanization of the European Colonies

The Nazis definitely planned to reduce subject populations to a level assuring permanent safety for the Teutonic minority in Central-Eastern Europe. Statistics indicated clearly that, unless drastic measures were taken, Slav pressure on German frontiers could not be resisted.[48] The measures decided upon included: (1) an attempt to Germanize all persons of Teutonic origin and those willing to become Reich nationals; (2) to move out or destroy Slavic populations incapable of assimilation who lived in sections adjacent to Germany proper and to replace them with German colonists; (3) to destroy the intellectual class of each conquered nation and the culture which they helped to perpetuate; and (4) to educate many of the children as Nazis by sending them to Germany for special training. Some of the methods employed to achieve these ends have already been described in the sections on the eviction of Poles from Western Poland, the rationing of populations, and labor policies. Certain other policies should also be noted.

The Policy of Assimilation

The removal of 1½ to 2 million Poles from Western Poland left a void which was filled by about 500,000 German settlers brought from various parts of Europe. Prevented by the war and the opposition of German peasants themselves from dumping more colonists into the area, the Fuehrer was confronted with the fact that only 12 per cent of the population of the territory was German. In desperation, he resolved to attempt to Germanize the Poles themselves. The peoples inhabiting Western Poland were classified into distinct nationalities according to their various racial origins and certificates of nationality were issued to those who, by German standards, were assumed to be of "Germanic" origin. Thus, all inhabitants of Polish Pomerania and Silesia were placed by administrative decree in the category of German nationals. Kashubans and Mazurians were also treated in this way.

In the *Wartheland* (Poznan and parts of the provinces of Warsaw and Lodz), a *Deutsche Volksliste* was set up and all persons of German origin were invited to register. In spite of the special inducements of German nationality or "state citizenship" for Poles, there were few registrants. Lack of popular support forced German authorities

[48] Lynn, H. Z., *op. cit.*, p. 3, and Roucek, J. S., "The Minorities Problem in Czechoslovakia," *Journal of Central-European Affairs*, III:2 (July, 1943), p. 192.

gradually to lower their standards until anyone not a Jew or a Gypsy could sign up. The German theory of blood unity failed when applied to Poland—thus demonstrating once more that the ties of nationality are stronger than those of blood.[49] In spite of the policy of terror invoked against the Poles, population ratios were not substantially changed, except on paper, where Poles were arbitrarily counted as Germans. The *Volksliste* fell far short of converting the Poles to Germanism.

The original Nazi idea of making the Government General a dumping ground for all Poles and Jews was not carried out. As early as 1939, the Germans began to try to minimize the number of "real" Poles in that area and to make hairsplitting distinctions based on tribal origins to prove that many of these tribes were not true Poles. Efforts were made to prove German origins for some of them. Early in 1940, a Governor-General's decree enabled Poles to become German nationals by a mere confession of faith.

Steps were then taken to split Polish populations apart by creating German islands among them, composed largely of renegade Poles. Villages of so-called "Germans" were isolated from Polish elements and subjected to an intensive program of German *Kultur*. Polish children were sent away to the Reich for schooling and Germanizing courses were organized for adults. Turncoat Polish families were given the farms of loyal Poles, who were forcibly evacuated. By 1942, it was estimated that from 70,000 to 100,000 persons in the Government General had been given certificates of German nationality.[50]

The small returns evidenced by these figures shifted the emphasis in German calculations to the alternative policy of exterminating the Poles biologically. In the case of the Jews, the policy of outright murder was systematically carried out until, by 1944, practically every Polish Jew had been "liquidated."

In the case of the Poles, more subtle methods were employed. In addition to starvation rations leading to high disease and mortality rates, Polish women in Western Poland were forbidden to marry if under 29 years of age. Those who violated this order were denied ration cards for themselves and milk for their babies. Most young Poles of both sexes were placed at compulsory labor under onerous conditions and prevented from marrying. Death penalties for many petty violations of regulations were mercilessly enforced. The shooting of hostages for violation of military regulations led to the death

---

[49] *The Quest for German Blood* (London: Polish Ministry of Information, 1943), pp. 8-22.
[50] *Ibid.*, pp. 35-46.

of thousands. Yet it became clear that the attempt to annihilate a considerable proportion of a large nation was a time-consuming business.[51]

A parallel policy was followed in Slovenia. Schools, theaters, museums, libraries, and musical entertainments were Germanized. Young Slovenes were compelled to join Nazi youth and military formations. German language courses were required for the entire population. A well-knit German propaganda unit operated in Slovenia to direct Germanizing activities. Even the names of streets, buildings, public monuments, and cemeteries were changed to German.[52]

De-Culturizing the Occupied Nations

In the German view, Poles were fit only for destruction, body, mind, and soul. Those left alive were considered capable only of manual labor. Hence they needed no education except in elementary and trade schools. In pursuance of this doctrine, the Nazis proceeded to destroy all Polish schools and colleges on the secondary and higher levels. University and school buildings were torn down, libraries burned, expensive laboratory equipment and museum pieces destroyed or carried away. All Polish colleges and universities were closed. The students were transported to compulsory service in the Reich.

In the annexed provinces, Poles were deprived even of elementary education or were subjected to humiliating discrimination. In the elementary schools of the Government General, Polish textbooks were confiscated, Polish history and geography were banned from the curriculum, and pupils were required to study German. School terms were shortened, fuel was not supplied in wintertime, and buildings were requisitioned for various military purposes. As a result, school attendance fell off drastically.

The teaching staffs of Polish schools were singled out for special persecution. Teachers colleges were closed. Many teachers were imprisoned and others were dismissed. Very few remained available to teach Polish children.[53] Polish university faculties were broken up and the professors were sent to concentration camps, where they were mistreated to such an extent that many died. Others were shot.

A deliberate attempt was made to destroy all traces of Polish culture. In Western Poland, all Polish signs and street-names were changed to

[51] Lynn, H. Z., *op. cit.,* pp. 3-5.

[52] Furlan, Boris, *op. cit.,* pp. 22-24.

[53] Ponikowska, M. S., and Jurkowa, M., *Polish Youth* (London: Polish Students' Association in Great Britain, 1943), pp. 21-27.

German. National monuments were destroyed. Polish theaters, newspapers, and periodicals were suppressed; libraries and bookshops were confiscated. All Polish radio sets were seized and listening to foreign programs was prohibited.[54]

In Czechoslovakia, the German aim of destroying all cultural and intellectual life was also in evidence. Czech universities were closed. Students who resisted were shot or imprisoned. University faculties were disbanded and the professors executed or sent to concentration camps. Czech elementary and high schools were closed in winter, while German schools were allowed to remain open. Czech cultural courses were prohibited and the German language was required.

Similar measures were employed by the Germans and Bulgarians in Yugoslavia and Greece. Native schools were closed and German schools encouraged. Teachers were shot or sent to concentration camps. In Croatia, Pavelitch permitted only Ustachi youth and Moslems to go to school. All schools were abolished by the Germans in part of Slovenia. Italians and Germans coöperated in "liquidating" practically all Slovenian teachers. In Serbia, hundreds of teachers and professors were killed. Even school children were massacred by the hundreds. In occupied Russia, the story was very much the same, except that the German culture-wrecking campaign was carried out on a grander scale.[55]

Persecution of the Churches

German destruction of all centers of resistance succeeded in the case of all private associations except the Churches. The importance of religion in preserving national cultures and keeping up the spirits of the oppressed was becoming clearer every day. So the Nazis also attacked the Churches and attempted to replace them with German religious leaders, beliefs, and institutions.

The initial attack was aimed at the clergy and prominent Christian leaders. Czechoslovak clerics and leaders were tortured, murdered, or sent to concentration camps, where they were shamed and mistreated. Theological seminaries were closed. The shortage of ministers made it difficult for many churches to remain open. Ministers were forbidden to speak on political subjects. In many cases German clergymen were forced upon the congregations. In Greece, many

[54] Godden, G. M., *Murder of a Nation* (London: Burns Oates, 1943), Chs. 1-4.
[55] *Axis Oppression of Education* (New York: United Nations Information Office, 1942), pp. 6-9, 11-14, 22-24; *Information Bulletin, U.S.S.R. Embassy*, No. 16 (February 13, 1943), p. 5; and No. 82 (July 27, 1943), pp. 9-10.

clergymen were shot and churches and religious monuments were desecrated.

In Poland, the Nazis evidently planned to exterminate the Catholic Church completely. Hundreds of priests were executed without trial, murdered, or tormented to death in concentration camps. There were wholesale massacres of priests in some sections. The Gestapo and prison guards subjected priests to the most degrading and shameful tasks, and administered brutal beatings to them. Church cathedrals, monuments, and chapels were destroyed or desecrated. Many churches were used as business offices, stables, gymnasia, and so forth. Those not destroyed were closed and looted. Similar measures were taken against churches and clergy in the U.S.S.R.

In Croatia, the Ustachi set out deliberately to exterminate all Serbian members of the Orthodox Church. Orthodox priests were killed or driven out of the country. The Orthodox and Jewish religions were refused official recognition—only the Catholic and Moslem religions were tolerated.[56]

Mass Murder

The German purpose in the mass murder of populations in Central-Eastern Europe was fairly clear. In the case of the Jews, the Nazis had marked them for obliteration from the beginning. Poles and Russians were to be removed in order to reduce the density of populations in areas destined for agriculture; to increase the percentage of Germans vis-à-vis the Slavs; to quell resistance; to simplify the task of policing by small garrisons; and to prevent any future resurgence by these enemy peoples in the future.

Jews were made the first victims of the extermination policy. Starting slowly at first by imposing various kinds of discriminations on the Jews, depriving them of their property and positions, the pace of persecution was gradually stepped up until wholesale slaughter of Jews became the rule. These tactics were employed in Czechoslovakia. After the Jews were completely dispossessed, they were organized into labor battalions and carried away to Germany or to Poland. In 1941, a Jewish "home" was established at Terezin in central Bohemia and 10,000 Jews were concentrated there. Then, in 1942, mass deportations of Jews to Poland were inaugurated. Compelled to leave all but a few personal possessions, they were shipped in cattle trucks to Lublin, where they were ultimately put to death in

---

[56] *Religious Persecution*, III (New York: United Nations Information Office, 1942), pp. 3, 7-9, 11, 18-23.

great murder factories. Under pressure from the Reich, the Slovakian quisling government passed a law providing for deportation of all but a few Jews to Poland. By the end of 1942, 75,000 Jews had been sent to Polish murder camps.

In Poland, after being deprived of all their possessions and rights, the Jews were segregated in ghettos in the large cities, where they were compelled to stay without food or means of support. Finally, they were shipped at the rate of 7,000 to 10,000 per day to the slaughter camps at Chelm, Belzec, and other centers. In the Russian Ukraine, Jews were slaughtered by the thousands and buried in mass graves which they themselves were compelled to dig. Similar measures were employed in Yugoslavia. The Ustachi in Croatia killed all Jews. In Serbia, the Gestapo carried out this grisly task, but in this case more refined methods of slow death by torture were used. Only in Greece were the Jews able to escape complete extermination, due to an uprising of the Greek people in protest.[57]

The campaign to eliminate as many actual and potential Polish leaders as possible had been prepared in advance. Aided by local Germans, the Gestapo had lists of victims composed of prominent people, landowners, religious leaders, and professional men. The Gestapo arrested these persons on slight pretexts and executed them in the presence of the assembled local population. Authorities estimate that at least 25,000 Polish leaders in Western Poland were killed in this way in 1939. Their families were then herded into concentration camps. Hundreds of thousands of young people were deported to work camps or scattered in small towns and villages. Carried in crowded, poorly ventilated, unheated cars in mid-winter, many died of exposure on the journey, especially women and children.

As a result of the increased severity of the laws and application of the death sentence for almost all types of offenses, thousands of Poles were executed. A system of hostages was set up by which Polish leaders, or even persons chosen at random, were selected in groups of 50 or more and held as surety for the good conduct of the population of a given area. Failure to observe German demands resulted in the massacre of the hostages. The practice was deliberate and designed not only to enforce German authority but to kill as many Poles as possible. Shooting of hostages became a daily occurrence and was continued throughout the period of occupation. By 1943, mass arrests and executions were being carried out by the Germans. Polish un-

---

[57] *Persecution of the Jews,* VI (London: Interallied Information Committee, 1942), pp. 3, 5-7, 9-10, 15-20.

derground resistance gave an excuse for greater terrorism, which seemed designed to prod the Poles into uprisings as a pretext for wholesale slaughter.

In Czechoslovakia, prior to Heydrick's arrival, German policies were relatively mild. A number of prominent political, military, educational, and religious leaders were shot and the Gestapo practiced its ruthless police methods, but nothing was attempted comparable to the Polish massacres.

After 1941, Heydrick attempted to overcome Czech resistance by a policy of utter ruthlessness. Summary political courts were established and a state of emergency was decreed. Intellectuals and army officers were singled out for persecution and the courts and Gestapo worked night and day handing out death sentences. Extensive purges of government officials were instituted. At the same time, Czech workers were favored with extra rations and pay allowances to try to win them over.

In Greece, the principle of "collective responsibility" was enforced. Hostages were killed and often whole villages were burned and their inhabitants massacred for aiding Greek irregular forces.

In Yugoslavia, the Nazis in Serbia killed 50 hostages for each German soldier killed by Serbians. In Croatia, similar practices were followed. In Slovenia, Slovene leaders from prepared lists were murdered and deported; prisoners in concentration camps were tortured and beaten to death; the hostage system was extensively applied; villages were exterminated in reprisals for resistance; and not only the intellectuals, but the entire peasant class were deported under barbarous conditions of transport.[58]

Resistance Movements in Central-Eastern Europe

For centuries, the peoples of Central-Eastern Europe have had to resist foreign invaders and reactionary governments. In consequence, they have developed mature and comprehensive methods of resistance to oppression. In World War II these took the form of counter-action to the attempts of the Germans to destroy national unity and economic organization; methods of national and social conspiracy; and belligerent resistance.

The most complete system of resistance to the Nazis was developed

---

[58] *Extermination of the Polish People and Colonization by German Nationals* (New York: Polish Information Center, 1941), pp. 5-15; *Polish Review,* III:2 (January 11, 1943), p. 15, III:14 (April 12, 1943), p. 3; *Four Fighting Years, op. cit.,* Ch. XI; *The Axis System of Hostages* (New York: United Nations Information Office, 1942), pp. 2, 4-5, 7-8, 12-15.

in Poland. Passive non-coöperation was combined with guerrilla warfare. In Austria, the movement took the form mainly of passive non-conformity. In occupied Russia, guerrilla warfare behind the German lines assumed enormous proportions. Passive resistance was the principal technique employed in Czechoslovakia, whereas in Yugoslavia armed insurrection by the Chetniks and later by the Partisan bands under Tito developed into nationwide combat with the invaders.

Underground resistance reached its most highly developed form in Poland. A widespread popular conspiracy against the government was organized and operated by means of secret communications. The system amounted to a secret state within a state. Its leaders either resided abroad or were unknown to the enemy. By means of this organization, the political, social, and cultural life of the people was maintained to some degree. In time a Polish underground army was created and was able to play havoc with the enemy. German reprisals against Poles were followed by Polish reprisals against German soldiers, villages, and communications. The long lines of German communications to the Russian front offered a favorable opportunity to tear up rails, destroy roads and supply trains, ambush isolated military contingents, capture secret documents and transmit them to the Allies, and hamper German activities in other ways. Large German forces were compelled to remain in Poland to deal with these acts of the underground.

The Polish underground, acting under instructions from the government-in-exile in London, coöperated actively with Russian Partisans, many of whom were dropped in Polish territory by plane. Misunderstandings between the two groups arose because Soviet Partisans wanted the Poles to rise immediately against the Germans and create a second front against them without regard to its effect on the Poles. General Bor's ineffective uprising in Warsaw, in the summer of 1944, illustrated the futility of this technique both for the Poles and for the Allies.[59]

Czech resistance was manifested in the form of *Svejk-action*, i.e. betrayal or the "doublecross", the slow-down, and sabotage.

[59] Malinowski, W. R., "The Pattern of Underground Resistance," *Annals,* CCXXXII (March, 1944), pp. 126-133; and "The Polish Underground Army," *Polish Fortnightly Review,* LXXXIV:84 (January 15, 1944), pp. 1-8.

Conclusion Regarding the German Occupation

Given sufficient time and success in the war, the Nazi plunderbund might well have succeeded in its ambitious and bloody attempt to reorganize completely the institutional and social life of the Central-European nations. Partial success accompanied German efforts at political and economic reconstruction, but the Nazis failed utterly in their population policies. The aftermath of their campaign of pillage and murder leaves Europe in a state of complete political and economic disorganization. Its peoples are disunited and scattered, suffering from starvation and decimation, and imbued with unrelenting hatred of their erstwhile oppressors. It will require years to heal the wounds inflicted by the invasion of the hordes of the modern Attila.

Bibliography

(See bibliography at end of Chapter XXIX.)

CHAPTER XXIX

CENTRAL-EASTERN EUROPE UNDER RUSSIAN OCCUPATION

Russia Takes Over Eastern Poland

GERMAN preparations for war after Hitler came to power caused the U.S.S.R. to look well to its defenses. The Kremlin feared a German attack by way of Eastern Poland, or alternatively through the Baltic States of Estonia, Latvia, and Lithuania. Finland was also a possible base of German operations against the Leningrad area. In Southern Europe, German columns, aiming at the Ukraine and Caucasian oil, might cross from Czechoslovakia into Romania and use that country as a supply center for a drive into Southern Russia.

Expansionist motives doubtless figured in the Soviet scheme of things, too, since Red leaders had always resented the manner in which the Allies, Poland, Finland, and Romania had taken advantage of their military weakness after the 1917 revolution to wrest territory from pre-war Russia.

After Munich and Hitler's seizure of Czechoslovakia, the Polish question naturally came to the fore. Germany was now in an ideal position to attack Poland and make that nation also a satellite of the Reich, settling the problem of the Polish Corridor at the same time. This objective, however, was blocked by Soviet opposition and the Franco-British guarantee of Poland's integrity. To break up this combination, Hitler employed his familiar tactics of divide and conquer by entering into negotiations with the Kremlin for the re-partition of Poland and the division of Eastern Europe into spheres of influence between Russia and Germany.

British attempts to thwart this move were rendered futile by the refusal of the British government to guarantee the Baltic States from German attack, and the Soviet conviction that British appeasers were determined to sell out Poland to Hitler.[1] Moscow also felt that

---

[1] Dallin, D. J., *Soviet Russia's Foreign Policy, 1939-1942* (New Haven: Yale University Press, 1942), pp. 66-67.

Britain and France were all too willing to save themselves from Hitler at Russia's expense.

The result was the famous non-aggression pact of August, 1939. Accompanying this treaty was an even more fateful secret agreement which divided Central-Eastern Europe between the two powers. The contents of this document purported to be as follows: (1) Hungary, Romania, Yugoslavia, and Greece were to come under German hegemony; Turkey and Bulgaria under Russian control; (2) the U.S.S.R. was to be given a free hand in the Baltic Countries; (3) Poland was to be divided between the U.S.S.R. and Germany; and (4) Bessarabia was to be restored to Russia. The U.S.S.R. agreed not to annex or bolshevize the countries in her sphere of influence or to spread communist propaganda in the German sphere. However, eastern Poland was to be annexed outright and bolshevized. Lithuania was at first claimed by Germany, but was finally included in the Russian sphere at Soviet insistence. Exchanges of population were included in the arrangements.[2]

On September 17, two weeks after the war began, the U.S.S.R. abruptly broke off relations with Poland, asserting that the Polish-Soviet Non-Aggression Pact of 1932 was no longer valid because the Polish State, by reason of its defeat at German hands, had ceased to exist. Alleging the need to protect Russian populations in Poland, Red Army troops crossed the border. Polish resistance was weak and Germany and the U.S.S.R. divided Poland between them five days later. The line of the pre-1914 partition was followed fairly closely, except that Germany obtained more of Central Poland, including the large cities of Warsaw and Lodz. Russia obtained most of Eastern Galicia, which formerly belonged to Austria. Somewhat later the U.S.S.R. conceded an additional strip of Polish territory in Central Poland in exchange for relinquishment of Nazi claims to Lithuania. In all, the U.S.S.R. acquired 76,500 square miles of Polish territory containing 12,800,000 people.

Absorption of the Baltic States by the U.S.S.R.

Cloaking her action with specious excuses, Russia compelled Estonia, Latvia, and Lithuania to enter into pacts of mutual assistance with her under threat of invasion in the fall of 1939. These agreements gave the U.S.S.R. the right to maintain naval bases and flying fields on the territory of these states, and to garrison them with land and air forces of limited size. After the Red Army entered the three Baltic States, its

---

[2] *Ibid.*, pp. 58-63.

relations with their governments were mutually unsatisfactory. The Baltic regimes were hostile to Communism and attempted to carry on foreign relations as if the Red Army was not in their midst. Citizens were forbidden to fraternize with Russian troops and there was some evidence of a tendency to prefer German to Russian intervention. Germany's success in Western Europe forced the U.S.S.R. to take further steps to safeguard her western flank against a Nazi attack before the *Wehrmacht* had completed its task in France.

Berlin was notified in June, 1940, that Stalin had strengthened Red Army forces on the frontiers of the Baltic States, preparatory to taking full possession of them. After some hesitation, the Nazis, unable to act at the moment, withdrew their opposition.

Accusing the Baltic governments of conspiracy and other hostile acts against the U.S.S.R., Stalin then ordered Red Army troops across their borders. "Democratic" governments replaced the existing regimes, Communist organizations were released from legal restraints, the armies of the three powers were re-organized along Red Army lines with political commissars, and finally the parliaments were dissolved and new elections dates were set. Only Communist candidates were permitted to run. The result was that the Communist tickets in all three countries were elected by majorities of over 90 per cent. Shortly afterward the newly elected parliaments met and voted to join the Soviet Union. In August, 1940, the Supreme Council of the U.S.S.R. voted to admit them into the union.[3]

The Seizure of Eastern Karelia from Finland

Finland's fear of Russia led her to incline toward Germany after World War I. Feverishly preparing for the German war she knew was coming, the U.S.S.R. realized that, with Germany's powerful fleet in control of the Baltic, Finland could be used as a base of operations against the great industrial area of Leningrad. After signing the non-aggression pact with Hitler, Stalin turned his attention to this problem. Frontier incidents multiplied and in November, 1939, the Kremlin abrogated Russia's non-aggression pact with Finland, demanding that the Finnish government withdraw its troops 25 kilometers from the Karelian frontier. In spite of Finnish efforts to compromise, the Kremlin, using new frontier incidents as pretexts, ordered the Red Army on November 29 to attack Finland. Instead of declaring war, the Soviets set up a "People's Government of Finland" in Moscow, under Otto Kuusinen and other Finnish expatriates, and

---

[3] *Ibid.,* pp. 80-93, 246-259.

made an agreement with it to cede part of the Karelian Isthmus and naval bases to Russia. This pseudo-government failed to function, but its establishment enabled the Kremlin to evade action by the League, to which Finland had appealed.

Pressure on the U.S.S.R. from both Germany and the Allies to end the war finally resulted in peace negotiations. The peace treaty ceded the entire Karelian Isthmus, including the city of Viipuri (Viborg) to Russia. In March, 1940, the U.S.S.R. organized the Karelian territory into the Karelo-Finnish Union Republic.[4]

Russia Takes Bessarabia and Northern Bukovina

The Russo-German secret agreement had allotted Romania to Germany's sphere of influence, but Romania's complete acceptance of Nazi domination in the spring of 1940 brought home to the Kremlin the extreme danger to the Ukraine of a fully prepared Germany based on Romania. Accordingly, Foreign Commissar Molotov notified Berlin on June 24 of the U.S.S.R.'s intention to annex Bessarabia, formerly a province of Russia, and Northern Bukovina, adjacent to it but to which Russia had previously made no claim. Berlin protested but decided to give in at Russia's insistence.

Two days later, Molotov demanded the return of Bessarabia as a former possession and the cession of Northern Bukovina as ethnically a part of the Soviet Union. These demands were accepted by Romania as the Red Army moved in on June 28. Russia thereby gained nearly 20,000 square miles of territory containing nearly 4,000,000 people, the bulk of whom are Romanians. The U.S.S.R. organized the Moldavian Union Republic out of part of this territory. The remaining sections were incorporated into the Ukrainian Union Republic.[5]

Soviet Policies in Occupied Poland

The Russians based their claim to the occupied territory of Eastern Poland on the contention that it had been obtained from the Soviets by violence under the Treaty of Riga, in 1921, when they were weak and unable to fight back. They also claimed that a majority of the population are ethnically Russians. Both of these claims were denied by the Poles.

As to the Treaty of Riga, the Poles maintain that it was moderate, in that they had refrained from demanding territories to the east and south which they had held in past centuries. They also presented evi-

---

[4] Hanč, J., *op. cit.*, pp. 234-235.
[5] *Ibid.*, pp. 235-237.

dence to indicate that Soviet leaders agreed willingly to the terms of the Treaty. On this point, however, the opinion of detached observers tends to be skeptical.

As to the ethnic character of the population, Polish spokesmen present statistics to show that the largest single group among all the racial elements is Polish, ranging from 32.1 per cent in Northeastern Poland to 47.1 per cent in Southeastern Poland (Eastern Galicia), with an average of nearly 40 per cent for the whole disputed territory. They also point out, with considerable cogency, that the fact of racial origin is not necessarily indicative of the nationalistic predilections of Slavic groups.

The Kremlin, on the other hand, claims that all White Russians, Ukrainians, and Ruthenians in the territory are Russians and therefore, by racial right, should belong to the U.S.S.R. These three groups combined constitute an unquestionable majority of the population. Red leaders also contend that the Poles, especially large Polish land-owners, oppressed the Russian peoples in this section, depriving them of adequate schooling and economic advantages and inflicting cruelties upon them.

Polish spokesmen argue that the Soviets acted illegally and unjustly in incorporating Polish territory into the U.S.S.R. When the Red Army entered the area, they assert, all Polish Army men, police, government officials, war veterans, owners of land and businesses, active members of non-Communist parties, and leaders of trade unions and other types of associations were arrested. Tens of thousands of others were detained on the word of informers.

Instead of holding a plebiscite, the outcome of which might be doubtful, Red leaders decided to sponsor an election to national assemblies of the "Western Ukraine" and "Western White Ruthenia," as they called the two parts into which they had divided Eastern Poland. Election committees were set up consisting of Soviet-appointed officials; the country was divided into election districts on short notice, so that the people were not fully informed of the purpose of the election; candidates were placed on the voting lists by Soviet authority; no opposition candidates were allowed to file, and voting was interfered with by election officials. The results of the elections, which gave the single list of candidates a vote of over 90 per cent in both cases, are therefore declared invalid by the Poles.

The elections were held on October 22, 1939. Soon afterward, the national assemblies met and voted to join the U.S.S.R. and to sovietize the country. In November, 1939, the Supreme Council of the U.S.S.R. voted to grant these requests and changed the federal constitution and those of the Ukrainian and White Ruthenian Union Republics in order to incorporate the two territories into the U.S.S.R. and the two Union Republics. Steps were then taken by Soviet authorities to nationalize all large-scale business and large landed estates and to redistribute the land among the peasants. According to Polish sources, large numbers of Poles were deported from these areas into Russia.

After Germany's attack on Russia on June 22, 1941, a Soviet-Polish treaty was consummated on July 30, under which Russia recognized that the German-Russian partition of Poland had lost its validity. By implication, Russia, through this treaty, gave up her claim to the disputed territory. The Agreement of August 14, 1941, which provided for the raising of a Polish Army on Russian soil, seemed to point to the renewal of amicable relations between the two powers.

As the German menace became less pressing, however, disputes again arose. Finally, as a result of Polish attempts to use the Red Cross to inquire into the circumstances of a grave of thousands of Polish officers uncovered by the Germans at Katyn, near Smolensk, Stalin broke off relations with the Polish government-in-exile, alleging that members of this government were hostile to Russia and that Polish action in the Katyn affair was an insult to the U.S.S.R.

Subsequently, a "Union of Polish Patriots" was organized in Moscow destined by the Kremlin to become the government of Poland in place of the London regime. As Red Army troops pushed the Germans back across Polish frontiers, the U.S.S.R. again laid claim to the previously occupied territory on ethnic grounds and as a part of the Soviet Union.

Stalin offered to establish a frontier at the so-called "Curzon line" and to compensate Poland for its territorial losses in the east by grants of German territory on her western borders (an arrangement later confirmed by the "Big Three" at Yalta). When the Polish government-in-exile requested British-American mediation of this question, the Kremlin refused to have any further dealings with the Polish government-in-exile on the grounds that it was hostile to the U.S.S.R. Though the government in London made changes in its personnel to try to satisfy the Soviets, the latter remained unmollified. Finally, when the Red Army crossed into German-occupied Poland, the "Union of Polish Patriots" followed it and began to organize the country under its auspices. All attempts of the government in London to achieve a *modus vivendi* with the Moscow-sponsored regime have failed.[6] Its future status is very unpromising since the Warsaw regime was reorganized in accordance with the Yalta formula.

The Baltic States

After the Baltic States of Estonia, Latvia, and Lithuania were overrun by the Germans in 1941 and the Russians were driven out, nationalists in those countries hoped again that, when Germany was defeated, the Allies, under the Atlantic Charter, would intercede with Russia and restore their independence. Events, however, appear to have decreed otherwise.

On recovering these territories from the Nazis, Soviet spokesmen stated that, in the Russian view, the Baltic States no longer exist. They added that not only are these states an indissoluble part of the U.S.S.R., but the 1917 treaties which created them were unjust to Russia. The people never desired independence from Russia. Besides, these areas are strategically necessary to the Soviet Union. These views seem to have the open approval of the British government and the tacit backing of the United States. Hence, there seems little likelihood that these nations will be given their freedom. Their aspiration to freedom is shown by the statements of their nationals who are not under Soviet control.[7]

Finland

Pressure by Germany and bitterness of the Finns at seizure of Finnish territory by the U.S.S.R. in the war of 1939-1940 led to Finland's entry into the war on Germany's side. In 1944, the Kremlin, desiring to make terms with the Finns in order to concentrate Russian forces against Germany, offered fairly easy peace terms, but the Finns held on until the Allied invasion of Normandy demonstrated the hopelessness of the German position. They then entered into an armistice with Russia, the terms of which required them to give back the territory granted to Russia by the 1940 treaty, to force evacuation of all German troops from Finland, and to allow the Red Army to enter Finnish ter-

---

[6] *Polish Facts and Figures*, 2, "The Polish-Russian Controversy" (New York: Polish Information Center, 1944); Dean, V. M., "The U.S.S.R. and Post-War Europe," *Foreign Policy Reports*, XIX:11 (August 15, 1943), pp. 128-129; "The Western Ukraine," *Information Bulletin, U.S.S.R. Embassy*, IV:18 (February 12, 1944), pp. 5-6; and "The Byelorussian People," *loc. cit.*, pp. 3-4.

[7] Vakar, N. P., "Russia and the Baltic States," *The Russian Review*, III:1 (Autumn, 1943), pp. 45-54. See also the articles on the Baltic Nations in *The Annals*, CCXXXII (March, 1944), pp. 39-42, 43-46, 49-51.

ritory. Resistance of Nazi troops to Finnish evacuation orders resulted in coöperation between the Finns and the Red Army.

The post-war prospects for Finland present a dismal picture. Permanent loss of Eastern Karelia is less important than the fact that Finland is predestined to become a satellite of the U.S.S.R., with consequent loss of her freedom of action as an independent state and unpredictable results upon her formerly democratic and capitalistic institutions.[8]

Bessarabia and Bukovina

Bessarabia and Bukovina have been completely absorbed and sovietized by the U.S.S.R. As an ally of Germany, Romania has undoubtedly forfeited any claim to them and the prospects are that they will pass into the permanent possession of the Soviet Union.

Post-War Prospects

By 1945, Nazi forces had been driven out of the occupied areas of Central-Eastern Europe and the European phase of the war ended in Germany's unconditional surrender. Red Army forces freed Poland, Yugoslavia, and parts of Czechoslovakia, and drove the Germans out of Finland, Romania, Bulgaria and Hungary. Their Red banners marched into Austria and the inner citadel of Germany itself. Establishment of Soviet garrisons in these regions raised questions of how long the Russians proposed to stay and, when their forces were evacuated, what influence the Kremlin expected to wield upon the small nations released from Nazi bondage. Was it to be their fate to win freedom from the Reich only to be subjected to Russian domination?

The answer to these questions was in process of solution even before the end of the war. Soviet determination to organize a "security sphere" on her western flank was made clear by Russia's adamant insistence upon incorporating the Baltic States, Eastern Karelia, Eastern Poland, Bessarabia, and Bukovina as integral parts of the Soviet Union; by the treaty of friendship and coöperation with Czechoslovakia consummated early in 1944;[9] and by the comparatively easy armistice terms imposed upon Romania and Bulgaria. The expropriation of Bukovina and Bessarabia from Romania was a blow, of course, but in view of the previous seizure of Bessarabia by the Romanians and their

[8] Saari, J., "Finnish Nationalism Justifying Independence," *The Annals*, CCXXXII (March, 1944), pp. 33-38; and "Finland's Dilemma," *The New York Times*, March 5, 1944, review of the week.

[9] "The Soviet-Czechoslovak Treaty," *Information Bulletin, U.S.S.R. Embassy*, IV:2 (January 6, 1944), pp. 7-8.

collaboration with Hitler in the attack on Russia, it was not unexpected. Moreover, the U.S.S.R. restored Transylvania to Romania
in compensation.

Reparations of $300,000,000 in goods were exacted from Romania,
and Romanian military resources were placed at the disposal of the
Soviets. The terms to Bulgaria were even easier. No territory was
taken; payment and restitution for war damage was to be made but
no specific amounts were named; and all Bulgarian troops and civilians
were to be withdrawn immediately from Greek and Yugoslav territories, except those under Soviet command. Hungary was compelled
to yield Transylvania and repay war damages.[10]

Even if these terms extended to Germany's satellites were not exact
criteria of the peace terms, they disclose Russia's settled purpose to
obtain coöperation by mild measures in the establishment of a solid
bloc of friendly states extending from the borders of the U.S.S.R. to the
frontiers of Germany.

However, this does not necessarily mean that the Kremlin intends
to absorb the entire Danubian area into the Soviet Union. The agreements at the Yalta Conference in February, 1945, conceded to Russia
a sphere of influence in Central-Eastern Europe, but the stipulations
concerning Poland indicated that the Anglo-American partners are
unwilling to allow Russia to absorb all of these territories or even to
set up puppet governments. If the Polish example is followed elsewhere, governments will be chosen within each nation by free elections
jointly supervised by representatives of the Soviet, British, and American governments.[11]

This of course would not prevent some of these states from voluntarily entering the Soviet Union after such regimes are established.
The recent change in the Soviet constitution to permit member republics to maintain standing armies, exchange diplomatic and consular
officials, and negotiate diplomatic agreements; and the re-establishment of the Greek Catholic Church in Russia both indicate the
Kremlin's desire for such a consummation.[12]

Meanwhile, the nations now unshackled from the Nazi yoke are
obviously deeply concerned in the decisions of the victorious powers

---

[10] Betts, R. R., "The European Satellite States," *International Affairs*, XXI:1 (January, 1945),
pp. 25-29.

[11] "Decisions of the 'Big Three': Settling Peace and Strategy," *United States News*, XVIII:6
(February 9, 1945), p. 12.

[12] "New Steps Toward Development of the Foreign Relations of the U.S.S.R.," *Information
Bulletin, U.S.S.R. Embassy*, IV:19 (February 15, 1944), pp. 6-7; and Eulau, Heinz H. F., "The
New Soviet Nationalism," *Annals*, CCXXXII (March, 1944), p. 30.

which will determine the fate of Germany. Needless to say, their principal concern is for security, a concern which reaches the proportions of an obsession. They demand that the "Big Three" shall take all necessary steps to make sure that the agonies they suffered at Germany's hands can never again be repeated. The security they seek will, in their judgment, be obtained only through a "hard" peace. This means the detachment from Germany of strategic and industrially valuable territories (such as the Rhineland, Silesia, and East Prussia); the destruction, removal, or control of German heavy industries, thus weakening Germany's war-making potential; a long period of occupation of the Reich by Allied garrisons, during which time all recoverable stolen goods will be restored or paid for by reparations; and the policing of the German nation for generations to come by the Allied powers to prevent rearmament and moves toward another war.

To secure these ends, the freed nations demand a voice in determining the terms of peace. They concur heartily in the leadership of the "Big Three" and in their avowed intentions to punish all war criminals, but they refuse to distinguish between the Nazis and the German people. The latter, they feel, should also be made to suffer for their support of the criminal acts of the Nazi leaders.

As for the proposal to partition Germany, opinion in the recently occupied areas considers it futile. But these countries do favor regional decentralization, especially if a considerable proportion of the German people can be made to agree. Along with political decentralization, there is a tendency to favor the splitting up of large landed estates and redistribution of the lands to the peasantry. Large-scale business should be broken up and scattered among the various regions of the Reich or delivered to Germany's neighbors. If this were done, the nations previously destined by Berlin to become agricultural plantations to feed the industrialized Reich would turn the tables completely and make of Germany an agrarian economy supplying raw materials for the highly industrialized countries surrounding her. Such a course, however, is probably favored by Russia but not by the Western Allies.[13]

The romantic projects of certain groups in Britain and the United States to re-educate the German people, to allow them to organize democratic institutions, and to remove military controls at the same time that they are welcomed into the family of peace-loving and

---

[13] Dallin, D. J., "Soviet Russia and the Peace with Germany," *International Postwar Problems*, II:1 (January, 1945), p. 73.

democratic nations, thereby persuading the Germans to forget any warlike plans they might have for the future, are viewed very skeptically by the victims of German oppression. They are firmly convinced that any such plans would only lull the Allies into relaxing their vigilance again and enable German leaders to rearm once more behind a smoke-screen of democracy and peace.

They believe that Germany will certainly seek revenge. Therefore she must be permanently deprived of the means of wreaking it upon the states of Central-Eastern Europe. These attitudes on the part of the victimized states will undoubtedly influence the tone of the peace and the post-war treatment of Germany by the victorious powers.[14]

Bibliography

(for Chapters XXVIII and XXIX)

Adamic, L., *My Native Land* (New York: Harper, 1943). Shows vividly the effects of Germany's bloody treatment of the people of Yugoslavia.

Clissold, J., *The Slovenes Want to Live* (New York: Yugoslav Information Center, 1942). Informative and fairly comprehensive.

Einzig, P., *Europe in Chains* (New York: Penguin Books, 1941). Filled with concentrated information.

Dallin, D. J., *Soviet Russia's Foreign Policy, 1939-1942* (New Haven: Yale University Press, 1942). Relates in detail the story of Russia's imperial expansion from 1939-1942.

Dean, Vera M., "The U.S.S.R. and Post-War Europe," *Foreign Policy Reports,* XIX:11 (August 15, 1943), pp. 122-139. An excellent brief survey of Russia's relations with her neighbors in recent years.

Europe Under Hitler, In Prospect and Practice (London: Oxford University Press, 1941). Valuable as a check against Einzig's booklet.

Four Fighting Years (London: Hutchinson, 1943). Recapitulates Nazi activities in Czechoslovakia during the period of occupation. Edited by the Czechoslovak Ministry of Foreign Affairs.

Furlan, Boris, *Fighting Yugoslavia* (New York: Yugoslav Information Center, 1943). Tells of Nazi operations in Yugoslavia, especially in Slovenia.

Godden, G. M., *Murder of a Nation* (London: Burns Oates, 1943). Describes in detail the Nazi attempt to destroy Polish culture.

Hanč, J., *Tornado Across Eastern Europe* (New York: Greystone, 1942). Traces the growth of the German "Greater Reich" in Central-Eastern Europe.

Hediger, E. S., "Nazi Exploitation of Occupied Europe," *Foreign Policy Reports,* XVIII (June 1, 1942), pp. 66-79. An excellent brief analysis of Germany's gains in occupied Europe. See also his "Nazi Economic Imperialism," *loc. cit.* (August 15, 1942), pp. 139-146.

---

[14] For a more detailed statement of the demands of Central-Eastern states for a "hard" peace with Germany, see W. N. Hadsell, "What Kind of Peace with Germany?" *Foreign Policy Reports,* XX:17 (November 15, 1944), pp. 210-219.

Kraus, Réné, *Europe in Revolt* (New York: Macmillan, 1942). Depicts German methods of exploitation and how they were resisted.

Munk, Frank, *The Legacy of Nazism* (New York: Macmillan, 1943). Ably relates Nazi economic policies in the occupied regions and their results.

Poland, The Black Book of (New York: Putnam, 1942). Documents and exhaustively examines the facts of German activities in Poland under the occupation.

Polish Facts and Figures, "Polish-Russian Controversy," 2 (New York: Polish Information Center, 1944). Ably and briefly defends the Polish side of the conflict.

Rabinavicious, H., "The Fate of the Baltic Nations," *Russian Review,* III:1 (Autumn, 1943), pp. 34-44. Reviews events leading to seizure of the Baltic States and argues for restoration of their independence.

Tirana, R., *The Spoils of Europe* (New York: Norton, 1941). Fairly detailed and clearly written.

Vakar, N. P., "Russia and the Baltic States," *Russian Review,* III:1 (Autumn, 1943), pp. 45-54. Argues in favor of retention of the Baltic States by the U.S.S.R.

Xydis, S. G., *The Economy and Finances of Greece Under Axis Occupation* (Pittsburgh: Hermes Printing Co., 1943). An aid to comprehension of Nazi economic policies in occupied Greece.

CHAPTER XXX

GOVERNMENTS-IN-EXILE AND POSTWAR PLANS FOR CENTRAL-EASTERN EUROPE*

Governments-in-Exile

ON SEPTEMBER 1, 1939, German tanks rolled across the frontier into the heart of Poland. Thus began a new chapter in the history of the traditional, almost mystical, German *Drang nach Osten*.

Despite unequal forces and armaments, the Poles fought back. Soon it was realized that Poland had lost the first round of the war. This was made especially clear when Soviet troops, acting in accord with Germany, invaded Poland from the east. But still Warsaw resisted the Nazis, and still, despite the fact that the commander-in-chief, Rydz-Smigly, and many high ranking officers had left Poland, the army and the people fought on.

After military resistance had collapsed, an underground organization was established to continue the fight in Poland. A large Polish army under General Sikorski was recruited in France from emigrés and other Polish citizens abroad. After the fall of France, the Polish army was the fourth largest in the United Nations camp. The fight was thus continued under the Polish flag in Poland and abroad.

Although they lost control of their territory, the Poles remained faithful to their French and British allies. Thus, the Polish government-in-exile was established to continue the struggle of a nation which did not lose its sovereignty.

After the war started, and the first country which resisted was temporarily occupied by Germany, a sharp line was drawn between the various states of Central-Eastern Europe according to their attitude toward Germany and the Nazis.

These attitudes were shaped by different factors. Certainly, one important factor was whether the influential political parties and the tendencies of the people of a given country were democratic or fascist,

---

* This chapter was written in August, 1944.

but traditional historic elements also played an important role. The example of the Poles is not an exception. The Yugoslavs and the Greeks followed the same pattern. Yugoslavs who fought against five hundred years of Turkish domination and who never became reconciled to Habsburg rule followed the tradition of their forefathers. They went to the mountains with Mikhailovich, and later with Tito, and continued to fight their enemies in a way which recalls the most glorious days of the Serb struggle against the Turks.

The Greeks also upheld their tradition of fighting the conqueror, with heroism equal to that which was an inspiration to Lord Byron more than a hundred years ago.

The Poles were experienced in underground activities before the underground was organized in 1939, because they followed an age-old tradition with which every literate Pole was familiar. They did what their forefathers would have done, repeating the examples of 1831, 1863, 1905, 1917, and a couple of other tragic and unsuccessful revolutions.

The Czechoslovaks also followed an old pattern of resistance and sabotage, as they did during the First World War. In the Tatra and the Carpathian Mountains, the Czechoslovak resistance movement resorted to guerrilla warfare. In the late summer of 1944, the Slovak army also rebelled against Germany and the Tiso puppet government.

Thus, history has played an important role when nations have had to decide which way to choose at crossroads of future history. It has always played and is still playing a much more important part in Central-Eastern Europe than is generally realized. An eastern European man of politics thinks largely in historical terms, which is most essential for intelligent people of this region. At decisive moments they look to the past for guidance and moral strength. They recall traitors as well as heroes. Collaborationists in Serbia during the war were compared with those who collaborated with the Turkish Sultan in the fourteenth century after Serbia was subjugated. The name of "Targowica," a place where a group of Polish nobles and aristocrats had formed a "Union" at the end of the eighteenth century to collaborate with the Tsarist Russia of Catherine the Great, reappeared in Polish emigré and underground papers as a symbol of treason and decadence. The word did not require an explanation, for every Pole knew what it meant.

World War II imposed a basic choice on all the nations of Central-Eastern Europe. Either they could help Adolf Hitler in his campaign of conquest, or they could fight for freedom and democracy against fascism and nazism with Great Britain and France, and later with all the United Nations.

Czechoslovakia, Greece, Yugoslavia, and Poland chose to fight with the Allies, forming governments-in-exile which represented their peoples on foreign soil, since their own was occupied by the enemy. Bulgaria, Hungary, and Romania followed Germany and appeased the brutal political pattern of Nazism.

Hungary joined the Axis camp without much of a struggle. Reactionary tendencies have always been strong in the ruling group; the fascist movement was growing and the aristocracy was afraid of losing its riches. In internal affairs, Horthy, although a reactionary, attempted to be more decent than Hitler until the government of Hungary was taken over by extreme fascists in 1944.

Romania under the boy-king, Michael, and Premier Ion Antonescu, also became a German satellite. Romania had a fascist movement of nazi type represented by the Iron Guard, which had great influence on the nation's ruling circles.

Bulgaria became the third satellite of Germany. Tsar Boris III was himself a representative of a German dynasty, and the government of Prime Minister Filoff was trying to expand Bulgarian territory. The Hungarians in Yugoslavia, the Romanians in Russia, and the Bulgarians in Greece were all excellent disciples of Hitler's incomparable cruelty.

In the United Nations camp, the people remained mostly sympathetic with the goals of their governments-in-exile. But new quisling regimes were set up on their soil by Germany.

Quislings, in fact, were established in all conquered European countries except Poland, where the Germans were unable to impose a fascist puppet regime. Despite the cruelest kind of persecution, no candidate for the job of Polish quisling could be found.

We are not going to discuss the satellite states in this chapter, nor are we going to devote much space to the quisling regimes. The reader will find information on these problems in earlier chapters which deal with single countries. Let us discuss here only governments-in-exile.[1] Their fate will figure largely in the post-war settlements.

---

[1] Many articles on governments-in-exile have been written in daily papers and periodicals. For more detailed information on governments-in-exile, see Daniel Bell and Leon Dennen, "The System of Governments in Exile," *The Annals* of the American Academy of Political and Social Science, CCXXXVII (March, 1944), pp. 134-147; Andre Visson, *The Coming Struggle for Peace* (New York: The Viking Press, 1944).

Legal problems are discussed in F. F. Oppenheim, "Governments and Authorities in Exile,"

Czechoslovakia

After Austria was occupied, Czechoslovakia became the next victim of German imperialism and European indifference. This most democratic country of Central-Eastern Europe was partitioned at Munich in 1938. Shortly after the Munich conference, Eduard Beneš resigned as President. Emil Hácha became President of the Republic and the Agrarian Party assumed leadership in the government. President Beneš later left Europe for the United States, where he occupied the chair of philosophy and sociology at the University of Chicago.

The model republic of Central-Eastern Europe became a German colony with Hácha, a quisling, as the head of the puppet regime. Bohemia was transformed into a "protectorate" and Slovakia into a puppet state, entirely controlled by German overlords.

In 1939, President Beneš started a movement in the United States for the liberation of Czechoslovakia. After the outbreak of the Second World War, a national committee was formed, which he headed. At first the committee met in Paris. After the military collapse of France, it moved to London. In 1940, a Czechoslovak government was formed out of this committee, which was recognized by the British Government.

President Beneš took over the Presidency of State, and Monsignor Šrámek was appointed Prime Minister. The most popular among the members of the government was Jan Masaryk, son of the late great President of Czechoslovakia, who became Minister of Foreign Affairs and Vice-Prime Minister.

In international politics, there is such a thing as political credit, a very precious thing for a country to have. A lawful, democratic, and well-administered country has always received political credit in Western Europe and the United States. Denmark, Sweden, and Norway could be mentioned among the countries which enjoyed a great deal of such credit. Thanks to its excellent democratic record, Czechoslovakia had the highest political credit of all the Central-Eastern European countries for over 20 years. Because of this fact, the Czechoslovak government-in-exile soon achieved a respected and important political standing among the United Nations.

American Journal of International Law, XXX (October, 1942); also *Czechoslovak Yearbook of International Law* (London: Czechoslovak Section of the International Law Association, 1942). A penetrating analysis of the problem was given by Raimund von Hoffmannsthal in his *European Resistance* (New York: 1942). It is unfortunately a mimeographed and not a printed memorandum issued by the Postwar Department of *Time, Life,* and *Fortune* magazines for their members.

The former Prime Minister and leader of the Agrarian Party in exile, the late Milan Hodža, and Štepan Osuský, an able diplomat who was former Czechoslovak envoy to France, opposed the Beneš government.

Greece

Greece did not possess too much political credit because of General Metaxas, dictator of Greece and foe of the greatest Greek statesman of this century, the late Venizelos. The heroic struggle of the Greek people and the guerrillas within the country eventually won for Greece the prestige she deserves. But two issues became a real obstacle: the controversy over King George II and the internal feuds of the guerrillas.

In 1935, King George II came back to Greece after twelve years of exile. In 1936, General Metaxas' dictatorial regime was established in Greece with the support of King George, who gave his signature to the dissolution of the parliament and the suspension of the constitution.

Greece did not yield to the Axis in 1941. The Greek people gallantly fought the fascist and nazi invasion of their fatherland. After Greece was occupied, King George went with his government to London, and after several changes had been made in his government, he appointed Emmanuel Tsouderos (a Venizelist) as Prime Minister. Later on, the son of Eleutherios Venizelos, Sophocles, took his place.

But the royal issue has not been solved. In fact, it has become more acute since the government returned to Greece. King George has been repudiated by the liberal and democratic Greeks who have constantly reminded the world of his collaboration with Metaxas and who resent British interference on the king's behalf.

The second issue was the feud between the EAM (the Liberation Front) and its partisan group (the ELAS) and the guerrillas of Colonel Napoleon Zervas, the EDES. The former was supported also by the Communists and had the sympathy of the Soviet Union.

These two controversies became a grave problem to the Greek government-in-exile and were still unsolved, after liberation, in the summer of 1945. But neither the royal issue nor the internal feuds should overshadow the heroic resistance of the Greek people and their strong stand against fascist and nazi aggression.

Yugoslavia

After the assassination of King Alexander of Yugoslavia in 1934 in Marseille, Prince Paul took over the regency for the boy-king, Peter

II. Prince Paul, supported by the Yugoslav reactionaries finally sided with Nazi Germany. In March, 1941, he sent his Prime Minister and his Foreign Minister to Vienna to join the Axis, of which Bulgaria, Romania, and Hungary had become satellites. Two days later a group of Yugoslav officers and democrats effected a *coup d'état* and seized power in Belgrade. They acclaimed the youthful Peter as king, dismissed Paul, and arrested his ministers. Shortly thereafter, German tanks moved across the borders of Yugoslavia. In spite of heroic resistance, the fight was soon lost. The democratic Yugoslav Government went into exile and moved to London. Part of it established its headquarters in New York City.

The Yugoslav Government-in-exile was soon torn by political controversies. As early as 1941, some of the democratic Yugoslav ministers urged a fundamental change of policy and closer Croat-Slovene coöperation with the Serbs. But the cruelties of the Ustashis in Croatia against defenseless Serbian peasants and priests had a marked influence on the government-in-exile. Serbian nationalists abroad started political activity directed against all Croats. The result was a cooling off in the relationship between the Croats and Serbs in the government itself. The government was changed, but no essential improvement of Serbo-Croat relations was achieved.

The situation became serious because of the fratricidal struggle between Mikhailovich, War Minister in the government-in-exile, and Tito, who accused the guerrilla hero of the Second World War of coöperating with the Germans and Italians. On the other hand, the great successes and the heroic fight of Tito and his Partisans were evidence of the growing resistance movement among the Croats and Slovenes, who formed the bulk of the Partisans.

This internal dispute caused a further split among Yugoslav emigrés. Some of them defended Mikhailovich, others sided with Tito.

A compromise was finally achieved in 1944. As noted in Chapter XXIII, the Ban of Croatia, Ivan Subasich, formed a compromise government, dismissed Mikhailovich as War Minister, and went by plane to see Tito in order to make the necessary political arrangements. The Subasich Government has in turn been accused by certain groups of Serbs of having no support in Serbia proper.

Before the war, Yugoslavia did not receive too much sympathy from abroad because of its autocratic king and internal feuds. The *coup d'état* of 1941, the war against the Axis, and the new democratic leadership were sufficient to redeem this gallant country in world opinion. Unfortunately for the whole of Central-Eastern Europe, traditional feuds among Yugoslav nationalities were revived to the detriment of all concerned.

Poland

After the military collapse of Poland, the democratic parties, which for years had opposed the ruling groups, assumed leadership. The former opposition parties took the lead in the underground, and those of their representatives who managed to escape formed a democratic coalition government. In September, 1939, the President of the Polish Republic, Ignacy Moscicki, at that time interned in Romania, acted in accordance with the Constitution to appoint his successor. His first proposition was not acceptable to the parties, but they finally agreed upon President Wladyslaw Raczkiewicz. He in turn appointed General Wladyslaw Sikorski, a moderate democrat who was one of the irreconcilable opponents of the Pilsudski regime, as Prime Minister.

The government was formed of representatives of the four major parties: the Polish Socialists (PPS), the Polish Peasant Party, the Christian-Democratic Party, and the National Party. The first two parties represent a decisive majority of peasants and workers. The government-in-exile was first established in Paris, then in Angers, and later, after the fall of France, it moved to London. After Sikorski's tragic death in a plane crash at Gibraltar (1943), Stanislaw Mikolajczyk, a representative of the Polish Peasant Party became Prime Minister, and Jan Kwapinski, a Polish Socialist, became his deputy. In 1944, Tomasz Arciszewski, a Polish Socialist underground leader, was taken out of Poland by the underground and became president-designate in place of General Sosnowski. It is beyond the scope of this chapter to discuss all the changes within the Polish government-in-exile. It is more important to analyze the forces which were and are behind that government.

First of all, the government has under its command a large army which has been fighting on many fronts, an air force which played an important role during the "Blitz," and a small but gallant navy and merchant marine. The government in London kept in close touch with the Polish underground. Contact was maintained by radio and by couriers who travelled to Poland and back. In Poland itself, a whole underground state was organized, controlled by a political council composed of the representatives of the four major political parties. The Polish Government within Poland was represented by a Deputy Prime Minister, the delegate of the London regime. The commander-in-chief of the underground forces coöperated closely with the Polish government-in-exile and with the Polish general staff in London. Therefore the Polish government-in-exile did represent the great majority of the resistance movement. Only insignificant groups were not linked up with it.

Some elements of the government-in-exile, notably including former Premier Mikolajczyk, joined forces with the regime originally established in Moscow to form a new government in Warsaw in June of 1945. At Russia's insistence, the Arciszewski cabinet in London was not represented in it. It remains to be seen what role the London group will play in the future.

Free Movements

Besides the governments-in-exile, emigré liberals from the pro-Axis countries established or tried to establish "Free Movements," a representation of democratic elements sympathetic to the United Nations. Romania, Hungary, and Austria organized Free Committees in London and New York City, and some attempts were made to establish a Bulgarian Committee.

Plans for Federation in Central-Eastern Europe[2]

Long-range plans for Central-Eastern Europe were outlined at the beginning of this war when the military situation was still grave and peace seemed very far away. International politics was visionary and hopeful at that time. A federation of Central-Eastern Europe was then proposed, although today it is far from realization. This project still forms a most interesting nucleus of post-war ideas for Central-Eastern Europe and may yet have some influence on future developments.

The idea of federation is not new. It was advanced long ago in the history of Central-Eastern Europe, as far back as the fifteenth and sixteenth centuries. The modern concept of close collaboration originated as early as 1848. The famous Czechoslovak statesman and historian František Palacký, the leader of the Hungarian revolution Louis Kossuth, and his compatriot Wladislaw Teleky envisioned the necessity for such coöperation. This realization came to Kossuth after he lost the fight against the Habsburgs.

Within the Austro-Hungarian Empire, too, there were strong efforts

---

[2] This part of the chapter is a somewhat shortened contribution already published in *The Annals*: Feliks Gross, "Peace Planning for Central and Eastern Europe," *The Annals* of the American Academy of Political and Social Science, CCXXXII (March, 1944), pp. 169-176. See also Feliks Gross, *Crossroads of Two Continents* (New York: Columbia University Press, 1945).

made to transform the monarchy into a democratic federation. The
Austrian Socialists in particular, such as Karl Renner (who wrote
under the pseudonym of Springer) and Otto Bauer, tried to promote
as much national autonomy as possible within the framework of the
monarchy. In 1906, Aurel Popovici attempted to present a plan for
a transformation of the Austrian monarchy into a federal body. All
of these plans within the monarchy pointed to two facts: first, that the
nationalities under the Habsburg yoke were struggling for freedom;
second, that most of the statesmen, even those of the smaller nations
within the monarchy, realized that some kind of close coöperation
among them was necessary to surmount economic and political difficulties.

The idea of close coöperation received new impetus from the great
Czechoslovak statesman and thinker, Thomas G. Masaryk. Masaryk
fought hard for the liberation of the small nations under Austro-
Hungarian rule, but he realized that the liberation must be followed
by a system of close collaboration among all the small nations in the
area. He presented these thoughts in his *New Europe,* written during
World War I, and in the Philadelphia Manifesto of 1918 which he
signed. After the Treaty of Versailles, the nations which were under
the Habsburg monarchy were freed, but strong regional coöperation
was not achieved. The nearest approach to it was the Little Entente,
a loose system that included Czechoslovakia, Romania, and Yugoslavia.

The Little Entente was directed primarily against Hungarian revisionist tendencies but it also had deep economic significance. Experience has shown that economic coöperation in this agricultural
basin is necessary for all the countries of the Danubian region, and
such coöperation was really established in the nineteen-thirties. But
when Germany exerted heavy pressure, neither the Little Entente nor
the Polish-Romanian Alliance proved strong enough to produce even
the most elementary solidarity of the countries menaced. Czechoslovakia was left all alone. Even later, the nations in that region and
in the Balkans did not comprehend the necessity for uniting to fight
the common enemy—Nazi Germany. The ties between them proved
very weak.

After 1939, many thoughtful people felt that the system of small
and unrelated national states in Central-Eastern Europe was one of
the reasons why it was so easy for the Germans to subjugate this part
of Europe. In the underground and in exile, in Paris, London, and
New York, statesmen, journalists, soldiers, and scientists widely dis-

cussed the causes of defeat and the way toward a solution of the situation. In the gloomy days of the superiority of the German war machine, many representatives of these nations came to understand how small were their differences and how petty their quarrels compared to the fate of the occupied territories. The necessity for close coöperation was more and more appreciated and political thinking became more lucid.

Until, let us say, 1940, there were plans and programs for some kind of international coöperation, vaguely expressed in 1848, limited to the concept of transformation of the Austro-Hungarian monarchy before 1914, clear as a necessity for close regional collaboration in Masaryk's writings. After 1940, the plans became more definite in their federal concept of international coöperation in this area.

The first sign of this was the Polish-Czechoslovak declaration issued on November 11, 1940, whereby both governments decided that Poland and Czechoslovakia should form a confederation after the war. The details were discussed in Paris for a long time; then in London; and finally, on January 23, 1942, a Polish-Czechoslovak agreement was signed confirming the formation of a confederation.

Simultaneously, the exiled governments of Greece and Yugoslavia worked on a Balkan union, reaching an agreement in London on January 15, 1942. Some common institutions were even outlined. This idea was cordially greeted by the confederated Poles and Czechoslovaks.

Another formal step in this direction was made on November 5, 1941, at the International Labor Conference in New York. The delegations from Czechoslovakia, Greece, Yugoslavia, and Poland issued a common declaration about Central-Eastern European regional solidarity. Consequently, in January, 1942, the Central-Eastern European Planning Board, composed of representatives of these four states, was formed as a planning and research agency in New York.

The formal treaties had plenty of background. Articles and booklets were written about this idea by political emigrés in the political centers of the United Nations. Speeches were delivered and the problems involved were studied and discussed.

In some countries the underground took an active part. In the Polish underground press, the idea of a confederated Central-Eastern Europe found wide support. All shades of political opinion from the radical labor movement to the moderates were responsive. In an article published by an underground Polish radical paper of January 21, 1942, commenting on the New York declaration of November 5,

1941, we read: "The federated Europe must be composed of federated regions. The Central and Eastern European confederation is regarded as a necessary step."

Many other underground editorials were written in the same strain, stressing security and economic problems as those which must be committed to a federation. On November 19, 1942, at the Polish National Council (which is a kind of Parliament-in-exile) representatives of the Polish Labor Party and the Polish Peasant Party jointly presented a project on post-war Poland. This entire project was prepared in the Polish underground by delegates of both of these groups and transmitted to London through underground channels. In this plan, the basic premise of Poland's foreign policy is the formation of a federation of the Central and Eastern European states as a part of a European Commonwealth.

What should be the extent of the proposed federation? There are many more or less conflicting plans. Broadly speaking three possibilities exist. The first is the formation of a large federation composed of Greece, Albania, Yugoslavia, Bulgaria, Romania, Hungary, Austria, Czechoslovakia, and Poland. The second introduces two federal groups—the southern one composed of the Balkan States and the northern composed of the rest. The third proposition envisages a northern group of Czechoslovakia and Poland; a middle-Danubian group of Austria, Hungary, and Romania; and a southern Balkan group.

The idea of federation gained in importance when the democratic leaders of Czechoslovakia and Poland, Eduard Beneš and Wladyslaw Sikorski, identified themselves with the plans. Beneš, in his original project, envisaged the eventual development of a natural bridge between the northern (Czechoslovak-Polish) and southern (Balkan) confederations, and believed that this would be a logical step toward the consolidation of the whole of Europe.

Sikorski, in his plan, advocated one large federal grouping. But many authorities felt and still feel that several federal groups in this area would work out better in practice.

The constitutional problem is also important. Certainly the difficult nationality problems of this region preclude a classic federal system like that of the United States, for the historical development of the latter is in no way comparable. A more feasible formula would be to adopt salient provisions from the United States, the Swiss confederation, and the British Commonwealth of Nations, and apply them to local situations. The Polish underground, in a paper which discussed the "Program for a People's Poland," pleaded for a close union on the pattern of the United States.

An interesting project is presented in the London Danubian Club plan. It contemplates the creation of a political system based on two chambers, a government of the union, and a presidency. The first chamber of the union, or, as the authors call it, the "Council of the Union," should consist of deputies elected on the basis of one deputy for a given number of citizens throughout the union. The second chamber, described as a "Council of the States," would contain an equal number of representatives from each member state, appointed by the government of such a state. In this way, a common platform could be developed in the first chamber for the main political groups— for instance, for the peasant or labor parties of the whole region. The interests of the states would be protected in the second chamber. The federal government should deal with foreign affairs, foreign trade and customs unions, finance and taxation, money and credit, exchange and banking, transport, policies of economic development, collective security, and other functions. According to this plan, the presidency should be a rotating office.

Somewhat different plans were presented earlier by the Polish diplomat Anatol Muhlstein, and later on still another plan was offered by the former Czechoslovak Prime Minister and Agrarian leader, Milan Hodža. Both plans are based largely on Austro-Hungarian experience. Hodža especially had long experience within the Hungarian Parliament, and drew some conclusions from it. Muhlstein proposed that the federation should possess legislative, executive, and judicial organs necessary for the exercise of its functions. Its legislative body, called by him the "federal senate," should be composed of delegates of the federated states. The delegates (senators) should be elected by the national parliaments of the respective states. This is reminiscent, in some respects, of the parliamentary delegations in the Austro-Hungarian monarchy.

Hodža brings forth some interesting ideas in his project. Among others, he proposes a federal Ministry of Coöperation. This would be a special body designed to encourage coöperation among the member states and to strengthen mutual friendship and understanding.

Economic Reconstruction

Economic reconstruction on a regional basis in this area has attracted even more attention. There are also many plans drawn for the region as a whole, in industry and in agriculture.

The main issues are the agricultural problem and the surplus population. Agriculture is still backward in most of the area, and it is a region of peasant economy. Land reform is essential in some countries. Land reform here means the breaking up of large estates and the consolidation of small holdings. As far as Poland is concerned, all political parties in the underground, perhaps with minor exceptions, acknowledge the necessity for a radical land reform which would strengthen and extend the reforms of the period between the wars. The labor movement, in particular, proposes "Agrarian reform" in its program for a People's Poland. Great landed estates will be expropriated and turned into land reserves for breaking up. These expropriated estates will be placed under the supervision of communal and district committees for land reform."[3]

But land reform will not solve all problems. It must be followed by adequate economic development. There are plans to make agriculture in certain areas more efficient. Peasant coöperatives, already successful in this region, are regarded in all plans as a basic system to promote the mechanization of agriculture and the increase of milk and food production. Finally, proper progress in agriculture requires cheap electricity. Plans are being made by eastern European experts in London for the electrification of the whole area of Central-Eastern Europe on a regional basis, and the TVA is cited as an example to be copied eventually.

An economic and political program for the peasantry was formulated by the peasant leaders of the Central and Eastern European countries in London, 1942. It is one of the most important documents on this subject. This program in general contemplates the above-mentioned lines of agricultural reform and is based on the regional concept of a peasant Central-Eastern Europe. It stresses peasant ownership, agricultural coöperation, agricultural credit and insurance, stability of prices, agricultural improvements, agricultural education, rural welfare, and industrialization.

Industrialization is needed in this area to raise standards of living and to give employment to a large jobless population. Before the war, there were many people in the villages who made a subnormal living. They were not needed for agricultural production, but could not find employment elsewhere. According to a Polish economist, J. Poniatowski, at least one-third of the rural population of Poland could be withdrawn from agriculture without reducing production. Egoroff for Bulgaria and Bicanic for the Croatian part of Yugoslavia have come to

---

[3] *Program for People's Poland* (New York: Polish Labor Group, 1943).

the conclusion that, on the average, one-third of the agricultural population represents a surplus which is, in fact, a burden for the stage of development already attained by agriculture and prevents its further advance.[4]

Most of the experts agree that emigration alone cannot solve the difficult population problem in this area. They mostly agree also that even a drastic land reform and the improvement of agricultural output will not be able to absorb all of the unemployed. Industrialization is thus regarded as a helpful solution, and some groups in London and New York are working out plans to that end.

Educational and Social Reconstruction

Plans for post-war reconstruction in Central-Eastern Europe also embrace the educational and social fields. Culture and education have been cruelly destroyed, and their reconstruction is a big problem. The Central and Eastern European Planning Board in particular has been active in this respect. A general plan of educational reconstruction for the area is envisioned by Vojta Beneš, an outstanding Czechoslovak expert on education. Plans for student and professor exchanges and mutual help in educational reconstruction were widely discussed in a special institute at New York University in April, 1943, organized by the Central and Eastern European Planning Board, the United States Committee on Educational Reconstruction, and New York University.

Furthermore, it is accepted as a basic principle that this federation can be organized only as a democratic and progressive union. An equalization of social standards is therefore needed, as Jan Kozák rightly points out.[5] A peasant country in eastern Europe could hardly unite with one ruled by big landowners. Therefore the introduction of socially progressive democratic patterns is needed in the whole area to form a true democratic federation.

Further development in this direction would probably also require some adequate plans concerning the regional organization of social security systems and a proper adjustment of living standards.

Role of the Great Powers

As can be seen from this short survey, planning activities for Central-Eastern Europe are quite prolific and often imbued with enthusiasm

[4] Bicanic, Rudolph, "Agricultural Overpopulation," *Yugoslav Postwar Reconstruction Papers*, No. 3, Vol. 1 (New York: Office of Reconstruction and Economic Affairs, Government of Yugoslavia, 1942).

[5] Kozák, Jan, "America and the Postwar World, Our Relations with the Countries of Central and Eastern Europe," *Oberlin Alumni Magazine* (December, 1942).

and good will.   But their materialization does not depend only on the nations involved.   It depends rather on political realities determined by foreign policies, above all by the three big powers, the United States, Great Britain, and the Soviet Union.

A favorable approach to a regional federal project in Europe was clearly expressed by Winston Churchill in his speech of March 21, 1943, in which he gave his support to the idea that the small nations should form groupings of states or a confederation.   The Soviet Union, which would be the nearest neighbor of such a confederation, is a very important factor.   There is no official Soviet statement on this subject, but an opinion was expressed in an article which appeared in the Moscow periodical, *War and the Working Class,* whose author, Mr. Malinin, took an unfriendly attitude toward any federal idea in eastern Europe.

A democratic and progressive federation of Central-Eastern Europe could not be hostile towards the Soviet Union.   It could not possibly exist if it were.   Moreover, it could form an important bridge between the Soviet and western Europe by developing an attitude of friendship and collaboration with both.

From Idealism to Realism

Besides the federal trend in post-war planning, there has also been a tendency towards realism, a tendency which has been growing stronger since the second half of 1943.

Realism here means that post-war plans have to be adjusted to the interests of the great powers, even if those interests are somewhat detrimental to the small states.   In a realistic approach, they have to find the best solution for themselves within the framework of an order which is principally designed for the benefit of the strong.

Soviet Russia is necessarily a dominant factor in all calculations about the future of Central-Eastern Europe.   For example, the mere fact that there were bad relations between the Soviet Union and Poland, and, on the other hand, friendly relations between the Soviet Union and Czechoslovakia, was bound to have an influence on the Polish-Czecho-slovak confederation.

Plainly the Soviet Union is able to exert a decisive influence in Central-Eastern Europe.   Since the U.S.S.R., at least for the present, is opposed to federation plans, it is evident that there is no real possibility for the creation of a federation unless and until Moscow's attitude changes.

The Soviet plan for Central and Eastern Europe was revealed by the

Moscow agreement between Czechoslovakia and the Soviet Union in December, 1943. As President Beneš explained, the agreement[6] is to lay the foundation for a permanent close alliance between the Soviet Union and Czechoslovakia, eventually to include Poland. A Soviet, Czechoslovak, and Polish union is envisaged in this scheme as a permanent defense against the German *Drang nach Osten*.

In his message to the State Council in 1944, President Beneš stressed the importance of Polish-Czechoslovak collaboration, recalling the mutual declaration of confederation of November 11, 1940. This also means that a Czechoslovak-Polish confederation within the Soviet-Polish-Czechoslovak system is still a feasible plan. This attitude has been confirmed by President Beneš in his recent article which appeared in *Foreign Affairs* (Vol. XXIII No. 1, pp. 26-37).

The more idealistic plans for a European federation are thus replaced by the realistic concept of spheres of influence which implies the division of our globe into orbits among the Great Powers.

There are some variations of this concept. Walter Lippmann predicts, rather than projects, three regional orbits: the Atlantic Community, the Russian orbit, and the Chinese orbit.[7] The United States and Great Britain would have dominant influence within the Atlantic Community; Eastern Europe would be a part of the Russian orbit; and the Far East would belong to the Chinese sphere.

The whole idea of spheres of influence is the outcome of a realistic approach to the distribution of political power in a global sense. The United Nations organization has to take account of this reality. The concept of spheres of influence substitutes some kind of domination of the stronger over the weaker for the coöperation of equality. This domination can vary in degree, and the degree will depend chiefly on the democratic tradition of the dominant factor. The dangers of spheres of influence can only be avoided by the establishment of an international world order based on the coöperation of all nations.

Central-Eastern Europe has become, in fact, a sphere of influence of the Soviet Union, and post-war plans for this area will be made according to this reality.

At first, the Soviet Union will use its influence in this orbit to satisfy its territorial demands. This means that it will incorporate into its territory Lithuania, Latvia, Estonia, and the eastern provinces of Poland and Bessarabia.

---

[6] Beneš, Eduard, *Czechoslovak Policy for Victory and Peace* (London: Czechoslovak Ministry of Foreign Affairs, 1944), p. 20 ff.

[7] Lippmann. Walter, *U. S. War Aims* (Boston: Little, Brown and Company, 1944), pp. 187 ff.

In turn, the Soviet Union will support Polish claims to the eastern provinces of Germany and to a part of East Prussia (a part will probably be absorbed by the Soviet Union); Romanian claims to Transylvania; perhaps Yugoslav claims to Fiume, Trieste, and maybe the whole of Istria and a part of southern Austria inhabited by the Slovenes.

Is there still hope for a federation? Yes, if the Soviet Union will agree. A federation of Central-Eastern Europe in friendly collaboration with the Soviet Union would be a firm barrier against German aggression. If the Soviet Union intends only to defend herself against the possibility of future German aggression and has no other plans, the federation is an adequate solution.

Bibliography

Bell, Daniel, and Dennen, Leon, "The System of Governments in Exile," in *The Annals* of The American Academy of Political and Social Science, CCXXXII (March, 1944), pp. 134-147.

Cave, Floyd A., "Axis Domination in Central and Eastern Europe," in *The Annals* of The American Academy of Political and Social Science, CCXXXII (March, 1944), pp. 116-125.

Gross, Feliks, *Crossroads of Two Continents* (New York: Columbia University Press, 1945), bibliography, pp. 139-153.

Stavrianos, L. S., *Balkan Federation* (Smith College, Northampton, Mass., 1944). A most complete presentation of history of the Balkan cooperation and an excellent study of political trends.

Visson, Andre, *The Coming Struggle for Peace* (New York: The Viking Press, 1944). A very readable summary of the problems which plague Central-Eastern Europe.

CHAPTER XXXI

ECONOMIC PROBLEMS OF CENTRAL-EASTERN EUROPE

Agricultural Economy*

THE economy of Central-Eastern Europe is predominantly agricultural. It is true that the oil fields in southeastern Poland and Romania are the richest in Europe and that the steel industries of Czechoslovakia, Austria, and southeastern Poland are among the most important on the continent. Other industries are also scattered through the region, but industrial production on the whole is relatively low in this area as compared with Western Europe, Great Britain, or the United States—low in output and in number of workers.

Yet despite the outstanding importance of agriculture, this part of the world is agriculturally underdeveloped, as shown by a comparison of the yields of the principal crops with those of Western Europe. The yields of Central-Eastern Europe are relatively poor not only because of primitive farming methods, but also because these countries were so often destroyed by wars and so much exploited that capitalization did not take place to the same degree as in the West.

The leaders of the small nations in the region are entirely aware of the hopes of their peoples that the Second World War would not only do away with Nazi slavery but that the peace to follow would also produce a more prosperous economic society. The basic economic problems of Central-Eastern Europe are discussed in this chapter.

Political Background of Economic Problems

In order to comprehend the economic ills of Central-Eastern Europe, it is inevitably necessary to understand the political setting and the political forces prevailing in that area.

Whether these forces threw detrimental shadows from the outside,

---

* This chapter was completed in the summer of 1944. The population figures as well as raw material resources of the individual countries are mentioned as of January, 1938.

or whether they came into being because of internal conditions, they all had one primary consequence. The nations of the region discussed here, with the possible exception of Czechoslovakia, "lived—economically speaking—a dead man's life." Feudalism and the guild organizations of the Middle Ages were dead, but their decaying bodies were political and economic obstacles to every endeavor of the people to advance along the road of welfare and progress on which the masses of Western Europe and America were marching.

It is our hope and the hope of the people of Central-Eastern Europe —who fought such a stubborn and costly battle for their freedom— that with the destruction of Nazi bondage they will also get rid of all those remnants of past ages which have hampered their strivings for genuine political and economic progress.

Let us then view from this angle the economic problems these people face and the tools they have at hand with which to solve them. In the crucial social problems of Central-Eastern Europe, the economic aspects naturally cannot be divorced from the political aspects. However, since the political factors in Central-Eastern Europe have been analyzed in previous chapters, we will refrain from discussing them here with the humble reminder that the economic salvation of this area can be achieved only in a sound political framework.

Population Factors

The greatest asset and at the same time the biggest problem of Central-Eastern Europe is its growing population. In 1920 this population was not more than 100,000,000 (excluding Russia), whereas in 1940 the number of people had increased to 116,420,000[1] and the population curve is still vigorously ascending.

Under these circumstances, the problem which the governments of these nations must face is to supply productive employment for the ever-growing population. Until 1914, a great stream of surplus popu-

---

[1]

Country:	Population:
Albania	1,100,000
Austria	6,660,000
Bulgaria	6,320,000
Czechoslovakia	15,300,000
Greece	7,180,000
Hungary	9,160,000
Poland	35,200,000
Romania	20,300,000
Yugoslavia	15,200,000

Data taken from Frank W. Notestein and others, *The Future Population of Europe and the Soviet Union* (Geneva: League of Nations, 1944), p. 56.

lation left this area yearly either for overseas—notably for the United States—or for Western Europe. Through this process—socially a costly one—the population pressure in the native lands was eased and the low per capita income of the population remaining at home was augmented by remittances from emigrants.[2] These remittances from overseas countries and from Western Europe played a considerable role in the national income structure of all these countries, especially in Greece and Poland. In 1928, total remittances sent to this area from the United States alone amounted to $65,000,000.[3]

After 1924, emigration became more and more difficult and so a growing number of people had to find employment in the home market, either in agriculture or in underdeveloped industry and commerce. At the same time, the income from remittances showed a declining tendency, due to the natural fact that emigrants gradually take root in their new homes, establish families, and lose their ties with their relatives in their native land.

Where then should the surplus population find its livelihood? The agricultural field is over-crowded. In the period between wars, this region had a natural increase of over 20,000,000 people, mostly in the rural areas.[4] For lack of adequate alternatives, over half of this increase had to be absorbed by agriculture, while emigration from the area removed less than 10 per cent of the natural increase. It is not surprising then to find that whereas the number of agricultural workers per hectare of cultivated land was 28.6 in Holland and 16.4 in Denmark, this number jumped to 58.6 in Bulgaria, to 41.1 in Romania, to 40.8 in Yugoslavia, to 28.6 in Hungary, and to 28 in Czechoslovakia.[5] At the same time, it must be stressed that the land under cultivation, insofar as its fertility is concerned, is far below standards considered marginal in Western Europe and the new continents.

One might assume that the great density of the rural population would result in a higher crop yield per hectare. Unfortunately, due to various reasons to be discussed later, the opposite is true. In Denmark, with an average employment of 16.4 people per hectare, the yield in wheat is 31.3 quintals. In Romania, known for its wheat

[2] In most of these countries the annual national per capita income was as low as $85.00. For details, see Agrarian Problems from the Baltic to the Aegean (London: The Royal Institute of International Affairs, 1944).

[3] Hanč, Josef, Eastern Europe and the United States (Boston: World Peace Foundation, 1942), p. 11.

[4] Notestein, Frank W., and others, The Future Population of Europe and the Soviet Union (Geneva: League of Nations, 1944), p. 166.

[5] Basch, Antonin, The Danube Basin and the German Economic Sphere (New York: Columbia Press, 1943), p. 234.

exports, employing 41.1 people per hectare as noted above, the average yield is only 9.1 quintals. In Yugoslavia, it is 11.1 quintals with an employment of 40.8 people.[6] The ratio in Poland is no better.

The productivity of agricultural labor in the Balkans, in a large part of Poland, and in the eastern part of Czechoslovakia is about one-third of that in France, Germany, or Denmark.[7] This is certainly not due to any lack of intelligence or energy on the part of the people themselves, since the same men whose small productivity in Central-Eastern Europe we deplore proved a valued help on the farms of France and were found to be dependable, versatile, and diligent workers in the factories of the United States.

Low productivity is due partly to the lack of capital employed in agriculture, roughly less than one-half of that used in Western Europe and, of course, considerably less than is employed in the United States and Canada. Other factors are the lack of fertilizer and also of higher educational standards which would make the people more flexible and alert to new processes of production and enable them to use the scientific findings of their respective agricultural institutes.

Diversification of Crops

It is evident that a structural change in agricultural production, as envisaged in the conclusion of the United Nations Conference on Food and Agriculture,[8] namely the replacement of grain production by systems producing more of the so-called "protective foods," would ease the situation of the rural population of Central-Eastern Europe.

Such a change would require more labor, more fertilizer, and above all better husbandry. The most important result, however, would be a far higher yield per acre as well as per man than in grain production —which would provide a higher income for the agricultural population. Not only would there then be an absolute increase in agricultural income, resulting from the increased productivity of the rural population, but at the same time this would also have a cumulative effect on the income of the rest of the population as a result of the increased purchasing power of the rural section. The area as a whole would be afforded an opportunity to utilize its plants and trade facilities fully and ultimately to expand them in the light of new demands.

---

[6] Basch, Antonin, *The Danube Basin and the German Economic Sphere* (New York: Columbia Press, 1943), p. 234.

[7] For further details, see D. Warriner, *Economics of Peasant Farming* (London: Oxford University Press, 1939).

[8] Hot Springs, U.S.A., May, 1943.

The importance of developing a balanced economy in this area, in order to increase the purchasing power of the peasant population, can be seen from the fact that, except for Czechoslovakia, over 50 per cent of the people of the region derived their income from agriculture.[9] The share of agricultural revenue in the total national income of these countries was far below the percentage of people earning their livelihood by farming. For instance, 81.8 per cent of the Bulgarian population was employed in agriculture, but the percentage of national income derived from agriculture amounted only to 53.5 per cent. The other countries were no better off in this respect.[10]

A fundamental change in agricultural production is imperative also for the simple reason that, even with ample capital and a properly adjusted monetary policy, it is hardly feasible for these countries to compete in the open markets of Western Europe with cereal producers from overseas. As far as protective foods are concerned, however, due to the greater amount of labor required for their production, Central-Eastern Europe would be able to compete in those markets without all the artificial stimulae which proved to be such a hindrance to an orderly expansion of foreign trade among the nations of Europe. Moreover, an increase in cash income of the rural population, resulting from such a diversification of agricultural production, would ease the pressure on the peasants of Central-Eastern Europe to sell their cereal products at the cost of an extremely unsatisfactory diet. This in turn would mean that wheat and maize, produced at high cost in Central-Eastern Europe, would virtually stop competing with the same products produced at extremely low cost overseas.

The possibilities of agricultural diversification can be seen from the fact that, before the Second World War, about one-third of the agricultural area of Western Europe was devoted to protective foods against less than one-seventh in Central-Eastern Europe.[11]

Naturally, to achieve positive results in this direction, a far-reaching long-range program is imperative. The diversification of agricultural production will have to be adjusted to the fertility of land in the various sections of this region. Better grades of land are more suited to the production of livestock and crop diversification than are areas with

---

[9] Hungary, 53.2 per cent; Romania, 78.1 per cent; Yugoslavia, 76.1 per cent; Bulgaria, 81.8 per cent; Greece, 53.6 per cent; and Czechoslovakia, 36.5 per cent.

[10] For detailed comparison of the ratio of employed people in agriculture to the share of national income derived from farming, see *Agrarian Problems from the Baltic to the Aegean* (London: The Royal Institute of International Affairs, 1944), p. 50.

[11] Basch, Antonin, *The Danube Basin and the German Economic Sphere* (New York: Columbia University Press, 1943), pp. 240-241.

poor soil. Furthermore, certain technical improvements must be made and the forces of nature must be brought under control and utilized for human welfare. This was clearly recognized by agrarian experts and representatives of the peasant communities of Central and Southeastern Europe who met in London on July 9, 1942. In the program they adopted for an agricultural policy in their respective countries, they stressed as prerequisites of a new era in Central and Southeastern Europe the necessity of:

"(a) land drainage, water conservation, irrigation and the vital supply of hydro-electric power both for town and country, for which an initial survey on a national scale will probably be required;

(b) measures of soil improvement, including the use of manure and appropriate fertilizers;

(c) the provision of technical equipment, many forms of agricultural machinery and implements;

(d) the improvement of all kinds of seeds, and the improvement of the breeding of livestock." [12]

It should be emphasized, however, that even a completely successful fulfillment of the program outlined above would be only a partial solution of the problem of over-population and low standards of living. A thorough land reform, which was already under way in all the countries under discussion except Hungary, will be an additional positive factor in the achievement of the goal. Nonetheless, assuming the absence of emigration into Western Europe and overseas, agriculture, even at the highest point of efficiency, could not fully absorb and productively employ the ever-growing population. In fact, if the agriculture of Central-Eastern Europe is to work efficiently, it is essential that some other field of productive employment should drain off the surplus population of the rural areas.

Industrialization

The only real solution then, combined with a progressive agricultural policy, is industrialization. The interest of these countries and, indeed, of the whole world, is not merely to employ their population at starvation wages but to increase their standard of living. We say the whole world because it is evident that, if living standards in this area

---

[12] "Program of Popular Liberation and Progress for Peasant Communities in Central and South-East Europe," reprinted in *Agrarian Problems from the Baltic to the Aegean* (London: The Royal Institute of International Affairs, 1944), pp. 19-27.

remain low, while they rise in Western Europe or overseas, increasingly bitter complaints would be heard against the wealthier countries and strong pressure would be brought to bear against the immigration barriers of more advanced nations.

Moreover, it is a recognized truth that in every region of the earth, income levels are higher where the proportion of the working population engaged in agriculture is lower. Professor Eugene Staley, in his new book *World Economic Development*,[13] quotes an unpublished paper by Louis H. Bean: "Industrialization, The Universal Need for Occupational Adjustment Out of Agriculture," to the effect that "the low per capita incomes of (e.g.) China and India could be doubled if, with more efficient use of human and natural resources, only 15 per cent of their working population were shifted from food production to other pursuits . . . additional shifts of less than 10 per cent would treble income."

This thesis seems especially valid for Central-Eastern Europe and makes the development of manufacturing and mining industries there essential. The people of Yugoslavia, Romania, Bulgaria, Hungary, and Poland have seen an example of the application of this theory in Czechoslovakia. The latter is endowed with the same climate and roughly the same natural resources as its neighbors. But, with nearly 40 per cent of its population employed in industry and mining and only some 36.5 per cent in agriculture (as against 50 to 80 per cent in other countries), it had more population per square mile of total land surface and per 100 acres of cultivated land, and its population enjoyed the highest living standard in Central-Eastern Europe.

Education of Industrial Workers

In the foregoing discussion, it was stated that the only remedy for the over-population problem in Central-Eastern Europe is industrialization. The question immediately arises whether there are natural conditions for such a process, particularly if it has to be undertaken on a large scale. A second question, since the necessary capital has to come from the West, is whether or not such development would be detrimental to established industrial enterprises in the West. In other words, would the Western countries, by supporting the development of industries in this area, be causing unemployment and lower living standards in their own countries?

Even a superficial glance at a map of the natural resources of

---

[13] Staley, Eugene, *World Economic Development—Effects on Advanced Industrial Countries* (Montreal, Canada: International Labor Office, 1944), p. 5.

Europe will convince the reader that two fundamental factors of production, raw materials and labor, are amply available in this area. (In fact, the over-abundance of manpower is the problem industrialization ought to solve.) It is true that the efficiency of the available labor is below that of America or Western Europe. In this respect industrialization will also have to do some educating.

The first task of such a project will be to provide for the training and "skilling" of labor which is to transform Central and Eastern European peasants into industrial workers. If this is done on a large scale, in the native language, it will be much simpler and even more successful than the "educational" process which the emigrants from this area had to undergo in such alien environments as Detroit or Pittsburgh before they became the exceedingly useful workers in the war industries of the United States which they are today. According to a survey made by the Office of War Information, some 60 per cent of the workers employed in American war industries are emigrants or descendants of emigrants from this part of Europe.

However, re-education has to be carried out on a national scale. The automatism of laissez-faire never worked properly in this respect. It broke down because it is not profitable for a private entrepreneur to invest in training labor. "There are no mortgages on workers—and entrepreneurs who invest in training workers may lose capital if these workers contact with other firms." [14] But such education, although not a good investment for a private firm, is the best possible investment for a state.

Preparation for war and contact with complicated war machines during the recent war has made the population of this area more machine-minded. Therefore the "re-education process" seems to us a much simpler one than is generally believed. This does not contradict the fact that for the first decade or so the West will have to send industrial engineers into Central-Eastern Europe to help organize, build, and run the new industrial enterprises. The point is rather that the problem of re-education will not be as insurmountable as some critics contend.

Raw Materials

As for raw materials, although geological formations are not yet fully investigated and a great number of natural resources are probably still undiscovered, the resources already known point to im-

---

[14] Rosenstein-Rodan, P. N., "Industrialization of Eastern and Southeastern Europe," *Economic Journal* (1943), p. 211.

portant potential developments. Let us therefore take country by country and analyze their resources:

(1) Yugoslavia: This country is known chiefly as a producer and exporter of agricultural commodities. Some three-fourths of the population were dependent on agriculture and forestry prior to the recent war. Maize and wheat were the main products, which were carried every autumn in long barges up the Danube to Czechoslovakia, Austria, and Germany. The yearly crop averaged around 4 million tons of maize and 3 million tons of wheat. Because of lack of capital and the trade restrictions of the importing countries, the wheat was not exported to foreign markets in the form of flour, but was left unground. Thus, Yugoslavia was deprived of the logical opportunity to develop a flour-mill industry.

As mentioned previously, after the outbreak of the agricultural crisis, the Yugoslav Government encouraged the shift from production of staple agricultural commodities to those of industrial use. Thus hemp, flax, and oil-seed plants became increasingly important in the Yugoslav economy and were developing into a valuable foundation for new domestic industries (e.g. textiles). However, the German economic policy (starting some time in 1936) reversed this healthy trend. Using the clearing system, the Germans paid such a generous price for Yugoslav wheat and maize that the farmers disregarded the government program and returned to their previous production system. Short-range German military plans won out over long-range Yugoslav needs.

Since nearly one-third of the country is covered with forests (or at least it was until the German occupation), one would expect to find many paper and wood-pulp mills and sawmills in Yugoslavia. Yet, except for sawmills, this industry was only in a primitive stage of development. This, then, was another opportunity for productive employment. It was not utilized, mainly due to lack of capital. Therefore this important raw material was exported mainly as timber, mostly for building purposes. As much as half a million tons a year went to Italy, England, Germany, and other countries, particularly to the Near East.

In spite of the fact that Yugoslavia is the richest and most important country of Central-Eastern Europe as a producer of minerals, only 27,000 people were employed in mining and only 2.5 per cent of the Yugoslav national income was derived from this source.[15]

Among the minerals mined in Yugoslavia are nearly all the essen-

---

[15] *South-Eastern Europe* (London: The Royal Institute of International Affairs, 1939), p. 211.

tial raw materials for the modern industrial age, including copper, lead, zinc, bauxite, iron, chrome, antimony, gold, and silver. Yugoslavia produced about 40,000 tons of copper and 71,000 tons of lead (or 4 per cent of the world output) per year. She also produced annually some 358,000 tons of bauxite (10 per cent of the world output). These products were mostly exported before being reprocessed. Yugoslav iron ore, too—nearly half a million tons a year—was exported to the steel mills of Hungary until recently. Now it is used by the state steel works at Zenica. Yugoslavia produced some 2,500 kilograms of gold a year, mainly as a by-product of copper.

In spite of these great riches in raw materials, only some 700,000 people were employed in manufacturing industries. These were chiefly consumption goods industries, such as milling, sugar, alcohol, jam, textiles, soap, candles, and simple drugs. It is probable that these industries—still in the early stages of development—were destroyed by the German occupants, who were more concerned with the requirements of their war machine than with the needs of the population.

(2) Romania: As in Yugoslavia, Romania has the paradox of great natural wealth coupled with extreme poverty of the people. The population is undernourished, yet the main exports are food products (wheat, maize, cattle, and poultry products) and raw materials, particularly timber.

According to the Romanian Institute of Geology there are still—in spite of the reckless exploitation of recent years—some 105 to 110 million tons of oil to be found in Romanian fields. Some 32.5 million tons of black coal, 13.5 million tons of iron ore, 7.8 million tons of manganese ore, and 26 million tons of bauxite await extraction and utilization. There are other mineral resources still unexplored and untouched. Romania also produces an average of some 4,000 kilograms of gold yearly. In spite of these riches, only some 800,000 Romanians were earning their living in industry and commerce.

(3) Hungary: This is a country well-endowed by nature to be an agricultural haven for its population. If, in spite of nature's bounty, the people did not attain the standard of life of, let us say, the people of Holland, Belgium, or Denmark, it is largely due to the socio-political structure which holds them in bondage.

Nowhere in Central-Eastern Europe is the distribution of land ownership so inequitable as in Hungary and nowhere else in Europe was the feudal system of economic (as well as political) organization so carefully preserved to this late date. This is the main reason for the extremely inequitable distribution of income and the backwardness of general economic activity. For Hungary more than for any other country in the Danube Basin, therefore, the prognosis demands a change in the political structure as a condition for economic advancement.

As of this writing, over 35 per cent of the country is still covered with estates of more than 700 acres. As a result, a large section of the population are landless laborers. According to the estimates of the British Royal Institute of International Affairs, half of the total farm population in Hungary has no land and 35 per cent of the farms are "dwarf" peasant holdings which cannot produce enough to support one family.

On the other hand, Hungary's secondary light industry was quite strikingly developed during the period between the two World Wars, especially the textile industry. The 152,000 industrial workers employed in 1921 doubled in number by 1936. High tariff and other protection helped to promote this development. But this industrialization did not greatly increase the total income level of the country because the social structure of Hungary remained unchanged while industrialization progressed. The bulk of the population did not benefit from the increase in national income associated with industrialization.

Industrial raw materials, notably the mineral resources of Hungary, are not important except for bauxite. The resources of bauxite are estimated at 250 million tons, nearly a quarter of the world's supply. In 1937, Hungary produced 500,000 tons a year, or some 14 per cent of world output.

Coal resources were estimated in 1914 at about 120 million tons, lignite resources at about 500 million tons, and iron ore resources at about 20 million tons. These are utilized in Hungary's own steel mills. A few years ago the American Standard Oil Company sank new oil wells here which have produced around 600 tons of crude oil yearly— about equal to the annual oil consumption of Hungary.

Only if and when the problem of the agricultural population (over 50 per cent of the total) is solved by a thorough land reform will the industrialization of Hungary rest on a firm foundation and benefit the whole area.

(4) Bulgaria: While this country is poor in mineral resources, its climatic and soil conditions readily permit a shift in agricultural emphasis from cereal production to more labor-consuming ("intensive") crops, such as tobacco, sunflowers, colza, soy beans, cotton, hemp, flax, and roses (for the famous Bulgarian rose-oil).

A negligible Bulgarian industry produces light consumer goods of cheap quality, mostly for home consumption. As to mineral resources, only coal and lignite are produced and these only in small quantities.

(5) Greece: This country is one of the most mountainous regions of the Balkans and only some 15 per cent of its total area consists of arable land. Yet the number of inhabitants per square kilometer of cultivated land is the highest. In 1931 it was 336 persons, as compared with 181 in Yugoslavia, 128 in Romania, and 147 in Hungary.

Greece is therefore by far the most over-populated country in Europe. Half of the territory is sterile and only 18 per cent is under cultivation. Moreover, Greek mineral resources are negligible. Yet the general living standard of the Greek people is considerably higher than that of their neighbors. The reasons for this unusual phenomenon are, first, the climatic conditions, which favor the production of such valuable crops as tobacco and currants. Second, foreign trade is an important source of national income. Some 680 ships sailed the seas under the Greek flag in 1937, representing a tonnage of more than 2,160,000. The Greeks are renowned for their commercial prowess.

In the nineteen-thirties, Greece started rapid industrialization. Efforts were made to reprocess export commodities before they were shipped abroad: e.g., cigarettes and various blends of tobacco. Textile and metallurgic industries also made rapid strides, as well as some branches of the chemical industry. Nonetheless, tobacco remains the lifeblood of Greek economic prosperity. It is a luxury commodity. However, luckily for Greece, it is little affected by the swings of the business cycle.

(6) Albania: Albania is a poor, hilly country with only 11.2 per cent of its area under cultivation. Its cultivated land, moreover, was for the most part held by the State or the Church. Because of this fact, the greater part of the population lived in the hills and was occupied in pastoral farming. Livestock was a major component of Albania's exports.

Even though more than a third of the country is covered with forests, Albania's timber resources were not developed before the war because of transportation difficulties. The only mineral resources of significance are asphalt and oil, which were being produced on an average of some 100,000 metric tons per year.

(7) Poland: Poland is known to the world as an agricultural state. Its mineral resources are comparatively little known. Yet this country is relatively rich in mineral resources: coal, iron, salt, oil, zinc, potassium, and so forth, are found there in considerable quantities.

Coal deposits are very large and have been estimated around 62,000,-000,000 tons. In 1936, the output of Polish coal mines amounted to 29,747,000 tons. This wealth of coal can provide a favorable basis for the development of large-scale industries in the future. Of the European countries, only Great Britain and Germany have larger coal deposits. In the meantime, however, domestic consumption of coal is five times smaller per capita than that of Great Britain and four times smaller than that of the United States.

Iron ore also is found in various parts of Poland. For the most part, however, it is low-grade. The percentage of iron is rarely higher than 36 per cent. Polish mines supply only a fraction of the requirements of the iron industry of Poland, which is well developed.

As a producer of zinc, Poland occupies third place among the nations of the world. The oil resources of the country, once substantial, are nearing exhaustion unless new wells are found and new processes of extraction developed, since the oil in Poland is rather deep in the earth. Nonetheless, they still will be an important factor in the economy of the region for years to come.

As to manufactures, Poland had great steel and textile industries which withstood all the structural changes in that area during the period between wars and possessed all requisites for further development. The same is true of Poland's new and still undeveloped chemical industry.

(8) Austria: Although Austria is better known to the Western world for its tourist hotels and beautiful summer resorts, it is one of the two industrialized countries of the region, the other being Czechoslovakia. Besides having a well-developed and diversified commerce and industry, Austria is rich in certain raw materials, such as timber and wood-pulp. Austrian production of iron ore was about 1.8 million tons in 1937 and this is not the highest output which can be economically achieved from Austrian mines. Moreover, Austria is the greatest magnesite producer in the world.

Austria's main problem in the period between wars (which was also Czechoslovakia's) was a lack of sufficiently large markets in the neighboring states for the full utilization of her industrial capacity, especially after the depression began. Austria did not have a big enough market to deal with the agricultural "hinterland" of Hungary, Yugoslavia, Romania, and Bulgaria on a barter basis. This was a type of trade which Germany—of course not for "purely" economic reasons—was only too willing to encourage.

Austria's industry expanded under Nazi domination. Due to its location, the German Government considered Austria the safest spot for the establishment of expanding war industries. There is still the question of how much of this new and old industry was wrecked by the bombs of the United Nations before Germany surrendered, and, of course, how far it will be possible to reconvert this industry for peacetime production. One thing seems certain. Given an increase in the standard of living in the neighboring agricultural states, and provided that free or freer trade practices are reinstated in this area, the Austrian people can not only regain their former prosperity, but raise it to a higher level.

(9) Czechoslovakia: Of all the countries discussed in this chapter, Czechoslovakia had the most stable and balanced economy. It had a productive agriculture which, particularly in the western provinces of the country, utilized the latest mechanical aids and the newest scientific methods of production developed in Western Europe and overseas. At the same time, it had great industries producing everything from complicated heavy machinery to the simplest needle. Czech steel mills made steel of such a quality that it was even exported to the United States. The same industry served as a basis for the Czechoslovak armament industry which, however, was well-equipped to serve peace-time needs also. Railroads in Iran, sugar factories in the Argentine, and bridges in Russia were produced by the Skoda and Vitkovice Iron Works of Czechoslovakia before the war. Similarly well-developed were the Czechoslovak textile industry and world-famous glass and toy industries. It would be difficult to enumerate all the industries which were profitably managed in Czechoslovakia, so manifold and diversified was the field in which Czechoslovak entrepreneurs and workers found profitable employment.

As a basis for this industrial development, one can cite Czechoslovakia's wealth of mineral resources, mainly coal—the yearly output of which amounted to 33 million tons. Large timber resources supplied the great wood-pulp, celluloid, and paper industries of the country with raw material. Above all, Czechoslovakia's greatest asset was skilled labor, well-trained and very efficient.

Czechoslovakia, like Austria, suffered greatly from the tremendous decrease in the purchasing power of the agricultural Balkan countries. Unlike Austria, it had the strength to seek and find new markets overseas, particularly in the United States, Latin America, and the British Dominions. Prior to the German occupation, Czechoslovakia developed a flourishing trade with these countries in spite of transportation difficulties (being a land-locked country) and the keen competition it had to meet.

(10) The Baltic States: As the Baltic States figured as independent states in the political structure of this area between the two wars, and as their history and political composition has been discussed in preceding chapters, it seems appropriate to mention in this chapter the economic situation of the peoples of the three Baltic Republics: Lithuania, Latvia, and Estonia. Since nature was rather stingy with raw materials in these countries, and since the climate is not the healthiest for cereal products, the Baltic States specialized in raising livestock (of excellent quality) and in the production of industrial agricultural plants like flax and hemp. These, however, were not enough to assure a prosperous livelihood for their population. By and large, their living standard was on the same level as that of Poland. The population pressure was equally as great.

Like the other countries in this area, the Baltic States suffered from lack of capital and thus from underdeveloped industry, although they have natural prerequisites for prosperous wood-pulp and textile industries.

Since 1940 these countries have been incorporated in the U.S.S.R. as autonomous states. It can only be hoped that this huge economic unit will see the potentialities of the peoples of these countries and provide them with the necessary tools to develop their own welfare.

The Need for Capital

From what has been said, it can be seen that the countries of Central-Eastern Europe possess the necessary raw materials as well as the manpower to assure a healthy industrialization. The chief needs are capital and a workable long-range plan of industrialization. These needs can be measured by the fact that the value of Hungary's industrial production, for example, was about 14.5 per cent of Germany's. The comparable figure for Yugoslavia was 7.8 per cent; for Romania 6.9 per cent; for Greece 5.9 per cent; for Bulgaria 3.5 per cent. The value of machinery per capita, except in Czechoslovakia and Austria, was at most 10 per cent of that in the more industrialized countries of Europe, and the number of motor vehicles per square mile from 5 to 10 per cent.[16]

Earlier in this chapter we questioned whether capital investment in

---

[16] *Agrarian Problems from the Baltic to the Aegean* (London: The Royal Institute of International Affairs, 1944), p. 82.

this area by Western nations would not endanger their own industrial enterprises; in other words, whether industrialization of this part of the world would hurt the industrial West. It seems to the author that the opposite is true. In fact, industrialization should make Central-Eastern Europe a better trading partner for the rest of the world. As Wendell L. Willkie stated in a speech at St. Louis, on October 15, 1943: "well-being is a multiplying and not a dividing process." The Post-war Committee of the National Association of Manufactures ex-pressed the same idea by stressing the point that "it must always be remembered that the economic value of trade between the United States and other countries increased in proportion to the development of those countries with which we trade . . . It follows, therefore, that world-wide efforts to raise the standard of living of the underdevel-oped people through the more intensive uses of their natural resources are bound to be beneficial to the people of the United States (and other capital exporting countries) as well as those whose opportunities are thus broadened." [17]

It would be a misstatement, however, to say that the Western coun-tries would not lose markets for some of their products by the indus-trialization of Central-Eastern Europe. They would lose markets for cheap, low-quality goods which will be produced first in the course of industrialization. They would, on the other hand, maintain and even enlarge their exports of goods of finer quality and complicated design when the scale of values and tastes rises because of a higher living standard in these countries.

A real danger to the Western countries from industrialization of this area would develop only if the newly established industries undertook production of goods solely or chiefly for foreign rather than home con-sumption, or if the bulk of the population did not benefit from the increase in national income resulting from industrialization, as hap-pened in Hungary.

Under such conditions, the lack of an increase in the purchasing power of the population of Central-Eastern Europe would lead to an attempt to export the produce of newly created industries and a de-crease of imports of consumer goods. This is the reason why Mr. H. Frankel, in his article "The Problem of Industrialization of Backward Areas", urges that "plans for international investment and export of capital should be linked up with plans for social improvement to be

---

[17] "Jobs, Freedom, Opportunity in the Postwar Years. Preliminary Observations by the Postwar Committee of the National Association of Manufacturers" (New York: 1943), pp. 35, 38.

undertaken there simultaneously with industrialization, thus creating larger markets for foreign goods and lessening the tendency to export abroad the produce of the new industries." [18]

It can therefore be safely stated that, given an intelligent industrialization plan, accompanied by proper social and economic legislation in the countries concerned, the West can only gain by investments in this area.

The capital needed for such a project will amount to a large sum even if we assume that industrialization (at least for the first ten years) will be concentrated on light industries which require relatively little capital equipment. According to a plan published by Professor P. N. Rosenstein-Rodan, an investment of 19.2 billion dollars would be needed in the next decade to achieve full employment in this area.[19]

Under present conditions it is hardly conceivable that the area itself will be able to provide this capital. Even though a rising standard of living will increase savings available for home investment, the bulk of the capital nonetheless will have to come from the outside, mainly from Great Britain and the United States.

Here the question arises how to accomplish such a large transfer of capital without overburdening the new and still vulnerable economies with huge service charges. Even before the war these countries had a big external debt, amounting to 24.3 billion Swiss francs. The external debt service totaled 1.3 billion Swiss francs per annum. It is not surprising therefore to learn that, in 1931-1932, Greece had to spend 49 per cent of her export proceeds for debt service, Hungary 48 per cent, Yugoslavia 29 per cent, Romania 28 per cent, Poland 24 per cent, Austria 22 per cent, Bulgaria 16 per cent, and Czechoslovakia 5 per cent.[20]

Even if we assume that German reparations in the form of capital equipment might decrease, to some extent, the sum mentioned in Professor Rosenstein-Rodan's article, the problem will demand a magnanimous and far-sighted solution. The two financial and monetary institutions planned by the United Nations Monetary and Financial Conference at Bretton Woods, New Hampshire, in July, 1944, and particularly the International Bank for Reconstruction and Development, will find their testing ground here and also a great challenge to serve humanity.

[18] *Economic Journal* (1939), p. 196.
[19] Rosenstein-Rodan, P. N., "Industrialization of Eastern and Southeastern Europe," *Economic Journal* (June-September, 1943), p. 211.
[20] Hanč, Josef, *Tornado Across Southeastern Europe* (New York: Greystone Press, 1944), p. 103.

Conclusion

In conclusion, it can be stated that, given an orderly and stable world monetary system, an expanding world trade, and, of course, a stable political system, Central-Eastern Europe will at last start her march on the road to prosperity and will assume an important role in the economic as well as the political life of future Europe. Insofar as it depends on these countries, they will play a constructive part, because they realize now more than ever that small countries are highly vulnerable to the protective economic measures of larger powers. Being large per capita exporters and importers, they know that policies of self-sufficiency and excessive protection, such as Germany advocated, might be a deadly peril to their national existence.

Bibliography

Armstrong, Hamilton Fish, "Danubia: Relief or Ruin," *Foreign Affairs*, X (1932).

Armstrong, Hamilton Fish, *Where There Is No Peace* (New York: MacMillan, 1939).

Basch, Antonin, *The Danube Basin and the German Economic Sphere* (New York: Columbia University Press, 1943).

Bidwell, Percy W., "Controlling Trade After the War" *Foreign Affairs*, XXI (1943).

Clark, Colin, *The Conditions of Economic Progress* (London: MacMillan, 1940).

Feierabend, L., "Czechoslovakia and Central Europe," *Journal of Central European Affairs*, II, 1943.

Frankel, H., "The Problem of Industrialization of Backward Areas," *Economic Journal*, 1943.

Gross, Hermann, *Südosteuropa: Bau und Entwicklung der Wirtschaft* (Leipzig: Noske, 1937).

Hanč, Josef, *Eastern Europe and the United States* (Boston: World Peace Foundation, 1942).

Hanč, Josef, *Tornado Across Eastern Europe* (New York: The Greystone Press, 1942).

Hopper, Bruce, "The War for Eastern Europe" *Foreign Affairs*, XX (1941).

Hubbard, G. E., *Eastern Industrialization and Its Effect on the West*, 2nd ed., (New York: Oxford University Press, 1938).

International Institute of Intellectual Coöperation, *The Development of Hungary's Foreign Trade between 1920 and 1936* (Paris: 1939).

Jászi, Oscar, "The Economic Crisis in the Danubian States," *Foreign Affairs*, XV, No. 1 (1935).

Jászi, Oscar, "Feudal Agrarianism in Hungary," *Foreign Affairs*, XVIII (1939).

League of Nations Publication, *Considerations in the Present Evolution of Agricultural Protectionism* (1935).

League of Nations Publication, *Commercial Policy in the Inter-War Period* (1935).

League of Nations Publication, *Europe's Trade* (1941, II.A.1).

League of Nations Publication, *The Future Population of Europe and the Soviet Union,* Frank W. Notestein and others (Geneva: 1944).

League of Nations Publication, *The Land Tenure System in Europe* (Conference on Rural Life, 1939).

League of Nations Publication, *Network of World Trade* (II.A.3, 1942).

League of Nations Publication, *Population and Agriculture with Special Reference to Agricultural Overpopulation* (Conference on Rural Life 3, 1939).

League of Nations Publication, *Preliminary Investigation into Measures of a National or International Character for Raising the Standard of Living* (II.B.4, 1938).

Machray, Robert, *The Struggle for the Danube* (London: Allen & Unwin, 1938).

Pasvolski, Leo, *Economic Nationalism of the Danubian States* (New York: MacMillan, 1928).

Rosenstein-Rodan, P. N., "Problems of Industrialization of Eastern and Southeastern Europe," *Economic Journal* (June-Sept., 1943).

Roucek, Joseph S., *The Politics of the Balkans* (New York: 1939).

Royal Institute of International Affairs, *Agrarian Problems from the Baltic to the Aegean* (London: 1944).

Royal Institute of International Affairs, *Europe Under Hitler* (1941).

Royal Institute of International Affairs, *The Problem of International Investments* (London: 1937).

Royal Institute of International Affairs, *South-Eastern Europe* (1939).

Staley, Eugene, *World Economic Development* (Montreal: International Labor Office, 1944).

Tasca, H. H., *World Trading Systems* (Paris: International Institute of Intellectual Coöperation, 1939).

Wright, F. Ch., *Population and Peace* (Paris: International Institute of Intellectual Coöperation, 1939).

League of Nations Publication, Commercial Policy in the Inter-War Period (1945).

League of Nations Publication, Europe's Trade (1941, II.A.1).

League of Nations Publication, The Future Population of Europe and the Soviet Union, Frank W. Notestein and others (Geneva: 1944).

League of Nations Publication, The Land Tenure System in Europe (Conference on Rural Life, 1939).

League of Nations Publication, Network of World Trade (II.A., 1942).

League of Nations Publication, Population and Agriculture with Special Reference to Agricultural Overpopulation (Conference on Rural Life 3, 1939).

League of Nations Publication, Preliminary Investigation into Measures of a National or International Character for Raising the Standard of Living (II.B.4, 1938).

Machray, Robert, The Struggle for the Danube (London: Allen & Unwin, 1938).

Pasvolski, Leo, Economic Nationalism of the Danubian States (New York: MacMillan, 1928).

Rosenstein-Rodan, P. N.; "Problems of Industrialization of Eastern and Southeastern Europe," Economic Journal (June-Sept., 1943).

Roucek, Joseph S., The Politics of the Balkans (New York: 1939).

Royal Institute of International Affairs, Agrarian Problems from the Baltic to the Aegean (London: 1944).

Royal Institute of International Affairs, Europe Under Hitler (1941).

Royal Institute of International Affairs, The Problem of International Investments (London: 1937).

Royal Institute of International Affairs, South-Eastern Europe (1939).

Staley, Eugene, World Economic Development (Montreal: International Labor Office, 1944).

Tasca, H. H., World Trading Systems (Paris: International Institute of Intellectual Coöperation, 1939).

Wright, P. Ch., Population and Peace (Paris: International Institute of Intellectual Coöperation, 1939).

PART VI

PART VI

CHAPTER XXXII

RUSSIA OVER CENTRAL-EASTERN EUROPE

Pattern of Power

IN THE vastness of the Allied victory and Germany's tremendous defeat (in the spring of 1945), one curious and significant fact was overlooked. "Never before in history have Western Europe and Eastern Europe faced each other except across a buffer of German or Austrian power. For some 500 years the history of Europe has been a series of variations, mostly tragic, on this geographic and political fact." The German surrender has finally destroyed this historic pattern. "Henceforth Western Europe and Eastern Europe must live face to face." [1]

For the first time, Central-Eastern Europe and the Balkans (with the exception of Greece) traditionally the most turbulent regions on the continent and those most subject to the rivalry of the Great Powers, were in a sense united under the political domination of a single power, Russia. The transformation was brought about by a combination of force and guile employed in a way not open to the Allies in the politically developed west. The technique was rather simple. When the Soviet Army occupied such states as Bulgaria, the Communist party immediately popped up from the underground as the leader in some such organization of leftists as the so-called "Patriotic Front." The next step was for the local Communists to gain power by taking key positions in the government, notably those involving control of the police and means of expression. After that, the local Reds proceeded to "purge" their political opponents.

As a result, in Yugoslavia, Bulgaria, Romania, and Poland, the governments were openly Communist or largely dominated by Communists. Communists held important government posts in the spring of 1945 in Austria and Finland. In Hungary, the regime was apparently under Soviet military domination. Besides exterminating their opponents, the new governments attempted to obtain popular support by

---

[1] *Time*, May 14, 1945.

agrarian reform programs and by a strong appeal to Pan-Slavism in Slavic countries.

Each of the new governments was being tied to U.S.S.R. by a network of treaties, both directly with Moscow and among the Central-Eastern and Balkan States themselves. In addition, Russia was redrawing national boundaries. Poland was apparently to be expanded to the Oder and Neisse Rivers. Transylvania was awarded to Romania. Bulgaria and Yugoslavia had been united in a customs union and may yet be combined in a single Slav state.

In redrawing the map, the Soviets gave major consideration to strategic frontiers. Vital points in Finland had been occupied. The Warsaw Polish regime had accepted the Curzon Line frontier in the east. Ruthenia had seceded from Czechoslovakia to join the Soviet Ukraine. The Soviets had taken Bessarabia and Bukovina from Romania. The Baltic States had vanished and Russia was ready to annex part of East Prussia, including Königsberg.

The Soviets had thus extended Russia's frontiers from 100 to 300 miles beyond where they were before 1939 and annexed territory inhabited by more than 14,000,000 people. A powerful revolutionary state was thus taking a forceful position in the world, a development which would inevitably bring to bear new strains, all the more severe because more were bound to develop. The presence of Russian troops in Norway's arctic Finnmark, of others on Denmark's island of Bornholm near the vital Kiel Canal, a Soviet blast at Stockholm for a Swedish newspaper's jibes at Stalin—all these signified the U.S.S.R.'s interest in the Baltic area and its outlet to the Atlantic. In part, the jockeying for position in occupied Germany also reflected Russia's Baltic concerns. From Poland, where Stalin refused to give an inch in May, 1945, to the Dardanelles, Turkey's outlet from Russia's Black Sea, the pattern of power tightened. The results were seen at the end of 1945, when Turkey was confronted with Russia's territorial demands.

There is much resentment in some American circles at what is called Russia's pathological preoccupation with her own security. But is our preoccupation with our security any less intense? Is Russia, for instance, less justified in insisting on securing her western frontiers after the bitter experience of recent years than we are in insisting on adequate bases in the Pacific after our experiences in this war? And if you ask Russia to put her entire trust in the machinery of the new security organization to protect her western frontier, cannot we be asked to forget the Pacific bases and place all of our trust also in the new League?

Russia's Reasons for Mistrust of the West

The Russians have a new regime, but they are a very old people. They think in long historical periods, not in decades. In approaching the issues of peace and world security, they bring fixed recollections of the age-old struggle between Slav and Teuton on the continent of Europe as well as of their sufferings in the latest manifestations of this historic conflict.

More recently, they recall the fruitless diplomacy at Geneva during the stronger days of the League of Nations and the years in which the democratic governments treated the Soviets as a pariah. They also know there is a latent fear in America and in the British Commonwealth of their European and Asiatic ascendancy which they think might produce another pro-German attitude such as existed in these countries between World War I and World War II.

Soviet Russia is inclined to coöperate with the United Nations in a system of collective security, but she is not entirely convinced that the other great powers may not try to turn the proposed League into a sort of capitalistic alliance against her. The Kremlin remembers very well that the League of Nations, dominated by France and Britain, kept Soviet Russia out of its councils for years. Moreover, although the League never seemed to be able to get the necessary "unanimity" to take action against Germany or Japan, it was able to get the necessary support to ease Soviet Russia out of the League at the time of the first Finnish war.

Furthermore, Soviet leaders cannot forget that, even as recently as late 1939 and early 1940, the British and French had prepared an expeditionary force to send to Finland's aid against her. And the "capitalistic bogey" in Russia is still as lively as the "Communist bogey" is in the West.

Russia's Need for Friendly Neighbors

The Soviet Government, moreover, is determined not to have "unfriendly" regimes in the states near her frontiers, just as the United States is concerned about unfriendly governments in Central and South America. The German attack on Russia in the Second World War through Poland, Finland, the Baltic States, and Romania has merely confirmed Russia's desire to regain the "secure boundaries" which she feels were taken from her unfairly after the last war.

Unless the Soviet Union has those "safe boundaries," part of which she had attained by May, 1945, and the rest of which she was in process

of acquiring, and until she is convinced that "the West," including the
United States, is prepared to take effectual collective action to prevent
any aggression, she is going to have reservations about relying too
much on the United Nations organization.

The Diplomatic Roots of Russia's Extension of the Sphere of Influence

It appears that the pattern unfolding in Central-Eastern Europe can
be traced to the Teheran agreements. There the leaders of the three
major Allied powers, the United States, Britain, and Russia, reached an
agreement as to the scope and timing of operations which were to be
undertaken "from the east, west and south." Before that happy result
was achieved, according to testimony now available,[2] there was considerable bargaining between Russia and Britain, while the United
States maintained what was described as a neutral attitude. Stalin
would not agree to coördinate the Red Army's operations with those of
his western allies until he had definite assurance that Britain would
support Russia's claim to Polish territory as far west as the Curzon
Line.

There was also considerable discussion between Churchill and Stalin
on the delineation of spheres of influence in the Balkans, with the result
that Premier Stalin agreed to let Britain have a free hand in Greece
and to make Yugoslavia a kind of ideological testing-ground of western democracy in exchange for British acquiescence in a similar Russian experiment in Romania. As a result, Poland will come out of the
war minus nearly half the territory with which she entered it, although
she will get compensation in the form of German territory.

Through the past century and more, Russian policy toward Southeastern Europe has consisted of two main strands, one positive and
one negative.

The positive strand was her own need of outlets to the open seas:
hence the perennial temptation to acquire control of the Straits—to
which Constantinople, as the symbol of the old center of eastern
Christendom, added a mystical element attractive to the Russian temperament.

The Straits command the bottleneck of the Balkans connecting Europe and Asia. Of supreme importance to Russia, the Straits have also
had commensurate attention from the other Great Powers in the game
of power politics. Both Peter the Great—Stalin's favorite hero—and

---

[2] Daniell, Raymond, "Fate of Poland Determined at Teheran, Diplomats Say," *The New York Times*, December 18, 1944.

Catherine the Great turned Russian policy southward to the Black Sea. After a six-year war against Turkey, Catherine forced the Sultan to sign the Treaty of Kuchuk Kainardji in 1774. By that treaty, Russia gained control of a large portion of the northern shore of the Black Sea and forced the Turks to grant her certain vague rights as the protector of members of the Greek Orthodox Church in the Sultan's domain. After the Napoleonic wars, the Russians not only extended their influence in the Black Sea but throughout the Balkans as well. During a dispute over religious rights in the Holy Land, the Russians made such extreme demands on the Turks that Britain and France came to the Sultan's support; the Crimean War was the result. For Russia this invasion constituted the first great lesson in the importance of keeping the Straits closed to her enemies—but also in keeping them open for Russia.

This object lesson was again demonstrated to Russia in World War I. Despite the major military effort of the Gallipoli campaign, the Turks kept control of the entrance to the Black Sea and the Russians were denied badly needed supplies from their western allies—perhaps the most important factor contributing to the Russian collapse in 1917.

The same situation, in a somewhat modified form, was produced by World War II. Russia was unable, due to the refusal of neutral Turkey, to import lend-lease supplies through the Straits. Consequently they had to be imported by a much longer route via Persia (Iran). The recent maneuvers in Russo-Turkish relations indicate that sooner or later Russia will force the issue in regard to the Dardanelles.

The negative strand in Russia's policy is her anxiety to prevent any strong or unfriendly political power from establishing itself athwart the historical highways of Southeastern Europe—an attitude not unlike that which England has always taken in regard to the Low Countries and the French Channel ports. But though Russia was repeatedly and successfully at war with Turkey and thereby played a large part in the liberation of the nations of Southeastern Europe, it is important to note that, whatever the opportunities, she did not try to add those states to her Empire. The one exception was Bessarabia, which Russia seized in 1812 in order to control the mouths of the Danube. This step was repeated during the opening phases of World War II. For the rest, Russia only sought influence as a protector in those countries, and gained it chiefly by encouraging national independence.

In 1917, bitter dislike and fear of Bolshevism resulted in the anti-Soviet policies of the democracies which are still remembered in Russia today. Paris at that time deliberately sought to turn Russia's border countries into a rampart against their powerful and dynamic neighbor. Unhappily the effects of that policy are still in evidence today. Perhaps the most characteristic example was Yugoslavia, a Slav country, which owed her independence in no small measure to Russia and whose life is steeped in Russian culture. Due largely to French influence, Yugoslavia refused to have any relations with the Soviets until 1940.

In 1945, Russia was determined to have regimes on her borders which would be friendly enough and free enough not to become the tools of hostile interests or schemes. Clearly, Russia is not afraid of those countries. She only fears their use against her by others.

The Kremlin is frankly pessimistic about the prospects of durable peace. It does not accept the prevalent division of history of the last thirty years into war and peace periods, regarding it as a continuous series of upheavals in which the sharp edges of peace and war are blurred. Where Americans and Britishers look for the war to end definitely, Soviet leaders expect it rather to subside in greater or less degree. Hence Russia is unwilling to trust the pacific claims of other governments and accepts assurances of friendship skeptically, even with irony. Lacking faith in the durability of post-war alliances, the U.S.S.R. seeks to win strategic positions, territorially and politically, for her own protection. "Its long struggle with 'capitalist encirclement' has made Russia what Americans call 'isolationist' and 'Russia-First' in temper."[3]

Pan-Slavism

One aspect of this political maneuvering is the Pan-Slav movement, which has only a remote resemblance to nineteenth-century Pan-Slavism. There is no longer any mystic faith in the unique character of the "Slav soul," no emphasis on a special historic mission. It is rather an opportunist design to meet a current political situation arising from World War II.

The first All-Slav Congress was held in Moscow at the very beginning of the Russo-German war, on August 10-11, 1941. Not a word was said about communism or revolution by those who attended. The emphasis was on national survival under the big-brother protection of Russia. An All-Slav Committee was elected as a permanent body. The second All-Slav meeting took place on April 4-5, 1942, and a third

[3] Dallin, David J., "Russia's Aims in Europe," *American Association of University Professors Bulletin*, XIX (October, 1943), pp. 495-507 (reprinted from *American Mercury*, LVII, October, 1943).

meeting occurred on May 9, 1943, just after the break of relations between Russia and the Polish government-in-exile. This conference heard the announcement of the creation of a new Polish army, openly hostile to the Polish armies outside the U.S.S.R. The organ of the Pan-Slav movement, *Slavyanie,* began publication in Moscow in July, 1942, and described its purpose as aiding "the struggle for national liberation on the part of the Slav peoples, and also the liberating role of the Red Army." The paper soft-pedalled the role of America and Britain in World War II. Russian friendship was presented as the sole salvation of the Slavs and the editors consistently supported the pro-Soviet Partisan movements in occupied countries.

The Pan-Slav movement has several other ramifications. Admiration for the heroic resistance of the Red forces has enabled it to rally people of Slav origin in the United States, England, Argentine, and elsewhere to serve as pressure groups for Soviet goals. Radio broadcasts in all Slav tongues emanate from Russia. Pan-Slavism has been accepted with widespread enthusiasm, particularly in Czechoslovakia, Yugoslavia, and Bulgaria.

The point is that Pan-Slavism has always been uppermost in the mind of the Slav peasant. It is true that Pan-Slavism—at best a vague concept—had never worked out successfully in practice. Proofs of its weakness were the two wars between the Serbs and the Bulgars since 1912; the traditional hostility of the Poles to the Russians and vice versa; Czech seizure of Tešín from the Poles and Polish recapture of Tešín after the First World War and before the Second World War, respectively; and the anti-Russian policies of the Bulgars who, although not at war with the Soviets, were allies of Hitler in World War II.[4]

Furthermore, Pan-Slavism, as a political weapon of Tsarist imperialism, was inexorably opposed to the democratic aspirations of the Czechs, the Yugoslavs, and the Poles. The Pan-Slav advisers of the Tsar did everything possible to prevent the establishment of a Czechoslovak volunteer legion in the First World War, although its value as

---

[4] There is hardly any literature published recently on Pan-Slavism without a propaganda taint. Hubert Ripka, *East and West* (London: Lincolns-Prager, 1944) is written by the Czechoslovak Secretary of State; the official line is also propounded by V. Clementis, *Panslavism Past and Present* (London: Czechoslovak Committee for Slav Reciprocity in London, 1943); and by Janko Lavrin, "Some Notes on Slavonic Romanticism," *Review 43* (London), I, 2 (Summer, 1943), pp. 83-88, I, 3 (Winter, 1943-44), pp. 121-5. Current interpretations of Pan-Slavism can be found in the current issues of *The Slavonic Monthly* (New York City, 5 Beekman St.). The best work on pre-war Pan-Slavism is Alfred Fischel, *Der Panslawismus bis zum Weltkrieg* (Stuttgart & Berlin: Cotta, 1919); for other works, see F. T. Epstein, "A Short Bibliography on the Slavs," *The Slavonic and East European Review,* XXII, 60 (October, 1944), pp. 110-119.

a weapon against Austria was apparent, because they feared the democratic and revolutionary character of such a movement. Likewise, the Russian Pan-Slavists suppressed Ukrainian and Byelorussian literature and favored the wholesale suppression of Polish culture and national aspirations.

The new All-Slav movement is based on the theory that, under Russia's leadership, the friendly and equal collaboration of all Slav nations, small and large, is possible. At the same time, it is more than obvious that Pan-Slavism is an instrument of Soviet policy. The refusal of General Mikhailovich to accept the Pan-Slav formula made him the object of world-wide defamation. Broadcasts from Soviet soil warned against "the traitors, the Chetniks of Mikhailovich."

Particularly attractive to Czechoslovaks and Yugoslavs, and, to a lesser degree, to Poles and Bulgars, is the theory that World War II was a life-and-death struggle between Teuton and Slav.

In 1942 Russia's outstanding literary man wrote:[5]

". . . Never, never will the Slavs accept the German yoke. Death is better than that. The Nazi divisions must be caught in a gigantic pincers from front and rear. The whole of Europe, including all the Slav countries, must become a great guerrilla camp . . .

In the midst of the world war we must reconsider our history. We have helped to build European civilisation, just as other peoples have done. Our young blood brought new life and vigour to the senile Byzantines. But the Slavs did not destroy Byzantium as the Teutons destroyed Rome. Thanks to the Slavs, Byzantium was preserved to infuse feudal Europe with its ancient culture.

Diligent and freedom-loving, attached to the pursuits of culture and peace, the Slav peoples stood on the eastern frontiers, separating Asia's nomad empires, with their fantastic plans for world conquest, from the mediaeval empires of the west, with their equally unbounded, grandiose schemes. Aggressions from both east and west were broken by the tenacious and courageous Slav peoples.

The part played by the Slav peoples in creating the humane culture of Europe has still to be appraised. The Slav nature is intricate and rich, peace-loving and gifted. But woe to him who outrages it. He will find not meekness or dejection but only stubborness and ferocious struggle. The Slav will gladly accept death if by his death he can bring liberty and victory to the homeland.

---

[5] Tolstoi, Alexei, "Slav National War," *Central European Observer*, XIX (April 17, 1942), p. 119.

To arms, Slavs! Let us unite in coördinated, multiform, relentless struggle! May our just anger rise with the force of a hurricane!"

Use of the Comintern

The Treaty between the U.S.S.R. and Great Britain and the understanding reached between the United States and the U.S.S.R. in June, 1942, touched upon the obscure but embarrassing relationship between the Soviet Government, through the Third International, and the Communist Parties of the United States and Great Britain.

As explained to Parliament by Foreign Minister Anthony Eden, the Russo-British Treaty contained a provision pledging each of the parties to refrain from interference in the internal affairs of the other. As outlined in the cryptic White House announcement, the accord between Roosevelt and Maxim Litvinoff, under which Soviet-American diplomatic relations were resumed early in the New Deal, contained a mutual guarantee of non-interference. Soviet Russia promised to have nothing to do with the Communist Parties of the United States and Great Britain, both of which were, in essence, Russian pressure groups operating with legal sanction inside nations that were Russia's allies in 1942. Apparently at the request of his Allies, Stalin dissolved the Comintern in 1943.[6]

To judge from the Communist press of various countries in 1944, Communists in each country identified their interests with those of the working people of their own country and of every country. In Europe, their main emphasis was on participation in movements for national liberation. They played an important part, along with other groups under Marshal Tito, in the liberation of Yugoslavia, and in swinging Romania (August, 1944) to the side of the United Nations. In Greece and elsewhere in Central-Eastern Europe, the Communists took part in broadly based underground movements which aided in the freeing of these countries and in the subsequent formation of provisional governments.

The very fact that Communism as well as Partisan movements in Central-Eastern Europe developed a dependence upon Russia as the savior of that part of the world will be of importance in the near future. It is true that the U.S.S.R., in the spring of 1945, was maintaining a formally very correct attitude in disassociating itself from local Communist Party matters and was promoting its policy through the For-

---

[6] For the operation of the Communist parties, see Roucek, Joseph S., "International Movements and Secret Organizations as Instruments of Power Politics," Chapter 26, pp. 743-62, in T. V. Kalijarvi, Ed., *Modern World Politics* (New York: Thomas Y. Crowell, 1942).

eign Office, where the three main lieutenants of Premier Stalin and Foreign Minister Molotov in European and border areas were Col. Gen. Andrei A. Ghdanov for Finland and Scandinavia, Andrei Y. Vishinksy for Eastern Europe and the Balkans, and Sergei I. Kavtaredze for Turkey and Iran.

Former Comintern officials had, however, emerged prominently in local political groups. Many of them at one time or another had not only worked with Moscow but had lived there. Among these were Poland's Boleslaw Bierut, Yugoslavia's Marshal Tito, Austria's Fischer (who used to head the Comintern press section), and Bulgaria's Georgi Dimitrov. These men had helped to organize the national Communist movements and to build strong party blocs around them from nationalistic Leftist and patriotic resistance groups. The formula was similar in all Central-Eastern European countries. There were national liberation fronts in Greece, Yugoslavia, Albania, and Bulgaria, and similar coalitions in Romania, Hungary, Austria, Poland, and Finland, varying as local conditions demanded but always with intellectual Communist leaders and methods at the top. The outstanding example of how this system operated was, of course, Yugoslavia.

Soviet policies in all the Central-Eastern European lands were remarkably harmonious, aimed at accomplishing reforms which, while greatly needed in Poland, Hungary, and Romania, were not nearly so necessary in Bulgaria and Yugoslavia. Basically, these reforms were concerned with land distribution and the socialization of certain industries.

The first step was to equalize land holdings. By accomplishing land distribution, a broad class of minor capitalists—peasants—was created. At the same time, the regimes of these countries, dominated directly or indirectly by the Communists, were eliminating all opposition elements. These included collaborators and traitors. But some pro-Allied peasant leaders were also regarded as "oppositionists."

The Emerging Pattern

The problem of coördinating Anglo-American and Russian post-war strategies and aims is the most crucial problem confronting the Allies.

In the spring and summer of 1945, Yugoslavia and Poland comprised perhaps the main diplomatic knots that had to be unraveled by the three great Allied statesmen. Russia was seeking security through augmentation of its national power, regardless of the rights or interests of the other Allies. The other political entities which the Soviet Union treated as "governments," in contrast to the United States and Britain, were the three Baltic States and Austria.

The ability of the United States, Great Britain, and Russia to work out amicable agreements in regard to Central-Eastern Europe (as well as other problems) will be the determining factor in world politics in the years to come. The old fear of "capitalistic encirclement" is still a powerful influence in the Soviet Union. There is a reason for the persistence of such psychology, which many American critics fail to appreciate. In their own suspicion and distrust of Soviet moves in Europe, some people fail to understand how profoundly the war has invalided Russia and how much her insistence on maximum security grows out of her state of convalescence and the need for a long rest. Her methods of assuring the friendliness of neighboring governments, in which some see only aggression, stem in fact from a consciousness of vulnerability rather than a sense of power.[7]

The finding of a way to solve these problems, to assure Russian security in the post-war world, and to find a formula which will be satisfactory to all members participating in the new world security organization, is the supreme task of the world today.

[7] See: Prince, Charles, "Current Views of the Soviet Union on the International Organization of Security, Economic Coöperation and International Law: A Summary," *American Journal of International Law,* XXXIX (July, 1945), pp. 450-485; McCormick, Anne O'Hare, "How Can We Get Along With Russia?" *New York Times Magazine,* October 28, 1945, pp. 11ff.; C. L. Sulzberger's numerous articles on Russia in *New York Times,* 1945; Dennen, Leon, *Trouble Zone* (New York: Ziff-Davis, 1945); Lauterbach, R. E., *These Are the Russians* (New York: Harper, 1945); Dallan, D. J., *The Big Three* (New Haven, Conn.: Yale University Press, 1945); Scott, John, *Europe in Revolution* (Boston: Houghton Mifflin, 1945); Shotwell, James T. & Laserson, M. M., *Poland and Russia* (New York: Ling's Crown Press, 1945); Stalin, Joseph, *The Great Patriotic War of the Soviet Union* (New York: International Publishers, 1945); Mac-Curdy, J. T., *Germany, Russia and the Future* (New York: The Macmillan Co. 1945); Chamberlain, W. H., "International Communism, 1945 Model," *New Leader,* June 9, 1945; etc.

INDEX

INDEX*

A

"Activist" movement, in Finland, 171
Adler, Victor, 53
Adrianople, Treaty of, 196
Ady, Endre, 49
Aehrenthal, Count Alois, 56-57
Agricola, Bishop Mikael, 165
Agriculture, 377
  problems of, in Soviet Russia, 446-447
Aizsargi, 476
Åland Island, 457-458
Albania, to 1918, 214-217; (1918-1945), 531-
  538
  bibliography on, 217, 537-538
  geopolitical and economic factors, 531
  history, 214-215
  Italian occupation of, 535-537
  King Zog, 532-535
  nationalism, 215-216
  World War I and, 217, 255-256
Alexander, of Greece, 223
Alexander I, of Russia, 142, 143, 169
Alexander II, of Russia, 148-149, 170
Alexander III, of Russia, 151, 152, 170
Alexander, of Yugoslavia, 511
Alliances, in the Baltic regions (*see also* Bal-
  tic Entente), 261, 262
All-Union Congress of Soviet Russia, 428,
  432, 433
Andrássy, Count Julius, 49, 55
Anjous of Naples, 326
Anschluss, 253, 261, 273, 276, 305, 313, 314,
  317, 361, 574
"Anti-Locarno Pact," 263
Anti-semitism, 52
Antonescu, Marshal Ion, 296, 501, 502, 503
Arany, Janos, 49
Arbeiter Zeitung, 313
Arciszewski, Tomasz, 414, 415
Aristotle, 214
Armfelt, Gustav Magnus, 169
Arpád, 323
Arts, the (*see also specific countries*):
  in Finland, 464-465
  in Soviet Russia, 440-441
Assimilation, German policy of, 597-599
Atlantic Charter, 292, 293, 299
Augsleich, 49-52, 327, 328, 332
Augustus II, 20
Augustus, Stanislaus, 108, 112, 113
Austria (*see also* Austria-Hungary), (1914-
  1945), 267; (1918-1938), 305-322
  anachronism of, 31-32
  culture of, 46-49, 315-316

Austria (*Cont.*):
  German occupation of, 574-575
  German seizure of, 277-278
  organization of, 306-309
  political and economic problems, 310-314
  political history, 316-322
Austria-Hungary, 25, 31-59
  anachronism of Austria, 31-32
  Augsleich, 49-52
  Austria's culture, 46-49
  Habsburgs, 32-33, 34-37, 41-46
  Hungary's culture, 49
  Hungary's nationalism and constitutional-
    ism, 39-41
  modern monarchy, 37-39
  monarchy's search for international solu-
    tions, 55-58
  nationalities *vs.* monarchy, 53-55
  origins of Hungary, 33-34
  Pan-Germanism, 52-53
  proposed partition of, 240
Autarky, 360
"Autonomous development," 251
Axis:
  Danubian problems of, 289-290
  defeat of, 293-294
  occupation of Greece, 548-549
  Rome-Berlin, 276

B

Badeni, Casimar, 54
Badoglio, Marshal, 293
Baksheesh, 493
Balfour, 349
Balkan conferences, 266-267
Balkan Pact, 272
Balkan States, 6, 16, 188-230, 488-567
  Hitler's campaigns in, 291-292
  peace settlements in, 253-257
Baltic Alliance, 261-262
Baltic Confederation, 481-482
Baltic Entente, 272-273, 459
Baltic Sea, 4
Baltic States, 6, 14; to 1918, 160-180
  between the World Wars, 470-487
  future of, 486-487
  German withdrawal from, 470-471
  peace settlements in, 244-251
  Russian occupation of, 607-608
  submergence in Russia and Germany, 481-
    486
Bartel, Kazimierz, 397
Bartsch, Rudolph Hans, 315
Basanavichius, Dr. John, 180
Bauernfeld, Eduard, 48

* Compiled by Alice Hero, Hofstra College.